THE BEDOUINS AND THE DESERT

SUNY Press and the family of the author
would like to thank the
Diana Tamari Sabbagh Foundation
and the
Wahbe A. E. Tamari Fund
for their generous support for the
printing of this book.

THE BEDOUINS AND THE DESERT

ASPECTS OF NOMADIC LIFE IN THE ARAB EAST

JIBRAIL S. JABBUR

TRANSLATED FROM THE ARABIC BY

LAWRENCE I. CONRAD

EDITED BY

SUHAYL J. JABBUR AND LAWRENCE I. CONRAD

State University of New York Press

SUNY Series in Near Eastern Studies
Said Amir Arjomand, Editor

Published by
State University of New York Press, Albany

For information, address State University of New York Press, State University Plaza, Albany, N.Y., 12246

Production by Marilyn P. Semerad
Marketing by Theresa Abad Swierzowski

Library of Congress Cataloging-in-Publication Data

Jabbūr, Jibrā'īl Sulaymān.
[Badw wa-al-bādiyah. English]
The Bedouins and the desert : aspects of nomadic life in the Arab East / Jibrail S. Jabbur ; translated from the Arabic by Lawrence I. Conrad ; edited by Suhayl J. Jabbur and Lawrence I. Conrad.
p. cm. — (SUNY series in Near Eastern studies)
Includes bibliographical references (p.) and index.
ISBN 0-7914-2851-6
1. Bedouins. 2. Arab countries—social life and customs. I. Jabbūr, Suhayl Jibrā'īl, 1931- . II. Conrad, Lawrence I., 1949- . III. Title. IV. Series.
DS36.9.B4J3313 1995
953'.004927—dc20 95-31533
CIP

10 9 8 7 6 5 4 3 2 1

DEDICATION

To my town on the edge of the desert where I was born, raised, and came to know the bedouins, a town they deem a haven unequaled by any other on earth;

And to the memory of my brother Tawfīq, who died in recent days and has been buried there;

I dedicate this book in remembrance of the wonderful boyhood years I spent with him there.

CONTENTS

THE FIRST PILLAR: THE DESERT

THE SECOND PILLAR: THE CAMEL

THE THIRD PILLAR: THE TENT

THE FOURTH PILLAR: THE ARAB BEDOUIN

APPENDICES

List of Illustrations

List of Tables

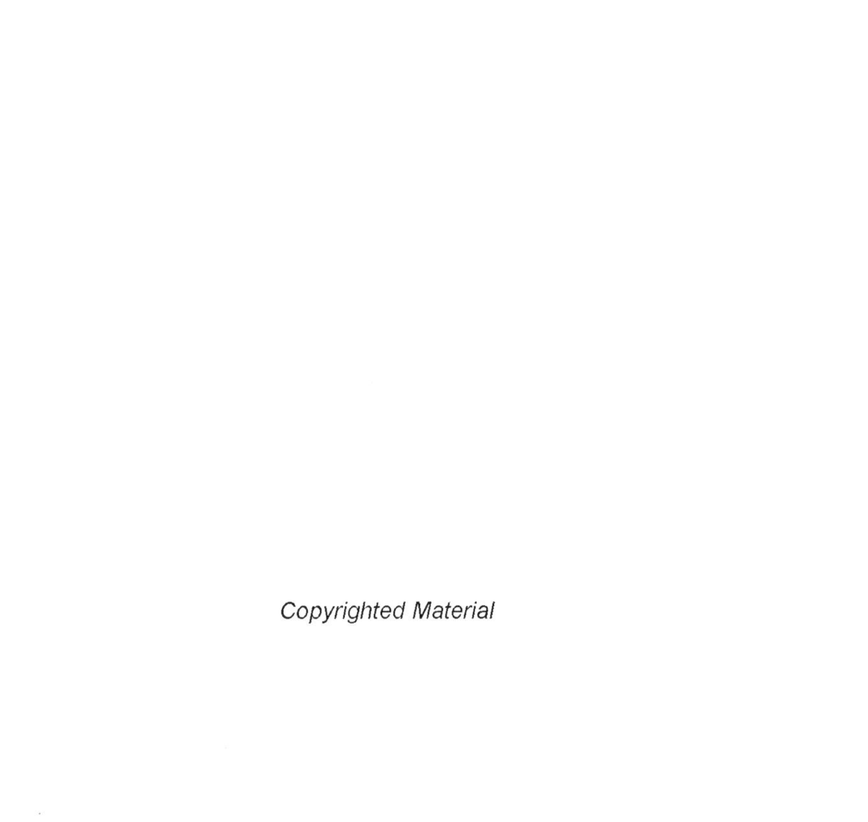

Translator's Note

THE AUTHOR OF THIS BOOK, Professor Jibrail Jabbur was a prolific scholar and very well known in the Arab world; but as he wrote for the most part in Arabic, he is less familiar to Western scholars.[1] A word of introduction might therefore be in order here. Born in 1900 in the small Syrian town of al-Qaryatayn, Jibrail Jabbur took his bachelor's degree at the American University of Beirut (AUB) in 1925 and began his professional career as director and vice-principal of the Ḥimṣ National Protestant College. Beirut soon beckoned, however, and after only a year he was appointed as Instructor in Arabic in the Department of Arabic and Near Eastern Languages at AUB. In 1929 he proceeded to King Fu'ād I University in Cairo, studied further with such renowned scholars as Ṭāhā Ḥusayn, Thomas W. Arnold, G. Bergsträsser, C.A. Nallino, and Joseph Schacht, and returned to take his master's degree at AUB in 1933.

Several promotions and numerous publications followed, and it was not until 1946 that he decided to seek his doctorate, this time at Princeton University. There he studied with Philip K. Hitti and achieved the distinction—never attained previously or repeated since—of completing a master's degree and a doctorate in a single year. Back in Beirut, in 1950 he was appointed Jewett Professor of Arabic at AUB, a position he was to hold for the next 20 years. Most of the graduate students of the department in these halcyon days were supervised by him, and he was also an active teacher at AUB's sister institutions, the Lebanese University and the Université Saint-Joseph. Upon his retirement in 1970, he was appointed Professor Emeritus of Arabic and continued to be an active researcher and teacher in graduate studies.

Through a career covering more than 60 years, Jabbur was to author close to twenty books and many more articles. His great work was a study of the Umayyad poet 'Umar ibn Abī Rabī'a. A first background volume on the era of 'Umar appeared in 1935, followed by a second in 1938 on the life of the poet himself; the third, an assessment of his

[1]See his autobiographical *Min ayyām al-'umr* (Beirut, 1991).

verse, was delayed by other commitments until 1971. An extraordinarily rich and wide-ranging work, this book of more than a thousand pages served to illustrate and expand upon Jabbur's conviction (also prominently displayed in the present work) that early Arabic poetry is a key source for understanding the spirit and *mentalité* of early Islamic times. He also prepared a number of useful editions of medieval Arabic texts: Najm al-Dīn al-Ghazzī's biographical dictionary of eminent personalities of the tenth/sixteenth century, published in three volumes between 1945 and 1959, and Ibn al-Jawzī's *faḍā'il* work on the merits of Jerusalem, published in 1979. A close friend of Philip Hitti, he also translated into Arabic several of the former's well known works: his *History of Syria* in 1958–59, his classic *History of the Arabs*, with much new material, in 1965 (with the author and Edward Jurji), the *History of Lebanon* in 1970, and *Capital Cities of Arab Islam* in 1991.

Such leisure time as Jabbur might have expected after retirement was soon consumed by work in the community. He lectured and wrote extensively on Arabic literature and medieval Arabic culture for popular audiences, and was also active within the Protestant church, serving first as an elder, then as President of the Board of Schools, and finally, at the age of 88, Executive Secretary of the Protestant Religious Court. In 1966 the World Bible Society, taking advantage of his background in Semitic languages generally, asked him to assume a leading role in their ambitious project for a new Arabic translation of the Bible from the original texts, and this was to occupy much of his time for the next 23 years.

In the spring of 1984, while on the faculty of the American University of Beirut, I was asked to look over the manuscript for a book on bedouin life by Professor Jabbur. The study proved to be a massive work based on a lifetime of contacts and experience with the bedouin tribes of the Arab east, an intimate knowledge of the bedouin dialects of Syria and northern and eastern Arabia, and decades of research in Arabic literary sources, modern studies and travelers' accounts, and foreign archives. The tribe of Rwāla and its *amīr*s of the al-Sha'lān family loomed large in the text, but while it thus invited comparison with *The Manners and Customs of the Rwala Bedouins* (1928) by Alois Musil, whom Jabbur held in very high esteem, this was clearly a different sort of book altogether. Aimed at a broader Arabic-speaking readership, it sought to familiarize its audience with Arab nomadism not as an abstraction to be analyzed and judged from without, but as a critical element in the Arab cultural heritage, brought to life against the background of the desert milieu and through an understanding born of life-long friendships and contacts.

Such a book clearly merited not only publication in Arabic, but also an English translation. Structuring of the Arabic text was basically complete by June 1984, revisions were well underway, and the translation was begun with a view to speedy completion. Unfortunately, this was not to be. Deteriorating security conditions resulted in my own departure from Beirut in June 1984 and obstructed the task at hand with a host of unanticipated difficulties, though some of these were alleviated by the appearance of the final published Arabic text in 1988. This was, however, one of the worst phases in the fighting in Lebanon, and the progress of the translation afforded a useful opportunity for incorporation of a significant number of corrections and revisions to the Arabic. Clarifications for the non-Arabic speaking audience have also been introduced. Almost all of the changes were discussed with and approved by the author and may be said to represent his work; further changes, almost entirely limited to a small number of additional notes, are set off in square brackets. In some cases, however, gaps could not be filled. Oppenheim's invaluable classic *Die Beduinen*, for example, was unavailable in Beirut at the time revisions were being made, and other more recent studies could not be acquired by the University Library under the circumstances prevailing in Lebanon.

In translating I have tried to adhere as closely as possible to the style and spirit of the original Arabic; and in particular, I have sought to render verse passages with some sensitivity to the fact that poetic forms and styles should not be entirely lost in translation. While claiming no particular merit for the results of my own efforts in this direction, I should say that the common tendency to translate what is often magnificent ancient verse into bald prose is surely to be deplored. A standard system of Arabic transliteration has been adopted, and this has also been applied where bedouin colloquial forms are concerned. To employ differing systems would pose the risk of considerable confusion, and in any case would not address the fact that among the bedouins themselves letters and words are pronounced in various ways. The rendering of the names of modern Arab tribes was also problematic; here an effort has been made to identify the most common form and to use it throughout.

It is always a pleasant task to acknowledge the contributions of others to the course of one's work. Professor Jabbur himself fielded a host of queries with the knowledge only he possessed, and commented upon the drafts of every chapter; I am grateful to him for his grace and patience, and the opportunity to work with him on this book. I owe an even greater debt of gratitude, however, to his son, Dr. Suhayl Jabbur, Professor of Physiology at the AUB Faculty of Medicine. It was Suhayl Jabbur who provided our work with its decisive impetus and attended to all the necessary details and arrangements. After my departure from Beirut he took over completely the task of finalizing the Arabic text and seeing it through the press, and assumed responsibility for assuring contacts between author and translator. He also read and reread every chapter in draft, pointed out many opportunities for improvement, checked references and provided copies of material not available in the UK, and tended to a host of procedural and technical matters—all with indefatigable enthusiasm and interest through some of the worst years of the civil strife in Lebanon. I am also grateful to Professor Fred M. Donner, the late Professor Albert Hourani, and Professor Michael G. Morony for their comments and suggestions, to Norma Jabbur for her stylistic comments, and to my research assistant, Leila Othman, for her help in locating and copying the Foreign Office documents used in Appendix II. At the Wellcome Institute, my thanks go to Freida Houser, Sue Hordijenko, and Jacqui Canning for their painstaking work in word-processing an unfamiliar and difficult text, and on the home front, as always, to Youmna, Mark, and Lisa for their love and patience.

Jibrail Jabbur, looking back over a long and distinguished career, found special satisfaction in the fact that what would probably prove to be his last major work would also be his first to appear in English translation. He passed away, however, on 11 May 1991, at the age of 91, shortly after sending me his comments on the last pages of the translation, and it is a source of deep personal regret to me that he did not live to see this work in print. But there is perhaps a certain poetic justice to be seen in the fact that one who, as a child, endured many of the less attractive aspects of life in close proximity to the bedouins of late Ottoman Syria, should, in his final years, play a leading role in nurturing a clearer understanding of the Arab nomads and their way of life, not only in his own culture and society, but in those of others as well.

Lawrence I. Conrad
London
24 April 1995

Preface

WHEN AS A STUDENT in the last two years of university I translated the book *The Girl Scout Guides* into Arabic, I remember that I sought the advice of my colleague Sa'īd Taqī l-Dīn on the matter of choosing a great writer to write the Preface. Sa'īd had just finished writing his first novel, *Law lā l-muḥāmī*, and had approached the great poet Khalīl Muṭrān to write the Preface to the work for him. Muṭrān did so, but did not deal graciously with him. Sa'īd thus said to me: "I would advise you to write the Preface yourself. You are more qualified than anyone else to present the book; and being a student like myself, you know that it would not be surprising for the author you chose to write the Preface to say that you are still an up and coming student, as was written about me, without actually having read everything you wrote and giving it a fair evaluation." I accepted his advice and wrote the Preface, the first one I composed for any of the books I had a hand in writing, editing, or publishing; and from that time onward I never asked anyone to write a Preface for any book I wrote.

It has been my custom since those days to show much of what I write to some of my colleagues at the American University for them to offer their comments before I give the book to the press. In fact, I showed some chapters of this book to my teacher and friend, the late Dr. Fu'ād Ṣarrūf. He was happy with what he read and said to me: "Were *Al-Muqtaṭaf* still under my direction, as it was in times past, I would have liked to publish some parts of this book in it." "What would you think," I asked him, "of writing the Preface for it when the book is published?" He smiled and nodded his consent. Many a time I have wished that he were alive at that moment, so I could entrust him with the task of writing the Preface and depart from my usual rule.

In the Introduction I have written what I wished to say of my connection with this research over the past 60 years and my study of the bedouins and bedouin life. Here I would like to point out that in arranging the parts of the book I have taken into consideration the principle upon the foundations of which the nomadic way of life is based. After setting forth in the Introduction what it was that prompted me to study nomadism and the bedouins, and surveying the most important works by Arab and foreign authors on this topic, I have divided the book into four main parts, which in my view represent the four pillars upon which the structure of nomadism is raised: desert, tent, camels, and the bedouin. Some of these parts contain multiple chapters, but I have numbered these chapters of the book consecutively from the beginning of these parts to the end.

Before continuing further, it remains for me to mention that the greatest credit for encouraging me to finish the book and send it to the press, and for helping me to read the entire text in proof and check it in its final form, goes to my son Dr. Suhayl Jabbur, Professor of Neurophysiology in the Faculty of Medicine at the American University of Beirut. I am also grateful to Dr. Lawrence I. Conrad, formerly Professor of Cultural Studies at the AUB and now Historian of Near Eastern Medicine at the Wellcome Institute for the History of Medicine, who helped me assemble the various parts of this work of many years, read the book in draft, offered many valuable comments and suggestions, and is now preparing an English translation.

I must also thank Dr. Charles Abou Chaar, Professor of Pharmacy at the University, who generously checked the table of plants compiling their names as known to the bedouins, and verified some of their Latin scientific names. I am also grateful to the Aramco Corporation, which collected for me some specimens of plants that grow in the region of the Aḥsā' oasis and wrote down their names for me. And I must express my gratitude to Muṣṭafā al-Qaṣṣāṣ, who read and corrected the proofs, and to Dār al-ʻilm li-l-malāyīn, which undertook to publish the book under its eminent auspices. This firm has played and continues to play an important role in the flourishing of literary and scientific activity in Lebanon despite the hardship the country has been and continues to be forced to endure through the recent years of strife.

I cannot forget the institutions that, before I left the University, made available to me many opportunities for visits to the Syrian Desert, and enabled me to visit the Jordanian desert and the desert of the Aḥsā' region. Nor do I forget the friendly reception I encountered from the leaders of these regions and states, be they kings, presidents of republics, *amīrs*, or tribal shaykhs. Of the *amīrs* I remember Amīr Nāyif al-Shaʻlān, who on more than one occasion did me the honor of receiving me in the reception area of his great tent, and on his estate (a lake in Roman times) on the edge of the desert. He allowed me to photograph the *'uṭfa*, the sacred litter or howdah of the Rwāla bedouins, and to take pictures of himself, of the *amīrs*, sons of Amīr Fawwāz, and of any scenes I wished of life in the desert. In this connection I am grateful to my friend, the photographer Manoug, who accompanied me on one of my trips to the desert and helped to enrich this book by contributing many of the photographs published in it.[2]

I make no claim that in this book, lengthy though it may be, I have covered every perspective on the subject of the bedouins and bedouin life. When I set out to prepare my own account, work on the bedouins in the modern social sciences was itself in its early stages. In subsequent years, it has produced a massive literature of its own on the subject. Readers of this book should bear in mind, however, that my own work is not a contribution of this kind. It rather comprises the personal observations of a historian of literature seeking to relate the ancient Arab heritage to the life of the bedouin tribes, especially in the Syrian Desert, in the first half of the twentieth century. At a more personal level, it springs from my hope that it will be worthwhile to record for posterity a summary of the bedouin ways with which I became familiar over many decades of knowing and living in contact with members of the various Arab tribes. To those who may query my infrequent reference to the social science literature, I would simply say that I have sought to write a different sort of book. If it stimulates an interest in bedouin life, and encourages the pursuit of more specialized reading from any of the numerous perspectives which have enriched our understanding of the bedouins, it will have served its purpose.

Jibrail Jabbur
22 November 1987

[2]All but three of the photographs published in this book were taken either by Manoug or by myself. These three are Figure 2, which was published as the frontispiece to the second edition of Charles Doughty's *Travels in Arabia Deserta* by Jonathan Cape (London, 1936); Figure 3, published as the frontispiece to Alois Musil's *Manners and Customs of the Rwala Bedouins* by the American Geographical Society (New York, 1928); and Figure 75, published in Max von Oppenheim's *Vom Mittelmeer zum Persischen Golf* by Dietrich Reimer Verlag (Berlin, 1899).

INTRODUCTION

The Desert and Bedouin Life: a Personal Perspective

My eyes first saw the light of day in a village environment, one in which the people for the most part made their living from agriculture. Located on the desert fringe, the village in which I was born and raised is in close contact with the desert; hence the spectacle of the bedouins, whom the village folk called *al-'arab*, "the Arabs," was familiar to me. I would see them when they visited the village, bought there the things they needed, and sold camels, sheep, butter, camel hair, and wool. We boys all used to whisper among ourselves that these simple "Arabs" in the village were the crudest of men and those most violently inclined to plunder, pillage, and murder. Thus we all shared in the village milieu's attitude of fear and loathing toward the bedouins. Indeed, we considered them the most evil creatures on earth, such fear and loathing probably representing an attitude rooted in the hearts of village folk from ages past, ever since they took up agriculture and sedentary life, leaving behind and despising the life of the wandering bedouin. What most frightened me, and most of the boys in our village, was the thought that we might venture out into the desert so far beyond the houses and fields of the village that, as the adults claimed when they wanted to make us afraid of the bedouins, we would risk being "stripped" by "the Arabs."[1]

I remember that once when I was a boy not yet ten years old, I was in a vineyard of ours separated from the houses in the village by

[1]When bedouin raiders in the desert encountered someone from the settled areas, it was their custom to accost him with the command, *Ishlaḥ yā walad*, "Strip, boy!," meaning that they intended to rob him of his clothing.

a broad plot of ground into which the village was beginning to expand and on which some people were building new houses. I was returning home from the vineyard just before sunset when, just as I was crossing this plot of ground, there suddenly appeared behind me a large force (*jaysh*)[2] of more than a hundred bedouin raiders on their thoroughbred riding camels, with their lances raised on high and their horses tied by their bridles beside them. Singing songs of victory and war, they charged toward the village to impose themselves as guests upon its people. I was almost stupefied with fear. I looked around me, but saw no shortcut I could take to reach the village before they did. So I threw myself into a deep, wide, round pit that one of the villagers had begun to dig by the roadside on the outskirts of the village to serve as a well in a house he wanted to begin building once water appeared in the well. I crouched in the shadow of the west wall of the pit next to the road, and I will never forget the sound of my heart pounding with fear as I saw the shadows of the lances passing across the east side of the pit. At that moment I felt as if I were counting the last few seconds separating me from death. But the raiders (or the *ghazū*, as we called them), rode past and continued on to the village to visit as guests. Not one of them turned in my direction; nor, indeed, did it even occur to them to do so. Then, when my fright had subsided and I felt safe from danger at their hands, I got up and quietly made my way back, far behind them, until I arrived at our house at the edge of the village, hardly believing that I was home safe and sound.

When I finished my elementary studies as a young student of my father, he sent me with my older brother to a boarding school in Ḥimṣ, the Ḥimṣ National Protestant College. A desert tract about 85 kilometers wide lay between our village and Ḥimṣ, and despite the small villages and farms scattered along the way, the road crossing this desert was desolate, dangerous, and subject in either direction to bedouin depredations and raiding parties from various tribes. The traveler had no sooner escaped from danger and the evil designs of the bedouins in one tribe's territory than he entered the domain of another tribe and exposed himself to the malice of other tribesmen. I will never forget the many times, during the four years I studied in Ḥimṣ, that bedouin raiders set upon

[2]The bedouins use the word *jaysh*, "army," to refer to a large group of raiders.

the caravan in which we were traveling and seized whatever it pleased their hearts to take from the provisions, fruits, merchandise, or money that it carried. I remember a time when my father was not with us and bedouins took us by surprise near a farm known as Umm Dūlāb. The people in the caravan suddenly began to shout, "The Arabs! The Arabs!" Sure enough, bedouins had surrounded the caravan from every side, and some of them began to close in and shout, "Strip, boy! Strip, boy!" My brother was so terrified that he began to cry, and the heart of the *'aqīd*—the raid leader in the bedouin dialect—was moved to pity for him. He began to walk his charger around the donkey we were riding, preventing his comrades from plundering us or even reaching us, and that day we alone were spared from plunder. The others were robbed of whatever the caravan carried, and some were stripped of their new clothing and given enough bedouin garments by the raiders to cover themselves.

Hence I grew up fearing these bedouins, loathing the desert, and hating its people, as did most of the boys in our village. Every one of them used to hear his mother try to frighten him by saying, "Tomorrow I'm going to sell you to the Arabs," or "Tomorrow I'm going to hand you over to the raiders." Indeed, when one of us wanted to play a trick on his friend, he would suddenly confront him with a bedouin pose and the command, "Strip, boy!"

As was the case for all the villages on the desert fringes, ours was sometimes the target for attacks by certain hostile tribes, the *qawm*,[3] as we called them. The young men of the village thus had to cope with the task of repelling raiders and fighting bedouins, and by virtue of their strength and great numbers they were able to resist domination from the desert. No bedouin raider dared to enter the village by force to loot anything from it, or to penetrate its nearby suburbs. But the village folk had much livestock—cattle, donkeys, sheep, and goats—and the herdsmen tending these animals were sometimes forced to graze them in pastures far from the village. Bedouins from the hostile tribes thus used to raid our district, pounce upon some of these animals, and

[3]The first thing you would hear from someone you encountered in the desert was the question, *qawm willā ṣāḥib*, meaning "Friend or foe?" Among the bedouins the word *qawm* has another meaning, that of *jamā'a*, "people." It is said, for example, "He is from the *qawm* of al-Sha'lān," i.e. from the people of al-Sha'lān.

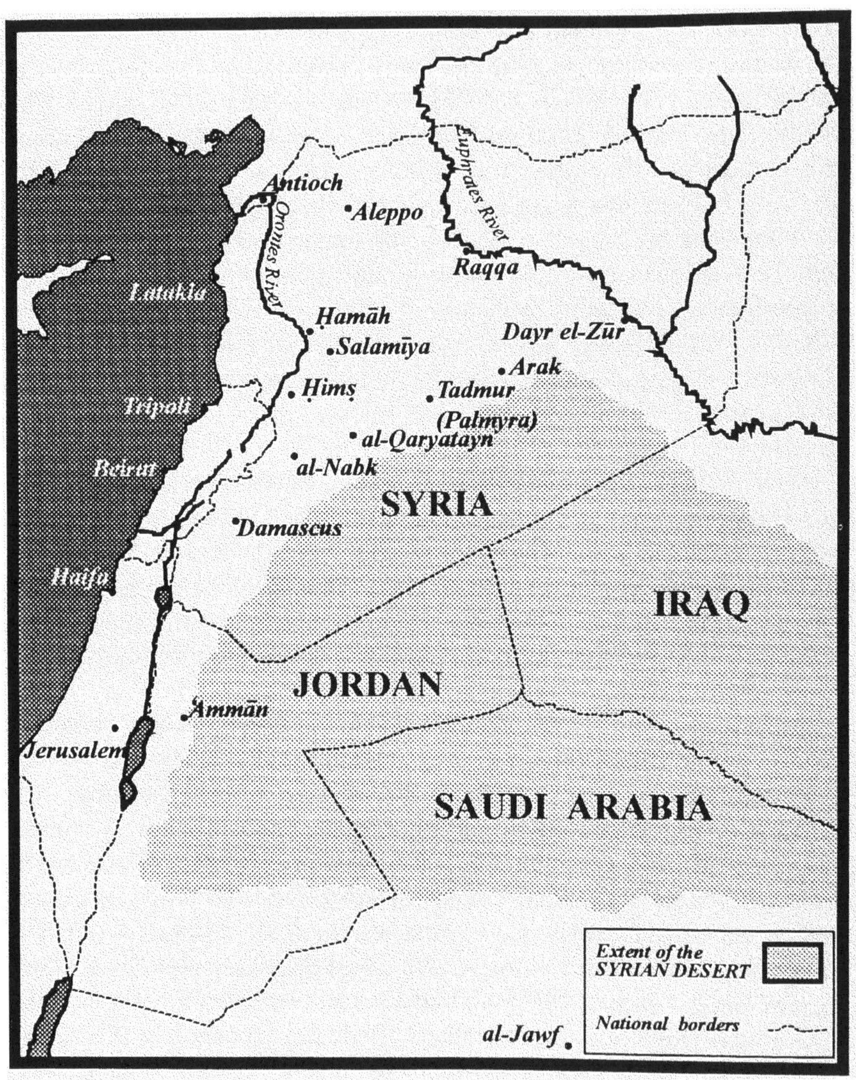

Figure 1: The Syrian Desert and surrounding lands.

drive them off before them into the desert as plunder. When news of this reached the local population, the men would rush to arms and hurry out, sometimes accompanied by elements of the army, to recover their animals from the enemy. Battle ensued when the force caught up with the raiders, and the village folk often displayed such intrepidity and courage that some lost their lives in clashes like this, regardless of whether or not the force succeeded in recovering the stolen animals. Matters finally prompted the late Fayyāḍ Āghā Fāris, *za'īm* of this village near the end of the nineteenth century, as I was told, to take action. A descendant of Arab shaykhs in the Jawf, he proceeded to train and arm some young men of the village, and to dispatch raiding parties against the desert folk themselves in order to deter and punish them. It was then that the Turkish authorities bestowed upon him his title of *āghā*.

After long experience, the people of the Syrian Desert came to realize that the people of this village, called al-Qaryatayn[4] ("the Two Villages," probably because it consisted in ancient times of two villages that merged), were a stern lot unlike other folk in some villages of the interior. Fearful of retribution from them, the bedouins began to form alliances with them, treated them with respect, and even called them *'iyāl majnūna*, "families possessed by the *jinn*," referring thereby to how they were *jinn*, or "demons," in battle.

It is in the bedouin's nature to despise civilization, cities, villages, and everything associated with them. But whether ally or adversary, friend or *qawm*, he made an exception in the case of the people of al-Qaryatayn, as I was told, and regarded them as if they were bedouins themselves. Some of the bedouin tribes even used to permit their daughters to marry young men from the village. Probably another underlying reason for this was that many people in al-Qaryatayn were of bedouin descent.

It happened that the *za'īm* mentioned above died in the first years after the turn of the century, as the power of the Ottoman Empire was also on the wane. The bedouins thereupon reverted to their old habit

---

[4]Al-Qaryatayn is located about 120 kilometers northeast of Damascus. See the photograph of the fields of this town, as seen by Max von Oppenheim in the late nineteenth century, in his *Vom Mittelmeer zum Persischen Golf* (Berlin, 1899–1900), facing I, 268.

of raiding the lands adjacent to the desert, and only ceased to raid the district of al-Qaryatayn after some of their shaykhs and the people of the village reached an agreement providing for the cultivators to pay a *khuwwa*, or "brother-right" to the bedouins. This *khuwwa* was paid to the shaykh of the tribe, who in return for this specified sum undertook to guarantee security from the men of his tribe to the people of al-Qaryatayn whenever they traveled in the desert or in the cultivated areas adjoining it. It became a tax designated for these shaykhs, who imposed it on the people of the villages close to the desert. It was paid as taxes were paid to the state, but it actually guaranteed the people security most of the time, and established between them and some of the bedouins a kind of symbolic brotherhood and friendship.[5]

When the First World War broke out the Ottoman Empire became fearful of an attack on Syria from its desert flank. It therefore began to cultivate the bedouin shaykhs and tried to entice them with grants of land so that they would support the Empire in its effort to suppress the revolt of Sharīf Ḥusayn. At the same time, it undertook the construction of an army post in al-Qaryatayn to guard the frontiers of the settled areas. Hence, our village became a hostel for many allied tribesmen, who were distributed among the local inhabitants. Several of them came to our house, and of their raiding tales, narratives, and evening story sessions I still recall a great deal.

In that same period al-Qaryatayn was also a general marketplace for many friendly tribes, who frequented it—as they continue to do to this day—on the eastward trip into the desert and the westward return from it, and bought from its various shops whatever merchandise or necessities they liked. Trade with the bedouins became an important element in the economic life of this little town and a source of livelihood for many of its people.

Although my father was not a merchant, he did lend money to two merchants in the village and so became their partner. I used to go

[5]In those days, from the death of Fayyāḍ until the beginning of the First World War, the people of al-Qaryatayn had to pay a *khuwwa* to the bedouins: 70 *majīdīs* to the Rwāla, 30 to the Wild 'Alī, 30 to the Ḥsāna, 20 to the Ghiyāth, 16 to the Sbā'a, 20 to the Fid'ān, and 30 to the 'Imārāt. The shaykh of the tribe took the money, and on his part undertook to return to the people of the town anything stolen from it by his tribe. See Alois Musil, *Palmyrena* (New York, 1928), p. 100.

to the shops of these two merchants—Sulaymān al-ʻAṭallāh and Mūsā al-Ibrāhīm—to help them during the summer, and watched them do business with the bedouins. Often I even took over adding up the bills and collecting from the customers. Hence, I talked and associated with the bedouins, became familiar with their dialect, and by experience came to know their simple good-hearted nature. I no longer feared these bedouins of whom every village woman tried to frighten her son; and the time came, when I was a young man, that I expressed my desire to visit them in their camps and to stay, if only for a few days, in the hair tents. I asked my father for permission to go with "Bṭayyin," a bedouin customer of our partners, to the camp of his bedouin kinsmen (I do not remember the name of their tribe) to buy some camels, as some of the village merchants used to do.[6] My father agreed, and I spent with the bedouins several days the impact of which still today cleaves to my soul. In the summer of that same year, I was entrusted with a responsible position in a camel-trading partnership with four other villagers, my task being to keep record of business accounts. We frequently visited the bedouin encampments, selecting camels we wished to purchase, bargaining with their owners over their price, buying them, and then selling them to traders who came from the cities to purchase them.

About a mile from the residential quarters of al-Qaryatayn there are a number of full-flowing springs that pour forth from the base of a small mountain near a large man-made tell, probably the remains of one or several successive ancient villages. The waters gushing from these springs collect into a small lake and then flow out as a river called Nahr Wādī l-ʻAyn, "River of the Valley of the Spring," which should have been called Wādī l-ʻUyūn, "Valley of the Springs."[7] It waters the

[6]It is said of Tagore, the famous Indian poet, that during his visit to Iraq in the reign of King Fayṣal I he averred a similar wish and spent a day in a hair tent among the bedouins. In his youth he declared his wish in a poem that began, "If only I were a bedouin."

[7]This was the largest source of water among the villages on the desert fringe. The Old Testament mentions the region in which it was located by the name of Ḥaṣar ʻAynān. Some modern historians refer to it as the town whose waters are the probable site for encampment of a large army, such as that of Zenobia when she set out to meet Aurelian. It is also possible that later, when Zenobia returned to her capital Palmyra, the town's waters were the encampment site of another great army, that of the emperor Aurelian himself, conqueror of Palmyra. See *Qāmūs*

villagers' farms, which stretch for a distance of five kilometers, and these springs and the river formed by them have been—even after the middle of this century—a favorite haven for bedouins from the desert regions during their westward and eastward migrations. They frequented its water sources when they came to the settled areas from the desert, and also when they returned, perhaps lingering around them for a few days or weeks. These water supplies are most copious, and here one could find thousands of camels on a single day, in one spot on the edge of the desert. The bedouins called this place Umm al-Qalāyid,[8] talked of its sweet, plentiful, and pure water, sang about it in their bedouin poetry, and esteemed it their one watering place equaled by no other. Encampment at these springs by friendly tribes during their eastward and westward migrations continued from those days up until the late 1960s, so it was easy for me to visit them every summer and to associate with them for as long as I liked.

As I grew older, I began to familiarize myself with my fellow villagers whenever I returned home from secondary school for the summer. I discovered that many of them were actually descended of bedouin stock from tribes of the Najd, and that some of them continued to take pride in this bedouin origin. This was particularly true of the *za'īm*'s sons, with whom I shared a relationship of affection and friendship; and though not of bedouin descent myself, I came to sense that merit of tracing one's ancestry to the desert. I still recall that when I entered the American University of Beirut in 1921, the first paper I wrote for the professor of Arabic dealt with desert life and was published that same year in the journal *Al-Mawrid al-ṣāfī*, which he edited.

---

al-Kitāb al-Muqaddas, ed. Buṭrus 'Abd al-Malik, John Alexander Thompson, and Ibrāhīm Maṭar (Beirut, 1964), art. "Ḥaṣar 'Aynān;" also William Wright, *Palmyra and Zenobia* (London, 1895), p. 141. See also Oppenheim, *Vom Mittelmeer zum Persischen Golf*, I, 271, where he cites the names of sixteen springs, most of which continue to be known to this day by those same names. These are the springs of Rās al-'Ayn, Qanāt Qāsim al-'Assāf, Qanāt al-'Awāṣī, 'Aynāta, 'Ayn al-Sukhna, 'Ayn Ḥaql al-Muhannā, 'Ayn al-Muḥammadīya, 'Ayn al-Ṣaghīra, Jubb Qaṭṭāsh, 'Ayn Shīḥa, 'Ayn 'Iṣām, 'Ayn Abū Jidār, Qanāt al-Jiftilik, Qanāt al-Naṣārā, 'Ayn Dayr Mār Ilyān, 'Ayn Jidya.

[8]By this they probably mean that it is a resting place for she-camels that have collars (*qalāyid*) on their necks, or for the herds that come and circle around it like necklaces encircle the neck.

After graduating from the university I spent a year in Ḥimṣ teaching at the school where I had studied in my youth. That was 1925–26, the year of the famous Syrian revolution; and I began to write, as a correspondent for the newspaper *Al-Aḥrār*, articles bearing a slogan borrowed from the desert life I knew and loved.[9] I signed my articles *fatā l-bādiya*, "Young Man from the Desert:"

> There are those whose pleasures in settled lands be,
> But in us, great men of the desert you see![10]

That year I also had the pleasure of coming to know the Ḥsāna shaykh Ṭrād al-Milḥim, one of the wisest and most sagacious of the bedouin shaykhs of that era.

I returned to the American University of Beirut in 1926. But desert life remained in my thoughts, I continued to visit various parts of it and to seek contact with its inhabitants every summer, and some of the desert shaykhs became close friends whom to this very hour I fondly remember and whose friendship I still pride myself on having enjoyed. Of these I particularly recall Amīr Nāyif al-Sha'lān and the late Amīr Fawwāz al-Sha'lān, grandsons of Amīr Nūrī al-Sha'lān, and similarly, Amīr Mut'ib and his brothers, all sons of Fawwāz, and Shaykh Hāyil al-Zayd.

In the University I read the works of Burckhardt, Palgrave, Wallin, Doughty, Musil, Dickson, and many others. And in the 1940s and after I had the pleasant opportunity of meeting Bertram Thomas and H. St. John Philby, the first two explorers to undertake the perilous adventure of crossing the Rub' al-Khālī, and both of whose books I admired. Once I was Thomas' guest for several days while he was director of the Middle East Centre of Arabic Studies established in Jerusalem by the British Army for officers to learn Arabic. I was Philby's colleague when the Department of Arabic Studies at the American University engaged him to give a series of lectures on Arabia, at which time he gave me some of

[9]Most of the articles I was able to gather together from those still in my possession were written for *Al-Aḥrār* between October 1925 and September 1926. I have given these to the library of the American University of Beirut.

[10]A verse by al-Quṭāmī in Abū Tammām, *Dīwān al-ḥamāsa* (Cairo, AH 1335), I, 135.

the books he had written. A third explorer, Wilfred Thesiger, followed Thomas and Philby in the exploration of the Rubʿ al-Khālī. I came to know him through his two books, *Arabian Sands* and *Desert, Marsh and Mountain*. I read his splendid description of how he undertook his adventure, feeling as though I were accompanying him as he crossed those silvery golden sands to which I was no stranger. I had walked along the crests of the dunes of the sand-desert of the Dahnā', which adjoins the Rubʿ al-Khālī, and I had experienced something of that trepidation he felt when he reached the crest of the sands in the region of the ʿUrūq al-Shaybā'.[11] And I understood the deep impression those desert lands had left in his soul when he said in his introduction to *Arabian Sands*:

> Since leaving Arabia I have travelled among the Karakoram and the Hindu Kush, the mountains of Kurdistan and the marshlands of Iraq, drawn always to remote places where cars cannot penetrate and where something of the old ways survive. I have seen some of the most magnificent scenery in the world and I have lived among tribes who are interesting and little known. None of these places has moved me as did the deserts of Arabia.[12]

This, then, is how I came to be attracted by the study of the desert and the life of the bedouins in it, and possessed by a desire to peruse what the desert explorers and travelers had written about it and its inhabitants. So I began to read any books I encountered, by both Arabs and Arabists, on this subject. I was impressed by the risks some of these explorers had faced and by the splendid and profitable works they had written about the desert. But at the same time I was surprised by what other Westerners allowed themselves to write about the bedouins, without a trace of scholarly criticism. After going through most of what these people had written, I was able to distinguish the useless works from the valuable ones, the liar from the man of truth. I realized that some authors were true scholars who had set down for us firm foundations for the study of the desert and the life of its people,

[11] Wilfred Thesiger, *Arabian Sands* (London and Colchester, 1959), p. 132.
[12] *Ibid.*, xiv.

while there were others who knew nothing of genuine desert life other than the little they had heard from some naive informants or from some of the shaykhs with whom they had camped. This was confirmed for me when I asked Shaykh Fawwāz al-Sha'lān about some of these later explorers, as his testimony corroborated the conclusions I had reached concerning them. It is no strange thing that among these Western writers one should find some that were objective and reliable. But even these lacked a knowledge of the dialect spoken by the bedouins and did not much participate in their unique way of life; hence they were unable to penetrate to the essential nature of bedouin life, missed important points, and drew erroneous conclusions.

Another point remains—what it was that compelled me to study nomadism and the life of its people since undertaking my work in the Department of Arabic at the American University of Beirut. As is well known, the Arabic language and classical Arabic literature, the fields in which I conducted research and taught at the American University, first emerged as the product of a wholly bedouin environment that comprised the foundation for Arab urban culture and the primary element that imparted to Arab life many of its distinctly bedouin features. I came to see that for the study of the special and unique features of the Arabic language and classical Arabic literature, it is essential to familiarize oneself with desert life and the various aspects of nomadism. I recognized the need to return to essentials and to proceed from the source itself. Unfortunately, none of the present-day Arab historians or students of our classical literature know much about the desert or are thoroughly familiar with the life of its people.

Fortunately for researchers, the desert areas of the Arab lands still remain the same, as does the life-style of their bedouin inhabitants. Also, the various bedouin tribes still speak dialects very closely related to those which their ancient forefathers spoke, and to the present day they continue to preserve many of the classical Arabic terms and phrases used by their ancestors. Even patterns of expression have remained unchanged for about 1500 years. This does not mean, as some may imagine, that the bedouins speak the classical Arabic that we write today, or that they used to do so. Rather, it means that many of the expressions, figures of speech, and literary devices which appear in the imagery, similes, and metaphors to which we are accustomed in modern literary usage, as well as many of the very words and phrases which we read in our Arabic literature, are borrowed from desert life and to a great extent remain current in the desert milieu. It is impossible to gain a complete and sound understanding of these usages in literary works or anthologies of poetry without familiarizing oneself with desert life and gaining an understanding of the nature of its people, plants, and animals.

With the experience of studying the ancient Arabic literature of pre-Islamic and Umayyad times, I saw that the way of life lived by those Arab bedouin authors was the same as that lived by their modern bedouin descendants, whose literature continues to give expression to desert ways just as that of their forefathers had done. These bedouins today live in tents similar to those which their ancestors have known for 2000 years and more: black goat hair dwellings like the tents of Kedar mentioned in the Old Testament. Stakes are driven in along the tent's sides, guy ropes are pulled taut upon it, and the tent is raised up on wooden poles. Then fires are lit inside to prepare meals for the guests, and in the open space before it meeting sessions are convened to relate news and tell stories. If herbage in the pastures is scarce, or if water disappears from the wadis or pools, the need for sustenance obliges the people of the tribe to move on. Ropes are untied and stakes pulled up, the tents are struck, the howdahs are made ready, burdens are loaded, and the noise rises to a din, with men shouting, horses whinnying, and camels growling:

> In dark night decided they all, kith and kin.
> And with them by dawn rose the noise to a din.
> From one who cries and then one who replies,
> From horses a'neighing, and o'er all camels braying.[13]

Even after they had abandoned their encampments and left their vestiges behind them, there would be another who would pass by the site and stop to examine it. His companion would do likewise, and together they would survey and inspect the remains, however meager, as if they were reading a letter written on an open sheet of parchment. Their

[13]From the *mu'allaqa* of al-Ḥārith ibn Ḥilliza. See al-Tibrīzī, *Sharḥ al-qaṣā'id al-'ashr*, edited by Charles C. Lyall (Calcutta, 1894), p. 129.

camps and what they left behind there when they went to search for food in another land—marks left by tent pegs, camel or horse droppings, holes dug around the tent, places where the camels had been rested and watered, and the vestiges and tufts of wool and hair scattered in the open areas of the remains—were no different from those described in the literature of the ancient poets. They resembled the ruined campsites of ancient poetry, for as time passed after they had been abandoned, the gazelles would return[14] and their droppings would be scattered over the area, just as Imru' al-Qays described the remains of his beloved's camp when he said:

> The dung of the antelopes its expanses adorn,
> Its lower reaches scattered with peppercorn.[15]

I also noticed that today's bedouin poet describes bedouin life just as his fellow poets in pre-Islamic or Umayyad times had done, and does not fall short of his ancient comrades in describing his docile, purebred, and bright-eyed she-camel. He portrays her as fleet-footed, firm in the forelegs, short-eared, and clear-eyed. She is adorned with new saddle gear with silken threads hanging from its sides and beautiful nose-cords tied to its pommels. Such a beast does not differ from those of his ancient colleagues, such as Ṭarafa, Labīd, al-Rāʿī, and Dhū l-Rumma. Just as they did, today's bedouin poet comes to the subject of his praise after first describing the deserts he has crossed and the hardships and travails he has encountered.

I further discovered that the various plants and trees familiar to us in the ancient poetry, such as wormwood, santolina, tamarisk, tragacanth, *samḥ*, acacia, lavender, *ḥawdhān*, and euphorbia, are still to this day well known in the desert. And it is impossible to gain a genuine appreciation of their import in the verse of the ancient poets if one has not actually seen them in their native environments today. Upon seeing them, one understands the imagery of such expressions as "a man of many ashes and of a high tent pole," "hotter than euphorbia coals," "it

---

[14] I witnessed such occurrences in the 1930s; but now, the gazelle has disappeared, or nearly so, from the northern part of the Syrian Desert.

[15] See his *muʿallaqa* in *Sharḥ al-qaṣāʾid al-ʿashr*, p. 3.

is more difficult than to strip the thorns off a tragacanth on a pitch-black night," "sweeter than the fragrance of lavender," and scores of other phrases. And the same applies in the case of desert animals and birds, as well as rainpools, dunes, wadis, and ponds.

All this prompted me to undertake a thorough investigation of the desert, and to write a modest study on bedouin life generally, and on the life of the bedouins of the Syrian Desert and the tribe of Ṣlayb in particular, based on my own personal experience and upon such information in the accounts of scholarly researchers and explorers as I could verify as correct. The Department of Arabic Studies provided me with the opportunity to pursue this research; so I spent a number of years studying the subject anew during the sabbaticals provided to me, visiting bedouin encampments in the lands of Syria and Jordan, and traveling in the desert region of the Aḥsā' along the Arabian Gulf. Then in 1960 I was destined to visit England where, in the Public Record Office, I examined the documents sent by the English consuls in Baghdad, Aleppo, Damascus, and elsewhere to the British Foreign Office concerning matters of trade and communications in the desert and other issues pertaining to bedouin affairs, movements, raids, and genealogies. These documents cover the last seventy years of the nineteenth century, certain earlier years, and some years of the early twentieth century. All of these are confidential reports which researchers were for many years unable to examine. In this study I have also included photographs taken by myself and some others taken by my friend, the photographer Mr. Manoug, who accompanied me into the desert one year.

Books and Studies on Desert Affairs

Before discussing nomadism and the bedouins, we would do well to note that the authors who have written books or studies in Arabic on the nomads and the desert, from the dawn of the era of the Arab Revival until the present day, are far fewer than those who wrote in languages other than Arabic. And of these Arab authors, fewer still actually penetrated the heart of Arabia and lived with its bedouins as the European explorer-scholars did. There were those whose official duties in various Arab lands compelled them to come into contact with aspects of the bedouin milieu, but even these did not live in the desert with the nomads or mix with them as some of the European scholars did. Nevertheless, it must be acknowledged that in the twentieth century there have appeared valuable Arabic books, however few, the contents of which are predominantly concerned with the investigation of bedouins and nomadism and with the study of the conditions of desert life in various regions. And this is not to mention the scores of articles that have appeared in newspapers and scholarly journals, as well as the many works of novelists, scholars, and political and literary figures who have written on the history of the Arab countries and on Arabian affairs. Among such works are the *Jazīrat al-'arab fī l-qarn al-'ishrīn* by Ḥāfiẓ Wahba (Cairo, 1925), Fu'ād Ḥamza's *Qalb jazīrat al-'arab* (Cairo, 1933), the *Khiṭaṭ al-Shām* of Muḥammad Kurd 'Alī (Damascus, 1925–28), and Amīn al-Rīḥānī's *Mulūk al-'arab* (Beirut, 1924–25).

There are other books whose authors have confined themselves to bedouin life in a general sense, or in a particular region. One of the earliest of these was Iskandar Yūsuf al-Ḥāyik's little booklet *Al-Badawī*, printed in Beirut. The work is undated, but it would appear from its contents that it was published in the early years of this century. It discusses the bedouins of Sinai and their manners, customs, poetry, and proverbs; and it appears that al-Ḥāyik compiled it from articles he had published in the newspaper *Mir'āt al-gharb*. Next to appear were two books by Khayr al-Dīn al-Ziriklī, *Mā ra'aytu wa-mā sami'tu* (Cairo, 1923) and *'Āmān fī 'Ammān* (Cairo, 1925); Archimandrite Būlus Salmān's *Khamsat a'wām fī sharqī l-Urdunn* (Ḥarīṣā, 1929), in which the author considered the administration of justice among the bedouins in Jordan and discussed their tribes and culture; and the work of 'Awda al-Qusūs, *Kitāb al-qaḍā' al-badawī* (Amman, 1929). 'Ārif al-'Ārif, *qā'im-maqām* of Gaza in the days of the British mandate, was the author of three books: *Al-Qaḍā' bayna l-badw* (Jerusalem, 1933), *Ta'rīkh Bi'r al-Sab' wa-qabā'iluhā* (Jerusalem, 1934), and *Al-Ḥubb wa-l-sharī'a wa-l-taqālīd 'inda l-badw* (Jerusalem, 1944). 'Ārif's works are particularly distinguished for their accuracy and scholarly method; in writing them, the author made use of many of the official documents and statistics available to him on the tribes around Beersheba. After him came the barrister 'Abbas al-'Azzāwī, who authored a two-volume work, *'Ashā'ir al-'Irāq*, the first volume (Baghdad, 1937) considering the ancient and modern bedouin tribes, and the second (Baghdad, 1947) discussing the Kurdish tribes. The first volume comprised a detailed comprehensive study of the bedouin tribes of Iraq, investigating their genealogies, sub-divisions, and customs, and became a source used by many who wrote after his time. It also contained a special chapter on the tribe of Ṣlayb, to which we shall have the opportunity to return. Al-'Azzāwī later went on to add to his book other volumes (Baghdad, 1956), which in the end totalled four.

There then appeared Aḥmad Waṣfī Zakarīyā's *'Ashā'ir al-Shām* in two volumes (Damascus, 1945–47). This book I will shortly discuss in some detail, for in my view it remains, even now, the most comprehensive Arabic work about the Syrian tribes and desert life. Zakarīyā was for seven years the director of the agricultural school he founded in Salamīya, a sub-district of Ḥimṣ. During that time he was destined to come into close contact with the life of the bedouins, especially those of the Mawālī and Ḥadīdīyīn tribes. After that he spent nine years traveling in government lands along the edge of the desert, and read many books by Western explorers, especially the French. He also wrote a two-volume work entitled *Al-Rīf al-sūrī* (Damascus, 1374–76/1955–57), in which he devotes further study to some of the bedouin tribes.

After that came the publication of 'Abd al-Jabbār al-Rāwī's book, entitled *Al-Bādiya* and published in a first edition and then a second with many additions (Baghdad, 1949). Al-Rāwī had been a desert administrator in Iraq since 1930 and then, in 1945, became a commisioner of police, in which capacity he compiled the above-mentioned book. The work's research revolves around the northern desert adjoining Iraq, Syria, Jordan, and Saudi Arabia, and consists of eight main chapters full of useful material, especially in the parts concerning the bedouins of Iraq and in the documents and texts pertaining to treaties and agreements. Oddly enough, the book makes no comment whatsoever about the tribe of Ṣlayb, although it was a tribe that had branches in Iraq and also special distinguishing features that attracted the attention of many researchers.

Next to appear was the work *Al-Badw wa-l-'ashā'ir fī l-bilād al-'arabīya* by 'Abd al-Jalīl al-Ṭāhir (Cairo, 1955), consisting of lectures which he delivered at the Institute for Advanced Arab Studies. This was followed by a thesis on the Syrian tribes and their settlement prepared by Aḥmad al-'Akkām in 1951 under the direction of Dr. 'Adnān al-'Ajlānī, accepted by the Faculty of Law at the Syrian University in Damascus and authorized for publication. The author later published a more complete and expanded version of his work, which contains important statistics, documents, and lists of some of the official directives issued in connection with the agreements concluded between tribal leaders and the local authorities from the Mandate period up until the author's own time. In it al-'Akkām gives a valuable account of the internal structure of the migratory tribes in different parts of the Syrian Desert, tribal organization, and the names of the most important tribes. He also discusses a number of criminal cases and the bedouin principles that govern legal proceedings in such instances. The book contains a long list of the wells, in various regions, from which the tribes water their livestock, and makes an appeal for their restoration. He also discusses directives issued by the Syrian government, beginning in 1944, when the Agency for Tribal Affairs was formally transferred to it. His book also contains a detailed draft bill of law pertaining to the tribes.

There also appeared a book by Makkī al-Jumayyil entitled *Al-Badw wa-l-qabā'il al-raḥḥāla fī l-'Irāq* (Baghdad, 1956). Al-Jumayyil was a director of records at Mosul in 1931, served as an administrator in various parts of Iraq, assumed in 1944 a post responsible for tribal commissary matters, and continued as an official of the state administration until 1950. His experiences inspired him, as he said, to write down his observations, the final product of which was a work dealing with topics covered in a symposium on social studies sponsored by the fourth session of the Arab League. These subjects were the bedouins and the tribes and the impact of their way of life on the evolution of living patterns, the sedentarization of the nomads, the social and health services available to them, and finally the organization of social welfare among them. He later wrote another book, *Al-Badāwa wa-l-badw fī l-bilād al-'arabīya* (Sirs al-Layān, 1962).

Among more recent writers are Father George Sābā and Rūkas ibn Zā'id al-'Azīzī, in the second chapter of whose *Ṣafaḥāt min al-ta'rīkh al-urdunnī wa-min ḥayāt al-bādiya* (Amman, 1961) we find an exhaustive study of desert affairs, family and social life among the desert folk in general, and bedouin culture as reflected in their proverbs and poetry. There is also Mu'ayyad al-Kaylānī, whose book *Muḥāfaẓat Ḥamāh* (Damascus, 1964) referred to the bedouin tribes that camp in the lands of that district, and to some of the wild animals that live there.

Finally, there is the book *Al-Badw wa-l-badāwa* by Drs. Muḥyī l-Dīn Ṣābir and Louis Kāmil Malīka (Sirs al-Layān, 1966). Its chapters (the first three by Ṣābir, and the last two by Malīka) discuss factors of cultural change in the bedouin way of life, settlement programs, newly established communities, the bedouin personality, and issues of psychological and social research in the field of Arab nomadism. These topics are generally treated in a modern scholarly fashion, but in certain places the book displays prejudice against most of the non-Arabs who wrote about bedouins and nomads, and neglects to mention many who were pioneers in the study of desert life and the bedouin personality. Dr. Ṣābir groups the authors into three categories, the first of which is that of the Orientalists and the Western explorers. Although such authors as Lawrence, Jarvis, Raswan, Thesiger, and Dickson spoke in solicitous terms of their friendship for the bedouins, their goal, Ṣābir claims, was to serve colonial interests. He states that most of their works revolve around the bedouin way of life, the structure of the tribe and of authority within the tribe, marriage customs, and nutrition; and he makes mention of their inclination toward such manifold subjects as beauty, the woman, life in the desert, and raids on caravans of merchants and pilgrims, their attitude in relation to governments, and so forth. Although Ṣābir concedes that this does not mean that everything they wrote was useless and devoid of merit, and that some of their material reveals keen insight and profound learning, he then goes on to say: "But of particular importance to an evaluation of what they wrote is the fact that this work was based upon the direct contacts between them and the bedouins, which comprised the relationship, as we have made clear, between colonizer and colonized."[16]

Although it is not my intention to defend Lawrence, Thesiger, Dickson, or Jarvis, whom he cites as typical authors of the first category, it seems to me that Dr. Ṣābir has been excessive in his judgment against them. Did all of the Western explorers who studied desert affairs un-

[16]Muḥyī l-Dīn Ṣābir and Louis Kāmil Malīka, *Al-Badw wa-l-bādiya* (Sirs al-Layān, 1966), pp. 124–25.

dertake their work in the cause of colonialism? Did Alois Musil write his books with the aim of serving colonial interests? At the time of his travels he was acting on behalf of the Austro-Hungarian empire, and with definite imperial tasks in hand; but he published his books as a Czech citizen beginning in the 1920s, after the demise of the Habsburg regime, and in English with the assistance of the geographical society of the United States, a country which did not yet have significant political or strategic interests in the Arab world. And in any case, it would be difficult to imagine what imperial interests would be served by the depth and range of scholarship set forth in these books. A similar case was Doughty, whom the British consulate in Damascus denied permission to undertake his dangerous project to study bedouin life; he proceeded at the risk of his own life, and bequeathed to us the most influential book on the subject. Analogous cases were those of H. St. John Philby, and the Finn George August Wallin. As for the individuals whom Ṣābir names and assigns to the second and third categories, I do not believe, despite my esteem for them, that they would consent to take precedence over those I have just mentioned in elucidating the bedouin personality as it really is. One should refrain from such generalizations and from recourse to flattery.

There yet remains *'Ashā'ir al-Shām*, the book to which I referred above. It is the most comprehensive of these works, and in it the author investigates the geography, history, and culture of the Syrian Desert, manners, customs, and law in bedouin society, and the genealogies and lore of the tribes in each administrative region and district. In his two volumes, Zakarīyā has cited many of the medieval Arab authors who composed studies about the bedouins in a general sense, or about their history, genealogies, and tribes. He did not neglect to mention the names of some of the European explorer-scholars and to point out their merit and precedence in this field of research. He had this to say in his long introduction:

> Even on these topics concerning ourselves, we are entirely dependent on the European explorers and Orientalists, for it is they who continually endure the hardships, dispute and discuss the issues, and pursue the evidence, historical events, and accounts of unusual occurrences. For the

> proof of this, it would suffice to peruse only the most outstanding topographical, historical, social, ethnographic, and other studies they have written. They left not one of our deserts without exploring it, not one of our tribes without visiting it, not one of our ruins without seeing it, and no lore, narratives, or poems about the bedouins and bedouin life without collecting them, explaining them, and commenting upon them—all that with an alacrity and interest that can only inspire admiration and respect. It is no secret that they were men with a burning desire for critical research and rigorous accuracy, striving to write and record, and readily willing to disseminate, publish, and provide useful information for others. These explorers and Orientalists wrote numerous books in various European languages, works which we will in due time enumerate. We have read them with much reflection and admiration. If only I could begin to list the names of these eminent scholars; to mention the places they penetrated and explored in the deserts of the Arabian peninsula, extending from one end to the other, even to the Rubʿ al-Khālī; to relate the hardships and perils they endured from rock and sand, heat and cold, hunger and thirst; and to describe the works they composed, graced with drawings, maps, and figures. To see for oneself how excellent their descriptions were and how accurate their interpretations, one need only scratch the surface of the topics they considered. I would say that were I to begin enumerating such details, the space of this entire book would be too confining for me to do so.[17]

His words reflect a great deal of fair-minded esteem for the services rendered by these explorers, although he is inclined to the sort of exaggeration required by his artistic and solicitous style. This is particularly true of his comments concerning the collection, elucidation, and discussion of bedouin poetry, of which I find few traces in most of the works the explorers left to us. In his introduction the author makes

[17] Aḥmad Waṣfī Zakarīyā, *ʿAshāʾir al-Shām* (Damascus, 1363–66/1945–47), I, 5–6.

special reference to some of these explorers: the Englishwoman Lady Anne Blunt and her husband Wilfrid Blunt, Miss Gertrude Bell, the Czech Alois Musil, the Frenchman Montagne, the German Baron von Oppenheim, the French Colonel Müller, Captain Raynaud, Lieutenant A. de Boucheman, the Dominican friars Jaussen and Sauvegnac, and the Jesuit priests A. Poidebard and Henri Charles.[18] Then, in a special chapter, he reconsiders this group and gives detailed accounts of them one by one, adding to them the Swiss traveler Burckhardt, whom he should have mentioned first since he preceded all the others.[19] And despite the esteem he shows for the deeds of these European explorer-scholars and his acknowledgment of their merit and precedence, there were many others whom he fails to mention, perhaps because he had not seen their works or was unaware of them.

Perhaps this would be the best place to mention the most important of those whom he passed over in silence. Among the most eminent of these was the man who in the view of many was the most famous author, without exception, ever to write about bedouin life, and who preceded most of the others: the greatest explorer of all, Charles Doughty. His great work *Travels in Arabia Deserta*, in two large-format volumes of about 600 pages each, is even now considered the best book ever written on bedouin life; and despite its age and high price, more than fourteen editions of the work have so far been published. Lawrence had this to say about it: "I have studied it for ten years, and have grown to consider it a book not like other books, but something particular, a Bible of its kind ....The more you learn of Arabia, the more you find in *Arabia Deserta* ....It is the true Arabia, the land with its goodness and evil, its smells and dirt, as well as its nobility and freedom ....Doughty's completeness is devastating."[20]

Also overlooked in Zakarīyā's book was another of the early travelers, W.G. Palgrave, who wrote a two-volume work entitled *Personal Narrative of a Year's Journey in Central and Eastern Arabia*. In his own time many Western newspapers carried the reports contained in these volumes, and there was controversy over certain matters which

---

[18] *Ibid.*, I, 6–7.

[19] *Ibid.*, I, 11–15.

[20] See Charles M. Doughty, *Travels in Arabia Deserta*, new edition (London, 1936), I, 17, and the rest of Lawrence's Introduction, pp. 18–28.

he mentioned in his book. There were also Carsten Niebuhr, author of *Travels Through Arabia* in two volumes; D.G. Hogarth, author of *The Penetration of Arabia*; and Bertram Thomas, who wrote *Arabia Felix: Across the Empty Quarter* and other works. De Gaury wrote *Arabian Journey and Other Desert Travels*; Colonel T.E. Lawrence compiled his *Seven Pillars of Wisdom*; and R.H. Kiernan authored the book *The Unveiling of Arabia*. We should also mention the work of Major Jarvis, *Three Deserts*, Christina Grant's *The Syrian Desert*, Carlo Guarmani's *Northern Najd* (translated from Italian into English), Robert Cheesman's *In Unknown Arabia*, and Douglas Carruthers' *Arabian Adventure: To the Great Nafud in Quest of the Oryx*. Richard Burton wrote his *Personal Narrative of a Pilgrimage to al-Madinah and Meccah* in three volumes in the first edition; William Wright discussed many aspects of bedouin affairs and history in his *Palmyra and Zenobia*; and Carl Raswan wrote a number of books and articles. There are also others which we will have occasion to mention in the text of this book; the reader will find references to the dates and places of publication for all of them in the bibliography.

It will be noticed that all of these works I have mentioned appeared in English. It would seem that Waṣfī Zakarīyā did not know this language, hence it was not easy for him to consult books written in it on the subject of bedouin life. But it must be noted that the gentleman realized this, for at the end of his study he says concerning the bedouin corpus: "There are probably other books and essays which I have not seen, but it will suffice for me to mention those I knew about and consulted." We must also point out that he cited a great number of books and articles written in Arabic from the earliest generations of Arab authors up until his own day.

It remains for us also to mention that there were other explorers, as well as scholars specialized in zoology, botany, and sociology, who wrote after Zakarīyā's time about life in the desert. Of these, David L. Harrison, Harold Patrick Dickson, H. St. John Philby (known to the Arabs as al-Ḥājj 'Abd Allāh Philby), William Lancaster, and Wilfred Thesiger are notable examples. There were also military men with close connections with bedouin matters who wrote books and compiled special reports, men such as Major Glubb and Major Jarvis, whom we mentioned above, Peake Pasha, and others.

Add to this the scores of important articles written by specialized researchers who visited the deserts and published their studies in well-known scholarly journals of both the West and the Arab world, in addition to the articles to which Waṣfī Zakarīyā refers. Among these are the articles of Carl Raswan and Henry Field in Western journals, and those of Ṣā'igh, Qasāṭlī, Makarius, al-Rīḥānī, 'Izz al-Dīn, and others in *Al-Muqtaṭaf* and elsewhere. Likewise, there are manuscript theses written for specialized diplomas or advanced degrees in some of the universities of Syria, Lebanon, and elsewhere in the Arab world, and secret manuscript reports submitted to several Western states by their consuls in the Arab East in the nineteenth and early twentieth centuries. Of these latter, those submitted by the British consuls in the Arab East to the Foreign Office are worthy of special note. For some years now researchers have been permitted to examine these documents, formerly kept at the Public Record Office in Chancery Lane in London and now available at the Foreign Office Archives in Kew. Last but not least, there is the *Handbook of the Nomadic, Semi-Nomadic, Semi-Sedentary, and Sedentary Tribes of Syria*, compiled by the British command during the Second World War to serve as a reference guidebook for the exclusive use of the military officers who drove the Vichy French out of Syria and Lebanon. The work contains accurate and important information on the bedouin tribes in Syria, some of this material having been taken, in my view, from *Les Tribus nomades de l'état de Syrie*, the book compiled by the French authorities in the Mandate period and referred to by Zakarīyā. The English work has an important introduction, perhaps from the pen of Colonel Glubb himself, who was known among the bedouins as Abū Ḥunayk, the "man with the (disfigured) palate," referring to the marks left by a bullet wound received during the First World War.

In closing this section I must emphasize the precedence and merit of these explorers and scholars, and reiterate the admiration for the efforts they made and the hardships they endured for the sake of their work, characterized by perilous adventures and adversities, and also by love of learning and research, that these works might be passed on to posterity. There are two worthy of particular admiration: Charles Doughty, whom the bedouins knew by the name Khalīl al-Naṣrānī, and

Alois Musil (Shaykh Mūsā al-Rwaylī); their books are unquestionably the best ever written on the subject of the desert.

It yet remains for me to refer to the writings of Carl Raswan, or Riḍwān al-Rwaylī, as he preferred to call himself, and especially to his book *The Black Tents of Arabia*. This work is full of confusion, fantasy, and deception. Much of his information has no foundation in truth, and some of the rest he copied from his predecessors and attributed to himself. I noticed this when the book was first published, and I asked Amīr Fawwāz al-Sha'lān about some of the statements made about him in Raswan's book and about the relationship between the two of them. Fawwāz denied all of "Riḍwān's" claims to a brotherly relationship between them, as well as the stories he told about going on raids with Fawwāz. This is in addition to his fantastic tale about Fāris al-Shammarī's love for the beautiful Ṭ'ayma—such stories deserve to be in fables and novels. It will suffice here for me to cite as examples his statements that Amīr Nūrī al-Sha'lān had 82 children, all but one of whom died; that the girl named Ṭ'ayma used to hunt gazelles; that Fawwāz raided the Sbā'a bedouin tribe and captured some horses from them, but then returned the animals to them because they had committed no act of aggression and because Fawwāz had not advised them of his intention to raid them. Raswan would further have us believe that Amīr Fawwāz sought the advice of soothsayers before setting out to hunt; that Fāris' mother wore clothes of cashmere; that the river of Tadmur (Palmyra) branches out from its source into hundreds of streams, gardens, and groves; that from the back of his charger the bedouin can cast a stone from his sling at a flying bird and hit it more accurately than he can with a rifle. All of these statements are untrue, and to them may be added his ignorance of the meaning of the few expressions he cites from the bedouin dialect. He claims that *ḥibbnī*, for example, means "O my beloved," while what it means in the bedouin dialect is "Kiss me." He also maintains that the word *qawwa*[21] is a bedouin greeting and means *kawwak*, that is *qawwāka*, "Strength to you." Similarly, he alleges that Amīr Nāyif, father of Fawwāz, was killed. The truth of the matter is that

[21]In reality, this is a greeting used by some in the region of the Aḥsā'. As for the bedouins of Syria, they use *kawwak*.

Figure 2: Charles Doughty (Khalīl al-Naṣrānī), author of the greatest book on the bedouins in general.

Photo credit: American Geographical Society Archives. Reprinted by permission.

Figure 3: The Orientalist Alois Musil (Shaykh Mūsā al-Rwaylī), Austrian author of many works on the bedouins and northern Arabia.

he suffered from a long persistent illness and died in the town of al-Qaryatayn, where he was also buried (his remains were later removed). It was during that illness preceding his death that I met him. It is strange that elsewhere Raswan states that Nāyif died suddenly in unusual circumstances, fulfilling a prophecy a woman had made about him.

I would not have bothered to speak of the writings of this man, had I not noticed that some researchers discussing desert affairs refer to his works and quote some of the things he says in them. I must also mention that while Amīr Fawwāz rejected the stories of Raswan, he was full of praise for "al-Shaykh Mūsā al-Rwaylī." Not content with this, he even sent for his uncle Saṭṭām so that he could tell me of Shaykh Mūsā's knowledge and veracity on bedouin matters.

I would also like to comment on the work of Harold Dickson. His book contains useful information on the life of the bedouins, and the author has made efforts to verify what he reports. But he is so inaccurate in his vocalization of well-known Arabic expressions, which he has taken orally from his informants and records in Latin characters, that he disfigures their pronunciation and betrays his ignorance of what he was reporting.[22] He is also mistaken when he claims that when the November rains fall in Kuwayt, bedouin boys dash out into the desert to dig up truffles.[23] As we shall see below, truffles do not appear until February.

There remains William Lancaster and his recently published work *The Rwāla Bedouin Today*. He too has committed a number of mistakes in relating information reported to him by the bedouins. He maintains, for example, that Ṣaqr ibn Mijḥim al-Sha'lān told him about the *khuwwa*, and that it accrued to this man because he used to own part of the town of al-Qaryatayn.[24] First of all, the *khuwwa* is not paid in consideration of property owned in a village, but rather in return for protection extended to the inhabitants of a village or to a clan. Furthermore, al-Qaryatayn is a town too large for any bedouin shaykh, whoever he may be, to own part of it. And when Lancaster

[22]H.R.P. Dickson, *The Arab of the Desert* (London, 1949), pp. 337–38.
[23]*Ibid.*, p. 60 (twice on this page).
[24]William Lancaster, *The Rwāla Bedouin Today* (Cambridge, 1981), p. 122.

asks to whom Ṣaqr sold a piece of al-Qaryatayn, I can assure him that al-Qaryatayn has never in its history been a property offered for sale.

These are some cursory observations on the most important sources and reference works that have appeared concerning bedouin life in Arabia, particularly in the north. There are also books describing the travels of employees of Western trading companies. These works provide important information on the history of the bedouins and their way of life since the sixteenth century, this in reference to the then-prevailing conflict between Holland, Italy, England, and France for control of the trade routes to India and a monopoly on trade with the East. By way of illustration only, we can mention four of the English travelers who in detailed essays, since then printed and published, described their journeys between Aleppo and Baṣra in the years 1745 to 1751. These were William Beawes (1745), Gaylard Roberts (1748), Bartholomew Plaisted (1750), and John Carmichael (1751).[25]

This would perhaps be the best place to indicate the reasons why Westerners, and especially the English explorers, took such interest in Arabia and its desert lands. When the Western states became aware of the treasures and products to be obtained in the Orient, they began to compete among themselves for ways to open trade routes to the east. It was then that England began to send its envoys to seek out routes across Arabia to India. The Suez Canal had yet to be opened, hence recourse to a land route was generally favored or chosen over the alternative of the long sea route around the Cape of Good Hope in southern Africa.

The Meaning and Character of Nomadism

The Arabic word for nomadism, *badāwa*, derives from the root *b-d-w*. Hence it is said in the classical dictionaries that a people "became bedouin" (*badā al-qawm badwan*), meaning that they went out to the desert (*al-bādiya*). The saying in Prophetic Tradition, *man badā jafā*, means that he who lives in the desert becomes of uncouth nomadic character. The verb *tabaddā* means that the man to which it refers went to live in the desert and became one of its people. The verb

[25]See the texts of these travel accounts in *The Desert Route to India*, edited by Douglas Carruthers (London, 1929).

tabādā denotes that he behaves like the desert folk. The *bādiya* is equated with the sand-desert, or similarly, the opposite of the settled lands; and the phrase *qawm bādiya*, "a desert folk," means nomads, a folk not settled. Nomadism, *badāwa*, means the way of life and living in the desert, the opposite of settled life. The bedouins, or *badw*, are the people of the desert, that is to say, the opposite of the settled folk.

Derivations from this root, in the sense pertaining to the desert, appear only twice in the Qur'ān. The first is in Sūrat Yūsuf (12), vs. 100, where Joseph says, "... when he brought me forth from prison and brought you out of the desert;" and the second occurs in Sūrat al-Aḥzāb (33), vs. 20, where we read, "If the confederates come, they will wish they were desert folk among the bedouins (*al-a'rāb*)." This word *a'rāb*, in the sense of "bedouins," occurs ten times in the Qur'ān.

Nomadism, or residence and life in the desert, requires much wandering from place to place in search of water and pasturage. The life of the bedouins in the desert is based on raising and tending livestock, and in past ages it also included raiding and plundering.

The scene of nomadism is the desert and the fringes of the adjoining regions around it. Life and animal husbandry in the desert oblige the bedouins to adhere to a special way of life, and impart to them distinctive customs and traits that must be appreciated in order to understand the variety of special problems that bedouins face. In other words, the life of the bedouin Arab differs from that of his brother, the settled Arab, despite the ties and relations between them. There is even a disparity of lifestyles and in certain customs among the bedouins themselves, between those who tend camels and those who raise sheep. The optimum living and reproduction conditions for the livestock of the camel-tending nomads are provided only through long-ranging searches for food and sojourns in the grazing lands of the desert during the winter season. The sheep-herding nomads and their livestock, on the other hand, rarely resort to the desert heartland as a source of food, and that only when the lands on the fringes of the settled areas dry up and there remains no pasturage for their animals. Even in this case the sheep-herding bedouin does not venture very far into the desert with his livestock, but rather hovers along its peripheries.

Types of Nomadism

Nomadism expresses itself in various degrees over a long graduated scale, the first level being in contact with settled life and occasionally having strong direct relations with it, and the other extreme being the type of nomadism so firmly fixed in the sand-desert that hardly any disruptive upheaval, however powerful, can dislodge it from its home territory. Although one who studies the nomadic life can distinguish many intermediate shades, there are three main types of nomadism. The first, at the lowest end of the scale, is a pure and firmly established type based exclusively on the raising of camels, those who practice it wandering rapidly back and forth between the desert and the fringes of the settled regions. It is at this level that nomads are most likely to disdain to submit to authority and order, and to reject any trend toward sedentarization unless it is forced upon them.[26] It is this form of nomadism that Ibn Khaldūn had in mind in his study of the phases of nomadism and man's natural inclinations, claiming that due to their inherently barbarous nature, these sons of the desert are "a people of pillage and ruination who plunder whatever they can lay their hands on without a fight or risk of danger, and then flee to their haven in the desert waste."[27] This natural inclination of theirs he regards as a negation of civilization and antithetical to settled life:

> The aim of all of their customary activities is traveling and the seizure of property, which likewise comprise the antithesis and negation of the tranquility from which civilization arises. For example, the bedouins' only need for stones is for something upon which to set their cooking pots; so they carry them from buildings, which they demolish in consideration of their own need for the stones. Likewise, their only

[26]In his book *Peace in the Holy Land* (London, 1971), p. 23, Glubb Pasha commits the same error that many contemporary historians and Bible commentators make when they consider that the greatest aspiration in the soul of every bedouin is to gain a piece of land to settle upon. This is entirely wrong, for even in the present day the nomadic way of life is deeply engrained in these people. Many governments have tried to settle the bedouins, only to encounter stubborn resistance.

[27]Ibn Khaldūn, *Al-Muqaddima*, edited by E.M. Quatremère (Paris, 1858), I, 269.

> need for wood is for something upon which to erect their tents and to make into tent-pegs for their dwellings, so they tear up roofs for that purpose. Hence, the very nature of their existence is the antithesis of building, which is the basis for civilization. Such is the general case with them. Further, it is their nature to plunder whatever other people possess, their subsistence consisting of anything across which the shadows of their lances fall. They know no limit at which they would stop in taking what other people possess; on the contrary, any time their eyes fall upon some property, commodity, or implement, they snatch it away.[28]

The second type of nomadism is one that for a variety of reasons developed from the first, and represents a form midway between pure nomadism and the semi-settled type. Such nomads make their livelihood from camels and sheep, and for this reason they wander and move about to a lesser extent than do their above-mentioned cousins who practice the pure nomadism.

The third type of nomadism is a semi-sedentary type, and is based on the raising of livestock consisting of sheep and goats and only a few camels. These bedouins have firm ties with the peoples in the settled villages and in the cities. Among them are those who have become only semi-nomadic and would readily take up settled life, or let us say, a semi-settled folk who have begun to see the positive aspects of sedentary life. They have begun to incline toward the equanimity, tranquility, and ease to be had in a settled existence. They have even tried to assimilate themselves to settled life, so that with the passage of no more than one or two generations their descendants will have fully incorporated to it and be counted among the sedentary folk. It is from this level of nomadism that the process of natural sedentarization begins. The scions of this level gain some rudimentary knowledge of agricultural skills; and some of them begin to purchase and exploit agricultural lands, having recourse to peasant labor from among the village cultivators in the first instance, and then to bedouins from their own tribe later on. Among the sons of this generation there emerges

[28] *Ibid.*, I, 270–71.

the circle of those who will become the shaykhs of later generations, men to whom the governments of various eras award grants of lands and wells along the desert frontiers. Today they reap great profits from these lands through agriculture, but in times past such lands and wells were farmlands subject to attack by raiders. It should be noted that the shaykhs of all the tribes were generally the bedouins most inclined to sedentarization. This was due to their control of certain agricultural lands, wells, and springs, as well as to their dealings with the towns and, if only for brief periods of time, to their living in them, especially in the cases of those shaykhs who represented their tribes on government representative councils or those who had agricultural contacts with the government and its various agencies.

The Ethnic and Social Significance of Nomadism

The life of the Arabs has strong roots in nomadism; and even today the Arab sedentary mentality is firmly bonded to that of the Arab bedouin. Hence, anyone trying to study the situation of the Arab world and to understand the peculiarities of the Arab mentality and the distinguishing features of Arab life must return to the sources of these traits and features in the desert and in bedouin life. The Arab does not know himself, or understand his unique qualities and the range of his capacity for development, if he does not know that the way he lives has its roots in the desert. The tribal spirit, and proceeding from it, family solidarity, ambitions of group leadership, personal inclinations, and disputes over access to authority and leadership—all these and other matters trace their origins back to the organization of the tribe and to the influence of bedouin life. Likewise, many Arab customs and conventions originate in well-known bedouin traditions still followed today. Among these are issues of vengeance, honor, hospitality, boasting, derogation, generosity, the sanctity of the guest, chivalry, and bravery.

Many Arabs dwelling in the villages on the periphery of the desert trace their ancestry back to well-known bedouin tribes, their forefathers having brought to these villages, where for one reason or another they sought refuge or were compelled to take up residence, many of their customs and conventions as well as certain features of their bedouin

Figure 4: A general view of a bedouin camp, with a market of white tents of the settled folk set apart from the rest of the tents.

dialects. The nature of nomadism in times past encouraged certain new bedouin elements coming from the desert to bring pressure to bear on the old bedouin elements closely attached to the settled lands, forcing them to settle down and to seek refuge in sedentarization. The entrance of many bedouins into the sedentary life is accordingly an enduring and uninterrupted process, as also is the influential impact of these newcomers on the way the settled folk live.

When Islam first emerged, it did not look favorably upon the *a'rāb*, the bedouins.[29] But the caliphs of early Islam and leaders of the factions were heavily dependent upon them in their campaigns of conquest and assimilated some of them to urban Arab life, and they became an important element in the early Arab polity. The caliph 'Umar ibn al-Khaṭṭāb is reported to have recommended them to his followers in

[29]Sūrat al-Tawba (9), vss. 97–98, 101; Sūrat al-Fatḥ (48), vss. 11–12.

these terms: "I bid the caliph who succeeds me to be mindful of God and solicitous of the early *muhājirūn*. . . .And I urge him to do well by the bedouins, for they are the root of the Arabs and the substance of Islam."[30] In fact, they comprised an important part of the armies of the conquerors, and also of the armies of such groups as the Khārijites, among others, that rebelled against the caliphs.

On the other hand, the bedouins were not entirely incorporated into settled life. In most Arab lands they still comprise a numerous social minority that must be taken into account in any study of Arab life, its current practices, and the problems that impede its advancement. Up until recent times, this social minority in certain regions accounted for a quarter or more of the total population. A minority of such magnitude in some places cannot be ignored by anyone trying to study the social and political problems of the Arab world. The number of bedouins is apparently not increasing as compared to the rate of population growth in the Arab countries. But it is not unlikely that with improved child care and the eradication of the various diseases from which they suffer, the proportion of bedouins will increase from what it previously had been, especially since the Arab countries themselves have taken an earnest interest in fighting some of the diseases that ravage both village and nomadic populations. One example is malaria, which is transmitted by a species of mosquito that breeds in the marshes frequented by the bedouins during the summer. If the causes of this and other diseases were eliminated, many bedouins would be saved and their numbers would increase.

Similarly, during the international campaign to eradicate smallpox, which succeeded in wiping out the disease in 1977, the bedouins themselves took the matter of immunization seriously and had their children vaccinated in the villages or by practitioners who made the rounds of the bedouin camps for this purpose. Many bedouin patients have even begun to come into the towns for treatment in local hospitals. The proportion of bedouins in certain hospitals close to them has risen so high that they account for almost a third of the patients in the entire

[30]Ibn Sa'd, *Kitāb al-ṭabaqāt al-kabīr*, edited by Eduard Sachau *et al.* (Leiden and London, 1904–40), III.1, 245–46. See also al-Jāḥiẓ, *Al-Bayān wa-l-tabyīn*, edited by Ḥasan al-Sandūbī (Cairo, 1351/1932), II, 35.

hospital.[31] Whatever the precise number of bedouins may be, the fact remains that they comprise a not insignificant proportion of the population in all of the Arab countries. It is impossible to promote reform, development, and advancement programs in the Arab world without taking this important social minority into account and subjecting it to full and comprehensive study. Such an investigation should seek to achieve an understanding of the nature of the bedouins' way of life and also consider the changes that have impinged upon that life, the way the bedouins have responded to the new attitudes and strange trends that have arisen in everyday life, and the impact that this new life has had upon them.

The Economic Significance of Nomadism

The sedentary population consumes large amounts of the meat of kinds of animals raised by the bedouins. Had the village folk in times past been granted conditions of complete security and sufficient water supplies in the areas adjoining the desert, they would have been able to raise all of the kinds of livestock required by their economy. But at any rate, the bedouins are better than settled folk at searching and exploring for places where water and pasturage can be found. And at times when certain kinds of this livestock comprised an important element in the diet of the settled population, the life of the desert had an important impact on economic life in general.

The meat eaten by settled folk is mostly of animals raised by the bedouins, especially mutton and goat meat, followed by that of the camel, which even today still comprises an important part of the village diet in certain parts of Syria and other Arab countries. It would be difficult to provide here specific figures for the amount of livestock the desert supplies to the settled areas in every Arab country, but up until recent years it undoubtedly provided a large part of what was consumed in settled areas. All of the Arab countries import meat from other nations, and had it not been for the bedouins and their livestock, this

[31]From the records of the district hospital in Nabk, Damascus district, Syria, for the years 1953–55. At that time the hospital was administered by Danish missionaries.

trend would have begun earlier and on a much larger scale. Indeed, some Arab countries, notwithstanding their own livestock production and imports from other Arab countries, still import a great deal more from neighboring nations such as Turkey and other countries, this in addition to the varieties of tinned or frozen meat they import from various foreign countries.

Modern agricultural equipment and means of transportation have served to diminish the importance of the camel for carrying loads, plowing, and threshing, but it still remains an important element in agricultural life in remote rural areas. And its meat is to the present day still a commodity in demand in some Arab circles. Its price, like that of such other kinds of meat as mutton and goat, is established in the price schedules imposed by municipalities on the butchers, even in some of the most important Arab cities.

The hair of the camel is of some use, but not enough to assign it much economic importance. Of the small amount collected in the desert areas of Syria, the bedouins use part to make the panels of their tents (the *khayma*), and sell the best hair to merchants in the villages. It is then carded, spun, and woven into beautiful camel's hair abas. For camel hides there is a brisk market. Large numbers of camels may be slaughtered on ʿĪd al-Aḍḥā; the bedouins take as many hides as they need to make *qurab* (their large waterskins), containers, and buckets, and sell the rest to town and village merchants, who tan the hides and make long-wearing shoes from them.

Sheep are of considerable economic importance, firstly for their meat and the meat of their young, large numbers of which are brought to the towns and slaughtered. Secondly, their wool is sheared every year, carded, and most of it exported to foreign countries.[32] Third, their milk is sold in curdled form in nearby villages; it is occasionally made

[32]The reports of the British consuls to their ambassador in Istanbul and to the Foreign Office in London make it very clear that in the mid-nineteenth century the British interest in bedouin matters was based primarily on two considerations. Firstly, they were anxious to guarantee security in the Arabian deserts in order to protect the trade route to India. Second, they sought to facilitate the purchase of wool by their own merchants, who would buy it from brokers for cloth merchants in Britain. They also wanted to facilitate the purchase of thoroughbred Arabian horses.

into cheese, but most often it is used to produce clarified butter, or *samn*. Indeed, many people in Syria, Lebanon, and Iraq until recently relied on bedouin *samn* for their cooked dishes. Nomadism thus has been of economic significance in that it has provided the sedentary population with much of the meat and milk products it needed for its diet. Consumption of meat in most parts of the Arab world has increased to such an extent that it has become necessary to increase livestock production in order to meet the demand.

Horses are now raised only in small numbers in the desert, although the bedouins are keenly interested in their breeds and pedigrees and some of them buy thoroughbreds.[33] The raising of horses has shifted to semi-nomadic lands and to certain settled areas near the desert where it is easy to feed them. There are two fundamental factors behind the camel-raising bedouins' current lack of interest in raising horses. The first is the cessation of raiding, once an important motive for acquiring horses. Secondly, during dry years it is a heavy expense to feed horses, this due to the rising cost of grain, especially barley, which must from time to time be fed to a horse to supplement its diet. Camels, on the other hand, receive everything they need from the pasturage upon which they graze in the desert.

Some bedouins raise goats, and some goatherds frequent the desert fringes; but it would be a mistake to think that the goat is an animal that can thrive and multiply in the desert. Goats are mountain livestock, and those who raise them are for the most part villagers or semi-nomads who have connections and ties with the villages, as one sees in the villages of Syria and Najd. But whether we count the goat with other desert livestock or not, it does have a considerable influence on desert life, since it is goat's hair that is woven into the panels that are sewn into tents for the bedouins. There are villages along the edge of the desert, and others within the settled regions, that base their eco-

[33]One can conclude from the consular reports that horses were quite numerous among the bedouins in the nineteenth century, as they offered the most efficient means to raid and plunder. They were also the bedouins' means for overtaking those who had raided or plundered them, in order to recover whatever they could of the camels and sheep that had been taken from them. Bedouin strength was for the most part gauged by the number of their horses. According to some of these reports, certain tribes had no fewer than 500.

nomic life on weaving, and especially on weaving goat's hair into cloth panels which they sell to the bedouins, who stitch them into tents. This is in addition to the wool they take from sheep and weave into abas that are sent for sale to the desert.

There is also the truffle, the fungal plant that grows in the desert and along its fringes. The bedouins collect truffles and sell them to the people of nearby villages and towns. In certain seasons they become so plentiful that they are either shipped or tinned—becoming a commodity of the canning industry—to be sold in all Arab cities.

The Military and Political Significance of Nomadism

One point pertaining to nomadism yet remains for me to consider, and that is its military and political dimension today. In both respects, it has been a significant factor in the history of the Arab countries, especially during early Islamic times. Political authority relied upon the support of the bedouins in the early decades, and then in Umayyad times was compelled to resort to their aid in its struggle against opponents rising against it in other regions, to curry the favor of the nomads in defense of the empire, or to fight them and subject them to its authority and influence. The desert and its people were accordingly of considerable importance in this respect. As we shall see when we consider the history of the tribes that came to the Fertile Crescent, the struggle between the bedouins and the political authorities of the settled folk was unceasing through the entire span of the Islamic Middle Ages until the first third of the twentieth century. In pre-Islamic times, the Roman emperor Augustus Caesar sent an army, led by Aelius Gallus and comprising 11,000 Roman troops and confederates, to suppress the bedouins and to subdue Arabia as far south as Najrān. The bedouins had only primitive weapons, but their deserts, with their sands, their level plains and rugged mountains, their heat and cold, and the ease with which their native sons maneuvered around the emperor's armies when they were forced to flee—all these factors compelled the Roman forces to give up the idea of remaining long in Arabia, and to withdraw in failure and defeat. Even in recent times, when Ibrāhīm Pāshā tried to subdue the desert and its warriors in the nineteenth century, his struggle against them continued for about twenty years, but to no avail. Indeed, it was the desert that could not be defeated.

Today, however, the desert has lost the influence it had in the days before the automobile and the airplane, and the military and political significance of nomadism has disappeared. There are but few exceptions to this. Bedouins allied to the political authorities in different Arab countries are sometimes used to guarantee the security of communications routes between them. The nomads help to protect nearly extinct wild animals, such as the oryx and the gazelle; to deter hunters, guard stations are built and manned by troops recruited from among the very bedouins who roam the desert fringes and heartlands. Bedouins are also used to guard the frontier region, of which the tribes have an intimate knowledge from grazing their animals on its pastures and migrating through its territories.

The Pillars of Bedouin Life

Pure archetypical nomadism is sustained by the tending of camels and is based upon four primary pillars. If any one of these collapses, the structure of bedouin life is shaken and its organization upset. These pillars are the following:

1. A desert area, the *bādiya* or *ṣaḥrā'*. I prefer the former term here, due to its affinity to the word bedouin—in Arabic *badawī*—recalling the bedouin's comings and goings across the whole expanse of the *bādiya* in search of pasture and water.

2. Camels (*ibil*, *jimāl*),[34] and she-camels, to transport the bedouin and his family and to carry his tent and its furnishings. He herds them from one source of sustenance to another in search of water and food, lives off their milk and meat, and warms himself over a fire fueled by their dried dung—the same fire over which he cooks the meals offered to his guests.

[34] [Deleted here is a note on the Arabic terms for "camel" used in the Arabic text, but which will not occur in this translation.]

3. A tent, the fabric of which is woven from goat's hair. It is in his tent that the bedouin takes shelter and finds protection from winter cold and the scorching heat of summer.

4. The bedouin himself, whose life is firmly bound to the first three pillars—desert, camels, and tent—and who turns them to his advantage.

It is impossible for there to be any genuinely bedouin life lest it uphold all four of these pillars simultaneously. There are those who claim that it was once possible to do without camels and to rely upon the donkey. But the pure bedouins in the Syrian Desert live primarily on the milk of she-camels, which is their essential source of strength. The camel also endures thirst in the desert better than the donkey, and moves more easily on its sandy ground. Hence, although the donkey is renowned among the Arabs for its sturdiness and ability to endure hardship, it is upon these four primary pillars that the structure of bedouin life is founded. I have accordingly decided to make my study in this book revolve around these pillars, which I will consider one by one.

THE FIRST PILLAR
THE DESERT

By the camp of one of my cousins,
In a distant wilderness of sand,
By her there sprout up *qayṣūm* and *shīḥ*
Over the expanse of low-lying land.

'Umar ibn Abī Rabī'a

CHAPTER I

THE DESERT HOMELAND

Defining and Describing the Desert

Because of the distinction drawn above between the terms *bādiya* and *ṣaḥrā'*, I do not think that the Arabic dictionaries can be of much use to us in defining what a desert is. Under the root *b-d-w* in the *Lisān al-'arab*, we read as follows:

> The *bādiya* is so called because of its open and uncovered character. A *barrīya* is also called *bādiya*, because it is open country in full view.

And under the root *ṣ-ḥ-r* we find:

> A place said to be like a *ṣaḥrā'* is expansive, and a people are said to be folk of the *ṣaḥrā'* when they go out to a vast open space where there is nothing to conceal them from view. A land called a *ṣaḥrā'* is generally level terrain, with both smooth and rugged places, but no prominent hills. When the people go out from the settled areas to the grazing grounds of the *ṣaḥrā'* lands, they are called bedouins (*badw*).

It is obvious from this that there is no great difference between the two terms. Indeed, some of the dictionaries draw no distinction at all between them; in such works we find that "the *bādiya* is the *ṣaḥrā'*, and the *ṣaḥrā'* is the *bādiya*."[1]

---

[1]See Ibn Manẓūr, *Lisān al-'arab* (Beirut, 1374–76/1955–56), under the roots *b-d-w* and *ṣ-ḥ-r*.

Figure 5: A hobbled mare and her colt in al-Daww, part of the Syrian Desert.

When one of these two words is mentioned, the first thing that comes to the mind of the Arab listener is a vast expanse of desolate arid land of shifting sands under the burning heat of the sun, of dunes or sandhills stretching for hundreds of miles. There are, in fact, vast sand-deserts in Arabia, Africa, and elsewhere in which there are only rare traces of life. No one comes to these unknown lands, except for certain bedouins forced by circumstances to live there, and a few daring explorers. On the other hand, there are deserts which, although not devoid of sands and dunes, are nonetheless inhabited by people and animals. Nor are they arid wastes. Rather, they contain plants and trees, and along their fringes there are oases containing an astounding array of vegetation and wildlife.

The alluring and fascinating qualities of some of these desert areas have attracted many seekers of knowledge or adventure. Eminent explorers and specialists in anthropology, zoology, and botany have been lured to the desert, risking their lives and exploring the unknown regions of many of these lands. There were those who survived, but some also who perished. So many memoirs have been recorded and books written that it has now become difficult for the researcher to gather together everything that has been written in the last two centuries on certain specific desert regions and the life in these lands.

Today the deserts are a focus of world attention because of their resources, primarily oil and petroleum by-products, and because of their vast extent, which according to some scholarly estimates comes to a total of approximately eight million square miles, or about one seventh of the land surface of the earth. If part of this land could be reclaimed, it would provide living space for hundreds of millions of people that will otherwise crowd the world in only a few years' time. This is a point of special importance now, when it has become possible for man to desalinate the waters of the seas near the deserts to produce fresh water for irrigating these lands. It is interesting to note that most of the great deserts—the Sahara in North Africa, the Rubʿ al-Khālī (the Empty Quarter), the Dahnā', and the Australian Desert, for example—lie along seacoasts. And oddly enough, most of the earth's deserts lie not at the equator, but north and south of it, at or beyond the Tropic of Cancer and the Tropic of Capricorn. And most of these deserts are in the Arab countries.

Returning to the terms *bādiya* and *ṣaḥrā'*, I should point out that in this study I will deviate from the definitions we find in the dictionaries. The word *bādiya* I restrict to the desert lands that are not all of sand, and where the ground in many places would be suitable for cultivation if water supplies were readily available. The term *ṣaḥrā'* I use only in reference to the sand-deserts full of dunes, where vegetation only rarely grows; if any plant life at all is to be found there it consists of the thorn tree, which lives on the plains and slopes of this kind of desert. Hence, and in accordance with this new usage, the *bādiya* is a vast expanse of open level steppeland, perhaps interrupted by occasional hills and prominences, with its soil sometimes mixed with and covered by a film of sand. In such terrain one finds no flowing streams, no extensive vegetation, and no trace of the cities and villages of settled civilized life except for those found here and there in the isolated oases.[2] But even in such desert land itself, one can still find good soil in which trees take root and grow tall enough to provide shelter for animals seeking

[2][In keeping with the distinction drawn by Professor Jabbur, this translation will render *bādiya* as "desert," and *ṣaḥrā'* as "sand-desert."]

protection from the sun. Plants grow in such shaded areas, and in certain seasons there is good grass that can support the camel and many other animals, especially such wild animals as the "wild cow," ostrich, gazelle, and onager. Indeed, there are plants that will take root even in the sandy lands of the desert, and some of these grow as high as large shrubs.

In his book *Three Deserts*, Major Jarvis said that he used to own three feddans of sandy desert land near the garden of his house in al-'Arīsh. He enclosed the land with a wall, and for a period of fourteen years protected it from goats and camels. Over the surface of that land there spread a variety of wild scrub bushes, some of them growing about eight feet high and twenty feet in diameter. The soil under and between the bushes was eventually covered by a layer of decayed leaves, with the result that the sand became so stable on the ground that the strongest gales did not move it. "This," Jarvis says, "gives one an idea of what Sinai must have been before the Arab came to lay it waste with his grazing flocks." He also observes:

> There is no doubt that the responsibility for the sand-dune area which has advanced over a mile on a 120-mile frontage during the time I have been in the Peninsula rests at the door of that accursed animal, the goat, ably assisted by his ruthless companion, the camel, and connived at by their feckless owner, the Beduin Arab.[3]

One of the usual characteristics of the desert is that rainfall is rare and occurs only on a few days during the winter season. Nevertheless, this small amount of rainfall is sufficient to water sprouting plants and trees, or to allow the seeds scattered in its soil to germinate and grow, presenting one with the radiant splendor of greenery spreading across the surface of the soft ground. Indeed, it is not uncommon for such rainfall to send torrential streams pouring down the watercourses, leaving pools of water behind them in the bends and depressions at the bottoms of the wadis. At some places in the desert, such torrents pour onto isolated expanses of level ground, where the water collects into pools called *khabrāt*. The bedouins, seeking water for themselves, their

[3]C.S. Jarvis, *Three Deserts*, cheap edition (London, 1941), pp. 152–53.

camels, and the other animals they own, come and camp around these pools.

The desert climate is harsh during the day, hot and dry, the relative humidity sometimes dropping as low as about seven percent. The level then rises during the night, and water vapor condenses as drops of dew that after dawn one can see soaking the ground and revitalizing the herbage. There is so much of this that plants can almost gain sufficient water from the dew collecting on their leaves. In spring, some women go out to places thick with herbage and collect the dew in their waterskins; and livestock that grazes on such herbage may sometimes go, if only for a short while, without finding water, as we shall see when we take up the subject of desert animals and birds. Some researchers claim that in certain deserts this dew condensed on the surface of the ground and on the leaves of plants reaches the equivalent of 25 centimeters of annual rainfall.[4]

The desert heat is intense, in the summer sometimes rising to more than 50° C. in the shade, and at night falling to about 20°. The combination of dry climate with the extremes and erratic fluctuations in temperature during the summer permits only certain special kinds of trees and plants to live in the desert. These are thorny or thorn-like types (if I may be permitted this term), the leaves of which do not have a large surface area through which water would evaporate during the intense heat of spring and summer. Animals must be of those particular species that can live from these plants, both green and dry, and that can go without water for a longer period of time than other animals can endure.

Over a long period of time, this harsh natural environment forces the animal or bird that lives in the desert to evolve and adapt, even with respect to the color of its skin or feathers. With its coloring having become similar to that of its surroundings, the weak is camouflaged from the strong, thus protecting the species or ensuring its survival. The gazelle, sand grouse, and ostrich, for example, are all protected by the similarity of their coloring to that of the ground in the desert. Even predatory animals, which would perish in the desert if finding food was inordinately difficult for them, have developed col-

[4]A. Starker Leopold, *The Desert* (New York, 1961), p. 102.

orings that enable them to catch enough prey to survive in the desert lands.

The desert environment may be harsh and life in it miserable, but its climate is generally salubrious. As al-Maqrīzī reports:

> ʿUmar ibn al-Khaṭṭāb related that he asked Kaʿb al-Aḥbār about the natural characteristics of the lands and the innate dispositions of those who lived in them. Kaʿb replied: "When Almighty God created things He made for each of them a partner. Intellect said, 'I am setting out for Syria;' and Discord said, 'And I go with you.' Fertility said, 'I am setting out for Egypt;' and Disgrace said, 'And I go with you.' Hardship said, 'I am setting out for the desert;' and Salubrity said, 'And I go with you.'"[5]

In the Umayyad period, the caliphs used to send their sons to the desert when pestilence broke out in the city. Hence, by reason of this harsh desert environment the bedouin himself is compelled to adapt his way of life to harmonize with his surroundings. This desert thus exerts its influence on his customs and manners, as we shall see when we consider bedouin matters in this book.

Deserts and Sand-Deserts of Arabia

In Arabia there are many desert areas suited to the life of the bedouin and from which he derives his name. As already mentioned above, one tends first to think of such lands in terms of sand-deserts. The largest of these is the Rubʿ al-Khālī (the Empty Quarter), the famous sand-desert in southern Arabia extending from ʿUmān in the east to the Yemeni frontier in the west and to Najd in the north. Its area is about twice that of all of France and many regions of it remain unknown, despite the writings about it by Western explorers, most notably Bertram Thomas, St. John Philby, and Wilfred Thesiger.[6] To

[5] See al-Maqrīzī, *Al-Mawāʿiẓ wa-l-iʿtibār bi-dhikr al-khiṭaṭ wa-l-āthār* (Cairo, AH 1324), I, 79.

[6] In former times its fearsome prospect was described in the verse transmitted from the poet al-Marār ibn Saʿīd al-Faqʿasī:

It was as if the hearts of its guides

the north it merges into the second sand-desert, the Dahnā', which lies to the west of the Aḥsā' region, runs parallel to it and to the Arabian Gulf, and connects the Rub' al-Khālī to the sand-desert of the Nafūd. Some geographers consider the Dahnā' as part of the Rub' al-Khālī. The third is the sand-desert of the Nafūd, which covers the northern Ḥijāz as far as the Gulf of al-'Aqaba. According to some estimates, there is enough sand in these deserts in Saudi Arabia alone to encircle the entire world with a belt of sand nine meters wide and one meter deep. There is also the sand-desert of Sinai, to the north and west of al-'Aqaba, and finally the northern sand-desert, the major part of which is called the Syrian Desert, or Bādiyat al-Shām.

Although it does contain broad expanses of sand here and there, the Syrian Desert is not a sand-desert comparable to the other four. Indeed, in many parts of it there is good soil, where many more kinds of herbage will grow than in the other sand-deserts, making it a paradise for the bedouin seeking a place to stop and graze his animals. The Syrian Desert spreads itself out in the form of a great triangle. One base angle lies above the Iraqi city of al-Baṣra on the Arabian Gulf, and is connected to the other, above the Gulf of al-'Aqaba on the Red Sea, by an imaginary line cutting across Iraq, the Kingdom of Saudi Arabia, and the Hashimite Kingdom of Jordan. The third great angle (in the shape of an arch) lies west of Tadmur in Syria and near the peripheries of the Euphrates in the Jazīra. As already suggested, this desert should more properly be called by this name in order to distinguish it from the sand-deserts mentioned above. Traditional Arab usage divides the northern desert into three desert zones: the Syrian Desert in southern Syria, the Jazīra Desert adjoining Turkey in northern Syria, and the Iraqi Desert in southern and western Iraq. In these three deserts there is little rain, the annual average not exceeding a few centimeters. It is more plentiful in the north than in the south, and usually occurs only in the winter, though some rain may occasionally fall in the autumn or early spring. Southeasterly or northwesterly winds are conducive to

---

Were suspended on the horns of gazelles.

See Aḥmad ibn Fāris, *Mutakhayyar al-alfāẓ*, edited by Hilāl Nājī (Baghdad, 1390/1970), p. 144. Here we read that the bedouins say of something that is unstable: "It is on an ill-fated footing," "It is caught amongst the claws of misfortune," and "It is on the horn of a gazelle."

rainfall; but when the wind shifts to the north, the clouds disperse and rain ceases.

All these desert lands are extremely hot in the summer, the temperature occasionally reaching the upper 50s on the Centigrade scale.[7] In winter it becomes cold and the temperature falls to nearly 0° C., especially in the north, where in some years snow falls and part of it lays. Musil mentions that he witnessed snowfall in the desert in early December,[8] and I know from my own experiences that one year in the 1960s the snow killed many head of livestock that were far from the camps of their owners. A similar disaster occurred during the winter of 1972–73. Within the same season there is considerable variation between the day and nighttime temperatures, particularly in the spring, when the difference can be as much as 30° C. At night during the summer, the temperature is moderate and there are refreshing breezes.

During the summer and late spring in some of these desert areas, there may occur storms and whirlwinds that blow the dust and sand with practically blinding force. Whirlwinds will sometimes rise in a column to a tremendous height from the ground, rapidly moving along and engulfing within themselves whatever vegetation and soil they may scour up from the ground. I have actually seen many such storms, but they are hardly of the force so eloquently attributed to them by Professor Waṣfī Zakarīyā:

> Between heaven and earth rage the whirlwinds and sandstorms of the desert, whirling like a pillar of tremendous height and stirring up a tempest of dust and soil. They are truly harrowing weather phenomena, and among the most frightening spectacles of nature that could ever rob one of his night's sleep. You see it approaching from the bowels of the sandy waste or the heart of the desert steppe, at first almost resembling a line drawn across the horizon, then rising and swelling into the air, its winds intensifying to driving blasts that carry the soil and dust away, whirling

[7]Dickson claims that in the desert of Kuwayt the temperature reaches 170° F., or more than 76° C., and in the shade 120° F., or about 49° C. See his *The Arab of the Desert*, pp. 258, 358.

[8]Alois Musil, *In the Arabian Desert* (New York, 1931), p. 20.

> it along the ground and lifting it up into the air, a twisting gale encompassing huge vortices of different hues, varying according to the color of the soil and the places where they originated. The storm blows and lifts soil from tens of kilometers away. It appears like a wall towering to the clouds in the sky, soaring, surging, and looming closer, and then suddenly it engulfs you and plunges you into a dark cloud, a deep sullen shimmering red. Caught out of doors, there is no possible way for you to avoid its horror and torment. By now you can hear the pattering of sand grains and the echo of their constant turbulent scratching. You see fine specks of soil surging and colliding together, grains and specks that lash the face like a whip, parch the throat, and sap the strength of one's soul. The rising dust blinds the eyes, and the animals wander in lost confusion... Those who live in Dayr al-Zawr and other such places in the lands of the Euphrates recognize the magnitude of these gales and storms by their characteristic features and the effects they have.[9]

I recall that once I took off on a flight from Baghdad as it was engulfed by a sandstorm; the storm eclipsed the city from our view, and we could see nothing but a cloud of sand. In the early years of this century, D.G. Hogarth claimed that the desert extended right to the settled areas, and that it even "licks the very walls of Baghdad."[10]

As I have already mentioned, the Syrian Desert is the desert with the most productive land, the richest plant life, the best pasturage, and the most people. There are many oases in the north, where it borders the settled lands of the Fertile Crescent, as well as villages known as the villages of al-Manāẓir. These oases were once populous villages or small towns, some of which have disappeared, their ruins obliterated and forgotten, while others survive to this day. One of these is al-Qaryatayn, which had a population of 4000 souls at the turn of the century and today has close to 20,000 inhabitants; and others are al-

[9]Zakarīyā, *'Ashā'ir al-Shām*, I, 31–32. In the 1950s, a storm of this kind caused a Syrian Dakota aircraft carrying about twelve passengers to crash south of Aleppo. All on board were killed, including the son of a friend of mine in al-Nabk.

[10]D.G. Hogarth, *The Nearer East* (New York, 1915), p. 260.

Sukhna and Arak. In ancient times, there were some desert settlements, such as Petra in Nabataean times and Palmyra in the days of Odenathus and Zenobia, that flourished to such an extent that they became the capitals of great kingdoms. Were it not for the constant conflict between nomadism and settled life, the continual depredations of the bedouins in centuries past, the menace they posed to security and settled life, their pillaging of fields and villages, and the resulting impoverishment and emigration of the villagers, there would have arisen in a large part of this desert an agrarian civilization similar to that in certain areas of the Fertile Crescent itself. In fact, the Romans exploited parts of this desert to the benefit and glory of their empire; and their example was followed by the Umayyad caliphs in Syria, who undertook building projects the ruins of which can still be seen today.

There is a Roman road (*stratum*) connecting Khān al-Shāmāt and al-Ruṣāfa and today known as *Al-Ṭarīq al-raṣīf*, "the Paved Way," many paved stone sections of which still survive and extend for long distances. There is another road, linking Damascus and Tadmur, that was built during the reign of Diocletian; and yet another road intersects the route of the pipeline north of the town of al-Ghunthur, between al-Furqulus and the T-4 pumping station. About 60 kilometers east of al-Qaryatayn there is a Roman dam stretching between the mountains of al-Bārida and al-Naqnaqīya. This dam once held back the water flowing down from the two mountains and the hills beyond them. It rises to a height of eighteen meters above ground level, with a width of 18.5 meters at its base in the wadi bed, and about seven meters at the top, easily wide enough for the passage of two cars. It extends for a length of about 320 meters between the two mountains, so that the waters flowing in from the mountains and the plains and trapped behind the dam would form a lake that, when filled, would amount to millions of cubic meters,[11] not 140,000 only, as Zakarīyā states.[12] These waters were used during the spring, summer, and autumn to irrigate the lands and fields of the settled regions downstream at al-Daww al-Fasīḥ, near Qaṣr al-Ḥayr al-Gharbī, and traces of the canals are still visible today.

[11]See the detailed study of this dam in A. Poidebard, *La Trace de Rome dans le désert de Syrie* (Paris, 1934), pp. 188–89.

[12]Zakarīyā, *'Ashā'ir al-Shām*, I, 65.

There are remains of other canals in other locations, and it is claimed that one of these connected with the Orontes River and was intended to irrigate some areas of the eastern desert. So it is surely not strange that some of the ancients should have populated and settled various parts of this Syrian Desert. Among them were those who dug the pits in the centers of the depressions where the rainpools form, features we can still see in the desert, where rain and floodwaters collect and where the bedouins come to water their livestock in the late spring months when rainfall ceases.

Today the dam and the land around it are owned by Amīr Nāyif al-Sha'lān, the grandson of Amīr Nūrī al-Sha'lān. When he gained possession of it, it was a desolate place called Kharbaqa.[13] With the passage of centuries, the outlets of the dam had become blocked, the lake bed had become filled with soil, debris, and silt, and water began to pour out over the top of the dam. Then it happened that the bottom of the dam was breached, with the result that water began to leak and pour through the wall of the dam and gradually to erode away with it some of the dirt and sediment. This created in the bottom of the filled-up lake a channel, with many twists and gullies, called the Kharbaqa. From end to end of the sediment in the lake bed, the channel widened until it became like a wadi, extending back from the dam for a distance of 200 meters or more, and bordered on both sides by accumulated soil to a height equal to the depth of the lake, or eighteen meters. As it was full of gullies, ravines, and twisting bends, the bedouins gave the place the name Kharbaqa, "the Fissured Land." I saw it while it was in this state, and noticed at the bottom of the inside of the dam an inscription from the Roman period and a well-constructed covered channel for fresh water flowing from a spring, probably the one today known as 'Ayn al-Bārida at the edge of the cultivated area. Amīr Nāyif concluded an agreement with some of the villagers allowing them to cultivate the part to which the gullies had not yet extended. This was rich soil and produced fine yields of cotton and other crops, and it therefore occurred to him to exploit the eroded area as well. So he closed the breach in the dam, and after some years the land began to refill with the soil washed into the lake bed by tor-

[13]Not Harbaqa, as Zakarīyā states in *'Ashā'ir al-Shām*, I, 64.

rential streams from the plains and hills. When I saw the lake bed after that, it was full of soil that had dried out in the summer, its surface cracking in beautiful geometric designs. The *amīr* considered taking up with the Syrian Ministry of Agriculture the idea of restoring the dam and the lake to their condition in Roman times and in the caliphate of Hishām ibn ʿAbd al-Malik, so as to provide water for the lands around Qaṣr al-Ḥayr al-Gharbī (excavated by the French archaeologist Schlumberger). This could be done by digging large outlets, causing all of the soil and silt to wash away and cleaning out the lake bed when the torrential streams were in flood. He then proposed to close the breaches and construct controlled outlets that would allow water to flow through to the expansive flatlands downstream during the summer.

This is a project worthy of the state's consideration, although considerable problems would be posed by silting during the winter floods and rapid water evaporation in the summer. In my view there is space to build still other dams in locations among the eastern mountains of Syria as a means of conserving the flood waters of winter for use during the summer to irrigate the lands of the nearby plains. It is worth noting that the ancients made use of similar dams, even in the heart of the Ḥijāz.[14]

This vast Syrian Desert includes regions that differ with respect to their soil, pasturage, and climate. Detailed consideration of Syrian desert geography and discussion of the distinctive features of each area are beyond the scope of this study. The explorer Alois Musil has already dealt with such matters in detail in his various books about the desert; he even went so far as to measure and record the temperature almost every day, summer and winter, that he spent in the desert lands. Waṣfī Zakarīyā also gave a general description of the desert in his book on the

[14]K.S. Twitchell states that near al-Ṭā'if he saw a dam, still in excellent condition, that had been built during the reign of the Umayyad caliph Muʿāwiya and his son Yazīd; it bears a Kūfic inscription dated 58 AH/677–78 AD. See Twitchell's *Saudi Arabia* (Princeton, 1947), p. 38. Similarly, Philby refers to the existence of two dams, both of which he described and one of which he photographed. These are the Ḥasīd Dam and the Qaṣr al-Bint Dam, in the mountains near Khaybar, about 165 kilometers from Medina. See his *The Land of Midian* (London, 1957), pp. 22–29.

Syrian tribes, and Professor Eugen Wirth has included much valuable information in his geography of Syria.[15]

Here, however, I cannot avoid commenting, albeit quickly, on the Jazīra region lying on the left bank of the Euphrates, east of Aleppo. This was an important area of the Syrian Desert that until recent times remained a bedouin domain and the scene for their raids; the strife between the various tribes, including ʻAnaza, Shammar, and others, was of such violence that in former times the area became practically, if not entirely, devoid of inhabitants. Today, however, with the introduction of modern agricultural methods, this Jazīra region of the Euphrates has begun to produce a harvest so rich that it has placed Syria in the forefront of the grain-producing nations of the Arab East. The same can be said of the al-Manāẓir region around the eastern oases—Arak, al-Sukhna, Tadmur, and al-Qaryatayn—where the village folk have begun to expand their fields into the vacant lands of the wadis and the dry beds of the torrential streams. There have also begun to appear certain state-sponsored industries. Phosphates, for example, are mined from the eastern mountains overlooking the desert close to ʻAyn al-Bārida, and farms and villages have been established nearby.

Among the principal areas of this desert are Wādī Sirḥān, which extends as far as the town of al-Jawf in Saudi Arabia, and the Ḥamād, the heartland of this desert and the area to which the bedouins come during the winter in search of pasturage. You can see them coming there from all the peripheral areas we have mentioned, and then returning during the summer when the rains stop, the rainpools dry up, and the livestock has consumed whatever plant life parts of the area had provided.

The ground of the Syrian Desert is for the most part calcic soil conducive to the growth of herbage and trees, although in certain places the soil is partially mixed with sand. In fact, in some regions of the desert I have seen during the spring season species of flowers the likes of which, before I began to frequent the desert, I would never have expected to see in that land. I have seen plant life at al-Daww, where during the spring the waters of torrential streams flow down from the mountains overlooking the desert and flood the land

[15]Eugen Wirth, *Syrien. Eine geographische Landeskunde* (Darmstadt, 1971).

to a depth of one meter, most particularly on the flatlands, where there accumulates a thick layer of sediment deposited there by the streams. At the bases of some of these prominences, such as Jabal al-Ghaṭṭūs, Jabal Kaḥla, Jabal al-Ṭiwāl, Jabal Khunayzīr, Jabal Qannāṣ, and 'Ayn al-Wu'ūl, there are many species of flowers, among them a variety of the lily of the valley that one botanist claims is not found anywhere else in the world. Some of the European explorers who visited these areas did not fail to mention the many kinds of plants they contained and to record their names in their writings. I have used a number of these to compile a table of the names of all those I could mention. There were those who discovered species previously unknown among Western scholars, and so gave them new names.

Doctor George Post, a professor at the Syrian Protestant College in Beirut, now the American University of Beirut, compiled late in the last century a two-volume work on the plants of Syria, Palestine, and Sinai. The book was revised and republished in 1932 by Professor John Dinsmore, and that edition listed about 4200 species of plants from about 1000 different families. Many of these the author says are found in the Syrian Desert. And this is to say nothing of the numerous observations made by other explorer-scholars about the plants and flowers that grow in this desert. I myself have seen there a kind of lavender (*khuzāmā*) similar to what we call *lāwandah* in Lebanon, and red anemones spread like a scarlet carpet in some areas. Among the hills overlooking and adjoining the desert near Tadmur, there is even a terebinth woodland on Jabal al-Bal'ās some trees of which are still growing to the present day, despite the number felled by both bedouins and settled folk in recent centuries.

On the desert fringe there are localities the current names of which suggest that they are places where many trees once grew. Al-Buṭmīyāt ("the Terebinths"), al-Khaḍrīyāt ("the Green Ones"), and Wādī l-Tīn ("Wadi of the Fig Trees") are all names that refer to the presence of trees in these places in earlier times. There are those who maintain that the truffle, which grows in the Syrian Desert after the autumn rains, only appears in land that had been covered with trees in ancient times, and now lives as a parasite on the decayed and disintegrated remains of tree roots.

Figure 6: The Kharbaqa Dam.

Figure 7: The bed of the lake, once the outlets of the dam had become blocked and the lake was filled with sediment from the flood waters.

Figure 8: The lake, its sediment-filled bed planted with cotton.

The sedentary culture of the Syrian Desert was destined, as we can see, to suffer setbacks and afflictions during the wars between the Persians and the Romans, and then through the subsequent bedouin onslaughts against the fringes of the settled lands in the centuries that followed. In these latter times the ruling power lacked the ability either to repulse or to deter the bedouins, who so ravaged and pillaged such areas, far removed from the capitals, entrepots, and great cities, that today nothing remains of the places but their names. One such place is the village of al-Baṣīrī, which Musil maintains is called Danābā in the ancient Arabic sources.[16] People of the villages of the interior will tell you about the village and its agriculture only a hundred years ago. It faded into oblivion, and today nothing of it survives but the ruins of an old church, looking like the remains of an abandoned encampment, and a well.[17] The same can be said of al-Bakhrā',[18] near Tadmur, which was a populous village when al-Walīd ibn Yazīd sought refuge and was killed there.[19] Today it is a desolate ruin. There are also al-Jabāh, al-Kamkūm, Ḥammāmāt al-Hummā (near al-Ghunthur), and hundreds of empty ruins scattered along the peripheries of the desert, all of which were once populous agricultural settlements. Even Tadmur itself, today a populous town, was practically devoid of inhabitants in the late nineteenth century.[20] Though situated in the heart of the Syrian Desert, it was once the capital of a kingdom that expanded its territory and extended its authority to such an extent that it subjugated Egypt and made it a dependency of Palmyra. Then sovereignty passed from Palmyra when its queen, Zenobia, was defeated by the emperor Aurelian.

---

[16]Musil, *Palmyrena*, p. 129.

[17]I was once told the name of a man from the family of Ḥabīb Ḥannah who owned a farm in the village, and I remember knowing him when I was a boy.

[18]Most of the European explorers misspell the name of this ancient town. This is because they displace it from the dialect of the bedouins, who pronounce no vowel after the *bā'* and *a* after the *khā'*. Some of the explorers even go to the extreme of writing it as "Bukhārā" [the name of a famous Islamic city in Central Asia].

[19]Sir John Bagot Glubb is mistaken when he claims that al-Walīd ibn Yazīd was besieged and killed in one of the villages of Damascus. See his [*The Empire of the Arabs* (London, 1963), p. 200 =] *Imbarāṭūrīyat al-'arab*, Arabic translation by Khayrī Ḥammād (Beirut, 1966), pp. 381–82.

[20]Lady Anne Blunt, *Bedouin Tribes of the Euphrates* (New York, 1879), p. 207.

There was a series of wars between the Persians and the Romans, fought mainly in Syria and the surrounding areas. First the Romans were defeated, then the Persians were defeated, but all the while the villages suffered the setbacks and afflictions of the wars and oppressive taxation as well. Finally, with the Arab conquest and the rising power of the bedouins, who gained mastery of the desert, settled life there eventually disappeared. Many of these centers on the desert outskirts were captured on terms of capitulation (*ṣulḥan*), and concluded treaties with the conquerors in order to save themselves from destruction;[21] but the bedouin spirit, which glorified raiding and martial exploits, was not particularly favorable to settlement in the agrarian districts, to life dependent upon agriculture, or to sedentary concerns relevant to it. Add to this the outbreaks of civil strife that occurred in early Islamic times in the later years of the caliphate of 'Uthmān ibn 'Affān and after his death; Mu'āwiya's rise to independent power as governor of Syria; the quarrels among the Arab tribes over issues between them and their division into the Qays and Yemen factions; the attacks launched against each other by opposing groups in the desert lands of Syria; the concern of the ruling authorities to alleviate the internal discord; the pursuit of conquests outside of Syria; the regime's need for troops, who were mostly men from the Arab tribes; and finally the transfer of the caliphate to Baghdad and the penetration of Persian elements in the 'Abbāsid regime—all these developments diverted attention from the protection of the desert fringes.

[21]See Donald R. Hill, *The Termination of Hostilities in the Early Arab Conquests: A.D. 634–656* (London, 1971), pp. 59–84. Shaykh Nāyif al-Sha'lān told me that when they were digging among heaps of debris on the site of a church in a field of al-Baṣīrī in the desert, they discovered a practically crumbling shoulder-blade bone on which were still visible some traces of words written in Arabic. Of these the name of the caliph 'Umar ibn al-Khaṭṭāb could be read, and also the word *'ahd*, "covenant." This was believed by some to be a covenant from 'Umar to the Christian inhabitants of the village, who preserved it in their church. As some of the bedouins told me, the church fell to ruin when the entire village was abandoned. The bone was given to Iḥsān al-Ḥuṣnī, a deputy in the Syrian Chamber of Deputies, in 1954. The story is of course doubtful, and the present location of the artifact is unknown.

The bedouins grew stronger in authority, but throughout the Umayyad caliphate and part of the reign of the 'Abbāsids, they were not sufficiently powerful to efface the landmarks of civilization on the peripheries of the desert.[22] But when the empire began to disintegrate, we hear from al-Mutanabbī himself how in the Ḥamdānid period Sayf al-Dawla pursued the remnants of a band of bedouin raiders and attacked them in the areas between al-Furqulus and Tadmur and at al-Jifār and al-Jabāh, as will be considered later.[23] From that era until the end of the First World War, it was the bedouins who held dominion in the desert and its adjoining areas, launching raids on the villages, plundering remote agricultural areas, ravaging the pilgrimage routes, and raiding each other as had been their practice in pre-Islamic times. As their poet said:

> On the camp of Ḍibāb and Ḍabba fell the force of our raid;
> For verily, the debt of a man's fate must be paid.
> And sometimes our onslaughts may turn on our brother,
> Should quest for a target avail us no other.[24]

The territory of the desert thus began to expand at the expense of the settled area,[25] and fine agricultural lands became part of the Syrian Desert. It was this that gained it a reputation for its excellent grazing, even in its heartlands, for many parts of it are rich in the kinds of herbage upon which camels and sheep thrive. In the summer of 1954 I met bedouins from tribes in the Najd whose land had been wasted by

[22] Abū l-Faraj al-Iṣfahānī mentions how the bedouins used to attack caravans in the desert. See his *Kitāb al-aghānī*, edited by Naṣr al-Hūrīnī (Cairo: Dār al-ṭibā'a, AH 1285), IX, 111.

[23] See al-Mutanabbī's ode rhyming in *rā'*:

> The long spears can naught but lose their length
> When against them you turn your arms to fight,

p. 418 in his *Dīwān*, edited by Naṣīf al-Yāzijī (Beirut, 1887). [The phrase comprises the first hemistich of the poem; see Chapter XIX, n. 48 below.]

[24] Abū Tammām, *Ḥamāsa*, I, 136. [The verses are from the *dīwān* of the pre-Islamic poet al-Quṭāmī. For an earlier citation from this same poem, see p. 19 above.]

[25] There are those who by way of exaggeration say that it was not the desert that gave rise to the bedouins, but rather the bedouins who gave rise to the desert and expanded its frontiers.

drought, forcing them to make their way to the lands of Syria in their quest for pasturage and water. The government of Syria allowed them to enter, and they spent about two months on its lands.

Conditions in the domain of the Syrian Desert differ from one part to another, but generally speaking it is possessed of very good soil, especially in the volcanic regions around the Ḥawrān, in the outlying districts of al-Qaryatayn, Tadmur, and the Jazīra, and in the heartlands of the Ḥamād. I have seen lands subject to flooding by torrential streams that benefit some people engaged in agriculture by making their lands more productive than any irrigated lands of the finest agricultural districts. I used to frequent certain of the desert fringe areas during the spring of some of the good years, and the herbage in some of the floodland areas came up to the knees of the horses. In such bountiful years as these, sheep herders could take the precaution of gathering up this herbage and storing it in desert warehouses built by the government for the dry years. I do not think that water supplies are lacking underground, if only the experts would drill for them. Because of the sloping of the desert toward the east and south it is easy to create artesian wells, as has in fact been done in many places.

As for the heartland of the Syrian Desert, although it has excellent soil in many places, it is among the dryest of desert lands, with hardly any water in the summer season. It is therefore extremely difficult, if not practically impossible, for any tribe to remain in the interior of the desert through the entire summer. Even certain wild animals in the desert heartland are forced to emigrate to the settled lands, or at least to their fringes, as we have already mentioned.

CHAPTER II

TREES AND PLANTS OF THE DESERT

IT IS BEYOND THE SCOPE of this book to enter into a detailed investigation of the various plants and trees to be found in the desert. What will concern us in this study are those to be found in Arabia and in the Syrian Desert in particular, and those that have some relation to bedouin life and to the life of animals that depend upon them for sustenance or live among them.

Fruit-Bearing Trees

The most important of fruit-bearing trees is the date palm, which grows in the oases of both desert and sand-desert heartlands, as well as in the villages surrounding these regions. This tree is regarded today as a symbol not just of nomadism, but of Arabism in general. In the Iraqi army, its intertwined fronds are depicted as symbolic recognition of honor and high rank. In the Kingdom of Saudi Arabia it appears as a symbol on many of the nation's products and manufactured goods, as the logo of its news media, and as an emblem on the gifts given by its kings and princes. And so it should be, for the palm is firmly bonded to Arab life throughout the peninsula. A tradition of the Arab Prophet reports him as saying, "Honor your aunt, the palm; for indeed, she was created of the clay from which Adam was created."[1] The fruit of the palm, the date, is just about the most delectable sweet in the bedouin's mouth; and in former times his foremost aspirations were to obtain *al-aswadān*, "the two black ones"—dates and water. A bedouin's tent is almost never devoid of dates, which comprise, after

[1] Al-Suyūṭī, *Ḥusn al-muḥāḍara* (Cairo, AH 1321), II, 255.

Figure 9: Plant life in one of the wadis.

the milk of his she-camels, the second constituent element of his diet. The bedouins buy dates from the oases to which we referred above, or from the villages surrounding the desert. They are also imported from Iraq or the Aḥsā', packed in palm-leaf baskets or hide containers, or, as has become common these days, in cellophane wrappers or cardboard cartons. It is not unlikely that the palm tree was transplanted into the desert and its various oases from Babylonia, where it was the most significant factor encouraging ancient man to settle there.[2] Nowhere in the world do dates grow in such enormous quantities as they do in the Arabian peninsula, particularly Iraq, where close to thirty million date palms are to be found.[3]

In historical terms, the date palm is apparently the most ancient of plants. In the state of Colorado in the United States of America, the fossilized remains of a palm leaf have been discovered which, in the

[2]See Philip Hitti, Edward Jurji, and Jibrail Jabbur, *Ta'rīkh al-'arab* (Beirut, 1965), p. 47 [an expanded translation of Hitti's *History of the Arabs*. For this passage, see the 10th edition (New York, 1971), p. 20.]

[3]*Kingdom of Iraq*, by a Committee of Officials (Baltimore, 1946), p. 46.

view of scholars at the Smithsonian Institution, dates from an era 160 million years ago.[4] Probably the paramount oasis in the peninsula for the date palm (if we do not count al-Baṣra as an oasis) is the oasis of al-Hufūf, the dates of which are known as *khāliṣī*, or "quintessent," and customarily regarded by the tribes as the most delectable of dates.

Because of the role played by the date palm and its fruit in the life of the Arabs, they use the Arabic word for it, *nakhla*, as a generic term for many kinds of trees. They also apply a great variety of names to the fruit of the palm. Today we find in the dictionary that the date is in its first stage of development called the *ṭal'*, then progressively the *khalāl*, *balaḥ*, *busr*, and *ruṭab*, and finally the *tamr*, the dried date.[5]

Following the date palm in importance to the bedouin is the grapevine. This is not a desert plant, but rather grows in the villages along the peripheries of the desert and in some of the oases. The bedouins regard the grapes picked from this vine as a most delicious fruit. They ripen in the summer, during early August in most of the places bordering on the desert. Their owners sell some of this fruit to the bedouins, for it is at this time of the year that the nomads draw close to the settled lands and pitch their camps near the villages in which grapevines are grown. But most of all, the bedouin longs for raisins, grapes dried in a special way, and then for the treacle made from raisins. Treacle and dates are the sweets most preferred among the bedouins.

The process for drying grapes involves dipping them into a solution of alkali and olive oil. The alkali is extracted from the ashes of saltwort, an astringent plant of the desert. Masses of green saltwort are gathered and burned, then the ashes are soaked in water and exposed for an extended period to the heat of the sun. The water is strained, and some olive oil is added to it to produce the right solution into which grapes can be dipped for drying. After the grapes have been so treated, they are placed on rough ground outdoors to dry in the sun for a week's time.

[4] *News Review* (Beirut), VII, no. 32, p. 5.

[5] See *Lisān al-'arab*, q.v. *b-l-ḥ* and *n-kh-l*. Date palms may all appear to be similar, but experts maintain that in Iraq there are about 350 different species, aside from the well-known species that produce fruit. These latter are only five: the *ḥalāwī*, the *khaḍrāwī*, the *sāyir*, the *khastāwī*, and the *zahdī*. See *Kingdom of Iraq*, p. 47.

In the villages adjoining the desert and in the oases there also grows the pomegranate tree, which is very frequently surrounded on all sides by grapevines. The bedouins favor the rind of the pomegranate for dyeing and tanning. Next in popularity among the bedouins, after the pomegranate, is the fig. This fruit they eat during the summer, when it is in season and the bedouins themselves are close to the settled lands. They buy figs from local cultivators, whose womenfolk in most cases go out to the bedouin camps to sell this fruit. The bedouins do not, however, store up dried figs as they do raisins and dates.

Non-Fruit-Bearing Trees

Also found in the desert and its oases are several varieties of prickly thorn-bearing desert trees that grow as tall as such large fruit-bearing trees as the almond and apricot and live for many years. The most familiar of these is a group of thorny shrubs collectively called the *'iḍāh*. There are many varieties of these, probably the best-known of which, as well as the most plentiful and most widely distributed, is the *ithl*, or tamarisk. The inhabitants of the oases use this tree, which thrives in most regions, as a means of protecting their date palms or fields from being covered with sand, planting tamarisk trees as barriers shielding their fields from damage by shifting sands. They set them around the field in parallel rows some meters apart, so that if the sands penetrate the first row, the second stands in their way, and so on. This makes the passage of sand so difficult that it rarely penetrates the fourth row of trees. The *ithl* variety of tamarisk, similar in appearance to another called the *ṭarfā'*, produces wood used by the Ṣlayb and some other Arab tribesmen to make wooden bowls; and from its branches craftsmen once fashioned fine yellow-colored arrows. The pulpit of the Arab Prophet in the mosque of Medina was made from the wood of the tamarisk.[6] Because of the height, straightness, and symmetry of the tamarisk tree, the poets compared a woman to it if she was of perfect build and erect stature. As Kuthayyir said:

Like a tamarisk she was, any time she rose,
Standing tall, and facing the evening breeze,

[6]See *Lisān al-'arab*, q.v. *'-th-l*.

Or nay, far finer; and if she turned,
A heifer in Jubba, in a thicket grazing at ease.[7]

How beneficial it would be if this tree were generally cultivated throughout the desert regions where growing it is possible, as it provides an excellent barrier against the sands.

Another member of the *'iḍāh* family is the lotus (*sidr*), a tree with broad round leaves that is of two types. The first is the *'ibrī*, which grows along the banks of rivers, and the other is the *ḍāl*, a steppeland type. The lotus is thorny and aromatic, and sometimes grows tall enough for man and animals to take advantage of its shade. Its wood is used for fuel.

There is also the *arṭā*, an aromatic desert tree with multiple branches growing from a single stem and a flower like that of the variety of willow known as the *khilāf*. It grows tall enough that beneath it animals can seek refuge, protection from the sun, and shelter from rain and cold. In his elegy for his sons, Abū Dhu'ayb said of a wild bull:

Refuge he sought there among the *arṭā* trees,
And security found from rain and chilling breeze.[8]

Euphorbia (*ghaḍā*) is a tree often encountered in Najd and in the sand-deserts of the Nafūd, the Dahnā', and the Rub' al-Khālī. Its trunk and branches are so solid that charcoal similar to that made from oak can be made from its wood. Hence the Arab tribesmen esteem it as the best fuel, and from its coals comes the proverb, "hotter than euphorbia coals." As the poet said:

Their expressions betray them as sour they turn,
And in their hearts coals of euphorbia burn.[9]

In the markets of some oases in the Aḥsā' region, I have seen heaps of euphorbia that bedouins have gathered from the Rub' al-Khālī. They bring it in lorries to the village markets of the Aḥsā' to sell it to the people as firewood.

[7]Kuthayyir 'Azza, *Dīwān*, edited by Iḥsān 'Abbās (Beirut, 1391/1971), p. 391.
[8]*Dīwān al-hudhalīyīn* (Cairo, 1385/1965), I, 11.
[9]See *Lisān al-'arab*, q.v. *gh-ḍ-ā*.

Also among the *'iḍāh* is the *ṭarfā'* tamarisk. It has long hanging branches like those of the *ithl*, and it is said that it is of different varieties, one of which is the *ithl*. It provides no wood. It sends up smooth and even branches, and camels eat it as the astringent vegetation (*ḥamḍ*) they need if there is none other available to them. Some claim that the *ṭarfā'* tamarisk is one of the *ḥamḍ*.

The variety of acacia called the *salam* (sing. *salama*), another of the *'iḍāh*, is a thorny tree the leaves, pods, and bark of which are used for tanning hides, and the leaves and pods of which are called *qaraẓ*. A certain place came to be well-known as Dhū Salam, "the Place of Acacia." Shaykh Muḥammad al-Būṣīrī mentioned it in his famous ode in praise of the Prophet:

> Is it because upon my neighbors
> At Dhū Salam my remembrance is fixed,
> That now my weeping eyes do well
> With tears with which blood is mixed?

The *salam* has a yellow flower containing a green aromatic pod, and when a skin has been tanned with the acacia leaf or pod it is called *maqrūẓ*, or "pod-tanned." If the skin is tanned with acacia bark, it is called *maslūm*, or "acacia-tanned." It is said that the origin of the term *taqrīẓ*, in its meaning of "panegyric," is a metaphor based on the tanning of hides, for the panegyrist, or *muqarriẓ*, adorns his boon companion with words just as the acacia tanner, the *qāriẓ*, beautifies his hide through tanning. In the history of Arabic literature there is a story about an acacia tanner (or two of them) of the 'Anaza tribe who went to gather acacia pods and never returned. This became the basis for a proverb referring to any absent person not expected to return: "the acacia gatherer will not come your way," or "the acacia gatherer will not return." Hence the words of Abū Dhu'ayb:

> Till the gatherers of acacia return safe and sound,
> And Kulayb for Wā'il is raised from the ground.[10]

[10] *Dīwān al-hudhalīyīn*, I, 145. [The second hemistich of the verse refers to Kulayb ibn Rabī'a, a famous figure of pre-Islamic lore. Legend tells of how his murder by a warrior from a related clan split the tribe of Wā'il and provoked 40 years of fratricidal strife, the famous War of al-Basūs, in the mid-sixth century AD.]

The bedouins cut and store acacia for firewood, and some of them supply it to villagers in the settled areas, where it is sold in the markets. The tree has roots that penetrate beneath the sands in search of moisture and water, and this may arrest the process of dune movement that occurs in most sand-deserts.

Another of the *'iḍāh* is the *ṭalḥ*, a thorny tree frequently found in the desert lands of Arabia, most particularly in the Ḥijāz. It is a stout crooked tree and grows very tall. It has only a few leaves, bright green in color, but its trunk is very tall and its branches quite large, and the trunk is so wide that if a man wraps his arms around it, his hands will barely touch. Camels are very fond of its leaves; and they, as well as wild beasts and people, seek refuge in its shade. The *ṭalḥ* is the tree from which the famous gum arabica is extracted.

The tragacanth (*qatād*), which some do not count in the *'iḍāh* group, is a solid thorny tree that grows in the Najd, the Tihāma, and the Nafūd. Sheep eat its leaves, but camels do not often do so. Some tragacanth trees are quite broad, while others are no wider than the space occupied by a seated person. Its branches, some of which grow as thick as the span of a hand, are spaced very close together, and each branch is full of thorns from tip to base. There is nothing more difficult or uncomfortable for a camel than to pass by night through a land in which there are tragacanths, for as the bedouins say, this plant causes scratches on the animal's feet and legs. This gave rise to the famous Arabic proverb in describing a difficult task: "it is more difficult than to strip the thorns off the tragacanth."

Desert Grasses and Shrubs

The trees mentioned above are not the plants upon which animals depend for their sustenance. Indeed, they are not the plants most commonly found in the various quarters of the desert: most of them are large trees rather than plants suitable for grazing, although camels do eat them. Camels and many other animals graze primarily on plants which the Arabs call *khulla* and *ḥamḍ*; as the bedouins say, "Grazing land all consists of *ḥamḍ* and *khulla*." Neither of these two are themselves particular plants, but rather are groups of plants. The bedouins consider *khulla* to include every sweet plant that is not astringent and that does not grow as a large tree. "*Khulla* is the bread of

Figure 10: *Ḥamḍ* plants.

camels," as the bedouin saying goes, "and *ḥamḍ* is their fruit." Probably the best-known types of *khulla* are *shīḥ*, *'arfaj*, *khulla* proper, and *qayṣūm*.

Shīḥ is practically the most common plant in the desert, and proliferates on hills, elevations, meadowlands, plains, and lowlands. Camels, horses, donkeys, and sheep consume it in all its forms, and do so with great relish, especially when it is ripe and tender. It is thorny in form, bitter-tasting, but quite fragrant. It is one of the most common and most widely distributed plants in both the wadis and more rugged areas of the desert, and the ancient poets frequently referred to it, usually in association with euphorbia and *qayṣūm*. One such poet and an astute commentator on desert life, 'Umar ibn Abī Rabī'a, said in one of his odes:

By the camp of one of my cousins,
In a distant wilderness of sand,

> By her there sprout up *qayṣūm* and *shīḥ*
> Over the expanse of low-lying land.[11]

When dry, *shīḥ* becomes an excellent fuel, catching fire like a match. Villagers use it as fuel and as tinder for kindling fires in home fireplaces and in the ovens in which they bake bread. Sometimes it is made into brooms, like those used for sweeping the streets in some Arab cities. Until recently, villagers used to gather it as fuel from the surrounding desert and load it like straw in bales on their pack animals.

'Arfaj is a supple and somewhat greenish dust-colored plant, aromatic like the *shīḥ* and bearing a yellow flower. Its roots spread widely through the ground and send up many shoots, and its leaves are slender and reed-like, similar to those of the saltwort. On its tips are buds in the heads of which is a kind of yellow down. Camels and sheep eat *'arfaj* both green and dry. When it is dry, the bedouins gather it for fuel. Its flame is of a redness so bright that it is said of a red-bearded man that his beard is as if it were an *'arfaj* flame.[12]

Khulla is a thorny shrub smaller than the tragacanth and the box-thorn. The desert folk call it the *shabraq*, "the one that tears to shreds," and it grows in gravelly or other rough ground. When camels eat the *khulla*, they give much milk.[13]

There yet remains *qayṣūm*, which is a plant of plains and lowlands. It grows on a stem that is tender and bright green when it is mature or when it first appears on the surface of the ground at the beginning of its season. Its leaves are long and dangling, like those of the young olive tree, but thinner. It bears a fragrant yellow-colored flower, and is one of the plants favored by camels. It is usually mentioned in association with *shīḥ* and euphorbia, hence the bedouins say of certain Arab regions that it is "a land in which *qayṣūm*, *shīḥ*, and euphorbia are found."

The *ḥamḍ* is another group, comprising any salty or astringent plant that grows in individual stalks and has no central stem. Its leaf continues to live under most conditions; and if squeezed, water bursts out of it. When camels eat these leaves, they are also drinking from them.

---

[11] 'Umar ibn Abī Rabī'a, *Dīwān*, edited by Paul Schwarz (Leipzig, 1318–20/1901–1909), II.2, 230.

[12] See *Lisān al-'arab*, q.v. *'-r-f-j*.

[13] *Ibid.*, q.v. *kh-l-l*.

We have already mentioned that the tribesmen say that *khulla* is the bread of camels and *ḥamḍ* their fruit, or as is also said, their meat. The largest of the *ḥamḍ* are about the seating space of a person in size, while the smallest is no larger than a fist.

Probably the best-known and most widespread of the *ḥamḍ* on the surface of the desert is the *rimth*, a tall, thin, drooping plant, similar to euphorbia, upon which camels and sheep graze. The Arabs say, "There is no shrub more common on a mountain, or more distracting to passing animals, or more fattening or better for their grazing, than *rimth*." This is because when camels become weary of *khulla*, they crave *ḥamḍ*. If they find a grazing ground with tasty plants like *rughl* and *rimth*, their appetite is restored and they return to the *khulla*, grazing well and enjoying their pasturage. But if they find no *ḥamḍ*, they graze poorly and lose weight. Hence the *rimth* is, so to speak, a kind of appetizer. When dry, it is also burned as fuel for fires. As al-Mutanabbī said in depicting the she-camel that brought him to Ibn al-ʿAmīd:

> Away from the homelands of *rimth*-smoke she turned,
> In quest of another land where ambergris burned.

That is, his camel left the lands of the Arab tribes, where they used *rimth* for fuel, and set out for Ibn al-ʿAmīd, who burns ambergris.[14]

Also among the *ḥamḍ* is the *rughl*. Like the *rimth*, it is a spreading plant with intertwining leaves. And also like the *rimth*, camels graze on it after eating *khulla*; it restores their appetite, so that their disposition for grazing returns. The *rughl* spurts water when handled or squeezed, and the nodules of its flower glisten like crystals because of the water they contain. Of this plant the poet said:

> She grazes in al-Ṣummān on fragrant fields,
> Staying where savory *rughl* satisfaction yields.[15]

Another of the *ḥamḍ* is *arāk*, a tall light-green shrub that grows in lowlands and valleys and has many leaves and branches. The tooth-cleaning stick (*siwāk*, *miswak*) is made from its stem. Some bedouins

[14] Al-Mutanabbī, *Dīwān*, p. 569.

[15] See *Lisān al-ʿarab*, q.v. *r-gh-l*.

accordingly call it the "*siwāk* bush" and do not consider it one of the *ḥamḍ*. They claim that its stem is better than that of any other plant for cleaning the teeth. In his famous ode rhyming in *fā'*, al-Farazdaq said:

T'was noontime already when the young girls arose,
The hot summer's day had then half slipped away.
They called for the *arāk* twigs chosen and gathered
In Na'mān by horsemen on the pilgrimage day.[16]

Livestock are particularly fond of its leaves, which leave a trace of *arāk* taste in their milk. Gazelles also graze on this plant, and are mentioned in association with it in ancient poetry. The *arāk* bush bears grape-like clusters of fruit called *mard* and sometimes *barīr*. The individual berry in such a cluster contains a small, round, hard pit, slightly larger than the usual *ḥamḍ* pit. As Ṭarafa ibn al-'Abd said:

Shaking the bush for its *mard*
Is the tribe's own dark-lipped fawn,
Adorning her neck two gem-strings
That pearl and crysolite hold.
In a thicket grazes a gazelle doe
That astray from the herd has gone,
The *barīr* boughs called her hither,
And enrobe her in their fold.[17]

Resembling the *arāk* is the *bashām*, a fragrant and pleasant-tasting bush bearing branches and leaves off a main stem. Its leaves are small ones, smaller than those of the olive tree but larger than those of the wild thyme bush. Sheep graze on the *bashām*, and when they chew off its leaf or break its branch a sticky, white, milk-like substance oozes forth. Its leaves are dried, pounded into a powder, soaked in water, and then mixed with henna to use for blackening the hair. Like the *arāk* bush, its stems are made into tooth-cleaning sticks. As Jarīr sang:

[16]See his *Dīwān*, edited by 'Abd Allāh al-Ṣāwī (Cairo, 1354/1936), II, 553.
[17]Al-Tibrīzī, *Sharḥ al-qaṣā'id al-'ashr*, p. 31.

> She polished her teeth left and right, if that time you recall,
> Blessed be the *bashām*; it needed no water at all.[18]

There is also *samḥ*, a plant that grows in great abundance in the northern regions of the Syrian Desert and in the steppeland of Taymā'. It has seeds that are ground into a flour made into bread eaten as a substitute for wheat bread. Philby reports that he ate such bread and found it excellent, that it is brown in color, and that the bedouins gather the seeds during the summer when they have matured.[19]

Also well-known in the desert is the *ushnān*, or saltwort, a plant or small shrub that grows as large as the space of a seated person. It grows in the streambeds and floodlands of wadis and on low-lying plains surrounded by the more rugged highlands. Saltwort is an alkaline plant with hanging intertwining leaves, like those of most of the other *ḥamḍ* plants. In the spring, its slender green stems are moist and tender, with no sharply defined heads; these dry up during the summer, then in the following season new ones grow. Neither camels nor other livestock graze on this plant, unless forced by hunger to do so or out of amusement or a desire for something salty. The bedouins and village folk, however, use it as a cleaning agent. They gather the leaves and fine stems, dry them, grind or pound them into a powder, and use it to wash their bodies and clothes. The ancient Israelites had used it for the same purpose since remotest antiquity. Its effectiveness as a cleaning agent became proverbial: in the Old Testament, God said to Jerusalem, through the words of Jeremiah, "'For though thou wash thyself with natron and cleanse thyself with much saltwort, yet thine iniquity is marked before me,' saith the Lord God."[20] The plant is common not only in the desert, but also in all of the regions adjoining it. Hence, many of the people in the villages scattered along the desert fringe join with the bedouins in gathering the saltwort and using it for cleaning. Some villagers even used to ship it into the settled lands, exchanging it for such grains as wheat and barley. It was a common thing to see such villagers, with no land of their own, seek to earn a living by devoting their efforts to cutting saltwort, drying and pulverizing it, and carrying

[18] Jarīr, *Dīwān*, edited by Nu'mān Amīn Ṭāhā (Cairo, 1969–71), I, 279.
[19] Philby, *The Land of Midian*, p. 102.
[20] Jeremiah 2:22.

Figure 11: Saltwort.

it on pack animals to the interior villages to exchange it for grain. When one set out on such a journey, people would say, "He went to change saltwort."

Saltwort turns yellowish when it dries, and clothes washed in it acquire a tinge of this yellow hue. The villagers also pull up this plant by the roots and burn it in the desert while it is still green, thereby deriving alkali from it. This alkali used to be sent to Tripoli, Nablus, and other towns, and was used in soap-making before the importation of lye, the Western caustic. Not surprisingly, some soapworks still use alkali in preference to lye. As we have already mentioned, this alkali is to this day still used in the drying of raisins. The alkali solution serves to clean the grapes and to draw out the water from them, so that they dry and turn into raisins. These are either stored for the following year or crushed and made into treacle.

Fungal Plants

Also known in the desert is a class of fungal plants. These have no stems, roots, branches, or leaves, and are of two types. One of them is the truffle, which the bedouins call the *faq'a* or *kimāya*. The truffle is an underground fungus, similar in shape to the potato, between one and five inches in diameter, and sometimes larger. On its underside is a knob from which fine threads extend out into the soil to supply the truffle with nutrients and water. There are various kinds of truffles: the white truffle, or *zubaydīya*, and the red and black varieties. The latter two kinds probably comprise only one: they are similar to each other in size, shape, color, and the solidity of their pith. In both, this pith is tawny brown in color, firm, and round, like a ball of dough. As for the white variety, its skin and pith are both white, its pith is softer, neither as firm nor as round, and larger in size. The large white truffles the bedouins call *shaykh* or *shuwaykh*, and when the bedouin girl is collecting truffles she sings, *Yammā kimāya ḥamrā yammā shuwaykh abyaḍ*, "Either red *kimāya* or little white shaykh." I personally saw a "white shaykh" in Wādī l-Buṭmīyāt, southeast of al-Qaryatayn, and dug it out of the ground with my own hands. It weighed more than 1400 grams and measured 24 centimeters in diameter; from a distance I had thought it was a large rock, since it lay exposed on the surface of the ground, as white truffles generally are when they are fully mature.

One effect of the autumn rains is to cause the truffle to grow underground, beginning from tiny spores or minute single-celled organisms scattered throughout the ground and on its surface.[21] When the earth begins to warm late in winter, these cells multiply and grow into a truffle the size of an apricot pit. On the surface of the ground, above its resting place, there begins to form a slight swelling accompanied by a cracking or loosening of the soil, practically invisible except to the individual experienced in the gathering of truffles. This is in early February,

[21]Local folk erroneously claim that growth of the truffle requires the occurrence of thunder to crack the land.

and not in early November, as Dickson supposes in his otherwise fine account entitled "An Autumn Study."[22] At this stage the experienced truffle gatherer uses a long sturdy stick, or an iron-tipped digger called a *ḥaffār*, to probe the place where he sees a kind of swelling or loosening of the ground. If he finds the soil crumbly, that indicates to him that in the middle of that inconspicuous swelling lies a truffle, which, in this small state, he then digs out with his *ḥaffār* or hoe. If the truffle is left to grow, the small swelling protuberence keeps growing with it and the cracks on the surface keep increasing, until it becomes a small spreading dome quite obvious to the eye. By that time there is no need for an expert to detect the truffle. The white truffle grows and appears earlier than its sisters, the red and black truffles, which do not appear until the month of February. If left ungathered, the truffle grows underground by leaps and bounds until it bursts through and appears on the surface of the ground. When it has reached its maximum size, it sometimes rolls out of the mouth of its little "volcano" and its skin begins to wrinkle a bit from exposure to the sun.

The seasonal rains having fallen in autumn and the truffle having grown by late winter, the bedouins, as well as the inhabitants of villages adjoining the desert, spread out over the places where truffles have been growing and gather them with their hoes and diggers from early February until late April, the beginning of the harvest time. Hence the proverb about the truffle: "the first in February and the last at the harvest." One commonly sees people with bags hung over their shoulders to put truffles into them, incessantly scrutinizing the ground so that no sign of a truffle will escape their notice as they walk from one place to another. One may happen upon a truffle and find another lying no more than a foot away, while on another occasion the next may be no closer than ten meters. Oddly enough, the harvester will return to the very same land from which he had been gathering truffles an hour ago, and will see new truffles that had previously escaped his notice. Thus, experienced truffle-gatherers rarely venture far from the places where they have already found truffles.

To dig up the truffle, the harvester cuts down with his digger along both sides of it, and then with his hoe lifts it out from underneath its

[22]Dickson, *The Arab of the Desert*, p. 60.

knob. Alternatively, he may dig down along one side, and then push the *ḥaffār* or hoe into the ground on the other side and push the soil containing the truffle back toward the dug out side, so that the truffle is lifted out intact, without being cut or broken. If the knob or the fine threads connected to it remain behind when the truffle is removed, and if rain falls shortly thereafter, then within a short time (not more than twenty days) a new truffle will grow in the hole. Hence, after a rainstorm, knowledgeable truffle-gatherers will go looking for them in the places where some have already been dug out. As they say, *uṭlubūhā fī maqāli'ihā*, "Seek them where they've already been dug out."

The bedouins and villagers live on truffles when they are in season, despite the fact that these plants are of insignificant nutritional value. They also ship them to the cities, where they are sold at high prices. Those they wish to eat they clean of any dirt or clay that has adhered to them, then wash them, roast or boil them, and eat them salted. Sometimes they cut them into thin slices, dry them, and store them up for the coming autumn months, when they sell them. In Damascus there are now processing plants that tin truffles, as mushrooms are tinned, in sealed cans.

As for the truffles that have grown, and yet escape the notice of the gatherers, these, whether below or above ground, dry out and fill the earth around them with tiny spores invisible to the naked eye. It is from these spores that truffles develop in the following year if the seasonal rains fall during the autumn; even in the absence of rain, they remain viable for many years. The spores are so light that the wind blows them across the surface of the land for great distances.

The desert also knows the mushroom, which is of the same family as the truffle, but differs from it in that the mushroom is neither a subterranean plant nor similar to the potato in shape. It is a flat, round, umbrella-shaped plant bearing many interior cavities containing the spores that guarantee the continuation of the species in the following year. The mushroom has a short stem of the same composition as the rest of the plant, and its cap varies in diameter between one and four inches. The mushroom also differs from the truffle in that it grows rapidly and appears suddenly; it is only gathered when it has already fully appeared on the ground. This mushroom is similar to the poisonous variety of the same family that grows in fields under the trees and during periods of continuous rain, but is shorter-stemmed, denser, and safe to eat.

There is another fungal plant called the *hawbar*, similar to the truffle but much smaller than it, varying between one and four centimeters in diameter. Its skin is pitch black, and it appears before the truffle does. Its season is not a long one, and the bedouins do not take as great an interest in it as they do in the truffle. They do, however, rejoice in its appearance, since this means that the truffle is probably soon to follow. A companion to all of these fungal plants is the *wasm*, a small non-fungal plant that usually appears prior to them or with the *hawbar*. The bedouins make no use of the *wasm*, but they take it as an indication that the truffle may appear in that same land during that season. It has small leaves like those of wild thyme and branch stems like those of sweet basil (*rayḥān*), and it grows between seven and twelve centimeters high. Obviously, the same autumn rains that promote the emergence of the fungal plants promote the growth of this *wasm* plant as well.

Desert Flowers

There yet remains the flowers that grow in the desert. One of these is the renowned red anemone, which at times covers vast areas like a scarlet carpet. Another is lavender, or as the bedouins call it. *khizām al-'arūs*, "the bride's nose ring." It is of the same family as sweet basil, and has small leaves. Its flower exudes a fragrant scent that, carried by the breeze, perfumes the entire area. As Imru' al-Qays sang:

> Like the much-prized wine and the cloud-borne shower,
> The fragrant scent of incense and lavender's flower.[23]

Lavender grows in such great abundance in some places that one sees the ground turning violet in color, as if it had donned a purple robe. Some claim that this wild lavender is the origin of the domestic lavender plant from which lavender perfume is extracted.

There are also types of lilies, especially the iris. One species of this flower was discovered in the southwestern parts of the Syrian Desert

[23]Imru' al-Qays, *Dīwān*, edited by Muḥammad Abū l-Faḍl Ibrāhīm (Cairo, 1958), p. 157.

around the mountains of Ghaṭṭūs, Kaḥla, and al-Bārida, and near al-Jabāh. In 1948 I had several specimens sent to Beirut to a Western enthusiast on lily-growing, and he told me that they were apparently unique of that species. Likewise, on the hills surrounding the desert from the south and west, there appear scores of species of plants and flowers that require detailed study to clarify their characteristics, colors, species, and uses. As I noticed on the highlands near the desert, some of them bear fruit underground, or more properly stated, have a root part of which is edible. When the plant is broken off, the skin of the buried root exudes a sticky white substance. If this root is roasted, it and its white liquid turn into a mastic softer and more elastic than any other. If this plant were domesticated, it would undoubtedly prove to be among the richest in rubber-like content. As for the plants upon which sheep graze, these are almost beyond counting. Waṣfī Zakarīyā cited the names of about twenty kinds, but gave no description or classification for them.[24] Musil devoted certain pages in his books to discussion of a broad range of the plants upon which camels graze. In view of the usefulness and completeness of these materials, I have collected all that I could from his scattered works and from other sources, and have organized them into a table providing the names of the plants in the bedouin dialect and their scientific Latin names. For ease of reference, this table has been placed at the end of the book as Appendix III.

[24]Zakarīyā, *'Ashā'ir al-Shām*, I, 41. [The Arabic text here quotes Zakarīyā's list of eighteen annuals, some of which cannot be identified. For those that can, see Appendix III below, nos. 25, 45, 114, 126, 153, 164, 172, 185, 226, 227.]

CHAPTER III

CARNIVOROUS DESERT ANIMALS

OF THE DESERT LANDS of the Arabian peninsula the Syrian Desert is probably the one richest in wildlife, containing such a broad range of animal species that it would be difficult to enumerate them all in this specialized study. Most of the explorers of Arabia gave due consideration to its wildlife. They also noted that many species that had once lived in the desert had since become extinct, and that other species were facing a similar fate.

The Lion

The lion, mentioned so frequently in the Arabic poetry of pre-Islamic and early Islamic times, is not to be found in the desert today. It is reported that someone who had seen a lion described it to the caliph 'Uthmān ibn 'Affān, who rebuked him since his portrayal was beginning to alarm the others present.[1] Mosaicists depicted the lion in the palace attributed to Hishām ibn 'Abd al-Malik (today called Khirbat al-Mafjar), as can be seen in the source cited below.[2] Al-Mutanabbī gave a magnificent description of the lion in his panegyric ode to Badr ibn 'Ammār: confronted by a lion, Badr made a dash for the security of his horse; with no time to draw his sword, he lashed the lion with his whip and knocked the beast to the ground.[3] In the time of the

[1]See also the description of the lion (*sab'*) in al-Damīrī, *Ḥayāt al-ḥayawān*, published by Muḥammad 'Alī Ṣubayḥ from the edition of Bulaq: Al-Maṭba'a al-amīrīya, AH 1274, II, 21–22.

[2]R.W. Hamilton, *Khirbat al-Mafjar: an Arabian Mansion in the Jordan Valley* (Oxford, 1959), Plate LXXXIX.

[3]Al-Mutanabbī, *Dīwān*, p. 145.

Crusaders, Usāma ibn Munqidh mentions seeing a lion near the town of Ḥamāh at a bridge close to the castle of Shayzar. It was crouching at the bank of the river, roaring and beating its chest on the ground, and Usāma charged at it and killed it.[4] Frequent references to the lion continue through the literature and attest to its presence in most parts of Arabia, especially in the northern regions where there are many thickets, until the nineteenth century, when the Finnish explorer Georg August Wallin reported an encounter with a lion in the sand-desert two days' journey from the tomb-shrine of 'Alī.[5] In her account of her travels in that same century, Lady Anne Blunt told of a lion that killed a bedouin named Būzān from the al-Khrāṣa clan of the 'Anaza tribe.[6]

Grant states that the lion was once a wild animal commonly found throughout Arabia, and particularly in the Fertile Crescent. "There are those who claim," she says, "that lions were unknown in Arabia before the time of the Roman emperor Decius, and that it was he who introduced them. He had a number of lions and lionesses caught in Africa and released them on the *limes* of Palestine and Arabia to intimidate the Saracens" (i.e. the bedouins).[7]

In this regard we must note that there are frequent references to the lion in the Bible. Some verses indicate its presence in the time of Samson, as occurs in the account of him confronting and slaying a lion, and in the story of Daniel when he was thrown into the lions' den.[8] In the Book of Job it is said, "The roaring of the lion, and the voice of the fierce lion, and the teeth of the young lions, are broken;"[9] and in Jeremiah we read, "Behold, he shall come up like a lion from

---

[4]Usāma ibn Munqidh, *Kitāb al-i'tibār*, edited by Philip Hitti (Princeton, 1930), p. 104.

[5]Georg August Wallin, [*Travels in Arabia (1845 and 1848)*, with introductory material by W.R. Mead and M. Trautz (Cambridge, 1979), p. 75; =] *Ṣuwar min shamālī jazīrat al-'arab fī muntaṣaf al-qarn al-tāsi' 'ashar*, Arabic translation by Samīr Salīm Shiblī (Beirut, 1971), p. 112.

[6]Blunt, p. 77.

[7]Christina Phelps Grant, *The Syrian Desert: Caravans, Travel, and Exploration* (New York, 1938), p. 15. See also Musil, *Palmyrena*, p. 247. Lady Anne Blunt (*loc. cit.*) indicates that the bedouins were very fearful of the lion.

[8]I Kings 13:24; Daniel 6:7.

[9]Job 4:10.

the swelling of Jordan against the habitation of the strong."[10] This is perhaps the most appropriate place for us to mention that the Bible is one of the oldest and most comprehensive sources for reports of wild animals in the northern part of the peninsula, including the Syrian Desert, Sinai, and the regions adjoining the desert. Among the habitats most favored by lions were the glens and thickets on the banks of the Jordan and the Orontes Rivers and near Lake Tiberias, and the thickets near the Euphrates and throughout the eastern steppe.

Whatever the case may have been in ages past, by the twentieth century the lion had completely disappeared. This was probably due to the introduction of modern firearms and the disappearance of many wooded areas.

The Wolf

The wolf is probably the most common, and most voracious, of carnivorous desert mammals. It has not become extinct in Arabia, as some have claimed; rather, in many areas it still roams the plains and hills by night in search of domestic livestock or wild animals upon which it preys. During the day it usually seeks shelter in hilly and mountainous terrain, and it makes its den in isolated caves and gaps in rock formations, where the female gives birth to her pups. The coloring of wolves varies: dark brown in the volcanic area of the Ḥamād desert, light brown in the Nafūd region, and ashen gray in the plains and flatlands along the fringes of the desert. The wolf is without doubt the most destructive animal in its attacks on livestock, causing more slaughter and injury than any other predator. Bedouin shepherds are accordingly very fearful of its depredations; they stand watch over their sheep by night and keep dogs specifically for the purpose of guarding them. In ancient times the Arab poet said:

> From him who owns no dogs does the wolf seek his prey,
> But from fierce-charging lion heart shies and slinks away.[11]

In the villages adjoining the desert, goatherds do likewise.

---

[10] Jeremiah 49:19.

[11] Some recensions have *al-ḥāmī* instead of *al-ḍārī* [both words meaning "fierce" in this context]. The verse is attributed to al-Nābigha in *Aghānī*, I, 37, 65.

Despite these precautions, wolves often catch the dogs by surprise and prey on the livestock. Some wolves may become so fearless, or so hungry, that they will occasionally creep up by night on houses on the outskirts of the villages and attack livestock in their pens. As one of the poets has said:

> If onto a land of claws and fangs
> One sets to graze his bleating fold,
> And o'er them does not keep his watch,
> He hands the wolf his crook to hold.

When a wolf attacks a flock of sheep or goats on the steppe, it seizes the ewe or goat's neck in its mouth and pulls her away; the confused victim hurries along at a rapid pace, unless the dogs detect the wolf. They claim that a wolf will often kill one ewe after another without stopping to eat them. One hears, for example, of an incident in which a wolf pounced upon a flock of sheep and goats and brought down about twenty (or *nayyib*, as they say "about twenty") of them and left them all dead or half-dead. But the investigations of those who specialize in the study of wolves refute this claim and indicate that wolves only attack animals they intend to kill and eat.

The wolf obviously cannot prey on camels or horses, but it can attack their young and may even bring down a donkey or cow if it finds one alone in the desert. Hence, when the bedouins or peasants have lost a beast in the desert and fear that wolves might attack it, they resort to charms to protect it from their depredations. Through these charms they seek, so they claim, to hold back the wolf. They recite passages in rhymed prose or verses from sacred texts, holding in their hands, as they read, an opened butchering knife or straight razor, and closing it as they reach the end of the reading. With this, they believe, the wolf will no longer be able to attack the animal. Many a time I have been told about how someone lost a head of livestock and held back the wolves in this way, or went to an expert to do so for him, and only then began to search for the beast. When he saw his animal, he found the wolf circling around it but unable to get close to it. What nonsense!

The wolf also subsists by preying on such desert herbivores as the gazelle and rabbit. A wolf will sometimes hide behind some of the shrubs among which gazelles graze, and then suddenly pounce upon one of them from behind and kill it. On moonlit nights gazelles avoid grazing in areas with plentiful plant life due to their fear of the wolf, for the hiding wolf can see the gazelle, but the gazelle cannot see him. It is therefore rare for a wolf to kill a gazelle, since it cannot get close to it. It is man that is responsible for the extermination, or near extermination, of the gazelle in the desert.

The bedouins also assert that by day the wolf seeks out the grazing grounds of the gazelle in the sandy lands, following their scent from downwind so that he can smell the scent of the gazelles while his scent does not reach them. He lies in wait until the gazelles have grazed and are satiated, and then suddenly attacks. He does not bring the hunt to an end by bringing one of them down at the moment of his attack, but rather continues to pursue the herd until one of the does tires and stops to urinate. When she does, the buck stops behind her, thus enabling the wolf at that moment to catch and kill the buck. Hence, as the bedouins claim, most of the gazelles caught by wolves in such situations are males.

If the wolf passes the night without finding game and by morning has still found nothing to eat, he howls in a special way from which the bedouins recognize that the one howling is hungry and *qalīl al-ghinā*, "destitute." Imru' al-Qays knew this long ago when he said of the wolf:

> When he howled, I answered him:
> "Oh, what a case we seem to be.
> Your prospects must be very dim
> If you are as destitute as me."[12]

If the wolf finds an easy prey to kill, he eats and fills himself, then retires to a cave and sleeps until late in the afternoon, when he gets up and returns to the hunt anew.

Wolves fear man and flee from him except in situations of extreme hunger during the cold winter season. I have seen wolves on many occasions during the summer in the hills adjoining the desert, and they fled as soon as they sensed the presence of man. Oddly enough, the bedouins eat the meat of the wolf and claim that it cures certain skin

[12] *Sharḥ al-qaṣā'id al-'ashr*, p. 21.

diseases.[13] Its skin is used to cover the rebab, and among the villagers it is used on tambourines and small drums.

The Hyena

The fringes of the desert are the prowling grounds of the hyena, which lives in the caves and grottos of the mountains surrounding the desert or adjoining the villages that lie along its peripheries. The bedouins erroneously apply the Arabic term *ḍab'* to the male; in the dictionaries this name refers to the female, the male being known as *ḍab'ān*. The pelt of the hyena is dark in color and striped with dark lateral lines. It stands about three feet high at the shoulder, and two and a half feet at the hindquarters. From its neck to its tail it has a mane that stands on end when it is aroused. The female gives birth to three or four pups in each litter.

The hyena is a kind of animal that is cowardly during the day, not daring to venture forth from its den. Many even claim that it is so cowardly that some brave bedouin and peasant youths can by day seek out the hyena in its lair. One of them will enter the cave, block the entrance behind him with an aba or a sack, and then slowly creep up on the hyena. He catches the hyena around the neck with a halter or a hobbling rope into which a loop has been tied, muzzles the beast, and then leaves the cave. Then he and his comrades pull out the hyena, which is ignominiously dragged cringing from his den and tied up like a camel. I have actually seen some live hyenas caught by hunters, muzzled, tied by a lead to a rock or tent pole, and put on display for spectators, who pay a fee to see them.

By night, however, this animal turns into a voracious predator, especially during the winter season. It boldly intrudes upon outlying villages and violates graves, digging up and dragging out corpses to eat them. It relishes carrion of every kind, and in some regions the villagers call it Abū l-Fuṭṭas, "eater of putrid carcasses." Village hunters set large traps around an animal carcass, the smell of which seldom escapes the notice of a hyena. When the hyena comes by night to feed on the carcass it is caught in the trap, which is fixed in the ground with iron chains and weights. In the morning, the hunters come and catch

[13] Doughty, I, 372.

the animal, muzzle it with an iron muzzle, and lead it on a chain back to the village.

The hyena still abounds in places in Arabia that have been known as haunts of this animal since ancient times, such as Jabal al-Ṭiwāl, east of al-Qaryatayn. I have seen some of them during my travels in the regions adjoining the desert. Once, while on a hunting trip, I saw one traveling across the steppeland; it had pulled loose a trap in which it had been caught during the previous night, and was dragging the trap behind it. When I followed it on horseback, the hyena broke into a run, with the chains and weights clattering behind him and the pebbles and stones flying and scattering in his wake. When I had drawn within rifle range, it fled into a rugged rock-strewn wadi, crossed it, and ran out the other side. When I saw it again it was a long distance away; and to my astonishment, it had left behind the trap, the weights, and part of its right rear leg, which had been caught in the trap. It continued to flee, hopping along at a high speed on its remaining three feet.

Hyenas very often frequent regions where gazelles abound, searching for a dead gazelle shot but not located by hunters, or one that moved on after being hit and then died, or an injured gazelle that has fallen behind the rest of the herd. It actually happened to some of my companions and me that we shot three bucks from a herd of six bucks and a doe, and followed the remaining three bucks without stopping to carry away those we had shot. When we returned fifteen minutes later, we found that a hyena had sneaked in to claim its share of our game. It had torn off one part of a gazelle carcass and was making off with it after having eaten both thighs of the animal. When our car suddenly appeared it dropped the piece it had on the ground and dashed away, but we followed it and killed it.

Despite its stench and the damage it causes, the hyena is useful in several respects. It is one of the elements—along with foxes, eagles, vultures, and the sun—that serve to cleanse the land and air of the desert of animal carcasses and their foul odor. For no sooner has a camel or donkey, for example, died in the desert and left a carcass in the open air, than you will see hyenas and jackals gathering by night around the carcass, devouring it as fast as they can gobble it down. Then vultures and eagles come by day to do the same with whatever the hyenas and foxes have left for them. The heat of the sun in turn does away with the remnants, so that no more than a week has passed when the carcass is no more. Nothing remains but a few bones scattered here and there.

Just as some of the bedouins eat the meat of the wolf, certain bedouins and people in the villages adjoining the desert used to eat the meat of the hyena, but probably in recent years have ceased to do so. From the teeth of hyenas the bedouins make necklaces for their children to protect them from certain diseases. They also claim that the bile of the hyena's gall-bladder, when mixed with water and drunk, serves to alleviate fever and to diminish its effects on the victim.

The Shīb

In the desert and in the villages along its peripheries, people speak of an animal they call the *shīb*. When a wolf mates with a female hyena, they claim, the result of the union is this strange animal. Some say that when the female hyena in heat is receptive to being mounted by a male, a wolf by chance encounters her and pounces upon her, so that she gives birth to the *shīb*. Others say that the *shīb* is rather the product of the mating of the dog and the female wolf. Whatever the case may be with this strange animal, which I have never seen, it is obviously of the wolf family or a special type of predatory wolf. The customary belief of the desert folk is that it is more destructive and malicious than either the hyena or the wolf: as they claim, it displays the courage and boldness of the wolf and the voracity and appetite of the hyena. The tales they relate about the harm and terrible deeds it perpetrates are legion, and go so far as to assert that nothing can stand against it or repel it. Musil discussed it in one of his books, called it the *sīb*, and did not doubt the stories told about it. He said that it is the result of the mating of the wolf with the female hyena, that the region in which it may be found is near Bi'r al-Shaqīq (al-Shajīj), and asserted that it attacks man without being aroused or provoked.[14] It seems to me that whether these stories are to be believed or dismissed,

[14]Alois Musil, *The Manners and Customs of the Rwala Bedouins* (New York, 1928), p. 22. And in *Aghānī*, III, 27, we are told that the *daysam* is the offspring of a wolf by a dog mother, that the *'asbār* is the offspring of a hyena by a wolf mother, and that the *sama'* is the offspring of a wolf by a hyena mother.

they seek to account for an animal rarely found in the desert, one that, like the mule, does not reproduce.

The Badger

In the desert there lives an animal larger than the cat, but smaller than the dog, which the bedouins call the *ẓarbūl*. This is the badger, which in the Arabic texts is renowned for its foul smell. Al-Damīrī describes it as follows:

> It has two auditory canals but no ears, and short paws with sharp claws. It has no spinal column in its back, nor vertebrae, but rather a single bone extending from a joint at the head to another at the tail. People sometimes catch it, but when they strike it with swords this has no effect, even if the blow falls on its nose. This is because its skin is similar to dried meat in hardness.[15]

The badger is grayish-yellow on its back and black on the belly, has a long tail, and lives on the flesh of jerboas, dhabbs,[16] and various other reptiles. With respect to its hunting of dhabbs, the bedouins claim that it sneaks up to the dhabb's hole and breaks wind into it; the dhabb comes out in dazed confusion from the stench, and so falls prey to the badger. They also claim that when the badger breaks wind into a bedouin's clothes, the smell remains until the garment falls to pieces. Despite its foul smell, some bedouins kill the badger and eat its meat. When Doughty discussed the matter, he denied that any such animal existed in Arabia and claimed that the badger was a mythical beast.[17] Musil, however, gave an accurate description of it, saying that it has teeth similar to those of a human being and a long tail.[18] It is said that in some regions the badger is called *al-gharīr* or *al-gharīrī*, "the

[15]Al-Damīrī, *Ḥayāt al-ḥayawān*, II, 153.

[16][On the lizard known as the dhabb (in Arabic, *ḍabb*), see Chapter VI below.]

[17]Doughty, II, 164. It is odd that when Doughty mentions the badger in Volume I (p. 371) of his book, where he calls it the "Thurbān," he says, "I do not know whether this animal is a real or mythical one." In Volume II he states that the bedouins described it to him as black in color and larger than the fox; nevertheless, he considers it mythical and calls it "eth-thurromban."

[18]Musil, *Manners and Customs*, p. 22.

deluded one;" and in the northern Syrian Desert, near the Euphrates, it is called *ḥaffār al-qubūr*, "the gravedigger."

The Fox and Jackal

In the desert and its peripheral areas there also live various members of the fox family, most notably the fox itself, which the bedouins sometimes call Abū l-Ḥuṣayn. The fox is widespread throughout the desert quarters bordering on the settled lands, and the bedouins eat its meat. Its fur is long, and its pelts are sold in most villages during the winter, when the animal is hunted. It too has a foul odor in the summer, as I discovered when I killed a fox during one of my travels. Of particular interest are the tales and stories the bedouins tell about the fox's tricks, and the legends concerning the fox, some of which we shall consider when we take up the topic of the superstitions commonly encountered in the desert.[19] The fox and the jackal, which in many respects resembles it, live on carrion, on such rabbits and birds as they may be able to catch, and whatever they may be fortunate enough to gain from powerful predatory animals willing to share with them the prey they have killed.

The Qurayṭa (Wildcat)

There is also a vicious and stealthy animal similar to the cat, but larger, and reportedly comparable to the panther in agility and ferocity. The bedouins call it the *qurṭa* or *qurayṭa*, and in Arabic texts it is called *ʿanāq al-arḍ*, "she-kid of the land." It is a dark tawny color and unspotted. In the desolate arid lands and in lands where dry vegetation is found, it lives among the thorn and *ḥamḍ* bushes where it can easily hide and suddenly pounce upon and kill such birds as the sand grouse, pheasant, and bustard. It may even fall upon rabbits and gazelles as its prey, as wolves do.

There appear to be three species of this animal, the wildcat. The first, small and olive-colored, makes its home in thickets and other scrublands. It is slightly larger than the domestic cat and preys on birds. The second is large-bodied, and, as we mentioned, dark tawny colored; its ears are black, with long hairs along the edges. This is

[19] *Ibid.*, pp. 23–25.

the species the bedouins call the *qurayṭa* or *qurṭa*. The third most closely approximates the panther in its coloring and spotting; and not surprisingly, the ancients used to tame it and use it for hunting. The female of all these species bears litters of from two to five cubs, like the domestic cat.[20]

The Panther

There yet remains the panther. Here we must mention that many apply to the *fahd*, or panther, the name *namir*, "leopard." Some Arabic dictionaries even err so far as to describe the panther and then say, "It is said that it is the product of the mating of the lion and the leopard." The animal to which we apply the name *fahd* is not the African leopard, which resembles the *fahd* in its spotting, but rather the Arabian panther, which is far smaller than the African leopard but larger than the wildcat, or *qurayṭa*. The panther is ashen white and speckled with large black spots. Until recent times it was found in abundance in most of the thickets along the peripheries of the desert and in various wadis in which trees grew. Not surprisingly, there so far remain a few panthers in certain areas of the Syrian Jazīra in the vicinity of the Euphrates, and east of Ḥimṣ in Jabal al-Bal'ās, where there are many terebinth trees. Many mentioned to me that they had seen panthers in some of these places, in Wādī Mūsā in Palestine, and in the thickets in the 'Alawite mountains. In my boyhood I saw a hunter who killed two panthers at Ghadīr al-'Uwayna north of al-Qaryatayn. He had taken up a position in a hunting blind (*nawja*) one summer night to hunt gazelles as they came for water, when he was suddenly confronted by two strange animals which he killed with two shots. They turned out to be a male and a female panther.

In times past the panther was caught while still young, trained and taught how to hunt by specialized handlers, and used to hunt the gazelle, oryx, and onager. The Arabic sources say that the first Arab to hunt with the panther was Kulayb ibn Wā'il during pre-Islamic times, followed by Yazīd ibn Mu'āwiya in the Islamic era.[21] Umayyad princes

[20]David L. Harrison, *The Mammals of Arabia* (London, 1964–72), II, 279–95.

[21]Al-Mas'ūdī, *Murūj al-dhahab*, edited by Charles Pellat (Beirut, 1966–79), V, 156; al-Damīrī, *Ḥayāt al-ḥayawān*, II, 317. They also claim that he taught it how to ride on horseback.

and rulers with a passion for hunting continued to pursue the training of panthers, and until the time of the Crusades the 'Abbāsids followed them in that interest. In the chapter on the chase in the *Dīwān* of Abū Nuwās, there is a *rajaz* poem describing the panther used by hunters to hunt the gazelle and other animals,[22] as well as five other *rajaz* odes attributed to this poet that all describe the panther. One begins:

> I arose in the early morning,
> With the sun in veil concealed,
> Allowing of its dressing gown
> Naught at all to be revealed.

and continues to describe the she-panther that hunted for him:

> Blessed be she, and he with whom she sets forth at dawn
> Proud riders both, and she on a mount by none despised.
> Like the lions of the thickets where she has gone,
> Gazing with a piercing eye in which I thought I espied
> Flying forth from her a bursting flame,
> Like unto the leopard in the way she creeps nigh;
> From decorated silk brocade her raiment came,
> Flashing on her flanks as she restlessly passes by,
> Like unto a lance as she stands erect, straight and tall,
> And a spotted snake whose glide no noise announces
> Swift as an eagle as her claws stretch forth and fall,
> And again, like the lion in the way she springs and pounces.
> No sooner had he set out than her keen notice found
> Herds of gazelles to which dust a light color had lent;
> She quietly slipped along as she ran them to ground,
> Devouring the surface of the land as she went.

and concludes to say:

> The fruits of her hunt do provide us our fill,
> While pleasures she offers to us as we will
> By virtue of granting her masters her kill.[23]

[22] Abū Nuwās, *Dīwān*, edited by Ewald Wagner and Gregor Schoeler (Beirut, 1378–1402/1958–82), II, 200–202.
[23] *Ibid.*, II, 285–90.

In Usāma ibn Munqidh's *Kitāb al-i'tibār* there are long accounts of hunting with panthers, and a detailed description of the animal's agility, courage, and superiority to greyhounds and other hunting animals.[24]

The training of panthers apparently remained common until recent times. Doughty mentioned that one of the bedouins told him about a certain bedouin shaykh who used to train a panther for hunting.[25] Before Doughty's time, Guarmani, in recounting the journey he undertook in 1864, reported that he saw a panther in the mountains near the Syrian Desert, that the bedouins used to hunt them on horseback, and that he actually pursued one on horseback until the beast tired, fell down panting, and was killed.[26] He does not, however, mention seeing any bedouin shaykh train a panther to hunt. So also is the case with Musil, who refers to the existence of the panther in the early twentieth century in the hills northeast of Wādī Sirḥān and in other places.[27] Raswan reports that one of the bedouins shot a panther in the early years of this century, and actually provides a photograph of it in his *Black Tents of Arabia*.[28]

I have inquired among many bedouin tribesmen and shaykhs, and have found not one in this era who has trained panthers for hunting or for any other purpose. Indeed, it too has probably begun gradually to die out in most parts of Arabia.

In closing, it must be mentioned that the panther is not the wildcat described above, and that it differs greatly from the leopard, which must have died out several centuries before our time. The ancient Arabs claimed that the panther is a cautious animal and sleeps with only one eye closed, the other remaining open and vigilantly watching out for enemies. Ḥumayd ibn Thawr al-Hilālī made reference to this:

> The panther's sleep was the rest I took,
> Against the grudging foe to guard,

---

[24]Usāma ibn Munqidh, *Kitāb al-i'tibār*, pp. 206–208, 212.

[25]Doughty, I, 373.

[26]Carlo Guarmani, *Northern Najd: A Journey from Jerusalem to Anaiza in Qasim*, translated by Lady Capel-Cure, with introduction and notes by Douglas Carruthers (London, 1938), p. 15.

[27]Musil, *Manners and Customs*, p. 20.

[28]Carl R. Raswan, *Black Tents of Arabia* (Boston, 1935), opp. p. 50.

And food I ate beneath his gaze,
Though hunger pressed upon him hard.
He slumbers with one eye alone,
The other has its watch to keep
For enemies that pass his way—
He's wide awake, yet fast asleep.[29]

[29]Ḥumayd ibn Thawr al-Hilālī, *Dīwān* (Cairo, 1371/1951), p. 105. In most recensions, the word *al-a'ādī*, "enemies," in the penultimate line above is replaced by *al-manāyā*, the "lots of death."

CHAPTER IV

HERBIVOROUS DESERT ANIMALS

IN THE DESERT there are wild animals that eat only vegetation. If the land is productive, they thrive in the desert, reproducing and increasing in numbers; but if the desert becomes barren and rain fails to fall, these animals become emaciated and breed poorly.

The Gazelle

The best-known and most common of these animals is the gazelle, the *ghazāl* or *ẓaby*, as the bedouins call it, and in the opinion of the Arabs one of the most beautiful of all creatures. In former times this gentle creature figured prominently in the literature of the Arabs, and especially in their poetry, since among the poets the figure of the gazelle was a metaphor for beauty. It was to a gazelle that they compared a girl in considering such attributes as graceful stature, the furtive glance, her eyes, and excellence:

> The white gazelle that prods her fawn
> On new-born wobbling legs to rise
> Has of features naught to match
> Of finer neck or more prominent eyes.[1]

The bedouins hunted the gazelle, however, as they continue to do until this day. They are very fond of its meat, which they rank among the most highly prized and most delicious of meats; they especially favor it roasted, and consider hardly any other meat comparable to it.

---

[1] ʻUmar ibn Abī Rabīʻa, *Dīwān*, II.1, 192; Jibrail Jabbur, *ʻUmar ibn Abī Rabīʻa* (Beirut, 1935–71), III, 409.

Figure 12: A gazelle grazing near the tent, with its mate near the entrance.

The gazelle spends the winter and spring seasons in the desert. Then, when water supplies fail, ponds and rainpools dry up, and pasturage becomes scarce, it begins to migrate elsewhere, heading toward the settled lands along the desert peripheries in search of water and pasturage. It is not true that the gazelle can live during the summer without water; and if water and pasturage remained available in the desert throughout the year, there would be no reason for the gazelle to leave its desert home. At al-Qaryatayn I have seen various hunters taking cover around certain water pools to hunt gazelles, which remain in the areas around the villages until late summer. At that time the gazelle watches for rain so that it can begin the return journey to the desert. In this respect it does not differ from the bedouin, living and wandering in the desert and migrating into and out of it.

Gazelles travel in herds. On the plains between al-Qaryatayn and Ḥimṣ during the First World War I saw close to two hundred in a single herd. Until the first years of the Second World War, some herds at times still numbered as many as forty animals. Every herd, however large it may be, has one animal, called a *najūd*, to lead it. This *najūd* (in most cases a doe) is mature, sharp-eyed and extremely wary, alert, lean and light, and always on her guard for the approach of danger from any direction. When the herd makes its way into a pasture or wadi, she grazes on whatever high ground may overlook the place where the herd is grazing, so that she can stand guard and watch out for any sudden danger or attack. If suddenly confronted by some source of peril, she beats the ground with her hoofs, calls out with an odd cry, and dashes off in fright in the direction she supposes will lead to safety. The herd follows behind her so quickly that hardly a moment passes before the entire herd has formed a single line behind her, like ivory beads strung on an open necklace in the middle of the desert. The *najūd* stays in the lead with the herd following in order behind her, turning wherever she does and following her every lead, until she has distanced the herd from whatever danger it was that she feared for the herd and herself. If it happens that the *najūd* is killed, her place is taken by another doe, usually the one following behind her as the herd flees or travels, or by the buck following her.

There are several kinds of gazelles in the deserts of Arabia. One of these is the gazelle called the *rīm*, or addax, a most comely and very white species well-known in the Syrian Desert. Another is the species called *'afrī*, a short-necked gazelle pale dusty-colored on the back and white on the belly; and another is called *ḥamrī*, an amber carnation-colored gazelle with a beautiful hide. There is a species of gazelle known as the *jāzī*, which the bedouins claim spends all of its time in the desert and only rarely migrates with the other gazelles during the summer. As they maintain, this is because the *jāzī* can endure lack of water; or as they put it, this gazelle pays no attention to water, neither drinking it nor seeking it. Who knows—it may be that the *jāzī* finds sufficient water in the small amount contained in plants, or in the dew that condenses on the herbage late in the night and lasts until sunrise, and hence quenches its thirst on the herbage rather than from water. There are bedouins who claim that the *'afrī* gazelle is identical to the *jāzī*, or similar to it in that it does not drink water. Some bedouins classify the gazelle into three types: the addax, the *'afrī*, and the *adamī*. The *adamī* gazelle they describe as having a long neck (as opposed to the *'afrī*), long legs, and a white belly.[2]

Usāma ibn Munqidh mentions this last type, says that it is large in size, and calls it the *idmī* gazelle. He hunted down one of these gazelles near Shayzar, and preferred it to the small white gazelles (which he compared to little fawns) caught by the panther they had with them.[3] This type is also mentioned by Harrison in his work on the mammals of Arabia. This gazelle, he says, lives in the mountains, at the bases of tells, and on the plains to the southwest; it thrives in regions in which the acacia tree (the gum arabica) abounds. It is beautiful, graceful, and nimble, and able to leap gracefully across rutted ground. It can go without water for long periods of time, as it satiates its needs with the moisture in the plants upon which it grazes. When tamed the *adamī* gazelle is playful. In the oasis of al-Buraymī in 1959 Harrison himself raised a doe that was a source of amusement and delight to them, playing with the cat, hiding itself from her, and then jumping out in front of her. In times of intense heat it would lick the perspiration from their hands and feet, due to its saltiness, and it liked all kinds of food. It would eat sausages, peas, potatoes, peaches, and the local bread, was particularly fond of tea and coffee, and sometimes would even eat cigarettes and paper.[4]

There is no doubt that the gazelle is amenable to domestication. Many bedouins used to raise them. Once I saw a gazelle wandering about with a herd of goats in one of the desert villages and returning with it to the house of the herd's owner. I also saw a woman of the tribe of Ṣlayb coming to the village with a gazelle fawn behind her, following her through the village lanes wherever she went, as a dog follows its master. Wallin claimed that some gazelles in the lands of Shammar used to mingle with flocks of sheep and graze with them, gradually become attached to them, follow them, and live together with them.[5]

Gazelles reproduce in the Nafūd and in the Ḥamād late in the winter season, and do not travel to the desert fringes in early summer unless their young fawns have grown. In good years the doe gives birth twice,

[2]Cf. al-Damīrī, *Ḥayāt al-ḥayawān*, II, 145.

[3]*Kitāb al-i'tibār*, p. 207.

[4]Harrison, *Mammals of Arabia*, II, 356.

[5]Wallin, [p. 75; = *Ṣuwar*,] p. 111.

and sometimes produces twins. The mother doe fears for her fawn from its first day, but by its third day it becomes difficult for her to catch up with the young one as it moves along. The mating season is in late summer and early autumn, as is the case of domestic goats. At this time the buck, called a *tays*, makes a bawling sound like the bleating of the male goat, and most of its sexual agitation occurs by night. I still recall that on one of my trips to the desert, in early autumn, I camped one night in the open air. There was a group of us, and we had no sooner gone to sleep than we were suddenly wakened by a sound that was none other than the sound of one or more bawling gazelle bucks. That bawling or howling continued for a long time that night.

The buck is distinguished from the doe by the large size of his body and the length of his antlers; those of the doe are small and bent at the tips. We shall discuss the methods used to hunt gazelles elsewhere in this book, but here we must mention that these days the gazelle has almost become extinct in the Syrian Desert. This is because of the toll taken by hunters, shepherds, bedouins, and members of the Ṣlayb tribe, all armed with modern weapons, and the failure of the governing authorities to prosecute and punish them. The coming of the bedouins in large numbers to the northern desert probably forced such gazelles as remained to seek refuge in other areas to the south, regions which offer little to encourage its proliferation there.[6] There is no doubt that if the hunting of gazelles were prohibited and the ban strictly enforced for only a few years, the animal would recover to something approximating the large numbers in which we were once accustomed to seeing it.

The Ibex

Following the gazelle among the herbivorous mammals is one that resembles it, the ibex, which the bedouins call the *bidin*. It differs from the gazelle, however, in that it is larger in size and has thick curved horns, approximately like those of the goat, curling toward its back. It lives in the mountains of the Syrian Desert and along its peripheries, as well as in the mountains of Sinai. It clings to its mountain refuges

[6]Even in the south it is almost extinct. In his *Forty Years in the Wilderness* (London, 1957), p. 200, H. St. John Philby mentions that it had become rare by his day, though there were once thousands and herds of the animal numbered in the hundreds.

and only descends to the plains when it is forced to do so by hunters chasing it from one mountain and compelling it to seek shelter on another one nearby. Hence, there are those who call it the *tays al-jabal*, or "mountain buck."

The Bible in many places refers to the ibex and the onager, indicating that both were plentiful in the mountain, wilderness, and desert lands familiar to the Israelites. In Job we find: "Knowest thou when the wild goats of the rock bring forth? Or canst thou mark when the hinds do calf?... Who has sent out the oryx; or hath loosened the bands of the onager?"[7] And in the Psalms we read that "the high hills are a refuge for the ibex."[8] The Arabs have known the ibex since ancient times, described it as *al-aʿṣam* ("the white-footed one"), and based proverbs on its inaccessibility and adherence to the mountains. Referring to these two characteristics, Kuthayyir said of his consort, ʿAzza:

> She turned away and deafness
> Was what received my calls,
> As if I'd cried to rocky peaks
> Where even the ibex falls.[9]

The ibex lives in the mountains around the desert, as we mentioned, such as Jabal Ṭubayq. This is the mountain where inscriptions dating back to the Stone Age were discovered. In one of these is the figure of a camel, and beyond it some distance in the background is the figure of an ibex, indicating that this animal had made its home on this mountain since the era of the Stone Age.[10] The ibex is also found on Jabal ʿĀd and on Jabal Rimāḥ to the south of Tadmur, and until recent times it lived in the mountains near al-Qaryatayn. I saw many hunting ibexes on the mountains of Ghaṭṭūs, al-Kaḥla, and al-Bārida, and at ʿAyn al-Wuʿūl. The animal is obviously at home in the mountain heights, where, when it becomes thirsty, it can find water in small springs and fountains.

---

[7]Job 39:1, 5.
[8]Psalms 104:18.
[9]*Aghānī*, VIII, 38–39.
[10]Philip K. Hitti, *History of Syria* (London, 1951), p. 52.

The ibex has long whiskers like those of the male goat, a short tail like the gazelle's, and two long brown horns,[11] thick and curved rearward in the form of a half-circle in line with its forehead. On the upper front surface of the horns are protuberances square or oblong in shape. When the ibex tries to hide itself behind some rocks, its horns frequently remain visible, like the diverging forks of a dry tree. The ewe has no horns. It is said that the age of the ram can be estimated by the number of rings on his horns.

It was said by hunters whom I met in those parts that the ibex is weak-sighted, but that it has excellent hearing and a strong sense of smell. It lives on herbage and the leaves of mountain trees and shrubs. Its meat is similar to that of the gazelle, but tougher and sometimes hard to digest. Hunters of the ibex go to the mountains and wait in hiding for it along the paths it usually follows. One group conceals itself in a high mountain defile while another chases the game downwind toward it. In the years following the First World War, the Egyptian prince Yūsuf Kamāl used to come from Egypt to Syria, with retainers, servants, friends, a doctor and nurse, and a convoy of automobiles, for the purpose of hunting the ibex in the al-Bārida and 'Ayn al-Wu'ūl region mentioned above. He would erect his pavilion near 'Ayn al-Bārida or in Tadmur itself and stay about ten days or two weeks, each day waiting at a spot in those mountains while hunters hired specifically for this purpose drove ibexes toward him, until a passing ram gave him the opportunity to bag one. Hunters were familiar with the mountain paths followed by the ibex, and could tell from its tracks and droppings whether one was in the area and in what direction it was going. They were sufficiently knowledgeable in these matters to outsmart the animal and force it to pass close enough to the concealed hunter for him to bag it. The hunter would hide behind a rock or in a depression in the ground, or would conceal himself in some dry brush.

The ibex was once found in great numbers on Mount Hermon and on the mountains of Palestine, and until the last century was even found on most of the Syrian mountains adjoining the desert. In his account of his journey from Jerusalem to 'Anayza Guarmani mentions that on his

[11]Doughty says (II, 164) that he was told of the two horns of one ibex, one of which was more than two feet long.

way back he camped and spent the night on a mountain overlooking the Ghawr Valley. He had hardly slept an hour when he was awakened by the sound of rocks falling from the heights around him. He looked closely, and there was a herd of ibex (*bidin*) walking along the mountain top above him.[12]

Today there are fears that this animal has been wiped out from the mountains surrounding the Syrian Desert, especially in the north, for goatherds from the interior villages who sometimes seek pasturage for their livestock in these mountains, the bedouins camping in the nearby desert, and especially the tribe of Ṣlayb, all pursue the ibex from one mountain to another for the sake of the hunt. At present it is to be seen seeking refuge in the most remote mountains of the south at Ṭubayq (its ancient homeland) or in the mountains of Sinai. These mountains offer it no defense, however; nor can it, in this age, find refuge there from modern weapons unless arrangements are made to protect it and people commit themselves to its survival and realize the value of preserving the progeny that yet survive of these rare animals. It is interesting to note that when caught young the ibex may be tamed (or at least does not flee back to the steppe) and becomes accustomed to living with goats or other similar domestic animals. Doughty mentions that he saw an ibex fearlessly following its owner from a palm grove to the coffeehouse in one of the oasis villages, just as the gazelle does when tame.[13]

The Onager (Wild Ass)

Another herbivorous desert animal on the road to extinction, if it has not entirely become so already, is the wild ass. This is the animal referred to in the Arabic sources as the *farā*—some authors make the

[12]Guarmani, p. 9. In his note to this passage, Carruthers is mistaken when he claims that the ibex in this region marks the northern limits of this animal's habitat, since until recent years some still lived in the mountains near al-Qaryatayn and Tadmur. These mountains are more than 200 kilometers north of Ṭubayq. In this region there is a place called 'Ayn al-Wu'ūl, "Spring of the Ibex," mentioned long ago by the Arabic sources and still known by that name to the explorers of the same period in which Guarmani mentions it. See Wright, pp. 40, 141, 200. My father told me that he bagged an ibex on the mountain where 'Ayn al-Wu'ūl is located, and this was at the beginning of the twentieth century.

[13]Doughty, I, 665.

extravagant claim that it lives for 200 years and more.[14] This animal became the basis for the proverb, "every kind of quarry lies in the belly of the onager," referring to the importance of this animal in the eyes of hunters and to how no quarry, regardless of how great it is, measures up to the onager. The Old Testament attests to its presence in the desert since the time of the prophet David, when he referred to it in his Psalms, saying: "He sendeth the springs into the valleys which run among the hills. They give drink to every beast of the field: the onagers quench their thirst."[15] The prophet Jeremiah makes mention of it when he describes drought and lack of pasturage, saying: "And the onagers did stand in the high places, they snuffed up the wind like the jackels; their eyes did fail, for there was no grass."[16] Daniel too refers to it when he speaks of Nebuchadnezzar and the loss of his kingdom and his life as an outcast: "His dwelling was with the wild asses: they fed him with grass like oxen."[17] Isaiah mentions it in his prophecy on the fate of the earth, saying: "The forts and towers shall be for dens forever, a frolicking ground of wild asses, a pasture of flocks."[18] In like manner, Job speaks of it, saying: "Behold, as wild asses in the desert go they forth to their work; rising betimes for a prey: the wilderness yieldeth food for them and for their children."[19] So far as the wild ass is concerned, the only information we gain from any of these passages is that the animal lives in the barren wastes, wanders like the bedouin in search of pasturage and water, and without these two cannot survive.

If we consult the Arabic sources we find that al-Ṭabarī speaks of an occasion when the cavalier Sasanian prince Bahrām mounted his charger, rode out to hunt wild asses, and then shot one and pursued it. Then he saw a lion pulling down another and killed this one too. At a session of his court he vividly described what had happened to him during this incident.[20] We then encounter Labīd ibn Rabī'a al-

[14]Al-Damīrī, *Ḥayāt al-ḥayawān*, I, 376.

[15]Psalms 104:10–11.

[16]Jeremiah 14:6.

[17]Daniel 5:21.

[18]Isaiah 32:14.

[19]Job 24:5.

[20]Al-Ṭabarī, *Ta'rīkh al-rusul wa-l-mulūk*, edited by M.J. de Goeje *et al.* (Leiden, 1879–1901), I, 857.

'Āmirī, the author of one of the *mu'allaqāt*, embarking on an account and description of the onager, comparing his she-camel both to it and to the "wild cow."[21] Later Abū Dhu'ayb al-Hudhalī mourned the death of his sons in an ode, finding solace for their loss in three scenes drawn from bedouin life. The first is that of a wild ass with his mate and young ones, all grazing serenely in a grassy field, feasting on lush pasturage and drinking the waters of limpid pools, when all of a sudden a hunter surprises them and spreads death among them:

> Decree of death he hurled fast,
> Spread among them each and all:
> One to limp and gasp his last,
> Another felled to lay and bawl.[22]

Here he also associates the wild ass with the "wild cow" (the oryx), making the latter the subject of the second scene and consoling himself with its death from the hunter's arrow.

For as long as hunting has been known among the Arabs, the wild ass, or onager, along with the "wild cow," has been the quarry most highly prized by hunters in the desert. And indeed, of the two the former was perhaps even more highly esteemed, as is illustrated in the oft-cited proverb, "every kind of quarry lies in the belly of the onager."

The onager used to be seen in most parts of the Arabian peninsula, especially in the hills, adjoining the desert, where pasturage and water are plentiful. Hence, it was the northern region of the Syrian Desert, from the limits of Damascus to the Jazīra region along the Euphrates, that was the richest in onager population. The Arabic sources mention that Yazīd ibn Mu'āwiya used to go to the region of Jarūd, between Damascus and al-Qaryatayn, to hunt the wild ass and the ibex;[23] the hills there are rich in pasturage and not far from certain springs and pools. One still today comes across the remnants of arrows shot at game by hunters in the days when arrows were the only lethal hunting weapon they had.[24]

[21] *Sharḥ al-qaṣā'id al-'ashr*, pp. 73, 76.

[22] *Dīwān al-hudhalīyīn*, I, 9.

[23] Al-Damīrī, *Ḥayāt al-ḥayawān*, I, 376; quoting from Ibn Khallikān, *Wafayāt al-a'yān*, edited by Iḥsān 'Abbās (Beirut, 1968–72), VI, 354.

[24] This is confirmed by information reported by Doughty (I, 613).

From some of the paintings left behind at Qusayr ʻAmra in Jordan by the Umayyads in the time of al-Walīd ibn ʻAbd al-Malik, it is clear that wild asses were so numerous that they traveled in herds. Here we also see that hunters used to drive them along until they forced the animals to seek refuge in enclosed places where other hunters waited in hiding to kill them with lances or spears. Some hunters used to pursue them on horses until they drew close enough for a lance or arrow shot.[25]

The wild ass remained plentiful even in areas close to agricultural lands and villages, and especially in the Syrian Jazīra and in the districts of Ḥamāh and Shayzar near the Orontes River. In the chapter on hunting tales in his memoirs, which he committed to writing in the twelfth century AD, Usāma ibn Munqidh refers to the existence of the onager in abundance in the surrounding Syrian Desert. He describes how one day, when he was a young boy, he and his father went out to hunt gazelles:

> When he (Usāma's father) reached Wādī l-Qanāṭir, he suddenly encountered some black brigands waiting to rob those passing down the road. So he seized them, tied their hands behind their backs, and turned them over to a troop of his retainers to be taken to the prison in Shayzar.

He continues:

> As for me, I took a javelin (*husht*) from one of them and we went on to the hunt. Suddenly there appeared a herd of wild asses, and I said to my father, "Sir, I have never before today seen wild asses; so, by your leave, I will gallop ahead to look at them." "Go ahead," he said. I had under me a sorrel mare, the finest thoroughbred, so I galloped off, carrying in my hand the javelin I had taken from the brigands, until I reached the midst of the herd. I cut one of the asses out of the herd and began to thrust at it with the javelin; but because of my weak arm and the bluntness of the spearhead, the beast suffered no harm. So I turned

[25]Martin Almagro *et al*, *Qusayr ʻAmra: residencia y baños omeyas en el desierto de Jordania* (Madrid, 1975), pp. 170–73, 176–78, 180.

> it around and drove it back to my companions, who then captured it. My father and those with him marveled at the way that horse ran.[26]

It is clear that the onager has been dwindling to extinction in the Syrian Desert since the late nineteenth century, for only a few of the European travelers mention seeing it. Palgrave, who penetrated to the heart of Arabia in 1862–63, mentions not a word—not even a passing reference—about this animal, nor does Doughty. Guarmani, who undertook his journey to central Arabia in 1864, has this to say in Appendix XIV to the account of his travels: "When winter is past, many of the Saleib cross the Euphrates to hunt the wild ass in Mesopotamia, there being no more of these now in the Hammad" (i.e. in the Syrian Desert). He then says that Ṣlayb takes a certain number of these asses alive and raise them to breed with their own donkeys.[27] The male offspring are castrated, and when they reach the age of two years are sold for 200 Austrian thalers each.[28] On the other hand, Musil, the traveler closest to our own time, refers in one of his books to how his guide in the Middle Euphrates region told him that he had once seen a large herd of wild asses, about 60 in number, and that he had shot one of them near the Khābūr River in the Jazīra.[29]

---

[26]*Kitāb al-iʿtibār*, p. 220.

[27]Among those villagers and Ṣlayb tribesmen whom I queried on this matter, I found no one who confirmed it. However, Ḥusayn Bey Ebesh, who ranked among the Syrians most renowned in the sport of hunting in the first half of this century, wrote to me that some of the Ṣlayb do claim this, but that he is not certain of the veracity of this allegation. Still, he pointed out, many domestic donkeys still show on their hides black lines similar to those that characterize the wild ass. These are sometimes to be seen on the hindquarter, other times on the shoulders or at the neck or tail.

[28]Guarmani, p. 120. In a note appended to the aforementioned report, Carruthers says that contrary to the claims of recent writers, this report is correct. He then goes on to say that the wild ass had disappeared from the Syrian Ḥamād, but was still to be found in the desert north of the Euphrates in the vicinity of Jabal Sinjār. Similarly, Lady Anne Blunt (p. 240) mentions that the Yazīdīs eat the meat of the wild ass, which is found in abundance in their lands.

[29]See Alois Musil, *The Middle Euphrates* (New York, 1927), pp. 74, 156. The same report appears in two places, but in differing versions. It would not be surprising if this proved to be a fabrication concocted by the guide, especially since Musil does not seem to be sure of its veracity.

I myself have inquired with many bedouins, and none of them declared that he had ever in his life seen a wild ass. I also asked others, people who live or work in the Jazīra, and one of them mentioned that although he himself had never seen a wild ass, he could name some elderly individuals who had seen the animal in the late nineteenth century. These informants did not think it unlikely that some might still survive today. An elderly herdsman told me that in the late nineteenth century he had sent a wild ass to Fayyāḍ Āghā, *za'īm* of al-Qaryatayn, who in turn sent it as a gift to the governor of Damascus, Aḥmad Pāshā al-Sham'a. The ass used to be hunted in the region surrounding the village of al-Furqulus near the present-day pipeline.

Douglas Carruthers mentions that the onager had been wiped out from the Ḥamād in the nineteenth century, when modern firearms came into the hands of the bedouins and the Ṣlayb. The animal then sought refuge in the Euphrates region, thus causing many tribesmen of Ṣlayb to cross the river during the winter in pursuit of onagers to breed with their female donkeys.[30]

The bedouins claim that the onager lives to an extremely old age; and Kushājim states that asses have no sexual desire until they reach the age of thirty months, that the female cannot be impregnated until the end of the third year, and that the animal was domesticated to such an extent that it was said that wild asses that had been domesticated produced meat superior to that of those still in the wild.[31] In al-Damīrī's *Ḥayāt al-ḥayawān* we find that Ibn Khallikān saw the head of a wild ass killed by a bedouin, and on its ear found a brand dating from the time of the Persian king Bahrām Gūr (r. AD 420–38).[32] This is an utterly bizarre tale, probably a fabrication by its transmitters.

The Oryx, or "Wild Cow" (Wuḍayḥī)

Also ranking among these wild animals is the so-called "wild cow," the oryx, or *mahā* as it is called in Arabic literary works and poetry. The bedouins call this antelope the *wuḍayḥī*, the "bright one," because of its whiteness. Until recently it was found in all of the deserts of Arabia,

[30] Douglas Carruthers, *Arabian Adventure* (London, 1935), p. 149.

[31] *Al-Maṣāyid wa-l-maṭārid*, edited by Muḥammad As'ad Ṭalas (Baghdad, 1954), pp. 156–57.

[32] *Ḥayāt al-ḥayawān*, I, 376; from Ibn Khallikān, *Wafayāt al-a'yān*, VI, 354.

even the Syrian Desert, where Guarmani reports having seen it in the mid-nineteenth century.[33] Citing an informant, Harrison says that after the First World War the "wild cow" was to be seen during the autumn in the hills near the village of Jarūd,[34] which is not more than 60 kilometers from Damascus. The Museum of the American University of Beirut holds a preserved specimen dating from the late nineteenth century. Carruthers in 1938 even referred to the "wild cow" when he commented on the above-mentioned passage in Guarmani, and stated that the "wild cow" was still found in the Ṭubayq region, which was, he says, its last refuge in northern Arabia.[35] Doughty too mentions its presence in the territories of the Sharārāt tribe along the pilgrimage road, and states that some of them raised a "wild cow" that had been caught by the bedouins; in fact, the animal was sent to Damascus and from there on to Istanbul.[36] Doughty further reports that in the late nineteenth century he saw a doe and a buck held by others at Ḥā'il.[37] He also says that the horns of the "wild cow" are commonly found at Taymā', where bedouins of the Sharārāt bring them and give them as presents to the people of Taymā', who use the horns to break up bunches of dates that have stuck together in their containers. And it is from Doughty that we hear that the bedouins of Ṣlayb sometimes use the horns as pegs for their tents, and likewise, that the hides are used for the soles of sandals.[38] Musil, one of the explorers from the early years of this century, refers to the presence of the oryx and its frequent appearance in the Nafūd region during the summer, especially when there are not many bedouins there to see it, so few that it even grazes during the day. During the rainy months, on the other hand, its fear allows it to graze freely only at night.[39]

When hunters began to slaughter the "wild cow," thanks to their modern weapons, the animals that remained took refuge in the Rub' al-Khālī. Wilfred Thesiger thus claimed that during his crossing of the

---

[33]Guarmani, p. 74.
[34]Harrison, II, 346.
[35]Carruthers, *Arabian Adventure*, p. 149.
[36]Doughty, I, 98.
[37]*Ibid.*, I, 372, 644.
[38]*Ibid.*, I, 613.
[39]Musil, *Manners and Customs*, p. 26.

Figure 13: The oryx, or "wild cow".

Rub' al-Khālī in 1948 he once saw a herd of 28 "wild cows," in addition to those he had seen previously.[40] The Aramco company used to keep a buck and a doe in a preserve it established in the Aḥsā', and then presented the two animals as a gift to the preserve of the Saudi ruler. More recently, the ruler of Qaṭar, Amīr Qāsim ibn Ḥamad Āl Thānī, founded a small preserve specifically for the raising of the oryx. In it he assembled a herd of about twenty animals caught, as mentioned above, in the Rub' al-Khālī. One can see from photographs taken in that preserve that the "wild cow" obviously reproduces in captivity and that its young look exactly like the calves of domestic cattle. Similarly, special wildlife preserves have been established in Oman, Jordan, and Saudi Arabia; "wild cows" have been imported and have begun to breed in captivity there.

The "wild cow" is similar to the ibex in size, and even larger; but it is distinguished from the latter by the shape of its head, the color of its hide, and its horns. The ibex, like the gazelle, is sandy-colored; but the "wild cow" has an ivory-white hide and a black spot on its face. It also has a cloven hoof and a tail like those of the cow, and both the

[40]Wilfred Thesiger, *Desert, Marsh, and Mountain* (London, 1979), p. 54.

buck and the doe have long horns that can sometimes reach two feet or more in length. These horns are nearly straight, thin, curved from the base to about a third of their length, and then straight to the end. The tip of the horn comes to a fine sharp point, like the tip of the spit used to skewer meat for roasting. The "wild cow" uses its horns to protect itself from hunting dogs and other animals that may attack it. Al-Nābigha was probably not exaggerating when he described the horn of a "wild cow" protruding from the hindquarters of a dog a hunter had set against him:

> A needle run through 'neath the shoulders is what he feels,
> Pierced as by the farrier when the upper leg he heals.
> As if there was protruding through its hide-covered frame
> A drinker's skewer forgotten and left aside the fire's flame.[41]

There is no doubt that it is the oryx that is mentioned in the Bible by the Hebrew term *ri'm*. The same term is rendered "gazelle" in the Arabic and erroneously translated as such in Deuteronomy 14:5, the same term being used in Numbers 23:22, 24, and 24:8. In Job 39:9–12 it is rendered as "wild ox." The author of the article on the *ri'm* in the *Qāmūs al-kitāb al-muqaddas* is mistaken when he claims that the animal has disappeared from the north and supposes that the term refers to the oryx.[42] In Deuteronomy 33:17, the blessing of Moses upon Joseph has the former saying: "His horns are like those of the *ri'm*;" and in Psalms 22:21 we read: "Deliver me from the mouth of the lion, and from the horns of the wild cow." It is interesting to note that Deuteronomy records the names of most of the animals and birds of the desert, including the ibex, onager, "wild cow," ostrich, eagle, vulture, and crow, and even the lioness and the horse. It is said that the meat of the onager is the tastiest of wild game, and that it is superior to that of the ibex.

The "wild cow" is a wide-eyed animal, and the Arab poets were quite taken by this, comparing young women to the oryx in their poetry and characterizing girls as having the eyes of the oryx. As 'Alī ibn al-Jahm said:

[41] *Sharḥ al-qaṣā'id al-'ashr*, p. 154.

[42] *Qāmūs al-kitāb al-muqaddas*, p. 391.

Twixt al-Ruṣāfa and al-Jisr, stirred by oryx eyes,
Passion caught me unaware and in my breast did rise.[43]

The eyes of the oryx are most beautiful and make the deepest impression on the observer when the doe bends over her new-born fawn and tries to remain alert to protect it. As 'Umar ibn Abī Rabī'a said in comparing his maiden to such an animal:

The dark-eyed oryx stares through thicket-home,
Seeking some place for her new fawn to roam.[44]

The "wild cow" is of special interest as a species that has recovered from extinction in the wild. Lee Merriam Talbot wrote in 1955 that the "wild cow" was being hunted to the point of extinction in Arabia, and that only about a hundred "wild cows" survived in the Rub' al-Khālī.[45] By 1962 the animal had became so endangered that the zoos of Phoenix and London embarked on a program to breed it in captivity. The last six oryx surviving in the wild were shot in Saudi Arabia ten years later, but by then the American and British breeding programs were achieving good results. In 1982 the "wild cow" was reintroduced into the wild in Oman, and further stocks of animals have been supplied to preserves in Jordan and Saudi Arabia.

In times past the bedouins of Ṣlayb were the most destructive hunters of the oryx. The Ṣlayb hunter, wearing white or sandy-colored clothing or a garment of gazelle skin, could hide behind his white donkey and close to within rifle-shot of a "wild cow" without it seeing him or sensing his presence, provided that the wind was blowing from the animal toward the hunter. But if it sensed his presence it would flee, and its fear would drive it to run for tens of miles before it stopped or felt secure. In more recent years, however, there was no prospect of safety since hunters could pursue the oryx with motor vehicles, or if the situation required, with airplanes. And the most ominous factor behind the extermination of the Arabian oryx was the fact that the

[43] *Nuzhat al-abṣār bi-ṭarā'if al-akhbār wa-l-ash'ār*, compiled by 'Abd al-Raḥmān ibn 'Abd Allāh ibn Dirham (Beirut, AH 1345), II, 405.

[44] 'Umar ibn Abī Rabī'a, *Dīwān*, I.1, 5; Jabbur, *'Umar ibn Abī Rabī'a*, III, 409.

[45] *Time*, 21 (November 1955), p. 32.

same species existed nowhere else. A colleague from the southern Sudan told me that the oryx is still found in the Sudan, but its horns differ from those of the Arabian oryx. These curve rearward, since the animal lives in woodland regions; it is as if nature or the environment had been a factor in their formation.

The Roebuck

Today the bedouins know no animal in the desert that bears this name. In his memoirs, Usāma ibn Munqidh mentions that he used to hunt the roebuck (*yaḥmūr*) near Bāniyās, which indicates that it lived in dense woodlands and scrublands. This is made quite clear when Usāma says:

> In the days of Shihāb al-Dīn Maḥmūd ibn Tāj al-Mulūk I used to go hunting around Damascus for birds, gazelles, wild asses, and roebucks. One day I saw him, and we set out for the wood of Bāniyās, where the ground was much overgrown with underbrush, hence we killed many roebucks. We pitched our tents in a circle and made camp; then a roebuck that had been sleeping in the underbrush stood up in the middle of the circle, and was taken amongst the tents.[46]

From what he says it seems that roebucks are animals distinct from wild asses, and that they are animals resembling the goat (as is stated in the dictionary[47]) or a kind of ibex or stag that differs from the goats of the mountains near the desert. Anyone who reads Harrison's work on Arabian mammals will realize that there are various kinds of wild goats in the peninsula, and it may be that the roebuck was one of them.

The Wild Boar

Another herbivorous animal of the Syrian Desert is the wild boar. This beast is found in large numbers in Wādī Sirḥān, where there is abundant herbage and water, in the western mountains lying along the peripheries of the desert in the Tadmur region from the outskirts of Jarūd up to

[46] *Kitāb al-i'tibār*, pp. 193–94.
[47] *Lisān al-'arab*, q.v. *ḥ-m-r*.

the Jazīra in the north, and in the wooded regions near the Euphrates. The boar lives on the stems, stalks, and roots of certain wild plants, such as the *tummayr* (stork's bill), *qaf'arūr*, and other similar plants. On occasions it may trespass into outlying fields, eat the yellow corn growing there, and destroy part of the cultivators' source of livelihood. As is well-known among Muslims, the meat of the boar is forbidden, and no villagers other than Christians will eat it. And even some of these join the Muslims in considering it taboo to eat of its meat. In the desert, however, certain bedouins do not hesitate to eat its meat, led to do so by their need, poverty, and ignorance of the tenets of their faith. They even treat their wounds and those of their horses and camels with its fat.

The boar is a fearsome and ferocious animal, especially when it is wounded or cornered. It has two sharp curved tusks with which it can cause serious injury, and it can even inflict wounds on a man if he does not know how to take precautions against injury from them. I knew a hunter who was gored in the buttock and thigh by a boar, and the wounds left him bedridden for about six months before he recovered completely.

The boar prefers marshes and lands where trees abound, so it now proliferates in parts of Iraq that are close to water. The Rwāla bedouins refer to the male of this animal as *shiḥl*, to the female as *shība*, and to the young as *qarnūṣ*.[48] They used to regard it as an evil omen to see a boar if they had set out to move from one place to another, or if they were on their way to undertake a raid.

The Porcupine

The porcupine is a small animal that resembles the boar in form, but is actually a very different species. It lives in rugged terrain and on rocky mountains, where it takes naturally dug out places for its den, or if it finds no such place, digs one itself, as a rabbit would do. It has a long nose or snout, short ears, and is the size of a cat, but stands taller and is thicker through the body. Its hair is like that of the boar but closer to that of the hedgehog in that the animal's back is covered with a type of long quill. This quill is longer and thicker than that of the hedgehog.

[48] Musil, *Manners and Customs*, p. 28.

One may reach 30 centimeters in length and a centimeter or more in diameter at the base, and the tip comes to a point as sharp as that of a pack needle. These quills are hollow and marked with wide black and white bands, and when we were students in the villages we used to use them as finger grips for quill pens. In the villages and in the desert they claim that when the porcupine is wounded out in the desert, or when it is cornered or sees something that frightens it, it curls up and trembles, its quills stand erect, and it makes a frightening sound. Then it turns its back toward its adversary and lunges forth at him, so that if the latter ventures close to him, some of these quills will stick to the attacker and penetrate his body like arrows.[49]

The porcupine has talon-like claws in a paw like the hand of a small boy, and when someone comes too close or corners it, it will bite and scratch. Similarly, its fangs can strike right to the bone and can cause serious injury. When a porcupine is killed it is not skinned; rather, its quills are scraped off and the skin that remains is eaten along with the meat, for the skin is a fatty gelatinous layer, somewhat like the skin of the pig.

The porcupine lives off of plants, and it eats, or so they claim, a bitter type of wild colocynth said to cause severe diarrhea in anyone who eats its leaf.[50] It also eats turnips, potatoes, onions, and carrots if the fields where these vegetables are grown are close to its dens.

The porcupine abounds in the al-Qaʻara area of the Syrian Desert, where there are many holes, dens, and hollowed out rocks, and also in the regions along the peripheries of the desert, especially in the large wadis and the hills and mountains where caves overlook the surrounding area. Between al-Ghunthur and al-Qaryatayn there is a wadi known as

[49]Doughty (I, 173) claims that this is one of the fables and legends of the Arab nomads; but as I understood from many who have seen the porcupine with their own eyes and have hunted it, this is apparently what the animal does. Some of these quills, which the bedouins call "feathers" (*rīsh*), will usually fall at the slightest shaking of the porcupine's body, but this does not mean that the animal "shoots" them like arrows. Its quills are often to be seen scattered around the entrances to its dens in the mountains near al-Qaryatayn, where porcupines abound. The late Ḥusayn Ebesh, one of the most renowned enthusiasts of the hunt in all the East, wrote to me that after hunting porcupines by night, his hunting dogs frequently return with porcupine quills still stuck to their bodies.

[50]*Ibid.*

Wādī l-Niyāṣa ("Wadi of the Porcupines"), mentioned to me by a man who had caught more than one porcupine there. He said that the best way to catch the porcupine is to go by night to the caves or crevices in the rocks where the porcupine takes shelter during the day, since during the night the animal goes out to feed. The hunter gathers some thorny plants, such as the tragacanth, and places them at the narrow entrance to the cave or crevice so that the porcupine's way in will be blocked when it returns at the end of the night. When the porcupine comes back to the cave from its roamings, it sees the thorns in the entrance and tries to get inside, but cannot do so because its face cannot stand the pain of the thorns. It remains standing at the entrance, at a loss as to what to do; and at dawn the hunters surprise it and kill it—with sticks if they wish, for during the day it cannot escape.

The Marmot

Living in dens among the rocks in the mountains is a strange and rare animal mentioned by David in the Psalms when he said: "The rocks are a refuge for the marmots."[51] It is the size of a young rabbit, resembles it in form, and eats the fresh herbage that grows in the sandstone mountains at the furthest limits of the Syrian Desert, as well as the leaves of the acacia, the tree from which gum arabica is derived and one which the marmot can easily climb. It is speckled and sandy colored, closely approximating the color of the rocks among which it lives, has a soft pelt, and has paws like those of the rabbit, with four toes on the forefeet and three on the back. It ruminates, or more precisely, moves its lower jaw as ruminating animals do, but does not have a cloven hoof, and for this reason the Jews were forbidden to eat it. The bedouins eat and enjoy its fatty meat. Its toes have round claws somewhat like sharp talons, and it also has sharp teeth that can deliver a painful bite to anyone who tries to catch it.

It lives in small groups which, it is claimed, set out a guard to keep watch from an elevated place and to sound a warning if it senses any danger.[52] Doughty claims that he saw marmots living together in groups of pairs—two, four, six, eight, or ten.[53] The animal has keen

[51] Psalms 104:18.

[52] *Qāmūs al-kitāb al-muqaddas*, p. 1016.

[53] Doughty, I, 371.

senses of sight, hearing, and smell, and during its mating season in the spring the males like to fight. Its gestation period lasts from seven to eight months and the female gives birth to three or four young in a single litter.[54]

Solomon described the marmot in an adage, saying:

> There be four things which are little upon the earth, but they are exceedingly wise: the ants are a people not strong, yet they prepare their meat in the summer; the marmots are but a feeble folk, yet make they their houses in the rocks; the locusts have no king, yet go they forth all of them by bands; the spider taketh hold with her hands, and is in kings' palaces.[55]

The Hedgehog

The hedgehog is a small animal familiar in both the desert and the villages, and is known as *Umm al-shawk*, "Mother of Thorns." There is probably more than a single kind, each differing from the other according to the region in which it lives. It is most often to be seen at night, when it ventures forth in search of food. It is the size of a large rat, and it can hide itself in its prickly pelt so that none of its limbs are exposed to view. It tends to do this whenever it is cornered and finds no means of escape, and when it does so it becomes an immobile prickly ball of thorns. When the bedouin sees the hedgehog, he pokes his stick into the animal's belly, which may be concealed in its prickly pelt, and forces it to expose its head, limbs, and abdomen. Some of the bedouins slaughter the hedgehog, eat its meat roasted, and consider it quite delicious. From its pelt they make amulets which they tie for at least a month around the necks of she-camels that show fear or shy away from anything. This, they claim, will allay the camel's fear.

The Jerboa

In the Syrian Desert, along its peripheries in the steepelands surrounding its villages, and especially around al-Qaryatayn, Tadmur, and in the

[54]Harrison, II, 320.

[55]Proverbs 30:24–28.

Syrian Jazīra, there is small strange-looking animal that, not surprisingly, is also found elsewhere. This is the jerboa, which the bedouins and settled folk call *jarbū'* and which the Arabic dictionaries refer to as *yarbū'*. It is rat-like in appearance and about the same size. But its forelegs are extremely small in proportion to its hind legs, for while the former do not come to more than five centimeters in length, the latter measure about ten. It is of two kinds. One has a long tail which it holds up high, as the squirrel does, when it runs, and which has a tassel-like tuft of hair on its end. It has long ears, its color is similar to that of the gazelle or wild rabbit, its pelt is soft like that of the rabbit, and its head also resembles that of the rabbit. The other kind is similar, but lacks the tuft of hair on its tail. Some of the bedouins claim that there is a third variety, which they call the *jirdī*. It is like the first, but larger, and has five toes on its foot.[56]

The jerboa makes its home underground in plains of sandy soil. It digs deep passages inward, and among these passages there are air holes which the jerboa can block whenever it wishes, so that even the rains of winter do not penetrate the burrow and reach its den. The bedouins claim that the jerboa never drinks and has no need of water. They eat its meat, which is white and resembles the breast meat of a chicken, and consider it quite delicious. It seems that the falcon also enjoys the meat of the jerboa, and so stoops on it whenever it ventures forth from its burrows. Indeed, hunters use the flesh of jerboas as bait in their snares when they are trying to catch adult falcons.

One desert fable has it that the jerboa boasts and says, "I am Jerboa, son of Marbū', on whom ten could fill themselves for dinner and still leave bits of me dangling in the brush. Were my front legs as long as my back legs, no thoroughbred *'ubaya* mare could catch me."[57] The *jirdī*, on the other hand, boasts of how he can unseat the greatest warrior from his charger by digging burrows into which the horse stumbles, thus throwing its rider to the ground. According to bedouin tradition an aged jerboa gave this advice to his child:

> Flee by yourself if destruction you fear,
> And leave the home for its builder to wail.

[56] On its varieties and distribution, see Harrison, III, 408.

[57] Musil, *Manners and Customs*, p. 29. An *'ubaya* is a kind of horse.

Now as for the home, its better you'll find;
But a soul like yours you'll seek, and fail.[58]

The Rabbit

The rabbit is a well-known animal and its wild variety is found in all parts of the Syrian Desert, from the Nafūd to the plains that lie between the Syrian villages. It is to be found in various kinds and colors, depending on the environment in which it lives. The bedouins seek out and hunt it with falcons. They regard it as a good omen, and when they see one they say: "You expose us to good fortune, while we expose you to the birds." The procedure for hunting rabbits will be discussed when we take up the subject of hunting practices.

[58] *Ibid.*

CHAPTER V

DESERT BIRDS

THE DESERT KNOWS many kinds of birds—so many that there is no space here to study or speak in detail on all their species or varieties. In the winter many water and other kinds of birds frequent the open expanses and pools of the Ḥamād. These include geese, ducks, doves, pigeons, partridges, Egyptian vultures, francolins, pelicans, storks, ravens, hoopoes, bee-eaters, larks, orioles, bustards, and the different varieties of sand grouse. Similarly, one also sees many predatory birds, such as eagles, griffon vultures, falcons, sparrow hawks, shahins, and black vultures. In his book *Al-Maṣāyid wa-l-maṭārid*, the poet known as Kushājim, Abū l-Fatḥ Maḥmūd ibn al-Ḥusayn, a bard of the tenth century AD, goes to great lengths in discussing the birds generally known to the Arabs in the desert. He refers to no less than 70 varieties in addition to those mentioned above (leaving out the repetitions), and some he describes with a meticulousness not found in the most comprehensive ornithological compendia.[1]

Nevertheless, to my knowledge there has so far been no sound scholarly study published in the Arabic language about birds of the desert, and in particular, about the birds of the Syrian Desert, which is so rich in oases and pools. Long ago, the Hebrew University sent out expeditions to collect specimens of desert birds and their eggs and deposited them in its museum in Jerusalem, and it probably preserves the best collection of stuffed specimens of these birds. The museum of the American University of Beirut used to hold a somewhat similar collection dating from the time of the college's founders, but now there

[1]Kushājim, *Al-Maṣāyid wa-l-maṭārid*, pp. 265–86.

is no one at the University to undertake the continuation of this task. It would not be surprising to find that the desert knows other kinds of birds not mentioned by Kushājim and perhaps rarely found in other places.

The Old Testament enumerates the birds forbidden for eating. These are the griffon vulture, buzzard, eagle, kite, all kinds of hawks and crows, the ostrich, sea gull, all kinds of falcons, the owl, cormorant, crane, pelican, jackdaw, Egyptian vulture, stork, all kinds of herons, the hoopoe, and the bat. Since the particular aim of this study is to survey such matters as concern desert life, I will discuss only the birds, including those both forbidden and allowed for consumption, that have some bearing on the bedouins and desert life.

The Sand Grouse

The sand grouse (or *qaṭā*) is the best known and most common bird in the desert and flies in large flocks. Were it not already stated in the Old Testament that the quail was the bird upon which the Israelites lived in the Wilderness of Sinai, I would say that it was the sand grouse, which so far as I know is far more numerous than any other bird, even the quail. In addition, it is the bird of ancient Arabic poetry, and the poets refer to it more frequently than they do to any other bird. Majnūn Laylā immortalizes it in his lines:

> I wept as a thick swarm of sand grouse flew by,
> And said, as it surely behooves me to cry:
> "Oh sand grouse, would one of you lend me your wing,
> To fly off to someone who makes my heart sing."[2]

Al-Shanfarā mentions it in his famous *lāmiya*, when he claims that he came and drank the water from a pool before it was visited by the early-arriving flocks of sand grouse, which thus drank the remainder he had left for them:

> By night come dusty sand grouse to drink of what I leave,

[2]See Majnūn Laylā, *Dīwān*, edited by 'Abd al-Sattār Aḥmad Farrāj (Cairo, 1959), p. 137.

In thirst they flock together as their ribs all knock and heave.[3]

Al-Ma'arrī speaks of the bird in his elegy for his father, referring to its wretched life and to how it nevertheless does not wish for death:

Eschewing death are dusky birds that fly five days,
Only to drink at brackish pools where water lays,
Or wandering into falcons' paths any night or day,
And finding themselves to curling talons falling prey.[4]

This bird is called a *qaṭā* because it calls out: "*qaṭā, qaṭā*!;" hence its name is derived from its call. And from this we get the Arabic proverb: "more veracious than the sand grouse," since it pronounces its name when it calls out. As al-Nābigha said:

It calls out "*qaṭā*," and the name it has reflects its cry.
How truthful it is: to give its name when men pass by![5]

The sand grouse is found in several varieties, among them the common variety today known to many as the *ṣayyāḥ*, "the crier," this being the one that makes the call "*qaṭā, qaṭā*." It is similar to the partridge in coloring, but is smaller, about the size of a pigeon. This variety is so numerous that its flocks fill the skies, especially in the summer when it migrates westward from the desert, leaving its breeding grounds for the waters of the rivers and pools of the desert peripheries adjoining the al-Manāẓir region. Some of the young ones may be seen with the mature birds coming thirsty to the watering place for the first time, swarming around it so thickly that they are immersed, and wetting their feathers so much that some of them cannot fly until they dry. The male has a ring around his neck, and his feathers are more brightly colored than those of the female.

[3]Al-Zamakhsharī, *A'jab al-'ajab fī sharḥ lāmiyat al-'arab* (Cairo, AH 1300), p. 50.

[4]Al-Khūwī, *Sharḥ al-tanwīr 'alā siqṭ al-zand* (Cairo, 1342/1924), p. 260.

[5]See al-Nābigha al-Dhubyānī, *Dīwān*, edited by Shukrī Fayṣal (Beirut, 1968), p. 177.

There is another variety of sand grouse known as the *ḥurrī*, which is sandy colored and does not make much noise, as the *ṣayyāḥ* does, although it does sometimes utter a call approximating its name. Another variety is called the *suktī*, "the silent one" (this is probably the variety that Musil calls *qirwān*[6]), because it utters no call. A fourth variety is called the *kudrī*, "the dusky one." It is the largest variety of sand grouse, approximating the size of the partridge, and its meat is the tastiest. It is dusty colored, with multicolored chest and back, black under the wings and on its primary feathers, and a yellow throat. It has a long feather on its tail, and it utters no cry. It is distinguished from other sand grouse by how very early in the morning it goes out to look for water—so early that it has become proverbial for these morning excursions. It can be seen leaving its nests at the break of dawn, flying out to the watering places, and returning to its nestlings and its resting grounds before sunrise. We used to conceal ourselves near some of the pools to hunt this variety of sand grouse when they came for water at dawn, unlike the *ṣayyāḥ* variety which always came to drink during the period from sunrise until just before noon. Al-Damīrī claims that there exists a variety which he calls the *jūnī*, and that it goes out to seek water earlier in the morning than does the *kudrī*. He quotes the words of the poet addressing his beloved and boasting of how she made him go out to see her earlier than this *jūnī* seeks his water:

T'was you who forced me thither,
From my tent out late at night,
While al-Jalhatayn's *jūn* grouse roosted,
Not yet roused to take to flight.[7]

During the season when the birds take turns nesting on their eggs, it is the habit of the *ṣayyāḥ* sand grouse for the male to go out for water in the morning and the female in the afternoon. Before this time the birds fly out in pairs, a male and a female, indicating that the time for the females to lay their eggs is approaching. The pairs explore various

[6]Musil, *Manners and Customs*, p. 40.

[7]See al-Damīrī, *Ḥayāt al-ḥayawān*, II, 358; *Aghānī*, XV, 155. In al-Damīrī it is stated that the poet is ʿAntara, but the correct attribution is Ibn al-Dumayna, as mentioned in the *Aghānī*.

areas searching for places where there is brush where the female can lay her eggs, and plants with dry seeds to guarantee nourishment for her nestlings. The scooped-out nesting spots in a single place may be so numerous that the bedouins can gather and eat large numbers of eggs.[8]

The sand grouse waddles in short steps, and when it walks near a watering place you can see it waddling along, the entire flock jostling each other as they make their way to the water. The ancient Arabs compared the way overweight women walk to the waddle of the sand grouse. As al-Munakhkhil ibn al-Ḥārith al-Yashkurī said:

> This buxom beauty swaggers about,
> Trailing her garments of silk soft and cool.
> I pushed her gently, but she strutted off,
> Like a waddling grouse as it walks to the pool.[9]

When searching for sources of water, the sand grouse, especially the *ṣayyāḥ*, usually flies from its nests in flocks, lands near the water, and then waddles and jostles the rest of the way and drinks its fill. If it gulps the water down it will not be satisfied to drink once, but will stand around the pool and drink several times, or fly and glide around it for awhile, return to gulp a second time, and then fly and return yet again, all the while calling, squawking, and making noise. If it is left undisturbed at the pool for a long period, so many scores of sand grouse will flock around the water and along its banks that the ground will be completely covered with birds—as if a swarm of locusts had arrived or a colorful carpet had been spread over it. The clamor raised by their voices resembles the din raised when thirst brings a clan of bedouins and their camels to camp at a watering place. As al-Shanfarā described them:

> It was as if the uproar raised all around, to left and to right,
> Had come from bands of traveling tribesmen camped for the night.
> Together they gathered around and so displayed its luring might,

[8]Musil says that in certain wadis more than a thousand of this bird's nests may be found. See his *Manners and Customs*, p. 39.

[9]Abū Tammām, *Ḥamāsa*, I, 210.

As a watering place draws in camels of a herd scattered
from sight.
They drank their fill in great hasty gulps, then took off in
flight,
As if they were riders of Uḥāẓa fleeing at morning's first
light.[10]

As the birds are so numerous, it is easy for bedouin boys to kill some of the grouse in the flocks with their slings.

The sand grouse nests in the spring and lays three or sometimes four white eggs speckled with black. Hence the Arabs called it *umm al-thalāth*, "mother of three." For its nesting places it chooses a level gravelly spot in rough hilly terrain, and while incubating the eggs it will only take leave of its nest if a man walks or rides nearby. Then it suddenly flies up, striking its nest rather roughly with its feet, perhaps in order to conceal traces of its location. The bedouin compares the bust of his beloved to the egg of the *kudrī* sand grouse.

It is strange that despite the distances it covers in search of water, the sand grouse can find its way back to its nest. It recognizes its chicks when the eggs break open, and gives them water it has stored in its craw, which is located in the forepart of its breast and large enough to hold a handful of seeds or water. When bedouin boys kill a sand grouse they remove this part, blow it full of air, and tie the ends shut, thus making an inflated ball about the size of an orange.

The Arabs have coined proverbs about the sand grouse's ability to find its way and say: "better guided than a sand grouse." In lampooning the tribe of Tamīm the poet al-Ṭirimmāḥ said:

Tamīm on the route to vile deeds
More than sand grouse knows the way.
But in the quest for noble exploits
You'll soon find they've gone astray.[11]

[10] Al-Zamakhsharī, *A'jab al-'ajab*, pp. 52-53. [Uḥāẓa is the name of a tribe.]

[11] *Dīwān al-Ṭirimmāḥ*, edited by F. Krenkow (Leiden, 1927), p. 132. See also al-Damīrī, *Ḥayāt al-ḥayawān*, II, 358; Ibn 'Abd Rabbih, *Al-'Iqd (al-farīd)*, edited by Aḥmad Amīn, Aḥmad al-Zayn, and Ibrāhīm al-Abyārī (Cairo, 1359–69/1940–50), II, 468.

The bedouins have stories, some of them beyond belief, that they tell about the sand grouse's sense of direction. One of these has it that a bedouin made camp one night on a hill where some sand grouse had nested, and unknowingly startled one bird from her nest. He pitched his tent and planted his lance in the ground in front of it, and about an hour later heard the sound of fluttering wings. He got up to see what had made the sound, and there was a sand grouse impaled on the head of the lance. He looked down at the base of the lance where it was implanted in the ground, and there he saw a sand grouse nest with three small nestlings in it. Unable to leave them unattended for a long time when she had been disturbed into flying away, their mother had returned by night to look for them. The extreme darkness had prevented her from seeing the lancehead, which consequently pierced her chest and killed her.

In years of famine and drought the sand grouse migrates from the desert before summer and makes its way to the fields of the villages along the desert peripheries to eat in the fields after the harvest. The villagers take this as an evil omen and say: "In the year of the sand grouse comes the selling of the covers."[12] The bedouins also take this as a bad sign, and say: "The sand grouse have arrived with a tumultuous cry—may God not invoke His blessing on them."

The bedouins and the villagers who live close to the desert have various ways and means of hunting the sand grouse, which we shall discuss in Chapter XV, on bedouin hunting practices.

The Ostrich

We may now consider the ostrich, a bird still found in the desert, and which the Old Testament in many places associates with the desert. Job said: "I have become the brother to the wolf and companion to the ostrich."[13] The prophet Isaiah said: "The beasts of the desert—wolves and ostriches—will glorify me;"[14] as well as: "Ostriches will live

[12][That is, a year in which the sand grouse come in large swarms implies a lack of rain and hence a bad harvest and famine, which will force people to sell everything, even their bed covers, to obtain food.]

[13]Job 30:29.

[14]Isaiah 43:20.

there and wild goats will frolic there."[15] In the view of the present-day bedouins its importance and status are no less than that of the gazelle. The entire *'uṭfa* of the shaykh of the Rwāla is adorned with the soft feathers of the ostrich, and until recently the bedouins of the tribe of Ṣlayb used to sell ostrich feathers to merchants in cities throughout Syria, from where they were sold to other regions. Hunting the ostrich affords bedouin horsemen a pleasure and delight unrivaled by hunting any other quarry, and they speak of it in their literature and their stories. The ancients—'Antara, al-Ḥārith ibn Ḥilliza, and others—likewise used to refer to it, coining proverbs about its agility and speed and comparing their thoroughbred racing camels to it. In its nature they recognize the same traits that the ancient Arabs did: strong senses of smell and sight, cowardice, and a propensity for fleeing. As their proverbs have it: "a better nose than an ostrich," "deafer than an ostrich," "quicker to run than an ostrich," and "their ostrich is upset."[16] And as the poet said: "a better nose than an ostrich, a better guide than a partridge." Likewise:

> To me you feign the lion's might,
> But war will find you gone from sight –
> A black-plumed ostrich, fled so soon,
> At the sound of the whistler's tune.[17]

They also say: "further astray than an ostrich," since, as they claim, the female will at times leave her eggs and sit on those of another; and "more brutish than an ostrich," because it is absolutely wild. In the laments of Jeremiah it is said: "As for the daughter of my people, she is as brutish as an ostrich in the desert."[18] The ostrich has no visible ears; and as the bedouins say, the ostrich went out to seek two horns, but they cut off its ears and it came back without them. Hence the proverb referring to someone who returns unsuccessful: "He came back like the ostrich." They also describe the bodies of their beloveds as "delicate

[15]Isaiah 13:21.

[16][I.e. "they are gone," or "they disappeared," alluding to the timidity of the ostrich.]

[17]*Aghānī*, XVI, 155.

[18]Jeremiah 4:13.

as the eggs of the ostrich," as the Arab poets used to do long ago, and in their evening story sessions they tell many tales about ostriches, hunting them, and how swiftly they run.

The male ostrich is called *ẓalīm* ("dark") due to the blackness of its feathers; the female is called *rabdā'*, and the young *rīlān*. The ostrich lays 10–30 eggs per season in the early spring, choosing a nesting place (*udḥī*) in the sand and beginning to incubate the eggs when the first one is laid. The Rwāla claim that the female takes turns with the male in tending to the eggs: he stands watch over them during the day and leaves them exposed to the heat of the sun while the female roams and feeds, and at night she returns to the nest while the male in turn goes out in search of food. At night the female sits on the eggs and warms them with the heat of her body, all, that is, except for three or four, which she rolls some distance away from the nest. When the eggs hatch 21 days later, the male pecks open one of the discarded eggs with his beak and the female pushes her nestlings over to it for them to eat its contents. When the first is eaten the male pecks open another, and so on until the chicks have finished all of the discarded eggs. Their mother then takes them to the grazing ground, and they become a small flock led by the mother and guarded from behind by the *ẓalīm*, who defends it as best he can should it be attacked by a hyena, wolf, or eagle.[19]

The bedouins claim that the ostrich may abandon her own eggs and nest upon those of another ostrich. As one of the poets sang:

> Like one who leaves her eggs to weather,
> To clothe another's with wing and feather.[20]

The ostrich used to live in the desert even in the summertime, which may have caused observers to wonder at its ability to endure the lack of water when rainfall ceased there. Some have claimed that the ostrich drinks from the drops of dew that collect on vegetation in the morning, which in their view explained the phenomenon of the bird's tendency to gather up with its beak every glistening seed.[21]

---

[19] Musil, *Manners and Customs*, p. 38.

[20] Kushājim, *Al-Maṣāyid wa-l-maṭārid*, p. 222; al-Damīrī, *Ḥayāt al-ḥayawān*, II, 502.

[21] R.E. Cheesman, *In Unknown Arabia* (London, 1926), p. 341.

The Syrian Desert has over the past four centuries been the home for many flocks of ostriches. In his account of his journey from al-Baṣra to Aleppo in 1750, Plaisted said that he saw an ostrich crossing the road ahead of them. A group of men from the caravan pursued it, but it was too fast for them and they could not catch up with it. Carruthers notes the great interest of this passage and begins to name those who saw ostriches before and after Plaisted. He indicates that Teixeira saw some ostriches in 1604 two days' journey from al-Baṣra. He also mentions General Coote and says that in 1771 he saw some ostriches about two days' distance from Tadmur. Then there was Eyles Irwin, who in 1781 found a nest midway between Tadmur and the Euphrates. John Taylor saw a flock of ostriches and a nest near the place where Plaisted had seen a bird. Then there was Olivier, who recorded that he saw ostriches in 1797 south of Dayr al-Zūr. Carruthers also mentions that Abraham Parsons collected fifteen eggs from an area that was probably the northernmost homeland for the ostrich in the Syrian Desert.[22] About 60 years later, at the end of 1862, Palgrave came and mentioned that he saw a flock around al-Jawf. Never in his life, he says, had he seen a bird as cowardly as the ostrich. He tried very hard to get close to the flock, but it took to flight while he was still far away and ran off in one long line, one bird following another.[23] Guarmani mentions that the ostrich may be found around Jabal Shammar.[24] De Gaury says that he saw the ostrich, but that it had become rare. "They say that there are some twenty survivors in a bay of the volcanic rock east of the Wādī Sirḥān," he notes, and indicates that he himself saw four at a place not far from there, and that some eggs were given to him as presents.[25] Doughty reports that the bedouins brought him an ostrich egg which they broke, mixed with flour and clarified butter (*samn*), and fried into an omelet, producing a tasty dish.[26] He claims that bedouin hunters

[22] *The Desert Route to India*, p. 81, n. 4.

[23] William Gifford Palgrave, *Narrative of a Year's Journey Through Central and Eastern Arabia, 1862–63*, 3rd edition (London and Cambridge, 1866), I, 43.

[24] Guarmani, p. 92.

[25] Gerard de Gaury, *Arabian Journey and Other Desert Travels* (London, 1950), p. 23.

[26] Doughty, I, 173.

eat the breast meat and save its fat and sell it as a remedy for many diseases.[27]

One of the more recent of the explorers of the Syrian Desert, Alois Musil, says in his book on the Rwāla that the ostrich was still to be found in the desert in northern Arabia until the early twentieth century. They are found primarily in the region of the Nafūd, most particularly in its northwest part, and in the summer season they may move northward, as the gazelle and even the bedouins themselves do, going as far as the environs of Tadmur.[28]

Riḍwān al-Rwaylī (as he liked to call himself) does not fail to report his hunting of the ostrich in a manner consistent with most of his exaggerations. He relates that he and a group of his companions went out hunting, and reports how they killed a panther and its cubs, and how one of the hunters cut open the animal, plucked out its heart, and sucked out its blood so that his strength would increase. He then goes on to relate how they killed an ostrich and caught three of its young. However, he fails to provide us in his book with a photograph of the ostrich or its young, even though the ostrich is a rare and beautiful bird, and despite the fact that his book contains 72 pages full of photographs.[29] I fear that he was simply trying to avoid omission from his book of any animal that had some connection with the desert. Jirjīs al-Khalīl, one of the best-known hunters in the town of al-Qaryatayn, in the district of Ḥimṣ, told me in the first half of this century, after the First World War, that the Hebrew University was able to collect two ostriches from the Syrian Desert, one alive and the other killed and stuffed. And Ḥusayn Bey Ebesh, from al-Hayjāna in the Ghūṭa district of Damascus, wrote to me saying that he had seen with his own eyes the ostrich killed by one of the sons of the family of al-Sha'lān. This was probably one of the two mentioned above. Likewise, I have heard someone claim that he saw a tribesman of Ṣlayb kill an ostrich at the dawn of this century. Major Cheesman, a zoologist, said in his book *In Unknown Arabia*, published in 1926, that the sultan of Najd (not

[27] *Ibid.*, I, 174.

[28] Musil, *Manners and Customs*, p. 38.

[29] Raswan, *Black Tents of Arabia*, pp. 67–71. On this author and his book, cf. the assessment above, pp. 24–27.

specifically named, but presumably 'Abd al-'Azīz ibn 'Abd al-Raḥmān ibn Su'ūd) gave two ostriches to Sir Percy Cox.[30]

Finally, it should come as no surprise that the ostrich too, like the oryx, began to seek refuge in the Rub' al-Khālī in order to preserve itself. In the old days hunting the ostrich required great skill (or even great horsemanship), especially among the bedouins of al-Sharārāt or Ṣlayb, who only pursued it on foot and could catch it only through recourse to trickery and concealment. Today, however, there is nothing to boast about in chasing the ostrich from an airplane or by using other modern deadly methods.[31] We will return to this subject when we take up the topic of hunting.

The Falcon

Just as the lion is the noblest and strongest of the predatory mammals, the falcon is regarded as the strongest and noblest of birds. As the poet Ilīya Abū Māḍī said on this subject:

> If you would be wild, then fierce lion be;
> Or flying on wing, a falcon let's see.[32]

In praise of the falcon they used to say: "The best of images is that combining three features—a falcon on the hand of a man on the back of a horse."[33]

Boasting of himself, the Umayyad poet 'Umar ibn Abī Rabī'a speaks of a visit to one of his female companions:

> Nought will surprise them like those cream-colored camels,
> With riders and packs as they came up the hill,
> And a horseman with falcon whom they pointed out to her
> With compliments fine, saying, "Look, if you will."[34]

---

[30]Cheesman, p. 341.

[31]See Musil, *Manners and Customs*, pp. 38–39. Philby, meanwhile, has reported in 1955 that the ostrich is entirely absent from the deserts of northern Arabia, and that the automobile was the instrument of its annihilation at the hands of merciless hunters. See his "The Land of Midian," *Middle East Journal*, 9 (1955), p. 125.

[32]Ilīya Abū Māḍī, *Dīwān* (Beirut, 1982), p. 462.

[33]Kushājim, *Al-Maṣāyid wa-l-maṭārid*, p. 51.

[34]'Umar ibn Abī Rabī'a, *Dīwān*, I.1, 13.

One of the Arabic sources says that Ptolemy, the successor of Alexander the Great, was the first to acquire and amuse himself with falcons and to use them to hunt game; other Greek, Arab, and Persian rulers then did the same.[35] It is said that the first Arab to use falcons for hunting was al-Ḥārith ibn Mu'āwiya ibn Thawr ibn Kinda, who one day met a hunter who had set a snare to catch some sparrows. An *akdar* (a kind of falcon) swooped down on one of the snared sparrows, was caught along with it, and began to eat the sparrow. Amazed at all this, the king brought the falcon back with him. The bird had a broken wing, so he tended it in a corner of a room, and noticed that it was becoming tame and did not leave or flee. When the falcon's food was thrown to him he ate it, and when he saw a piece of meat he flew up onto the hand of his master. He even answered when called and was fed on his owner's hand. They used to amuse themselves carrying the falcon about, until one day it spied a pigeon, flew up to it from the hand of the person carrying it, and ate the pigeon. So the al-Ḥārith ordered that the falcon be taken and used for hunting; and when he was out one day shortly thereafter, a rabbit came in sight and the falcon flew out and seized it. With that he began to use it to hunt birds and rabbits, and the Arabs after him did likewise.[36]

However one wishes to take such tales, it is evident that the Arabs have been familiar with hunting with falcons since their pre-Islamic days. It is said of Ḥamza, the uncle of the Prophet Muḥammad, that once (before his conversion to Islam) when he had just returned from the hunt with a falcon on his hand, a woman said to him: "If only you had seen how Abū l-Ḥakam treated your nephew today," referring to how the Prophet had been insulted by Abū Jahl. Ḥamza went immediately, found Abū Jahl, hit him so hard over the head with his bow that his skull was fractured, and announced that he accepted Muḥammad's religion.[37]

[35] *Kitāb al-bayzara*, by the master huntsman of the Fāṭimid caliph 'Azīz bi-llāh, edited by Muḥammad Kurd 'Alī (Damascus, 1371/1952), p. 4.

[36] Kushājim, *Al-Maṣāyid wa-l-maṭārid*, pp. 84–85.

[37] *Kitāb al-bayzara*, p. 40. It is odd that Ibn Hishām should mention this account but make no reference to the falcon on the hand of Ḥamza; see his *Sīrat Rasūl Allāh*, edited by Ferdinand Wüstenfeld (Göttingen, 1858–60), I.1, 184–85. The detail may, however, be a later addition.

The Arabs divided the falcon into five varieties: the *bāzī*, the *zurrāq*, the *bāshiq*, the *baydaq*, and the *ṣaqr*,[38] to which some added the *shāhīn*. Of these types the modern bedouins are interested only in the bird they call the *ṣaqr*, and they probably use this name in reference to more than one of these varieties.

The Arabs took to widespread training of predatory birds for the hunt after the conquests and their intermingling with the Persians and Byzantines. In the Umayyad age, mention of the falcon came generally to be associated with the life of ease and luxury enjoyed by poets, princes, and singers, as we find, for example, in the verse of 'Umar ibn Abī Rabī'a when, mounted on his charger and carrying his falcon, he gazes at his female companions. Yazīd ibn Mu'āwiya also acquired panthers, dogs, and falcons, and made so much use of them for hunting that he was called "Yazīd of the panthers and falcons." When we proceed on to the time of Hishām ibn 'Abd al-Malik, we even find that this caliph had a "master huntsman" (*bāzyār*), a man named Ghaṭrīf ibn Qudāma al-Ghassānī, the title of whose occupation was associated with the falcon (*al-bāz*). The poet al-Farazdaq, a contemporary of Hishām, anticipates 'Umar al-Khayyām when he expresses to his Lord his wish to be alone with his beloved in the desert, accompanied only by fine wine from the juice of unpressed grapes. But then he adds his wish that they should also have some cold water and pieces of meat from a bustard caught by a falcon they had trained and tamed:

Of victuals but two leftovers fine:
Of unpressed grape its finest wine,
With water crystal clear and cold
As e'er a billowing cloud did hold;
Of bustard meat in strips, a dish
Before us laid when e'er we wish,
By bird of prey that's trained and tame
And swoops to pounce on hunted game.[39]

[38]Kushājim, *Al-Maṣāyid wa-l-maṭārid*, pp. 73, 78; al-Damīrī, *Ḥayāt al-ḥayawān*, I, 160. As for the bedouins, there are those of them who differentiate between falcons according to their colors: *ashhab* (grey), *aḥmar* (reddish-hued), *aṣfar* (yellow), and *akhḍar* (green).

[39]From al-Farazdaq's famous ode (*Dīwān*, II, 555) that begins: "You withdrew from A'shāsh, and had no sooner done so. . . ."

Power had no sooner been transferred from Damascus to Baghdad, and the 'Abbāsid caliphs begun to enjoy this new heritage, than they took to imitating the ancient Persian kings. Hunting became a highly organized and extremely important affair: the raising of falcons became a specialized art known as *bayzara* or *bazyara*, and as mentioned above the master of the hunt came to be known as the *bāzyār*. The poor bedouin did not stop hunting, but it was not within his means to bear its costs in pursuit of either pleasure or livelihood to the extent that the ruler or *amīr* did, although both were as one in the satisfaction they derived from the enjoyment of a successful hunt. Modern-day bedouins may be proficient in the training and use of birds for the hunt, but unlike the falconers about whom we read in the Arabic falconry texts these men left to us, the bedouins do not know how to treat their birds when they fall ill. Indeed, most bedouins do not keep any birds of prey other than falcons.

The nomads sometimes call the falcon *al-ṭayr*, "the bird," and refer to the better ones as *al-ḥurr*, "the noble free-born one," this variety being either light grey or reddish brown (treacle) in color. Likewise, they call the most superb falcons *al-naddāwī*—the name derives, so they claim, from the Arabic word for dew, *al-nadā*—because this type of falcon hunts in the early morning and detects its quarry even if it is hiding or concealed under dew-covered herbage, while other birds will only search out the game after the dew has evaporated and the quarry has left its hiding place. The largest falcon chick in a nest they refer to by the name of *zayn al-nādir*, the "rare beauty," and claim that this one in most cases proves to be the most attractive and swiftest chick, followed in strength by the second largest chick, then the third, these being called *al-nagl* (with *jīm* as pronounced in Egypt), or "the scion." Male falcons they refer to as *shabbūt*, and the female as *shayhāna*.

Falcons spend their winters in the desert and migrate westward, so they say, in the summer. They prefer the meat of jerboas, hence one can observe that they spend long periods of time in areas full of jerboas, which they hunt during the day. Bedouins even hunt jerboas for falcons, which they train and feed on jerboas. If it happens that a feather in a falcon's wing breaks, they pluck it out so that a healthy one can grow in its place.

Acquisition and Training of Falcons

The bedouins purchase falcons from village folk in the settled lands adjoining the desert in Syria,[40] Najd, the Ḥijāz, and Kuwayt, as do *amīrs* and shaykhs in most of the Arab emirates. The aeries of falcons are to be found in rocky heights and mountains, where you can see experts in such matters searching the rocky mountain tops until they find their way to the birds' nests, or climbing a cliff where they see a falcon's aerie so they can collect its chicks while they are small. There are usually three chicks per nest, and these the collectors take before they leave the nest to fly.

Bedouins may sometimes catch live adult falcons. They set a net in places among the rocks frequented by falcons, and the hunter hides behind a rock that will conceal him from view. He carries with him a live crow tied with a strong cord, a clump of feathers fashioned to imitate a bird killed by the crow, and a tame pigeon. The crow is placed on a rock near the net and food is set out for him, so that when he senses the presence of a falcon gliding overhead he begins to caw. The hunter pulls the crow back toward himself and throws out the pigeon, which is tied to a place under the net. The falcon swoops down on the pigeon, and when he seizes it the hunter pulls a cord attached to the net and the falcon is caught in it. The hunter then takes the falcon, sews its eyelids shut, and leaves it like that for three or four days until the bird calms down and becomes submissive. The hunter then cuts the stitches from the falcon's eyes and allows it, while tied, to see the light. Then he begins gradually to train the bird, despite its adult age, until it becomes accustomed to its master and makes a habit of returning to him when turned loose. Another method approximating this one is to dig, in an area frequented by falcons, a hole about half a meter deep and wide enough for one or two persons to sit in it, and to build around it a small stone wall about half a meter high, leaving openings through which one can see. The hunter then covers himself in the blind with some branches and brush, ties fast a crow held on a fine lead about 100 meters away, and lets it flutter about. When it

[40]The town of al-Ruḥayba, between Damascus and al-Qaryatayn, is famous for raising falcons and selling them to hunters from among the bedouin shaykhs and *amīrs*.

Figure 14: The falcon.

does, then if there is a falcon in the sky it will think that the crow has caught a pigeon and will dive down to take the pigeon away from it, thus causing the crow to caw in fear. At that point the hunter releases a pigeon that is also tied, but with nylon cords tied into slip-knot loops on its wings and back. When the falcon tries to seize the pigeon its claws are caught in a loop and it is captured alive.[41] When an adult falcon is caught its eyes are sewn shut, as we have mentioned, and depending on the training it takes about 40 days before the stitches are cut and the bird becomes accustomed to staying in the tent. The bedouins may set the falcon free after the hunting season ends; the bird regains its freedom, and in some cases the same bird may be caught a second time.

The falcon can catch most kinds of birds, such as the pigeon, partridge, francolin, sand grouse, and others like them; but the largest bird it can kill is the bustard. It can also catch all kinds of rabbits, and some bedouins even go so far as to claim that the falcon hunts the gazelle. In fact it does sometimes help in gazelle hunting if trained to do so. When the hunter sees the salukis chasing a gazelle he sends up the falcon, which flies over the gazelle, swoops down on its head as it runs before the dogs, and obstructs its vision by flying in front of it. Or it may land on the gazelle's head and strike it with its beak, thereby impeding its progress so that the dogs can catch up to it and kill it.[42]

---

[41] Usāma ibn Munqidh mentions in his memoirs (*Kitāb al-i'tibār*, p. 200) how falcons were caught alive in his time. This was a method not much different from that we have explained, and it is apparently still practiced in the 'Alawite Mountains up to the present time. Among the rocks a small chamber, large enough for a man to sit inside, is built of ordinary uncut rocks. It is then roofed with branches and covered with debris and brush, and an opening is made in the chamber. The man sitting inside then takes a pigeon, holds its feet together on a stick, and ties the bird to it. He then pushes the stick out through the opening and shakes it, so that the pigeon moves and flutters its wings. The falcon sees this and descends to seize the bird; and when the hunter feels that the bird has struck he pulls the stick back to the opening, reaches out with his hand, grabs the falcon, pulls it down into the chamber, and sews its eyes shut.

[42] *Ibid.*, p. 225; *Bayzara*, p. 99; al-Qazwīnī, *'Ajā'ib al-makhlūqāt wa-gharā'ib al-mawjūdāt* (Beirut, 1978), p. 453. In this note I am compelled to continue by commenting on the ignorance of a modern Syrian author who discusses the falcon in a study on desert affairs. There he makes the claim that "men of the bedouin tribes still use the falcon to hunt other birds, especially domesticated birds whose meat

Sometimes it is possible for one falcon to provide enough food for the people of a bedouin group consisting of seven or eight tents. One bird may catch about ten bustards in a single day, provided that there are large numbers of these birds in the area where the bedouins have camped, or about ten rabbits. It has been said of some falcons that they caught more than this in one day.[43]

The acquisition of falcons and their use in hunting is not limited to bedouin common folk or their poor. One can see many shaykhs doing this, but for the most part they rely on their servants or attendants to raise and train the birds and take the servants with them on hunting trips. The master huntsman makes ready for himself a special glove that he puts on his hand so the falcon can perch on it, or has a special wooden stand—called a *markab* or *markaba*, "vehicle," by the bedouins—prepared for the falcon to "ride" upon. This perch is covered with stiff leather, or something rough and hard like dry leather, and mounted on a pointed iron staff implanted in the ground. The perch stands about a third of a meter above the ground, and on it sits the falcon with his feet fastened to a chain reaching to the ground, so that the bird can jump to the ground and return to his perch if he wishes. They use a leather hood to cover part of the falcon's head so that it masks his eyes, if they want to prevent light from reaching them. The falcon may molt (*qarnaṣa*, in the bedouin parlance): that is, some of its feathers begin to fall out. If this prevents the bird from

is eaten." He then says: "The falcon kills its prey with its sharp beak, using it to sever the jugular vein in the neck in a way absolutely identical to slaughtering the game by cutting its throat with a knife. After that, the falcon carries this prey of his to its master, then dashes off again to return to the attack." See Mu'ayyad al-Kaylānī, *Muḥāfaẓat Ḥamāh* (Damascus, 1964), p. 85. It would seem that the author of this book is ignorant of the meaning of the word *dājina*, "domesticated," and exaggerating in the extreme in his claim that the falcon carries his prey to his master so he can return to the attack. And this is not to mention his errors in asserting that the Rwāla form a branch of the Mawālī bedouin tribe (p. 88), that the bedouins use as their dwellings tents that they weave from the wool of their sheep (p. 87), that in the al-Ḥaffa region there are panthers that people encounter from time to time, and that some of these panthers attack populated areas when they are extremely hungry (p. 83).

[43]Musil, *Manners and Customs*, p. 34; Dickson, pp. 35, 367. Dickson claims that the falcon may catch 20 rabbits in a day.

hunting it is kept in isolation and cared for until its new feathers begin to appear.

The bedouins have stories about falcons and how they hunt that in some cases are almost beyond belief. One bedouin told me about a falcon whose owner set the bird on a rabbit. The bird circled overhead watching the rabbit until it saw its quarry flee for refuge under a small boxthorn tree. Then it dove down from the sky on the rabbit and struck with the claws of one of its feet where the latter was hiding, with the result that its foot became caught in the rabbit and in a branch of the firmly rooted boxthorn tree. With a burst of strength it flew up into the sky trying to carry the pelt of the rabbit in which its foot had been caught, and suddenly, there it was flying along with only one leg. They will also tell you how the falcon makes a single pass over the rabbit and with its talon flays the rabbit's back open from tail to head. On the other hand, the bedouins claim—and rightly so—that in scrublands hunting rabbits is generally more difficult for the falcon than hunting bustards, because in most cases the rabbit can evade it and conceal itself from his sight. The falcon is one of the fastest of birds, and its flying speed may reach over 200 miles per hour.

Just as al-Farazdaq wished that he were together with his beloved, his drinking cup, and a falcon to catch a bustard so the two of them could eat pieces of its meat, so the Rwaylī poet wished that he had a falcon and a hunting dog to turn loose to hunt as he stood near some beautiful girls about to break camp:

> Would that a hound and a bird were mine,
> And saddle cinched on a young camel fine.
> Twixt guard and tribe would fall our pace,
> To call the hound while bird does chase.

That is, he wishes that he had a greyhound hunting dog (*jarw*), a hunting bird (a falcon), and a young thoroughbred racing camel on which to fasten his saddle. He would then seek game to hunt between the tribe's warriors riding far ahead and the others following behind with the pack train, and would call the hound and send it out while the falcon pursues the quarry. The poet's intent is to be close to the pack train—that is, the young maidens setting out in the howdahs—so that he might see his beloved among them. Thus, this bedouin does not differ from his fellow bard, the medieval Umayyad poet al-Farazdaq, or from his comrade, the later Persian poet 'Umar al-Khayyām.

The Eagle and Vulture

This is perhaps the best place to discuss the *'uqāb* and *nasr*, which the books and other writings of the Arab tradition regard as the two largest and strongest birds. Amīn Ma'lūf has noted that modern Arab writers and authors do not distinguish between them. The *'uqāb*, or eagle, however, is a predatory animal that hunts, while the *nasr*, or griffon vulture, does not hunt and instead eats carrion, despite which it enjoys particular esteem among the bedouins.[44] The ancients realized this and used the eagle to hunt those animals that were difficult for the falcon to catch. Kushājim mentioned that the eagle "serves as a hunting animal for people. They train it when it has been tamed and grown accustomed to them, and sometimes it hunts the wild ass."[45] Probably going to extremes in his assertion, he claims:

> When it sees an onager, it throws itself into the water until its wings are soaked, then comes out and lands on the dirt and carries away a load of sand [stuck to its feathers]. Heavily laden, the eagle flies and lands on top of the onager's head, and flaps its wings in its eyes until they are so full of dirt that the onager cannot see and is taken.[46]

However one judges this report of his, the fact remains that the eagle was once used to hunt just as the falcon was, although I have neither known nor read of anyone using the eagle to hunt in the desert in our own times. The vulture's benefit to the desert is that, as we have already mentioned, it cleans it of carrion, which it joins other birds and predators in consuming. Feathers from its primary plumage are used as picks to play the oud. Its neck is completely featherless.

---

[44] Amīn Ma'lūf, *Mu'jam al-ḥayawān* (Cairo, 1932), p. 93. See also Kushājim, *Al-Maṣāyid wa-l-maṭārid*, pp. 93–94.

[45] Kushājim, *Al-Maṣāyid wa-l-maṭārid*, p. 95.

[46] *Ibid.*

The eagle is referred to as *laqwa* ("crooked jaw") because of the capacity of its jaws, *khudārīya* ("the very dark one") because of its black color, and *ṣawma'a* ("hermit's cell") because it always flies up to the loftiest place it can reach. A desirable eagle is described as having a sturdy build, firm legs, reddish hue, deeply set eyes, white markings, a white head, and black plumage mottled with white or other colors. They claim that if it is hungry, the wolf is not an impossible quarry for it. It may watch falcons from high above them, and if it sees them catch something it dives down on them and seizes their prey as the falcons flee. As the poet said:

> Like an eagle watching falcons from its vantage point high,
> So that if their hunt succeeds then for their game it may
> vie.[47]

The Bustard

The sand grouse may be the most common bird in the desert, and the ostrich the most outstanding and so well known that the bedouins claim that it can claim equal renown with the camel, but there is another bird called the *ḥubārā*, or bustard, smaller than the ostrich but larger than the sand grouse, that hunters covet and prize for its meat more than they do either of the other birds. The plural of *ḥubārā* is *ḥabarī* (m.) and *ḥubārayāt* (f.), and the word *ḥubārā* is also used for the masculine, feminine, and plural forms. It is a bird the size of a small turkey[48] and its meat is just as good. It is to be found in most parts of the Arabian peninsula, from Kuwayt to Wādī Sirḥān in Jordan, and abounds in the al-Daww region around Tadmur and the villages of al-Manāẓir. It lives on green plants and the seeds that fall from them. Al-Damīrī was especially impressed by its endurance:

---

[47] *Ibid.*, p. 97.

[48] In his *Black Tents of Arabia*, pp. 195–201, Raswan does not fail to recount the hunting of the bustard. He says that to hunt a single bird there was mobilized a force of twelve of the slaves of the Amīr Fawwāz, a band of *amīrs*, 200 horsemen, and 300 men mounted on camels some distance from the falcon. All of the slaves were carrying falcons. They then proceeded to bag a single bustard. He then states further that he and his comrades killed an ostrich and caught three of its chicks, which were kept by the shaykh. Before Raswan, al-Damīrī was fond of telling strange stories, sometimes including tales that passed beyond belief.

> It is said that of all birds it is the most vigorous flyer and the one that covers the greatest distances: one killed at al-Baṣra was found to have among the contents of its craw the green seed of the terebinth tree native to the Syrian frontier. Hence they say in the proverb: "more venturesome than the bustard."[49]

Its coloring is beautiful—that of the male particularly so—as is the case with other birds of this genus. But while God may have endowed it with beautiful multicolored plumage, it enjoys no security from the depredations of either the falcon or man.

Because of their weight bustards fly close to the surface of the ground and do not rise to any great height above it; and for the same reason they do not fly very far even if stirred up from their place. You see it fly, then land somewhere else and run along the ground for a long distance. Thus it is difficult to get close to a bustard, and detecting one is easy only for the falcon, which no sooner sees the bustard in the air than it hovers and then dives down on it. If it only wounds the bustard while it is airborne, the latter throws itself on the ground, or else lands out of fear of the falcon. The falcon then descends to pounce on the bustard and kill it while it is sitting on the ground, and either remains nearby until its master the hunter arrives, or perches on its prey and tears at it with its beak and talons. When the hunter reaches the game he chases the falcon away from it, cuts the bustard's throat, and carries it off. The village hunter may give the falcon something from the bird, but the bedouin hunter only gives the falcon a share of the game in the tent.

God has endowed the bustard with a way to defend itself. Sometimes, when it is flying through the air and finds itself ahead of a falcon, it can play a trick on the latter. When it notices that the falcon is directly behind it and has almost caught up with it, it voids excrement on its pursuer, seeking to wet its feathers. The falcon thus drops back immediately, and due to the ill effects of this excrement may not be able to fly all the rest of the day; for that day the bustard and other animals are safe from the falcon's mischief. If it can, the bustard also

[49] Al-Damīrī, *Ḥayāt al-ḥayawān*, I, 334.

does this when it is on the ground. Fear may be the immediate reason for this; but as the bustard has no other means of saving itself from the falcon, instinct compels the bustard to void in such a situation in order protect itself and the species.

As the Arab poet said, reproaching his adversary for being cowardly and quick to flee:

> They have left you more incontinent than a bustard
> That has seen a falcon, quicker to flee than an ostrich.[50]

The bustard forms the basis for proverbs on stupidity and foolishness. Bedouins claim that the saying "more stupid than the bustard" derives from the fact that if it leaves its nest, it forgets where it is and broods on the eggs of another, as the ostrich sometimes does.

The Francolin

Another bird, the francolin (*durrāj*), is still to be found in many places along the peripheries of the desert, especially along the upper reaches of the Euphrates. This bird too the bedouins hunt with falcons, and in fact the Arabs were fond of hunting it ages ago; Usāma ibn Munqidh mentioned it in many places in his memoirs, and referred to the enthusiasm of hunters for hunting this bird. Francolins are attractive birds the size of pigeons, with multicolored plumage, long legs, and straight beaks. They walk by running quickly along the ground, hence their name, *durrāj*, the "runner." The male is called *ḥayqutān*. Its meat is quite delicious.

Cranes and Herons

Among the birds that pass across the desert and frequent its peripheries are cranes (or *karākī*). The crane is a large bird close to the goose in size, with a clipped tail, grey plumage, and a black luster on the sides of its face. A single bird is called *kurkī*. As for the heron, this is a white bird, with a moaning-like call, that lives in the Ḥijāz. Of this bird ʻUmar ibn Abī Rabīʻa said:

---

[50] *Ibid.*

My companions holding council
Were a'moaning, one and all,
Like the heron leaving lush lands
That cries out its mournful call.[51]

The Stork

One of the largest birds that pass through the desert and winter in all parts of Arabia is the stork, a bird known among the bedouins as *abū sa'd*, the "bringer of good fortune." The Arabic sources call it *ḥajj laqlaq*, the "clatterer," and in many parts of the Arab world it is referred to as *lajlaj* (pronounced *laklak*), the "stammerer," the name in both cases deriving from the sound it makes, just as the sand grouse, or *qaṭā*, is so named after its call. It is considered a "non-Arab" bird, and among the Iraqis its agnomen is *abū ḥudayj*.

The stork eats snakes and many insects, especially locusts. Village folk rejoice at the sight of this bird when their fields are inundated by swarms of locusts, for the stork gobbles down locusts and annihilates both their swarms and their young (when these are on the ground), as also does the *samarmar*, a bird with a long straight beak, white feathers, and black wings.

The stork migrates to northern Europe for the summer, then returns at the beginning of winter. It flies in large flocks that circle high overhead, and makes several circuits in the air before it suddenly sets out on its long eastward or westward journey. It nests on the roofs of houses in Europe; and before the rainy season begins it leaves the northern regions and in early autumn arrives in the lands of the Syrian Desert on its way south. So long as the sky is cloudy and it hears the sound of thunder, the stork keeps moving southward where there is less rain and cold. At such times the bedouin boys can be heard singing, in reference to its migration:

O stork, see: the thunders roar,
While worms fill up your ass full sore.

[51] 'Umar ibn Abī Rabī'a, *Dīwān*, I.1, 173.

Other Birds

There are many other birds, among them the *qandara*, a brightly colored bird the size of a chicken and found only in the Nafūd, especially in certain lowland depressions. There is also the raven, a well known bird of which three varieties may be found, one of which follows the camels to eat the ticks off them. The *ṣabrī* is a bird that eats insects and the young of the jerboa, and there is also the owl and the *qāq*, a water bird. The *qaṭrā* is larger than the bustard and does not fly much. If attacked by a falcon, it turns over on its back and begins to defend itself with its claws. The *ṭarshī* is the size of a small duck and lives in pairs, like the dove. There is also the *bawwa*, which is approximately the size of the partridge and probably a kind of sand grouse resembling the *kudrī*. The partridge frequents the mountains, highlands, and lowlands of Wādī Sirḥān and lives in flocks. The *samakmak* lives near the water and eats fish.

Aside from the stork, already discussed above, migratory birds include the Iraqi goose and several kinds of ducks that frequent the rain-pools and the expansive ponds of water in the oases, not to mention a large category of small and medium-sized sparrows like the hoopoe. The bedouins call this bird "the slaughterer of its mother and father," and some villagers on the desert fringe refer to it as *shubub*. There are also such birds as the *ṣaffar* (an oriole), *warwar* (bee-eater), *samarmar*, *mulahhiyat al-ru'yān*, *fusaysa*, *zarzūr* (starling), *sunūnū* (the common swallow), *jarjara*, *umm ṭuwayq* (turtledove), *qabba*, *umm fkayr*, *umm sālim* (a kind of lark), and *duhayyin*, among others.[52]

[52] Cf. Musil, *Manners and Customs*, pp. 39–41.

CHAPTER VI

DESERT REPTILES AND INSECTS

MANY KINDS of reptiles and insects are to be found in the desert, including various species of snakes, although most of the snakes in northern Arabia are non-poisonous. The worst of these creatures are the scorpions; but the sting of the scorpion does not kill, and one rarely encounters a villager or bedouin who has never—not even once—suffered the sting of a scorpion. I remember that one late spring day in the desert, in an area of not more than a square mile, I saw not less than a hundred scorpions. Almost all of them were hiding under camel dung out in barren country, and one could hardly turn over a piece of debris on the ground without finding a large scorpion wiggling about underneath it, and sometimes a group of small scorpions. Snakes abound in the hot regions of volcanic soil. Legged reptiles such as skinks and gechoes also abound, as do many other species, the one most renowned among the bedouins being the dhabb. This is the reptile most closely connected to bedouin life, for the bedouin regards its meat as very appetizing.

The Dhabb

The dhabb resembles the crocodile and has a long tail like it, but is a smaller animal and terrestrial by nature. Its tail is covered with rough knobs and has become the basis for a proverb: "knobbier than the tail of a dhabb," which is said of any difficult problem. The length of the dhabb from its head to the tip of its tail comes to about 70 centimeters, comprising more than 20 segments or knobbed sections. Its back is blackish with green spots, and its flat broad belly is yellowish. It lives in dens or burrows that it digs in the ground and where it stays throughout the winter months. When a region of the desert abounds with dhabbs they call it a "dhabb-filled land" (*ḍabiba*, *maḍabba*), in the same way that they refer to a region that is full of lions (*ma'sada*), predators (*masba'a*), wolves (*madh'aba*), or jerboas (*marba'a*). The bedouins claim that of all animals the dhabb is the one that best endures starvation, as well as the one most cowardly, the most deceitful, and the most simple-minded. They thus apply to it many proverbs: "further astray than the dhabb," "more undutiful to kin than the dhabb" (because they claim that it devours its own young out of hunger), "madder than a dhabb," "more simple-minded than a dhabb," and "more deceitful than a dhabb" (this perhaps because, as they say, it changes color in the heat of the sun, as the chameleon does).[1] They also claim that when it ventures forth from its burrow it finds it so difficult to find its way back that it betakes itself to another one. It lives on certain plants that it relishes or finds attractive, especially the savory fragrant *'arfaj*, and may eat certain insects, including grasshoppers. In jest the bedouins call it "Shaykh Ḥāmid" and they say that it is humanoid or humanlike (similar to the daman, or *zalama*) since its feet resemble the human hand in having five digits. The female dhabb lays about 70 eggs, as they claim; and when the young hatches it is called a *ḥisl*.[2] They claim that the dhabb does not come to water, hence the proverb, "I won't do it until the dhabb comes to the water."[3] It is also said that it urinates one drop every 40 days.[4]

Bedouins eagerly hunt the dhabb and eat its meat roasted in a fire. When they see a dhabb entering a burrow, you will see them head for water, if there is a pool nearby, and use it to flood the burrow, thus forcing the dhabb to come out where they can catch it. If no water is available, they push a long stick with claws or a hook on the end into the burrow and drag out the dhabb, cut its throat and skin it, lay it either on glowing firewood coals or directly on the sand, and burn a fire over it until it is well cooked. They eat all of the animal except for the

[1]Al-Damīrī, *Ḥayāt al-ḥayawān*, II, 110.

[2]Kushājim, *Al-Maṣāyid wa-l-maṭārid*, pp. 242–43; al-Damīrī, *Ḥayāt al-ḥayawān*, II, 110.

[3]Kushājim, *Al-Maṣāyid wa-l-maṭārid*, p. 242; al-Damīrī, *Ḥayāt al-ḥayawān*, II, 109.

[4]Al-Damīrī, *Ḥayāt al-ḥayawān*, II, 110.

feet and tail, and camel tenders use its skin to make a small container for camel's milk. Al-Damīrī mentions many uses for the skin and fat of the dhabb, but there is more folklore than truth to this.[5] This may be one of the reasons why simple village and town folk hang dhabb skins stuffed with straw in their shops, as I have often observed.

The Locust

The desert knows many insects other than those we have mentioned, but the most important one is the locust, which of all of them has the greatest impact on the life of the bedouins and of the people in the villages adjoining the desert. When it hatches from the egg the locust is called a *qummaṣ*, or "hopper," then when it begins to crawl it is a *dabā*, or as the villagers and bedouins call it, a *zaḥḥāf*, or "creeper." Then when its wings appear and it grows larger it is a *ghawghā'*, or "clamorer," and when its adult colors appear and it reaches maturity it is called a *jarād*, "locust." There are numerous varieties of locusts, some of those in Arabia differing from those in North Africa.

The insect is mentioned in many places in the Bible, sometimes in metaphorical usages based on its great numbers and at other times in reference to the damage it causes. Thus in Isaiah 33:4 we find: "Your plunder is harvested as if by locusts"; or in Exodus 10:4: "Tomorrow I will bring locusts across your borders." In Joel 2:1–11 there is a passage in which the term "locust" is not mentioned, but which in my opinion refers symbolically to the locusts apparently set upon the Israelites by God to chastise them. In this passage the swarm of locusts is described as an unconquerable army of which it is said:

> Let all of the people of the land tremble, for the day of the Lord is coming: yea, the day is nigh—a day of gloom and darkness, a day of clouds and mist. Like the dawn there spreads across the mountains a vast and mighty host, such as no one has seen since time immemorial, such as will never be seen again for epochs to come. Before them a fire devours, behind them a flame burns. The land is like the garden of Eden before them and a desolate waste behind

[5] *Ibid.*, II, 114.

> them, and from them there is no escape. They look like horses, like chargers they gallop, with the clatter of chariots they hurtle over the mountain tops, with the hissing of a blazing fire devouring the stubble, like a mighty army lined up for battle. The people tremble on their account, and every face pales. Like heroes they issue forth, like warriors scale the walls: each keeps to his path and they divert not from their ways. They do not crowd each other, each keeps to his way: they pass among the weapons, but do not break ranks. They rush upon the city, they leap onto the walls, climbing to the house tops, and enter through the windows like the thief. Before them the earth trembles, the skies shudder, the sun and moon grow dark, and the sparkling of the stars is obscured.

Although this description does reflect the penchant of Joel's imagination for exaggeration, locusts are in fact a frightful spectacle. During the First World War I witnessed clouds of them that almost obscured the sky from view, and saw a swarm that consumed every plant in the fields and then, like an endless black carpet, began crawling down the streets. The locusts climbed walls and spent the night on the wooden guttering of the roofs, where they gnawed at the wood when there was nothing else for them to eat.

The ancient Arabs claimed that when God created the locust he endowed it—despite its weakness, small size, and ignoble reputation—with ten features of the great and mighty animals: a face like a horse's, eyes like an elephant's, a neck like a bull's, antennae like the horns of a stag, a chest like a lion's, a belly like a scorpion's, wings like an eagle's, hindquarters like a camel's, legs like an ostrich's, and a tail like that of the snake. In describing the locust the *qāḍī* Muḥyī l-Dīn al-Shahrazūrī said:

> It has the camel's haunches and the ostrich's legs,
> The eagle's wings and the breast of the lion.
> Its belly was donated by the snakes of the ground,
> And its head and mouth were gifts from mares fine.[6]

[6] *Ibid.*, I, 278.

The place where the locust grows to maturity is the desert, from where it migrates to the settled lands in certain years, devastating their fields and sparing and leaving nothing. Locusts sometimes migrate in consecutive years, and there is no sound foundation for the claim that they only migrate once every seven years. It appears that locusts only take leave of the desert in noticeably large numbers when they become too numerous for the desert to contain them, or when they no longer find sufficient nourishment in its plant life and the greenery of its oases, at which time they develop into swarms and begin to migrate together in search of food. Waves of migration occur during dry spells and on hot dry days. As the body temperature of the locust rises it takes to flight, and as flying and the exercise of its muscles cause its temperature to rise further, its urge is to keep flying without stopping and a single journey may cover hundreds of miles. Some swarms of locusts have been witnessed flying over the sea at a point more than 1200 miles from the nearest landfall. If the weather turns cold or rain falls, or with the approach of night, the locusts stop flying and land on the ground, and there are many of them that come down in the sea and perish. Swarms of locusts may throng together in the sky to such an extent that they fill an area of about 2000 square miles, as occurred, according to the testimony of some experts, in 1889 when swarms crossed the Red Sea to Arabia.[7]

The locust may lay eggs in some of the places where it lands, and these hatch after about 20 days.[8] The young locust (the "creeper") has no sooner hatched than it begins to cover the ground and devour whatever vegetation is around it, allowing no plant life on the ground to survive and then crawling onward to attack whatever fields may lie nearby, where it devours every green plant—trees, vines, and standing crops. The natural banes of the locust are hail and the bird called the *samarmar*; and when the village folk try to drive the flying locusts

[7]See the article "Locust" in *Encyclopaedia Britannica*, 15th edition (Chicago, 1978), *Micropaedia*, VI, 293.

[8]This is the incubation period for the eggs of the *najdī* locust. As for the Moroccan *ziblī* or dung locust, in most cases it lays its eggs when it migrates to the Syrian Desert and adjacent regions in early June, and its eggs remain buried underground until late March of the following year. This locust secretes a substance on the eggs to protect them from decomposing.

away from their fields by banging on metal pots and other resonating containers, you will see them shouting: "Move on, move on, O locusts! The *samarmar* and the hail are coming for you!"

I have seen the *samarmar* swoop down on locusts, and a small flock of ten birds or less no sooner reaches a swarm of locusts than it either annihilates it or drives it away. Many a time I have seen a flying locust drop impotently at the mere sound of the call of the *samarmar*, before the latter has even reached it, and when the bird catches locusts crawling on the ground it begins either to gobble them down or to peck and kill them with its beak. The locusts are cleared so quickly that one would think that they had evaporated from that place. Another bird that wreaks havoc on locusts is a large migratory bird we have already mentioned, the stork. The stork is fond of insects, particularly the locust, and eats many of them in the evenings and mornings. The stork does not, however, frighten the locust as the *samarmar* does.

The locust may compete with the bedouins' livestock for food and deprive it of plant life upon which to graze, but at the same time it is a food item that the bedouin lives on in certain seasons and feeds to his horses to fatten them. In this sense, the locust is both a misfortune and a source of sustenance.

The locust favored by the bedouin is the female of a special type called the *najdī*, or Najd locust, and in the particular phase of its life cycle before it has laid its eggs in the ground. In reality, the parts of the locust that the bedouin eats are the egg case in the rear part of the insect, the thin covering around it, and the breast. The head, wings, entrails, and legs of the locust are all discarded, although some bedouins may occasionally eat the head as well.

The bedouins roast the locust a bit, or else scald it in boiling water and then set the boiled insect aside until it dries out. They then remove the appendages, head, and entrails and eat what remains. I have myself sampled locusts, both roasted and boiled, and I did not find their flavor much different from that of certain kinds of fish.

Locusts are usually collected in the early morning, just after they have spent the night crowded together on the leaves of small scrub plants in the desert and are too sluggish to move. The bedouin collectors pick them off these bushes and put them into sacks, the mouths of which they tie shut so the locusts cannot fly when the temperature rises, and then drop them into large pots of water boiling over a fire. Among both bedouin and village folk I have seen boiled and dried locusts stored in sacks, just as grain is stored. In the markets of certain villages in North Africa, I have been told, locusts are sold as grain is sold.

For laying her eggs the female locust usually chooses moist ground. There she digs a hole large enough for the egg case, inserts her back end into this narrow hole to a depth of about ten centimeters, and lays her eggs, which adhere together in a glutinous fluid. Some claim, out of ignorance, that she remains attached to the egg sack until she dies, while some entomologists hold the view that she does not die and claim that the male of certain varieties eats his mate while she is still in the hole, a view which I do not think can be substantiated. Locusts lay their eggs in groups, hence it is easy for their enemies to collect the eggs and destroy them.

According to bedouin tradition locusts follow a leader or leaders, taking to flight whenever the leader does so and landing when he lands, much as migrating bedouins do. This behavior may seem strange and there is no definitive proof for it; but I have seen swarms of locusts descending on a plot of ground *en masse*, and no sooner has one of them taken to the air than the entire swarm begins to follow it, without delay or hesitation. It may be the locust's instinct to move as a swarm and to land as a swarm. The fact that they take to flight together may even be explained by the locusts reaching a specific temperature at which they can no longer remain on the burning hot ground, and so take off in swarms. The locust flies only during the day and when the heat becomes intense. People in the villages and agricultural areas therefore welcome hot days when locusts come to call, for at such times it is easy for them to stir up and drive the locusts from their fields by shouting, making noise, and banging on metal containers, hoping that the locusts will fly away and not return.

Nothing, however, can turn back or stop locusts in the "hopper" stage of development. You see them like a black carpet spread across the ground, wiping out any greenery they find in their path so completely that they leave not a trace of it behind. In former times people used to combat hoppers by digging trenches across their path and erecting smooth sheets of plain or galvanized tin along the facing edge of the trench. As soon as the locusts crossed the trench and began to climb the wall of metal sheets, they would slip off, fall back into the trench, and accumulate in piles, where they could be killed by throwing dirt over them, trampling them underfoot, or crushing them by hand. Today, the land where locusts hatch is sprayed with insecticides, and if some survive after eating the poison they are dealt with and destroyed with flame throwers. If it has laid its eggs in a place near the settled areas, people collect the eggs or they plow the ground, thereby exposing the eggs to the heat of the sun, cold, and the open air, and destroying most of them. A single egg reaches the size of a fine withered grain of wheat, and the egg case of the *najdī* locust contains anywhere from 60 to 80 eggs. There are probably types of locusts that lay a greater number of eggs, and one explorer mentions that there is a locust the female of which lays about 200 eggs. As for the Moroccan locust known as the *ziblī*, or dung locust, the female of this variety lays only a few eggs, probably not exceeding 40.

CHAPTER VII

DOMESTICATED ANIMALS IN THE DESERT

THERE CAN BE no doubt that the domesticated animal most renowned among the bedouins is the camel. Indeed, their name is so closely associated with the camel in history, as well as in many of the inscriptions that make reference to bedouins, that the bedouin is not mentioned without reference to the camels accompanying him. But as the camel has been considered one of the pillars of bedouin life in our study, we have decided to devote a special chapter to it and to discuss here the other domesticated animals that have some connection to the life of the bedouin.

The Horse

We begin with the animal most closely linked to the bedouin after the camel, and the one that takes preference over the camel as the thing dearest to him. This is none other than the horse, the name of which is so closely associated with the Arabs that their horses are called Arabian horses (*al-khayl al-ʿirāb*). The horse was of great influence in the life of the Arabs in general and the bedouins in particular, and played a significant role in the military successes achieved by the Arabs in their long history. The camel, as we shall see, may have been a mainstay of nomadic life, but it was the horse that both settled and bedouin Arabs prized, and about whose merit, usefulness, strength, and devotion they spoke. They lavished such attention on horses and showed them such tremendous affection that this animal ranks as the one best-loved by the bedouin. As they said: "Their backs are a source of protection (*ḥirz*) and their bellies a store of treasure (*kanz*)." And such was their attitude both in pre-Islamic times and after the rise of Islam since the days of the Arab Prophet. Al-Damīrī reports that a bedouin came to see the Prophet and said: "I am fond of horses. Are there any horses in Paradise?"[1] Their attachment to horses reached the point, they claim, that they only took pleasure in the birth of a boy, the foaling of a mare, and the rise of a poet to eminence. For tying up their horses they used spots nearby, in the places between the tents, and called the horses tethered there *muqarrabāt*, "the ones kept close by." The bedouin poet Zayd ibn al-Muhalhil al-Ṭā'ī, known as Zayd al-Khayl ("Zayd of the horses"), said of his horse al-Haṭṭāl:

I keep al-Haṭṭāl tethered at a nearby spot,
For I see the years bringing explosions of war.
I treat him like 'Urwa to share winter's lot,
And compared to my wife, I value him more.[2]

And Ibn 'Abbās said:

Their feelings for horses waxed fond and endured;
By their might and their beauty to them they were lured.
Though some may slight them with harm and neglect,
We keep them to show them a kinsman's respect.
Each day subsistence with them do we share,
And their head cloths and blankets betray how they fare.[3]

Sufficient proof of their importance is the verse found in the Qur'ān: "Prepare for them what you can of force and strings of horses, that you might thereby strike fear into God's enemies and yours."[4] Al-Damīrī even claims that it is sufficient honor for the horse that God Almighty has taken an oath by it in His Book, saying: "By the snorting chargers," referring to "war horses that make chesty sounds, or snort, when they

[1]Aḥmad ibn Ḥanbal, *Musnad* (Cairo, AH 1311–13), V, 352; al-Damīrī, *Ḥayāt al-ḥayawān*, I, 463.

[2]'Abd Allāh ibn Ḥamza, *Ta'rīkh al-khuyūl al-'arabīya*, with the commentary of his son Aḥmad (Sanaa, 1979), p. 33. ['Urwa was the poet's son.]

[3]Al-Damīrī, *Ḥayāt al-ḥayawān*, I, 461.

[4]Sūrat al-Anfāl (8), v. 60.

gallop."[5] It was also said: "The angels are present at no amusements, save three—the amusement of a man with his wife, horse racing, and battle,"[6] and that the Prophet himself raced horses.[7] In Prophetic tradition we read: "Benefit will lie knotted in the forelocks of horses until the Day of Judgment, so long as their owners are attentive to them; so stroke their forelocks and appeal to them for blessing."[8] The Arabs even devoted their attentions to the genealogies of their horses, carefully preserving their pedigrees (or their *arsān*, as the bedouins say), and went to great lengths to try to ensure that thoroughbreds did not mix with non-thoroughbreds, so that the pedigrees of the former would remain absolutely pure and unblemished by any defect. When they discussed their horses, they would speak with caution, just as they would in discussing affairs of honor. They would not speak of matters that might blemish the pedigrees of their horses, and they sought God's absolution from anyone who spoke ill of a horse's pedigree unless what he said was well known to be true.

Medieval Arab authors took account of the importance and eminent status of the horse, and so wrote books about it to such an extent that one can hardly find a famous author known for the multitude of his works without also finding that one of these works is about horses. Ibn al-Nadīm, a scholar of the fourth century AH/tenth century AD, mentions the names of many third/ninth-century scholars who wrote on horses. Ma'mar ibn al-Muthannā, known as Abū 'Ubayda, wrote three books: one on horses, which we have used, another on geldings, and a third on names of horses.[9] Al-Aṣma'ī composed a *Kitāb al-khayl* ("Book of Horses");[10] and Ibn Durayd wrote two such works, the first the *Kitāb al-khayl al-kabīr* ("Large Book on Horses") and the second the *Kitāb al-khayl al-ṣaghīr* ("Small Book on Horses").[11] Al-Qāsim ibn

[5]Al-Damīrī, *Ḥayāt al-ḥayawān*, I, 459.

[6]*Ibid.*, I, 463.

[7]*Ibid.*

[8]Al-Bukhārī, *Al-Jāmi' al-ṣaḥīḥ*, edited by Ludolf Krehl and T.W. Juynboll (Leiden, 1862–1908), II, 213, *Jihād* nos. 43–44; Ibn al-Kalbī, *Kitāb ansāb al-khayl fī l-jāhilīya wa-l-Islām wa-akhbārihā*, edited by Aḥmad Zakī Pāshā (Cairo, 1946), p. 9.

[9]Ibn al-Nadīm, *Al-Fihrist*, edited by Gustav Flügel (Leipzig, 1871–72), I, 53–54.

[10]*Ibid.*, p. 55.

[11]*Ibid.*, p. 61.

Figure 15: A bedouin horseman on his sorrel mare.

Ma'n[12] and Ibn Qutayba[13] both wrote books about horses. Hishām ibn al-Kalbī also compiled such a work, this probably being the *Kitāb ansāb al-khayl fī l-jāhilīya wa-l-Islām wa-akhbārihā* ("Book of Pedigrees and Accounts about Horses in Pre-Islamic and Islamic Times") edited and published by the late Aḥmad Zakī Pāshā.[14] Al-Madā'inī had a *Kitāb al-khayl* ("Book of Horses") and a *Kitāb al-khayl wa-l-rihān* ("Book on Horses and Wagering Stakes"),[15] and al-Riyāshī too wrote a book about horses.[16] Al-Naḍr ibn Shumayl composed a book *Fī khuluq al-faras* ("On the Nature of the Mare"),[17] and both Abū 'Amr al-Shaybānī[18] and Muḥammad ibn Ḥabīb[19] wrote works on horses. Even Ibn Sallām, famous for his book *Ṭabaqāt al-shu'arā'* ("Classes of Poets"), is mentioned by Ibn al-Nadīm as author of a book entitled *Kitāb al-ḥilāb wa-ijrā' al-khayl* ("Book of Race Horses and Horse Racing").[20] He also assigns a book on attributes of the horse to 'Alī ibn 'Ubayda al-Rīḥānī,[21] and another book on horses to the poet al-'Utbī.[22]

Not surprisingly, some of the contents of these books, most of which are lost, have come down to us in some of the works of later authors, as we see in the book *Ta'rīkh al-khuyūl al-'arabīya* ("History of Arabian Horses"). The author of this work, to which we referred at the beginning of this chapter, was a writer of the seventh/thirteenth century. In his book he discusses the strains of horses, their colors and names, and the passages in poetry and prose in which horses are mentioned. The work also contains a complete *rajaz* poem on horses. And he is not content—when describing their colors, for example—to mention such ordinary well-known colors as sorrel (*aḥmar*), bay (*ashqar*), or pitch-black (*adham*), but rather subdivides each color into many hues. He says, for example, that chestnut (*kumayt*) "is divided into eight

[12] *Ibid.*, p. 69.
[13] *Ibid.*, p. 78.
[14] *Ibid.*, p. 96; see also Ibn al-Kalbī, *Kitāb ansāb al-khayl*.
[15] *Ibid.*, pp. 103–104.
[16] *Ibid.*, p. 58.
[17] *Ibid.*, p. 52.
[18] *Ibid.*, p. 68.
[19] *Ibid.*, p. 106.
[20] *Ibid.*, p. 113.
[21] *Ibid.*, p. 119.
[22] *Ibid.*, p. 121.

varieties." The primary color comes in "four hues: blood chestnut (*al-kumayt al-mudammā*), red chestnut (*al-kumayt al-aḥmar*), marginal chestnut (*al-kumayt al-muḥlifa*), and golden chestnut (*al-kumayt al-mudhahhab*)." To these he adds four others, arranged according to their shading: the first is called deep sorrel (*aḥmar aḥamm*) and russet chestnut (*al-kumayt al-aklaf*), a color in which red is dominated by black, etc.[23] Of yellow sorrel (*aṣfar*) he distinguishes light yellow sorrel (*aṣfar a'far*), pure yellow sorrel (*aṣfar nāṣi'*), and bright yellow sorrel (*aṣfar fāqi'*),[24] and even the whinnying of horses he divides into different varieties.[25]

Arabian horses have been renowned throughout the world since remote antiquity. Horse breeders in many areas outside the Arab world have begun to import and breed Arabians, and have striven to mix the strains of their horses with Arabian blood; as a the result, one now only rarely finds beautiful throughbred horses whose blood lines are not mixed with those of the Arabian. Information in the reports of the English consuls to the Foreign Office in the nineteenth century, as well as in the works of the explorers and adventurers who followed the desert route across Syria and Iraq to India and the Arab Gulf from Aleppo to al-Baṣra, confirms how keen the Europeans—especially the English—were to buy Arabian horses from the Arab lands and to transport them back to their own countries. Indeed, some of these travels were undertaken with that goal alone in mind.[26] And in recent years the United States has begun to hold long-distance races for Arabian horses. Experts several decades ago estimated the number of thoroughbred Arabians there at 10,000, but it seems that the demand for them now is not as high as it was previously.[27]

Since ancient times the Arabs have recognized the advantage and effectiveness of the horse and its superiority over the camel in the hit-and-run tactics used in their raids, which in all of their campaigns, and especially in close-quarter fighting in battles, demanded the advantages of speed and surprise. Even when they expanded in their conquests

---

[23]'Abd Allāh ibn Ḥamza, *Ta'rīkh al-khuyul al-'arabīya*, p. 132.
[24]*Ibid.*, p. 137.
[25]*Ibid.*, p. 148.
[26]See *The Desert Route to India*.
[27]*News Review*, vol. 10, no. 42 (15 October 1959), p. 4.

during Islamic times the horse was a steady support that helped them to achieve their victories and to penetrate that vast area of land spreading across three continents. In boasting about the acquisition of horses and about bedouin life, while disparaging the life of the peasant cultivators of fields, vineyards, and gardens, Ṣa'ṣa'a ibn Mu'āwiya al-Sa'dī said:

On the *dāliya*'s arm my funds would not sway,
From stump-top a'pouring its water on clay.
The daughters of A'waj, all straining at reins,
O'er cucumbers and figs mark far higher gains.
That horses adorn men, the Prophet agreed,
But he commented not upon gardens in seed.
Round cities of tyrants they've pounded on hoof,
To bring down in ruins each proud lofty roof.[28]

There is no image that reflects the Arab sense of pride as beautifully as does the image of an Arab on a thoroughbred horse. Indeed, the word *furūsīya* ("horsemanship") in the Arabic language, and its connotations of gallantry, nobility, might, and fortitude, are derived from the terms for the mare (*faras*) and the horseman (*fāris*), and the word *fāris* has also come to mean "hero." As their poet said:

If hero you'd be, then be like 'Alī;
Or if poet you'd be, then be like Ibn Hānī.[29]

They also transmitted traditions stating that it was permissible to pray on horseback in time of war, and to go on pilgrimage on horseback and to travel by horse among the ritual stations in Mecca.[30] The Arabs claimed that the horse is by nature disposed toward pride, arrogance,

[28]'Abd Allāh ibn Ḥamza, *Ta'rīkh al-khuyūl al-'arabīya*, p. 30. [A *dāliya* is an irrigation device for lifting water to the fields, in this case an upright member to which is fastened a transverse arm with a bucket hung at one end. In tribal lore, A'waj was a renowned stallion considered more famous than any other and the one that had sired the most progeny.]

[29]This is a famous verse, but I have found no information on its author or any source mentioning it. [By 'Alī, the fourth caliph, 'Alī ibn Abī Ṭālib, is meant; Ibn Hānī was a renowned Andalusian Fāṭimid poet, d. 362/973.]

[30]'Abd Allāh ibn Ḥamza, *Ta'rīkh al-khuyūl al-'arabīya*, p. 16.

self-esteem, and devotion to its master, and that it will not eat the fodder left by another horse.[31] Al-'Arjī gives an extravagant account of his stallion's arrogance and its reaction to his courtesy in pulling the animal's saddle cloth off its back. Claiming that it was like performing a courtesy for a king, he says:

> When we drew off his cloth, what a flattering deed:
> Like unto a king pranced that proud strutting steed![32]

They once did and still do point out the superiority of mares when launching a surprise attack by night or making a raid, since mares whinny very little.[33]

The Origins of the Horse

In his book on the horse, Simpson claims that it appeared with the emergence of early man, and that man's contact with the horse in the Early Stone Age did not differ from his contact with the other animals that he hunted for their meat.[34] The horse did not have an auspicious place in this relationship, as it played the role of the slaughtered victim. In 1866 excavators in Solutré-Pouilly, in the Mâcon region of France, uncovered many horse bones among the debris left behind by Stone Age man there, a fact that leaves no room for doubting that the horse was hunted for its meat just as were such other wild animals as the gazelle, rabbit, ibex, and oryx.[35]

It should come as no surprise that horses were first domesticated for the same purpose that domestic cattle, sheep, and goats are raised

---

[31] Al-Damīrī, *Ḥayāt al-ḥayawān*, II, 299.

[32] Al-'Arjī, *Dīwān*, edited by Khiḍr al-Ṭā'ī and Rashīd al-'Ubaydī (Baghdad, 1375/1956), p. 17.

[33] Al-Damīrī, *Ḥayāt al-ḥayawān*, II, 299.

[34] G.G. Simpson, *Horses* (London, 1951), p. 24.

[35] Although the most complete fossil remains of horse skeletons have been found in North America, it is clear from the statements of scholars that the horse originated in Asia and in successive waves migrated from there to North America. It lived there throughout the Pleistocene Age, then subsequently became extinct and was unknown until the Spanish conquest. See A.W. Podhajsky, "Horse," in *Encyclopaedia Britannica*, 15th edition (Chicago, 1978), *Macropaedia*, VIII, 1088.

today—to be fattened and then slaughtered for their meat. When the Arabs first came in contact with the horse they ate its meat, as we can see from their stories about slaughtering their horses for their guests; and indeed, there are reports informing us that they continued to eat horse meat up until the time of the Prophet.[36] It is evident that the early domesticators of horses already recognized other useful features in the horse: its ability to carry heavy loads, its swift pace, its friendly disposition, its loyalty, and its fondness for life with man. They accordingly began to spare the horses and to take advantage of these qualities. Not surprisingly, it was the early skirmishing and fighting among groups of men that illustrated this dimension of the horse's merits and benefits, and horses thus became animals that men relied upon for both attack and flight. Whatever the reasons for it may have been, it is evident that the date for the domestication of the horse is not a very remote one, and is probably not much earlier than 2500 BC. In all probability it was first achieved on a broad scale in Central Asia, perhaps among certain bedouins who recognized the advantage the horseman had over a man on foot in both military engagements and in the search for places possessed of pasturage and water.

It must not have been difficult for man to domesticate the horse. This probably involved only catching a stallion and a mare, allowing them to become tame and accustomed to captivity, and leaving them in a spacious corral to breed. Alternatively, one could catch a young colt and filly and raise them until they reached adulthood and produced young of their own. One of the theories on the origins of the domestication of the horse is as follows. The first person to domesticate a horse was a boy who took a colt as a plaything with which to amuse himself, just as other boys kept puppies. When the colt grew older he began to ride it, and suddenly noticed that the horse made the finest, fastest, most obedient, and noblest mount. Thus the idea spread: people began to domesticate and acquire horses, and the horses began to breed and proliferate in captivity. Not surprisingly, this process occurred in different parts of the world at the same time; hence, many different kinds of horses were domesticated at various places in the world in the

[36] Abū ‘Ubayda, *Kitāb al-khayl* (Hyderabad, AH 1358), p. 8; al-Damīrī, *Ḥayāt al-ḥayawān*, I, 468; II, 307.

same era. From that period onward domestication began to spread and these different types of horses developed into distinct breeds, each manifesting its own distinctive traits and qualities.

Man evidently began to take advantage of this swift and powerful beast in his quarrels and conflicts with his fellow men established in other regions, and the horse accordingly became a factor of great significance in military history. After Central Asia, its most important domain was probably the lands of the Near East, where ancient civilizations clashed and where the most important battles between the armies of various peoples occurred. It was used in battles to pull war chariots, or in raids, in which context the Bible mentions it in many accounts. It was also used for hunting, as we see in some of the bas-reliefs and paintings left behind by the Egyptians and Assyrians, as well as in the Book of Job, where Job refers to the ostrich, saying: "When she betakes herself to the highlands, she laughs at the mare and at its rider."[37]

It would seem that the first Arabian horses acquired by the Arabs of the Arabian peninsula were not originally from Arabia, but more probably came from the Fertile Crescent, where they had already gradually moved in with peoples coming from the north, either from Iran and Central Asia or from beyond Asia Minor, from one of the regions bordering the Caspian Sea. These Asiatic horses were the original stock from which the Arabian, Turkish, and African horse all developed. They were also the original stock of most European horses, and spread to Europe either directly from the East or later via Spain. It is not unlikely that there are European horses of other origins. Arab tradition has it that the horse was originally a wild animal and that the first man to ride one was Ishmael, for which reason it was named "Arabian" (*'irāb*). From the Prophet they relate a tradition in which he says: "Ride horses, for they are the legacy of your father Ishmael."[38] The

[37]Job 39:18.

[38]Al-Damīrī, *Ḥayāt al-ḥayawān*, I, 463. There is a legend that some claim has been transmitted by tribes in the Syrian Desert concerning the first thoroughbreds. This tale has it that they were wild animals roaming about after the bursting of the Ma'rib Dam; five bedouins resorted to stratagems to capture them, and they came to be called *al-jiyād al-khamsa*, "the five thoroughbreds," famous by their own individual names. See the newspaper *Barīd al-sharq* (Cologne), 10 February

Prophet bought mares (sources differ as to their number and names); one, purchased from the bedouins, was named al-Sakb and was the first mare Muḥammad rode in his campaigns. Others were named al-Subḥa, al-Murtajiz, Lazāz, Liḥāf, and al-Ward, this last one reportedly given to him by Tamīm al-Dārī.[39]

The earliest mention of the horse in the Fertile Crescent probably goes back to the Babylonians, who used it for chariots and other vehicles about a thousand years before Christ. Earlier they had used donkeys to pull chariots.[40] They had become familiar with the horse from, as we mentioned above, the peoples of the north, who were already using it to pull chariots. The Babylonians thus referred to it metaphorically as the "mountain ass," since it came down to them with the mountain peoples.

The earliest Old Testament reference to the horse appears in the Book of Judges 4:2–18 and 5:22–28. This goes back to the time of Japin, king of Canaan, and Sisera, commander of his army, who they claim had 900 iron chariots that were destroyed by his enemies. Then in II Samuel 8:3–4 we find in the reports of the Prophet David's war with Hedadezer, king of Zobah, that along the Euphrates River David captured 1700 cavalrymen and 20,000 foot soldiers from him and hamstrung all of the chariot horses, sparing only those for 100 chariots. Solomon then followed his father and began to acquire horses: the Bible has it that he had 40,000 feed troughs for his chariot horses and, so they claim, 12,000 cavalrymen. And for the horses they used to bring straw and barley.[41] The Qur'ān refers to the horses of Solomon in Sūrat Ṣād (38), vs. 29–32, and speaks of how the standing steeds were shown to him and distracted his attention from prayer. Saddened and angered, he began to stroke their legs and necks. In the Book of Job there is a precise description of the charger, its fortitude and courage, and how it leaps like the locust and feels no fear in battle.[42] From the story told about him, however, it appears that Job himself did not own horses,

1969. I have never heard this legend from any bedouin, however, though I have asked many of them about it.

[39]Al-Damīrī, *Ḥayāt al-ḥayawān*, II, 308–309.

[40]H.R. Hall, *The Ancient History of the Near East* (London, 1952), p. 213.

[41]I Kings 4:26–28.

[42]Job 39:19–25.

nor are any mentioned among the various kinds of livestock he is said to have lost.[43]

While it may be true that Job was an Arab, horses did not figure among his possessions. Indeed, horses are not even mentioned among the presents that the queen of Sheba brought with her to Solomon. She arrived with a very great procession, but the Old Testament story makes no specific mention of horses in this procession, while it does mention camels bearing spices and vast quantities of gold.[44] This probably indicates that southern Arabia was not familiar with the horse in this period.

On the other hand, we can see that the horse was well-known in Egypt even before the exodus of the Israelites. In the accounts of Joseph we read that when Joseph was an overseer for the Pharaoh of Egypt, the Egyptians brought their livestock to him and he gave them bread in exchange for their horses, their sheep and cattle, and their donkeys.[45] And in II Kings there is a reference to the Israelites' attempt to convince the Egyptians to reinforce them with chariots and horsemen in order to confront the king of Assyria. When the king of Assyria conquered them and wanted to conclude a truce with Hezekiah, king of Judah, he offered Hezekiah 2000 mares if he could find riders for them.[46] Some historians are of the opinion that even in Egypt the horse was unknown before the eighteenth century BC.[47] Some claim that it was the Arab shepherd kings (the Hyksos) who introduced the horse into Egypt when they occupied Lower Egypt in the seventeenth century BC. This was in the wake of the intrusion of the Aryans from Iran and the Anatolian peoples from Asia Minor into northern Syria and Mesopotamia, driving southward the Semitic inhabitants, including the shepherd kings, who thus came to Egypt. In spite of this, there are those who claim that Egypt knew the horse before the era of the Hyksos, and that an archaeological expedi-

---

[43]Job 1:1–22.

[44]I Kings 10:2.

[45]Genesis 47:17.

[46]II Kings 18:23–24.

[47]Much useful information on this and other aspects of the history of the horse is collected in E.D. Brickwood, "Horse: History," in *Encyclopaedia Britannica*, 11th edition (Cambridge, 1910–11), XIII, 717–23.

tion has discovered the skeleton of a horse dating back to the Middle Kingdom.[48]

Whatever the fact of the matter may be, the shepherd kings were the first Arabs to be acquainted with the horse. And it would come as no surprise to find that at the same time that the horse passed with the Hyksos into Egypt, it also spread southward with other Arabs into Arabia. The Greek geographer Strabo, however, denies that the horse was to be found in the Arabian peninsula prior to the first century BC, and he apparently bases his verdict on the statements of the Roman general Aelius Gallus, who mounted an expedition into Arabia in 24 BC.[49] When we turn to the Arabic sources, the first mention of the horse among the Arabs is to be found in pre-Islamic poetry, as we see, for example, in the *mu'allaqa* of Imru' al-Qays:

> The birds in nests were roosting still when forth from camp I came
> On a mighty short-haired beast that outruns the fastest game,
> That in one move will hit and run, will charge and yet will fly,
> Like a bouncing rock cast down by torrents from on high,
> A chestnut steed whose saddle cloth comes sliding down his side,
> Just as water slips past pebbles in rainstorms' streaming tide.[50]

And in the *mu'allaqa* of 'Antara:

> "Antara," they cried out, and the lances were like
> Well-ropes sunk into the chest of the jet-black steed.
> I kept charging them with the wound in his neck
> And chest, until he was drenched, such did he bleed.

---

[48]See the journal *Al-'Ālam* (London), May 1959, pp. 3–4, in an article on an Egyptian fortress built 4000 years ago.

[49]Cf. Hitti, Jurji, and Jabbur, *Ta'rīkh al-'arab*, p. 48 [= Hitti, *History of the Arabs*, p. 21.]

[50]*Sharḥ al-qaṣā'id al-'ashr*, pp. 21–22.

He staggered from the blows of spears in his chest
And complained to me with tear and whinny of his need.
Had he known how to argue he would have complained,
And had speech been his, he'd have made me take heed.[51]

In an ode by Khālid ibn Ja'far ibn Kilāb he mentions his mare and refers to his solicitude for it and his exhortation to his two herdsmen to favor it with milk:

In terms of my life do I think of her cost,
And cover her up with my cloak in the frost.
To favor her both herdsmen their orders I gave,
That *khalīya* and *ṣa'ūd* milk for her they should save.[52]
Mounted on her, God may to me concede
A manifest triumph o'er Zuhayr and Asīd.[53]

Indeed, the poet al-A'raj al-Ma'nī scolded his wife when she reproved him for preferring to give the milk of his she-camel to his mare Ward rather than to her:

I see there Umm Sahl tormenting me still;
Her trouble I know not, but fault me she will.
For granting al-Ward milk she hurls forth blame,
Though Ward when war beckons would put her to shame.[54]

It is said that a king coveted a mare named Sakāb, owned by a man of Tamīm, but as the horse was of such noble nature her owner withheld her from the king and said:

Risk not a curse, for Sakāb is a beast most dear,
So precious that of loan or sale I could not hear,

---

[51] *Ibid.*, p. 105.

[52] The *khalīya* is a she-camel whose milk is left for the dog, the *ṣa'ūd* one that gives birth to its young prematurely, yet has abundant milk.

[53] Abū 'Ubayda, *Kitāb al-khayl*, p. 10. His father had been killed, his sister and mother had been taken prisoner, and they sold his father's mare. When he grew up and became a young man, he raised horses and gained revenge for his father.

[54] Abū Tammām, *Ḥamāsa*, I, 136–37.

A well-fed steed—a pampered mare—that casts the lot
That family should go hungry so that she might not.[55]

Horses are also mentioned in the accounts of al-Muhalhil and al-Ḥārith ibn ʿAbbād in the War of al-Basūs, when al-Ḥārith sent his son to al-Muhalhil in order to reach agreement on retaliatory killing as vengeance in the matter of Kulayb, whom Jassās had killed. Al-Muhalhil killed al-Ḥārith's son, saying: "Die, as blood vengeance for the toe-thong of Kulayb's sandal." When the news reached al-Ḥārith, he called for his mare al-Naʿāma and clipped its forelock and docked its tail. He was the first Arab to do this, and from that time the Arabs adopted this as a custom practiced when someone dear to them was killed. Al-Ḥārith then went out to fight al-Muhalhil. In this story of al-Muhalhil there is a reference to the wounding of horses and the shattering of lances, and in the poetry of al-Muhalhil there are many references to horses.[56] Similarly, we see that the war that broke out between ʿAbs and Dhubyān was reportedly caused by a dispute between them over a race between the two mares Dāḥis and al-Ghabrā'.

It is beyond doubt that the horse had already begun to spread into most parts of Arabia in pre-Islamic times, and that the Arabs had begun to make use of it in their raids and in their famous "battle days" (*ayyām*). It also played a role in their conquests and military expeditions. Abū ʿUbayda said:

> In pre-Islamic times the bedouins protected and pampered none of their possessions as much as they protected and pampered horses, due to the power, force, and strength that horses gave them over their enemies. A bedouin would even remain starving while his mare ate its fill, and show it preference over himself, his kinsmen, and his children by giving it buttermilk to drink while everyone else drank plain water. They upbraided each other for the neglect and mistreatment of horses and for allowing them to become emaciated, and referred to such matters in their poems.[57]

[55] *Ibid.*, I, 74.
[56] See the story of al-Muhalhil in *Aghānī*, IV, 143–47.
[57] Abū ʿUbayda, *Kitāb al-khayl*, p. 2.

With the advent of Islam the Qur'ān urged that horses be taken and readied for the *jihād* against the enemy, and the Prophet encouraged the Muslims to rely upon them. Indeed, the Prophet himself ranked among those keenest on and most solicitous toward horses, and most emphatic in his deference, love, and admiration for them. He used to run races between horses and to wipe the face of his mare with his robe, and in dividing spoils gave the horseman two shares and the foot-soldier one.[58] And as already mentioned, it is still an emblem of pride, fortitude, nobility, strength, and beauty among the Arabs. They have also used it in hunting since their earliest times, as did other peoples, and on it have given chase to the gazelle, oryx, onager, and ostrich.

The Arabs were supremely fond of horses and claimed that when God made it subservient to man and put its sustenance in his hands, the horse beseeched God to make it dearer to man than his kinsmen and children, a request that God granted.[59] They cared for, raised, and trained horses, and as al-Kumayt said:

> We teach them: "Back," and "Come," and "Give way;"
> Weaned foals are adopted, and in our tents stay.[60]

Among the Arabs, the first man to become famous for his horses, so they claim, was Zayd ibn al-Muhalhil al-Ṭā'ī. He owned many horses, so many more than anyone else in his tribe that he was called Zayd al-Khayl, "Zayd of the horses." He survived into Islamic times and came to visit the Prophet, who then named him Zayd al-Khayr, "Zayd of the good deeds." Among his many horses were al-Haṭṭāl, al-Kumayt, al-Ward, al-Kāmil, and Lāḥiq.[61]

Until recent times the bedouins remained among those most solicitous of and deferent toward horses. They say: "The backs of horses are

---

[58] *Ibid.*, p. 4. The text would appear to refer to "the mare" (*al-faras*) and "the man" (*al-rajul*); but the long *alif* is often dropped in medieval manuscripts, and the words originally intended are probably "the horseman" (*al-fāris*) and "the foot-soldier" (*al-rājil*).

[59] Al-Damīrī, *Ḥayāt al-ḥayawān*, II, 297. They even claim that on the Judgment Day their urine and dung will be as fragrant as musk.

[60] Al-Kumayt, *Shi'r al-Kumayt*, edited by Dāwūd Sallūm (Baghdad, 1969–70), II.1, 128.

[61] Al-Damīrī, *Ḥayāt al-ḥayawān*, I, 327. See also the accounts recorded for us by Abū l-Faraj al-Iṣfahānī in *Aghānī*, IV, 143–47.

a source of power (*'izz*) and their bellies a store of treasure (*kanz*)," and their saying is probably derived from a Prophetic tradition: "You must have the females of horses, for their backs are a source of protection (*ḥirz*) and their bellies a store of treasure (*kanz*)."[62] It was upon the horse that they depended in surprise attacks and important expeditions. The bedouin would withhold nothing for the sake of the care, welfare, and comfort of his mare: it would not be surprising to see him sometimes denying his sons the milk of his she-camel if his mare stood in need of that milk, or denying himself, his wife, or his son water if his mare was thirsty.[63] In dry spells, when the Rwāla bedouins headed west toward the settled regions, they made sure to assign to each mare a she-camel with suckling young so that the mare could drink its milk. And indeed, they claimed that the horse would perish were they not more concerned for their horses than for their own children.

Bedouins made a point of preserving the pedigrees and genealogies of their horses, and they did not allow their thoroughbred mares to produce young from any but a thoroughbred stallion. They were thus experts at raising horses of pure pedigree, and there accordingly appeared among them thoroughbreds that were agile and fast, that did not tire easily, and that endured hardships well. They even claimed that there were horses that would not urinate or defecate so long as their riders were mounted on their backs, and others that knew their masters so well that they allowed no one else to ride them. And as mentioned above, thoroughbred horses were so closely associated with the Arabs that they were called "Arabian" horses (*al-khayl al-'irāb*). At present there are a number of famous thoroughbred strains among the bedouins, the most important of which are these five: the *kuḥaylān*, the *'abayyān*, the *saqlāwī* (or *ṣaqlāwī*), the *ḥamdānī*, and the *hadbān*, the mares of which are called *kuḥayla*, *'ubayya*, *saqlāwīya*, *ḥamdānīya*, and *hadba*. Among certain tribes there are other strains regarded as thoroughbred, such as the *umm 'arqub*, the *mu'anaqīya*, the *khlāfa*, and others. These strains are in turn subdivided into others: there

[62]Ibn Qutayba, *'Uyūn al-akhbār* (Cairo, 1343–49/1925–30), I, 153.

[63]Abū 'Ubayda, *Kitāb al-khayl*, p. 2; Hitti, Jurji, and Jabbur, *Ta'rīkh al-'arab*, p. 48 [= Hitti, *History of the Arabs*, p. 21]. Doughty (I, 304) mentions that the bedouins used to designate a milk camel for every mare, due to the shortage of grain, and devote special attention to the care of horses.

are, for example, the *kuḥaylat al-kharas*, the *kuḥaylat al-'ajūz*, and so forth.[64]

Lady Anne Blunt mentions the five thoroughbred strains and says of the *kuḥaylān*:

> This strain is the most numerous and, taken generally, the most esteemed....The Kehílans are the fastest, though perhaps not the hardiest horses, and bear a closer resemblance than the rest to English thoroughbreds, to whom indeed they are more nearly related....Its subdivisions are very numerous...[and among them] are the Kehílan Ajúz, the Kehílan Nowag, the Kehílan Abū Argúb, and Ras-el-Fedawi.

As for the *saqlāwī*:

> One strain of this blood, the Seglawi Jedrán, is considered the best of all in the desert; and the Seglawis generally are held in high repute. They are, however, comparatively rare, and exist only in a few families of the Anazeh. Among the Shammar there are Seglawis, but no Seglawi Jedráns....The four strains, Jedrán, Obeyrán, Arjébi, and El Abd, are identical in origin, being descended from four Seglawi mares, sisters—but only the first has been kept absolutely pure.

As for the *'abayyān*:

> The Abéyan is generally the handsomest breed, but is small and has less resemblance to the English thoroughbred than either of the preceding. The Abéyan Sherrák is the substrain most appreciated, and an Abéyan Sherrak we saw at Aleppo, bred by the Gomússa, could not have been surpassed in good looks.

The *ḥamdānī*, she says, "is not a common type either among the Anazeh or Shammar. Most of the animals of this breed I have seen have been grey." Her statement is an accurate one, for the *ḥamdānī* horses I

[64]Musil, *Manners and Customs*, pp. 371–73.

have seen have all been grey. We used to own a grey *ḥamdānī* mare—one of the noblest and fastest of horses—that was killed under my brother during a race through the lanes of the village. Blunt also says: "But a very handsome brown horse was shown to us by the Gomussa. This was a Hamdáni Simri, which is the only substrain recognized as *hadúd*."

The *hadbān*, the fifth of these thoroughbred strains, is "also uncommon among the Anazeh, the best having formerly been possessed by the Roála, this being the Hádban Enzekhi." Lady Anne describes a mare of this substrain in al-Dayr that was "full of fire" and carried her tail very high, and claimed that it resembled a race horse. The other two substrains are the *mshayṭib* and the *furruḍ*, but these are not as highly esteemed as the *anzayjī*. Finally, she mentions: "Besides these five great breeds—all the [sixteen] breeds except for the last six have at least one substrain, whose name is added to that of the breed, and these substrains only are used in choosing sires."[65]

Characteristics of the Horse

The bedouins distinguish the best thoroughbreds of these strains by special traits which they enumerate concerning most of the external members of the body. Probably the most prominent of these desireable features are a white spot (*najma*) on the mare's forehead, or rather, a blaze extending down as far as its upper lip—so that it "drinks" with the mare, as they say—and feet that are white except for the right

[65]Blunt, pp. 437–40, there listing the other sixteen strains referred to above—the *mu'anaqī*, *su'dān*, *daghmān*, *shūmān*, and the rest—and giving long descriptions of each of the five strains mentioned above. See also the observations on this subject by Doughty (I, 252–53), whose comments are repeated by many later writers. See also Nabīl 'Abd al-'Azīz, *Kitāb al-khayl wa-riyāḍatihā fī 'aṣr salāṭīn al-mamālīk* (Cairo, 1976). This work contains a long-winded account (pp. 20–23) describing the features the bedouins consider to be indicative of a fine mare, as taken from a manuscript work by Abū Khizām ibn Ya'qūb al-Khaylī on horsemanship and farriery, discussing the features and illnesses of horses. It also discusses types of horses (pp. 34–36) and their colors (pp. 37–47), but does not mention the thoroughbred strains acknowledged by the bedouins by the names given by Lady Anne Blunt. See also William R. Brown, *The Horse of the Desert* (New York, 1929), pp. 95–117.

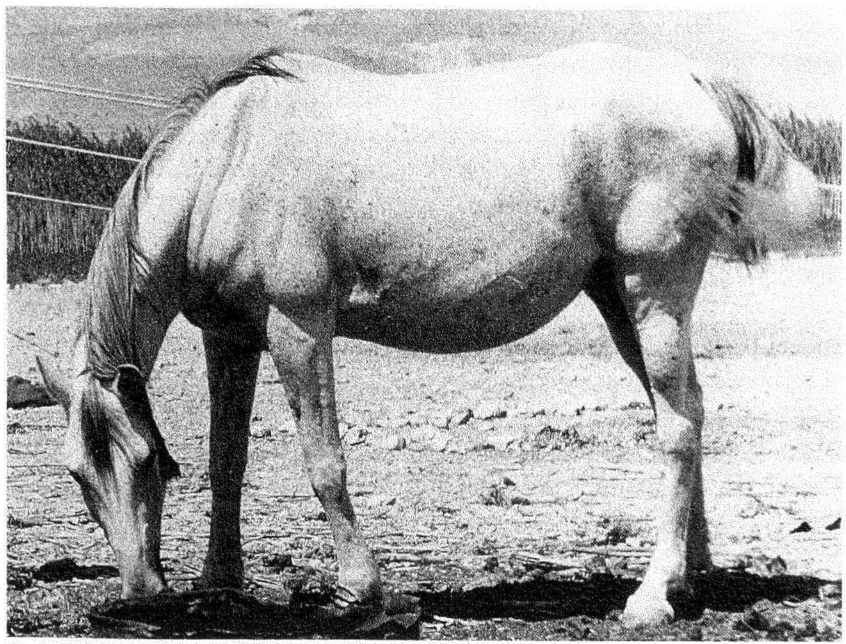

Figure 16: A pregnant thoroughbred mare.

foreleg, of such a horse it being said: *mḥajjalat al-thalāth maṭlūqat al-yamīn*, "white of foot on three, absent on the right." They show no enthusiasm for a mare that is not white-footed on the left. It should also have long ears, legs, and neck, a large nose and eyes, a broad chest, a wide prominent forehead, an arched breast, and a thick tail and mane; it should also hold its head high and raise its tail when it runs. Arabian horses are of various colors, among them sorrel (*ḥamrā'*), pure white (*ṣafrā'*), white with fine black hairs (*zarqā'*), black (*dahmā'*), off-white (*waḏḥā'*), and so forth. They are extremely expensive, and a single thoroughbred Arabian used to be sold for not less than a hundred camels. In fact, the Arabian is today the finest and most pure-blooded breed of the Oriental horse, and the one of greatest influence in the pedigrees of other horses. Probably their most prominent features are their heads: the way they regard you reflects an obvious intelligence—even personality—that can only arouse one's admiration.

Among the bedouins it is taken for granted that the entire family is at the service of the mare. The wife gathers greenery for it if herbage is in short supply round about the tents, and fetches water for it from distant wells or pools if there is none nearby. The son takes it to the nearby grazing grounds and guards and protects it there. The master of the household makes sure that the mare is covered with a blanket at night in cold spells, or when the animal is perspiring, and that it is groomed and has the feed bag hung on its head for it when necessary. He may even reserve camel's milk to quench its thirst if water is unavailable.[66] Were it not for the bedouins' extreme solicitude, many of their horses would perish.

The bedouins in most parts of the Arabian peninsula are still fond of horses and keen on acquiring them. But the security established (thanks to the current governments) from the end of the First World War until today, the political stability achieved and consolidated by the authorities when they began to prevent the bedouins from raiding and to crack down on lawbreakers, the high cost of grain for feeding horses from the Second World War until today,[67] the introduction of modern instruments of war that would render the horse superfluous even if raiding were possible, and the diminished demand for horses in world markets—all these factors have contributed to the decline in the status and importance of the horse among the bedouins, and have discouraged the continuation of bedouin horse-raising. The horse is of no use to the bedouin beyond amusement and hunting, and as he does not live a life of such ease and luxury as to acquire horses for the sake of amusement and hunting, the tribesmen have begun to sell their horses and to refrain from having their own reproduce. Hence, the large numbers we used to hear about among the bedouins or read of in the works of the travelers[68] have dropped substantially, though the horse has not yet disappeared. Today one can find well-known tribes whose

[66]Doughty, I, 304; Musil, *Manners and Customs*, p. 374.

[67]According to Kiernan, Wilfrid Blunt claimed that the Nafūd region solved for him the mystery of horsebreeding in central Arabia, for in the harsh sand-desert there is nothing a horse can eat. The Nafūd, however, is rich in pasture and herbage. See R.H. Kiernan, *The Unveiling of Arabia* (London, 1937), p. 281.

[68]Guarmani, pp. 32, 39, 40, 42. As for Palgrave, he mentions (II, 92–93) that in a single stable of the Sa'ūdī prince Fayṣal ibn 'Abd al-Raḥmān he saw about 300

horses can be counted on no more than the fingers of both hands; and if we omit the households of certain shaykhs, then it can be said that the bedouin encampments are today gradually being emptied of horses. Before long, we will have seen all the bedouins giving up the raising of horses and leaving this to wealthy village folk and farmers.

Among the strangest tales recorded by some of the European explorers on the number of horses owned by certain bedouins is the story told by Varthema when he visited Syria and some parts of Arabia more than 400 years ago. He claimed that the numbers owned by one of the *amīr*s near Mzayrīb came to 40,000 mares, 10,000 stallions, and 300,000 camels. These figures are undoubtedly exaggerated, but they indicate the multitude of such animals that were owned by certain *amīr*s at that time.[69] And there is a certain degree of exaggeration in Burckhardt's statement that the Arabian peninsula was full of horses, for there are far fewer in the south than there are in the northern regions where water is plentiful.[70]

Whatever the case may be, horses still play an important role in the life of the bedouin and in the stories he tells, be they tales relating accounts of their ancient raids and expeditions or concerning aspects of horses' dispositions and temperaments and their habits in their relationships with the masters who have raised them. To horses are attributed the qualities of fidelity, endurance, courage, devotion, and other traits that many recognize in the dog. Some Western explorers tell stories about Arabian horses that one would find difficult to believe of other horses. One such story reported by Dickson has it that one mare traveled 160 miles across the sand-desert during the summer without tasting water.[71] Among the familiar tales cited in children's readers is one that tells of how a horseman fell from his mare in battle; he was taken prisoner, and his horse was seized from him as booty. That night the mare heard the sound of her rider groaning in the tent, broke her reins with her mouth, and came to her master. There he

---

horses and a similar number in the pasture. He estimates (II, 95) that the horses in all of Najd did not come to more than 5000 head.

[69]Kiernan, p. 56.

[70]John Lewis Burckhardt, *Notes on the Bedouins and Wahábys* (London, 1831), pp. 50–53.

[71]Dickson, p. 360.

was, bound in chains, so she carried him away from the tents with her mouth, without anyone noticing her, and galloped away with him until she reached the camp of his tribe.

Palgrave did not fail to describe the Arabian horse, and devoted about five pages of his book to the subject. In his account he says, in his splendid style, that the appearance of the Arabian horse surely justifies everything said of their reputation and value, and all of the poems composed about them.[72]

One of the most marvelous accounts I have ever read about the endurance and stamina of the bedouin horse is a passage to be found in the memoirs of the *amīr* Usāma ibn Munqidh, whom those who study his works regard as a factual writer who neither exaggerates nor deliberately deviates from the truth. Usāma reports:

> A good example of the endurance of the horse arose when Ṭirād ibn Wuhayb al-Numayrī took part in fighting with the Banū Numayr. They had killed ʿAlī ibn Shams al-Dawla Sālim ibn Mālik, governor and ruler of al-Raqqa, and the war was between them and their victim's brother, Shihāb al-Dīn Mālik ibn Shams al-Dawla. Ṭirād ibn Wuhayb was riding a stallion of his, the finest of thoroughbreds and one of great value, when the horse was gashed in its side. Its entrails protruded from the wound, so Ṭirād bound it with the saddle strap so that the horse would not tread upon the entrails and tear them. He fought until the battle ended and then took the stallion to al-Raqqa, where it died.[73]

Of his own experiences with horses Usāma says:

> A stallion was wounded beneath me during some fighting at Ḥimṣ. The thrust pierced his heart and several arrows struck him, but he carried me forth from the battlefield, his nostrils gushing blood like water from two spouts. I noticed nothing amiss with his performance, and after I reached my companions he died.[74]

---

[72]Palgrave, II, 93–97.

[73]Usāma ibn Munqidh, *Kitāb al-iʿtibār*, pp. 98–99.

[74]*Ibid.*, p. 97.

He also states:

> A horse on which I was mounted and fighting, in the region of Shayzar during the war with Maḥmūd ibn Qarājā, was thrice wounded beneath me. And by God, I did not know that he had been wounded since I noticed nothing amiss with his performance.[75]

In the section on Arabian horses and common hackneys, he says of his father:

> He (may God have mercy upon him) used to pursue roe-bucks in the land of Ḥiṣn al-Jisr, and once brought down five or six while mounted on a black mare of his named Faras Khurjī ("the mare of Khurjī") after the name of the owner who had sold it. My father had purchased her for 320 *dīnārs*. Anyway, he was chasing the last of the roe-bucks when the mare's leg fell into a pit, one of those dug to catch wild boars. The mare tumbled over on top of him and he broke his collarbone, then the mare got up and ran for about 20 cubits, while he lay prostrate on the ground. She thereupon returned, stood by his head, and bawled and whinnied until he got up and the servants came to mount him on the horse. Such are the ways of Arabian horses.[76]

Among the bedouin customs pertaining to horses is that if one of their horsemen killed a horseman from another hostile tribe during a raid and made off with the latter's mare, he would clip off a piece of its forelock and hang it on a pole of his tent to boast of his feat. They would emaciate their horses before a raid so that they would be better able to endure hardship and would run faster during close combat and hit-and-run encounters. They did not allow the mares to mate prior to the raid, so that they would remain strong. If a mare had recently foaled they would only ride her on a raid if necessity forced them to do so, for in the mare's absence her young might die.

[75] *Ibid.*

[76] *Ibid.*, p. 214.

The Rwāla bedouins prefer horses of a pure white color[77] untinged by the slightest trace of any other color, and refer to such horses as *ṣafrā'* (lit. "yellow"). Among the Rwāla these are the mounts of the *amīrs*; as they say: *al-ṣufr markūb al-amārā li-l-naẓāra*, "pure white horses are the mounts of the *amīrs* for public occasions." They would not use these horses for the raid, since they stand out clearly by both day and night. They hold that horses of a pale yellow color (*shuqr*) are the fastest in short races, consider no horses superior to their Arabian horses, and make use of the bridle only on attacks.[78] Some bedouins claim that horses were created from the south wind and call them *banāt al-rīḥ*, "daughters of the wind." In the *Ta'rīkh al-khuyūl al-'arabīya* we are told that historians agree that God Almighty created horses from the wind, while others hold that they were created as other animals were created, that they were first to be found among the settled folk, and that the bedouins took them from the settled folk.[79] They would regard as an evil portent a horse that returned from the fight spattered with the blood of its owner, and such a horse was soon sold. If in a battle they would capture a mare without knowing who killed its owner, the mare was the share of the *'aqīd*, or raid leader. If the one who killed the owner of the mare was known, the horse was his and no one else had any claim upon him for a share in it. If one of them was able to kill a horseman and make off with his mare, he was a hero. The mare involved in this case was called a *qilā'a*. If young men were not known for reckless courage on raids, the bedouin women would rebuke them, saying: *'umrak mā jibit qilā'a wa-lā l-bīḍ iḥmadinnak*, "In all your life you have never come forth with a mare whose owner you have killed, nor have women praised any deed of yours."

The mare can conceive in every season, but she is receptive to the stallion once each month and at that time submits to him immediately. He covers her once in the morning and once in the evening (though

[77] Cf. Revelation 19:11, 14, where we read: "Then I saw heaven open, and there was a white horse, and seated upon it one called The Faithful, The True; with justice he passes judgment and wages war... and the armies that were in heaven, dressed in pure white linen, were following him on white horses."

[78] See Guarmani, p. 13.

[79] 'Abd Allāh ibn Ḥamza, *Ta'rīkh al-khuyūl al-'arabīya*, p. 6; see also al-Damīrī, *Ḥayāt al-ḥayawān*, I, 467; Musil, *Manners and Customs*, p. 371.

one covering may suffice) in exchange for a fee set by the owner of the stallion. The foal, which is born a year after conception, stays with his mother. His pedigree is traced through hers, even though the father may sometimes be of a nobler strain than the mother. If the father is not a thoroughbred, however, he may blemish the reputation of the foal. The stallion is usually not broken to the saddle before it completes the second year of its life. He remains strong to the age of 20, and may survive longer than that.

In concluding this section, it is worth mentioning that today the finest thoroughbred Arabian horses are found not in the desert, but in the West—in Europe and America—and in the settled regions of the Arab world. Wealthy horse enthusiasts began to import them at exorbitant prices, and established special stables for them where they were raised and trained for participation in races held at urban race tracks, in Beirut in particular. And we must not fail to mention also the thoroughbred horses acquired in the lands of Najd and elsewhere by the Saudi royal house and some of the sultans, *amīrs*, and shaykhs of the Arabian peninsula.

The Donkey

Among the other domesticated animals is the donkey. There are those who claim that the Arabs in the desert lands of the Arabian peninsula knew the donkey before they knew the camel, and that they were dependent on it in the first stages of their nomadic existence.[80] Today, donkeys are for the most part bought from the ʻArab al-Shawāyā bedouins, that is, those who raise sheep and goats and do not venture very far into the desert heartland. With each shepherd you see a donkey which he loads with his supplies and rides at the head of the flock from one place to another. On it he may also carry a lame or sick ewe or a kid born in the desert and unable to walk along with its mother. Similarly, donkeys are bought along the desert fringes by groups of *nawar*. These are neither bedouins nor Arabs, but rather a band of gipsies who earn their living as dancers, singers, and practitioners of certain handicrafts, and travel on their donkeys among the villages adjoining the desert.

---

[80] William Foxwell Albright, *From the Stone Age to Christianity* (Baltimore, 1940), pp. 120–21. We have taken this reference from Hitti, *History of Syria*, p. 66.

There is, however, another type of donkey among the tribe of Ṣlayb, the Ṣlaybī donkey which they still ride up to the present day. Not surprisingly, certain clans of this tribe have adhered to the principle of relying on the donkey to move about among the regions of the desert, dispensing with the camels used by other tribes. These Ṣlaybī donkeys are special donkeys the best-known of which are white in color. Agile, spirited, and strong animals, they differ from the donkeys of the farmers, the shepherds of the 'Arab al-Shawāyā, and the *nawar*. They resemble the donkeys of the Aḥsā' region,[81] but from what I have seen they are stronger and nimbler. Some hold the view that these donkeys, which among the Ṣlayb are called *shahāra* (sing. *shahrī*), have acquired their strength through crossbreeding, and claim that they are offspring of the domestic donkey and the onager. One of the donkeys owned by the Ṣlayb was left out in the open while she was in heat, they say, and the onager came by night and mounted her.[82] We shall take up this question in some detail when we consider the tribe of Ṣlayb. There is another variety called the *ḥaqāra* (sing. *ḥaqrī*), which resembles the local donkey common among the peasant cultivators, but is stronger and livelier. In times past the Ṣlaybīs used to raise white donkeys and sell the males and some of the females to wealthy men in the villages and towns, where they reproduced. Those who acquired such donkeys in the towns and villages used to boast of and take pride in owning them just as the bedouins took pride in owning horses.

The Ṣlaybī donkey has a special way of moving along that cannot be described as either walking or running, and perhaps closest approximates what is known among equestrians as *hadhb*, a "quick trot." The donkey may sometimes run, proceeding in a manner like the trotting of a horse; but at its normal pace, its speed is evident from the fact that its feet are moving so quickly that you can hardly see them. The bedouins have marvelous stories, some of which we will come to later in our study of Ṣlayb, that they tell about the swiftness of the Ṣlaybī donkey.

[81]In all of the Arabian peninsula, this is probably the region with the most white donkeys. These days they are very expensive. People make use of them to fill various needs, and sometimes they dye their feet and legs with henna.

[82]Guarmani, Appendix XIV; Musil, *Manners and Customs*, p. 197.

The other donkeys are the shepherds' donkeys mentioned above. These are the ones from whose submissiveness the proverb has been coined: "None patiently submits to injury, except the tribe's donkey and tent peg."

The Guard Dog

Shepherds and goatherds buy dogs to guard their livestock from wolves. These dogs are of the common type, known among the bedouins as the *kalb ra'y*, or "watchdog," and one will find two or three of them with each flock. Similarly, the bedouins buy dogs to guard their homes—the hair tents—regardless of whether their owners are tenders of sheep or camels. Only rarely will one pass by a band of bedouins camped somewhere, however few in number they may be, without seeing dogs of this kind among them. Indeed, it would probably be no exaggeration to say that there is no bedouin tent without a dog. If a stranger approaches the tent, these dogs rush from their resting places in front of the tent and come barking and running toward him. They stop and stand nearby when they get close to him, until their master calls them and their howling and growling comes to a stop, especially when they see that the stranger approaching the tent of their master is coming as the bedouin's guest. As Ḥassān ibn Thābit said in praise of the Ghassānids, who received many guests:

> So visited they were that no dog did growl or bark at all
> They asked not if a stranger approached and came to call.[83]

They are thus the night watch for the camps of the bedouins, keeping guard through the night while their masters sleep, and catching a few hours of sleep during the day around noontime. These dogs travel with their masters when the latter move on, and on hot days they walk with the pack train in the shadow of the camels. If the intensity of the heat makes them tired or overheated and they see a bush along their way, they stop and rest awhile in its shade, panting to relieve the enervating effects of the heat, and then return to follow the pack train and its retinues, each dog with the gear of its masters, until the group stops to

[83]Ḥassān ibn Thābit, *Dīwān*, edited by Walīd 'Arafāt (London, 1971), I, 74.

make camp. When the people of the household begin to pound in the tent pegs and pitch the tents, the dog finds himself a spot beside the tent and lays down there, after having scraped off the surface layer of hot earth in an effort to cool himself.

Of all the creatures in the desert, there is probably none whose lot in life is more wretched than that of this camp dog. He is an outcast not allowed to seek refuge inside the tent even on extremely cold or hot days. A filthy squalid beast, he is not permitted to lap the water in the family's containers and is kept from eating anything aside from the scraps left over from their food, this perhaps not amounting to more than some shreds of bread if they have been baking, or some bones to gnaw if they have slaughtered an animal.

The Saluki

The bedouin fond of hunting will buy a saluki to help him hunt gazelles and rabbits. The bedouins claim that the saluki originally came from the town of Salūq or Salūqīya in Yemen: concerning this town, Yāqūt said that *salūqī* chain mail and saluki dogs are said to have originated there. These dogs have been commonly used in hunting since the time of the poet al-Quṭāmī in the Umayyad period. Referring to them in his poetry, he says:

> With them were hunting dogs from Salūq,
> Like steeds roaming about dragging their reins.[84]

Indeed, Zayd al-Khayl made reference to them when he came to see the Prophet and asked him what he thought of hunting with salukis. It was then that verse 6 of Sūrat al-Mā'ida was revealed: "They will ask you what is lawful for them; say: Lawful for you are the good things, and such predators as you train, as instructors in the ways of the hunt (*mukallibīn*), teaching them as God has taught you." The term *mukallibīn* means "trainers of dogs,"[85] and in the remains left by the Umayyads at Quṣayr 'Amra there are images of salukis, including several scenes of them pursuing onagers.[86]

[84] Al-Quṭāmī, *Dīwān*, edited by Jacob Barth (Leiden, 1902), p. 17.
[85] Al-Ṭabarī, *Jāmi' al-bayān 'an ta'wīl āy al-Qur'ān* (Cairo, 1373/1954), VI, 88–89.
[86] Almagro, *Qusayr 'Amra*, pp. 176–77.

Figure 17: A bedouin woman baking on a bread tin (*ṣāj*). In front of her are two dogs: a saluki for hunting and a regular dog for guarding.

The saluki was thus an important factor in the hunting of the gazelle, onager, oryx, and rabbit. As we have seen in the verse of al-Quṭāmī, it was compared to the thoroughbred; and the bedouins even claim that the qualities appreciated in the parts of the thoroughbred's body are also appreciated in salukis. This reached the point that they began to trace their pedigrees as they did with horses, and to describe some of them by their pedigrees and names.[87] As they said:

> Al-Qanīṣ and Salhab, Siḥām and Baqlā',
> Al-Sirḥān and al-Mutanāwal and Ḥadlā':
> Born of two salukis by which his life was made,
> He died when they did, and survives as a shade.[88]

Salukis are thin, graceful, beautiful animals, and can outrun the gazelle.

When the hunter sees game he turns loose the salukis on it, and they block its avenues of escape and impede its movements until the hunter draws close enough to kill it. If the dogs see that the quarry is a long way off and are unable to bring it down themselves, they approach it obliquely, forcing it to run in a circle that eventually brings it close to the hunter, who conceals himself at the place where the dogs were turned loose.

Salukis were a steady source of assistance to medieval hunters in their quest for the oryx, which has disappeared from the Syrian Desert today. Ancient Arabic poetry teems with passages describing these dogs as they pursued the oryx and the risk of danger and death they faced when the oryx turned on them with its sharp horns. The horn would pierce the side of the dog like the skewer pierces a piece of spitted meat. As al-Nābigha said:

> As if there was protruding through its hide-covered frame
> A drinker's skewer forgotten and left aside the fire's flame.[89]

In the past the hunter, carrying his bow and arrows, used to ride his charger to overtake the quarry being harassed by the dogs or held up

[87] *Al-Bayzara*, p. 140.
[88] *Ibid.*; Kushājim, *Al-Maṣāyid wa-l-maṭārid*, p. 131.
[89] *Sharḥ al-qaṣā'id al-'ashr*, p. 154.

by the falcons. He would boast of how his steed had galloped to bring him up to the herd of oryx or gazelles, so that he could bring down as many in the herd as he wished and he and his companions could enjoy the most delicious roasted meat:

> Quickly it ran twixt a buck and a doe,
> To pounce, and no sweat at all did it show.
> Then cooks took to roasting some slices o'er flame,
> While fast-bubbling pots they filled up with game.[90]

One finds that most enthusiasts of the hunt select a saluki for purchase from among those suitable, as we have said, for hunting rabbits and gazelles. As for dogs that assist hunters in their quest for birds, such as the partridge and other similar game birds, these are not commonly found in the desert and I have never seen anyone buy dogs for such a purpose.

Most of the bedouins who buy salukis are such hunters as *amīr*s, other notables, and tribesmen of Ṣlayb, a tribe of which we have already taken note more than once in this book. Hunters in the villages adjoining the desert take up the task of raising and training salukis, and some of these are sold to *amīr*s and other desert enthusiasts of the hunt.

Saluki females are more agile than the males, faster to train, more alert, and live longer, about 20 years. The gestation period is about 60 days. The largest litter the female can produce is eight, but this occurs only rarely; sometimes she will give birth to only a single puppy. The puppy remains blind for about twelve days.

Among the attractive features sought in a fine saluki are the following. There should be a long distance between the front and hind legs, the back should be short, and the neck should be long and thick. The ears should be floppy and set far apart, and the eyes should be blue with large eyeballs and prominent pupils. The snout should be long, the jaw wide, and the forehead prominent. The front legs should be short as compared to the length of the hind legs, and the chest should be long, large in girth, and protruding toward the ground. The throat should be prominent. The upper front legs should be thick, the forelegs

[90] *Ibid.*, pp. 24–25, from the *mu'allaqa* of Imru' al-Qays.

straight, the toes closely set so that no dirt or clay can get in between them, and the joints along its sides and between the tops of the thighs widely spaced. The thighs should be long, the muscles firm, the tendons taut, and the waist thin. The animal's body between the thigh joints and chest should be long, the hind legs straight except for the bend at the knees, the leg shanks short, the tail short, thin, and hard as a piece of wood, and the fur soft, which is also mainly esteemed in birds and quadruped animals.[91] The bedouins claim that if the puppies are taken while they are still small and have not yet begun to walk, and are put in a damp place, then any of them that walk on all fours without falling too frequently must be the most agile of the puppies and will be the strongest of the litter.

No less than other dogs, salukis are devoted to their masters and when separated from them show a strong sense of awareness of the route to their homes. Munīr Āghā Fayyāḍ, one of the elders of al-Qaryatayn, told me that in the days of the Mandate he gave a saluki as a present to a French officer who was a counselor (*mustashār*) in the town of Sweida in the Jebel Druze. He fastened a collar around the dog's neck and took him with him to Sweida, but some time later the dog ran away and arrived—thin and emaciated—back at the home of his former master, the elder in al-Qaryatayn, after covering about 200 kilometers and passing through more than ten villages along the way, including three in the Ghūṭa region around Damascus.

Sheep, Goats, and Cattle

Sheep, goats, and cattle are familiar livestock and do not call for discussion in any detail. Nevertheless, it must be pointed out here that the sheep in the Arabian peninsula are of a type distinguished by their large fat tail and the softness of their wool. As we have already mentioned, they have an impact on the economy of the region in view of the clarified butter (*samn*) extracted from their milk and the meat of their lambs. In 1953 the number of sheep in Syria alone was estimated as about 2,800,000 ewes, and goats were estimated at about 1,200,000.[92]

[91]Kushājim, *Al-Maṣāyid wa-l-maṭārid*, pp. 136–37.
[92]See the report by Munīr al-Sharīf in the newspaper *Al-Ḥayāt*, 1953, no. 2094.

Figure 18: A flock of sheep belonging to Shawāyā bedouins camped near the water.

Figure 19: A flock of sheep, with one shepherd at the front of the flock and another at the rear.

As for goats, their hair is spun into the thread woven into the black tent cloth with which the bedouin name for the tents—*buyūt al-sha'r*, "houses of hair"—is associated. Hence the goat's great importance in desert life. From the statements of scholars who have studied the history of animal domestication, one may conclude that the goat was one of the first animals to be domesticated. This probably occurred about 10,000 years ago, originally in the mountains of Syria, Lebanon, and Palestine. There are still wild goats in the mountains of Anatolia. As for domestic goats, they are prevalent in every Arab country in Asia and Africa.

True bedouins do not know cattle, but semi-sedentaries who have begun to settle in villages and farms in certain seasons of the year do raise cattle, and are known as *al-'arab al-baqqāra*, "cattle-raising bedouins," to distinguish them from the other bedouins. The number of cattle in Syria alone is about 400,000 head.[93] The best are those known as the *shāmī*, or "Damascene" cattle, and these are found in large numbers in the Ghūṭa region around Damascus. In the late 1940s Syria was beginning to import from Denmark strains of cattle that give much milk, in order to spread and improve the strains of dairy cattle in the region.

Here we conclude our study of the desert and its plants, animals, insects, and reptiles, except for the camel, the next pillar of bedouin life. In the following pages we shall devote a special chapter to it.

[93] *Ibid.*

THE SECOND PILLAR
THE CAMEL

Night falls, and the riding saddle is cinched on fast
To a land-ship whose reins 'neath my cheek are passed.

Dhū l-Rumma

CHAPTER VIII

THE CAMEL[1]

The Origins and Habitats of the Camel

The Rwāla bedouins in the Syrian Desert relate a curious legend about the origins of the camel, according to which it was the Jews, and not the bedouins, who had camels in remote antiquity. The Jews lived in the mountains of the Ḥijāz, while the bedouins lived in the deserts. The bedouins kept horses and rode them in their raids, but they avoided climbing the mountains for fear of losing their way in the mountain ravines and winding passes or falling with their horses into the chasms. For some reason, the bedouins were once compelled to mount a raid on

[1]Most of this chapter appeared in 1967 in an article of mine published in *Kitāb al-ʿīd*, edited by Jibrail Jabbur (Beirut, 1967), before any full study on the camel with respect to its connection with bedouin life had appeared. Since then many books have appeared, the most important of them two works in English: Richard W. Bulliet, *The Camel and the Wheel* (Cambridge, Mass., 1975), and Hilda Gauthier-Pilters and Anne Innis Dagg, *The Camel* (Chicago and London, 1981). The first considers the relationship between the camel and the cart as a means of transportation, and hence does not deal much with the camel's connection with bedouin life in the Arab countries. It is, however, rich in information on the history of both the Arabian and the Bactrian camel and on the history of the wheel, and contains a wealth of photographs of ancient representations of both. The second work is confined, or almost so, to the camel in certain parts of North Africa. It is, in addition, a scientific work dealing with the physiology and life cycle of the camel and all sorts of topics relevant to the life of the camel. I will refer to both of these works when I deal with them in this chapter. There have also appeared three articles by Michael Ripinsky in *Archaeology*, 36.3 (May-June, 1983), pp. 21–27; *Antiquity*, 49 (1975), pp. 295–98; 56 (1982), pp. 48–50. These provide a full study on the origin of the camel and its domestication in Egypt, the African Sahara, and the Arabian peninsula.

the Jews in the mountains, and took with them a guide who claimed to know every mountain and location in that region. But they had no sooner penetrated the region than the guide went astray and no longer knew how to direct them. They thus began to proceed aimlessly from one ravine to another, from one defile to another, until, reduced to desperate straits, they became so starved that they slaughtered some of their horses. Their wandering about among these mountains then brought them to a ravine where they encountered a traveler, whom they queried about the camps of the Jews. This traveler then led them by night among the winding defiles to a plain, surrounded by hills, across which were spread the tents of the Jews. And there in front of the tents were strange animals, the like of which the bedouins had never before seen—these were camels (*al-bil*). So the bedouins hid on the heights until sunrise, then descended with their horses and attacked the Jews on the plain by surprise. The latter fled by every possible means, and with them their she-camels (which the bedouins call *maghāṭīr*), so that none remained in front of the tents except for the *zurq* camels, those in which their white coats are mixed with some black hairs. These did not flee, so the bedouins seized them and marveled at how they had not fled with their masters. They were loathe to keep these camels, and their leader said: "May God grant no blessing by you!," and ordered his men to slaughter them because they had remained behind their masters—it was then that the bedouins took to slaughtering white camel calves with black hairs. Then the bedouins hurried on in pursuit of the fleeing Jews, caught up with them, defeated and plundered them, and made off with all of their white she-camels. Henceforth the Jews no longer had camels to raise, and instead became farmers or tenders of sheep and goats. But they still await the return of their camels to them; hence, the legend goes, every Friday before evening they fill containers with water and wait for the camels to come back to be watered. But they never have and never will. From this comes the bedouin proverb for something one does not expect to attain or achieve: *rajw al-yihūd min al-bil*, "the Jews' hope for the camels."[2]

Whatever the truth may be concerning this legend, zoologists today do confirm its content in part: i.e. the camel is not of Arab origin

[2]Musil, *Manners and Customs*, pp. 329–30.

despite its connection with and impact upon Arab life. They maintain that in its earliest times, before its domestication, the camel was unknown throughout Arabia.[3] Its original habitat was America,[4] where in the Pleistocene Age there were wild animals with something akin to padded feet that belonged to the genus of the camel we know today and from which the latter has descended. Many ages before the advent of recorded history, the camel moved from America across the steppes of Alaska, which in the Pleistocene Age was connected to Asia.[5] From the northeast tip of Asia the camel passed on to other parts of the continent and from there on to Africa and Europe.

For reasons unknown to us the camel became extinct in America, while in South America its brother the llama survived. In Tulāl al-Sawālik in India, and in Kashmir, fossilized remains of camel skeletons dating back to the Miocene Age have been discovered. Similarly, other remains dating to the same period have been uncovered in Algeria in North Africa.[6]

Scholars state that the earliest known representation of the camel dates back to the Stone Age. This is found in two carvings in a place called Kilwa in Jabal Ṭubayq on the frontier of Jordan. In one of the inscriptions the camel appears clearly in the background behind an ibex, and is of the same single-humped variety known today as the Arabian camel.[7]

Domestication and References in Ancient Records

It is not known when man first took to domesticating the camel, and on this question scholars disagree. Some claim that domestication began in

[3]Most modern studies, however, maintain that Arabia knew the wild camel before its domestication, and that the Arabs were the earliest men to domesticate it. See Gauthier-Pilters and Dagg, *The Camel*, p. 115. Likewise, Albright, *From the Stone Age to Christianity*, p. 120, maintains that it has come to be taken as certain among scholars that the wild camel was common in Arabia before its domestication.

[4]Hitti, Jurji, and Jabbur, *Ta'rīkh al-'arab*, p. 50 [= Hitti, *History of the Arabs*, p. 22].

[5]Alfred Sherwood Romer, *Vertebrate Paleontology*, 2nd edition (Chicago, 1945), p. 459.

[6]Arthur G. Leonard, *The Camel* (London and New York, 1894), p. 2.

[7]Hitti, *History of Syria*, p. 52, with a reference to the source from which he has taken this account.

Figure 20: Sculpture of an Arab in the days of the kingdom of Palmyra, with a riding camel behind him. Thus was the Arab associated with the camel long ago.

the fourth millennium BC, while others maintain that it did not begin before the second and cite as evidence for their view the fact that the camel is never mentioned in any of the Assyrian texts, amounting to tens of thousands of letters and economic narratives dating from between 1800 and 1200 BC.[8] On the other hand, however, we note that there is a reference to domestication in a picture of a camel, with a rider on its back, found in the ruins of Tall Ḥalaf in Iraq, which go back to between 3000 and 2900 BC.[9] Likewise, small Egyptian figurines of camels that date back to about 2500 BC have been found at Byblos (modern Jubayl, in Lebanon). This establishes that in that era the camel was a domesticated animal.

[8]Harold A. McClure, *The Arabian Peninsula and Prehistoric Populations* (Miami, 1971), p. 49. See also Gauthier-Pilters and Dagg, *The Camel*, pp. 115–16.

[9]M.F. von Oppenheim, *Der Tell Halaf* (Leipzig, 1931), p. 140. This reference we owe to Hitti, *History of Syria*, pp. 52–53.

The oldest report on the camel in written records is probably the one found in the Old Testament and concerns Abraham, when he and his wife Sarah were in Egypt. Here we are told: "So he did good unto Abram for her sake, and he gained sheep, cattle, donkeys, slaves, slave girls, asses, and camels."[10] It may be noted here that camels are mentioned at the end of the list, a point that has led some to maintain that it was added to the text at a later date. However, we see that when Abraham returned to Canaan he sent one of his slaves to Aram Naharaim (northwest Mesopotamia). The slave took ten of his master's camels and went to Aram, to the city of Nahor, to ask for a girl's hand for his master's son Isaac. He made the camels kneel down to rest at a well outside the city; this was in the evening, at the time when the women came out to fetch water, and there at the well he encountered a young woman whose hand he requested for his master's son.[11]

But to continue, we find camels mentioned in the stories about Jacob, son of Isaac: he possessed many sheep, slave-girls, slaves, camels, and donkeys, and his wife Rachel took along idols when they moved, and placed them in the camel saddle and sat on them.[12] So also we find them in the story of Joseph and the caravan of the Ishmaelites (that is, the Arabs) in which their camels carried tragacanth gum, spices, balsam, and myrrh to Egypt.[13] Later we read that the meat of camels is forbidden to the Jews because the camel does not have a cleft hoof.[14]

Reference to the camel later appears in Old Testament war narratives. We hear of the Midianites, Amalekites, and the people of the East settled in the valley like the locusts in multitude, while their innumerable camels were like the grains of sand on the shore of the sea in magnitude.[15] We read of how Gideon killed two of the leaders of the Easterners and took the crescent-shaped ornaments that were on

---

[10]Genesis 12:16.
[11]*Ibid.*, 24:10–11.
[12]*Ibid.*, 30:43; 31:34.
[13]*Ibid.*, 37:25.
[14]Leviticus 11:4.
[15]Judges 7:12.

the necks of their camels.[16] Elsewhere we read that the camels of these Easterners had collars on their necks.[17]

It would seem that these bedouin Arabs used to attack the Israelite agriculturalists in such great numbers that it was said of them that they and their camels were beyond counting. Reference to camels in the Old Testament continues after these periods, and the animal is mentioned on most of the occasions in which the "people of the East," or the Arabs, are mentioned. They appear in the account of the queen of Sheba, and in that of Job, who had 3000 of them before his catastrophe,[18] and 6000 afterwards.[19] The Old Testament also mentions that the Reubenites and Gadites and half of the tribe of Manassa plundered 50,000 camels from the Hagrites.[20]

Our concern here with the camel is the fact that it came to be associated with the Arabs and inseparable from the bedouin Arab. Or, more appropriately, we should say that from remote antiquity the bedouin was inseparable from the camel. One singular point of agreement is that the oldest inscription bearing a reference to the Arabs mentions the camel in association with them. This inscription has been left to us by the Assyrian king Salmanasser III, and bears an account of his campaign into Syria and his clash with the armies of its rulers at Qarqar, north of Ḥamāh, in 855 BC. Enumerating the things he captured and the destruction he wrought on his enemies, he says: "ten thousand camels of Gendibu (Jundub) the Arab."[21] It is clear that from remote antiquity the Arabian peninsula ranked as one of the most suitable habitats for the domestication and raising of the camel; and in all the world today it is probably the region most famous for the raising of camels[22]—especially fine thoroughbred dromedaries—if not the region richest in camels so far as numbers are concerned.

[16] *Ibid.*, 8:21.
[17] *Ibid.*, 8:26.
[18] Job 1:3.
[19] *Ibid.*, 42:12.
[20] I Chronicles 5:18–21.
[21] Hitti, Jurji, and Jabbur, *Ta'rīkh al-'arab*, p. 66 [= Hitti, *History of the Arabs*, p. 37].
[22] See *Arabia*, Foreign Office no. 61 (London, 1920), pp. 72–73.

The Camel as an Important Pillar of Bedouin Life

Whatever the truth of the matter may be concerning the camel and its original habitat, it comprises a pillar of bedouin life critical to nomadism in the Arabian peninsula. The barren deserts of the region are like the sea, which cannot be crossed without a vessel. The camel has been this vessel, and long ago the Arab poet called his she-camel *safīnat al-barr*, "the land-ship." Of his she-camel Ṣaydaḥ, Dhū l-Rumma said: "a land-ship whose reins 'neath my cheek are passed."[23]

Were it not for the camel, it would be impossible for the bedouin to live in the desert and move about from one part of it to another. It carries for him his tent, with its panels of cloth, poles, ropes, and pegs, and whatever amenities, supplies, and furnishings it contains. The bedouin woman can ride in a howdah on the camel's back and make a cloth cover for the howdah to protect her from the heat in the summer: the camel carries her along, and it is as if she were in her tent. Camels are associated with these litters in the Qur'ān, where one reads:

> And indeed, in the livestock there is example offered: we give you what is in their bellies to drink, and in them there is much of use to you; you eat of them, and upon them and on the ships (*fulk*) you are carried.[24]

The camel is endowed with such an ability to tolerate thirst for long periods of time, and to content itself with tough thorny shrubs as its food, that it easily endures life in the desert. Provided with wide padded feet and slimly built legs, it travels easily among the desert regions with their soft sandy or calcic soil. Similarly, its lip, covered, as it is, with tough stiff hair, permits it to nose through thorny plants and root them out or break them off, while its mouth is specially adapted to chewing and ruminating them. The camel has thus come to depend upon and to content itself with those kinds of plants that live in desert and barren lands. Furthermore, it is satisfied with little water, when compared to the amounts needed by other animals of similar size found in such a hot desert climate.

---

[23]Dhū l-Rumma, *Dīwān*, edited by Carlile Henry Hayes Macartney (Cambridge, 1919), p. 638; al-Damīrī, *Ḥayāt al-ḥayawān*, I, 21, under the entry *ibl*.

[24]Sūrat al-Mu'minūn (23), vss. 21–22.

Figure 21: The pack train on the move with the camel herd in search of a new grazing land. In the howdah is a woman, her child, and some of the furnishings of the tent.

It is thus the camel that has made it possible for the bedouin to live in the desert; and indeed, it is probably the camel that has led him to do so. The camel is the progenitor of the genuine pure nomadism and the reason for its continued survival; and deprived of the camel, bedouin life would fade into oblivion. The bedouin has become a parasite of the camel: he lives on the milk of the she-camels when they give birth, and indeed, sometimes finds no nourishment or drink except for this milk. One scholar has claimed that the bedouin lived in the desert before he knew the camel as a domesticated animal in its vast expanses, and that he made use of some other animal, probably the donkey.[25] If this were true, then we would have to maintain that the bedouin depended on the milk of donkeys,[26] otherwise he would have been forced to keep sheep in order to live on their milk. In either case, we should not suppose that the bedouin's search for food would have taken him as frequently or so far into the desert as occurs among the camel-raising bedouins of today.

Types of Camel

Today camels are divided into two main varieties, the two-humped camel known as the Bactrian (*Camelus bactrianus*), and the Arabian one-humped camel known as the dromedary (*Camelus dromedarius*). The Arabian peninsula and North Africa know only the latter type, which is known as the Arabian camel to distinguish it from the Bactrian. If a she-camel is covered by a bull of the other variety, this may produce crossbred young with two connected humps, the dip between them becoming so indistinct that they look like one long hump with two small domes on it.[27]

The Arabian camel is in turn divided into two types. One is the common camel that comprises those of the many herds raised for their meat and to carry loads, and the other is the pure-blooded thoroughbred.

[25]Albright, *From the Stone Age to Christianity*, pp. 120–21.

[26]Here reference must be made to the fact that the tribe of Ṣlayb, which we shall take up in a special chapter, keeps donkeys in the desert but does not drink their milk. Rather, they keep sheep and live on their milk and on hunting, which has become a professional vocation for most of their men.

[27]See Gauthier-Pilters and Dagg, *The Camel*, Plate 50.

Although the predominant color of the Arabian camel is an amber brown, there are many white camels (which the Rwāla call *maghātīr*[28]) and black camels in both the common and thoroughbred types. And if we wished to elaborate in bedouin fashion, we would mention many colors. It is common practice among the bedouins to name their camels according to their widely differing colors; thus we hear of black (*malḥā'*), light brown (*ḥamrā'*), gray (*shahbā'*), pure white (*waḍḥā'*), white with black hairs (*zarqā'*), smoke-colored (*dakhnā'*), dark (*ghabshā'*), white (*bayḍā'*), and white with a pinkish tinge (*shaqḥā'*). These they pronounce by ignoring the *hamza* and sometimes turning them into diminutives, thus saying *buwayḍā*, *ḥumayrā*, *ghubayshā*, and so forth. Or they may name their camels according to their qualities, thus saying *'ajlā* ("the fast one"), *'awjā* ("the curving one"), *ṭayyāḥa* ("the wanderer"), *sharhā* ("the voracious one"), *'alyā* ("the tall one"), *jarīda* ("the bald one"), etc. One of their proverbs advises *asāmī l-bil bwujūhihā*, "the names of camels should accord with their qualities."[29] As for the bedouin names of the most important parts of the camel, these are as follow: *sanām*, the hump on the back; *ṣulb*, the back; *ghārib*, the shoulders; *'aḍud*, the front leg above the knee; *farsam*, the foot; *khuff*, the sole of the foot; *'arnūn*, the bridge of the nose; *khashm*, the nose; *burṭam*, the snout; *ḥijāj*, the area above the eye; *manḥar*, the lowest part of the neck; *ḍar'*, udder; *shabīb*, tip of the tail; *ḥalama*, teats of the udder.[30]

Attributes of the Camel

As we have mentioned, one of the most important attributes of the camel is its toleration of thirst, or more correctly, its ability to endure lack of water. During the winter it may be able to remain about 50 days without being watered, while in the summer it may remain five days without water.[31] The reason for this is that in the winter it grazes on many green plants containing enough moisture to enable the camel

[28] Musil, *Manners and Customs*, p. 335.

[29] *Ibid.*

[30] *Ibid.*, p. 330.

[31] And it may possibly go longer than what we have mentioned here. See Knut Schmidt-Nielsen, "The Physiology of the Camel," *Scientific American*, 201.6 (December 1959), pp. 140–51.

to do without water. This is probably not a matter of choice on the camel's part, as some people imagine.[32] In reality, it is the desert (or the sand-desert climate and its inhabitants) surrounding it that imposes this behavior on the camel. Left to its own natural inclinations, it would come to the watering place every day in the summer and perhaps once a week during the winter. And so far as the camel is concerned, the best time for it to come to drink is of course when it is thirsty. I have seen camels, returning from their grazing to drink, three days after their last watering, which when they sense the presence of water rush to the watering place from a hundred meters away, like someone crazed with fever. When the camel reaches the watering trough and something obstructs its access to it, it fights and struggles to such an extent that it almost throws itself into the vessel or well from which it is drinking. And when it has drunk its fill a look of satisfaction and contentment appears on its face. I have no doubt that were it to be given water every day during the summer it would happily drink, and perhaps even be inclined to return repeatedly for more. As al-Buḥturī said long ago:

> How different—drinking but every fifth day, or the life of
> ease
> In which they come to the water whenever they please.[33]

One will notice from this verse of al-Buḥturī that camels that have been far off in the pastures are watered once every five days in the summer. However, the custom today among most of the bedouins who keep camels, including the tribe of Rwāla, is to water their camels once every three days during the summer. They usually bring them from their pastures in the afternoon, the animals are watered at the sources by which the bedouins camp, and they settle down for the night in front of the tents of their owners. Camels watered in this way are called *khamīr*. They drink again on the morning of the second

[32]In the article cited above, Schmidt-Nielsen states that he saw camels in the African Sahara that had not drunk water for two whole months, and that when he offered them water they did not drink it because they were not thirsty. We fear that his story is rather exaggerated. Some herdsmen may have misled him; or perhaps he has no first-hand knowledge of the matter himself, but rather relied upon what camel-owners said.

[33]Al-Buḥturī, *Dīwān*, edited by Ḥasan Kāmil al-Ṣayrafī (Cairo, 1963–64), II, 1153.

day, and afterwards depart for their distant grazing grounds, to return again three days later. If the owners of the camels are camped far from a watering place, the herdsmen will water the camels, send them out to graze for about an hour, and then bring them back to drink a second time and take them back to the distant pastures where they usually graze.

When the camels are far from sources of water and if it has been a long time since their last watering, they become so thirsty that their eyes fill with tears, they refuse to graze, and they begin to moan. One sees the restless beasts trying to urinate from time to time, and at that point it is absolutely essential that the herdsman take them to water. Some scholars have observed that the urine of camels in this condition is meager and thick, and that thirsting camels become emaciated and lose so much body fluid that they lose about a quarter of their body weight. But they remain sufficiently active to be able to move from place to place, and do not lose more than a tenth of their blood fluids. In a similar situation, man would lose about a third of his blood fluids, his temperature would rise, and he would die.[34]

When thirsty the camel drinks about 80 liters of water in one session, and may bring this total to 100 liters or more when it is watered on the following day. The sources from which camels drink in the desert are not flowing streams, but rather the waters that have collected together in rainpools, ponds, or wells. The two authors of a work on the camel have observed that if a camel has been thirsty it can drink between ten and twenty liters of water in a single minute, and that one camel once drank 27 liters in a minute.[35] Oddly enough, the authors also state that camels entirely refuse water throughout the six or seven-month period when rain may fall, even if it is offered to them.[36] I am afraid that they were mistaken in accepting such a tale as this from the mouth of one of the bedouins.

The *khabrāt* rainpools of the desert comprise the rain water that collects in some of the depressions in the desert during the winter. In early spring, some of these pools in the Syrian Desert are large

[34]Schmidt-Nielsen, p. 141.
[35]Gauthier-Pilters and Dagg, *The Camel*, p. 57.
[36]*Ibid.*, p. 50.

Figure 22: Thirsty camels at the beginning of their watering, upon their return from the pasture.

enough to water tens of herds at one time. In the summer they dry up completely. The *ghudrān* pools comprise the waters that collect in the beds of flood streams after the passage of a torrent, and are located close to the settled lands. In most of them one finds that the water level is so much lower than the level of the ground that it becomes necessary to raise it up out of the pool to water the camels. Here one can see the water carriers, having tucked their garments up from their forearms and feet and doffed their cloaks,[37] beginning to lift the water out in their waterskins and pour it into troughs made of leather or

[37]Hence the words of the Arab poet when the *sāqī*, the one who helps his camels to drink, did not water the camels well:

> Sa‘d watered them, but was still wearing his cloak.
> Camels are not to be watered thus, O Sa‘d.

Sa‘d was Sa‘d ibn Zayd Manāh, the brother of Mālik, who owned more camels than anyone else of his time. Mālik was married and was busy consummating his marriage with his wife, so his brother Sa‘d watered the camels. He did not take good care of them or provide them with enough to drink, however, which prompted Mālik to recite this verse. See Ibn ‘Abd Rabbih, *Al-‘Iqd (al-farīd)*, III, 108.

some other material. Each herdsman begins to call his camels to his trough with a call they will recognize and so come to him and drink. While the camels are being watered one will hear the herdsman's voice repeatedly calling out: *Ṭirr, ṭirr, ṭirr*, "Come on, let's go!" Or one may hear him taking turns with another herdsman in singing out short ditties (*ḥadāwī*) from bedouin poetry. The bedouins repeat these when the camels are being watered so that the latter will drink, quench their thirst, and feel satisfied.

Some used to claim that the camel has a special sack or a special "fifth stomach" for the storage of water, and that it was this that prompted the bedouins or other Arabs to slaughter camels when they were thirsting, in order to drink from the beast's paunch. But modern science confirms that the camel has no fifth stomach. I pursued this question myself when I watched butchers in al-Qaryatayn and bedouins making their sacrifices on the 'Īd al-Aḍḥā as they slaughtered camels and skinned them. When their stomachs were emptied I saw no stomach with the particular function of storing water. In recent years this has been confirmed by scholars studying the physiology of the camel.[38] The truth of the matter probably does not amount to more than the fact that in its first and second stomachs there are certain sections or cavities in which a certain amount of water can be held aside without being much mixed with food, as is the case with ruminants other than the camel, since most of the food immediately runs out via passage on to the third stomach. Historians cite Ashurbanipal as having said that on certain occasions the Arabs slit open the bellies of their riding camels to get out the water and quench their thirst.[39] And in the history of the Arab conquests one reads how Khālid ibn al-Walīd, ordered by Abū Bakr to go from Iraq to Syria to assist the Muslim armies there, marched until he reached Siwā. At this point in the account there is a clear reference to how Khālid, fearful lest his army perish from thirst

[38]Gauthier-Pilters and Dagg, *The Camel*, pp. 69–71. See also Leopold, *The Desert*, p. 98, where it is reported that Pliny was the first to conjecture that the camel has an extra stomach for water. Later writers took this up from him.

[39]Daniel D. Luckenbill, *Ancient Records of Assyria and Babylonia* (Chicago, 1927), II, 317–18, no. 827. We owe this reference to Hitti, Jurji, and Jabbur, *Ta'rīkh al-'arab*, pp. 205–206, in the notes [= Hitti, *History of the Arabs*, p. 149, n. 6].

Figure 23: The camels have drunk and had their fill, and the expression of contentment is on their faces.

as it crossed the desert, proceeded to allow the riding camels that were with him to go thirsty, then watered them and cut their lips so they would not ruminate. Setting out across the desert, he slaughtered these camels one after the other, as al-Balādhurī tells us, and he and his companions drank the water from their stomachs.[40] Many have denied that this is accurate; but the fact of the matter is that it is possible, and that there is nothing to cast doubt upon such claims. I discussed the matter with many who live in the Syrian Desert, and they told me that it was a familiar custom there. Indeed, some of them claimed that on more than one occasion thirst had forced them to drink the water from the stomach of a slaughtered camel. Such also was the situation observed by the Orientalist traveler Alois Musil, as he mentions in his two books *Arabia Deserta* and *Manners and Customs of the Rwala Bedouins*.[41]

Similarly, St-John Philby, known among the Arabs as al-Ḥājj ʿAbd Allāh Philby, states in his book on the Rubʿ al-Khālī that when the water ran out he asked one of his bedouin comrades traveling with him in the desert: "Supposing one was very thirsty... could one make shift with the urine of camels?" "No," the bedouin replied, "but we do sometimes get a deal of drinkable liquid in another way. We take the undigested food from a camel's cud and squeeze the water out of it."[42]

Having seen this water myself, I must comment here that it is not clear, as some may imagine, but a filthy coffee-colored liquid that is

---

[40]See al-Balādhurī, *Futūḥ al-buldān*, edited by M.J. de Goeje (Leiden, 1866), p. 110. See also the similar accounts in Ibn Qutayba, *ʿUyūn al-akhbār*, I, 142; al-Ṭabarī, *Taʾrīkh*, I, 2111–13.

[41]Alois Musil, *Arabia Deserta* (New York, 1927), p. 570; *idem.*, *Manners and Customs*, pp. 94, 95, 368. In his book on the manners and customs of the Rwāla (pp. 94–95), he mentions that his guide Mandīl al-Qaṭʿī had drunk this kind of water eight times in his life. He also states (p. 368) that one only rarely finds a Rwaylī of advanced age who has not drunk of this water at least once in his life, and that Miḥjim ibn Jandal attacked the Sharārāt in the region of al-Khanfa and captured many herds returning from the pastures. Fearing that the Sharārāt would beat him to the wells along his way, he took about 50 of the camels with full bellies, slaughtered them, and filled the waterskins with the water taken from their stomachs. He avoided the route past the wells and returned to his tribe at al-Nuqra, south of Damascus 1000 kilometers from al-Khanfa, without suffering any loss.

[42]H. St. J.B. Philby, *The Empty Quarter* (New York, 1933), p. 306.

undrinkable unless strained through a finely woven cloth or left in a container to stand motionless until the filthy materials in it settle to the bottom.

The study on the camel and its endurance of thirst undertaken by Schmidt-Nielsen in the African Sahara and published in a specialized article indicates that the camel retains moisture in its body more so than do the other large terrestrial animals, and that moisture does not evaporate from its hide through perspiration to the extent that it does in other animals. Further, the camel has a special ability to alter its body temperature during the summer by up to 12° F: at night it falls below the average to 93°, and during the day it rises to 105°. When it rises the difference between the body temperature of the animal and the temperature of its surroundings decreases, hence the water which would have evaporated through perspiration instead remains in its body—this if it is not possible for it to obtain water when it wants it. Schmidt-Nielsen further holds that the fur of the camel helps it to retain moisture in its body, so that it does not perspire as it would were the fur to be sheared off its hide.[43] This probably explains why the bedouins wear woolen clothing even in the summer. In addition, when a camel is thirsty part of its hump wastes away: part of the hydrogen contained in the fat of the hump is released, and combines with oxygen absorbed by the camel to create water to replace what the animal needs when it is thirsty.[44]

The Diet of the Camel

One of the distinguishing traits of the camel is that when it is in the confines of the desert it needs no food beyond the plants which the surface of the ground offers up to it. It thus puts the bedouin to no trouble other than that involved in protecting it and taking it to land where pasturage and water are to be found. Unlike wild animals, however, the camel does not know the places where pasturage may be found, which is why the bedouin has developed a superior ability to select fertile grazing grounds for his camels, as has the scout who is familiar with

[43]Schmidt-Nielsen, pp. 140–51.

[44]Leopold, p. 98.

Figure 24: The camels after they have been watered and have spread out to graze.

the land from prior experience, knows which places will be right for his camels, and then sets out for them to seek food for his herd.

The camel has certain particular grazing habits, one of them its fondness for one particular plant above all others, such as *ḥamḍ*. One will see a camel grazing on patches of this plant from one place to another with such aimless abandon that it sometimes becomes lost from the herd, while another camel has no sooner eaten a bit of *ḥamḍ* it has seen than it wearies of it and longs for other plants of the *khulla* type, which are quite different from the *ḥamḍ*. Camels grazing in the pastures may roam about in small herds not exceeding ten animals, or large herds of more than 100. Each herd has a herdsman who tends the camels, collects his wages from their owners (if he himself is not the owner), and almost becomes a member of his employer's family. He stays with the camels in their grazing grounds, and at night makes them kneel down in their resting places on the steppe until morning.

If their owners are nearby, he finds the camels places to sleep at their camp. He may hobble the camels after he makes them kneel down, and in the morning he unties the hobbling ropes, gives them back to the owner, and then sets out with the camels for their grazing grounds. The best vegetation for camels to graze on is *ḥamḍ*, and of this the bedouins mention such varieties as *arṭā*, *uraynba*, *ḥinwa*, *rughl*, *rimth*, *rawtha*, *zrayqa*, *sha'rān*, *ṭaḥma*, *ḍamrān*, *'ajrām*, *'arād*, and *ghaḍrāf*.

When the heat becomes intense in the summer, some camels feel an urge to roll in the dirt. When they pass by a patch of land with soft earth they kneel down in it and begin to roll back and forth on their backs. One camel may begin to roll, and no sooner does it rise than another takes its place. The place in question may become a great rolling ground in which many of the camels grazing in the desert will roll when they pass by it. One will see a camel passing nearby approach it, sniff the ground, kneel down on the ground, and begin to turn over on its back and neck, its feet up in the air, as if it is trying to bathe in the dust as the heat intensifies. Camels will frequently crowd together in a single rolling ground, so expanding its size that it sometimes covers an area more than 100 meters in diameter. The bedouins claim that this rolling strengthens and soothes the joints and has somewhat of a cooling and relaxing effect on the camel's body.

Its Endurance and Strength on the March

The camel is characterized by its ability to travel great distances and to walk for a long period of time. It is commonplace for it to cross barren deserts in search of pasturage and water, and to move about from one area or region to another within a single season of the year if it does not find suitable pasturage and water in its own territory. In the summer of 1954 I witnessed clans migrating with their camels from Najd to the lands of al-Qaryatayn in the district of Ḥimṣ in Syria. They remained in these retreats about a month or more, and then returned to their own country.[45] The camel-raising bedouin tribes in Syria migrate with their camels once each year to the desert in the autumn, and return

[45]In such a case the government of the state in which the tribe seeking new grazing grounds is located asks the government of the neighboring country for permission for the tribe to enter the grazing lands within its territories.

to the settled areas in the summer. Indeed, when in the desert they have hardly camped in a place for a week or two than they move on in search of pasturage somewhere else. One notices that their camels are in constant motion even in their grazing grounds, for these afford the camels sufficient pasturage only if they move about from place to place. In general, the female surpasses the bull in its endurance, sturdiness, strength, and tolerance of the hardships of a long journey.

Thoroughbreds

We have said that the Arabian camel is divided into two types, the common and the thoroughbred. The latter is distinguished from the former by its noble pedigree and its descent from well-known distinguished blood lines and from well-known regions. Such camels are bred simultaneously by most of the bedouin tribes. These she-camels are called *hujun* and *mahārī*, and in the singular one is also called *dhalūl*. Today thoroughbreds are bred among most of the bedouin tribes, but the most famous of them are the *'umānīya* (from Oman, bordering the southern end of the Arab Gulf), the *qaṭarīya* (from Qaṭar), and the *mahrīya* (from Mahra in southern Arabia; to this region are attributed the *mahārī* thoroughbreds, from which the French take the term *méharistes*, in the sense of "troops mounted on camels"). In former times the *maharīya* and *'umānīya* were recognized among the bedouins as camels of thoroughbred origin. There are also thoroughbred strains called the *sharārīya*, *htaymīya*, and the *tīhīya* (referring to the tribes of al-Sharārāt, Htaym, and Tiyāha), and these are not inferior to the *maharīya*, *qaṭarīya* and *'umānīya* in speed or strength. Some bedouins call the *sharārīya* thoroughbreds *banāt wuḍayḥān*, "white daughters." Some claim that thoroughbreds are the descendants of a common she-camel: she was left by her herdsman to sleep overnight out in the open country, and a wild undomesticated bull came and covered her. There is no foundation of truth to this, and the story is rather only a well-traveled fantasy. In the deserts of the Arabian peninsula there are no wild camels except for those domestic ones that become agitated and run away from their herds, and these perish within the year if they are not caught. It was on such thoroughbreds that the bedouins depended in their raids, just as the Arabs long ago depended on them in their great conquests and in their dazzling victories over the Persians

Figure 25: A thoroughbred riding camel and a herd of common camels.

and the Greeks. Indeed, it was probably these camels that facilitated the Arabs' ascendancy in many of their campaigns and wars, especially during the days of summer, and it was on thoroughbreds that messengers were dispatched on important missions. It is such camels as these that are described today in bedouin odes, just as they were described in the past in the verse of the *mu'allaqāt* and other ancient odes.

If the bedouin was the substance of Islam, as related in a report handed down from the caliph 'Umar ibn al-Khaṭṭāb, then the bedouin's thoroughbred she-camel and his mare were—in my view—the substance of the conquests. The Arab would not have achieved his conquests with the facility he did, had it not been for the superiority of his camel mount, the like of which was not available to his enemies, the ease with which it carried him along on its back, his use of it even when he took horses along on his expeditions, the capacity he had for launching surprise attacks on his enemies and slipping away if the situation required, the ability of his she-camel to remain without water for long periods of time, its contentment with the nourishment it received from whatever plant life it encountered along its way while it was in the desert, and its ability to cross deserts and barren wastes. It escapes me why modern-day historians of the Arab conquests have not paid heed to the impact of thoroughbred camels in the achievement of these conquests. Although thoroughbreds have lost their military value today, in some regions close to the desert they remain useful for limited patrol and guard duties, as we see in the Camel Corps in some Arab lands. Up until the first quarter of the twentieth century thoroughbred camels remained the most important element upon which the bedouin relied in raids and for preserving a certain degree of autonomy. On many occasions raiders would ride their thoroughbreds doubled up (*mardūfatan*), with one warrior behind another on the back of one camel, or would ride the camels while leading horses alongside them to use for the final attack.

The bedouins have stories and tales on the subject of the swiftness of their riding camels. They will tell you dubious stories about a thoroughbred that traveled more than 200 kilometers in a single day; about another that carried a letter-bearing messenger to a region and returned so quickly with its courier to the *amīr* who had sent him that the *amīr* had his suspicions until the messenger handed him a letter from his friend in that very region;[46] and about a third that, although carrying two riders, neither ate nor drank until it had covered more than 100 kilometers. Such tales filled the books of the daring explorers and travelers. Though hardly credible as literal fact, there is some truth to the general sense of the content of these stories. No domesticated animal will go the distance on long journeys faster than a thoroughbred camel, and no animal, however well trained, can equal its ability to endure lack of water and food and tolerate the mid-summer heat. Schmidt-Nielsen tested this distinctive trait on a common camel by depriving it of water for eight days during the summer season. The animal lost a quarter of its body weight, its belly contracted and shrank, and its muscles shriveled; but it neither died nor stopped moving about, and when offered water it drank and its vitality and weight were restored.[47]

[46] Alois Musil, *Northern Negd* (New York, 1928), p. 145.
[47] Schmidt-Nielsen, p. 141.

Traits of Thoroughbred Camels

The bedouins take great interest in preserving the pedigrees of their thoroughbred riding camels, and do not allow them to come into contact with any but thoroughbred bulls. They cite witnesses to attest to the covering of their thoroughbred she-camels by a thoroughbred bull, and refer to the thoroughbred as *ḥurr*. Both parents of such an animal must be of thoroughbred pedigree. If the sire was a thoroughbred and the dame was not, then, if the calf is female, the line is recognized as thoroughbred only after four generations in which the female descendents from this calf are all covered by thoroughbred bulls. If the calf is a male, then the line is recognized as thoroughbred only in the ninth generation. Among the features expected in a thoroughbred she-camel are ears that come to sharp points, shining eyes, husky shoulders, an erect neck, small feet and upper breast, prominent shoulder blades, a broad chest, and thighs tightly covered with flesh. The animal should be narrow in the loins, and her hump, depending on how slender it is, should be evenly centered and distributed over her body.

As for the statements made about the strength of the camel's senses of sight and smell, whether in thoroughbreds or others, I fear that these are exaggerated. Indeed, the faculties of smell and sight in the camel are probably weaker than those of many other domesticated animals. On numerous occasions I have actually seen camels standing near water sources without sensing their presence, and have seen them looking down over places in which there were many camels, without making the slightest movement to indicate that they were seeing what we were. And although the waters of some of the springs where I have seen camels—thirsty camels—being watered emit a sulfureous odor that can be smelled from afar, I have not seen these camels manifest any awareness or recognition of their proximity to the water until they come to within about 200 meters range of it. The bedouins told me that a camel in its grazing ground may become separated from its herd by, for example, entering a wadi where it spies a shrub or plant that it likes and beginning to graze up or down the course of the wadi. Sensing nothing but the fact that it has strayed away from the herd, it becomes entirely lost and has no idea how to rejoin its herd until the herdsman comes looking for it, finds it, and takes it back to the others.

Benefits of the Camel

Probably the most important of the camel's benefits is that it is the best animal for traveling in the sands and empty desert wastes and the one best able to endure lack of water, thus making it easy for the bedouin to live in the desert and to move about in it from one place to another. Were it not for this, it could not comprise an important pillar of bedouin life. In these abilities it is unique among the common domesticated animals, and among wild animals it has no equal other than the ostrich, which only lives in sand-desert lands. The bedouin uses the camel to cross the desert: on the day he breaks camp he carries his wife and children on the backs of his camels and loads his baggage onto them; the camels carry his tent, poles, and whatever household effects and foodstuffs he has, and set out with him for the new grazing lands to which he is going.

Were it not for the thoroughbred riding camels, which can travel great distances, the bedouin would not be able to scout out new grazing lands before breaking camp. It is a customary bedouin practice to send scouts out on thoroughbred riding camels to explore the various quarters of the desert searching for water or pasturage until they find them and return to their tribe and show them where they should march to reach them. The bedouins also send out messengers into the desert mounted on fast strong riding camels, which thus serve as courier camels. As we read in Sūrat al-Naḥl (16), vss. 5–7:

> And the livestock—He created them for you, and in them is warmth and various benefits. You eat of them, there is beauty in them for you when you bring them in to rest and send them forth to graze, and they carry your burdens to a land you would otherwise never reach, except with hardship to yourselves. Indeed, your Lord is All-Benevolent, All-Compassionate.[48]

In Sūrat al-Zukhruf (43), vss. 12–13, it is stated:

> And He who created the pairs, all of them, and made for you ships (*fulk*) and the grazing animals that you ride, that

[48] See also Sūrat al-Naḥl (16), vs. 80.

> you might be mounted on their backs and then remember the grace of your Lord when you are seated upon them, and say: "Glory be to Him who has made this subject to us when we ourselves were not equal to the task."

And in Sūrat Ghāfir (40), vs. 78, we find: "God, who made for you the grazing livestock, that you might ride some and eat some."

Another benefit the bedouin derives from the camel is easy access to the basic nourishment upon which he subsists—milk. Indeed, this milk itself to a great extent replaces the water the bedouin would otherwise need to quench his thirst. The milch camel is milked once in the evening. Were it not for the milk of these she-camels, the bedouin would need to drink many times more water than he does. Some bedouins slaughter the she-camel's calf so that their children and mares can live off its milk, and if it does not yield much milk they bring her the calf of another she-camel so that nursing this calf will increase the flow of milk. Sometimes they gather three or four she-camels together with one calf to increase their flow of milk. And if they do not slaughter the calf they still share in the milk, leaving one side of the udder to it and milking from the other side. Milking a she-camel is done in various ways: with the entire palm of the hand (a method called *ḍaff*), with the thumb and all of the fingers wrapped around the udder (*ḍabb*), with the tip of the thumb and the index finger (*bazm*), or with the tip of the thumb and the tip of the index finger (*faṭr*).

Those who have studied the milk of she-camels have noted that it contains a higher proportion of Vitamin C than cow's milk, and a higher ratio of fat, protein, and mineral content than either cow's or goat's milk.[49] It is possible to make butter or cheese from any milk; but contrary to what some think, it is not common practice for the bedouins to make butter from the milk of their she-camels. I know no one who told me that he had eaten butter made from camel's milk. Here we must point out that the blocks of stuff, resembling dry cheese, that the bedouins sometimes make, is usually made from the milk of sheep and goats and is only rarely made from the milk of she-camels. And the fermented milk with a special leavening to it is not curdled

[49]Gauthier-Pilters and Dagg, *The Camel*, p. 164.

milk, as some believe. In his study on the camel, which the reader may consult, Wilson indicates the amount of fat and other substances in camel's milk, compared to that in human milk and the milk of some other animals.[50]

Volney is mistaken when he claims that the camel supplies the bedouins with butter,[51] as are many others who have taken information from him. The bedouins make butter from the milk of sheep and goats, not from that of she-camels.

The camel also provides the Arabs—both the bedouins and the settled folk—with a readily available source of meat, which in Arab towns is called *laḥm al-jazūr*. Its price is fixed just as the prices of other meats are fixed, and is recorded in the price lists published by the municipalities and distributed to butchers so they can set their prices accordingly. Camel meat, especially that of the young camel, does not differ much in taste from beef.[52] Dagg and her colleague Gauthier-Pilters have stated that camel meat has a higher ratio of protein than that of beef, and less fat than beef. They also indicate that since the modern world is threatened with future prospects of hunger, scientists have begun to expand their search for sources of nourishment to include the meat of the camel.[53]

Here it must be pointed out that *jazūr* (the camel slaughtered for its meat) is a term applied to both male and female camels that have not been used as beasts of burden. Hence their meat is not tough, like that of the camel that lives in the villages and is used for ploughing, harvesting, transportation, carrying loads, and other tasks of settled life. When a bedouin wants to honor his guest the greatest sign of esteem he can make is to slaughter a *jazūr* for him, and Arabic poetry is full of verse in which bedouins boast of their efforts to outdo each

---

[50]R.T. Wilson, *The Camel* (London and New York, 1984), pp. 154–58.

[51]C.-F. Volney, *Travels Through Syria and Egypt, 1783–1785*, translated from the French (London, 1787), I, 390.

[52]Guarmani (p. 15) notes that the meat of the camel is not as insipid as many imagine. So also Doughty (I, 499), who describes camel meat as delicious, tender, and not much different from veal, especially if the meat is that of a young camel calf. We find Musil (*Northern Negd*, p. 10), however, describing it as tough and devoid of fat, and for this reason not good to eat.

[53]Gauthier-Pilters and Dagg, *The Camel*, p. 163.

Figure 26: A migrating pack train searching for a new grazing land.

Figure 27: The method used by the woman for riding on camels.

Figure 28: A young man with his braided hair hanging down, and near him a large calf hobbled for slaughter.

other in offering meals to guests and slaughtering camels in their honor. When the land is fertile and the pasture plentiful and the bedouins slaughter such *jazūr* camels, they save the fat from their humps. One will see camel-raising bedouins melting this fat and keeping it as cooking fat for their food, thus replacing the clarified butter used by settled folk or sheep-raising bedouins.

The bedouins slaughter many camels on ʿĪd al-Aḍḥā, this as a sacrificial gesture in memory of those of their people who have died. A family that has lost one of its loved ones will, on the first or any subsequent ʿĪd al-Aḍḥā after the death of the deceased, slaughter a camel in his memory. On one of the days of the Feast,[54] one will see the

[54] Among most of the Rwāla, the sacrificial slaughtering usually takes place on the second or third day of the Feast, when the bedouin has ascertained that the Feast

master of the household prepare the camel for sacrifice, hobble it, then make it kneel down and slaughter it. In passing by one of the camps of one of the large tribes on the second or third day of the Feast, it is not unusual for one to see that the tribe has sacrificed about 50 camels for the sake of the individuals they have lost. Should it happen that the bedouins be camped near a village at the time of ʻĪd al-Aḍḥā, the people of this nearby village will be sated with the meat acquired—without payment—from the sacrificed camels whose meat was distributed among them when they took part in the slaughtering during the Feast. The bedouins may store some of the meat after cooking it and rendering the fat out of it, or cutting it into long thin strips that dry and keep for a long time. As for the tribes that keep sheep, they sacrifice some of their sheep.

From the hide of the camel the bedouin makes containers in which to keep water, buckets in which to raise water from wells or pools, or a trough to fill with water for the camels to drink when he lifts water from the wells. From the hide he also makes sandals for himself to wear when the sands make his feet sore, or when the burning heat of the ground forces him to wear sandals; and from it he also cuts off strips to serve as straps for these sandals. From the camel's foot pads he sometimes fashions shoes or soles for his sandals. Indeed, from camel hide he makes many of the things he needs and furnishings for his tent. Some bedouins in southern Arabia use camel hides as covering material for their tents.

The fur of the camel he uses to weave bags in which grain or flour is stored, to make tentcloth panels for flaps for protection from the wind, or to make an aba for the master of the household or a cover for the saddle of his mare. Among the Rwāla and the bedouins of the Syrian Desert the fur is not sheared at a fixed time of the year, as, for example, the wool of sheep is sheared. Rather, the fur is only taken as it is shed from the bodies of the camels during the summer. The women collect it before it falls out, and often some try to hide part of it from their menfolk and sell it secretly so they can buy bits of cheap jewelry.

---

is underway. In regions where the first day of the Feast is known, the slaughtering occurs on the first day. This custom will be discussed in fuller detail in Chapter XVI.

Figure 29: A camel slaughtered on ʿĪd al-Aḍḥā, its hide split open at the hump.

Figure 30: The camel after slaughtering and the removal of its hump.

Camel dung the bedouin uses as fuel for the fire over which he warms himself during the winter, prepares his food, heats his drink, or bakes his bread. Camel dung was and continues to be the primary fuel not only in the desert, but in certain villages adjoining the desert. In many peasant homes, even in the unirrigated villages close to the cities, there are special rooms for storing the dung of camels, sheep, goats, or cattle, so that it can be used as fuel throughout the year. When the bedouins camp in agricultural lands, the dung and urine of their camels, rich as they are in ammonial salts, serve as fertilizers to enrich the land. These salts are probably what prompts many of the bedouins' daughters and wives to wash their hair with camel's urine, for this protects it from infestation by vermin and gives it a reddish hue. Indeed, among the bedouins there are those who sometimes drink this urine as a medicine to cure certain diseases.

When the bedouin breaks camp he sets a howdah on the back of his camel and makes it a tent in which his wife sits. Along with her she has some of her food, drink, clothing, pillows, and cushions, just as if she were in her tent. Over this large howdah she sets up an awning, and in this shade the children are protected from the sun. With all this burden the camel walks along, patient and content.

The camel penetrates to the heart of the economic life of the bedouin, for it is his essential source of wealth. Until recently, the monetary worth of everything in the desert was established in terms of this unit—the value of a camel. The *diya*, the wergeld or restitution paid for someone who has been killed, to this day continues to be paid in numbers of camels, as it was in pre-Islamic times. By this means compensation was made for wounds and the wergeld was paid for those killed. As Zuhayr ibn Abī Salmā said:

> Each one I see coming to pay the wergeld for him,
> With flawless camels ascending a mountain peak.[55]

The *mahr*, the dowry given to the bride, is paid by a fixed number of camels, depending on the social standing of the bride and her family or the bridegroom's ability to pay. A statement handed down over the generations and attributed by some to the Prophet says: "Do not revile

[55] Al-Zawzanī, *Sharḥ al-mu'allaqāt al-sab'* (Beirut, 1382/1963), p. 85.

Figure 31: A bedouin woman collecting camel's urine to wash her hair.

camels, for through them the flow of blood ceases and the dowry of the noble woman is paid;"[56] that is, they are given as wergeld payments, thus sparing lives and stopping bloodshed, and as the *mahr* paid to the women. Even horses are sometimes valued in numbers of camels. And once, when I was a young man, I saw a delegation from Shaykh 'Awda Abū Tāyih, the famous companion of Lawrence, offering one of the bedouins three camels in payment for a pair of binoculars 'Awda knew the man had.

If he is from a camel-raising tribe, the bedouin assesses his fortune and wealth by how many camels (*ḥalāl*, literally, "lawful possessions") he owns. They say: "So-and-so owns so many camels;" but until recently you would never hear anyone say: "So-and-so's possessions are worth such an amount of money."

The taxes that the state today receives from the bedouin who lives within its borders, and the *zakāt* (alms tax) that he used to pay in early Islamic and Umayyad times, are paid in camels. Until recently, the shaykhs of the tribes used to gather together their camels, a fixed number of which were cut out of the herd for the state. Now, however, government revenue officials are the ones who collect these taxes from the bedouins: on the basis of the number of camels owned by each member of the tribe, an equivalent rate in cash is assessed. And a final use for the camel is that it is sold to the settled folk, either for slaughter, for carrying loads, or as a means of transport. For the price of a camel the bedouin is able to buy whatever he wants by way of commodities, equipment, and foodstuffs. The camel is indeed something precious to its owners.

Some of those studying the camel have tried to compare it to the wheel pulled by horses among non-nomads in the history of civilization. According to their view, the camel is superior to the wheel and in most situations surpasses the other animals able to pull wheeled vehicles, such as the ox, mule, and donkey. Hence the camel's eminent standing in the history of transportation. One scholar sums up the reasons for the superiority of the camel over cart-pulling oxen in a number of points.

[56] Al-Damīrī, *Ḥayāt al-ḥayawān*, I, 21, in the article *ibl*, there citing the tradition: "Do not revile camels....." This tradition does not appear, however, in any of the six authoritative collections of Prophetic tradition.

The most significant of these are that a camel can carry or pull twice as much as a single ox, is faster than the ox, and covers daily a greater distance; that it can travel about 25 miles without stopping and make a greater number of journeys in a single year; and that it lives and works four times as long as the ox. It can traverse ground into which a cart would sink and ford a river impassable to a wheeled vehicle, and it has a greater ability to tolerate hardships and endure hunger and thirst than any other beast of transport.[57]

Disadvantages of the Camel

The disadvantages of the camel can almost be reduced to two points. The first is that being a pillar of bedouin life, it obstructs the sedentarization of the bedouins. By virtue of the fact that they raise camels, they are compelled to lead them to the desert and to remain bedouins, rather than settle down. The camel cannot be used in agriculture and farming as the cow is used, since it involves more trouble than it is worth, while in the desert it involves no burden beyond the wages for the herdsman entrusted with a large herd. The second point is that in the summer, when it approaches the lands of the settled regions, it eats up all the land's vegetation that would be suitable for the peasants' livestock, and tramples under foot the small plants that remain, thereby either killing them or halting their growth.

It is odd that the authors of *The Camel*, a book rich in useful information, physiological data, and other details, should claim that plants grow more when camels graze on them and that the camel causes no damage to plants in the desert, and indeed, actually preserves them. They then say: "It is clear to both of us that vegetation grows more in a place where camels have grazed than it does in a similar place where camels have been prevented from grazing."[58] Jarvis, on the other hand, as we have already mentioned in our study of the desert, maintains that the camel and the goat are the enemies of plants in the desert. When he fenced off a plot of land in the Sinai Desert from camels and goats, plant life in the plot flourished; tall shrubs grew, and growing conditions began to improve because of the dry crumbled leaves that

[57]Bulliet, *The Camel and the Wheel*, pp. 22–27.
[58]Gauthier-Pilters and Dagg, *The Camel*, p. 33.

fell on the ground there.[59] I do not deny that the damage amounts to little when camels are grazing far from one another in broad expanses of desert, but can their grazing be of any benefit to the plants? And what would happen if camels were to graze in large numbers in a single spot?

The Temperament of the Camel

Above all else, the camel is an animal that prefers life with a group of its own kind, hence it travels in herds, as sheep and goats do. If for some reason a camel becomes separated, one will see that its first concern is to rejoin its herd. If one wishes to cross a river or go through a pass or a dangerous area of treacherous footing with a herd or train of camels, and the herd or train refuses to come along, he has only to force one of them to proceed and the others will readily join it. Even the camel that had been the first to refuse to cross the spot in question will, when it sees the rest of the herd crossing, cross in turn behind it so as to keep up with the group and remain part of it.

The camel is also, despite all that is said about it, a mild-mannered animal, except in certain cases during the mating season and when it is being loaded. It is not in its nature to be cross or spiteful, as many imagine, and it does not begin with a hostile attitude to anyone. It is sociable and friendly towards one who treats it with kindness and affection and puts it out to graze. I have seen many bedouin boys and adults stroking and petting their camels, which enjoyed the company of those who were doing so. Once I watched a boy petting one of his family's she-camels and scratching her neck, and the animal raised her head high in her contentment and satisfaction. Then I heard him say to her: *Ḥubbah*, "Kiss," so she lowered her head down to the boy's face and kissed him with her rough lips, and he gave her one in return. He repeated this several times in front of me, and the she-camel was quite pleased with this affectionate attention. Some of those who have spoken of the ill-temperedness and crossness of the camel are probably only familiar with the village camel, which is subjected to such traveling in caravans and hard work in the fields that life has become a misery for it. They do not know the free-roaming camel that grows up with

[59]Jarvis, *Three Deserts*, pp. 152–53.

the bedouins, or the well-trained thoroughbred riding camel—described so well by such ancient poets as Labīd, Ṭarafa, al-Rāʿī, and Dhū l-Rumma—accustomed to travel with her masters in the lands of the desert and the attacks of raiding expeditions, the likes of which are still used today in the Camel Corps of the desert patrol forces in many of the Arab countries.[60]

The camel is easily led, this to the point of stupidity, and is accordingly the animal most prone to mishap in dangerous places and predicaments. It cannot be trained as one would train a donkey, dog, or horse, since it is less attentive than these other animals. Hence, it can be driven or led into any situation by its nose, so to speak. In former times they used to insert a ring through its nose, so that it would be an easy matter for any boy to tie a rope to the nose ring of his camel and lead it by the rope. The Arabs knew how easy it is to lead a camel: in a letter that Muʿāwiya ibn Abī Sufyān sent to ʿAlī ibn Abī Ṭālib, he says, after a long discourse: "In all that you are led like the camel with a ring in its nose."[61]

In his *Dīwān al-ḥamāsa*, Abū Tammām long ago related a poem many verses long, by ʿAbbās ibn Mirdās, on the submissiveness and weakness of the camel, despite the large size of its body. The poem begins:

> A thin man you see and so deride,
> But a crafty lion his garments hide.

and in it the poet says:

> The camel grows large but becomes not wise,
> And is not enriched by its large size,
> Toward any point the boy turns its face.

[60]Cf. the account of Lady Anne Blunt, pp. 355–57. There she provides a long commentary on the attributes and temperament of the camel and refers to its superiority for travel over the thoroughbred horse, not for its speed, but rather for its ability to tolerate and endure hardships and its lack of complaint. Of its braying and bawling when burdens are loaded onto it, she says that this is a means of expressing how it had to be loaded. She then says: "Much as I love horses, I hold them on both of these points below the camel."

[61]Ibn ʿAbd Rabbih, *Al-ʿIqd (al-farīd)*, IV, 335.

And hobbles restrain it in disgrace.
The little girl pummels it with sticks of cane,
While no zeal or protest will make it complain.[62]

The camel is also a cowardly animal, and among the large animals there is none more cowardly than this one. Were I permitted to formulate a theory on the question of its domestication, I would maintain that this did not occur by the hand of ancient man himself—as we conjure up in the image of some hunter finding a small wild camel calf and bringing it to his son, who raises and domesticates it—but was rather the work of the camel itself, seeking to guarantee its security from wild predatory animals. Not only is it the weakest and most cowardly of the large animals, but also nature does not help it to protect itself. Thus it sought refuge in the desert, where the dry barren environment protected it from predators accustomed to thick vegetation and unable to endure lack of water as well as the camel. Then, when the desert did not provide it with the security it sought, it took refuge with man, who protected it and used it to his advantage. One result of this protection was that the protector of the camel became its parasite. If this theory is sound, or at least partially so, then it will come as no surprise that it is the camel that led man to the sandy desert lands and to life in such regions.

Here it is interesting to note that the creator of the story of Kalīla and Dimna considers that among all the animals upon which the lion can prey, none is of greater servility, weakness, and cowardice than the camel. He then makes it an image of sacrifice in the story. Our view that the camel is a coward is probably confirmed in the famous address of al-Ḥajjāj ibn Yūsuf, when he refers to his fortitude and courage and says: *innī wa'llāhi mā yuqa'qa'u lī bi-l-shinān*, "By God, no waterskins are banged together in front of me." For when a bedouin wants to upset or frighten a camel, he bangs *shinān* (tanned leather waterskins that have dried out) together in front of the animal, so that it runs away from the sound.

[62]Abū Tammām, *Ḥamāsa*, II, 15–16. In al-Ḥuṣrī's *Zahr al-adab*, edited by 'Alī Muḥammad al-Bijāwī (Cairo, 1372/1953), I, 355, the last three verses are attributed to the poet Kuthayyir, with some variation in the reading. They are also found in Kuthayyir's *Dīwān*, p. 530, with some variation in the last two verses.

The she-camel is most fearful when it has just borne young; one sees her restless and agitated, especially when she is separated from the herd or, when roaming about to graze, she realizes that she is all by herself. It may sometimes happen that while a camel is grazing about with the herd, something appears that frightens it. A wolf or hyena or some other frightening animal may suddenly appear before it from a den in a wadi, or a swarm of locusts may suddenly fly over the ground in front of it.[63] Filled with terror the camel runs off, followed by the herd, and then by other herds grazing nearby. One sees the herds fleeing over the desert, leaving columns of dust behind them. Their fear does not abate nor their composure return until either they become exhausted from running or their herdsmen catch up with them on horseback.

Bull camels become fearful in particular situations, i.e. during the rutting season when they are looking for the females. One sees these bulls raising their heads skyward, braying loudly, frothing at the mouth, and perhaps extruding from their mouths a red membrane, called a *shiqshiqa*, about the size of a fat orange. Rutting bulls become more agitated when they are competing amongst themselves for the females, and they eat very little.[64]

The traditional view of the bedouins has it that the she-camel is the animal with the greatest yearning for and attachment to its young and the one that grieves most when she loses it. Indeed her yearning is such that it has become the basis for proverbs, and ancient Arabic poetry as well as modern bedouin verse teems with descriptions of the she-camel's attachment to her young one, her yearning for it if she finds herself separated from it, and her anguish if she loses it:

> My she-camel yearns for what lay behind, and I for what lay ahead,
> She and I aiming in different ways, in opposing directions led.

[63] Palgrave (II, 138) maintains that of all timid creatures, none equal the "ship of the desert" in cowardice. See Musil, *Palmyrena*, pp. 26–27, 183.

[64] Al-Damīrī, *Ḥayāt al-ḥayawān*, I, 22. See also the photographs of bulls in their state of sexual arousal, in Gauthier-Pilters and Dagg, *The Camel*, between pp. 84 and 85.

Figure 32: Both white and black camels are prized among the bedouins.

When yearnings unite, both yours and mine, you feign a limping gait,
As if your failing legs cannot stand to bear the heavy load's weight.[65]

When the bedouins slaughter a calf, it is their custom to relieve the mother's grief for the young one she has lost by stuffing the calf's skin with dry straw or hay and placing it in front of her so she can sniff it and take comfort in the smell of the calf's skin. This they call a *baw*. Alternatively, they take the suckling calf of another she-camel and give it to her so she can take comfort in it for the loss of her own. Two nursing mothers thus share an attachment for a single suckling calf, so if this second one in turn either perishes or is slaughtered, both she-camels—the natural mother and the "foster" mother—will grieve for it.[66] The grief and moaning of a bereaved she-camel may last for a month. As 'Amr ibn Kulthūm said long ago:

None like unto mine is the grief of the she-camel that has lost her new-born,
Who murmurs and cries out with long trembling calls her bereavement to mourn.[67]

Doughty maintains that when the she-camel has lost her calf at birth, she continues grieving for about ten days, then forgets and gives all her milk to the members of the family.[68]

Concerning the lore told about the attachment and yearning of she-camels, the bedouins also claim that the camel is of a brutish nature, but say that despite this it is fond of tunes and melodies and listens to its master's voice when he sings songs or camel ditties (*ḥudā'*) to it. A story handed down over the generations has it that there was an Arab camel driver, named Sallām, who sang so well to camels that he became the basis for a proverb. "They used to let the camels go thirsty for days, and then water them," it was said, "and Sallām would

[65]'Urwa ibn Ḥizām al-'Udhrī, *Dīwān*, manuscript in the author's possession.
[66]Musil, *Manners and Customs*, pp. 194–95, 209.
[67]*Sharḥ al-qaṣā'id al-'ashr*, p. 111.
[68]Doughty, I, 369.

Figure 33: The she-camel's affection for her calf, and its devotion to her.

stand behind them singing to them, and the camels would leave the water and come to him."[69] Their poets did not neglect to mention this tale. Indicating that the voice of the singer could make camels led to the watering place forget all about drinking, they related that one such singer said:

> That melodies are of both use and avail
> Is a viewpoint which you may now slight.
> Yet look to the camels, which compared to you,
> Are surely more brutish by natural right.
> They harken unto the voices of drivers,
> So that traverse the waterless wastes they might.
> That they should go thirsty for five days, or four,
> Is surely a nigh well remarkable sight.
> And so when they begin to drink from the troughs,
> And gulping down water their thirst to requite,
> And yearn for a driver to sing them a song,
> Their attention upon him to pause and alight,
> They forget the water in which they'd revel,
> With its cool relief from their thirsting plight,
> Longing for the song whose air and tune
> Fills them with joy and enraptured delight.[70]

The Breeding of She-Camels

The breeding of she-camels begins in the winter, though some go into heat earlier and are bred in the late autumn. Pregnancy lasts for an entire year. Camels are sometimes wary of human beings during the mating season; the male and female move away from the tents, but do not shun the herdsman or their owner. The best time for mating is from early December to late January. One will see the rutting bull, which is described as a *hadūr*, or "braying one," murmuring, foaming at the

[69] Buṭrus al-Bustānī, *Muḥīṭ al-muḥīṭ* (Beirut, 1867–70), I, 988, article *s-l-m*.

[70] See Kushājim, *Dīwān*, edited by Khayrīya Muḥammad Maḥfūẓ (Baghdad, 1390/1970), pp. 324–25; *idem.*, *Adab al-nadīm* (Cairo, AH 1298), p. 21; Abū Ḥayyān al-Tawḥīdī, *Al-Baṣā'ir wa-l-dhakhā'ir*, edited by Wadād al-Qāḍī (Beirut, 1408/1988), II, 110–11.

mouth, and braying as he stretches his head upwards. He begins to pursue and flirt with the she-camel, and tries to make her kneel down until, eager and aroused, she drops to her knees, kneels down, spreads her hind legs, and urinates. The bull then crouches over her, throwing himself onto her and stretching his two front legs around either side of her belly. Seven days later she is led to the bull again, and if she refuses to kneel or raise her tail it is considered that she has become pregnant (*'ashsharat*). During her pregnancy the bedouins prevent her from eating *kurb* plants, since these, as they claim, would cause her to miscarry. According to bedouin custom, when a she-camel becomes pregnant she is deemed to be one of the *'ishār*, the "young-bearing ones," and after two months she is called one of *al-niyāq al-laqaḥ*, the "bred she-camels." Camels give birth to twins only rarely, and although I have been told of she-camels that have done so, I have never seen one with twin calves. One bull is sufficient for breeding a herd of about twenty she-camels during the mating season, and two or three years may elapse before the she-camel gives birth to another calf.

Stages in a Young Camel's Life

When the she-camel feels labor pains she begins to murmur, and if out grazing at the time she tries to take refuge in some wadi or in a low spot behind a hill to give birth. But the herdsman follows her to stay close to her, or brings her back to the vicinity of the tents, if they are close by, to bear her young there. When the time for throwing the calf approaches, the she-camel quickly kneels down on the ground: the forefeet of the young one appear first, then the head and the shoulders.[71] When the entire body falls to the ground, the mother rises from the spot where

[71]Doughty claims (I, 369) that when the she-camel drops to her knees she throws herself over on her side without a sound or a moan, and when the foot of the calf appears the herdsman pulls the young one out with all his might and places it, dead-like, before its mother. She sniffs the calf, then rises to her feet and begins to lick it. The herdsman claps his hand on the young one's upper breast, placing his palm underneath it. The calf thus revives and tries to stand on its own—tottering, rising, and falling. After only three hours of such attempts it is able to stand and reach for its mother's udder without any assistance. On the second day it can follow its mother to the pasture. At birth the calf has a hide as soft as silk and a weak voice. Its suckling period lasts for twelve months, but when only some weeks old it can graze on the tender tops of plants.

she had been crouching and turns to nuzzle, sniff, and lick the calf; she may also cut the umbilical cord with her teeth if it has not broken of its own accord or if the herdsman has not cut it. After about two hours the young one rises to its feet. The bedouin teaches the calf to suck from his finger by smearing it with butter, clarified butter, or milk, and putting it to the calf's mouth so he can suck it. When the calf is accustomed to sucking the finger, he puts it to its mother's udder for it to suck, and then leaves the two of them together. The calf remains free to nurse from its mother whenever it wishes for three months, and then is kept away from its mother so that it can only suck three times a day and will become accustomed to grazing on small plants. He continues thus until he is a year old, or sometimes a year and a half, and at that time is weaned from the mother and becomes a *faṣīl*, an immature but weaned camel. By this time it has become accustomed to grazing on the various plants and shrubs upon which camels feed. The she-camel's udder has four teats, two of which are usually tied with two small sticks in order to save their milk until the evening, so that the family can drink it. The other two teats are left free so that the calf can nurse from them.

In each year of its life, as the calf grows, it takes on a new bedouin name. When it is a year old it is called a *ḥiwār*, then at two it is a *labanī*, at three a *ḥajj*, at four a *jadh'*, and at five, when it changes its teeth (*thanāyā*), a *thanī*. At six it is called *rub'ī*, and here its growth is complete. The male becomes a *jamal* and the female a *nāqa*; the latter is called *rub'* and can now be bred and bear young. In the seventh year it is called *sudās*, in the eighth *shaqq al-nāb*, in the ninth *qāriḥ*, and in the tenth *mufṭir* or *fāṭir*. The bull is called a *qu'ūd* until the sixth year, then after that a *jamal*. As for the she-camel, she is a *bakra* until the sixth year, then a *fāṭir* until the tenth. The names applied to camels between the third and the tenth year vary among certain tribes.[72]

It is appropriate that we conclude this study of the camel by noting that there is no animal that equals the camel in the attention devoted to it by philologists or the status it enjoys in Arabic dictionaries and in Arabic literature. The terms for the camel and its attributes are so

[72]Doughty, I, 401; Musil, *Manners and Customs*, pp. 333–35; G. Boris, *Le Chameau ches les Marâziq* (Tunis, 1951), p. 63.

Figure 34: A calf nursing from its mother, despite the barrier placed over her udder to prevent him from doing so.

Figure 35: Beauty (*jamāl*) in the camel (*jamal*).

numerous as to be counted in the hundreds. The ancient poets went to great lengths in describing it; many similes, metaphors, and parables revolve around it; and they associated it with things that were good and beautiful. The lexicographical compendia held that the camel's name, *jamal*, is derived from the word *jamāl*, "beauty," since the bedouins consider the camel a fine beautiful animal. In a Prophetic tradition it is said: "He brought a fine beautiful (*jamlā'*) she-camel," and in another we read: "Then a fine beautiful (*jamlā'*) woman appeared before him."[73] And who knows, perhaps the word *jamāl* ("beauty") is itself derived from *jamal* ("camel"), since the latter is the source of goodness and life for the bedouin. Desert life decreed that the bedouin woman should be of slender build, due to the great amounts of moving about, traveling, and working that she did, which kept her something short of plumpness and corpulence. Hence, if she became plump and soft-bodied, like a camel (*jamal*) fills out when it becomes fat, then they would refer to her as *jamīla* and *jamlā'*, "beautiful."

Al-Kisā'ī said that *jamlā'* is of the same meaning as *jamīla*, and sang:

> She is comely (*jamlā'*) as a full moon on the rise,
> Surpassing all human beings in her beauty (*jamal*).[74]

The description of she-camels—especially thoroughbreds—in ancient Arabic poetry practically overwhelms everything else, and in many cases it monopolizes most of the ode, as we see in the poetry of Ṭarafa, Labīd, al-Rā'ī, Dhū l-Rumma, and others. Hence the importance we have assigned to camels for the study and understanding of bedouin life, for this is the most expedient means to facilitate students' proper understanding of ancient Arabic literature.

---

[73]See the article *jamal* in Ibn Manẓūr's *Lisān al-'arab* and al-Bustānī'a *Muḥīṭ al-muḥīṭ*.

[74]Al-Bustānī, *Muḥīṭ al-muḥīṭ*, I, 289.

THE THIRD PILLAR

THE TENT

A tent through which the breezes sigh
Is dearer to me than a palace high.

Maysūn bint Baḥdal

CHAPTER IX

THE BEDOUIN'S TENT

THE THIRD PILLAR of bedouin life is the tent—the bedouin's home, made of goat's hair. The bedouin calls it a *bayt*, "house," and it is undoubtedly from this sense of the word that the term *bayt* was borrowed to refer to the house built of brick or stone. And from *a'mida*, the poles of the hair tent, the same word was borrowed to refer to the pillars of temples, and perhaps also in the expression "the seven pillars of wisdom," mentioned by Solomon and used by the famous T.E. Lawrence as the title for his book *The Seven Pillars of Wisdom*. Anyone who today sees the tent of the al-Sha'lān *amīrs* of the Rwāla bedouins as I have seen and photographed it, pitched with its seven large poles on the outskirts of the village of 'Adhra near the Ghūṭa of Damascus,[1] cannot help but conclude that the compiler of the proverbs of Solomon, the wise man whose people in their earliest times lived the life of bedouins, refers to a hair tent and not a stone temple when he says: "Wisdom has built her house; she has hewn (*naḥatat*) its seven pillars."[2] In our view it would have been more appropriate for the Arabic translator to have used, instead of *naḥatat*, the word *iqtaṭa'at*, "she has cut," or some similar word amenable to wooden tent poles, especially since Solomon was as familiar with the black tents as the Arabs were and sang of their beauty. In the Song of Songs ascribed to him, we find him saying: "Black I am, and beautiful, O daughters of Jerusalem; black like the tents of Kedar, like the cloth panels of Solomon."[3] Indeed, when

[1]See the photograph on p. 255 below.

[2]Proverbs 9:1.

[3]Song of Songs 1:5. The "cloth panels of Solomon" are black hair tents.

Figure 36: The simple one-room tent, home for all the members of the family.

one compares the shapes of the letter *b* in Arabic, Hebrew, Aramaic, Ethiopic, South Arabian, Phoenician, Sinaitic, and Latin, in all their different forms, they do not differ in shape from the configuration of the hair tent, and in most of these languages the pronunciation of the letter approximates that of the term *bayt*.

The Bedouin Tent

The shape of the hair tent is an extended cube the roof and sides of which consist of cloth made of black goat's hair, and the front side of which is open along the entire face of the cube. It is raised on wooden center poles that vary according to the number of rooms the tent contains, and on secondary poles that support the sides (that is, the *arwiqa*) and the front. The length of the tent varies from four to five meters, if it consists of one room and one center pole, and may extend to about 40 or 50 meters if it has many rooms and stands on a large number of center poles.[4]

The hair fabric panels are unrolled, then stitched together into a rectangular shape, and then the tent is raised onto the poles. The guy ropes tied to these panels around the edges of this rectangle are then stretched out several meters, where they are tightened and tied onto pegs pounded into the ground, thereby stablizing the tent.

The principal constituent of the bedouin household is a tent, or *khayma*, which has been inseparable from the Arab nomads and has figured in their accounts as far back as bedouins have existed. In the Book of Isaiah, when the prophet predicts that Babel will be destroyed and become a desolate waste, he says: "No bedouin will pitch a tent there."[5] The tent is made up of panels of goat's hair fabric, wooden poles, guy ropes, and pegs. If the family is fairly well off, the ropes are purchased from the settled areas—from the villages near the desert or from the large cities—and are made of hemp. Otherwise, the women of the household twine them together from various kinds of threads and wools. As for the pegs, these are made from any sturdy wood, and the tribe of Ṣlayb may make them for the bedouins from the wood of some of the trees in the desert. Among poor folk in small tents, or among the Ṣlayb, the pegs may be replaced with heavy stones, and in former times in some Ṣlayb tents, with oryx horns. As mentioned above, the cloth panels are usually made of black goat's hair. Such has been the case since remotest antiquity, as recorded in the Old Testament in its mention of the black tents of Kedar.[6] This cloth is made in specific well-known villages, the most important of which we shall discuss below.

The hair of the goats is sheared in the spring, and then is carded, spun into thread on a spinning wheel, and woven on a loom. This

[4]A tent could be extended for a longer distance and erected on more poles, but would be difficult to lift and transport. It is not unusual for the number of poles to reach eleven with certain shaykhs, as some of them told me concerning a tent in the Syrian Jazīra. In such a case, the tent probably remains set up throughout the year and is not struck, since its owners remain in the lands surrounding the settled areas.

[5]Isaiah 13:20.

[6]Song of Songs 1:5, Exodus 26:7. One makes cloth tent panels from goat's hair and not from camel's fur, as Volney claims (I, 390), except, if necessary, for some parts of the back wall.

Figure 37: Goat's hair panels before they are stitched together.

process produces panels of fabric called *shiqāq* (sing. *shuqqa*), which vary in width from two-thirds of a meter to one meter and in length from ten to twenty meters. These panels are then stitched together side to side to attain the required width. The length of the panels is generally the length of the desired roof, or a bit longer, and the woman in the tent takes up the task of stitching the panels together. As for the sides (*arwiqa*), these are usually made of lower quality fabric; or their upper part may be made of goat's hair, and the lower part may be a composite fabric woven from a variety of hair, fur, and other threads.

The two-room tent requires about eight panels, each ten to twelve meters long and 60 or 70 centimeters wide. About twelve meters more are required for the upper part of the back of the tent, and a similar amount of inferior fabric for the lower part. The two sides (*kisr*) of the tent also require about eight meters. The height of the tent is generally about two meters, except among the wealthy, where the head of the household is *rafī' al-'imād*, a man "high of tent pole." As for the edges that touch the ground, these are strengthened with cheap fabric about half a meter wide. Among some sheep-raising bedouins the tents may be lined with linen fabric.

Tent Fabric

The primary fabric for roofing the tent is made from goat's hair and is of three kinds. The first is that of the pure unmixed hair taken from the goats when they are sheared in the spring. It is the longest hair and cleaner than the other two varieties, and hence is more expensive. Few of the bedouins buy it, and it can be obtained from Lebanon, Syria, Jordan, and Iraq.

The second type is a blend of sheared hair of short length and hair collected from tanneries in Syria and Lebanon, or imported from tanneries in Turkey or North Africa. The hair in these tanneries retains a certain degree of its strength; hence, the fabric made from this blend is regarded as sturdy and serviceable, though not equal to that made from pure goat's hair.

The third type of hair is the *kambak* hair imported from tanneries in India or elsewhere, and is shorter than the previous two types. It seems that the tanneries there use lime and dyes when the hides are tanned, thus reducing the strength of the hair and changing its natural

Figure 38: A two-room tent.

color. The cloth made from this kind of hair is for this reason the cheapest of the three types. Here we must note that the hair prevents the penetration of rain during the winter and keeps the tent warm, while in the summer the fibers stretch out and the panels extend about an extra ten percent, though this does not keep the tent any cooler.

The bedouins who make use of the cloth woven from the first type of hair are very few. The most widely used cloth is that consisting of a blend of 25 percent clean sheared hair, 25 percent of the second type, and 50 percent of the third type, and even this mixed type is only used for roofing the tent. As for the back wall, which the Rwāla call the *riwāq*, and the side walls (which they call *kisr*), the cloth for all these is generally made from inferior types that contain only a slight amount of pure sheared hair. The cloth used for the back wall and sides may even include fur or cheap wool threads, which show an ashen or sandy color.

As for the carding of the hair, this is done with two long flat carding combs, the surface area of each which is about a half foot square and covered with sharp teeth about a centimeter long. Each comb has a handle. One places the hair between the two combs, takes a comb in each hand, and rubs them back and forth with the hair in between them. In this way the hair becomes separated and carded. The hair may alternatively be carded by using a comb with two long rows of teeth fastened to a wooden board. The hair is passed back and forth over the teeth using both hands together.

If the hair is of a cheap variety it is carded in the following manner. Four or five ropes, each about two meters long and five to eight millimeters thick, are tied at one end to a handle and at the other end to an iron or wooden stick fixed in the ground, leaving about 15 centimeters between one rope and the next. The hair is then placed under the ropes about 30 centimeters away from the stick or post, and beaten with them. The worker can also use two combs of this type at one time, using both hands together. All he has to do is beat the hair with these fixed ropes, and it separates and is carded enough to be easily spun.

Women then spin the hair on special wheels while seated, as seen in the photograph below. It can also be spun by the men on wheels differing from those the women use: they stand and move backward, thereby turning the wheels to which the threads are tied, and simultaneously spinning the threads by twisting them with their fingers as they move. The spun thread is then woven on hand looms into panels of cloth of various lengths, some of which reach 40 meters, and also of varying widths, some up to a meter. The most commonly encountered widths are 40, 50, 60, 70, and 100 centimeters. The width of some panels may be as narrow as 20 centimeters; at this point they are called *mukhallāt* rather than *shiqaq*, and are used either to connect some of the panels or to strengthen certain parts of the tent.

The tent made from pure goat's hair fabric may be used between 15 and 20 years before it wears out. If the fabric is a blend of pure goat's hair and hair from the Syrian tanneries, the tent will last seven to ten years. If it is a mixture of all the various kinds, it will survive five to seven years; and if it is made entirely of *kambak* hair it will not last more than five years. The durability of the tent is thus determined by the kind of hair used in the fabric of its panels: the more pure goat's hair it contains, the longer it will last and the more serviceable it will be. The size of the tent may also affect its longevity: the smaller the tent is, the longer it will last.

Figure 39: A village woman from Yabrūd spinning goat's hair into thread for weaving into panels.

Black goat's hair is generally stronger than spotted or white hair, and the hair of goats that live in mountainous or cold regions is generally stronger than the hair of those that live in lowland or warm regions. And generally speaking, goat's hair is stronger and warmer in winter than are either sheep's wool or camel's fur. Furthermore, goat's hair keeps rain water from seeping through the fabric—the water slides off its surface as if it had been rubbed with wax—and in winter keeps heat inside the tent. In summer the threads stretch and the interstices in the weave of the fabric broaden, although the tent nevertheless remains warmer than it would be had it been made of white cotton.

Some may find it odd that the bedouins should live in black hair tents during the summer; but in fact, the reason for this is their poverty. Wealthy bedouin shaykhs replace most parts of the tent with cotton during the summer, and Amīr Fawwāz al-Sha'lān at this time used to replace his entire tent and erect in its place another one of white cotton, since a tent made of cotton is cooler in the summer.

If the tent has one center pole and one room, has been made from fabric of medium quality, and does not use up more than 100 kg. of fabric, then these days, in the early 1980s, it will not cost its owner more than 1200 Lebanese pounds (about 300 US dollars). In times past it would not have cost more than 150 dollars.

In most cases the bedouins purchase the cloth panels from merchants in the villages that lie along the peripheries of the desert, or from well-known traders who accompany the bedouins, travel with them, and camp where they camp. These traders set up the goods they offer for sale to the bedouins in round white tents entirely different from the bedouin hair tents, and congregate in one place where they pitch their tents and which they call "the market" (*al-sūq*). If they set up their market in the al-Sha'lān camp, however, they call it "the market of al-Sha'lān" (*sūq al-Sha'lān*). This market is usually held either in 'Adhra, where the al-Sha'lāns own a share in its agricultural land, or at al-Qaryatayn, regarded by the bedouins as an outstanding camping site. In this market the bedouin can find all the kinds of goods he requires, including tent-cloth panels, poles, tent pegs, ropes, saddles, clothing, axes, sandals, abas, and stocks of coffee, tea, sugar, and the like. There are well-known markets in Syria in the villages and towns near the desert, the most important of which have been Ṣadad, east of Ḥimṣ, for abas, and al-Qaryatayn, followed by Ḥimṣ, Ḥamāh, and Aleppo in the north, al-Ḥsāja, Tadmur, and Dayr al-Zūr in the northeast, and Damascus in the south for all kinds of goods. Others similar to these are to be found in Iraqi and Jordanian cities near the desert.

If the year has been a prosperous one for the bedouins they refit their tents, buy new ones, and purchase new supplies, or repair their old tents and are generous with themselves in purchases of food and clothing. If it has not been a good year, they make do with what they have and are parsimonious with themselves until the following year.

Probably the most important center for the production of tent-cloth panels is the town of Yabrūd in the region of al-Qalamūn in southern Syria, about halfway between Damascus and Ḥimṣ. In this small town there were about 2000 people who earned their living making tents. There are about 300 looms there, and these supply the bedouins of Syria and export to Jordan, Iraq, Najd, Kuwayt, and the oil companies. Among the particular advantages of Yabrūd are that the worker's wages there were, until recently, relatively low, and that pure goat's hair is readily available due to the town's proximity to the mountains of al-Qalamūn, the mountains richest in fine goats—the hair of goats in cold regions being longer and stronger. Most of the workers are Christians who have inherited this craft from their forefathers ages ago, and it would not be surprising if this extended as far back as the tentmaker, the Apostle Paul. Yabrūd produces about 200 tons of this cloth per year—that is, about half of Syria's annual consumption and an amount sufficient to erect more than a thousand fine medium-sized tents. The industry flourishes in fruitful and rainy years: it is then that the bedouins, their livestock having fattened and produced many young, have money to spend and so refit their tents.

The second-ranking town in the weaving of tent-cloth panels is Shḥīm in Lebanon, overlooking the road between Beirut and Sidon, which produces about ten percent of the cloth consumed. Shḥīm used to weave hair into filters used for straining sweet oil, and then began to weave it into tent-cloth panels as well. The remainder of the annual consumption of panels is produced in Ḥimṣ, Ḥamāh, Aleppo, Damascus, and the villages surrounding some of these towns, in Kuwayt, and in some villages in Iraq. I would not be surprised if some of the cheap panels purchased by the bedouins in eastern Arabia proved to be im-

Figure 40: Weaving tent-cloth panels in Yabrūd.

Figure 41: A bedouin woman weaving wool into a panel for the back of the tent.

ports from India. Philby mentions that in the spring of 1947 King 'Abd al-'Azīz pitched his tents on a site in the al-Qasīm region that consequently turned into a city of tents. When these tents began to wear out he wanted to purchase new ones from Kuwayt, but found them excessively expensive. Philby was able to buy him better ones from India at half the price,[7] but does not indicate that they were of goat's hair. This is perhaps the best place for us to mention that the number of tents in Arabia alone may be in excess of 100,000. Anne Blunt mentions that in 1879 the tents of the Rwāla alone came to about 12,000. And the use of hair tents is not limited to Arab bedouins, but rather is widespread from the heart of Afghanistan in the east to the Atlantic coast in the west.[8]

If the bedouin has the means to purchase cloth for a new tent he will do so, otherwise he is satisfied to buy enough to roof his tent and to use the old cloth for the sides and back. Poor bedouin women may undertake the task of weaving the back and sides by hand on primitive looms that they set up in the open air when they camp and remain in one place for a long time, as can be seen in the photograph. Here we would do well to note that it is the bedouin woman who in many cases weaves what serves for the back and sides. It is she who generally pitches the tent for the man, and she who pounds in the pegs, raises the poles, and "strikes the ropes," as they say. When camp is made, the man's only responsibility is to choose the site where he decides his tent should be pitched.

The Bedouin Camp

Among the bedouins of the north the tent is normally pitched facing east, especially during the winter, in order to take advantage of the heat of the sun. In the other seasons the bedouin takes into account the direction of the winds, the lay of the land, and the direction of the light. If the tent is of two rooms or more, one room, called the *rub'a*, is restricted to receiving guests and making coffee, and in it is dug the pit in which the fire for coffee will be kindled. This reception room is in the right part of the tent (that is, to the south) among the Rwāla and

[7]Philby, *Forty Years in the Wilderness*, p. 224.
[8]C.G. Feilberg, *La Tente noire* (Copenhagen, 1944).

Figure 42: The camp, in almost parallel lines.

Shammar,[9] and in the left part among the Fawā'ira and Banū Khālid in Syria and the tribe of Ḥarb in Najd. Some expert bedouin observers may recognize the remnants of the shaykh's camp, after he has moved on, from nothing more than the fire pit.

In the summer the back wall of the tent is raised to relieve the heat by allowing the air to circulate. During the winter dirt is thrown back onto the edges of the back and sides that touch the ground, in order to prevent the penetration of water from the hard rains, to keep the cold air out, and to conserve heat.

There yet remains the question of how the tribe or clan sets up its camps, or rather, how the camps are organized when the tents are pitched. This is a matter that varies among different tribes. A powerful tribe like the Rwāla, for example, stipulates no specific organization and its members set no store by how the tents are laid out. Since it fears no enemy among the other tribes, it does not adhere to the circular alignments in which tents are lined up in half-circles or ovals. Rather, the tents are scattered about randomly in the camp, though they do keep to something of a disposition in lines, with specific intervals between one line and the next so that one can pass easily between them without tripping over the ropes extending rearward and forward. The tents of the Htaym tribe, on the other hand, are pitched close to one another.

A camp containing fewer than ten tents is called a *farīq*; if it has between ten and thirty, it is called a *najī'*; and a camp larger than this is referred to as a *nazl* and has its tents laid out in approximately parallel lines. As for the tent of the shaykh, he himself specifies its location. Indeed, it is he who designates the place where the tribe or clan will camp when it moves from one grazing ground to another. When it moves he is the last to depart, and when it reaches the new grazing ground he is the first to unpack.[10]

---

[9]Dickson (p. 80) errs when he claims that the men's reception room is always in the eastern side, irrespective of which direction the tent is facing. Musil, however, is correct in stating that the *rub'a* is always in the right side of the tent; see his *The Northern Hegaz* (New York, 1926), p. 17. I noticed this myself among the bedouins of Syria generally, but I would not be surprised to find that the situation differs among some of the tribes of other lands. One must thus beware of generalizations.

[10]Musil, *Manners and Customs*, p. 77.

Figure 43: The tent of the al-Sha'lān *amīrs*, showing the "seven pillars."

The front of the tent is generally oriented to face the sun, except when the wind is blowing strongly from the east, in which case the back of the tent is turned towards the wind. The back may be raised in the summer, when the heat becomes intense, to facilitate air circulation. The tent thus reaches the point where its back is in the same form as its front, with the air and light passing right through it. The men's reception room is set up to the left of one entering the tent, although not among all tribes, since among some this room is to the right.

In the men's reception room a pit is dug for the fire for making coffee, tea, and related items. From this fireplace, one stopping later at the traces of the tents will judge the generosity of the shaykh and his standing among the shaykhs of the tribes: the broader and larger the heap of ashes is, the more generosity and expense it indicates.

There is a special sanctity to the bedouin's tent, especially if a fugitive or stranger seeks refuge there. In such a case it is the obligation of the owner of the tent to protect him. Similarly, a visitor would be reproached if, coming to stay with the people of a camp, he passes by a tent without staying as a guest there, as this would be regarded as a blemish on the honor of the people of the tent. I remember that one time when a group of my companions and I wanted to camp with a tribe, we saw a fire in a large tent and headed towards it to stay as guests there. We passed in front of the first tent in the camp without asking its owner, a woman living alone in it, if she would accept us as guests. She herself blocked our path and rebuked us for passing in front of her tent without staying with her; so we apologized and asked for her permission to stay with the one tending the kindled fire, since we did not intend to stay long.

THE FOURTH PILLAR
THE ARAB BEDOUIN

There are those whose pleasures in settled lands be,
But in us, great men of the desert you see!

'Umayr ibn Shuyaym al-Quṭāmī

CHAPTER X

THE ARAB BEDOUIN AND HIS TRIBES

Who is the Arab Bedouin?

There remains the Arab bedouin, the last of the pillars of desert life and the most important of them all. His name, "bedouin" (*badawī*), is derived from the term for the nomadic way of life (*badāwa*), and the way he lives is tied both to nomadism and to the camel. The milk of the latter comprises his food and drink, and the camel itself helps him to move about among the various parts of his desert territory. Unlike his brothers, the Arabs living as settled folk, he only rarely mixes with other peoples.

The bedouin today is of several types. One keeps to his nomadic ways, searches for pasturage far out in his desert territory, and raises no livestock other than camels and a few horses.[1] Another type has some contact with the villages and towns near the desert. He has already begun to depend on the raising of sheep more than he does on the raising of camels, thus his dependence on sheep-raising prevents him from venturing as far out into the desert in search of pasturage as his camel-tending cousin does. The third type keeps to the desert peripheries and the lands near the villages and towns, and restricts his migrating to those regions and lands located among these villages

[1]These are the pure bedouins, and there are those who claim that the Arab is not a bedouin unless he fits into this category. Also, when I say "a few horses" I do so in comparison to the camels and in light of the circumstances the bedouins have faced in recent years. But as we have seen in our study of the horse, horses were so plentiful in the Nafūd region of Arabia in the nineteenth century and earlier that certain explorers claimed that these animals numbered in the thousands.

Figure 44: A bedouin prepared for a long-distance journey on some mission.

and towns adjacent to the desert. He depends on sheep-raising for his living and keeps horses to protect himself from the powerful tribes, devoting no more attention to the tending of camels than that required to maintain a number sufficient to carry his household effects, tents, and furnishings when he migrates from one grazing ground to another. At the same time, he establishes a certain degree of contact with the people of the towns and villages so he can sell the lambs, butter, and wool of his sheep, and he lives most of his days near the towns, visiting them often. His contact with the townsfolk sometimes reaches the point that he concludes an agreement with one of them for joint ownership of the sheep, and it becomes an easy matter for him to settle down should necessity in time lead him to become one of the sedentary folk.

There are groups of bedouins that fall between these categories I have just mentioned, sharing some features with a certain category on one side, and other features with another category on the other side. Most bedouins are now in the course of shifting to a perspective that is distancing them from nomadism and drawing them closer to settled life. This is occurring in many Arab lands, especially in Jordan, Saudi Arabia, Iraq, and in some parts of the Jazīra.

There are other tribes in the desert that are deeply rooted in their nomadism, but these are not of ancient descent, inasmuch as one finds that the other tribes do not consider them of such genuinely bedouin origin as themselves. Among these tribes are the Badūl in Jordan, the Sharārāt, and the Ḥwayṭāt. Still, it is recognized that some of these other tribes have produced great warriors and raid heroes who played important roles in intertribal strife.[2] And there is a particular tribe, that of Ṣlayb, to which we shall devote a special chapter since it differs in its origins and descent and is erroneously regarded by some as descending from the Crusaders.

It was once possible to divide the bedouins generally into two main groups, as many researchers have done: camel-tending nomads, and the sheep-herding bedouins known as the ʻArab al-Shawāyā. But I know of tribes that until recently were tenders only of camels, but which today combine the raising of both camels and sheep. For this reason I have preferred to categorize the bedouins according to three main groups, as above. Here it must be pointed out that according to bedouin tradition those who tend camels are, generally speaking, the most ancient Arabs and the ones of most noble descent, although this does not deny nobility of descent among some other tribes that have begun to incline toward sheep-raising and so are gradually coming to be counted among the ʻArab al-Shawāyā. There are also bedouins that have begun to settle in villages and farms and to turn their attentions to agriculture, working in the fields themselves. These have passed outside the nomadic community and have come to be counted among the settled folk and agriculturalists, despite their continued adherence to many bedouin manners and customs.

The Origin of the Arab Bedouin

The Arab bedouin is Semitic in origin, from the Caucasian race of mankind. According to the traditional view of Arab historians the bedouin traces his descent from southern and northern Arabia, hence the practice of the genealogists generally to trace descent back to two origins, northern and southern, or ʻAdnānī and Qaḥṭānī. This tracing

[2]Such as ʻAwda Abū Tāyih, who was known for his heroism and became famous in the days of the First World War. He was a bedouin of the Ḥwayṭāt tribe.

of descent is sometimes generalized to include the settled Arab as well. Today one sees dark or extremely black skin in individuals of certain tribes, especially in the south. This is the result not only of the influence of the environment, but also of intermingling between the Arabs and other peoples of eastern Asia and Africa. Through the course of history both before and after the advent of Islam, trade and pilgrimage resulted in Arabia establishing contacts to the east with India, Indochina, and Pakistan, and to the west with Somalia, Ethiopia, Eritrea, the Sudan, and Egypt. In many parts of the peninsula, such contacts of course involved the bedouins.

Since intermingling is not possible in the desert environments among some of the bedouins of Najd and the Syrian Desert, people are white in skin color so long as they have not had much exposure to the sun, as I witnessed among many men and women from these tribes. This phenomenon did not pass unnoticed by some of the European explorers who visited the Syrian Desert and Najd and dealt with their people at first hand. Burckhardt mentions that he saw the body of a bedouin woman he was treating for an illness, and states that her body was no different in skin color from the body of a European woman.[3]

In a camp along the peripheries of the Syrian Desert I myself saw the daughter of a bedouin of the Ḥadīdīyīn tribe who did not differ in her appearance, the proportions of her face, or the shape of her nose and eyes, from any European or even Scandinavian girl, as the reader will see in the photograph on the next page. It may be appropriate that I mention here that some modern studies deny that nomadism arose in southern Arabia or passed from there to the north. Rather, one finds that in its earliest phases it was already known in the north. This conclusion is based on the study by some scholars of ruins and carvings they discovered; these scholars push the first appearance of nomadism back to the third millennium BC.[4]

Bedouin Solidarity and Pride in Descent

Circumstances under which the bedouin lives have obliged him, with time, to maintain an intense solidarity with his family and tribe, and

[3]Burckhardt, *Notes*, I, 52.

[4]W. Dostal, "The Evolution of Bedouin Life," in *Ancient Bedouin Society*, edited by Francesco Gabrieli (Rome, 1959), pp. 21–25.

Figure 45: An almost Scandinavian looking bedouin girl (on the left) in a bedouin tent with her sister.

he thus began to take pride in his relationship with them and to spurn settled life. Up to our own time, then, he continues to identify himself with clans or tribes that for ages have devotedly upheld their lines of common descent and have adhered to them with a fierce tribal solidarity. This continues despite their wanderings among various home territories in the deserts of Arabia, despite the movement of some of them away from their ancient tribal homelands and their separation from some of their brothers in other lands, and despite the fact that they have sometimes assumed and come to be known by new names due to the status and renown attained by some of their shaykhs in recent times.

The division of the bedouins into tribes or clans and their devotion to a common line of descent became one of their most prominent distinguishing features, and this solidarity had an influence on Arab life in general. Since pre-Islamic times they have devoted their attention to their genealogies, and anyone ignorant of them they view with suspicion and regard as deficient in ambition and culture. Islam tried to curb the Arabs' adherence to this spirit of tribal solidarity and their attachment to their tribal line of descent. It is claimed that the Prophet said: "The glorious deeds of the pre-Islamic era are inventions, so do let its haughty attitude and boasting of ancestors fade away." In another tradition we read: "O people, God has removed from you the arrogance of the pre-Islamic past and its boasting of ancestors. The Arab has no basis for priding himself over the non-Arab, save in his God-fearing piety."[5] The tribal spirit continued to prevail, however, and allegiance to the tribe remained predominant among the Arabs. And from another viewpoint, one can see from other statements of his that despite Islam's call for the renunciation of tribal solidarity, the Prophet himself apparently did not intend for the Arabs to be ignorant of their lines of descent. Also passed down on his authority is this statement: "To dissociate oneself from a descent line, even if one is but a slave, amounts to disbelief in God, and to lay claim to an unacknowledged descent line amounts to disbelief in God." He is even reported to have once said, in boasting of ancestors: "We are a tribe of Naḍr ibn Kināna; and indeed, God has made the Arabs into clans, and so made me the best of them

[5]Ibn 'Abd Rabbih, *Al-'Iqd* (*al-farīd*), III, 408.

Figure 46: Bedouin girls of the ʻAqaydāt tribe, with a boy standing in their midst.

Figure 47: Bedouin youths of the ʻAqaydāt tribe.

with respect to his clan affiliation." Another time he said: "I am the Prophet—that no one can call a lie. I am the son of 'Abd al-Muṭṭalib." He also stated: "Learn those of your genealogies that establish your kinship connections, for the connection of kinship engenders affection within the family, encourages the accumulation of wealth, and provides solace at the moment of death."[6]

During early Islamic times one of those most learned in genealogy was Abū Bakr al-Ṣiddīq, who used to relate to Ḥassān ibn Thābit al-Anṣārī, the poet of the Prophet, the genealogies of those Qurashīs who opposed Muḥammad so that Ḥassān could lampoon them. A report handed down from 'Umar ibn al-Khaṭṭāb has him saying: "Learn your genealogies that establish your kinship connections, and be not like the peasants of the Sawād. If one of them is asked: 'From whom are you?,' he replies: 'From the village of such-and-such.'"[7] Taking note of this tendency in the history of mankind, Ibn Khaldūn said: "[Concern for] kinship connections is a natural phenomenon among mankind, with very few exceptions."[8] In fact, such ties were so strong among the Arabs that they turned knowledge of genealogy into a branch of learning and were probably the first to refer to it as such. One of the most compelling proofs of the importance of genealogy among the Arabs and their interest in it is that many of their medieval scholars composed books on the subject. The *Fihrist* of Ibn al-Nadīm mentions many of the genealogical works written by such authors as al-Zubayr ibn Bakkār, Abū 'Abd Allāh al-Jahmī, 'Umar ibn Shabba, al-Balādhurī, Muḥammad ibn Sallām, and Abū l-Ḥasan al-Nassāba.[9] This last author is described as being one of the scholars of genealogies. When Ibn 'Abd Rabbih al-Andalusī wrote his *'Iqd* on the history, culture, and sciences of the Arabs, he devoted one of his 25 chapters to genealogy. In this chapter he gives an account of the genealogies of the Arab tribes of both the 'Adnānī and Qaḥṭānī lines, and of their various subdivisions from great tribes (*qabā'il*) to sections of tribes (*'amā'ir*, *buṭūn*, *afkhādh*), to

[6]See *ibid.*, III, 312: "And in *ḥadīth*: Learn such genealogy as you need to familiarize yourselves with your noble descent lines and to establish your bonds of kinship."

[7]*Ibid.*; Ibn Khaldūn, *Muqaddima*, I, 237.

[8]Ibn Khaldūn, *Muqaddima*, I, 235.

[9]Ibn al-Nadīm, *Fihrist*, pp. 111–14.

clans (*'ashā'ir*) and families (*faṣā'il*), and in some cases goes so far as to list the families' famous shaykhs.[10] In this discussion he says: "He who does not know genealogy does not know the people, and he who does not know the people is not to be counted among their kin."[11]

We would do well to note that the bond of kinship, or *nasab*, is something that had a distinct specificity to it among the Semitic peoples or in the early Semitic environment. The Old Testament confirms this through its recounting of the genealogies of kings, prophets, tribes, and others. It is therefore obvious that the attachment of the Arabs in general and of the bedouins in particular to the issue of descent, and their boasting of their genealogies, comprise a deep-rooted phenomenon the origins of which go back to the bedouin Semitic milieu. Even today the bedouins continue to adhere to such attitudes, clinging to their common descent lines and priding themselves in their Arab origins. This inclination faded out among the settled Arabs, with a corresponding fading away of their spirit of tribal solidarity; but as Ibn Khaldūn said, it survived among the bedouins.[12]

Though some of them laid claim to false lines of descent, it would be inaccurate for it to be said that the genealogies of the Arabs were fabrications of their own creation. The history and customs of the bedouins confirm that the tie of common descent was and continues to be the strongest bond to which the bedouins could adhere in order to preserve their existence, despite their division and dispersal into tribes, clans, sub-tribes, and sections. Long ago their poet said:

> I am but of the clan of Ghazīya, going astray
> If it errs, and led right if it keeps to the way.[13]

Another said:

> Protect your nearest kin, for upon your life
> The right is theirs to divide man from wife.[14]

---

[10]Ibn 'Abd Rabbih, *Al-'Iqd (al-farīd)*, III, 312–17.
[11]*Ibid.*, III, 312.
[12]Ibn Khaldūn, *Muqaddima*, I, 236–37.
[13]Abū Tammām, *Ḥamāsa*, I, 343.
[14]Al-Mubarrad, *Al-Kāmil fī l-lugha wa-l-adab*, edited by William Wright (Leipzig, 1864–92), I, 229.

Most of the explorers of Arabia noticed this phenomenon, and tried in their research on nomadism and the desert to become acquainted with the genealogies of the various clans and sub-tribes and to record these in the studies they left behind. Hence we find that most of them prepared detailed tables of the names of the various tribes, the clans into which they were divided, then the sub-tribes, if possible, down as far as sections and families. In fact, tables of most of the bedouin tribes have appeared in many of the explorers' books published up to the present day.

For my part, in this work I have attempted to provide a complete table of the names of all the tribes known today in Arabia, or at least in the northern part of the peninsula. I consulted some of the bedouins themselves and also used the most important works that set forth the names of tribes in detail, including Müller's *En Syrie avec les bedouins*, Aḥmad 'Akkām's *'Ashā'ir al-Sūriya wa-taḥḍīruhā*, the various works of Musil, Fu'ād Ḥamza's *Qalb jazīrat al-'arab*, Waṣfī Zakariyā's *'Ashā'ir al-Shām*, al-'Azzāwī's *'Ashā'ir al-'Irāq*, the *Mu'jam qabā'il al-'arab* by Riḍā Kaḥḥāla, and other works.[15] I found that the large tribes number more than 40, including some that contain more than 30 clans, but I regret to say that in most of them I encountered no agreement when I came to the subject of their sub-divisions—that is, the clans (*'ashā'ir*), sub-tribes (*buṭūn*), or sections (*afkhādh*). Some promote the sub-tribe to a clan or demote it to a section, while others placed the clans on the same level as the tribes or sub-tribes. Nor did I find agreement among these books with respect to the branching out of the tribes according to a fixed basis, and this also holds true for the information handed down by many of those familiar with the affairs of some of the bedouins.

I tried to collect whatever I could myself, directly from certain bedouins who were renowned for their knowledge of the genealogies of the Arab tribes of Syria. I found much disagreement among the various accounts, and perhaps it would be appropriate for me to cite a tangible example. For the Ḥwayṭāt bedouins there is mention of about 40 clans in some books and of 15 clans in others, while in yet other

[15]Oppenheim's *Die Beduinen* was not available to me during research for this book.

works the number of clans does not even come up to this lower figure. The names in one table differ from those in another. Much the same can be said of the tribes of Ṭayy, Banū 'Aṭīya, Banū Ṣakhr, and even 'Anaza itself, the reports on which fill volumes and the affairs of which have been discussed by many researchers. There was discrepancy among the tables of the clans of 'Anaza, as well as among the subdivisions and sections of these clans. And add to this the discrepancies in names and the inaccuracy in the way they have been vocalized by Arab authors, some of whom have taken their tables from the works of the European explorers, as well as by European authors who have passed on these names as they heard them from the bedouins. The bedouin *jīm* is written as *j*, but sometimes as *k*; the *ẓā'* is written as *d* because its pronunciation is close to that of *ḍād* and is expressed by a dotted *d* (*ḍ*) in the Latin character, but then passes as *dāl* back into the Arabic, thus resulting in the obfuscation of the real name of the tribe. Much the same could be said of tens of others examples of this kind, involving such letters as *ḥā'*, *khā'*, *hā'*, and *'ayn*. By way of illustration only, I can mention the clan of Mshāṭa (from Wild 'Alī), one of the sections of which is written by one in the form "al-'Awāḍ," by another as "al-'Awāẓ," and by a third as "al-'Awād." Another clan is here written as "al-Ṭulū' ," and there rendered as "al-Ṭulūḥ." There are tens of other examples, even in the *Mu'jam qabā'il al-'arab*, the compiler of which depended on such error-ridden sources.

Finally, one must take into account the change that continually occurs in the names of some of the clans from one generation to the next. A shaykh may become famous and his clan be named after him—'Arab al-Sha'lān for example, while formerly the clan was known as al-Mur'iḍ. There are those who call all of the Rwāla bedouins by the name 'Arab al-Sha'lān, although the Rwāla comprise about 30 clans other than those of al-Sha'lān. In this way, many of the old names for some of the tribes or clans have changed and have been replaced by new names, despite the above-mentioned attachment of the Arabs to the common descent line and their social bonds to the tribe. The important thing is not so much the name as it is the tribal family bond.

Among the names of the tribes there is sometimes a single name borne by two different tribes. The al-Jumlān, for example, are a sheep and camel-raising sub-tribe (*baṭn*) of the Ḥadīdīyīn located south of

Aleppo, while among the bedouin tribes near Dūmā there is another al-Jumlān, a tribe of origin unknown to the genealogists and now semi-sedentary, living on agricultural lands in tents. In the tribe of Bū Ḥasan there are three different sub-tribes or sections known by this same name and two other sections known as Abū Ḥasan.

To illustrate the confusion and chaos in these tables of tribes and subsections of tribes, we may mention what we have found in the *Mu'jam qabā'il al-'arab* of Riḍā Kaḥḥāla. This is a large compendium in which the author has sought to collect the names of all the tribes and clans, with their subsections, in three volumes and two supplements. He took everything he could find from the works of the genealogists, explorers, travelers, and others, and deserves the greatest appreciation for the efforts and labor he devoted to his work. Still, he was not able to avoid mistakes: he overlooked the names of many tribes, clans, sub-tribes, or sections, and in most cases his mistake originates in the sources from which he took information. By way of illustration I will cite the Banū l-Khirashāt. They are known by this name, and it is generally recognized that they are part of the clan of al-Ka'ābina from the tribe of Banū Ṣakhr; they branch out into nine sub-tribes, and these are al-Ḥanīf, al-Quḍāt, al-Ḥamd, al-Ḥammād, al-Tamd, al-'Ayṭ, al-Ṣāliḥ, al-Ghudra, and al-Sulaymān. On the other hand, in the *Mu'jam* we find reference only to a tribe that Kaḥḥāla calls al-Khrasha (in bedouin customary usage there is no difference between the two names). But as given in the *Mu'jam* the tribe is part of Banū l-Karak, has six sub-tribes rather than nine, and the names of these are al-'Anātīr, al-Salmān, al-Shamā'īn, al-Marājīn, al-Sakhkhān, and al-Jīlāt. If al-Khirashāt and al-Khrasha are the same tribe, then there are no points of correspondence among their sub-tribes other than al-Salmān and al-Sulaymān; if they are not the same tribe, then—which is worse—the *Mu'jam* has neglected to mention the al-Khirashāt clan of the Banū Ṣakhr bedouins. But I must also mention that in the book there are no fewer than 10,000 names of clans, sub-tribes, or sections, extending from the earliest times in which Arabs were known up until today. And similarly, the same state of affairs would hold true were we to collate the tables of some of the European authors. Musil, for example, lists a total of eleven clans of al-'Umūr, while Müller mentions no more than three of them.

This has thus obliged me not to go into lengthy detail on tribal branches and the vocalization of their names, an almost impossible problem despite my knowledge of the dialect of some of the bedouins in northern Syria and their special pronunciation of certain letters. Nevertheless, I have decided against omitting a list of the names of the best-known tribes. I had prepared a chart for detailing the clans branching off from these well-known tribes; but again, despite my contacts with some of the 'Anaza bedouins in the desert and my reliance on two genealogist informants sent to me by one of the shaykhs so I could take the names of the tribes from them, the discrepancies among the versions mentioned made it difficult for me to ascertain the correct form of many names.

As it happens, among the documents to be discussed at the end of this book I discovered in a report by one of the British consuls a detailed table of most of these tribes in the Syrian Desert in the nineteenth century. To avoid repetition I decided to make do with what was in that table, and here I will make mention, if only by way of summary, of some few details on each of the well-known tribes. Particular attention will be paid to the clans of 'Anaza, for it is the largest tribe in numbers in all of Arabia, has the most clans, sub-tribes, and sections, and is one of the earliest to be mentioned in the works of the historians and explorers, especially when they came to be firmly established in northern Arabia in the desert lands adjoining Syria, Jordan, and Iraq. They are also the tribe most closely attached to the camel, the important pillar of desert life, to such an extent that a certain 'Anaza tribesman found it difficult to decide whether God created the camel for them or them for the camel. Others maintain that had God created 'Anaza before camels, 'Anaza would have been like ordinary people. But since God created camels before he created 'Anaza, he was obliged to create 'Anaza to protect and tend the camels. And here it must be noted that many of the names of the clans and sub-tribes within 'Anaza and other tribes have, with time, changed from what stands in the table referred to above, and that the cited numbers of tents and warriors have also changed.

Despite this, the genealogists are agreed that the bedouins of 'Anaza branch out into two main parts, Muslim and Bishr. The tribesmen of each of these two parts are referred to as *ḍanā*, or "offspring," hence the bedouin tribesman of 'Anaza is either from Ḍanā Muslim or from Ḍanā Bishr. Bishr then divides into two branches, al-'Imārāt and 'Ubayd. 'Ubayd is widely distributed in the Syrian Desert, while al-'Imārāt is to be found in the desert of Iraq, hence it has also come to be said of the 'Anazī bedouin that he is either from Ḍanā Muslim or from Ḍanā 'Ubayd. To demonstrate the importance of these two great tribes—Muslim and 'Ubayd—it is sufficient for us to state that until recently they were represented by five deputies in the Syrian Chamber of Deputies, three from Ḍanā 'Ubayd and two from Ḍanā Muslim, and that some of the smaller clans that gathered around them and some of the villages located along the peripheries of the desert used to pay the *khuwwa*—a protection tax—to the shaykhs of the large clans branching off from these two tribes.

Some of the Best-Known Tribes

I will begin with the tribe of al-'Imārāt, who are from Ḍanā Bishr, though not as numerous as Ḍanā 'Ubayd, and have in recent years been making their camping grounds in the desert of Iraq.

The 'Imārāt (from Ḍanā Bishr)

Though most of the 'Anaza have made their camping grounds in the lands of Syria adjoining the desert, the tribe of al-'Imārāt is established along the Iraqi frontiers and hence is counted as one of the tribes of the Iraqi desert. Its territories extend from the banks of the Euphrates near Karbalā' in the north, to the Nafūd region far beyond the territories of Shammar, and in their migrations they at times used to go as far as certain parts of Najd. Explorers and researchers differ on the numbers of their tents, camels, and horses, but agree that they had in excess of 3500 tents and owned about 20,000 camels and many horses. In his book *Al-Bādiya*, 'Abd al-Jabbār al-Rāwī maintained that in al-'Imārāt there are two sub-tribes, al-Dahāmsha and 'Arab al-Jabal, and estimated the number of tents in each branch as 4000.[16]

[16]Al-Rāwī, *Al-Bādiya*, pp. 112–14.

The Sbā'a (from Ḍanā 'Ubayd ibn Bishr)

The name of the tribe is pronounced with no vowel after the *S*, hence some write it "al-Isbā'a." It has two large clans, al-'Bāda and al-Qmāṣa. Some claim that the two clans are al-'Bāda and al-Buṭaynāt, and that al-Qmāṣa is a branch of al-Buṭaynāt and became so well-known that its name replaced that of the original tribe. The two clans had many branches ranging the northern Ḥijāz to the Syrian Desert in the early years of the nineteenth century. Until the middle of this century these sub-tribes owned about 20,000 camels, about 30,000 sheep, and many horses.[17]

The Sbā'a were among the first to migrate to the Syrian Desert, and included those who limited themselves to the raising of camels and others who raised both camels and sheep. There were clashes between them and the bedouins who had come before them in the Syrian Desert, and some of these conflicts found mention in the documents we will discuss at the end of this book.[18]

The Fid'ān (from Ḍanā 'Ubayd ibn Bishr)

This comprises two clans, al-Khrāṣa and al-Wlāda, each of which has about 4000 tents. Here I leave out certain other sub-tribes that have so closely affiliated themselves with these two clans that the *Mu'jam qabā'il al-'arab* states that the Fid'ān with its dependent groups comes to about 6000 tents. The number of their camels is estimated at about 20,000 and their sheep at about 60,000,[19] although these figures vary in years of plenty and with the locality. They also had many horses, once estimated at about 2000, but fewer now. The Fid'ān are established in most parts of the Euphrates valley, and in the winter some of their clans venture as far as the Ḥamād region.[20]

---

[17]'Umar Riḍā Kaḥḥāla, *Mu'jam qabā'il al-'arab* (Damascus, 1368/1949), I, 19–20.
[18]See below, Chapter XIX and Appendix II.
[19]Kaḥḥāla, *Mu'jam qabā'il al-'arab*, III, 910.
[20]*Ibid.*

Ḍanā Muslim

The Ḍanā Muslim part of 'Anaza branches out into two great tribes, al-Jlās and Banū Wahb, each of which has many subdivisions. Banū Wahb divides, in the first instance, into two clans, al-Munabbih and Wild 'Alī, and al-Munabbih is distinguished by the fact that it includes the clans of al-Ḥsāna and al-Masālīkh, from which it is said the Saudi house is descended.

The Ḥsāna (from Ḍanā al-Husayn ibn al-Munabbih, from the Banū Wahb branch of Muslim)

The name of this tribe is also pronounced with no vowel after the *Ḥ*, hence some write it "al-Iḥsāna." They camp on the outskirts of Ḥimṣ around Lake Quṭayna, and along with those from other tribes affiliated to them they now number about 600 tents; and in view of the fact that some of them have turned to settled life, in times past they were more numerous than this. In the days of the Syrian revolution I knew their shaykh, Shaykh Ṭrād ibn Milḥim, and had discussions with him; he had studied in his youth and was a man of distinctive character and culture. On its eastward migration to the fringes of the Ḥamād, his tribe used to camp on the outskirts of al-Qaryatayn, the town in which I grew up. The Ḥsāna were probably among the first of the bedouins to descend upon the Syrian Desert, where they came into conflict with some of the long-established tribes there. They defeated these tribes and in the end established themselves in the finest regions around Salamīya and Ḥimṣ. At the same time, they were forced to confront many tribes of 'Anaza and others that began to arrive after them. They thus lost many of their men and notables, and as I have mentioned, some of them began to incline toward sedentarization.

The Rwāla (from the al-Jlās branch of Muslim)

The name is, again, pronounced with no vowel after the *R*; some transformed the tribe's name by adding a vowel after the *R* and then a long *ā*, so that the name became Ruwāla. Others tended to call it the Rulā, as we observe in the opening line of an ode by the modern poet Qayṣar al-Ma'lūf:

> The Rulā are bedouins whose palaces are tents,
> And whose dwelling places are Ḥamāh and Damascus.

In some Arab towns the form Rulā became a common girl's name.

The Rwāla is the tribe that has come to play the leading role among the tribes in the Syrian Desert, because of the multitude of its clans and the authority of its shaykhs. In the middle of the first half of this century, their shaykh Nūrī al-Sha'lān enjoyed such standing among the mandatory powers and among the shaykhs of the other tribes that it practically made him the unrivaled leader among the bedouin shaykhs. And Alois Musil wrote a book, limited to the Rwāla and their customs, that is used by most researchers on the Rwāla and their traditional practices. Recently, in 1981, William Lancaster wrote a book entitled *The Rwāla Bedouin Today* that discusses the tribe and the evolution of bedouin life. The son of Amīr Nūrī al-Sha'lān, Amīr Nawwāf, could well have become shaykh after him, but the son died before the father and the position of shaykh passed to Nawwāf's son Fawwāz, and after him to his son Mut'ib. Amīr Nāyif, the brother of Fawwāz, became the tribe's deputy in the Chamber of Deputies when Mut'ib was still a juvenile, and enjoyed such standing in the Chamber that most of the deputies from the tribes rallied around him.

Researchers disagree on how many tents this tribe has, as well as how numerous the Rwāla are and the numbers of camels and horses they own. I recall that once I myself asked Shaykh Fawwāz about this, about some of the figures for their numbers that I had read in various books, and about the data in official records during and after the Mandate. He laughed and said:

> Most of these figures they pass on from the shaykhs of the tribes, and these shaykhs provide them with figures that suit their own interests. If the aim was to collect the taxes on camels the shaykhs would reduce the number, and likewise of people; while if the idea was to distribute something, for

Figure 48: Amīr Nāyif al-Sha'lān, one of the shaykhs of the Rwāla. He was a deputy from his tribe and other clans in the Syrian Chamber of Deputies.

> example, they would cite a higher figure. The fact of the matter is that it is not within our power to make an accurate count.

Whatever the truth of the matter may be, the Rwāla are numerically one of the largest tribes, and their subdivisions include about 50 subtribes, each branch known by a particular name, as one can see in the tables recorded by the researchers.

It appears that the Rwāla have no fewer than 100,000 camels. They are the bedouins richest in camels, horses, and sheep, and have the most tents—no fewer than 5000. Burckhardt mentions that there were more horses in Rwāla possession than among any other tribe of ʿAnaza, and says: "In 1809 they defeated a body of six thousand men sent against them by the Pasha of Baghdad."[21] They are also distinguished by the fact that they have preserved the *ʿuṭfa*, the emblem of their might and glory to which we shall devote a special chapter. In the early 1880s, as some mention, the Rwāla comprised 3000 tents or slightly more. One sees them occupying the most expansive tracts in the Syrian Desert and in Najd, and their camel-raising members search for pasturage in the desert of the Ḥamād, reaching right to the heart of the desert in the winter season. Hence, they rank among the tribes that venture the furthest in foraging in the heart of the desert, that adhere the closest to bedouin life, and that keep to desert life and bedouin customs in the greatest numbers.

The Ḥadīdīyīn

The Ḥadīdīyīn are probably the tribe best known to the settled folk. The Syrians in general are fond of a kind of fatty substance in their food that is called *samn* ("clarified butter"). After butter is made from sheep's milk, it is then boiled over a fire and stored. They mix their food with it when it is cooked or fried. This type of *samn* is called "Ḥadīdī butter," *al-samn al-ḥadīdī*, and until recently it was sold in all the markets of geographical Syria, even in the city of Beirut, and Arabic pastry shops were proud to publicize the fact that their products

[21] Burckhardt, *Notes*, I, 6–7.

Figure 49: The *amīrs* Mut'ib and Sulṭān, sons of Amīr Fawwāz al-Sha'lān.

were made with Ḥadīdī butter. The territories of this tribe, which is a large one, lie in northern Syria adjacent to those of the Mawālī, and the consequent wars and conflicts that frequently broke out between the two tribes have come to an end only since the time of the French mandate.

The Ḥadīdīyīn depend for their livelihood on the raising of sheep, and also raise some camels which they use for their migrations. It would come as no surprise to find that they were compelled to raise sheep and to come in close to the villages in the wake of their struggle with ʿAnaza, which was stronger than they were. Such has occurred in many cases in which certain tribes, challenged by stronger ones, are unable to maintain their position in their territories bordering the desert. Other small clans affiliated themselves with the Ḥadīdīyīn, bringing their number of tents to about 4000.[22]

Some of them began to establish farms on the outskirts of the villages; these thus came to be semi-nomadic, and with them the process of sedentarization began. This occurred when they found in agriculture a better source of livelihood than sheep-raising. At the same time, one sees that when tranquility and security came to prevail some of them began to raise camels and were inclined to become absorbed in nomadic life. And in the winter it became necessary for them to venture far out into the heart of the desert in search of pasturage.

Banū Khālid

There is a tribe similar to that of the Ḥadīdīyīn in that they devote themselves to the raising of sheep and have solid contacts with settled folk and settled life. This is the Banū Khālid, which, it is said, migrated from the region of the Aḥsāʾ. They spend the summer period in the region extending from the district of Ḥimṣ to the east of Ḥamāh. Some of them do not reach the distant heart of the desert in the winter, but rather go as far as the limits of Tadmur and the peripheries of the Ḥamād. With the arrival of spring they begin to return to the settled regions to sell the lambs, butter, and wool they have produced, and

[22]See Selah Merrill, *East of the Jordan* (London, 1881), p. 471, where he states that at that date their tents numbered about 3000 or more.

to put their sheep and livestock out to pasture. They do this in the harvested fields belonging to the people of the villages, after reaching an agreement with them and especially with those who had contracted a partnership with them in the sheep or fields. The mother tribe is very large, but scattered in different regions. The Banū Khālid did not rank among the tribes fond of raiding, since they earned their livelihood raising sheep and so favored peace and stability. In the past, however, they were forced to defend themselves against the tribes of ʿAnaza and the Mawālī. They bred horses and raised their sons to be mounted warriors, and in the last century it was within their ability to muster more than 2000 warriors from their ranks.

The Fawāʿira

There is also the tribe of al-Fawāʿira in the region of Ḥimṣ. Like the Banū Khālid, they devote themselves to the raising of sheep and have strong contacts with the settled folk of Ḥimṣ and the villages surrounding it, where they have a partnership agreement with the local folk in the raising of sheep and the proceeds from sheep products. One part of the tribe still searches for pasturage as far as the Ḥamād with the tribe of al-Ḥsāna and other bedouin tribes that raise sheep. In the summer its members spread out around the villages on the desert peripheries east of Ḥimṣ, and indeed, there are those who sometimes reach the plains west of Ḥimṣ among the settled lands in al-Baqayʿa and ʿAkkār. Also like the Banū Khālid, they were forced to defend themselves from attack by the other bedouins—even by their neighbors the Banū Khālid and by the Mawālī in the north. The author of the *Muʿjam qabāʾil al-ʿarab* states that the history of the Fawāʿira from the mid-thirteenth to the mid-fourteenth centuries AH brims with accounts of the catastrophes and misfortunes that have befallen them in their fighting with the tribes of the Rwāla, the Mawālī, the Ḥadīdīyīn, Banū Khālid, the Fidʿān, the Turkī, the Ghiyāth, the tribes of the Jebel Druze, the Ḥwayṭāt of Jordan, and the ʿImārāt of Iraq.[23]

[23]Kaḥḥāla, *Muʿjam qabāʾil al-ʿarab*, III, 932.

The Mawālī

Of non-'Anaza origin, the Mawālī are considered to be one of the earliest tribes to have established themselves in northern Syria, though researchers disagree on their origins and on the number of their tents. They were one of the tribes that played a major role in the conflicts that broke out among the tribes, and, as is evident in the documents written by the English consuls, between the tribes and the Turkish government in the nineteenth century. They are divided into northerners and southerners, and their territories in the summer are in northern Syria from the vicinity of the village of Salamīya to the area north of Aleppo. The number of tents varies in the various accounts from 1200 to 2000, and in the winter their search for pasturage takes them as far as the area north of Tadmur. The most comprehensive account of them is probably that of Waṣfī Zakariyā in his book *'Ashā'ir al-Shām*. He aptly concludes that their origin is to be attributed to the Ḥiyārīyūn of the Āl Muhannā, who enjoyed high standing and authority in the Syrian Desert and its villages and were descended from the Āl al-Faḍl of the fourteenth century AD. Many references to them are to be found in the history of the successive periods which follow, and recently accounts have emerged of their struggle with the tribes that had begun to come to the desert. These included the Banū Khālid, for example, who migrated from the Aḥsā' region; the Mawālī repelled them after killing, it is said, about 100 of their warriors, including 40 young men of marriageable age. Other intruders were the Murr bedouins, who came in from Najd after the Banū Khālid. They too were repulsed.[24] As the number of migrating tribes increased, the Mawālī were finally obliged to abandon some of the southern regions and to withdraw northward. One of their *amīr*s in the late eighteenth century was Muḥammad al-Kharfān, who is mentioned many times in local histories. The French traveler Volney met him when he came to the outskirts of Ḥamāh, and claimed that the sum total of his warriors was estimated by some at 30,000 horsemen.[25] He has probably exaggerated greatly in giving this figure.

---

[24] Zakariyā, *'Ashā'ir al-Shām*, I, 107–108.

[25] *Ibid.*, pp. 108–109. The author is mistaken when he dates his visit to 1099, probably a printer's error.

Banū Ṣakhr

The Banū Ṣakhr are one of the great tribes that migrated from the Ḥijāz to the lands around al-Karak in about the early sixteenth century and clashed with the bedouin tribes already living there. They then shifted to al-Balqā' and came into conflict with its bedouins as well, moved yet again to the outskirts of Gaza, and from there went on to other areas in Jordan, where they finally established themselves in the Jordanian Desert in the regions that used to control the pilgrimage route. Mention of them is made in accounts of pilgrimage caravans in the Arabic sources, where it is described how in the late twelfth/eighteenth century they attacked and plundered the Egyptian caravan and killed its *amīr*. The *amīr* of Gaza thereupon mounted a campaign against them; he killed many of them and seized their camels and horses, so they returned to the Balqā', concluded an alliance with its tribes, and fought the 'Anaza when the latter emerged from Najd.[26] Khayr al-Dīn al-Ziriklī claims that the Banū Ṣakhr used to be able to set out for battle with 3000 armed warriors. Today their territories lie south of Amman.[27]

It seems that after the efforts undertaken by the government of the kingdom of Jordan, some of the tribesmen of Banū Ṣakhr began to acquire certain agricultural lands along the peripheries of the desert, and to build some stone houses. Although the sons of the shaykhs study in the government schools and wear urban-style clothing, as I noticed when I visited them in the 1960s, the tribe remains a long way from definitive commitment to settling down. They have very close contacts with the Jordanian royal family and also with the Saudi ruling house.

Shammar

Shammar is regarded as one of the large tribes of Arabia. Not related to 'Anaza, they clashed with the latter over a long period that lasted until the middle of this century. The tribe is spread out in Najd

[26]Kaḥḥāla, *Mu'jam qabā'il al-'arab*, II, 634–35.
[27]*Ibid.*, in the note to II, 634.

Figure 50: The sons of the shaykh of the Banū Ṣakhr, who at that time were studying in government schools.

and the deserts of Iraq and Syria, the largest part of it established in the desert of Iraq itself. In recent times it has been under the leadership of the al-Yāwir family. The tents of those in Iraq are estimated at no fewer than 10,000, those in Najd have about 5000 tents, and those in the Syrian Desert have a similar number. Among the renowned Shammar shaykhs in Iraq was Shaykh ʿAjīl al-Yāwir, whom I was privileged to meet in Beirut in the first half of this century at the home of the president of the American University. I saw in him a man thoroughly conversant with world political issues, highly articulate, and possessed of an imposing personal character. It was then my good fortune to teach his son, Shaykh Ṣfūq, at the same university before leadership of the tribe passed to him. In the documents to be considered at the end of this book I will discuss some accounts of Shammar in the Syrian Desert and their conflict with the ʿAnaza bedouins.

The ʿAqaydāt

This is a large tribe branching out into many clans established in various regions—in the Dayr al-Zūr and Abū Kamāl regions of the Euphrates valley, in the districts of Ḥimṣ and Ḥamāh in northern Syria, and in the Ghūṭa region around Damascus. These clans have continued to keep the name of the tribe, and some of them have begun to settle down and to acquire agricultural lands. Generally speaking, the 'Aqaydāt rank among the tribes that are richest in sheep and that have the greatest contact with agricultural life, due to the fact that in the lands of the various districts where they establish themselves they in most seasons make their homes near the villages. They number almost 10,000 tents, and their tribal loyalty in general is to the al-Sha'lān family of the Rwāla in the Ghūṭa and to the Mawālī in the district of Ḥamāh.

The Wild 'Alī

There is also the tribe of Wild 'Alī, from the Ḍanā Muslim branch of the 'Anaza. They were among the earliest tribes to come to the Syrian domains, and were under the leadership of the family of Ibn al-Smayr. When their shaykh died they split into two clans, one under the leadership of one of the shaykh's kinsmen and the other under the leadership of Sulṭān al-Ṭayyār. Sulṭān was a bedouin shaykh famous for his courage and heroism in the raiding days prior to the First World War. He was not on good terms with the Rwāla shaykh Nūrī al-Sha'lān, hence his clan did not, as the other clan did, follow the Rwāla when they went in search of pasturage to the Ḥamād. With time this tribe lost much of its standing and joined the clans dependent on the Rwāla. It spread out into many parts of northern Arabia, with the result that some sections of it became bedouins of Najd, others assimilated to the Iraqi tribes, and one part became Syrian. When the *Mu'jam qabā'il al-'arab* turned to give an account of this tribe, it placed it under the name 'Alī. This is a mistake, for it is widely known as the Wild 'Alī. Of its divisions the *Mu'jam* mentions one clan that circulates in Najd, enters Iraq, and has about 800 tents; another that roams from place to place in Jordan and the Ḥijāz; a third affiliated to the Ḥadīdīyīn that has 100 tents; and a fourth of 500 tents that owns 3500 camels and 6000 sheep. This last clan the compendium also divides into sections. It states that when it is time to migrate in search of pasturage the Wild 'Alī affiliate themselves to the Rwāla, marching behind the Rwāla rear guard to Jabal 'Anaza in the Ḥamād or to the Jawf, while in the summer most of them remain in the Jawlān. Finally, Kaḥḥāla takes from Waṣfī Zakariya's *'Ashā'ir al-Shām* the names of the sections of Wild 'Alī as Zakariyā copied them from other sources, as well as the name of a fifth family, numbering 60 tents and based at Manbij (one of the administrative districts of Aleppo), part of which goes in search of pasture to Jabal Bishrī.[28]

[28]See *ibid.*, II, 813–14.

CHAPTER XI

THE TRIBAL ORDER

BEDOUIN LIFE is governed by a particular tribal order. The natural configuration of the Arabian peninsula, surrounded by seas and sands on all sides but the north, and the fact that it encompasses one race of mankind speaking a single language, would suggest that the inhabitants of Arabia all combine together to form a uniform whole. The real situation, however, is otherwise. Since ancient times, and continuing today, there has been regional conflict among the various parts of the area. There has also been conflict among the various tribes, and this too continues. Thus the number of Arabian tribes and clans increased, enmities proliferated, and among the various tribes a particular order came to prevail. Unity came to be confined within the individual tribe, and sometimes within the individual clan isolated in one particular area, a region beyond which it does not move except when forced to do so in search of water and pasture when these are not available in its own region.

The Family: the Foundation of the Tribal Order

The foundation of the tribal order is the family, or *ḥumūla*, and the highest aspiration of the bedouin is to be the father of many sons. He can become more powerful through them, and pride himself in them when they grow up to form a large family of which he is the master (*rabb*). Then when they marry and the family becomes larger, the eldest grandfather becomes head of an extended family, or shaykh of a small clan descended from himself. If, by virtue of his noble-minded generosity, wealth, and courage in battle, he is able to gain the devotion of another family of his relatives and the respect of its members, he becomes shaykh of a larger clan. Among the bedouins, then, the tribal order is their political order—known as long as the bedouins of the desert have been known. According to this system, peoples divide into tribes, the tribe into clans, the clan into sub-tribes, the sub-tribe into sections, and the section into extended families, until we reach the nuclear family and its single head—the foundation of the tribal order.

The bedouins are not familiar with this nomenclature we have mentioned with respect to sub-clans and sections, but they are accustomed to subdivision of this kind. The names used for it differ with the variant usage of certain tribes; one thus finds such terms as *ḥumūla*, *'ashīra*, *badīda*, and *qabīla*. In most cases in which they are few in number, one sees the members of the individual clan living together in one place, migrating and camping together, and searching for water and pasturage together. To lead them they have one shaykh—the one with whom they take refuge when misfortunes strike, their commander (their *'aqīd*) in wars and raids, and on many occasions their judge. Some tribes may become large and gather around a great shaykh, as did the Rwāla and their allies from the tribes of 'Anaza when they confirmed Nūrī al-Sha'lān as shaykh in the days of the First World War.

Descent-Group Solidarity

This special tribal order obliges the members of the tribe to commit themselves to each other through the bond of common descent, which, as we have already mentioned, has an important psychological influence on them. It is from this that there arises that intense group feeling for the tribe, a sense of solidarity that is enjoined by life in the desert and has become the foundation of tribal society for the bedouins.

The tribe branches out into clans (*'ashā'ir*), and the clan into sub-clans (*buṭūn*), sections (*afkhādh*), or sub-groups (*badā'id*, as some call them), down to the nuclear family, as we have mentioned. This is the foundation of tribal society. The bedouin's sense of solidarity is thus directed, before anything else, to his family, which has first claim on his loyalty and love: if he is a minor, to his father and brothers and then paternal uncles; if he is an adult, to his sons and brothers. After his loyalty to his family, he directs his group feeling to the clan or section that includes his family members and uncles and their relatives, and finally to the tribe that encompasses these and their kinfolk.

This feeling of group solidarity or loyalty forges the strongest of bonds with the welfare and interest of the tribe, and the latter has taken on such moral, social, political, and philosophical meaning that everywhere in the desert life is solidly based on tribal foundations, with most of the bedouins' ethical, cultural, political, and social institutions being dictated by the constraints of group feeling and the demands it makes on the individual and on society. In sum, bedouin society has come to focus on the tribal order, in which, to a great extent, individual interest has melted away and become transformed into that of the tribe—it is left to the tribe to determine what the individual's interest and rights are. It is thus the tribe that is the exerciser of rights, and the tribe itself that bears responsibilities. If a tribesman commits a crime against an outsider, for example, his tribe or clan is regarded as the perpetrator of the crime—regardless of whether or not they have taken part in the offense. In this case the tribe is forced to bear the responsibility and hence to defend the guilty party or to help him pay the wergild and compensation. And if anyone commits a crime against a member of the tribe it is taken as if the entire tribe has been wronged, and it has the right to act to protect its reputation and to avenge itself on the perpetrators. So long as the crime or offense occurred within the tribe, it is the clan that stands as the party wronged for one of its members, and likewise at the level of the sub-clan, section, or even the family, which assumes the same role with respect to its members and the protection of its own and their interest, while trying at the same time to redress the injury so that the bonds of tribal unity will not be disrupted.

This sense of solidarity thus encompasses, in the first instance, loyalty to the family, then to the section or sub-tribe, then to the clan, and finally to the tribe. The tribe might sometimes take the further step of an alliance of tribes, but in such a situation no loyalty is required other than assistance in case of war or defense of pasturing grounds or sources of water.

At times it may happen that one of the members of the tribe seeks protection and refuge with some other tribe; his loyalty is thereupon owed to the latter. He may seek refuge with one of that tribe's members, and if this man protects him the refugee proffers his loyalty to him and to his kinsmen, rather than to his own tribe.

The tribe is also generally responsible for its members, and likewise, the family is particularly responsible for its sons. The master of the household bears the primary responsibility and is the highest authority to which one can refer. In this system sons grow up according to the traditional customs inherited from their fathers. They are imitators of their fathers' example, and these traditions enjoin upon them respect for the master of the family, who in some tribes attains such standing that he holds absolute authority over his sons and would not be held accountable even were he to kill one of them. One sees the bedouins in general holding fatherhood in deep respect and reverence, esteeming old age, and obeying their elders.

Tribal Territories in the Tribal Order

Each of the large tribes in bedouin society has territories which are recognized as its own. It does not trespass beyond these territories, and were it to do so it would be subject to attack. These lands it acquired by virtue of its strength, and it maintains control of them by virtue of its strength: when a tribe weakens, a stronger one will incorporate the weaker tribe's territory into its own. Anyone who studies the history of the migration of the bedouin tribes to the Syrian Desert, some of which have reached the agricultural regions, will see how the rights of certain tribes in many of these territories were wrested away and the lands occupied by other tribes. The present-day territories of the Mawālī, for example, were not theirs previously, likewise the territories of the Ḥsāna, the Rwāla, and so forth. But what is important for us to point out here is the fact that for the last 60 years at least, the bedouins have been moving about within recognized, practically demarcated territories, and have the right to camp on any spot within them that is not someone's private property. Naturally, most of these tracts are in desert lands; if they camp in the settled lands they do not camp on agricultural lands without the consent of their owners, and in that case only for a limited time.

When they make camp their tents are usually arranged in lines, each line about 60 meters from the next, so that there will be space for the tent ropes and for the passage of camels between them. A single camp may sometimes be as large as 300 tents, if the available water supplies can support such a number and if the tribe is this large. Among the Rwāla and many of their allies the tents are usually oriented eastward, facing the sun. There are, however, tribes of ʻAnaza that orient their tents northward.

In the desert one rarely sees any crowding, such as we encounter when the bedouins camp near the villages in the settled regions. Usually each *farīq* camps in its own spot. The *farīq* consists of families related to one another in descent, for when a family grows in the number of sons it has, it is customary for the sons, when they erect new tents, to take up living in their own tents near their family in the same row. The same will occur with another large family in another row, and so on, even in a *farīq* of six or seven or more rows, depending on the size of the tribe.

If anyone seeks refuge with the shaykh of the tribe, or with one of its members, and is obliged to live among them for an extended period of time, he asks to pitch his tent near that of his protector and becomes his *jār*, his "protégé" or "neighbor." In the bedouin dialect the protégé is called a *qaṣīr*, and one thus says of himself: "I am the *qaṣīr* of Shaykh So-and-So," for example.

The Master of the Household

The *rabb al-bayt*, or "master of the household," thus has the first and last word; his order admits of no dispute, and all are obliged to obey him. In times past it was he who went on raids and provided for his family, and his standing increased in proportion to his power, courage, noble-minded generosity, and descent. The people of the household are obliged to do his will, but this does not mean that the master of the family rules as a despot or without taking the opinion of his family. In reality, if his wife is a sensible woman he will consult her in most of the matters he decides. Similarly, if his sons have reached the age of majority and have become men, they may well participate in many of the decisions he takes. But the general custom is that the last word belongs to the elder man of the family so long as he remains rationally competent. His decision prevails in the raising of his sons, and if one of them does something wrong his father will reprimand him, but rarely beat him, especially when he has become a boy over ten years of age, or when the boy's father is elderly and will in his coming years need someone to support or take care of him in his old age.

If the people of the tribe want to move from one place to another in search of water and pasturage or in fear of a powerful band of raiders, they gather together around their shaykh and deliberate. When they decide to move, they fix a day for this and the head of every tent notifies his household to prepare for departure. Then, on the morning of the appointed day, they watch the tent of the shaykh. When they see that his household is beginning to strike his tent for departure, the people of the tribe all begin to strike their own tents.

When they reach the land where they are going to camp, they wait until the shaykh selects a place to pitch his tent. Then the tribe spreads out around him and the master of every household selects a place to pitch his own tent.

The Mistress of the Household

In the bedouin household it is the woman who is in charge from a practical standpoint. She is, first of all, the person who is entrusted with the task of pitching the tent. The man selects the location, and she does the work: sometimes she and her daughters finish the task by themselves, at other times she has the help of the herdsman or her sons. She pounds in the tent pegs, ties the guy ropes to them, then spreads out the tent and raises it on the poles. It is she who strikes the tent when the tribe departs, and she who stitches the panels together to make the tent.

Similarly, it is her responsibility to gather camel dung and other things as fuel for the fire, to prepare the food, and to perform other services the household requires, such as weaving cloth for the back of the tent or sewing bags for provisions when the master of the household lacks the money to purchase such items. If he has no herdsman for his camels, she frequently walks with them to water them. She fills the waterskins with water from the rain or flood pools, or from the springs if they have camped close by them, and carries the skins to the tent on her back. She tans hides to make waterskins from them, and pounds down pomegranate peels for the tanning.

Despite all this, however, she is not burdened, as some of her village sisters are, with the execution of heavy and difficult tasks. The excep-

Figure 51: A tent encampment near the settled regions.

tion here is the carrying of water, for some bedouin women carry skins of water the like of which village women would find difficult to handle. Similarly, it must be said that when she is first married the bedouin sees nothing wrong with assisting her in many of the tasks required of her, such as pitching the tent and other tasks, especially when there is love and devotion for her in his heart. In certain situations he himself may rush off to pull up *shīḥ* and other shrubs for fuel, and carry it back to the tent to lighten her labors.

The bedouin woman has few prerogatives which are hers by right. The most important of these is that she may receive a guest in the absence of her husband and is regarded as the master of the household while he is away. It is also she who names her children, and with only rare exceptions this is a right that is hers alone. She usually chooses the name befitting the circumstances under which her child was born. She will name him Sahl ("smooth," "easy") if her delivery was a routine one, or Suhayl if the star Canopus (Arabic *suhayl*) was ascendant, or Maṭar ("rain") if it was a rainy day, or Zā'al ("anger") if she was upset with her husband. In doing so she acts in accordance with the earliest eras of Old Testament tradition, where we see that most names were given depending on the occasion in which the birth occurred.

When the time arrives for a bedouin woman to give birth, her husband does not call for a midwife and it suffices that one of her neighbors or relatives be on hand. Similarly, if the tribe is leaving and she feels labor pains and the birth is imminent, she asks one of her relatives to remain with her and for a short while the two are left behind the pack train with their camels. When the woman gives birth to her child, her relative assists her and then the two set out and catch up to the pack train. It may happen that the woman is traveling only with her husband and sons, with no one accompanying them who can help her when the labor pains begin. In such a case she does by herself everything that is required, ties the baby's umbilical cord herself, mounts her camel, and proceeds with the others.

Most bedouin women carry their children on their backs while they walk. The bedouin woman arranges something like a pouch with two side extensions that she ties under her neck to prevent the pouch from coming open and the baby from falling.

Figure 52: How bedouin women carry their children on their backs.

Marriage

Nomadic life makes it easy for women to intermingle with men, and the bedouin woman is not kept isolated as is her settled sister in the town and even many of her village sisters. Thus, if the clan lives in a single camp site she is familiar with most of the men of the clan who live with her, for they migrate together, camp together, and frequent the bedouin market together. This may hold true more for the bedouins of the north than it does for some of those of the south.

Where marriage is concerned, a woman's first cousin on her father's side has the first right to marry her. If neither he nor any of his brothers have any desire to do so, then she is freed from this restriction and the cousin must make it clear that he has relinquished his right so that she will have the freedom to marry whom she wishes. If the woman does not want to marry her cousin or has fallen in love with another young man, she asks her cousin to give up his right. This he may do, especially if he is not interested in her or is offered a present from the suitor who seeks her hand. If the cousin does not consent, then she will never be able to marry someone she loves unless she runs away with him. In such a case her connection with her tribe is severed and the cousin can avenge himself on her, if he wishes to do so.

The right of the cousin excepted, she is usually free to love and marry whomever she wishes. Most marriages among the bedouins are thus marriages of love—even between cousins—in which the young man and the young woman come to a mutual understanding beforehand. In the introduction to his book on the desert, Glubb speaks of a person he knew who married a girl after a love affair that had lasted for eight years, something that would be practically unheard of, so far as the length of the waiting period is concerned, in the villages and towns. Her family had raised opposition throughout this period, but in the end they were unable to change her mind.[1]

The bride prices vary depending on the tribes and on the families of the bride and groom. But among the bedouins of the north they are generally not excessive, and sometimes the amount is not specified, and left to the inclination and means of the groom. It is customary for the

[1]John Bagot Glubb, *Handbook of the Nomad, Semi-nomad, Semi-sedentary and Sedentary Tribes of Syria* (British Ninth Army, 1942), xii.

groom to give the bride's family a camel, which is usually kept for her, so that if she returns divorced to her family, the camel remains hers. As for those bride prices that, as some have maintained, range as high as tens of camels or a hundred pounds in gold, there is no trace of this today.

Divorce is a right of the man only, but he does not have the right to insult or abuse his wife. If he is not happy with her or her disposition he divorces her, but were he to beat her he would be subject to reproach. Also, if the husband abuses her it is permissible for her to leave his tent and to return to that of her family until the two reconcile or he divorces her. Until he does so, it is not permitted for her to marry someone else.

Because of their poverty there are not many bedouins who marry numerous women, although there are many who take two wives. On many occasions a woman is widowed and so marries another man, becoming a second wife in addition to his first. Whatever the case may be with plural marriages and divorce, especially among wealthy shaykhs coming from well-known families, the prevailing custom is that the first wife, who is in many cases her husband's relative, is not divorced as easily as the other women are. Rather, she remains the first lady of the household and the leadership of the family passes to her eldest son.

There are some tribes that pride themselves on their noble descent and so do not marry their daughters to men from any other tribe. Once when I was in the desert my travels brought me together with a bedouin named Sālim al-Manāḥī, from the ʻArab al-Ghushūm. We began to talk about the tribes, and he maintained that his tribe, which did not number more than twenty tents, forbade their daughters to marry men from any other tribe unless they had been widowed or divorced. He told me that a girl's bride-price was paid to her father, and that if it happened that the father asked for a dowry higher than the man desiring the girl could afford, the best thing for the suitor to do was to take all of his she-camels and make them kneel down in front of the bride's tent, leaving her family to choose whatever they wanted from them. He then said that in this situation custom obliged them to be fair in what they took; they would not take a large number of she-camels since by his action the suitor demonstrated that he was a noble and generous man. He also told me that if a long time passed and a girl remained unmarried, her father would summon together her paternal cousins, both close and remote relatives, and warn them that if none of them had any desire for her she would be free to marry anyone else she wanted. He further claimed that there was one man who married seven of his paternal cousins; he married one, then divorced her and married another, and so on with the others in succession. Among some of the bedouins the divorced woman is not bound by Islamic law's regulation that after divorce a woman must wait a specified period (the *'idda*) before remarrying. Some of them are pregnant when they remarry, and the members of the tribe find no fault in this. If she is not pregnant, then when she is divorced the Rwāla bedouins oblige her to wait at least six months, her *'idda*. If she proves not to be pregnant, then at the end of the *'idda* she has the right to marry another man.[2] The divorced woman also has the right to take with her everything she owns in the tent—furnishings and clothing—and to return to her family. As soon as she reaches her family's tent she is deemed to be divorced and comes under the custody of her father, or if her father has died, her eldest brother, or if she has no immediate family, her nearest male relative. Among the Rwāla bedouins the husband may divorce his wife with an exclusion provision in which he designates a specific man and stipulates that she may not marry him, if he has not demanded the return of the price he has paid to her family.[3] So far as the children of the divorced woman are concerned, they remain with her until the age of seven. After that the father has the right to claim custody, and in most cases this is what occurs.

Boys and Girls

The mother gives her daughters chores to do and teaches them the affairs of the home, i.e. the tent. They help her to fill waterskins and carry them to the tent, to gather firewood, and to tend to other household tasks. In the women's gatherings, bedouin girls learn from their mothers much about the social and personal lives they will lead in the future when they in turn become mistresses of households.

As for the boys, when they become older they frequent the men's circles, where they listen to the discussions of the adults. At the same

[2] *Manners and Customs*, p. 236.
[3] *Ibid.*, p. 233.

Figure 53: A girl carrying a waterskin.

time, they are entrusted with certain camp tasks, such as taking care of the horses and watering them when it is time for them to drink, or taking them to the spring or pool when they have camped close by one.

Before governments began to prevent the bedouins from raiding, boys were sometimes charged with learning to shoot. When he reached the age of fourteen a boy was expected to gain raiding experience; and if he wished to do so, or if he displayed particular ability when put to the test on his first raid, he was in a position, once he reached sixteen, to participate in major raids with the adults. Once I actually saw a band of raiders that included three brothers, one of whom was not yet fifteen years old. A clash occurred between these raiders and government forces; one of the brothers was wounded, and the young one had his camel killed and was captured and imprisoned.

Bedouin Justice

The bedouin has no written law to which to conform, no recorded code to which to refer; nor does he recognize the authority of these written laws, religious or civil, except when they accord with his own unwritten law. This is the law of tradition and custom to which he has adhered for as long as bedouins have known their nomadic way of life. Fortunately for him, Islam arose in a milieu familiar with bedouin life and firmly bonded to it. Hence, it confirmed many of nomadism's institutions and customs.

The bedouin regards this unwritten law with the greatest respect, and is bound by precepts it imposes upon him through institutions dictated by the ways of desert life and the manners and customs of desert folk. Hence, he does not deviate from established custom. If he does, scrupulously administered justice brings him back to the straight path; otherwise, his tribe is obliged to bear on his behalf the penalty prescribed by customary practice.

Among the bedouins, judges consist of a group of generally irreproachable men and seldom make mistakes; and if they do err, they make good their mistakes when they are advised of the proper course of action. One sometimes sees the judge allowing the defeated party to appeal against his decision. I have witnessed some of their judicial sessions: the highest respect is shown for the proceedings, as well as for the opinions of all the litigants if there is evidence to substantiate their views. Some of them informed me that once one of the litigants objected to the ruling of the judge, and the latter replied: "This, my brother, is my ruling in this case. If you cite me a precedent contradicting this ruling and produce witnesses that will corroborate your position by affirming that in a case similar to this one some other judge has ruled differently than I have, then I will retract my verdict and rule in conformity to the precedent."

Even the people of the villages and towns that surround the desert view bedouin justice with respect and hold bedouin judges in high regard. Indeed, they maintain that bedouin justice is the most impartial and fairest of judicial systems.

The law of established tradition and custom is not as harsh as the legal systems we are accustomed to seeing in some primitive ancient nations, or in some advanced modern nations. One who commits murder, for example, is not sentenced to death; rather, he and his kinsmen are sentenced to payment of wergild (the *diya*), which is set at a huge amount. In cases of theft the perpetrator is not sentenced to having his hand cut off, as prescribed by Islamic law, but must return the stolen property and pay a fine. There is no "eye for an eye," no "tooth for a tooth," as in the Mosaic law, but rather payment of a *diya* (or price) set for the value of the eye in compensation for that eye, and the value of the tooth in compensation for the tooth, and so forth. On the other hand, in the case of murder the victim's relative has the right in blood vengeance to exact revenge for his relative on the murderer or on his kinsmen, or to hamstring the horses and camels of the murderer or his family for the first three and a third days after the crime. These in turn return for vengeance of their own, thus resulting in those endless hatreds in men's souls, those acts of vengeance, those continual wars among the tribes for as long as tribes have existed, and those tendencies to seek revenge for the sake of honor and reputation. As the poet Zufar ibn al-Ḥārith al-Kilābī said long ago:

> Pasture may sprout on a moist manured plain,
> But the hatreds in men's souls will always remain.[4]

In judicial proceedings it is important that the plaintiff produce unequivocal proof or witnesses. If there is no clear proof or no witnesses and the accused persists in denying the charge, the judge will oblige him to swear an oath. The principle agrees with Islamic law, which is sometimes based on pre-Islamic bedouin custom, in this case the rule that "the plaintiff must produce the evidence and the accused must take the oath." They have special expressions by which they sometimes swear in their oaths, drawing lines on the ground with a stick as they recite the oath. In some important and serious matters the judge occasionally used to resort to the *bash'a*, or "licking," especially if the plaintiff lacked clear proof and witnesses and requested this. In this procedure the accused was summoned, and if he denied the charge it would be proposed that he submit to the *bash'a*. The plaintiff and the defendant would be brought to the judge's tent, and the latter would proceed to the fire before him in the open space in front of his tent and thrust into it an iron implement similar to the handle of the Arabic roaster in which coffee beans are turned as they roast, or one such handle itself. This consists of an iron rod about 65 centimeters long—round

[4] *Aghānī*, VII, 176.

at the tip, thin, and solid. The tip of this instrument would remain in the fire until it was hot or glowing slightly red. When it was hot, the suspect was told to open his mouth and stick out his tongue so he could touch the rod with it. If the rod left no mark on his tongue he was innocent, otherwise he was guilty. If he proved to be innocent and the judge announced this, girls beside the tent would proceed to call out the *zaghārīd*, shrill trilling calls of joy, to proclaim the news, and would collect compensation for this from the defendant. The plaintiff paid the fee for the ruling. In such a case as this it is obvious that the judge made use of physiognomy and psychology, and based his decision on the conclusions to be drawn from the behavior of the accused, his reaction to the influence of these proceedings, and his composure. If he was innocent, then he would show no fear, his mouth would not dry up or his saliva cease to flow, and hence the quick lick would have no effect on his tongue. But if he was in fact guilty, then naturally he would be afraid, his saliva would dry up, apprehension would show on his face, the hot iron would mark his tongue, and the judgment would go against him. Here we must mention once again that the *bash'a* occurred in court proceedings only on rare occasions. Indeed, the Arab governments have prohibited it wherever possible. There is no need for lengthy study of this subject, since many have already written about it.[5]

The Office of Shaykh Among the Bedouins

The office of shaykh is not one that must necessarily be an inherited post assumed by the son from his father or uncle, though this is usually what occurs. Rather, the customary procedure is that the shaykh makes arrangements on the matter and prepares the kinsman who will succeed him. This is generally one of his sons, or if they are still young, one of his brothers. Disagreement among the candidates for succession sometimes leads to controversy and conflict over the shaykhship and the splitting

[5]See 'Ārif al-'Ārif, *Kitāb al-qaḍā' bayna l-badw* (Jerusalem, 1351/1933); 'Abd al-Jabbār al-Rāwī, *Kitāb al-bādiya* (Baghdad, 1368/1949), pp. 277–302; 'Awdat al-Qusūs, *Kitāb al-qaḍā' al-badawī* (Amman, 1936). See also M.J.L. Hardy, *Blood Feuds and the Payment of Blood Money in the Middle East* (Beirut, 1963), pp. 82–97.

of the tribe, with the tribe generally favoring the strongest contestant, especially if he is endowed with noble traits of character.

It is thus expected that the shaykh be generous when people come to him and camp on the ground around his tent, that he be a valiant warrior when he raids or protects his domains, and that his sense of honor be quickly aroused when his aid and protection is sought. If he possesses these qualities a man has the right to nominate himself for the shaykhship. Indeed, if signs of these qualities manifest themselves in him while he is yet a juvenile, he will gain support and notice before others do and his kinsmen will all prefer him for the shaykhship over other contestants.

In former times the shaykh was accountable to no one from his tribe; he was the legitimate ruler until his tribe renounced his authority. Today, however, most of his powers have been abrogated and have passed to the state on whose lands the tribe lives. Since becoming independent the various Arab states have enacted laws for the tribes, codes that to a certain extent conform to the life and customs of the bedouins. Many Arab states have even established a special bureau, known as the Bureau for Tribal Affairs (*Dā'irat maṣlaḥat al-'ashā'ir*), to supervise matters and affairs pertaining to the bedouins. Thus, if one of them commits a crime, for example, while he is in the towns or villages, he would be judged differently than if he were in the desert.

There can be no doubt that it is difficult for the bedouins to endure submission to urban institutions and legal codes before they have submitted to sedentarization and the life-style of the settled folk.

The Search for Water and Pasturage

One of the requirements of bedouin life is that one roam from place to place. This wandering is not a caprice or the result of mere habit, but an obligation enjoined by desert life. In the first place, water is available in certain rain or flood pools; a tribe has no sooner camped around it and begun to use it than the pool's supply of water is exhausted and the pool dries up, and the people of the tribe are forced to move on to another place where supplies of water are available. Likewise, in an area of a few kilometers surrounding their tents, there may be pasture sufficient for their camels for several days. But when these days have passed, the camels will have eaten up all its plant life and the bedouin

Figure 54: The bedouins, as they search for water and pasturage along the peripheries of the settled lands in early summer.

will be forced to seek pasture lands for his camels elsewhere. This alone explains the migration of the bedouins from one place in the desert to another. The fact of the matter is that plant life is so meager and scattered that a small group of bedouins has no sooner camped in a spot than the camels eat up this greenery, and the tribesmen thus move on to another grazing ground. There may pass a succession of years in which almost no rain falls, and when one sees no sign of vegetation in most parts of the desert. In this situation the bedouins' camels live on what little remains of the dry plants left from past years; the camels become emaciated, and many of them die. If pasturage disappears from its grazing grounds, the tribe may be forced to migrate to lands far away from its own territories or those where it usually camps. Before the First World War, a tribe in such a situation would raid the lands in which it found grazing grounds and either join the current occupants or drive them out of the area and occupy it. In the last 50 years it has become necessary for a tribe to seek the permission of the other tribes to migrate into their territories. The domains of the second tribe may lie in a neighboring country, in which case, as I have already mentioned, the men of the tribe leave it to their country to ask the other's permission for them to move onto its territories.

The bedouin does not generally remain in one spot for a long time, even in periods of rain and abundance and on fertile lands. Camels may spoil a pasture if kept in a limited area; so the bedouin moves on to another place where the pasture is untouched, and so keeps wandering from one spot to another.

The Greater Quest—if we are allowed this expression—takes place in the winter and summer seasons. In general terms, one sees the bedouins leaving the desert in the summer when the heat becomes intense and water supplies dry up, and heading for the settled regions—or the lands adjoining the settled areas. They spend the entire summer there and wait until the rains fall in the autumn and some of the rain and flood pools in the desert fill up, and then begin to return to the desert. Each tribe has a *dīra*, or recognized territories within which it wanders throughout the winter and spring seasons until the water supplies dry up. The bedouins then head for the lands adjoining the settled regions and the oases that lie along the desert peripheries. One must not suppose that whenever the bedouin penetrates deep into the

Figure 55: Returning to the desert at the beginning of winter.

heart of the desert he ends his journey at lands mostly parched, full of sands, and possessed of very little pasturage and water. The land of Najd, which lies in almost the center of Arabia, is one of the areas most amply supplied with water, and in the oases of the Aḥsā' there are springs practically equal to the fullest flowing springs in Lebanon. I saw the spring of Umm Sab' in the Hufūf with my own eyes, and branching off from this spring were seven canals each of which would drown a young boy who did not know how to swim. In the land of the Nafūd, for example, there is, despite the vast extent of its sands, such plant life as to render it, in the opinion of one of the explorers, the best of places for raising horses. Quoting Wilfrid Blunt, Kiernan says that when the former visited the Nafūd region and saw how much plant life there was there, it finally solved for him the puzzle of how horses could live in the heart of Arabia.[6]

Whatever the case may be, when the tribe decides to seek new grazing and watering lands, it does not proceed there before making sure that the water and pasturage there are better than that in the land

[6]Kiernan, p. 281.

they currently occupy. For this reason, then, one will see the shaykhs, before they move on, sending out scouts to explore the land for the tribe. On many occasions the large tribes count on the assistance of the tribe of Ṣlayb when the move is to be to a distant land, the Ṣlaybīs providing them with information on the area and about its pasturage and water supplies.

CHAPTER XII

THE BEDOUIN CHARACTER

THERE IS NO TASK more difficult than that of defining precisely the distinguishing characteristics of a particular people and describing their qualities of character with the accuracy required in a scholarly study. The researcher may misrepresent the character traits of the Arab bedouin if he relies heavily on the statements of some of the Arabs and European explorers who studied these features, since in both groups there are those who disagree with one another on many points which they describe, as well as much which represents misleading ethnic stereotyping. Here I shall attempt to give an account, as close as possible to where I consider the truth to lie, of the most prominent features of the character of the bedouin in general, and especially of the influence he has had on the life of the settled folk today.

Endurance and Patience

In general, the bedouin is calm and even-tempered, contrary to the claims of some European travelers, and despite the manifest speed with which he is overcome when he rushes forth to seek and take vengeance on one who wrongs him, as we shall see, in order to protect the honor and dignity of his family. It is probably the desert environment that has taught him endurance and tolerance of hardship; and indeed, he has probably learned endurance from the camel, which shares his life and nourishes him with its milk. Proverbs were based on the endurance of the camel, since it was one of the few animals that could endure life in the desert, going without water for days on end. When the quality of endurance and patience (*ṣabr*) was endowed with one of the greatest descriptive epithets in the Arabic language, the term used to do so was derived from the name of the camel, *jamal*. Just as the word for beauty, *jamāl*, is so derived, as we have seen in the chapter on the camel, the quality of superlative endurance and patience is called *ṣabr jamīl*, "fair patience." Islam laid great stress on the quality of *ṣabr*, and the Qur'ān promotes it in more than a hundred places and compares it with all that is good, virtuous, and highly regarded. In Sūrat al-Baqara (2), vs. 153, one reads concerning patience: "O you who believe, for aid rely upon patience and prayer; for God is with the patient ones." In Sūrat Āl 'Imrān (3), vs. 200, we find: "Be patient, vie with others in it, be steadfast, and be mindful of God." In Sūrat al-Ma'ārij (70), vs. 5, one is told: "Reflect the quality of fair patience;" and in Sūrat Yūsuf (12), vss. 18 and 83: "Your souls have tempted you to a certain deed, so come, fair patience." In Sūrat al-Naḥl (16), vs. 126, we find: "If you are patient, better it is for those who are so." This attribute in the soul of the righteous man so appealed to the Arabs that they gave sons the name Ṣābir ("the patient one"), a custom widespread among both the bedouins and the settled folk.

Once I saw a bedouin raider who had fallen wounded, struck by a bullet that passed through his foot and killed his she-camel. He pretended to be dead, then at night arose, covered his wound with ashes, and bandaged it. Summoning all his powers of endurance, he walked by night for three days on one foot, dragging the other and going without water or food until he reached a village about ten kilometers from the place where he had fallen. Such is defiance, in the face of adversity, with endurance and obstinacy. Were the bedouin not so composed, patient, and capable of enduring so much that is harmful to him, he would probably be unable to find satisfaction in the life that he leads. Indeed, because of this one European explorer went so far as to describe the bedouin as characterized by "a great obtuseness in the general nervous sensibility."[1] At the same time he is sharp-witted and quick to make up his mind, especially where intuitive matters are concerned. Once I saw a bedouin woman in a large truck with village-folk passengers who began to mock her and the bedouins, and she spontaneously responded with a single well-chosen expression so powerful in its import and so

[1]Palgrave, II, 35.

eloquently phrased that it left them all dumbfounded and silenced. The bedouin is also a simple and innocent man sometimes carried away by his innate disposition to believe the superstitious tales and fables that are told to him. And many a time he changes sides because of his weakness: depending on the circumstances, one day he sides with you, but the next day he will side with someone else if he realizes that it is more to his benefit to do so.

Courage and Combat

The bedouin is a reckless and brave man who in former times was raised to love looting and plunder and the undertaking of raids for the sake of such brigandage. It is in the nature of bedouin life to build courage in a man; and as Ibn Khaldūn asserted in his *Muqaddima*, the bedouin folk are more courageous than the settled folk.[2] Deprivation and poverty are probably the two factors that in the first instance impel the bedouin to this, for there is nothing in the desert to gain him a prosperous livelihood. In times past, when there was a succession of years in which no rain fell, drought and dearth spread over the land, and the livestock upon which he lived died, then he would recklessly turn to raiding and head off for regions in which he could pounce upon the livestock of others.

The love of raiding became so deeply engrained in his soul that for him it became like a sport engaged in for enjoyment, while it simultaneously provided a source of livelihood. He would plunder other groups belonging to some other tribe, but if he found none of these he would raid one of the other clans of his own tribe. Describing his people's love of raiding and mounted attack on the tribes, including that of his own brother if no other target were to be found, a bedouin poet long ago said:

> On the camp of Ḍibāb and Ḍabba fell the force of our raid;
> For verily, the debt of a man's fate must be paid.
> And sometimes our onslaughts may turn on our brother,
> Should quest for a target avail us no other.[3]

---

[2] *Muqaddima*, I, 231.

[3] Abū Tammām, *Ḥamāsa*, I, 136.

Hence the bedouin's fondness for battle and raiding—not a love of killing and bloodshed, but rather a predilection for plundering the property of others, even if they be from another clan of his own tribe. And hence the sporting way he enjoyed this life style: for indeed, if he emerged victorious and found it easy to plunder and pillage someone else, the keenness of his desire for the booty waned and he would distribute shares of it to his kinsmen and companions.

It is this that explains the low level of fatalities in the early wars between the various Arab tribes in pre-Islamic times. This has been noticed by researchers on pre-Islamic Arab history, especially those who studied their popular folklore and the early literature describing their heroic wars. We are moved by the descriptions of battles in some of the narratives of the ancients, and by the accounts of hit-and-run tactics and other clashes, but we marvel at the low number of fatalities, even in wars (such as the War of al-Basūs) that they say lasted about 40 years.[4] The same holds true for them in the raiding campaigns they staged, even in the early years of this century.

Many years ago one of the bedouins told me that a bedouin mounted on his charger may be following an adversary fleeing before him on his horse, and reach the point where he can run him through with his lance, reach him with his sword, or slay him with a bullet. But rather than kill him, he asks him to surrender and offers to spare his life if he will hand over his horse.

Individuality

The bedouin loves to be free and to keep himself clear of the systems of regulations that fetter mankind. He cherishes his independence to such an extent that no one holds authority over him, not even his shaykh. He does defer to the shaykh to the limited extent required to uphold the latter's honor, and harbors a feeling of devotion for him since the shaykh symbolizes his own pride and freedom. But if the shaykh oversteps his bounds and inclines toward behaving like an autocrat, the bedouin will give up obeying him if he can, or will oppose his shaykh and defend his freedom as best he can verbally. I actually attended a council session

[4]See Reynold A. Nicholson, *A Literary History of the Arabs* (London, 1907), pp. 55–60.

in the tent of Amīr Fawwāz al-Sha'lān, and at that session there was a bedouin who had come to defend himself on some matter. Because I was there with them the *amīr* tried to prevent him from speaking and began telling him *Bass*! *Bass*!, "Enough! Enough!," but the bedouin persisted. The bedouins used to pay a tax on their camels to the shaykh each year, and the *amīr* suspected that this man had lied in giving the number of his camels when paying his taxes. Amīr Fawwāz finally allowed him to speak, so the bedouin began to do so in daring words and to claim that he had only sixteen camels. The *amīr* replied: "You lie! They are eighteen." At this the bedouin responded to the *amīr*: "No, by God!, I have not lied, and you have only to send your slave this very instant in order to verify which of us is the liar," a reply which was as much as to say that it was either the *amīr* or the tax collector who was the one not telling the truth. Fawwāz did not become angry, but rather responded: "If you have told the truth I shall exempt you even from the tax on the sixteen, and if you have lied you shall pay the tax at double the rate this year." From witnesses present at the session it proved in the end that the bedouin owned only sixteen, and he was exempted from paying the tax on his camels that year.

Generosity

The bedouin is a generous man who loves to entertain guests and prides himself on doing so, and when he invites someone to be his guest he is not niggardly with anything he has. He loathes stinginess in people and extols those who are generous. This trait of bedouin character is probably attributable to the fact that the bedouin originated in an environment shaped by want and deprivation. The traveling stranger was not able to carry enough to sustain him on his wanderings, hence it became necessary for him to stop as the guest of others. The practice became a reciprocal one and a custom commonly recognized among the bedouins, and with time generosity became a habit so deeply rooted in the bedouin's soul that it became a disgrace for one of them not to be seen as a generous and hospitable host. I remember one time when I was in the desert with a group of people from my town. We called at a camp in one tent of which there was a circle of men sitting around coffee and a fire, and on our way there we passed in front of the tent of a woman, who rebuked us for passing in front of her tent without stopping, despite the fact that at the time there was no man in her tent. We proceeded to offer her the excuse that we saw no man at her tent, and she replied: "If you were to stop I would call my husband from that meeting session, so you could be his guests." Bedouin narratives and folk tales confirm this character trait of theirs, which is so strongly impressed upon them that it has become an attribute inseparable from them and a general habit for which they are well known. Their poetry since remotest antiquity brims with accounts of their generosity, to the point that some accounts are almost beyond belief.

There is no room here for relating the many extraordinary tales told concerning their generosity by the town, village, and settled folk who frequent their camps. The history of the Arab bedouins teems with accounts of generosity and generous men, and there is probably no other nation whose literature extols profuse generosity and the giving of presents to guests to the extent that Arabic literature, and especially Arabic poetry, does. Of the Arab bedouin it was even said:

> Astride the way their tents they raise
> At feeding guests they aim to duel.
> Their hearth near starts on its own to blaze,
> With zeal for the guest-meal as its fuel.[5]

In praising the generosity for which the Ghassānids were known, Ḥassān ibn Thābit said:

> So visited they were that no dog did growl or bark at all;
> They asked not if a stranger approached and came to call.[6]

Qays ibn 'Āṣim refused to eat alone. They claim that he married the daughter of "Zayd of the horsemen" (i.e. Zayd ibn Muhalhal al-Ṭā'ī); and when, in the evening of the day after their wedding night, she brought him something to eat, he said: "Where is my dinner companion?" She did not know what he wanted, so he composed a poem, saying:

[5]Two well-known verses the author of which I have been unable to ascertain.

[6]Ḥassān ibn Thābit, *Dīwān*, edited with commentary by Muḥammad al-'Inānī (Cairo, AH 1331), p. 247.

O daughter of 'Abd Allāh, O daughter of Mālik,
O daughter of he with two cloaks and bay mare:
When you prepare my meal, make sure you entreat
A dinner companion—alone I'll not eat;
Any man passing or in a tent near,
For later tales' censure—'tis that which I fear.

So she sent a witty slave-girl of hers to look for a dinner companion, and the girl also composed a poem, saying to [a man she found]:

Qays refuses to taste any food from the pan
Without a companion — what a generous man!
Alive you'd be blessed for your kindness profound,
And also when dead beneath stones in a mound.[7]

Probably the most eloquent image evoked of generosity in Arabic poetry is that composed by Ṭarafa ibn al-'Abd. Here he writes of how he rose and went with his sword to his she-camels resting on the ground. The animals shied away from him because they knew that he would not suddenly confront them with sword in hand unless to slaughter some of them for his guests. When he began to hamstring the she-camels that had run off and fled and was about to cut their throats, his guests tried to stop him. But one of Ṭarafa's companions replied to them, saying: "Leave him be. If you raise objections with him he will hamstring and slaughter even more of them. How he reaps the benefit of his camels is for him to decide." This is when he said:

My camels kneeling through the night,
Now rose and shied, so much afraid
To find themselves facing the plight
Of my approach with naked blade.

and so forth until he has his companion saying:

Leave him; their use is up to him to say
Lest he spare not even those kneeling far away.[8]

---

[7] *Aghānī*, XII, 150–51.
[8] Al-Zawzanī, *Sharḥ al-mu'allaqāt*, p. 68.

The generosity of the sheep-herding bedouins is no less than that of those who keep camels. A poet of theirs claims that he reduced his sheep to such a desperate situation that the animals would have preferred to be tended by the wolf rather than by their generous herdsman. The reason for this was that their herdsman would slaughter some of them every day, while the wolf would come to visit them only once in a very long time:

I left my sheep wishing for the wolf to tend their needs
And yearning not to see me while any soul has life.
Through long times but once the wolf comes and feeds,
While every day they see my hand on my slaughtering knife.[9]

Indeed, the Arab bedouin's sense of generosity even induces him to humble himself before the guest, like a slave in front of his master or like a servant when he unpacks his tent. Al-Muqanna' al-Kindī said:

The servant of the guest I am while at my tent he'll stay;
In no other situation at all do I have this role to play.[10]

Al-Hudhlūl ibn Ka'b al-'Anbarī said, in addressing his wife:

By your father's good life, a servant I'll surely be
To my guest, but if mounted then a warrior you'll see.[11]

In the history of the Arabs generally, and of the bedouins in particular, the worst thing for which a man can be ridiculed is greed and niggardliness; in the bedouin's eyes, he can be blamed for nothing more repulsive than this. At the same time, the best thing for which he can be praised is generosity. Most of the European explorers who have frequented the desert lands in recent centuries have recognized the generosity of the bedouins and have marveled at this trait in the disposition of the bedouin, who at the same time is fond of raiding and the booty and plunder that it gains him.

[9]Verses by an Arab poet in the *Ḥamāsa*, II, 245.
[10]*Ibid.*, II, 34.
[11]*Ibid.*, I, 296.

When you are a bedouin's guest, it is his custom to take it upon himself actually to wait upon you, and when you partake of his food to make sure that you get the finest meat from the carcass of the animal he has slaughtered for you. If he is unable to slaughter an animal, then he will offer you the best dates and butter that he has stored away. It is perhaps worth recording here that the contacts that some of the bedouins made with settled life have today begun to change many of the forms of their customs, or at least the customs of some of them.

Solicitude for Kin and Protégés

Next to the bedouin's love of generosity is his solicitude for the welfare of those close to him, a sentiment which in its broad sense includes kinship in the home or protection of anyone seeking refuge with him. This distinctive trait was known among the Arabs both before and after the rise of Islam; it is mentioned that the Arab Prophet used to place so much stress upon protection and respect for the commitment to protect others that he once said: "[The angel] Gabriel kept exhorting me to do well by the protégé, until I considered that he was going to give the latter a share of the inheritance."[12] It would come as no surprise were it to prove that a commitment to such protection (*jīra*) was the first custom that arose to protect the weak from the strong and to put a limit on the exercise of violent force and acts of vengeance. If someone committed a crime, whether intentionally or unintentionally, and was not strong enough to confront his pursuers and repel them, he would take refuge with a powerful benefactor to seek his protection. At this point the law of the desert—the law of tradition and customary practice—obliged the man whose protection had been sought to grant such protection, even if the one seeking it was from another tribe, and even if the fugitive was one of those upon whom the protector himself had the right to take vengeance.

It is thus also possible for us to maintain that no other nation acknowledges the sanctity of the covenant of protection as do the Arabs, and the bedouins in particular. In the literature of no other nation I know is such commitment to protect others raised to the grand and glorious levels that are conceded to it by nomadism and the Arab spirit

[12] A prophetic tradition.

in Arabic literature. As Ḥātim al-Ṭā'ī, their poet famous for his generosity, said of the covenant of protection and generosity together:

> If only two things I had, O Umm Mālik,
> T'would be for my protégé to take his pick.[13]

Indeed, the Arabs used to boast that the protégé, while under their protection, would become as immune and invulnerable to harm as the ibex on a towering mountaintop where no one could reach it. In praising the tribe of Banū Shaybān for generosity and protection of the protégé, Yazīd al-Sakūnī said:

> Such generosity they show in a sterile barren year
> That their protégé knows well he has nothing to fear.
> He resembles the ibex that atop the towering peak rests,
> While far beneath him one finds the griffons' nests.[14]

Bedouin Eloquence

The bedouin is furthermore an eloquent man who loves to talk, is stimulated by discussion, and speaks very well, holding forth with superb coherence when the situation calls for well thought-out speech. When written without voweling or inflection, some of his speech comes closest of all in its grammatical construction to the classical Arabic, or *fuṣḥā*. When we hear him, however, what distances his Arabic from classical Arabic is the way he pronounces the words. He says *manta rāyiḥ* when he means *lasta rā'iḥan*, "you are not going," the original form being *mā anta rā'iḥ*. He also says *jayf antā* for *kayfa anta*, "how are you," as well as *'asāj ṭīb* for *'asāka ṭayyib*, "I hope you are well," and *mālī bihā shān* for *mā lī bihā sha'n*, "I have nothing to do with it." But he also uses expressions to which we find nothing analogous

[13] *Aghānī*, X, 127, 128.

[14] *Ḥamāsa*, I, 115. In this work Abū Tammām devotes a large number of his poetic selections to verse in praise of generosity and munificent individuals, amounting to 111 pages in his chapter on guests and panegyric. This indicates the esteem with which the Arabs viewed generosity and generous individuals. [In these particular verses the sense is that the protégé is so well treated that he forgets that he is not a member of the family.]

in the classical Arabic dictionaries, such as *hīn* in the sense of *hunā*, "here," to cite one of many possible examples, and so says *ilḥaq li-hīn*, "come here." At the same time, he uses classical expressions which we find in the dictionaries but do not use ourselves, for example, *fihr* in the sense of *ḥajar*, "stone." I think that there is ample room for undertaking a scholarly study on sentence structures and terms among the bedouins and their proximity to the styles used by the writers of classical Arabic with respect to their conciseness of expression and the classical elements in their phrases and individual terms. Long ago the bedouins were renowned for their eloquent Arabic; and in the chapter on "The Speech of the Bedouins" in his *'Iqd*, Ibn 'Abd Rabbih devoted a large section of some scores of pages to the eloquent and concise way in which bedouins—both women and men—spoke Arabic.[15]

Loyalty

The bedouin is known for his loyalty, but his loyalty is before all else to his tribe or to its shaykh (since he is the tribe's leader), or to someone he esteems and with whom he has some connection. He cleaves to his tribe with the utmost devotion, whether in right or wrong:

> I am but of the clan of Ghazīya, going astray
> If it errs, and led right if it keeps to the way.[16]

Anyone who reads, for example, Jarvis' book *Arab Command* on the life of Peake Pasha, especially the last chapter, on how the man was bidden farewell by his comrades from among the bedouins under his command, will grasp the extent of the love and devotion that they felt for him. The bedouin is also a faithful man who appreciates and remembers a good turn and fosters deep affection toward one who treats him similarly.

At the same time, however, he is capricious in his political inclinations and has no loyalty to any political principle or party. Hence, we sometimes see him siding with the strong so long as he remains strong; but if he finds that the latter has become weak or has been put to flight, he will abandon him and perhaps help to finish him off. This pattern

[15]See Ibn 'Abd Rabbih, *Al-'Iqd (al-farīd)*, III, 418–98.

[16]Abū Tammām, *Ḥamāsa*, I, 343.

has manifested itself in many of the contacts the bedouin tribes had with the ruling authorities in the Arab lands during the final decades of Turkish rule, and in the days of al-Ḥusayn's revolt and the Mandate. Who knows; this characteristic trait in the bedouin's soul may be attributable to his esteem for and glorification of strength.

Circumspection

The bedouin is circumspect and reserved. He does not divulge information he has unless he knows that what he says will cause no one harm; when he speaks in a discussion session he does not raise his voice, as many of the village folk do; and he seldom laughs in public or private sessions. I do not remember having ever in my life heard loud boisterous laughter in any tent, though it may be that bedouins do laugh this way among themselves. If the bedouin laughs, he only does so in a scoffing and scornful fashion and is not fond of witticisms or inclined to indulge in amusement to relieve a tense situation. In most cases, then, the bedouin meeting session is calm and composed. Shaykhs are particularly distinguished by their composure, as I myself noticed in the council sessions of Shaykh ʿAjīl al-Yāwir, Shaykh Ṭrād al-Milḥim, Amīr Nāyif al-Shaʿlān, Amīr Fawwāz and his sons, Shaykh Hāyil al-Zayd, and others. It was known of Shaykh Amīr Nūrī al-Shaʿlān that he was never seen laughing in any meeting session, and one of the Arab bedouins informed me that the *amīr* was nicknamed or described as *aḥmar al-ʿayn*, "red-eyed," or "one with red unresponsive eyes," referring to his perpetually composed and austere countenance.

The bedouin is a man of self-esteem and is proud of his ancestry and his nomadic way of life, but he is not arrogant. Some of the good qualities that distinguish him—generosity, dignity, manly virtue, and courage—are probably attributable to his sense of pride in himself. He wants it to be said of him that he is a generous, courageous, and heroic man, a source of help in one's hour of need. If you were to seek refuge and protection with him while a fugitive under pursuit, he would protect, shelter, and defend you, for you would be under his wing, *bi-wajhihi* (lit. "in his face"), as they say, and he would be obliged to protect you. The bedouin also has such a keenly discriminating eye that some claim that he can identify a boy's father from a mere glance at the child's features. He is also patient, as I have already mentioned, and his patience is unequaled save by that of his camels; it is as if they were created for hardship and distress and exist together so that the one might find solace in the other.

The bedouin is fond of the bedouin poetry (known among them as the *qaṣīd*) that he composes in his own special style, in which he differs from the style of classical Arabic poetry and from the common poems familiar in the village and urban milieus. An unusual aspect of this bedouin poetry is that many of the poets of the villages near the desert imitate it in pronunciation and vocabulary, a fact that indicates the power of bedouin life and its cultural domination of the settled folk. It is clear that the *amīr*s and shaykhs do not consider themselves above composing *qaṣīd*s. In his book on the Rwāla and their customs, Musil quotes a *qaṣīd* by Amīr Nūrī al-Sha'lān himself, a poem he and his scribe composed in praise of Musil and his learning and in which the *amīr* spoke in glowing terms of Musil's knowledge of the affairs and conditions of bedouin life.[17] We shall come to this poem when we turn to study poetry among the bedouins. But here we must mention that when the bedouin composes a *qaṣīd* he does not do so for the sake of financial gain, as the bedouin of Ṣlayb does or as some of the poets frequenting the courts of kings used to do. The bedouin poet despises those who compose verse for profit.

The Bedouin's Zeal for Vengeance

Among the particular features of the bedouin's character is his passion for vengeance and the fiery zeal with which he rushes forth to avenge himself upon one who has wronged him, especially if one of his kinsmen or family members has been killed. In such a case he will furiously rush forth to quench his thirst for blood and to kill, if he cannot lay hands on the killer himself, anyone he sees from the killer's family or clan. His right to avenge himself is not limited to the killer and his family, but rather extends beyond them to the killer's relatives as far removed in kinship from him as five generations, so as to include grandfathers or grandsons and paternal cousins. In the law of the desert, known through tradition and custom, this vengeance period lasts for three full days and the first third of the fourth! In this period one sees the seeker

[17] *Manners and Customs*, pp. 289–92.

of vengeance trying to kill any relative of the killer who falls into his hands, or any camels or horses of theirs that he sees—this if mediators do not intercede and gain the avenger satisfaction through the payment of wergild or the surrender of the killer in order to spare the blood of the others. If no kind of agreement is reached and none of the slain man's relatives is able to avenge his death, then they feel shamed and disgraced for not having exacted vengeance and a hateful yearning to do so long persists in their hearts, as we have already mentioned concerning one of the poets:

> Pasture may sprout on a moist manured plain,
> But the hatreds in men's souls will always remain.[18]

The spirit of retaliation and vengeance has manifested itself in the souls of the descendents of the Semitic peoples, including the Arabs, since remotest antiquity, and this has had its influence on the laws that have been established. These enjoined an eye for an eye, a tooth for a tooth, and killing for the killer, and it became a disgrace for one to be bereaved unless he avenged himself and exacted vengeance for his lost kinsman. Anyone who examines the history of the Arabs in both pre-Islamic and Islamic times will understand what an influence the love of vengeance has had on their souls. Many of the battle-days (*ayyām*) of the Arab tribes in pre-Islamic times were retaliation for incidents that had occurred, such as the War of al-Basūs, the killing of Kulayb, and how al-Muhalhil set out to exact vengeance from Jassās and his tribe, resulting in a war that lasted 40 years, as they claimed. The same occurred in Islamic times. When 'Uthmān ibn 'Affān was killed, Ḥassān ibn Thābit began to appeal for vengeance by saying:

> They slaughtered a grey-beard marked by prostration in prayer.
> Who interrupted the night in praising God and reading Qur'ān.
> In their homes, you'll soon hear the call resounding there:
> "God is most great, O for the vengeance for 'Uthmān."[19]

[18] *Aghānī*, VII, 176.

[19] Ibn 'Abd Rabbih, *Al-'Iqd (al-farīd)*, IV, 284, 298; Ḥassān ibn Thābit, *Dīwān* (al-'Inānī), p. 339.

Indeed, the assassination of the caliph 'Alī ibn Abī Ṭālib would probably not have occurred had it not been for the spirit of vengeance in the heart of Qaṭām bint al-Shijna, the Khārijite woman who, as they claim, enticed 'Abd al-Raḥmān ibn Muljam to assassinate 'Alī because her father and brother had been killed. It is as if the Arab cannot tolerate harm and for this reason refuses either to suffer it or to inflict it. Through the mouth of al-Faḍl ibn 'Abbas, one of the poets of Banū Hāshim addresses the Umayyads and says:

> Go easy on the tribe of our uncles, and easy on our masters;
> Do not exhume that between us which has been laid to rest.
> And do not expect to be honored by us while you deride us,
> Or expect us to spare you while we suffer at your behest.[20]

Among the tales that illustrate the penchant for vengeance in the Arab's soul is that related about Qays ibn al-Khuṭaym. A man from the tribe of 'Abd al-Qays attacked and killed Qays' father al-Khuṭaym, Qays being a young boy at the time. Previously, Qays' grandfather 'Adī had also been killed, and al-Khuṭaym, his son, had been unable to exact vengeance for him. Qays' mother feared that her son would seek to avenge both his father and his grandfather and so, in turn, also perish, so she dug two graves for the father and grandfather in the open area beside the tent. Qays suspected no foul play in the matter and presumed that the two had not been killed, but rather had died natural deaths. The boy grew to become a strong man with powerful arms; and one day, when he was fighting with a young man from the tribe of Banū Ẓafar, the youth said to him: "By God, it would have been better for you had you directed the strength of your arms against the one who killed your father and grandfather." So Qays went to his mother and implored her to tell him what had happened; and when she saw how earnest he was about the matter, she told him. And from that time onward he never stopped seeking to avenge them until he finally did so. On this subject there is poetry of his in which he says:

> I stabbed the son of 'Abd al-Qays an avenger's blow
> That opened a cleft where light showed the way to go.

[20] Abū Tammām, *Ḥamāsa*, I, 82.

and then:

> Vengeance is mine for al-Khuṭaym and also for ʿAdī;
> Forsake I not an elder's charge when one is put to me.[21]

Thus one sees the fondness of revenge in the bedouin soul and the relish and pride he feels when he takes vengeance and "slakes his thirst for revenge," as they say; and were it not for the fact that vengeance-taking became a trait of the Arab character, it would be possible to consider this issue among the bedouins in the chapter on bedouin law.

What applies to the bedouin of former times still holds true today. In 1917, when I was a boy during the First World War, I heard of an incident that occurred near al-Qaryatayn. Raiders from the al-ʿAbd Allāh tribe attacked the two villages of al-Sukhna and Arak, between Tadmur and Dayr al-Zūr, plundered them of as much of their furnishings and household effects as they could, and headed back to their camps in the south. The Turkish authorities had placed an army garrison in al-Qaryatayn to protect the area from attacks by the bedouins accompanying Lawrence, should he attempt to enter Syria via Tadmur, and the garrison received news of this raiding party and its southward march. From one of the well-informed men in al-Qaryatayn, the commander of the garrison knew that the raiders would have to water their animals at a well known as Bi'r Ḥufayyir, located a few kilometers from al-Qaryatayn and surrounded by a chain of hills that runs between the town and the well. There the army could conceal itself behind the hills, so that when the raiders arrived at the well and began to water their animals the army would attack them by surprise and wipe them out.

The army included Circassian cavalry, Turkish infantry, and Arabs from settled areas. When the raiders arrived, they had no sooner begun to water their animals, making the camels kneel down and beginning to draw water, then the cavalry charged around from behind the hills to cut them off from the rear and the infantry began to shoot at them from the hills. A number of the bedouin raiders were killed, and the others surrendered. The next day, the people of al-Qaryatayn hastened to the battlefield to collect what they could of the plundered household effects, some of which were still lying around the well and on the hills

[21] *Ibid.*, I, 62–63.

where some of the bedouins had tried to flee and had been killed. Some days later the men of the raiders' tribe came to know of what the people of al-Qaryatayn had done and so remembered them in connection with the battle. Unable to avenge themselves on either the Turks or the Circassians, they resolved to take vengeance on the people of al-Qaryatayn. In fact, several months later they were able to catch sight of six of them out in the desert between al-Qaryatayn and Tadmur, and killed five of them while they slept; only a boy escaped to report what had happened to his innocent comrades.

Vengeance also enters into their bedouin folk tales. Woven into the bedouin tale one sees a love story between the hero of the tale and a girl whose father or brother has been killed by a well-known individual who has taken refuge with another tribe or has fled to a distant land. It is therefore stipulated that before the wedding the girl's beloved must take vengeance for her on the one who killed her relative. The hero does so, and the wedding takes place. Or alternatively, one of her kinsmen is a prisoner in the hands of a group of her tribe's enemies; it is thus stipulated that in return for her marriage to him, the one seeking her hand must try to free her kinsman from captivity and take revenge on his captors.

Morality

This leads me to comment on the behavior the bedouins generally display when it comes to morals and sexual relations. In the main, the bedouins differ significantly from the settled folk only in that they have a more pronounced sense of honor and are more protective of their good reputations. Few bedouin girls remain unmarried, and although in many cases it is easy for the bedouin to be alone with certain women, in general he regards the woman as a person whose sacred honor must be safeguarded, even if she is from an enemy tribe. After a clash between two quarreling tribes, the woman has the right to travel between the two sides, to see the dead or wounded, to tend to injuries, or to return to her people without anyone doing anything that would sully her good reputation. There is nothing to prevent her from loving whomever she wishes: her paternal first cousin has the first right to her hand, but if for some reason he prefers someone else to her she will marry another man whom she loves. Hence it is usually the case among bedouin girls that they have no experience with men before marriage. This virtuousness continues to typify her in her married life, and she will not be unfaithful to her husband. The usual case among men is to marry while they are still immature boys. If, because of differing inclinations and temperaments, the marital life of the young man is disagreeable to him, the two separate through divorce. The girl may be the offended party, in which case she may ask to return to her family and is respected and honored even if her husband has not divorced her, or she may return of her own accord without consulting her husband. All this, however, does not preclude the occurrence to a certain extent of sexual relations between a man and an unmarried woman if he loves her and the two are far from the watchful eyes of her guardians.

His Ability to Interpret Physical Signs

The bedouin has a sophisticated ability to interpret the traces and remains he sees in abandoned encampments, and hence this seems to have had an influence on his ancient poetry. In the opening lines of such poems we see the poet stopping at the camp site and examining the remains, and when he stops at such remains he can recognize the general time period when the people camped there had moved on and the place where the tent of his beloved had been pitched. If the traces are recent ones, footprints are clearly distinguishable on the ground and he can tell that of a woman from that of a man when the two are walking in bare feet. Indeed, he can distinguish the footprint of a pregnant woman from its impression in the soil, and similarly, can tell the footpad print of a male camel from that of a pregnant female. From certain external indications that he sees as he travels in the desert, he knows how to deduce many unseen matters that would be difficult for someone else to recognize. He sees a bird passing over a dune or hill, for example, and takes precautions lest there be a band of raiders or enemies passing behind that hill or dune, thus causing the bird to fly up from its nesting or perching place. This unique skill has so won the admiration of most of the explorers of Arabia that some of them have claimed that the bedouin's ability to interpret physical signs is something practically prophetic. In his book *Falconry in Arabia*, Mark Allen relates a story about a hunting trip in northern Arabia, near Jabal 'Unayza:

> The car shuddered to a halt with the driver standing on the foot brake, all jumped out and a heated discussion followed, held with faces bent over the ground. "Do you not see them?" "Well, no—what, where?" and then, pointed out with a finger, the faintest traces of footprints. A nail mark in the dust where the houbara's foot had been on pebbles, a clearer impression of one step a few inches further on and then, to my eyes, the trail was lost again in the gravel.[22]

Beyond all these skills, the bedouin is knowledgeable on storms, the locations of the stars and planets, and changes in the weather. This helps him to know how to proceed in the desert lands without losing his way, and how to organize the times when he will venture forth in search of water and pasturage.

In this chapter I have discussed the character of the bedouin in general, the good qualities that are to be recognized in him, and the other negative features enjoined upon him by his harsh environment and his primitive way of life. In closing I must say that most of the European explorers who lived for extended periods in close proximity to the bedouin, and experienced for themselves the life of the desert and desert folk, have not failed to point out the nobility and honor of the Arab bedouin. Burckhardt praised them and mentioned many of their virtues,[23] Doughty gave a fair account of them and did not neglect to recount some of their good qualities,[24] and Dickson did the same.[25] Glubb, however, exaggerated in glorifying them and extolling their loyalty to a friend, spoke in glowing terms of their courage, generosity, and nobility, and claimed that the European explorers had not given the qualities of the bedouin the full praise they deserved.[26] Even Palgrave, who did not view either the bedouins or their hardship-ridden lives with approval, did not hesitate to say that they were the noblest people in the world.[27] Probably the earliest of all these explorers to

[22]Mark Allen, *Falconry in Arabia* (London, 1980), p. 84.

[23]Burckhardt, I, 358.

[24]Doughty, I, 269, 303, 424, 446, 459; Kiernan, p. 18.

[25]Dickson, pp. 129–30.

[26]J.B. Glubb, *The Story of the Arab Legion* (London, 1948), pp. 155–56, 159, 235.

[27]Palgrave, I, 24.

make a point of the merits of the Arab bedouins and their nomadic environment was the Abbé Carré, an explorer who in 1672 described their manners and customs and then wrote:

> Such are the customs of these Arabs, whom we regard as savage and rough. They shame most of our rich Christians in Europe, who often refuse a piece of bread to poor pilgrims and strangers without means. Such are the manners and ways of living so different from those in our countries, where pomp, luxury and eagerness to amass wealth, blind so many of us. Come with me to this desert. I will show you a nation, Arab and barbarian, that can teach us the valuable lesson that we must rid ourselves of mad and extravagant ambitions for wealth, palaces, fine furniture, sumptuous clothes, perfumes, dainties and the like, which pervert the brains of the greatest men in European countries. Come, I say, to this land of our first fathers, come to Arabia. . . .[28]

[28]Peter G. Bietenholz, *Desert and Bedouin in the European Mind* (Khartoum, 1963), p. 8. In this treatise there is an accurate scholarly exposition on most of these early explorers.

CHAPTER XIII

BEDOUIN APPEARANCE, DRESS, AND ADORNMENT

Bedouin Appearance

Bedouins, especially those of the south, are in most cases light in weight and of slender build, and except in certain tents of the shaykhs I do not remember ever seeing a bedouin of above-average weight or as stout as one finds among settled folk. There are two main reasons for this. Firstly, the bedouin is constantly engaged in traveling, migrating, or moving about, mounted or on foot. Secondly, his diet contains few of the fat-rich items usually found in abundance in the foods eaten by the soft-living settled folk. The bedouin does eat clarified butter or melted fat on festive occasions when a banquet is held, but the amount he consumes of this in most cases does not exceed 200 grams per month—a meager amount which has no appreciable effect on his body and does not cause him to gain weight. The only exceptions to this general trend are certain shaykhs who hold many banquets in their tents, or other sheep-owning notables who have grown accustomed to lingering near the settled areas and pursuing a life of calm, tranquility, and ease.

The bedouin has strong white teeth, because he lives for the most part on milk, which is rich in calcium, and does not, as some imagine, eat much meat. Nor does he eat many sweets, which together with meat contribute to tooth decay. He pays special attention to his hair, and begins to do so in boyhood. He allows it to grow long, washes it from time to time with camel's urine (as bedouin women also do), and plaits it into braids which he allows to hang down on his chest, thus adorning himself with it in his boyhood and youth in the same way that the village girl does with her long hair.

Figure 56: Two youths, both showing a predilection for long braided hair.

Figure 57: Two elderly bedouins. Note the full set of teeth in the mouth of the one on the right.

Figure 58: A bedouin with long hair hanging down both sides of his chest, as is the habit with most bedouin youths.

Bedouins are of moderate stature, the northerners generally being taller than the southerners. Among tribesmen of Najdī, Rwāla, or other northern origin one will sometimes find men more than 175 centimeters tall. Some claim that bedouins are short; but while this applies to those of the south, it is not generally true of bedouins of the Syrian Desert.

Bedouin Dress and Adornment

Bedouins, especially those of the north, do not pay much attention to their attire. Or at best, those who do are limited to young men who have become of marriageable age and are anxious to attract the attention of the young women of their tribe, or sons of shaykhs whose material circumstances make it easy for them to turn out smartly dressed. Although it would be an easy matter to enumerate the styles and colors of clothing that the bedouin generally wears on his body, head, and feet, it would be a mistake for the reader to suppose that the bedouins have a uniform style of dress that the tribesmen of every region have agreed to don. Each tribe has a practically unique manner of dress that only the bedouin recognizes. It is true that most bedouins wear the *shamla*, or headcloth, and *'iqāl*, headcord, on their heads; but among many tribes the type of *shamla* and *'iqāl* differs, some even dispensing with the *'iqāl* and finding it sufficient to fold the *shamla* around the head in a style unique to themselves. The same must also be said of the style of shirt that the bedouin wears next to his body. Among some it is short and covered by another long enough that it almost reaches the ground, while one will see another bedouin wearing only a long shirt and above it a *ṣāya* (a white linen open-fronted robe), *qumbāz* (a striped silk robe, also open-fronted), or an aba mantle. Winter and summer attire differ, and the clothing worn by bedouin women of the Shawāyā tribe differs from that worn by women among their camel-herding cousins. Similarly, among some one sees long lappets hanging from the sleeves of their robes, while among others the lappets are missing. And while some wear drawers (*sarāwīl*) under their robes, most—both men and women—do not and consider this healthier for their bodies.

Some European explorers devoted a large part of their writings to the description of the various types of bedouin dress; but I see no need for a detailed account of this, and the photographs in this book of men and women from various tribes of pure bedouins and of the Shawāyā tribe will give a general idea of the clothing usually worn by the bedouins. Here it would be appropriate to mention the work of the French author Albert de Boucheman on bedouin clothing, utensils, furnishings, and the saddles and bridles they use on their camels.[1] The book contains photographs of all these items.

Bedouin attire has begun to change in recent years. Many sons of the desert have begun to dress like people in the villages near the desert, and many village youths—both young men and young women—have begun to adopt the attire of the town folk. Some shaykhs' wives have begun to wear robes embroidered and brocaded with gold and silver thread, as do some of the shaykhs' wives in the regions enriched by the presence of oil. Similarly, in the photograph in Figure 65 you can see my wife and niece on an occasion when they enjoyed the hos-

[1]Albert de Boucheman, *Matériel de la vie bédouine* (Damascus, 1934).

Figure 59: A bedouin with muffled face, wearing his *kūfīya* without an *'iqāl*.

Figure 60: Bedouin poverty—torn robe and exposed chest.

Figure 61: A handsome and well-dressed youth of the Shawāyā tribe.

pitality of Amīr Nāyif al-Sha'lān's wife, who ordered one of her servant girls to dress them in brocaded bedouin attire for me to take a photograph of them.[2] I also photographed the *amīr* himself dressed in his everyday attire, which was of the utmost possible cleanliness and neatness.[3]

In certain parts of the Arab world some of the sons of shaykhs began to wear European dress when they became students in official or private schools, but continued to wear the *kūfīya* and *'iqāl*, as can be seen in the photograph in Figure 50 of the sons of the shaykh of the Banū Ṣakhr in the Jordanian Desert.[4]

During the winter the bedouin may be forced to don another robe over his clothes, a coat (*farwa*) made from sheepskin, or an overcoat of thick broadcloth; and if he is from the Shawāyā tribe, he may wear a jacket like that worn by the settled folk. When bedouins used to plunder the settled folk of their property during raids, they saw no harm in putting on the very clothing they had just plundered, especially when their own was so old that it was about to fall to pieces on their bodies. Hence, at a given time you might see a group of men wearing different styles and colors of clothing.

However much their attire may differ in other respects, there is one point of general agreement. Every bedouin wears on his head the headcloth (*kuffīya*, or *kūfīya*), and over it may wind the headcord (*'iqāl*) around his head. The headcord is woven by himself or his wife from camel's hair or sheep's wool, or made of black goat's hair and purchased from a village or town merchant or a trader from the settled lands who has come to the bedouin camps. It is tightly woven and of various thicknesses ranging between two and five centimeters, while those of a century ago were generally thicker than those produced now. If no headcord is to be found, the bedouin is sometimes content to wind a simple kerchief (*mandīl*) over the headcloth to hold it in place on his head. Here we must note that the headcord woven by the bedouin himself or by his wife, and usually tied on his head, does not differ in form from the *'iqāl* cord he uses to hobble his camel around the knee

[2]See below, p. 339.
[3]Above, p. 276, Figure 48.
[4]See above, p. 283.

Figure 62: The bedouin holds his *kūfīya* fast with the *'iqāl*.

of its left or right foreleg. The term *'iqāl* in the sense of the headcord is probably taken from its meaning as the hobbling cord; and the word *'aql*, or "intellect," may itself be derived in the Arabic language from the term for the hobbling cord, for it is said that the intellect (*'aql*) "hobbles" a man in the sense that it restrains him from traveling in the ways of error.

On his body the bedouin wears a loose flowing robe, extending to the ground, usually made of either raw or beaten and bleached linen, and some may dye this robe with a dark yellow color so that it matches the color of the sands. Even his white undyed robe does not long remain on him before it turns a color more dusty hued than white. Under his robe he may gird himself around the waist with a belt (*zunnār*); and as we have already mentioned, bedouins do not generally wear drawers and only a few are familiar with them. The bedouin may don a second robe over the first, especially in the winter. Among some Rwāla tribesmen

Figure 63: Bedouin youths wearing abas over jackets. It is very common for a youth to wear his *'iqāl* tilted to one side.

the outer robe will sometimes have long lappets, each of which hangs from the sleeve opening in the shape of an acute triangle, the tip of which may reach the ground even if the arm is raised over the head, while the sleeve opening is broad enough to allow for easy movement of the arm. On many occasions the bedouin will tie his lappets together behind his back.

At times he also wears a woolen aba over his robe. In summer this will be a light one to protect himself from the noonday heat, or may be dispensed with altogether, while during the winter he will wear a heavy thick one to protect himself from the cold. For the northern tribes, abas are woven by the people of the villages adjoining the desert; and there is a Christian village in Syria called Ṣadad in which most of the inhabitants earn their living weaving abas and woolen mats on looms in their homes and sell them either to merchants or directly to the bedouins. Besides Ṣadad, there are other villages in which there are Christians familiar with the craft of weaving (an art passed down to them from their ancient ancestors) who sell what they make to both desert and village folk.

The bedouin only rarely wears shoes—and that in the winter. Those he does wear are in most cases a special kind of boot called *jazma* or *basṭār*, each of which has a shank extending several centimeters above the ankle-bone. Sometimes he wears sandals the soles of which are made of camel's hoof or rubber, and the straps of leather.

Women's Dress

The dress of the bedouin woman differs from that of the man in that she does not wear the *'iqāl*, but rather winds a kerchief (*mandīl*) made of soft black cotton cloth around her head. Above it, or at times underneath it, she may tie another silken kerchief, called the *ḥaṭṭa*, which she folds over in multiple layers to form a band about as wide as the palm of one's hand. This she winds around her head so that it shows on her brow and can be tied at the back, leaving the top of the head exposed. Some *ḥaṭṭa*s worn by the womenfolk of shaykhs are embroidered with gold or silver thread. Many women are tattooed on their chins and lower cheeks. This is particularly common among Shawāyā women, but is a feature that one only rarely sees on the face of a village woman. The woman's robe is in most cases dark in color, black or dark blue, with a hemmed border along its edges that may be colored among the women of some tribes, particularly if she is a young woman still unmarried. Over her robe she sometimes wears a broadcloth *durrā'a*, or loose sleeved tunic, the style and fabric of which differ according to the tribe and the wealth of its owner. It has hemmed borders decorated with cord sewn onto the edges of its sleeves, around its bottom hem line, and on its front and back. During the winter she wears *jazma*-style shoes, most often yellow or red, while in summer most women go barefoot.

Some women gird themselves with a belt over their robes, the belts varying among different women of different ages; for some of them it is an article of adornment. Some bedouin women of southern tribes wear an aba that covers the top of the head and hangs down to the ground. In the Najd this is also what women of the villages and towns wear.

Figure 64: A family of the Shawāyā tribe in their distinctive attire.

Figure 65: The author's wife (on the right) and niece wearing the precious brocaded clothing of the womenfolk of the shaykhs.

Figure 66: Two armed youths, and on the right the photographer Manoug, wearing an *'iqāl*.

Attentive to her adornment, the bedouin woman will buy various kinds of cheap jewelry, unless her man is wealthy. On her foot she sometimes wears an anklet, on her arm she wears a bracelet, and she puts rings on her fingers and earrings on her ears. Among some Shawāyā clans there are women who wear a *kh̩izām*, or nose ring. Most of the jewelry of bedouin women is made of silver alloy or copper, although some may be of gold if it is to be worn as a nose ring or earring.

The fondness of some bedouin women for adorning themselves with this jewelry is such that they will sell some of their household stores in order to buy their jewelry and clothing, or save camel's hair in order to sell it and use the proceeds to buy these cheap trinkets for adornment. Others gather truffles and sell them in order to buy the jewelry for which they yearn.

The bedouin woman of the north Arabian tribes does not wear the head veil (the *qinā'* or *burqu'*) over her face, as is commonly found among some southern bedouins. She sometimes leaves a braid of hair on both sides of her face. These braids play the equivalent role of the man's moustache: if need be, she can be distinguished by her braids just as the man is distinguished by his moustache. If she wishes to be modest, she wraps a veiling cloth (*khimār*) across the lower part of her face so that it covers it from the neck up to the nose. Worn in this fashion the cloth is called a *lithām*, or muffler.

Among the bedouins, the *lithām* is regarded as an indication of aloofness and staid dignity, and men may muffle themselves so as not to be recognized or in order to achieve a more effectively impressive image. Indeed, they have said of Nūrī al-Sha'lān that he passed most of his time wearing a muffler, even when he was in his council chamber.

Bedouin women generally apply kohl to their eyes. Kohl is a black powder made from lustrous antimony. It is first washed seven times with water, and then is placed in the middle of a lump of dough with a bit of oil and cooked in a baking pit (*tannūr*) or fireplace heated by a hot fire until the dough is baked. It is then removed from the center of the dough, some roasted olive and date pits and a bit of nutmeg are added to it, and all the mixture is pulverized or pounded down together into a powder. Before this, however, one must burn a piece of raw linen dipped in indigo dye and placed in a receptacle. A fine black dust from the smoke of the burned piece of cloth adheres to the

Figure 67: The nose ring adorns the nose of the bedouin woman. Note her long hair and the belt in which she has tied the key to her box of valuables.

Figure 68: The bedouins of Shawāyā are known for the raising of sheep, and their women are more attentive to their attire than are the women of the tribes that tend camels.

Figure 69: The forceful personality of the bedouin woman shows in the expression on her face, and she enjoys greater freedom than her sister in the village. Hence, the photographer encounters no difficulty in taking pictures of women without consulting their menfolk.

Figure 70: Village women carrying earthenware jars. Note how their attire differs from that of bedouin women.

Figure 71: The modest bedouin woman is wearing a muffler and has no objection to being photographed.

bottom of the receptacle, and is collected and mixed with the powder prepared as described above. This powder is then sifted through a very fine muslin cloth, thus becoming suitable for application to the eyes as kohl.

As for men, the only ones who apply kohl to their eyes are certain passionate youths and seekers of romantic adventure, and when one of the bedouin youths falls into this category the others call him *'ilq*, a "womanizer." In general, however, bedouin men pay little attention to the tidiness of their attire, to their adornment, or to their cleanliness, this being particularly true of those Rwāla bedouins who live a purely nomadic life. For this they perhaps have an excuse—lack of water.

CHAPTER XIV

RAIDING AND THE BROTHER-RIGHT

Raiding

We have already mentioned that the bedouin knows nothing of vocational skills: on the contrary, he looks down on every vocational trade, as well as on agriculture, with contempt. The bedouin woman who wishes to insult a man will find no more abusive epithet for him than *ṣāniʿ*, "craftsman," or *fallāḥ*, "farmer." Among the bedouins nomadism defines an exclusive aristocracy, the loftiest peak of noble life. But how does the bedouin earn his livelihood? How does he spend his time? Two ways of earning a living are open to him, the first of which is the raising of livestock. If he is a camel-owning nomad, then raising camels is his most important means and every year he will sell enough of their male offspring to enable him to live for the rest of the year. If he is one of those who have sheep as well as camels, he will raise both. Then, when he is close by the fringes of the settled lands, he will sell sheep products: lambs, clarified butter, and curdled milk. He will also sell truffles if the autumn rains have facilitated the emergence of truffles at the end of the winter. The other means, for decades now effectively denied to him by all of the Arab governments, would have been raiding and plundering—that is, warfare for the sake of gain or in defense of his livestock so that bedouins from another tribe would not plunder them.

It used to be that one rarely encountered a bedouin who grew to young adulthood without owning some kind of weapon. And although the government authorities in every Arab country have enacted laws to forbid raiding, the bedouins continue to carry arms and still fear that they will be raided. Indeed, they would still gladly mount a raid if the opportunity to do so presented itself to them.

In certain situations the tribes were forced to fight among themselves in defense of their grazing lands: when water supplies in the lands of a tribe dried up and the land became arid, the tribe would set out for territory belonging to another tribe in search of water and pasturage for its livestock, and so clash with the tribe to which that land belonged. Hence the strength and standing of the tribe were judged in terms of the strength of the tribe's manpower and weaponry, or rather, its horsemen and how well prepared they were to confront adversaries or to mount attacks and monopolize watering places and pasture lands. The pasture lands may be adequate at most times of the year for this plethora of tribes in the various parts of the Arabian peninsula, but watering places are limited to certain fixed sites and to well-known pools and wells. The bedouins compete with each other for use of these watering places and come into conflict with one another over this issue, much as they did in ancient times, when the strong tribe left no room for the weak tribe to gain an adequate share of the water:

> When we come to drink 'tis of clear water pure,
> While muck and the clay is what others endure.[1]

It was this need in former times that led some men of the tribes to become warriors. As of the 1930s, when security was established in the desert and raids and plundering were prohibited, it became essential that some outlet be found for the martial inclinations and fighting experience of these warriors. Beginning in Mandate times, and later under most Arab governments, some bedouins have joined the desert patrols of the countries adjoining their territories. In Syria in the days of the Mandate, for example, there were bases for camel-corps units in many of the villages along the peripheries of the desert, some of these units including individuals from this country's bedouin tribes, and in Jordan there were camel-corps units made up of the bedouin tribesmen of that region. After independence, some of the Arab governments began to court the affections of some of the bedouin tribes, for fear that they would shift their loyalty to another state. To some members of

[1]From the *mu'allaqa* of 'Amr ibn Kulthūm; *Sharḥ al-qaṣā'id al-'ashr*, p. 122.

the tribes the question of military conscription is one of a trade, nothing more, and the bedouin can bargain over his military service and so serve only where the most favorable treatment is available. This may well have been one of the factors that served to encourage the emergence and growth of a part of the Jordanian army composed of bedouin tribesmen. In medieval times, Arab rulers bent on military expansion used to rely upon bedouins in their expeditions, while these tribesmen gladly participated in the expeditions for the spoils and plunder they hoped to gain. It used to be that most of the bedouins in the armies were mounted on horses and camels, but today many of the bedouins have learned how to drive motor vehicles and have begun to serve in the motorized units.

The bedouin is no worse at marksmanship than anyone else, and were it as easy for him as for others to gain access to opportunities for practice he would rank among the best of marksmen. But the high cost of ammunition denies him the necessary practice, hence he cannot compete with the well-trained marksmen of the settled lands.[2] Nevertheless, there are bedouin marksmen who are as skilled with modern firearms as their ancestors were with bow and arrow. In his *Arabian Sands* Thesiger relates the story told to him by the bedouin who killed Ibn Dwaylān, "the Cat," who never missed his target when he fired. A raiding party from Ibn Dwaylān's tribe attacked the bedouin's camp, killed two of his fellow tribesmen, stole all their camels, and fled. The

[2]'Abd al-Jalīl al-Ṭāhir went to the extremes of exaggeration when he claimed in his book *Al-Badw wa-l-'ashā'ir fī l-bilād al-'arabīya* (Cairo, 1955), p. 54, that "when the bedouin reaches the age of fourteen he begins to shoot, accompanied by one of the members of the tribe. Every day for three months he spends three hours practicing his marksmanship; and if, at the end of this time, he hits the target 80 percent of the time, he is made a warrior (*fāris*), otherwise he remains a herdsman. When he reaches the age of twenty his marksmanship training is resumed for one month; and if he succeeds he is promoted to the rank of warrior, otherwise he remains a herdsman. At the age of 25 he trains a third time for a month, this being the last training session. If he succeeds he becomes a warrior, otherwise he spends his life as a herdsman." In reality, the 'Anazī bedouin with which I associated does not know such methodical arrangements as those mentioned here, and indeed, is in many cases ignorant of how old he is. I do not think that the bedouins of other tribes are any different. It is worthwhile for us to point out that Doughty (I, 173) claims that the bedouin is in general a poor marksman.

bedouin and eleven others rode in pursuit of Ibn Dwaylān and four of the other raiders, and at an area of low dunes covered with bushes there ensued a fight described by the bedouin as follows:

> They stopped there and fired on us. The plain was as bare as this floor, and we could only get near them from the north, where there were other dunes. They had already killed one of us. We could not see them. Do you understand? We got off our camels and ran towards them through the dunes. There was much firing. We killed three of them, and they had killed another of us and wounded two more. Then we killed another, and knew that there was only one left. He was somewhere among the big dunes, and every time one of us moved he fired, and he never missed. He had killed four of us, and still we could not see him, though we knew where he was. I realized that he was very close, with only the crest of a dune between us. I and my cousin crawled slowly up it towards him. Then my cousin lifted his head to look as we neared the top of the dune, and fell back dead beside me, shot through the forehead. I saw the barrel of a rifle jerking. By God, it was less than eight paces from where I lay! I realized that the rifle had jammed. I drew my dagger and leapt on the man before he could get to his feet. I drove my dagger into his neck and killed him. He was a little man and was armed with an English rifle.[3]

The bedouins are generally ignorant of many of the stratagems and means of deception in which the soldiers in the modern states have been trained. However, they do seek out information about their enemies' activities and movements and try to keep similar information concerning themselves from reaching their adversaries. They follow routes along which they will find water and pasturage and try not to reveal their presence there to their enemies, and they would traditionally recognize advantageous times at which to launch raids, such as a dark night, favorable climatic conditions, and so forth. They also have vanguards that they send out ahead to serve as their spies on their enemies, so that

[3] *Arabian Sands*, p. 226.

rather than encountering them unexpectedly they would already know a great deal about them in advance. And many times they would resort to tricking their enemy by shifting a group of their warriors to attack a band from another tribe or clan from one direction, and launching the main surprise attack on another band from another direction or on the livestock of the same band in its grazing grounds.

If raiders mounted a surprise attack on the herdsmen of a tribe and stole their camels, for example, they would split into two groups and send the stolen camels with one group to herd and continue on with them, and leave the other group waiting in ambush for the camel-owners' pursuit party, in order to obstruct its search for their livestock. When the ambush party retreated, some of its members would fall back, protected by others who remained in their positions until those who had withdrawn regrouped in a position behind them, after which the ones who had remained in place fell back to a position behind their comrades. This process of alternating stages of retreat continued until the pursuers became exhausted and the stolen camels were too far away to be overtaken. At that point the raiders reunited and drove the stolen camels before them back to their own territory. However, when they rose against governments, or disobeyed their ordinances and violated the rule of law, then despite their vigilance they frequently fell into the traps of the government forces. In our discussion of vengeance we have already mentioned the story of the raiding party, late in the First World War, that plundered the two villages of al-Sukhna and Arak and how it fell into the ambush set for it by the imperial army.

Raids in the desert took place only on camel-back. If the journey of the raiders was to distant lands, the camels would sometimes be accompanied alongside by horses: the raider rode his thoroughbred camel and tied alongside it a mare that he would ride during the final attack or, if the situation so demanded, in flight. At that point the force was called a *janīb*, after the horse (*janīb*) which was led by the raider's side. If the land where their adversaries were located was nearby, not more than one or two days' traveling distance from them, the bedouins might raid on horses only. When the people of a tribe decided to mount a raid on distant lands, it sometimes happened that two raiders, one owning a mare and the other a thoroughbred riding camel, would strike a bargain and travel together, both riding the camel and pulling the mare behind them. It was the responsibility of the horse's owner to provide the provisions and the saddle gear, and the owner of the camel rode behind his companion until they reached enemy territory. When they did, the horse was not tired. Upon their arrival the *'aqīd*, or raid leader, selected three sites where the camel-mounted men (*ziml*) gathered and awaited the return of the horsemen, who set out toward the enemy. The first of these three sites would be no more than a mile and half from the enemy camp, either in a wadi or behind a hill. If the horsemen did not return within the time limit specified, these others hurried on with their camels to the second site and waited a whole day there for the arrival of the horsemen. If the day passed and the horsemen did not return, the group moved on to the third site, a location chosen earlier far from the enemy's camp, where they were obliged to remain three or perhaps four days. If the time elapsed and the horsemen still had not returned, the camel-mounted men quickly returned to their own people.

If the horsemen were successful and made off with the camels and other livestock of their enemies, then each camel-owning partner was rewarded with a she-camel, even if the horseman had not succeeded in stealing more than one. But if the horsemen had been defeated, the partner lost nothing. On some long-distance raiding expeditions such as this, it could happen that all of the horse-mounted raiders would perish because their provisions had remained with the camels and their owners. When the horsemen attacked the camps of their enemies they were not as interested in the contents of the tents as they were in the *ḥalāl*, the camels and horses. However, if the enemy was close to the raiders' own camp, the attackers might also loot the tents and their contents. In such a situation it might happen that a courageous woman would be able to recover one of her husband's camels if she recognized the *'aqīd* and ran after him and implored him to return a camel to her since her people had now become destitute. She remained close by him until he gave her one from his own share. The raiders either divided everything out among themselves or left each person with whatever property or livestock he had been able to carry away.

The desert also knew a type of looting that was not raiding, but rather resembled burglary. The bedouins acknowledged it, but did not regard it as raiding. It was rather a strike after the fashion of commandos, and in a single operation no more than two or three men participated. By night they slipped into the camp of their adversaries and hid among the tents until there arose a good opportunity for them to steal a charger, a riding she-camel, or some sheep, then they slipped away without anyone becoming aware of their presence. These commandos were called not *ghazw*, "raiders," but *ḥanshal*, "footmen," and a large proportion of their bedouin tales revolves around accounts of the *ḥanshal* and their exploits. The plot lines of these stories are woven around the theme of love involving a girl and the hero of the story who proves to be one of the commandos. The *ḥanshal* pursue their exploits only at night and rarely go mounted. When they do go mounted their riding animals are camels, which they make kneel down far from the target camp and leave tied out in the open, guarded by one of their number if they are more than two or three, or unguarded if they are fewer than that. The tellers of *ḥanshal* stories frequently relate how participants in the operation disguised themselves. One of them would don a sheepskin and hide in a depression on the ground near the camp of his adversaries until the shepherds returned to the tents of their clansmen, then our friend slips in among the herd and crawls along with it until it arrives back at the camp. He then remains with the herd, lying down in front of the tent until he has an opportunity to steal something: a mare to jump on and ride away to safety, a riding she-camel to lead away quietly without anyone being aware of his presence, a sheep, or some other animal. In the bedouin tales the *ḥanshal* raiders are also asked to rescue *amīr*s' sons who have been taken prisoner and tied up at the camp of their captors for some reason or another.

In this connection we should mention that raids offered an opportunity for the adventure-seeking bedouin to display his heroism, courage, and martial skills. When the bedouin spoke of one of his exploits in this context, one would see him doing so with unequaled relish and delight. Raiding was a domain of activity involving not gain alone, but also the demonstration of valor and fortitude, and it thereby constituted a kind of refreshing diversion when the bedouin wearied of monotonous tent life in front of the fire and around the poles. If he was successful and returned with booty, he began singing songs of victory and glory and his reputation rose in the eyes of the sons and daughters of his tribe, especially in the eyes of his young lady, if he had fallen in love with one. Beyond this, the raid gave the bedouin—if he was a poor one—the means to achieve his aspirations for wealth; he would constantly hope for the day when good fortune on a raid would leave him rich and happy.

The "Brother-Right"

In the past the bedouins were accustomed to imposing on the people of the villages adjoining the desert a kind of tax in return for the bedouins' protection of or lack of aggression against the villagers. This tax was called the *khuwwa*, or "brother-right," and the bedouins also sometimes imposed it on the traveler crossing the regions where the bedouins were camped and which thus became part of their territory. In order to safeguard themselves, their property, and their trade, people made a habit of paying this *khuwwa* to the shaykh of the tribe or to one of its other influential members.

The tax consisted of a specified amount of revenue that sometimes consisted of certain gifts of clothing and supplies. Every village had its trade or business with the bedouins, or had livestock that was exposed to the bedouins' raids. Such settlements therefore came to an agreement with a notable in the tribe whereby it made that notable the village's *akh*, or "brother," and paid him the rightful due for this "brotherhood," that is, the *khuwwa*, or "brother-right." This tax was collected from most of the villages along the peripheries of the desert in Ottoman times and in early Mandate times, but subsequently the Mandatory authorities and the governments of the region were able to put an end to this and the people stopped gathering and paying this tax.

By way of illustration, I might mention the amount of *khuwwa* that the people of al-Qaryatayn were obliged to pay in the nineteenth century. Each year they paid to the shaykhs of each of these tribes the following amounts in *majīdīs* (the *majīdī* was worth approximately one-fifth of a gold Ottoman *līra*):[4]

[4]Musil, *Palmyrena*, p. 100.

Tribe	*Amount Received*
Rwāla	70
Wild 'Alī	30
Ḥsāna	20
Ghiyāth	20
Sbā'a	16
Fid'ān	20
'Imārāt	30

The villager was able to travel and move about without fear or dread in all of the lands where a certain tribe camped or pastured its camels, provided that the people of his village had paid the required *khuwwa* to its proper recipient, or to the tribal shaykh who had imposed this "brother-right" upon them. Even if this agreement was violated and one of the bedouins from the same tribe robbed the villager, the man receiving the *khuwwa* was responsible for making sure that whatever had been stolen from the villager was returned to him.

The amount of the *khuwwa* varied among different tribes and villages and, as we have seen, did not exceed a few gold *līra*s and some presents. As we have said, the *khuwwa* has now been suspended, except for special cases between certain individual bedouins and merchants. In this case it becomes something like an assist for the merchant, rather than a *khuwwa*, since it makes it easier for him to practice his vocation among the bedouins. Similarly, most of the tribes demanded the payment of a *khuwwa* not only from the people in the villages bordering the desert, but also from certain other low tribes that sought protection under their wing. The tribe of Ṣlayb, for example, used to have *khuwwa* agreements with fifteen powerful tribes to protect the lives of its people, and paid a "brother-right" to the shaykh of each of these tribes.

CHAPTER XV

THE BEDOUINS AND THE HUNT

IT IS REPORTED that Aristotle said: "The first of the essential vocations was hunting, then building, then agriculture."[1] The reason for this is probably that hunting was the vocation most closely bonded to the life of early man, who had no way to ensure his survival other than to prey upon animals weaker than himself and to eat their flesh. Even when he progressed in his development and his way of life came to be organized around the raising of livestock in a state of nomadism, hunting continued to be the vocation closest to him. This was because it was one of the easiest means of gaining his subsistence in his harsh primitive environment. He used to spare the livestock he had domesticated and for his nourishment relied upon their milk; only when compelled to do so did he slaughter them to eat their meat. If he had no source of sustenance other than his livestock at his disposal, he would continue to watch for wild animals and birds as a source of food for himself, and to resort to hunting in order to gain access to that source.

Furthermore, hunting was also a form of recreation, a diversion that in turn ranked as one of those in closest harmony with life in the desert—a life in which bedouins were accustomed to raiding and being raided by their neighbors and to having some members of the tribe who were fast runners, brave men, good shots, and fine horsemen. This form of recreation trained the bedouin to be a brave man or a good horseman; in fact, among the Arab bedouins the hunters, whether *amīr*s or vagabonds, ranked among the most renowned marksmen and

[1] *Al-Bayzara*, p. 20.

horsemen. In this they were comparable to their oldest ancestor Ishmael, who, as reports have it, was a marksman passionately devoted to hunting.

As the Arabs ranked among the nations most deeply rooted in a nomadic way of life, among them hunting was more widespread and a more general form of recreation than it was among other peoples who were settled. Thus we read of vagabond poets (the *ṣa'ālīk*)— al-Shanfarā, al-Sulayk ibn Sulaka, Ta'abbaṭa Sharran, and others—who lived on plundering and hunting. We also see chieftains of the pre-Islamic era, like Imru' al-Qays and others, priding themselves in this type of diversion and speaking of how they used to hunt ibex and gazelles. Indeed, in the oldest known carving in the desert we see an image of the ibex alongside one of the camels upon which the bedouin depended for his livelihood, as much as to indicate the strength of the bond between hunting and desert life.[2] Similarly, among Egyptian carvings we see a representation of the ibex alongside a hunting Amorite shaykh who traveled to Egypt in about 1890 BC. In appearance he does not differ from the bedouins.[3] The bedouins passed the tradition of this pastime down from father to son, and as we shall see, some of them even made of it a means of earning a living.

The sport of hunting was of assistance to the Arab conquerors, since hunters were among the best shots and such marksmen supported Islam. The Arab Prophet compared hunting to the riding of horses and classified it as dearer to him than the latter: "Shoot [arrows] and ride horses, but it is dearer to me that you should shoot than that you should ride." He also said: "Each diversion in which the believer engages is worthless, save three particular cases: shooting with your bow, training your mare, and amusement with your wife—all these have their rightful place."[4] There is even a clear reference to the permissibility of hunting in the Qur'ān, where, in Sūrat al-Mā'ida, it is said: "They will ask you what is permitted unto them. Tell them: Permitted unto you are the delightful things and the hunting dogs you train, training them as God

[2]Hitti, *History of Syria*, p. 52.

[3]Philip K. Hitti, *Lebanon in History* (London 1957), opp. p. 74, and his *History of Syria*, opp. p. 76.

[4]Abū 'Ubayda, *Kitāb al-khayl*, p. 10.

has taught you."[5] One also finds: "Fishing in the sea and its food are permitted unto you as a diversion and as a proper way, and hunting forbidden game is forbidden unto you so long as these remain unlawful. And be mindful of God, before whom you shall assemble."[6]

As for ancient and medieval hunting devices, there were arrows, which the hunter shaped and feathered and shot to bring down his quarry, or spears. He also used a horse to take him to places where game animals lived, a panther or dog that he would set upon the quarry to drive it back to him or prevent it from running away, or a falcon or hawk to help him hunt birds and small animals. Even today, remains of arrow fragments continue to be found in the foothills throughout the desert.

The main animals that the bedouins hunted were oryx, onagers, gazelles, ibex, and rabbits, while among the birds were ostriches, bustards, cranes, partridges, pigeons, francolins, and sand grouse. They used birds of prey to hunt most of these birds, and salukis, panthers, horses, camels, and Ṣlaybī donkeys to hunt the land animals. Arab life was overtaken by many changes, many of its modes of behavior were transformed, and some practices were replaced by others; but in this form of recreation the only significant change was in the means employed by man. The bow and arrow fell into disuse when gunpowder was discovered, and men instead relied on firearms. Today some people also resort to pursuing game with automobiles and airplanes instead of horses and camels.

It would seem that this form of diversion is one that God has made accessible to rich and poor alike, though they pursue it in different ways—at this point the rich and mighty king and the poor man in his shabby rags are in accord. It seems that it is the joy of triumph over the quarry that endears this sport to people, and it may well be that for the poor man there is further delight in that a successful hunt marks the gain of his means of subsistence. But the joy of pursuing the quarry and triumphing over it is the fundamental point. As was said long ago

[5]Sūrat al-Mā'ida (5), vs. 4. The *jawāriḥ* are beasts of prey used for hunting. The *mukallibīn* are those that train the animals to hunt: the term originally referred to those who trained and taught dogs (*kilāb*) to hunt, and then came to be used in reference to any beast of prey.

[6]Sūrat al-Mā'ida (5), vs. 96.

by the poet Maḥmūd ibn al-Ḥusayn al-Baghdādī, known as Abū l-Fatḥ Kushājim:

> What lends joy to hunting is pursuit of the game;
> So before I yet catch you, let's chase awhile first.
> This beverage sustains life, but lacks, all the same,
> A pleasureable taste 'til it slakes burning thirst.[7]

Indeed, there is nothing unusual in the fact that this form of recreation has a greater impact on the life of the bedouin today than it did in the past. This change occurred when the organized governments in all of the Arab countries began to bar the bedouin from posing a menace to the settled lands and sought to prevent the bedouin from engaging in raids and brigandage and mounting attacks. With his customary means for demonstrating his strength, courage, and martial skill no longer available to him, he turned to the diversion of hunting and raising dogs and falcons to achieve the sense of satisfaction denied to him when he was forbidden to mount raids. Renowned today among the bedouin tribes throughout the Arabian peninsula is one tribe so experienced at hunting that it has almost become a profession for most of the tribe's members. This is the tribe of Ṣlayb, the study of which we shall take up in a special chapter.

The animals and birds that the bedouins have raised and used for hunting are horses, camels, Ṣlaybī donkeys, salukis, panthers, and falcons. Using these, bedouins used to try to hunt the oryx, onager, ibex, gazelle, ostrich, bustard, rabbit, and various other kinds of animals and birds. In previous chapters we have had occasion to discuss these among the animals and birds of the desert, and in the pages to follow we will consider the hunting methods followed by the bedouins to catch these various animals.

The last point I would like to emphasize in closing these remarks is the matter of the hunters' proficiency in shooting with modern weapons. There is no doubt that in former times they were experts at drawing aim with bow and arrow and that they used to train their sons at this. But it is a different matter when it comes to modern firearms. If we leave aside the bedouins of Ṣlayb, most bedouin marksmen do not differ

[7]Kushājim, *Dīwān*, p. 389, no. 383.

much from the rest of mankind in how proficient they are at hitting the target. Most of them, however, and notwithstanding the claims of some (as we have already mentioned), lack opportunities for practice comparable to those available to hunters from among the settled folk. Because of this, Doughty, in speaking of a bedouin who aimed his rifle at an ibex and missed, ventures the judgment that bedouins miss the mark nine times out of ten.[8]

Hunting methods differ from one quarry to another and likewise among different hunters. The way the bedouin hunts varies from the practice of the villager living near the desert, and both of these are likely to differ in their hunting methods from the Ṣlaybī bedouin, who specializes in hunting. One feature the various methods share is their deplorable toll on desert wildlife. Some individuals, as we shall see below, have understood that unlimited slaughter will eventually wipe out a species, at least in the Syrian Desert, and so have limited the amount of game they take. But since the introduction of modern firearms and means of transportation, desert hunting in general has been characterized by the wholesale destruction of herds and flocks and an attitude obviously unmindful of concerns for conservation.

Gazelle-Hunting with the Trap Method

For hunting the gazelle there are numerous methods, the simplest of which is to set traps for it in the broad expanses of the desert steppe. Like the bedouins, the gazelle wanders across the desert from one place to another in search of pasturage and water. As we mentioned in our account of the gazelle, each year it undertakes two practically methodical journeys, one in the winter and one in the summer. Perhaps the main thing to be said in this regard is that the gazelle, like the bedouins, takes refuge in the settled lands in early summer, seeking water and pasture, and returns to the desert in early autumn, when the weather turns cold, rain falls, or it has less need for water. In its travels from the desert to the settled areas it follows well-known routes from which it almost never deviates, and as it approaches the settled lands its path is obstructed by rugged areas or high hills. It therefore makes its way to the narrow passes it sees from afar and tries to traverse the area

[8]Doughty, I, 173.

along these paths. And it is the gazelle's nature to travel in herds led by a doe called the *najūd*; if this doe senses danger it runs in front of the herd and all the others follow her.

Hunters who lived in the villages along the peripheries of the desert or in its oases were aware of this instinct of the gazelle, and also knew the routes that it usually follows when it makes its way from one place to another as it heads for the settled lands. In order to catch the gazelle, they therefore built traps for the animals to fall into behind the mountain passes and hills. The form of the trap and the method for building it are as follows. Using ordinary stones collected from the nearby hills and rocky areas, two walls about a meter or more in height are built in the middle of the plain across which the gazelles travel in order to reach the mountain pass they want to traverse. The beginning of the first wall is about a kilometer or less from the corresponding spot on the second wall, and the closer the two walls come to the mountain pass the nearer they draw to each other, so that finally there remains between them a distance of no more than ten meters as an outlet route for further progress. At this point the two walls both spread out and then rejoin to form a single circle about 100 meters or more in diameter. Outside the wall forming this circle six or seven pits, called *ābār*, "wells," each about three meters deep and about five meters in diameter, are dug along the circumference of the circle. These pits must be right up against the wall of the circle, in which there is a low spot opening onto the edge of each pit.

When the herd of gazelles, heading for the settled lands, tries to cross a rugged, hilly, or mountainous stretch that obstructs the herd's path, then, as mentioned above, it heads for the easily seen pass and proceeds unaware down the ever-narrowing space between the two walls. As the herd continues in its forward progress it is difficult for it to turn back the way it came, because the hunters have made inward-facing projections on each wall and have placed pieces of colored cloth on them. When a gazelle turns back, it no sooner sees these than it starts with fright, runs to push forward again, and gets itself into even more difficulty than before as it makes its way to the trap. When the herd reaches the narrowest place between the two walls, it runs faster and passes on beyond it into the circle we described above. Here, realizing that it is inside a circle and has no way to get out except by jumping over the low spots open in the wall to whatever lies beyond, the gazelles leap over these low spots and thus fall into the pits prepared to receive them. The hunters may also conceal themselves in hiding places at the entrance to the circle; and when they are sure that the herd is inside the circle they get up from their hiding places, stand in the opening behind the herd, and agitate it, thus causing the entire herd to stampede and rush for the above-mentioned low spots. Alternatively, the hunters may bring a dog with them and turn it loose behind the gazelles so that they will stampede and jump over the low spots. In many cases the animals falling into a single pit comprise most of the herd. This occurs when the herd keeps following the *najūd*, which jumps first into the pit: the rest, before the herd becomes too crowded, follow her and jump over that particular low spot.

With this method the gazelles remain alive, except for those that break limbs and so may be trampled to death by the other gazelles. In recent years governments have forbidden the hunting of gazelles in this way. The traps have been neglected and most of their walls have fallen to ruin; but despite all this, hunters in the early years of this century sometimes used to go out to these pits and find gazelles that had fallen into some of them.[9]

Gazelle-Hunting without Recourse to Dogs

Another method for hunting gazelles is the basic method followed by the bedouins of Ṣlayb, and proceeds as follows. Most important of all, the hunters try to disguise themselves: they don garments made of gazelle skin, and sometimes they even cover their rifles in gazelle hide. They work in pairs in different places, one (called the *qannāṣ*, or "marksman") carrying the weapon and the other (called the *ḥawwāsh*, or "driver") driving the game. If a herd of gazelles is seen at some point from afar—many hunters today use binoculars—the one delegated to drive the game, the *ḥawwāsh*, sets out in the direction from which the

[9]Philby saw these walls but did not know what their purpose was. He asked me about them in 1956, so I told him and drew his attention to what I had written on the subject in the journal *Al-Hilāl* in 1930. He translated the entire article into English, but I do not know whether he published it in a journal or book after 1956. Musil, however, had already referred to the walls in his *Manners and Customs*, p. 26.

wind is blowing. Placing the gazelles between himself and the hunter, he then begins to approach the herd so that it will smell him and run off in the direction of the *qannāṣ*, who will already have hidden in a low spot on the route the gazelles are traveling. They will not be able to sense the presence of the hunter because he is downwind from them; and since he has disguised himself by dressing in their hides, they will not be able to see him until they are quite close to him. He then suddenly confronts them and shoots as many of them as he can. It may happen that the herd passes over the hunter and sometimes tramples upon him before realizing he is there. The *ḥawwāsh* may also use a donkey to pursue the game, driving the donkey ahead of him or riding it.

Gazelle-Hunting with Dogs and Falcons

There is another method in which the hunter uses salukis or both dogs and falcons. The dogs help to drive the gazelles toward the hunter, or circle around them so that the hunter can take up a position in hiding along the path the gazelles will take as they flee from the dogs.

In his book *Falconry in Arabia* Mark Allen was puzzled that hunters use the falcon to hunt the gazelle. He considers that on this matter there is a difficulty that is not easy to accept, but he mentions the point nonetheless because it is found in the lore of the bedouins. He then states that he never met a bedouin hunter who told him that he had taken a gazelle by means of the falcon alone.[10] This is true, for it would be difficult for the falcon to kill the gazelle on its own. But the ancient hunters mentioned in the Arabic sources to which he refers used to resort to the falcon when the dogs they had turned loose on the gazelles were unable to overtake them. The hunters would then turn the falcon loose on the gazelles, and it would divert them from their course and make it easier for the dogs to catch up with them. Anyone who reads the memoirs of Usāma ibn Munqidh will find that Usāma referred to the falcon taking part in the hunting of the gazelle in several places in his book. One time he says of his father, whom he used to accompany on the hunt: "One day, when the ground was soaked with rain and thick with mire, he sent the falcons onto the gazelles."[11] He

[10] Allen, *Falconry in Arabia*, pp. 80–82.

[11] Usāma ibn Munqidh, *Kitāb al-iʿtibār*, p. 213.

then says: "The falcons and the dogs brought down the gazelle."[12] And in a third place he says: "If a gazelle was started it [was allowed to] run out beyond [the canebrake] so a panther could be set upon it. If the panther caught it, [well and good]; and if not, the falcons would be set loose upon it. Except by a twist of fate, it was very seldom that any game escaped from us."[13]

The bedouins also used to use horses to drive gazelles, and turned dogs loose to circle around them and to turn them back to the horsemen. They continued to do this until the last years of the nineteenth century, and proceeded similarly when hunting the panther.

Gazelle-Hunting with the Automobile

Today some of the bedouin shaykhs and certain hunting enthusiasts in the villages and towns use the automobile to hunt gazelles. They seek them out in their pastures in the middle of the plains and pursue them over terrain in which it is possible for automobiles to travel faster than the gazelles can run. When they overtake the herd fleeing before them, they open fire on the gazelles and kill as many of them as they can. This is a method of no less cruelty than the trap method discussed above. On level ground it is rare for one gazelle from the entire herd to escape, since, as we have said, the gazelles all follow the *najūd* and when they flee one sees them form a single line, like a string of pearls. When the automobile pulls up beside the herd, the hunters fire with their rifles at it, shooting one gazelle after another without stopping until they have wiped out the entire herd, or most of it. They then retrace their route to collect their quarry from the ground. Arab governments have also forbidden hunting by this method, but there is little enforcement, and indeed, there is no enforcement on certain government officials themselves and on some hunting enthusiasts who are men of influence.

Hunters may also undertake their search for game with their automobiles by night. They go out to the plains where the gazelles graze, and then shine the headlights of their automobiles in various directions until they meet with the eyes of the gazelles in the fields. Their eyes

[12] *Ibid.*

[13] *Ibid.*, p. 202.

glow in the dark and indicate where they are grazing, and when the lights of the automobiles are turned on them the gazelles freeze where they stand and move only slightly as the vehicles approach. They remain in position, dazed and bewildered and making no effort to move from their places, until the automobiles reach them and the hunters open fire. If they flee, the lights of the automobiles are in themselves enough to hinder or stop them.

Gazelle-Hunting from a Blind

There is another method that may be used, especially by the tribesmen of Ṣlayb and, following their example, some individuals from the villages adjoining the desert. By night at certain pools, the hunters take cover in blinds or in holes they have dug and surrounded with some stones to conceal themselves. They make sure that the holes are located downwind of the direction from which the gazelles will come, since for protecting themselves these animals rely more on their sense of smell than on their sense of sight. Then, when the gazelles come to drink at the pools, the hunters catch them by surprise and kill some of them. The hole is large enough to hold a man, or two men at most: it is dug to a depth of about half a meter, and then around it is built a wall of small stones, also about half a meter high, so that when the hunter sits in the hole no part of his body shows. In the wall he makes openings large enough for the muzzle of his rifle, so that he can open fire on the quarry when it approaches the water and comes within his range. The hole is called a *nūja*,[14] and it seems that its use goes back to an early age.

When bedouins are on the move, they consider the best place for hunting to be the area that lies between the scouts (*ṭalā'i'*) that go out ahead of the main party and the main party itself. Game, whether animals or birds such as ostriches or bustards, usually builds up in this area, which extends for about two miles. If they escape the hunters and run or fly in the direction of either those in the main party or the scouts, they are forced to turn back toward the hunters.

[14]Kushājim (*Al-Maṣāyid wa-l-maṭārid*, p. 241) reports that this blind was called a *qarmūṣ*, and says that it is a small hole that the hunter digs and builds up on all sides so as to conceal his body in it.

Hunting the Ibex

Ibex live in the mountains and take refuge on their highest peaks, and they have an amazing ability, equaled by hardly any other animal, to climb the rocky peaks and move about among them. Most of the mountains bordering the desert rise no more than 300 or 400 meters above the surface of the desert surrounding them and are not more than ten kilometers long, while in a long mountain range there may be six or seven mountains separated by lowlands or wadis. It is therefore easy for hunters to encircle a certain amount of game in a small area. On many of the mountains along the fringes of the desert one can find open springs where in the summer it is possible for the ibex to reach the surface of the water and drink. These springs or the land adjoining them have thus been a good place for hunters to hide to hunt ibex. It is interesting to note that the Arabs have given these springs names associating them with the ibex. In the eastern mountains near Tadmur there is a spring called 'Ayn al-Wu'ūl, "Spring of the Ibex" and in the mountains bordering the Nafūd region there is also a spring named 'Ayn al-Wu'ūl. The bedouins call the ibex *bidin*, hence every spring with the name 'Ayn al-Bidin is also a spring frequented, or once frequented, by ibex.

The best method for hunting ibex is for the hunter either to conceal himself near the spring along the paths used by the ibex, downwind of the direction from which he expects the animals to come, or to hide somewhere on the mountain and rely on others to drive the ibex from various parts of the mountain so that they pass by him within shooting range. In either case, the clothing of the hunter must be dust-colored so that the quarry will not see him, and the wind must be blowing from the same direction as that from which the animals are coming so that they will not catch his scent (since the wind is blowing from them to him). One of the ibex hunters in al-Qaryatayn told me that sometimes the ibex almost walked over their bodies as they hid among the rocks. Most of the mountains frequented by the ibex have rocky refuges where the ibex, when forced to do so, can flee and seek a safe haven. My father told me that once he shot and killed an ibex at the peak of such a haven on Jabal al-Bārida. But although they could see it hanging down one side of the high rock, they could not reach the top since none of them was able to climb it. They returned from the hunt and left the ibex, and the next day vultures and other birds of prey began to hover around the carcass.

During and prior to the inter-war period, the Egyptian prince Yūsuf Kamāl and some of the men of his entourage used to go out to the mountains near Tadmur and hunt ibex, and would hire a band of hunters from al-Qaryatayn and Tadmur to drive the ibex for them in the way described above. But here I must mention that Prince Yūsuf Kamāl did not permit any of his companions to shoot, and himself shot only male ibex and gazelles and on many occasions was satisfied to kill only one ibex. Once security came to prevail in these mountainous regions, however, they became grazing grounds for village goatherds and bedouin shepherds, with the result that most of the ibex in these areas were killed. Most of the remaining ones have moved off to the distant mountains, and if the herdsmen and bedouins continue in their tracks, it would not be surprising if this animal disappeared from the mountains of the desert.

Rabbit Hunting

Rabbits are hunted using automobiles by night, the same way gazelles are. The lights of the automobile are turned on the rabbit's eyes and, dazzled by the powerful light, it does not know which way to flee. Depending on the extent to which it is facing the light, the light reflects from its eyes and makes them shine. This reveals the rabbit's position to the hunters, who then open fire on it.

Rabbits are also hunted by day using salukis, which are turned on the rabbits when the hunters see them and which can also detect their hiding places behind small shrubs. Rabbits can further be hunted using falcons, which, when turned loose, circle and glide overhead until they see a rabbit, stoop onto it, and kill it. Hunters may also hunt rabbits without recourse to the dog or falcon, if the hunter is able to follow the rabbit from one crouching place to another and if his eyesight is sharp enough to detect behind which shrub the rabbit is hiding. The rabbit remains crouching in its hiding place until the hunter is quite close, and when it jumps out to flee from him the hunter shoots at it. If the rabbit is not hit it runs a long way and makes a large circle around the area in which it is accustomed to roaming or in which it has made its burrows.

After a time it comes back, and the experienced hunter can take cover behind the small shrubs among which the rabbit roams, waiting for it to return. When it does, it is an easy matter for the hunter to bag it. The best of the various methods is undoubtedly that followed by the bedouins—use of the saluki and the falcon together. The dog is better able to detect the rabbit's hiding place among the shrubs, and the falcon gliding overhead is better able to see it when it moves; both of them help the hunter to determine the rabbit's location and to bag it.

Bustard Hunting

The bustard provides one of the most gratifying and enjoyable forms of hunting. It is, firstly, hunted like the gazelle, with automobiles. The hunters go out to the plains, where the automobiles can travel at a high speed, and look for the bustard. If they encounter a flock or only a few of them flying ahead of them at a low height, then if the automobile can catch up with them as they fly, the hunters pass under the bustards and open fire on them with their guns.

This method, however, only achieves its most consummate form if the hunters have falcons with them to set on the bustards, and in this case the advantage and superior skill of the falcon in pursuing and catching the quarry is demonstrated. Nothing is easier for the falcon than to catch a bustard: the falcon no sooner sees a bustard in the sky than it circles over it, stoops down on it, and there it is between the falcon's talons on the ground. The bustard may sometimes evade the falcon in the air until it finds itself in front of the latter. Then, when it senses that the falcon is directly behind it and has almost caught up with it, it voids a loose stream of droppings on it and wets it, with the result that the falcon abandons the chase and is unable to fly all the rest of the day, leaving the bustard and its fellows secure from the falcon's depredations. If it can, it does the same thing when it is on the ground; it turns its tail in the falcon's direction as it circles, and if the falcon comes close to it the bustard voids on it. The bustard probably does this out of fear, and in this way nature has endowed it with a means of protecting itself and its species. Thus they claim that the falcon approaches the bustard from the sides, comes in, and pounces on it from above so that its droppings will miss it.[15]

Bedouins look for bustards in the plains used as grazing lands and use falcons which, as mentioned above, they have trained. It is the falcons that catch the bustards for them, just as used to be the case with the ancient Arabs. Most of the *amīr*s in the peninsula today buy falcons and use them to hunt the bustard in their desert lands. One sees that the master of the hunt has prepared himself a special hunting glove (*quffāz*) to put on his hand so that the falcon can perch upon it.

Hunting the Sand Grouse

We have already mentioned above that the sand grouse is the most common bird in the desert. It flies in flocks so thick that the bedouin can hit one of the birds with a stone from his sling. Bedouin enthusiasts of the hunt are not as keen on hunting the sand grouse as they are on hunting the bustard; and indeed, falcons are probably not able to catch the sand grouse with the same ease with which they catch the bustard. When it is alone, the sand grouse stays on the ground much of the time and is concealed in its hiding places from the falcon. The falcon is thus an excellent one if it can catch the sand grouse,[16] and for this reason the methods for hunting it differ completely from those for hunting the bustard.

The most widespread method among the bedouins is to hunt it on the ground when it lands in vast flocks, either in the fields where it feeds or at the water sources where it drinks. As for the people of the villages adjoining the desert, they hunt it using the blind we discussed where hunting the gazelle is concerned. The sand grouse, in all its different varieties, is by nature fond of water, especially during the summer season. One sees it heading for the rain pools and flowing springs in huge swarms, so the hunters take cover in the blinds already described and shoot them. The number hit by a single shot from a shotgun may come to about 50 or more, and I am not exaggerating when I say that

[15] *Ibid.*, p. 85. See also Usāma ibn Munqidh, *Kitāb al-i'tibār*, p. 217; Cheesman, p. 312.

[16] Kushājim, *Al-Maṣāyid wa-l-maṭārid*, p. 58.

sometimes the area around the blind is so thickly covered with sand grouse that none of the surface of the ground is visible. I still remember that once, when I was hunting sand grouse and was positioned in the blind, some sand grouse chicks were drinking water and so filled their craws and wet their feathers that they were unable to fly when we opened fire on the flock. The sand grouse chicks were not hit, and we collected them, cut the primary feathers on their wings, and left them alive. One of them lived for a long time with the chickens at the home of one of the villagers.

The hunter in the blind must conceal himself: he must wear only dust-colored clothing, and he must make no movement until the sand grouse are crowded around the water and raising a great clamor. He can then put his shotgun through one of the small openings in the blind, aiming at the place where the thickest concentration of sand grouse is located, and fire. If he wants to, he may be able to fire a second shot at them when the surprised and frightened birds fly up en masse over the surface of the water.

When the sand grouse thickly congregate around the pool or some other place where there is water and begin to drink, each bird will carry a bit of water in its craw and take to flight. As you sit in the blind, you realize that some of the water is falling from the beaks of the sand grouse onto you like a light drizzling rain. And in some seasons the sand grouse may proliferate and invade the dry-farmed fields of the village folk, covering the fields and devouring most of their grain. Hence their saying: "In the year of the sand grouse comes the selling of the covers."[17]

Some of the villagers also hunt the sand grouse by night in the areas where the birds roost in flocks overnight. Each of the hunters takes a she-ass along with him, drives it ahead of him, and hides himself behind it until he reaches the spot where he knows the sand grouse are roosting. As the donkey approaches the flock, the birds begin to cluster close together, until they are so densely packed on the ground that the hunter, seeking to kill as many as possible with a single blast from his shotgun, decides to open fire on them. I was told that the villagers in northern Syria also hunt the sand grouse using nets at night when the

[17][Cf. the explanation of this proverb above, p. 126, note 12.]

birds roost in recently harvested lands. So many are caught in a single net that the hunter is not able to carry it by himself.

As for the dark sand grouse (*al-qaṭā al-kudrī*), this bird is not as numerous as the common sand grouse. It is only hunted near the water and in the early autumn, for it is extremely alert and does not long linger at the water when it comes to drink. Rather, it comes suddenly in the early morning, drinks quickly, and flies off without tarrying. As mentioned earlier, this is the bird al-Shanfarā described when he said:

> By night come dusky sand grouse to drink of what I leave,
> In thirst they flock together as their ribs all knock and heave.
> I hastened, and they also, toward the water beckoning nigh,
> But I waded in ahead and rest with garments tucked up high.[18]

Hunting the Ostrich and Oryx

Hunting of the ostrich and the oryx has either entirely or almost entirely ceased throughout the Arabian peninsula. These two animals and the gazelle used to be the main quarry pursued by the Arabs, both settled folk and bedouins, as we find immortalized in their tales and poems.

The Arab used to rely on his horse to take him to or near to the places where the quarry lived, and used his salukis to prevent it from fleeing and if possible kill it. This kind of diversion, or means of gaining one's subsistence, did not reach the point where it involved annihilating the species and rendering the animal extinct. Until recent times the bedouins, and in particular the Ṣlayb, continued to hunt the ostrich and the oryx according to the method of the ancients. But when basic firearms were introduced, followed by such modern military weapons as the Mauser and its successors, the balance between the hunter and the prey disappeared. The ostrich and the oryx thus began to seek refuge in remote areas in the heart of Arabia where it was difficult to reach them, and the day is not far off when we will see no further trace of these two animals anywhere in Arabia.

[18] Al-Zamakhsharī, *A'jab al-'ajab*, p. 50.

Figure 72: A bedouin carrying the falcon he uses to hunt.

In any case, the modern methods for hunting them do not differ much from those formerly employed, assuming that they are not pursued with automobiles and airplanes, as some of the *amīr*s do today. Above all else, they depend on the wind blowing toward the hunter, so that it does not carry his scent to the quarry, and on the hunter wearing camouflage clothing so that he is not seen from afar and, if possible, from close at hand. If he plans to hunt in this way his clothing should be white or sandy-colored. Further, he will hide himself behind a camel or white horse so that the oryx will only become aware of his presence when it is already within his range. The hunters from the tribes of al-Sharārāt and Ṣlayb are the bedouins most skilled at and most famous for the hunting of the ostrich, oryx, and gazelle. These days, however, they are forced to be satisfied with hunting the few remaining and rarely encountered gazelles, since the oryx and ostrich have disappeared from the Syrian Desert.

CHAPTER XVI

THE BEDOUINS AND RELIGION

The Bedouin's Profession of Islam

The Arab bedouin today professes Islam, though there were once Christian Arab tribes. Descendants from these Christian tribes survived in Jordan up until the not so distant past, and those of them who settled down upheld the noble Arab traditions. These days the bedouin's adherence to religion varies, depending on the country in which he is and the tribe to which he belongs. In former times it was characteristic of the bedouins to fail to keep to all of the canonical observances enjoined by the faith. Hence the passage one finds in the Qur'ān: "The bedouins are more obstinate in unbelief and hypocrisy and more likely to be unaware of the bounds set by what God sent down upon His Apostle; and God is All-knowing, All-wise. Among the bedouins are those who take what is used up for a fine and wait for the turns of fortune to go against you. The evil turn shall be against them, and God is All-hearing, All-knowing."[1] And likewise: "The bedouins say: 'We believe.' Say: You do not believe; rather say: 'We submit', for faith has not yet entered into your hearts."[2]

Today it would be difficult for us to apply a general rule to the extent to which the beoduin adheres to the canonical observances established by Islam, for when he submitted to Wahhābism in Najd he demonstrated that he was a believer, an adherent to the canonical observances of his faith, and willing to rush to the cause of defending that which Islam enjoins. Today the bedouins of Saudi Arabia are probably

[1] Sūrat al-Tawba (9), vss. 97–98.
[2] Sūrat al-Ḥujurāt (49), vs. 14.

those that, of all the bedouins in the world, most closely adhere to their religion and abide by its requirements. But this does not hold true with respect to all bedouins, or in all ages. The explorers who lived with the bedouins in the last century and in the early years of this century differed in their views. Burckhardt, for example, remarked that most of the bedouins meticulously fast during Ramaḍān and adhere to most of the canonical observances established by Islam.[3] Palgrave, on the other hand, was of the opinion that Islam, through the course of the past twelve centuries, had had no influence on the bedouins, for better or for worse, or if it had any effect at all it was a slight one.[4]

We find Musil saying, from another viewpoint, that throughout the two years 1908 and 1909 he never saw a single Rwāla bedouin performing the prescribed prayers.[5] Volney records a discussion he had with a bedouin on matters of religion. When he commented that the latter did not fulfill the required duties, the bedouin replied: "How shall we make ablutions, who have no water? How can we bestow alms, who are not rich? Why should we fast in the Ramadan, since the whole year with us is one continual fast? and what necessity is there for us to make the pilgrimage to Mecca, if God be present every where?"[6] Dickson, on the other hand, claims that the bedouin believes in and observes all of the religious duties: if he would occasionally fail to pay the alms tax, it would only be in years of drought. By virtue of his nature and his way of life, he was compelled to commit his fate to God.[7]

I personally noticed that the bedouins of ʿAnaza in general and of the Rwāla in particular fail to adhere much to the regulations and duties enjoined by Islam, with the exception of those who have strong contacts with the settled folk and thus, to a great extent under the influence of their co-religionists in the towns, fast and pray. Even these, however, do not know much about Islam or about any of the particulars in many of the regulations and duties. By way of illustration, I recall that among certain tribes a woman, if divorced, could marry another man before her waiting period (*ʿidda*) was over; some of the settled

[3] *Notes on the Bedouins and Wahábys*, I, 99–106.
[4] Palgrave, I, 3, 8–10.
[5] Musil, *Arabia Deserta*, p. 427.
[6] Volney, I, 415.
[7] Dickson, p. 45.

folk thus condemned them when the divorced woman gave birth, since her son would not know who his father was. Sufficient proof that in centuries past they were not observant of the faith lies in the fact that they attacked the pilgrimage routes and plundered the Muslim pilgrims.

Similarly, on the matter of inheritance they do not adhere to the provisions of Islamic law or to the civil codes: a daughter is barred from the estate. Their administration of justice also differs in some of its provisions from both Islamic and civil law. Aḥmad Waṣfī Zakarīyā maintained: "Theft, whether outright theft or unlawful seizure, is among them not a shameful deed, as the settled folk conceive it and are taught: rather, it is considered a kind of heroic act."[8] A woman's consent to adultery absolves the adulterer of responsibility for his act, but the woman's kin will take vengeance on her.[9]

Palgrave on one occasion mentions that he began to discuss the issue of religion with a bedouin, and expressed to him his surprise at how he could face God on the Judgment Day after the way he had spent his life raiding, plundering, and looting. In such a case as his, did he expect there to be a place for him in Paradise? The bedouin replied: "We will go up to God and salute him, and if he proves hospitable (gives us meat and tobacco), we will stay with him; if otherwise, we will mount our horses and ride off."[10]

Sacrifices Among the Rwāla

The strongest manifestation of religion among the bedouins is probably their respect for the 'Īd al-Aḍḥā, the "Feast of the Sacrifice," and their concern for making sacrifices for their deceased kinsmen on that feast. In their view, 'Īd al-Aḍḥā, and not 'Īd al-Fiṭr, the "Feast of Fast-breaking," is their greatest feast; many of them do not fast during Ramaḍān and celebrate neither the Prophet's birthday nor the date of his *hijra*—nor indeed do they know the dates for these last two feasts. In general, Arab Muslims have only taken a particular interest in these two feasts in recent times, probably in imitation of the Christians.

'Īd al-Aḍḥā is of special importance to the bedouins because it is associated with the pilgrimage season and the sacrifices made for their

[8] *'Ashā'ir al-Shām*, I, 322.

[9] *Ibid.*, I, 327.

[10] Palgrave, I, 32–33.

dead. Custom has it that during the feast a family should sacrifice for the member it has lost in the year just past or earlier. The sacrifice itself is made from the livestock the bedouin possesses: sheep among sheep-herding bedouins and camels among camel-owning ones. On one feast in late July 1951 I witnessed many sacrifices of camels, among them these three: one for a bedouin shaykh by the name of Khashm al-Qa'qā', shaykh of the tribe of al-Qa'āqi'a, which had formerly held the leadership of the tribe of Rwāla; another for Shaykh Danḥān, shaykh of the clan of al-Duwayraj; and a third for a person by the name of al-Muhdhir. The last two had died late in the year immediately preceding the 'Īd al-Aḍḥā.

The slaughtering of the sacrificial animal usually takes place on the first day of the feast, but the bedouins prefer that the sacrificing occur on the morning of the second or third day of the four-day feast. A camel, usually chosen from among the best and fattest ones, is brought, made to kneel down, and hobbled by its front legs (and sometimes also the back ones). A saddlebag of white linen is brought and placed on the back of the sacrificial camel. As it lies facing the *qibla*, the direction of Mecca, the head of the camel is turned toward the east and the animal is slaughtered by plunging a knife into the lowermost part of the neck, where the chest begins, and opening the cut to a width sufficient for an ample flow of blood.[11]

In the saddlebag are customarily placed a small vessel or container full of water, and with it a supply, called a *dhahāb*, or "traveling kit," of dates, flour, or both. There may also be included certain implements that the deceased had carried or used during his lifetime, such as a pipe, flint and steel, comb, kohl jar, mirror, cane, and even some tobacco if he was a smoker. In many instances it also includes a riding stick, or *khayzurāna*.

In most cases the camel is slaughtered by one of the deceased's relatives, one of the oldest family members, or one of those closest to him—his son, brother, paternal cousin, or a representative of one of these. If they are close to the villages and the family performing the sacrifice has no one to undertake the task, they entrust one of the villagers with the job. The slaughterer says: "In the name of God,"

[11]See above, p. 220, Figure 29.

repeats "God is great" three times, and then addresses the deceased, saying: "Before you is your sacrifice, O So-and-so."

The sacrificial animal is skinned by first cutting from the rearmost part of the back to the top of the hump. The hump is extracted in two pieces, which are taken by the family of the deceased, then they and their relatives take what they wish from the tastiest cuts of the meat. The rest is given to those who skinned the animal and to the poor and needy who have gathered around it; many a time these needy quarrel over this matter and argue over the leftover parts of the sacrificed animal. The hide is then cut in half and made into two waterskins, or *rāwiyas*; the skin of the neck is also cut in half for making into what is called a *sarīd*, that is, a band or bands for stitching into receptacles.

In the view of the bedouins, the tastiest cuts of meat are, first of all, the *kharza*, which is behind the neck near the hump, then secondly the *ḥimāla*, which is the place where one rides from behind, near the tail at the top of the rear legs, and thirdly the foreleg, because its meat is, so they claim, "more tender" than the meat of the thigh. The neck is cut in two and each needy or poor person is given a piece from one. It may be that more than one animal is sacrificed for the deceased. Some bedouins are convinced that the deceased rides this sacrificial animal to Paradise on the Judgment Day—hence the supplies and the riding stick. If it happens that the family of the deceased has purchased the animal they offer for sacrifice, they brand it with the symbol of their brand, and others outside the family stand as witness to the fact.

The ropes with which the camel had been hobbled are cut when the animal is slaughtered, and are not untied. The items placed in the saddlebag may be distributed if the family of the deceased wishes to do so. As for the flour, it is mixed with water and kneaded into dough, baked, and distributed to those present. The heart and liver are finely chopped, and the minced meat is given to those who helped to skin the sacrificed camel and cut up its meat.

The Rwāla bedouins generally sacrifice during the year in which they lost the deceased, so long as it is possible for them to do so and if they have a camel they can dispense with and sacrifice for the sake of the deceased. They believe that through this sacrifice they are protecting the livestock they own. It may sometimes happen that the ʿĪd al-Aḍḥā finds the bedouins camped at a pool or in camping places near the villages adjoining the desert. This then becomes a festival for the villagers, for during the days of ʿĪd al-Aḍḥā they hurry to the camps of the bedouins so as to take the meat of the sacrificed animals free of charge, especially if it has been a year of plenty and there are many camels being sacrificed. Taking advantage of these festivals, the poor villagers stay close to the tents of the family of the deceased for whom the camel is to be sacrificed, help them in the skinning and meat cutting, and are given meat to compensate them.

I was once told that a villager was helping a bedouin and held the head of the sacrificial camel when the bedouin slaughtered it. Addressing his deceased father, the villager said: "Before you is your sacrifice, O Father," supposing that having done so God would be pleased and would accept from him this sacrifice which the bedouin himself was making for one of his kinsmen. As it happened, the bedouin heard him and said to him: "By God, it is not the sacrifice of your father. God knows how many dirhams I paid for it." (Apparently, not having camels of his own from which he could sacrifice, the bedouin had paid well for this one.) He was unwilling to accept that anyone else should share in this sacrificial camel, even if only in name.

The slaughter of animals on other festive occasions, such as a wedding, a circumcision, the birth of a boy, or for the sake of a guest, is not a requirement of religion or even part of general religious custom. Rather, it is general Arab custom and holds true for both bedouins and settled folk, although in the case of some traditions there may possibly be a religious foundation for them. Archimandrite Būluṣ Salmān gave a lengthy description of the various forms of such slaughterings as he saw them among the bedouins of Jordan—an account which the reader may consult for further details.[12]

The Markab, or Sacred Litter

Up to the present time the Rwāla retain a special sacred litter which they sometimes call the *ʿuṭfa* and sometimes "Abū l-Duhūr," "Father of the Ages." In general, they apply to it the name by which they refer

[12]Archimandrite Būluṣ Salmān, *Khamsat aʿwām fī sharqī l-Urdunn* (Ḥarīṣā, 1929), pp. 227–58.

to any litter, the *markab* (lit. a "vessel" in which one rides).[13] The *markab* is something familiar to all bedouins, especially the wealthy ones. It is a throne-like litter made of wood that is placed on the back of a she-camel or camel; it has poles made of thick sticks that project upwards, so that if a cloth is set up over it the litter becomes a small tent, or *kinn*, in which a woman can take shelter from the heat of the sun during the day's traveling. The bedouins have known these litters since the time of Imru' al-Qays when, referring to the litter as a *ghabīṭ*, he said:

> Ah, the day I entered the litter, that of 'Unayza,
> Who cried out: "For shame! A reason for walking's now
> shown."
> She said, as with us together the litter rocked:
> "You've wounded my camel, Oh Imru' al-Qays, so go and
> get down."
> But I told her: "Go on, and lighten your grip on the reins,
> And send me not away from your fruits of renown."[14]

For as long as the litter has been known it has been associated with women. It is particular to them, and if a woman rides in one both she

---

[13]There are bedouins who say that the word *'uṭfa* should be applied to the girl who rides in the litter and not to the litter itself. In his book *Notes on the Bedouins and Wahábys* (I, 144), Burckhardt claims that this litter is of two types: one called *markab* and the other *'uṭfa*. He then says (p. 311) that both kinds are unknown in the Ḥijāz, but rather are known only among the 'Anaza. He furthermore mentions (pp. 145, 146) that al-Ṭayyār, shaykh of the Wild 'Alī, has an *'uṭfa*, while what Ibn Sumayr and Ibn Faḍl have is only a *markab*. Guarmani says of certain tribes that they fight under a single flag, and then states: "I say flag and not *ootfe*; I do not find *ootfe* any longer in use in the Neged. In Syria only the Biscer [Bishr] of the Emir Heidal [Hadhdhāl] and the Ruola of Sceilan [Sha'lān] use it." Carruthers, author of the Introduction to Guarmani's book, adds in a note: "According to Burckhardt this ancient custom was dying out even in his day and is doubtless now extinct. The last one in use belonged to the Ruwalla." It would seem that Carruthers was uninformed on the history of the bedouins and their present circumstances, otherwise he would have mentioned that the *'uṭfa* survives today among the al-Sha'lān, shaykhs of the Rwāla. See Guarmani, p. 35 n.

[14]From the *mu'allaqa* of Imru' al-Qays; see al-Tibrīzī, *Sharḥ al-qaṣā'id al-'ashr*, pp. 9–10.

and the litter are called *ẓaʿīna*, "the journeying one." As Zuhayr said in his *muʿallaqa*:

Look hard, my friend; can you yet spy
The traveling maids that litters bring,
Who through ʿAlyāʾ their way do ply
O'er paths above the Jurthum spring?
Arising with the break of dawn,
Before the sun shines on the land,
In Wādī l-Rass they then were gone,
Just as the mouth receives the hand.[15]

ʿAmr ibn Kulthūm said:

Halt, before our paths shall part,
Oh damsel borne in litter's frame.
We shall bare to you our heart,
And you shall tell to us the same.[16]

The bedouin *markab* is of various kinds. One of them, in keeping with its name, is shaped like a small ship or boat set sideways on the back of the camel. Another type is oblong, and another is closer to a square in shape.

The *markab* of concern to us here, the *ʿuṭfa* of the Rwāla, is a wooden throne-like rectangle made of poles, similar to tent poles, interlocked with other poles at the top, middle, and bottom so that it looks like a topless cage. It measures about two meters in height, including the saddle placed under it on the camel, two and three-quarter meters in length, about 50 centimeters in width at the bottom and about 70 centimeters at the top, so that the face of the litter is wider at the top than at the bottom. It differs from other litters or *markab*s in that it is decorated with black ostrich feathers and to the Rwāla represents a sacred symbol that is used only in times of danger. It is always kept in the tent of the *amīr*, and leaves it only when the *amīr* is traveling with his tribe to the desert, which he seldom does these days.

[15] *Ibid.*, pp. 55–56.
[16] *Ibid.*, p. 110.

The *'uṭfa* represents the glory, might, and prestige of the Rwāla, and so resembles the large flag carried by an army's standard bearer in front of its commander. If the tribe was attacked and the battle was a clash that would decide its destiny and its standing among the other tribes, the shaykh would muster the horsemen and marksmen and motion to a virgin girl from among his or his family's daughters to ride in the *'uṭfa* on a camel, in most cases on a white one. The girls, if relatives of the girl in the litter, would rally around it to make trilling noises and call out rousing slogans to the warriors, and the horsemen from their tribe would circle around them and call out war cries to one another. Each one rises in the esteem of his woman and the rider in the *'uṭfa*, and the women would vow to die in defense of the *'uṭfa* rather than let a single one of the enemy reach it. The battle was thus a struggle to defend the inviolability, honor, sanctity, might, and dignity of the tribe.

Arabic poetry refers to situations in which the poets mention how their women followed behind them during battles, fanning the flames of valor in the warriors, encouraging them to keep fighting, and dissuading them from withdrawal or retreat during the battle:

> Behind us came damsels who were noble and fair,
> Whom we guard lest they stray or humiliation bear.
> They urge on their husbands and cause them to swear
> That when they meet squadrons whose dust fills the air,
> They'll seize flashing sabers and cloaks fine to wear
> And captives whose legs chains of iron will bear.[17]

The custom then began to crystallize among the bedouins and to assume a form with a certain religious coloring, until it became the tradition one currently finds among the Rwāla. For them, the *'uṭfa* is a sacred object with a connection to supernatural forces; it reinforces the tribe with power during battles and helps them to gain a great victory.

It is obvious that this custom—that of depending upon a girl or a woman to stir up the courage of the warriors in times of danger—was one well-known in the history of the ancient Arabs. The Day of Ḥalīma is probably the most famous example one could cite in this regard.

---

[17]From the *mu'allaqa* of 'Amr ibn Kulthūm (*ibid.*, pp. 122–23). Some recensions have *fawāris*, "horsemen," instead of *katā'ib*, "squadrons."

Figure 73: The *'uṭfa*, the tribe's symbol of its strength and honor. The Rwāla tribe still preserves its *'uṭfa* and has never lost it in any battle. In the photograph a young man is sitting in the place where a girl would sit in time of war.

This was a decisive day in the history of the tribe. Her brother Ibn al-Ḥārith had been slaughtered by his enemies as a sacrifice to their gods, so Ḥalīma appealed to her family for vengeance. She rode with the army encouraging valor among the horsemen and filling them with zeal for revenge and for proving the sovereignty of her father and the might of her tribe.

In the *mu'allaqa* of al-Ḥārith ibn Ḥilliza there is a clear reference to such an *'uṭfa* as this among the rulers of the Ghassānids when he says:

> When Maysūn's *qubba* at al-'Alāh he made to stand,
> Al-'Awṣā' was then of theirs the nearest land.[18]

It is reported that when the father of 'Amr ibn Hind was killed, 'Amr sent out his brother al-Nu'mān, who had mobilized as many men of his realm as he could, and ordered him to fight the Ghassānids and the rebels of the Taghlib tribe. When he reached Syria he killed a Ghassānid ruler, rescued his brother Imru' al-Qays ibn al-Mundhir, and captured one of the ruler's daughters in a "pavilion" (*qubba*) of hers. This was the Maysūn whom the poet mentions.[19]

The Battle of the Camel, in which 'Ā'isha, the "Mother of the Believers," came out exhorting the army during that decisive struggle between 'Alī and her two sons-in-law al-Zubayr and Ṭalḥa, was a crucial battle in the history of the internal strife among the Arabs in those days. It is claimed that her camel came to look like a hedgehog because of the many arrows that struck it. They did not reach her camel until a great number of her kinsmen and tribesmen had been killed around it; and when they reached her and hamstrung her camel and she fell into 'Alī's hands, the battle ended and the issue was decided.

---

[18] *Ibid.*, p. 137. Al-'Alāh (or al-'Alyā') is a place name. Here we would do well to note that the *qubba*, as this pavilion was known, figured in pre-Islamic Arab tradition and was one of the venerated items possessed by Quraysh. In his *Al-'Iqd (al-farīd)*, III, 314, Ibn 'Abd Rabbih claims that the tribe of Quraysh used to pitch it and in it collect supplies for the army. Father Henri Lammens, however, denies that it had this military signification and claims that the *qubba* marks a survival from pre-Islamic tribal custom. It contained symbols of their fetishes and was placed like a litter on a camel, which the chiefs and notables of the tribes took turns leading by its reins. See *EI*[2], III, 438, in the article "Mecca."

[19] See al-Tibrīzī, *Sharḥ al-qaṣā'id al-'ashr*, p. 137.

Today it is a bedouin tradition that should the *'uṭfa* be captured, the tribe will be defeated and forced to submit to its opponents and acknowledge their ascendancy and primacy. The *'uṭfa* is not returned, and the defeated tribe does not have the right to obtain another one.

For some reason the Arab historians do not have much to say about desert life after the era of the conquests. Hence, we do not hear reports about anything like this *'uṭfa* or about the special litters among the bedouins, except for what is mentioned concerning the *maḥmal* in the days of Queen Shajarat al-Durr. The *maḥmal* displays so many points of similarity to the *'uṭfa* that one could speculate that it is an offshoot from the latter. But it is not an *'uṭfa*, and it would be a mistake to regard it as equivalent to one.

European travelers in the last two centuries were probably the first to take note of this phenomenon in the military life of the bedouins. Burckhardt mentions the *'uṭfa* in his account of a battle that took place between the bedouins of al-Faḍl and Ibn Sumayr near Mzayrīb. During the battle Ibn Sumayr rushed into the midst of the army of al-Faḍl, where the *'uṭfa* was, putting to flight those defending it until he reached the camel carrying it, hamstrung the animal, and captured the *'uṭfa*. The battle ended with victory on the side of Ibn Sumayr.[20] Elsewhere he tells us that al-Ṭayyār, a shaykh of the Wild 'Alī, had an *'uṭfa*, and that the bedouins of 'Anaza are the only ones who possess such *'uṭfa*s.[21]

Palgrave also mentions an *'uṭfa* among the al-'Ajmān bedouins. He claims that they call it a *hadīya*, or "offering," and refers to a battle they fought with Najdīs from the bedouins of Fayṣal ibn 'Abd Allāh ibn Su'ūd in the mid-nineteenth century. The battle ended when the Najdīs reached the *'uṭfa* of the al-'Ajmān: a Najdī warrior whose name he forgot approached the young woman and struck and killed her with his lance, and because of this the al-'Ajmān were defeated.[22] Similarly, Dickson claimed that there were *'uṭfa*s in southern Arabia.[23]

As for Guarmani, he claims, as we have said above, that such *'uṭfa*s are no longer found, except among the bedouins of Syria: one possessed by Ibn Hadhdhāl of the clan of Bishr, and the other by the Rwāla

[20] *Notes on the Bedouins and Wahábys*, I, 135–37.
[21] *Ibid.*, I, 145–46.
[22] Palgrave, II, 71.
[23] Dickson, p. 104.

shaykhs of al-Sha'lān.[24] The same is maintained by Lady Anne Blunt, but she says that the reason for the disappearance of the *'uṭfa* from the other tribes is the scarcity of the ostrich feathers with which it is decorated.[25] This view is incorrect.

Musil mentions that the al-Masālīkh bedouins, a branch of 'Anaza, used to have an *'uṭfa* that was taken from them by the shaykh of the al-Qa'āqi'a.[26] Elsewhere he asserts that the Banū Khālid shaykh Turkī ibn Ḥumayd ibn 'Uray'ir had an *'uṭfa* when they were camped in the Ḥasā near the Arab Gulf. When the al-Fuḍūl bedouins attacked their herds they were unable to hold their ground, and so retreated before them to the tents and fell back on their *'uṭfa*. They seated a girl in the *'uṭfa* and mounted it on a camel, and the girl called out bits of poetry and incited the hearts of the warriors to fight bravely. The attackers overpowered them, however, and surrounded the tents and reached and captured the *'uṭfa*.[27] Some of the bedouins claim that every tribe used to have an *'uṭfa*, but that only two tribes, one of them the Rwāla, were still able to preserve theirs. Amīr Nāyif al-Sha'lān, one of the shaykhs of the Rwāla, told me that he believed that there was another *'uṭfa* belonging to a Najdī tribe which he did not name.

Shaykh Nūrī al-Sha'lān used to take the Rwāla *'uṭfa* with him on his eastward or westward migrations in the desert with his tribe. Musil referred to how, one time when he made the eastward journey to the desert with Nūrī al-Sha'lān, the *'uṭfa* went with them under the protection of his slaves, leading the pack train. The horsemen, however, were in the advance party of the cortege, usually at some distance from the pack train. If they went so far out ahead of the pack train that they could no longer see the *'uṭfa* behind them, then Nūrī, fearful lest the *'uṭfa* or the pack train be surprised by some opponent or raiders from hostile tribes and the slaves alone not be strong enough to repulse them, would order the advance guards to slow down or stop until the *'uṭfa* had drawn closer to them.[28]

[24]Guarmani, pp. 35–36.
[25]Blunt, p. 351.
[26]*Manners and Customs*, p. 396.
[27]*Ibid.*, pp. 214–15.
[28]Musil, *In the Arabian Desert*, p. 241; see also his *Manners and Customs*, p. 573.

Amīr Nāyif, grandson of Amīr Nūrī al-Sha'lān and the brother of Amīr Fawwāz, told me that the *'uṭfa* had helped the Rwāla to gain a great victory over the Druze in their war with them in 1895, and in commenting on this said that it had to be regarded as the standard or flag of the army, and that defense of it was comparable to defense of the flag, the symbol of the army's honor. Some men of his tribe, however, listened to what he said and smiled. During an evening session at the tent, one of these men told me that his father had participated in that battle and had seen the *'uṭfa* itself, together with its rider on the back of the camel, rock as though a spirit were moving it, with the result that the warriors became so inflamed with courage that they achieved such a great triumph as this. It was then Amīr Nāyif's turn to smile, and he said to me: "Do not think it extraordinary when I tell you that about 30 men from the tribe of this man speaking to you fell around the *'uṭfa* in that battle."

The story is often told of a hot still day when the ostrich feathers with which the *'uṭfa* is decorated fluttered due to a breeze so light as to be imperceptible. The bedouins, however, believe that at such times a spirit is moving around in it.[29] Some claim that the Rwāla, when they used to take it with them in their migrations between the Nafūd, the Ḥamād, and the settled lands, allowed themselves to be guided by the *'uṭfa*—or rather by the camel carrying it—in the route they followed, when and where they camped, and when they departed. If the animal stopped at a place, for example, and refused to continue traveling, the tribe would stop and pitch their tents there. They swear oaths by it, just as they swear by various other sacred things, and they claim that it is the *'uṭfa* that protects them. It is said that on 'Īd al-Aḍḥā they used to slaughter a camel in its honor and sprinkle its poles with the sacrificed animal's blood. Hence it is exactly comparable to the *qubba* that contained the deities and other objects worshipped by some of the tribes in pre-Islamic times, or to the Israelites' Ark of the Covenant.

On occasions in the history of the Rwāla when the lands in which they camped suffered from drought and pasturage and water there became scarce, they would set out for neighboring lands where these were available. In this situation, if they felt that the bedouins already estab-

[29]Musil, *Manners and Customs*, p. 574.

lished in these lands would oppose them, they took the *'uṭfa*, placed it on its camel, and sent it with the scouts surrounded by warriors from the various clans gathered under the leadership of the Rwāla. Each clan knew where to deploy its men around the *'uṭfa* when a battle was expected. If one occurred, a girl would be mounted in the litter and the warriors would be obliged to uphold the honor of the *'uṭfa* to the last man.

The Rwāla poets who composed bedouin *qaṣīd*s did not fail to refer to the importance of the *'uṭfa* and its influence in the battles into which the Rwāla plunged with other tribes. One of these odes, in which a poet named Khalaf ibn Zayd describes some fighting, was related to me:

> We set the litter forth and there we gathered around;
> And many shaykhs' heads were then cast to the ground.

The meaning is that they sent out the *'uṭfa* and then rallied close around it. They then attacked their enemies and cut off the heads of many of the shaykhs of the tribes that had been hostile toward them. Musil reported the poem of a poet named Yūsuf ibn Majīd, a warrior with Ibn Sha'lān:

> To the kindling of the flames of war is Abū l-Duhūr inured,
> While Thunderer's aid over armed men meant triumph assured.[30]

He also reports an ode by another describing how al-Sha'lān defended the *'uṭfa* in a battle between the Rwāla and the bedouins of the al-Muntafiq confederation in 1905:

> By morning they came, then took to mount the young Sha'lān band,
> Protecting the *markab* from any extending their covetous hand.[31]

The Rwāla consider that the shaykh who can bring the *'uṭfa* to his tent and keep it there is the shaykh who is the strongest and most

[30] *Ibid.*, p. 631.
[31] *Ibid.*, p. 623.

invincible. When Saṭṭām al-Sha'lān, shaykh of the Rwāla, died in 1904, his son Mish'al got up, announced that he was succeeding his father as shaykh, and transferred the *'uṭfa* to his tent. His uncles al-Nūrī and Fahd, however, decided to remove him from leadership. Al-Nūrī went to him and killed him and brought the *'uṭfa* to the tent of his brother Fahd, who thus succeeded Saṭṭām as shaykh. Then, it happened that one of the slaves of al-Nūrī killed Shaykh Fahd, and al-Nūrī became shaykh and moved the *'uṭfa* to his tent.[32] It remained with him and after the death of his son Nawwāf passed to his grandson Fawwāz. Up to the present it is in the possession of al-Sha'lān, and stands in the tent of the sons of Amīr Fawwāz in 'Adhra.

As for the claim made by one Westerner, to the effect that the Rwāla dislike having the subject of the *'uṭfa* raised with them,[33] this is simply untrue. Once when I was in the tent of Amīr Nāyif, along with a group of Rwāla tribesmen, most of the discussion revolved around the *'uṭfa* and its status. None of them objected to this; and indeed, when I wanted to photograph it and feared that there was not enough light inside the tent, Amīr Nāyif ordered his slaves to take it out into the sunlight, where I took the photograph reproduced in Figure 73.[34]

[32]Musil, *Arabia Deserta*, pp. 238–43.

[33]Robert Montagne, *La Civilization du désert* (Paris, 1947), p. 128.

[34]Above, p. 384. On the Rwāla *'uṭfa*, see Jibrail Jabbur, "Abu-al-Duhūr, The Ruwalah *'Utfah*," in *The World of Islam: Studies in Honour of Philip K. Hitti*, edited by James Kritzeck and R. Bayly Winder (London, 1960), pp. 195–98.

CHAPTER XVII

EDUCATION AND CULTURAL LIFE

Education and Instruction

Camel-raising bedouins know nothing of the educational matters familiar to the settled folk, even at the most elementary levels. They have no regular or primary schools, and indeed, no trace of any institution or system of education, and the written word makes its appearance in their life only under exceptional circumstances. When a bedouin is far from his kin in a settled area, or imprisoned, and is unable to reach them or send them news with a fellow bedouin who knows them, he will ask a townsman to help by writing a note for him saying how he is faring, where he is, and what he wants from his family. He sends it with a messenger to one of the settled folk who knows his family and has contacts with them, and when it reaches them they reply through that same person. I remember one time I wended my way, quite by chance, into a discussion session in a bedouin tent; and when those in attendance learned that I was from Beirut, one of them pulled from his pocket a piece of paper, folded up in a handkerchief, and gave it to me to read. It proved to bear word of a brother of his in Beirut who for some reason or other was connected with the 'Arab al-Maslakh bedouins on the outskirts of the city. He then said to me: "If you should know where the 'Arab al-Maslakh are camped in Beirut, please inquire about my brother for me and send me word of him through a merchant in al-Qaryatayn (whose name he gave me), so I can assure myself as to his circumstances and health. And when you see him, don't forget to tell him that we and all his family are well."

This state of affairs is not, however, absolute. Certain shaykhs of the large tribes may sometimes have a scribe (*kātib*) or religious spokesman (*khaṭīb*) who knows the basics of reading and writing. This happens especially in bedouin milieus that have begun to establish contacts with settled life, buying sheep and sharing the task of tending them with people from the villages and towns. But leaving aside such cases, one sees no trace of the pen and the book. There are accordingly no fixed or mobile schools in the desert; and while most Arab governments have established in their constitutions regulations providing for such schools, these laws for the most part still remain unenacted texts and the schools in question still amount to names with nothing to which to apply. In the past certain Arab states did actually organize some mobile schools and begin to send them to the desert, but these were of meager impact and short duration and I doubt that such schools as these would be able to penetrate to the heart of the desert. The benefit of these mobile schools was probably limited to the fact that at first, when they were in the lands of the sedentary zone near the towns, some boys began to visit them in order to see what the trucks carried and to listen to some of the teachings that the new instructor offered them, and perhaps began to learn to read the letters of the alphabet. But before long, weary of instruction and the teacher and bored with learning to read, they would leave the school. A school itself may be mobile, but it cannot carry knowledge to someone who does not want it.

Another situation one sometimes observes is that bedouin shaykhs who have seen for themselves the benefit of knowledge—especially those who live in the cities as deputies, even if only for a season or so per year—will oblige some of their sons to live with them in the cities, where the boys in turn receive schooling. There are other shaykhs who, having married city women, take a liking to the new life and so spend part of their lives in the towns and send their sons by their urban wives to school. Or one may see shaykhs who have recognized the value of reading and learning and thus send for teachers to instruct their sons and have them camp and live with them in the desert. But all this is of only rare occurrence, and the anomaly provides no basis for comparison. Where it does occur it is limited to the shaykhs, a tiny minority among the bedouins in general. I remember when I met Shaykh Ṭrād ibn Milḥim, shaykh of the Ḥsāna bedouins, more than 40 years ago: he was a self-taught man who read, wrote, and pored over newspapers, and in his *majlis* one sensed oneself in the presence of a man who valued learning. The same can be said of Amīr Nāyif al-Sha'lān, a Deputy in the Syrian Parliament and a self-taught man who perused newspapers and magazines and read books. When he was a Deputy he was able to rally around himself a throng of tribal Deputies in the Parliament who made up a bloc that wielded its own influence on the voting when many of the decisions taken by the Parliament were decided and, up until recently, was taken into serious account when it was time for the balloting. Amīr Nāyif's two daughters by his first wife (a kinswoman of his) studied in the schools of Damascus and were learning a foreign language. The *amīr* is now preoccupied with agricultural matters on his farm at Jabal al-Bārida, where he tries to apply what he can by way of modern agricultural methods.

The same also applies to his nephew Amīr Mut'ib, who was a Deputy from the Rwāla after his uncle and is the son of Amīr Fawwāz, chief of all the Rwāla shaykhs. He studied in some of the Syrian schools and hired a private tutor to go along with him, even in the desert. I met him in the desert in the *majlis* of his father, and Amīr Fawwāz asked me to speak with him in English so I could see how well he knew this language. I found that he knew it very well up to the level reached by the secondary schools that follow the American program in Lebanon. And about 30 years ago it happened that at the American University of Beirut I taught Shaykh Ṣfūq al-Yāwir, son of Shaykh 'Ajīl al-Yāwir, who, as I recall, was in the final year of the secondary section. I also met his father, Shaykh 'Ajīl, at the home of the President of the American University, and was astonished at the breadth of his grasp of the most important world political issues of his day, and amazed by how well he spoke and the power of his personality. But as already mentioned, all these are anomalous cases that provide no basis for broader generalization, and are restricted to the tents of the shaykhs. The general rule is that more than 99 percent of the purely camel-raising bedouins are still illiterate and know nothing of reading and education.

The Majālis as Centers of Education

Despite the bedouins' ignorance of writing—their illiteracy in the literal sense of the word—they are not so ignorant as to be called dolts or ignoramuses. Life in the desert has made it easy for bedouin boys sometimes to attend the adults' *majālis*, or "discussion sessions," in the late afternoon, evening, and forenoon, and to listen in on subjects being studied or discussed. The bedouin is by nature an inquisitive man who enjoys finding out about things, hence one sees bedouin boys lending highly attentive ears to the adults in these sessions, when they are permitted to attend, and receiving orally from them information of use to them. Much of what is discussed in these sessions concerns important matters with some connection to the history or raids of the tribe or world news. Anyone who has read the books of the European travelers will realize how these bedouins used to astound them with their grasp of affairs of the outside world and their knowledge of some of the details concerning them.

In these sessions the sons of the bedouins learn about their society, customs, and institutions, the narratives concerning personalities of their tribe, their system of justice, and their culture. Sometimes they also hear the cases that arise between two litigants and each party's defense of his rights, and in such sessions there are also repeated accounts of raids and heroism, love stories, curious accounts of individuals, odes by the poets of the desert folk, news about the settled folk and the governments in the towns, information concerning rain, the weather, pasturage, and water, and various other matters pertaining to these concerns. These sessions comprise the school of the desert, and sometimes they graduate men prepared for leadership should suitable circumstances arise. In a more restricted sphere something analogous occurs in the women's sessions for the girls: they learn how to become like their mothers in behavior, management of the home, discretion, generosity, and good speech.

The boys may learn bedouin songs from their elders in their private sessions, or from their poets, and before long these songs will have spread throughout the tribe. Some of these are composed in the wake of a particular incident of love or licentiousness that has become known and is now proclaimed in sung bedouin verse. Once I saw some bedouin boys playing together, and then they formed a line, joined hands, and began to sing a new song that at the time, right after some moral incident, had already become widespread. The song was not free from certain obscene expressions.

In closing this discussion I must say that this must not lead the reader to conclude that this state of affairs holds true for all bedouins everywhere. Rather, it applies only to camel-raising nomads and in particular to certain branches of the Rwāla up until the first quarter of this century. Today drastic changes have taken place in most of the tribes in the Arab countries, through the efforts of their governments and the bedouins themselves, as I shall indicate at the end of this book.

Cultural Life in the Desert

Cultural life in the desert manifests itself in two main ways, poetry and folk tales. As for bedouin verse, it is unquestionably held in high esteem. But even had it been set down in writing the same considerations would hold true for it that hold true for the old authentic Arabic poetry. That is, we can conceive of a certain degree of loss from our ancient original poetry in the time that elapsed before it was committed to writing, and similarly, I doubt that any bedouin today remembers a bedouin ode originating more than 200 years ago. Even the poets themselves can seldom remember all the verse they have recited. On many occasions when you ask one of them to recite some of his verse, he will repeat part of a *qaṣīd* (as he calls the bedouin ode) and then refer you to some other narrator or bedouin and tell you: "He knows the whole ode," or "He knows more of it than I do; I have forgotten most of it."

The literary output of the modern-day bedouins does not differ much, in its rhetorical expression, perspectives, and spirit, from much of the ancient Arabic literature that we consider the finest works of the cultural heritage bequeathed by the ancient Arabs. The explanation for this is simple: Arab life in the desert today is not much different from the life of the Arabs in the desert in pre-Islamic and early Islamic times. Indeed, it would probably be more appropriate for me to say that the bedouin way of life familiar to the pre-Islamic Arabs remained as it was through the course of the centuries up until our own times. The pronounced partisan attachment of the ancients to the tribe, their earnest solicitude for its honor and prestige, the ways in which they decided and passed judgment on legal issues, and their devotion to the well-established Arab values of pride, protection of the protégé, disdain, generosity, courage, self-esteem, and a strong predilection for martial skills and raiding—these are the selfsame attributes with which the modern-day bedouin is endowed.

Here I would like to make an important point that is not, I think, irrelevant to our subject. If a student of classical Arabic literature wishes to gain a proper understanding of this subject, if he wishes to comprehend its images and its various constituent metaphors and understand the way of life that it symbolizes, then I would say to him that if he seeks all this he must familiarize himself with modern bedouin life. It is perhaps the good fortune of the modern-day student of the ancient literature that the ancient bedouin way of life represented by the greater part of this classical heritage still continues in many places in the Arab world. The Arab student may not understand what it means to stop at the remains of an abandoned campsite, nor the aim of such a stop, if he has not seen such traces and does not know what sort of information the bedouin today can try to gain from them when he stops there. The remains comprise a book written without a pen and unintentionally by the people who had camped there, and left behind for the passing bedouin. When the latter stops there, he can, if he wishes, read in it whatever he wants to know of their important affairs.

The stones that had supported the cooking pot indicate one thing and the trench that kept water out of the tent another. The locations of the pegs to which the tent ropes had been tied, the places in their evening pastures where the camels had laid down to sleep, the camp's refuse, the location of the site in relation to the other sites in the place where the tents had been pitched, and the bits of cord or scraps or pieces of clothing or furnishings that lie scattered about here and there—all these and many other signs indicate things that the bedouin understands when he passes by the site and stops to examine it. In my journeys to the desert since my youth I have had many bedouin traveling companions, and I do not remember that we ever passed by an abandoned campsite without one of them stopping to "read" what was there and to "question" the traces about those who had left them. Similarly, the student of classical Arabic literature will not be able to comprehend properly many of the Arabic language's expressions, metaphors, and allusions if he is completely unfamiliar with modern-day bedouin life. Indeed, many of these splendid images in the classical poetry would stand out more clearly and more fully in the minds of today's students were it easier for them to familiarize themselves with bedouin life. The same applies to the phrases and words we find in classical poetry for meanings for which we find no parallels in our settled milieus; these terms cannot have the desired effect and impact on our souls when we do not recognize them and do not see what they mean. When one encounters references in the classical poetry to such fragrant desert plants as *'arār*, *shīḥ*, *qayṣūm*, lavender, *ḥawdhān*, *rand*, and *bān*, and thorny desert shrubs and trees like euphorbia, *qalām*, tragacanth, lotus, and *ḍāl*, it is impossible to understand the underlying reason for such references and comprehend their meanings and the objective sought by such citations if we do not recognize them as we recognize references, for example, to the violet, carnation, rose, jasmine, and other flowers and plants.

One must not suppose that today's literature of the desert is equivalent to the classical literature, for there are differences in expression, meter, and inflection that make modern bedouin literature sound strange to the townsman's ear. But despite this difference, it is very close to the classical with respect to its terminology, style, manners of expression, rhetorical figures, and certain poetic images, as well as with respect to the way of life it in general symbolizes. In early Islamic times (and earlier), the desert was the homeland of eloquent classical Arabic and a refuge for those learned in the language, a land to which the grammarians and litterateurs made their way in order to take sayings and reports from its residents and to listen to the narrators of its poetry. Indeed, Ibn 'Abd Rabbih devoted 80 pages of his book *Al-'Iqd* to the speech of the bedouins, doing so, as he says at the beginning of his discussion, "since it was the speech noblest in pedigree, fullest in splendor, most elegant in style, freest from affectation, clearest in its manner [of expression], and since it was the pivot around which all speech turned and the source to which it was traced."[1] He then cites scores of examples attesting to their eloquence and the elegance of their speech.[2]

Literary Genres—the Bedouin Qaṣīd

Literary genres in the desert today are concentrated into two main categories, the folk tale (*qiṣṣa*) and the ode (*qaṣīd*), to which one could add conversation in the *majlis* sessions, the pleading of one's

[1]Ibn 'Abd Rabbih, *Al-'Iqd (al-farīd)*, III, 418.
[2]*Ibid.*, III, 418–98.

case (*murāfa'a*) before the bedouin judges, riddles, proverbs, and poetic admonitions (*'atābā*), as well as the eloquence and purity of style subsumed within these secondary forms. Some of the desert folk rank them among their literary genres, and the styles of some of them will arise for our consideration below.

The bedouin ode, or *qaṣīd*, is the better known of the two main genres, but may be firmly bonded to the other genre, the folk tale or *qiṣṣa*. Hence on many occasions we find the folk tale linked with the *qaṣīd*, so that the latter closes the tale with an elegant poetic flourish. The *qaṣīd* covers almost all of the subjects that classical poetry does: it includes boasting and speaks in glowing terms of the poet's own tribe, describes battles that occurred during raids and the defeat of enemy raiders, and takes up panegyric, erotic description, elegy, and admonition; and while it dispenses with the subject of wine verse, it replaces it with verse on coffee, describing its cups, the aroma of its spices, how well it has been roasted, the way it has been pounded in the coffee mortar (*jurn*) with a musical beat, and how it has been heated and passed around to the guests. In bedouin poetry there are many small melodious pieces, ranging from the war poem that the warriors sing in order to fan the flames of valor in their hearts before the battle (and sometimes during it and when they return from the raid), to the love poem with which lovers console themselves when they are traveling far from their loved ones and wives, to the watering poem sung when one is watering his camels.

These poems, or *quṣdān*, as the bedouins call them, are composed in special meters. These are for the most part meters in which each half line is *majzū'* ("curtailed," i.e. it contains only two feet) and adheres to the following patterns of long and short syllables:

– – . –	– – . –	*mustaf'ilun mustaf'ilun*
– – . –	. – –	*mustaf'ilun fa'ūlun*
– . – –	– . –	*fā'ilātun fā'ilun*
. . –	. . –	*fa'ilun fa'ilun*

Odes in the "uncurtailed" (*ghayr majzū'*) modes adhere to special meters, the most perfect of which segment the line into the following rhythm patterns:

– – . –   – – . –   – . – –   *mustaf'ilun mustaf'ilun fā'ilātun*
– – . –   – . –   – –   *mustaf'ilun fā'ilun fa'lun*

In both the *majzū'* and *ghayr majzū'* meters there are many familiar variations in prosody (*'arūḍ*): *khabn*, *ṭayy*, *qabḍ*, *'aṣib*, and others.

Further, the bedouin *qaṣīd* bears a certain appeal for the children and provides them with many pieces to recite, something the like of which would not have come down to us from the pre-Islamic or Umayyad era. Most of these pieces are melodies that little girls sing in groups during evening discussion sessions. Each group sings in turn, with the women perhaps also joining in with them.

In most of its main forms the consummate bedouin *qaṣīd* takes up the description of the she-camel, as we see in the ancient poetry. Indeed, almost all of the first lines with which the classic bedouin ode of today opens are limited to the dispatching of a messenger, who mounts a she-camel upon which he is supposed to ride to whomever the author is praising, to his beloved, or to the person to whom the ode refers. The poet has no sooner mentioned the camel than he launches into a detailed description of it and an account of its pedigree. The beast is usually a thoroughbred raised by the Sharārāt tribe, the noblest and fastest thoroughbreds in northern Arabia (i.e. the equivalent of the thoroughbreds of Oman in the ancient poetry), then the poet describes its disposition, its color, the color of its saddle, how fast it runs, what kind of food it eats, the provisions of its owner, and other such matters, sometimes adding a description of the messenger who mounts it. More often than not such an ode will begin with *yā rākibin*, "Oh rider," paying no heed to whether the formulation is applicable or not, and then leaves the subject of the rider and turns to that of the she-camel. It may happen that the poet will begin with a first line differing from these, but he will rarely neglect to mention the she-camel and give descriptions of it. I know one ode in which its composer mentions eight messengers mounted on eight she-camels, each of which he describes separately in one or more verses differing from the descriptions given for the other camels.

It must be noted that throughout the Arab world much bedouin poetry, which some authors call *al-shi'r al-nabaṭī*, "Nabataean poetry," has been printed and published. Here, however, I have decided to select two *qaṣīds*, one of them from the book *Manners and Customs of the Rwāla Bedouins* by Shaykh Mūsā al-Rwaylī, as the bedouins called him, the Austrian-born scholar Alois Musil. I have frequently cited him in this book, and Amīr Fawwāz himself praised Musil when I met Fawwāz in the 1950s, after Fawwāz had visited Musil in Prague and talked to him about his relationship with Fawwāz's grandfather Nūrī al-Sha'lān. In this first *qaṣīd*, which Musil claims Amīr Nūrī composed himself in cooperation with his scribe, he praises Musil (Shaykh Mūsā) and enumerates the qualities and attributes by which he was graced. I see no reason to provide a commentary on it; to the bedouins it scans with elusive ease, and in it the two composers do not stray off into the rare vocabulary we see in many of the bedouins' poems.

In Praise of Shaykh Mūsā al-Rwaylī (Alois Musil)

With each new task remembrance of God my soul does fill,
Of the most glorious Lord, the Knower of things unseen:
O rider of a she-camel, a bay in her first teeth still,[3]
A thoroughbred swift which the Sharārāt tribe did wean,
For which an offered hundred cannot turn her owner's will,
A pampered beast which knelt-for load will ne'er demean;
On fringes of the healthful Najd she wanders at will,
Nibbling rose and blossom soft amidst the springtime green;
On her back a saddle with a gorgeous foot cushion is set,
And *safāyif* ribbons adorn her sides with silk most pure.[4]
Out she came from a tent sending forth the latest news yet
Of the shaykh whose great tasks do burden his mind full sore,
From Abū Nawwāf's tent, whose men pose the wolfpack's threat,
Who won such alms-spoils and the shield of the *majlis* bore.[5]

[3][I.e. the camel is not yet five years old, at which age she begins to grow new incisors. See Musil, *Manners and Customs*, p. 333.]

[4][The *safāyif* are long wide ribbons tied at the back of the saddle and allowed to hang down the camel's sides (*ibid.*, p. 292).]

[5]By "Abū Nawwāf" Nūrī al-Sha'lān himself is meant. [I.e. Nūrī al-Sha'lān protects those who gather around him and on raids takes spoils which he later intends to give away as alms.]

On her back rides a youth whom vast deserts give no regret,
Who to distant lands bears word which he carries afore.
If in such lands as these your travel's aim is to be met,
Begin with glad tidings and from us fair greetings assure.
Say: "From you a hunting falcon with a firm resolve came,
A star like unto Canopus, one that notice cannot but greet.[6]
Countries both settled and desolate do know the fair name
Of him of mind acute, unawed by what dooms others to defeat.
Shaykh Mūsā is one whose tidings come in unblemished fame,
On ages long since past he is a fount of knowledge replete.
No chaste beauty did ever give birth to another the same,
And among the bedouin chiefs no equal does he meet.
A ruler, a vizier—on all things does he shed his light;
None save Abū Zayd could in merits o'er him take the lead.[7]
What fair examples of his generous hand words set to flight;
To heavy loss or expense, like Ḥātim, he pays no heed.[8]
With a smile on his face and a will of indomitable might,
He advises in difficult times and all consuls does precede,
A great lion who draws not within the contemptible's sight,
And the stout armor that others cherish in time of need.
If God on high assists him and if his motives proper be,
He will surely come to you with precious tidings that,
Give news of nomads, settled folk, and herdsmen he will see,
Of Rwāla domains, of Fid'ān too, and those of the 'Imārāt,
Of Najd territory and barren wadis of population free,
Of the Sawwān country and lands in which roam the Ḥwayṭāt.
Of fame a cache and of learning and virtues a rolling sea;
Such are the works most perfect which his qualities begat."[9]

---

[6][I.e. Musil's eminence, unlike that of others, is beyond question, just as Canopus is too bright to be obscured, like other stars, on a hazy night (*ibid.*).]

[7][The hero of the medieval 'Antar tales.]

[8]*Ibid.*, pp. 289–92.

[9][Ḥātim al-Ṭā'ī was a pre-Islamic figure whose extraordinary generosity was the subject of many anecdotes in Arab popular and literary tradition.]

The second *qaṣīd* is a long piece by Muḥammad ʻAbd Allāh al-Qāḍī (d. 1285/1868), from the tribe of ʻAnaza, and comprises a section on coffee from a love poem. I have taken it from the book *Al-Shiʻr ʻinda l-badw* by Professor Shafīq al-Kamālī, a work in which he deals in detail with the subject of poetry among the bedouins and cites many examples of it. Due to the length of the *qaṣīd*, I have dropped the section in which the poet expounds on love.

On Coffee, Introducing a Love Poem

O you heart that no sooner mends from sore wounds past
Than there return the anxiety and beat of fluttering heart,
As if with a hawker displaying his wares it stood tied fast,
And to the slender-waisted one was for two years set apart.
It battles great hosts as into thought it plunges deep,
And shows from a box what it would have preferred to hide.[10]
Suddenly memories of loved ones dear over my soul do creep:
My dreams succumb to longing yet at which my heart has cried.
I brought you beans, chosen and bought at cost most dear,
Beans which must not mix with others, as you know well;
I asked you, friend, to put them on euphorbia thrice to sear,
So the market would be overpowered by their diffusing smell.
Beware of undercooking, but take care that they do not burn;
To shake the beans as they roast is the best method to try,
Until they sizzle and sweat and slowly yellowish turn,
Becoming like sapphires in sight of him who passes by.
It creates a smell of an aroma strong, a scent most fine,
Which when inhaled is like ambergris of fragrance profound.
Pound in a *jurn*, so that every yearner will for them pine,
So each heart will hear and rejoice in its crunching sound.
Pour into a shining copper pot close by the fire,

[10][I.e. the lover's troubled contemplation brings to mind secrets he would rather not recall.]

One shaming the crane's fair plume with hue of burnished lead.
Let its spreading aroma arouse the taste of discerning desire,
Rilling gem-like bubbles as its flavor attains a perfect head.
Its smaller bubbles shine and flash like emeralds come alive,
While it brims with larger ones like eyes serene and round.
Pour it into a serving pot with the spices of the colors five:
Cardamom and *mismār* of various kinds all together ground,[11]
Of saffron and *shamtarā* exactly the right amounts to use,[12]
And costly fine ambegris sprinkled liberally o'er all the top;
So that when these and the others blend together and fuse,
Pour it—and may no creature cause you to delay or stop–
Into a china cup beautiful to the eye as it gazes about,
Settling into its seat as the crane settles onto her nest.
You think it is the *shibrāq* when it pours from the spout,
Or the body's blood flowing forth free at its own behest,[13]
Like wine pouring forth from it to slip past one's lips,
Giving the taste of having been mixed with rose-water pure.
On tasting it one feels it is the most limpid wine he sips,
Enthralling to its taster, a cup of delight and rapture.[14]

There are also poems of admonition (*'atābā*), but I fear that they have fallen into disuse as a literary genre among the bedouins, though it was well known that they comprised a literary form among the villagers of Syria and Lebanon. They are still familiar to the villagers, and some of the most famous contemporary singers sing them.

One of them told me that in northern Syria there is a bedouin clan, the al-Jbūr clan, that is well-known among the tribes for this literary form. This informant claimed that this form is bedouin in origin and from the bedouins passed to the villages, and he told me the story of

[11] [*Mismār* is apparently a kind of brown-colored spice or herb. Al-Kamālī, p. 309 (as below, n. 14), states that *mismār* is a kind of carnation.]

[12] *Shamtarā* is a fragrant sweet-smelling herb.

[13] [I.e. the coffee is of a red color deeper even than *shibrāq* (an unspecified red substance) or blood.]

[14] Shafīq al-Kamālī, *Al-Shi'r 'inda l-badw* (Baghdad, 1384/1964), pp. 306–10. [In the Arabic text Professor Jabbur also acknowledges al-Kamālī for notes and commentary which have not been reproduced here.]

the man who first became known for admonition poems among the bedouins and from whom this type of verse spread to others. It would not surprise me if his account, which I shall give below, should prove to be true. I have encountered no mention of the *'atābā* in the medieval sources, and I would not find it unusual that the villagers should have taken them up from the bedouins, since the cultural life of the villagers 200 years ago was to a great extent influenced by bedouin culture. The *'atābā* are completely bedouin in their terminology, and the old ones are also bedouin in spirit and exemplify the life of the bedouins.

By way of illustration, I recall a story once told to me about a bedouin who saw the young maidens of his tribe drawing water from a distant pool or wadi by night, and so ordered his son to go and fill a small container for him from it. The boy tarried, probably distracted in conversation with the girls, so his father sang a verse from an *'atābā* poem in which he said:

> Throughout the long night I sit here and wait
> While you linger o'er earrings and curling plait.
> [Have you] no conscience? And why sit so late?
> In such broad springs are there no waters?

The meaning of the last two lines may be: "Have you no shame?" They say that his son used to compose *'atābā* verses like his father, and so sang and said:

> Me, I cinch fast my saddle up on high;
> On a thoroughbred camel my gear do I tie.
> "Whence is your water?" of the girls asked I.
> They told me: "A scoop from the dew."

The meaning of the verse is: I will fasten my saddle onto my thoroughbred she-camel and travel forth. I asked the girls from where they filled their containers, and they said that they had scooped the water from the dew fallen on the herbage.

As for my companion's story about the rise of the *'atābā*, I cite it although I am uncertain about its accuracy, since it may be a bedouin folk tale. It does, however, name its hero, and this man was one of the well-known bedouin shaykhs of the last century, Shaykh ʿAbd Allāh al-Fāḍil, shaykh of the Ḥsāna bedouins. He was famous for his generosity and martial skills and was delegated to protect the pilgrims, a service for which he received a fixed stipend from the Turkish empire. They claimed that when he was making the eastward migration with his bedouins during the rainy season he was stricken by smallpox. Fearing contagion, his kinsmen pitched a hair tent for him far away from the camp; and when he did not recover and they were forced to move on, they left him behind, leaving with him a slave girl to serve him, a dog named Shīr, and a she-camel. The slave girl had already had smallpox and thus was not afraid of being stricken by the disease, and with the two the man's kinsmen left a sufficient store of provisions. When, some weeks later, he recovered from his illness, he decided to stay until summer in the place where his people had left him.

Now it just so happened that there passed by that place a caravan of the tribe of ʿUqaylāt, who were bedouin traders, on their way to Damascus. Without telling them to what tribe he belonged he asked if he could accompany them, and then went with them until he reached the al-Nāṣirīya and Jarūd region. There he left the ʿUqaylāt, made his way to the tents of his tribe, the Ḥsāna, and arrived at his own tent, where he found his kin in a condition in which he was not accustomed to seeing them and noticed that the number of their camels had diminished. So he made his camel kneel down, made his way to the tent of his aged uncle, and began asking him, without identifying himself, about the shaykh of the Ḥsāna. His uncle told him the story of how the shaykh had been taken ill with the smallpox, how he had been left out on the steppe, and how, when the slave girl failed to return, they concluded that he had died. He also told him that his agent Ḥamad had betrayed him: this Ḥamad was the one who had taken over the leadership of the tribe and was collecting the stipend for protection of the pilgrimage. At this the shaykh flew into a fury and identified himself to them. Raging at how not one of his sons had received the position of shaykh after him, he desired to take vengeance on his perfidious agent. Sparing his people not a moment, he went straight to one of his uncle's mares which was tied in front of the tent, mounted it, and set out that same night, heading for Damascus to intercept Ḥamad, who had gone there to collect the stipend from the province's governor.

Suddenly Ḥamad appeared, on his way back from Damascus accompanied by an elite group of warriors. They claim that when Ḥamad saw Shaykh 'Abd Allāh from afar he said to his companions: "By God, had 'Abd Allāh al-Fāḍil not died I would say this is he; this warrior looks like him from afar, and his horse resembles that of 'Abd Allāh's uncle." When the warrior drew closer to them, Ḥamad, convinced that he was facing Shaykh 'Abd Allāh, began to tremble with fear. "On guard, you traitor," 'Abd Allāh cried out to him; "I will not grant you a respite and bring you to justice; rather, I challenge you to single combat."

He ordered the entourage accompanying Ḥamad to stand aside, and they obeyed him, for they realized that he was their shaykh. The two warriors, each mounted on the back of his charger, then began to fight with their lances, and before long 'Abd Allāh had transfixed Ḥamad through the head with his lance and thrown him down from the back of his charger. Turning to the warriors who had been with Ḥamad, he said: "Come with me and let us stone him, for he does not deserve better than that." So they stoned his corpse with rocks on a hill there, and the site is still there near the village of al-Ruḥayba, also known as Rajm Ḥamad, "the place where Ḥamad was stoned."

It is said that the *'atābā* composed by Shaykh 'Abd Allāh—the first known *'atābā* verses, as they claim—were verses he sang when he was ill and his kinsmen left him and set out on their eastward migration. Addressing his dog, named Shīr, he said:

> Your people have departed on kohl-colored steeds, O Shīr.
> And left to you some sheep bones to eat, O Shīr.
> Why do you howl o'er all of the hills, O Shīr?
> Hope not that your people will return to you.

Addressing the slave girl, whose name was Laylā, he said:

> O Laylā, covered so naught but your eyes you concede,
> I can but describe you as a doe which takes the lead.
> Your people left me in a waste, groaning with need,
> With no Luqmān to prescribe for me a cure.[15]

[15][Luqmān was a legendary sage renowned for his wisdom and knowledge of medicine.]

It is reported that, both boasting and complaining, he said:

> We clutched the rope [of hope], but it was cut in two.
> Then estrangement's herb reached the heart and grew.
> We would gulp sand from underfoot as our due,
> Rather than enter the abode of disgrace and stay.

One point concerning bedouin poetry yet remains, and that is the bedouin's attitude toward the poet. This differs from the attitude of the ancient Arabs as we know it from the historical sources, especially where the poet seeking favors or composing panegyrics is concerned. From the viewpoint of the bedouin (as also that of the Qur'ān) such a poet is a liar who says that which he does not do. Hence most of the panegyric poets are from low tribes, such as the Ṣlayb and their like. One usually sees them frequenting the camps of the shaykhs in certain seasons or circumstances, soliciting their rewards and stipends; the poet takes along with him his musical instrument—the rebab—to sing his poem to the rhythm of the tune he is playing.

If the poet is not a gift-seeker or a panegyrist, then his work is highly regarded and its author esteemed as a man of taste and talent; this is especially true where poets who speak of martial skills, heroism, lamentation for the dead, and noble love verse are concerned. Some shaykhs therefore see nothing wrong or offensive in memorizing the bedouin *qaṣīds*; indeed, one of them composes such poetry himself and prides himself on this when emotion moves him to speak of love, boasting, or lamentation. Well-known among the shaykhs who composed bedouin poetry in recent times was Amīr Nūrī al-Sha'lān, an ode of whose we have already mentioned, and in the nineteenth century or earlier there was Nimr al-'Adwān. Well-known poets in the Iraqi desert also included shaykhs and others whose verse has been set down in writing by some contemporary scholars.

Here it might be advisable for me to mention that Nimr al-'Adwān ranked among the most famous poets of the desert in the last 200 years. Tribal transmitters specialized in telling stories about him and memorizing much of his poetry, and some of it is still in circulation today, especially in Jordan, among the bedouin tribes of which they claim he came. Most of his odes are about his wife Waḍḥā: after her death, or so they claim, he composed about 365 odes, the number of days in a year, and would repeat one of them every day. It is love poetry similar to that of Shāh Jihān in its outstanding quality. In one ode he asks his sons to aid him and informs them that it is he, not they, who has suffered orphanage. In another one he consoles himself, and to the one trying to comfort him and suggesting that he take another wife he says that he could show preference to no woman in the world over Waḏḥā, and then consoles himself in the knowledge that one day he will meet her in the abode of divine grace.

Bedouin Folk Tales

Another literary form is the bedouin folk tale, which is similar to the genre of poetry in that the desert and the surrounding settled area know it only through oral transmission. There may be some in the towns and villages adjoining the desert who write down a *qaṣīd* and preserve it among their papers, but so far as I know there is no one who has written down a tale that has been told to him or preserved any part of it in written form. Naturally, then, many of the tales have been lost while some have been altered or modified upon the death of some of the storytellers. Nevertheless, the bedouin folk tale continues to preserve the coloring of its bedouin origin, stand in harmony with the bedouin spirit, and adhere to bedouin institutions and customs. Its aim is always to glorify valor, pride, and generosity and to protect the territory and honor of the tribe, in an effort to lend it assistance and support. In most cases the concern in such tales is to set forth the merit of adventure and the endurance of hardships and dangers.

The tales are of two main types. The first is a realistic type that portrays the way of life familiar to the bedouins in the days of wars, raids, and strife over water and pasturage, and is exactly comparable to the old narratives of the battle days of the tribes (*ayyām al-ʿarab*) in pre-Islamic times and the famous incidents in which they clashed over pools, water cisterns, and wells. The second type is the fantasy tale in which love plays a role and in which a woman participates. Both types, as mentioned above, are sometimes linked to the genre of the *qaṣīd* in that the story is in some cases concluded with a *qaṣīd* put into the mouth of the hero himself in which he reiterates the most important main events of the story. The two types have the same distinguish-

Figure 74: A bedouin telling a story.

ing features. The story is dominated by the element of surprise and characterized by exaggeration in its description of events, although the exaggeration does not extend to extreme hyperbole or the absurd and the tale may even be free from excess. It steers well clear of prolixity and garrulousness, since it will be told orally and not written down, but some parts of it are rich in fine detail, a feature characteristic of Arabic literature in general.

The objective of folk tales in Arabic literature was not mere artistic enjoyment. Rather, their aim was in most cases to strengthen certain virtues recognized in the Arab character, or to distract people from certain matters from which the authorities wished to divert their attention. Similarly, we find that folk tales in the desert today aim at various objectives other than the artistic enjoyment for which we find them so attractive.

For telling these tales, today there are special sessions that the bedouins hold on winter and spring nights around their fires. In summers some of their storytellers may travel to the villages near the desert and tell their people these stories. They revel in the hospitality of these villagers and how well they pay heed to the stories, and in this way they teach them something of their dialect and expressions. Even when these nomads return to their desert at the end of the summer, they leave behind them village storytellers who will tell you tales of the desert in the bedouin dialect. I still recall a session in a village on the fringes of the desert in which a village storyteller told bedouin folk tales in a bedouin dialect. It was as if this dialect had an influence so dominating the dialect of the villagers that the latter's mode of speech had collapsed before it, though the session was in a village and there was not a single bedouin among those listening.

The Subject Matter of the Stories

The subject matter of these folk tales usually revolves around one of three topics: raiding, love, and the thieves of the desert (the *ṣa'ālīk*), and in this they do not differ much from the ancient stories. In the raiding story one will find accounts of heroism and of the appearance of a warrior of unrivaled strength and courage, like 'Antara of old, but without the exaggeration evident in the well-known tale concerning him. In the *ṣa'ālīk* stories there are accounts of robbery, thievery, murder, and treachery, and the tales closely resemble those told by the storytellers about the *ṣa'ālīk* of the ancient Arabs—men like al-Shanfarā, Ta'abbaṭa Sharran, and Sulayk ibn al-Sulika—or the stories told in some of the *Maqāmāt* of al-Ḥarīrī and al-Hamadhānī. In the love story one encounters, for example, a tale about a young man who has grown up with a girl (usually his cousin), falls in love with her, and asks her father for her hand in marriage. His uncle, however, is only willing to accept him as a son-in-law if he pays an exorbitant bride price or after a test of his martial skills. So the young man goes on a raid, displays his courage, and returns loaded with booty, only to find that for some reason or another his consort has married during his absence or that during the night her family was plundered and she was carried off as a captive. The hero thus tries to wrest her away from her husband or to bring her back from captivity, and in most cases his struggle to do this takes a long time. His consort will have moved on to a distant land, so he sets out for that place. The means he uses to reveal his identity to his consort is similar to that set forth in the 'Udhrite story: while staying as the guest of his girl's husband while the latter is away, he asks for a drink of milk and then, after drinking from the vessel, drops into it a ring of his that the girl will recognize, or a piece of gold, so that when he returns the vessel to her all will become clear to her. The love stories sometimes differ from the 'Udhrite stories in the way they end: in the desert today the story concludes with the triumph of the lover, while in the 'Udhrite story the end is denial, pain, madness, and death.

The Aim of the Story

The objectives of the story are varied, but the pivotal point of the tale is the promotion of martial skills, heroism, adventure, generosity, manly virtue, the sanctity of the visitor, and the other Semitic qualities for which the Arab character has been distinguished since ancient times. Even in the thieves' stories one finds an affirmation of love of the good. A thief dresses in beggar's garb and takes up position along a desert route. A mounted warrior then comes down the road, and the thief deceives him and implores him to let him mount and to take him to his people. So the warrior seats the thief behind him and then, concerned for his horse, dismounts himself, leaving the thief to ride. At this point the thief gallops off with the horse, leaving the steed's owner abandoned in the sandy desert—but the story does not end here, for that would promote treachery and perfidy. Rather, the owner of the horse calls out to the thief: "Stop! Let me have a word with you. You got what you wanted: the horse is yours, and the trick you played on me has worked." So the thief halts, and the man implores him in the name of God and begs him for mercy, vowing that he will tell no one about what the thief has done so that the doing of good deeds will not cease in the desert and cause those in need to perish. Moved by his words, the thief comes back and returns his horse to him, saying: "I will not be less generous than you are." No *ṣa'ālīk* story is enjoyable unless it holds forth some example of daring and adventure.

The Bond between Story and Qaṣīd

Poetry was a factor in the formulation of the ancient folk tale; and similarly, today we find the bedouin *qaṣīd* entering many desert tales, uttered either by the hero of the story or by someone else. For example, a young man loved a girl and asked her father for her hand in marriage. The latter was agreeable to having him as a son-in-law; but the girl had learned from one of her relatives that the young man was of settled origin and descended from villagers, so she refused to accept him. When she was told that he was a warrior of highly esteemed descent, she said: "Do the villages give rise to noble-born warriors? The horseman of the villages is good for nothing but craftsmanship and trade." What she said spread among the women of her tribe, and the boys noised it about in the camp until it reached the ear of the young man. Now as it happened, on the afternoon of that same day the tribe was suddenly attacked by raiders who drove off their camels and so overwhelmed their menfolk that they forced them to seek refuge among the tents. They almost captured the girl herself and would have done so had it not been for the zeal of this visiting young man. He and his comrades were able to drive the raiders away from her, and then pursued them and recovered the tribe's livestock from them. Having witnessed the strength and courage he displayed, the girl regretted what she had said and went out to meet him, kissed his head, praised him, and advised her father that she would never accept any other man. The young man, however, thanked her for her appreciation and then sat down to rest after the battle. Looking to the side of the tent he saw a rebab hanging there, and taking up the instrument he began to sing his poetry in apology to her. He could not accept her now, he said, after she had rejected him and insulted him in front of the other girls by saying that he was a villager and claiming that the village horseman is good for nothing but craftsmanship and trade. Saying that it was therefore useless to praise him now, he began to sing:

> Earlier you showed us your back, pretty one,
> "A villager's for craftwork" is the slur you did cite.
> By God, how we've raided and thrown back the foe,
> And divided fine camels of those put to flight!
> Fighting is not only for the nomads to claim;
> To high thriving villagers it falls as their right.
> Both nomads and village folk—wherever we live—
> Each bears the blessed spirit in God's sight.

He went on to some flirting lines and said:

> O you of fine breasts, swelling like china cups,
> Buffeting the complaining heart with deadly might.
> No plums are they, no pomegranates, no ripening dates,
> Nor the apricots of al-Baṣra, nor apples' delight.

And then said:

> We would shun him who shuns us, even were he our guide,
> For praise gives the thirsters no cure for their plight.

Genuine Historical Events

In modern desert tales one notices that many of the narrators claim that their stories are based on events that have actually happened. Sometimes they trace the events in the tale back to well-known members of their tribes. The main character of the story just cited and the author of the *qaṣīd*, for example, was a youth well-known in the al-Baṣra region of Iraq; and the girl and her family were well-known persons to which the story attaches specific names, a feature we see in many of the ancient tales.

The bedouin is by nature realistic, and the bedouin tale is thus devoid of the bizarre spectacles conjured up by unrestrained imagination and free from accounts of jinn, demons, angels, and spirits. References to such things in bedouin lore are extremely rare. But at the same time, the bedouin does not view tales of the unexpected with doubt or suspicion. It seems that the regular and usually consistent character of the desert is not without unexpected turns of events, or perhaps encourages him to change and embellish certain developments. In his story the element of surprise is thus a familiar feature that the poet seeks to achieve, and sometimes makes the main point of the tale.

Examples of Such Lore

By way of illustration, I cite here a bedouin tale told in my own language so that the reader can understand it, and then follow it with examples of riddles.

It is said that three of the *ḥanshal*—those who specialize in plundering not by the familiar method of the raid, but rather by sneaking up at night and stealing whatever property or livestock they can—met together and prepared to mount a thieving operation against an encampment of a distant tribal group unrelated to their own tribe. Laying up a supply of flour, dates, and water and taking up their weapons, they set out walking in the dead of the night toward the region in which was camped the tribe from which they had decided to steal some horses or riding camels. At the break of dawn they made their way to a bend in a wadi where they took cover, made and baked their bread, ate, and rested until night approached, at which time they rose and continued their journey toward the camp they intended to rob, not neglecting to stop along their way by night at such water sources as wells or rain pools to fill the small waterskins they carried with them.

They continued this way for three days, until they reached the territories of the enemies whose camp they intended to rob. It was just after nightfall; and except for a bit of flour and water their supplies were all but exhausted and hunger had begun to take its toll on them. So they betook themselves to the foot of a hill that concealed them, and there they mixed the last of the flour they had into dough, made it into a single large, round, flat loaf, laid it in a fire they had kindled in a small hole to conceal it, and covered it with the fire's coals and ashes to cook—this being called a *tarmūs* among the bedouins.

There they were, then, when they suddenly realized that that very night a pack train of camels was approaching that very hill, and in fact had already come quite close to them. Having no time to dig into the fire and take out their *tarmūs*, they covered the embers with dirt and fled, hiding in a bend in the wadi at the foot of the hill so that when the pack train had passed they could return to the place where their *tarmūs* was buried. They waited, but the pack train did not move on. Instead, the people in it began to pitch their tents at the very foot of the hill. At this point the members of the *ḥanshal* party—with hunger gnawing at them and having no food supplies at all—began to deliberate among themselves over what they should do, and with that the youngest one got up and promised to bring the *tarmūs* back to them even if one of the tents had been pitched on top of it. The others lauded his daring, and our hero set out to carry out his mission.

When he drew near to the camp he turned the hide he was wearing inside out so he looked like a sheep, and began to crawl on his hands and knees, as if he was a sheep, until he reached the camp. He continued to wander among the sheep until he determined where the object of his quest was. Much to his astonishment, the *tarmūs* was in the women's room of the tent of the shaykh himself. So he crept under the *riwāq* into the tent and began to search for his *tarmūs*; but when he recognized its exact location, he found that the daughter of the shaykh and *amīr* had spread her bedding over top of it and had gone to sleep. So while she was sound asleep, our hero tried to pull her bedding—with her in it—off to one side without her noticing, so he could retrieve his *tarmūs*. While he was nimbly and lightly tugging at the bedding, she felt it, awoke, and tried to cry out for help to her family; but he covered her mouth with his hand and whispered to her: "Do not be afraid, O sister, for I mean you no harm. I only have something at this place over which you have spread your bedding, and upon it my survival depends." He then told her his story and that of his companions. Marveling at his courage she pulled aside the bedding; the spot was clear from the ashes, and the *tarmūs* was still hot. She then believed him and allowed him to take it, but only allowed him to go after making him swear an oath to return to them that next morning. So he swore the oath to her and left.

The girl told her father what had happened to her that night and of her wonder at the courage of that young man. This girl had a brother who was being held prisoner by some distant tribe, despite the efforts of her family and clan to free him. She hoped to get her brother back with the help of this brave young man, who had already found a favorable place in her heart and was regarded by her as her beloved.

That same morning the young man and his two comrades returned to the camp, where they were welcomed as brothers. The girl told the young man the story of her brother and asked him to free him from captivity, while her father allocated to him a number of camels and horses as compensation. These the young man refused, but he said to the father: "In deference to the honor of your worthy daughter, who has placed her trust in me, I will do as you wish." Her father smiled and said to him: "You have surely won her heart; and if you succeed in your mission and return safely, I would be happy to see her married to you."

The next day they saddled for him a Sharārī she-camel, one that could outrun the wind, and furnished him with a sufficient supply of provisions. With his heart still cleaving unto them, he bid them farewell and set out across the deserts and barren wastes, interrupting his journey only for a few short stops to rest his thoroughbred riding camel and to allow her to feed on a few plants. And so it continued until he reached the area where the enemy camp was located. Making his way to the foot of a hill that hid him from view from their tents, he made his camel kneel down, hobbled her, and at night left her and proceeded on toward the camp. Discerning the tent of the shaykh from afar, he crept up under cover of night until he reached the tent and could hear the talk of those assembled within. From this he realized that the prisoner was still alive, that he was confined in a hole covered by a carpet through which his head protruded, and that on each end of the carpet a hobbled camel had been made to kneel down so that he could not escape.

He kept quiet until the evening visitors had left and the people living in the tent had gone to sleep, and then heard a deep intermittent groaning sound interspersed with moans, signs, and certain words of which he could understand nothing but the phrase, "O sister." Fired up with courage, he drew close to the place from which he heard the groaning coming, where our hero found the scene described above. Placing his hand on his mouth as a signal to the prisoner not to speak, he came up, split the carpet crossways with his knife, pulled the prisoner up out of the hole, and then, carrying him on his back, began to crawl on his hands and knees until he was well clear of the campsite. Then he stopped, lowered the man to the ground, broke his fetters, hoisted him onto his shoulders, and then quickly ran for the place at the foot of the hill where his camel was hobbled.

But it seemed that fate insisted on standing in his way, for just as his hopes were on the verge of being realized, he looked for his camel, failed to find her, and so became convinced that one of the camp's herdsmen must have happened onto the beast and taken it as booty. He thus had no choice but to take the captive, hide him in a nearby cave, and then return to the camp in search of his own she-camel. He found it hobbled in front of one of the tents; and looking through the gaps between the cloth panels of the tent he could see that its inhabitants were still awake, though the scale on the balance of the night was already tipping toward morning.

Listening in on them, he could hear them discussing the question of the prisoner and learned that news of the rescue was already spreading. He had no choice but to act quickly; so, creeping inside between the cloth panels of the tent until he reached the large center pole holding it up, he pulled the center pole out to one side and the tent collapsed upon all those who were under it. At once he crept out to the place where his she-camel was tied, broke her hobbles, and rode her off in the direction of his comrade, whom he found waiting for him. He seated him behind himself and prodded the swift-running camel to fly forth, dashing across the countryside.

He kept going like this until daybreak, when he saw behind him a group from the tribe pursuing them, but, as his good fortune had it, he also saw some tents pitched by the edge of a wadi in front of him. He reached the tents, made his she-camel kneel down, proceeded to the tent of the shaykh, and kissed the tent pole to seek protection. So the shaykh rushed out, stood in front of the attackers, turned them back, and prevented them from getting to the young man. Our hero had no sooner rested than he thanked his host for his gallantry, mounted with his comrade behind him, and rode off for the captive's family. They were overjoyed to see him, gave him the shaykh's daughter in marriage, and gave him and his two comrades so many camels that it restrained them from any further thieving and *ḥanshal* raiding.

Other Bedouin Genres

There are also proverbs, derived from their bedouin way of life and from memorable events, but these do not go back to ancient times as do the Arabic proverbs that were recorded by the ancient transmitters and became a part of the Arabic literary heritage. In my association with the bedouins I never heard any one of them quote an ancient proverb, and not even a modern one based on their life in recent times. I thus recorded nothing about this, and of those who have written on their literary life I have found no one who has taken up this topic.

There are also riddles, a kind of literature most often made up of small segments of bedouin poetry or rhyming expressions, with which the men amuse themselves in their discussion sessions. Musil took up this subject in his book on the Rwāla, cited a few of them, and mentioned that the Rwāla like to solve such riddles. If this is indicative of anything, it would have to be guilelessness and simplicity, and to show how easy they are to solve one need only cite a few:

Riddle: Seven ones named I ask of you:
Not a one has error met,
Nor of them does one forget;
They all are old but still as new
Who walks, his foot in them does set,
Whether with life or death in view.

Answer: The seven days of the week.

Riddle: I ask you for five of lofty grade:
Not of horses or camels are these made,
Two in the sun and three in the shade.

Answer: The five daily prayers.

Riddle: I ask you for something that fills horses and she-camels with joy,
And cheers all the desert lands with love.
Fair women laugh for it,
While anxiety for it brings even the male sand grouse down from the sky.

Answer: Progeny (young, or children).[16]

In closing this chapter it remains for me to say that with the evolution of bedouin life, the acceptance by many of them of sedentarization and education, and the spread of reading, writing, and exposure to classical Arabic poetry, there will be a shift from bedouin poetry to

[16]Musil, *Manners and Customs*, pp. 327–28. On the meaning of *qarāniṣ*, Musil claimed that this referred to the "wild foes," meaning the falcon, but in returning to the matter stated that Jawād, the poet of Amīr al-Nūrī ibn Sha'lān, and another person both said that the *qirnāṣ* is the adult bird already feathered. But the bedouins I heard and those familiar with hunting the sand grouse said that the *qirnāṣ* is the male sand grouse.

classical Arabic poetry. One can already see this occurring in Saudi Arabia, Jordan, and among educated bedouin youths.

CHAPTER XVIII

NOMADS OF THE NOMADS
THE ṢLAYB

A Curious Tribe

Among the bedouin tribes of Arabia there is a curious clan—the tribe most intimately familiar with Arabia's deserts and oases, its wadis and pools, its mountains and dunes, its animals and plants. It is the tribe most proficient at crossing the desert wastes in these parts and the one most widely distributed in them. This is the tribe of Ṣlayb, or al-Ṣlāba as most of the bedouins call it;[1] some others call the tribe al-Ṣulbān or al-Khlāwīya. Despite the ability they display in dealing with desert conditions, Ṣlayb is a humble tribe that is not large in numbers. It is the weakest of the tribes in strength, the lowest in status, and the most inferior in terms of ancestry; indeed, one could with greater justification say of them that they have no line of descent recognized among the Arab tribes.

This tribe occupies no one particular area (a *dīra*, or "tribal territory," as the bedouins say) recognized as theirs, nor does it establish itself in the desert of a specific region or migrate and wander back and forth through it. Instead, it has branches scattered in most parts of the Arabian peninsula: in the north from along the fringes of the Syrian Desert at Tadmur to Mosul, in the Nafūd in the heart of the peninsula,

[1] In his *Mu'jam qabā'il al-'arab* (II, 646), Kaḥḥāla gives the name as "Ṣilaba," which is wrong. The bedouins pronounce it "Ṣlāba," some of them also saying "Ṣlūba." Some of the Ṣlayb say of themselves that they are *awlād Ṣlaybī*, "sons of a Ṣlaybī." [The written form in this book varies between "al-Ṣulaba" and "Ṣulayb," which in the English will both be translated by the well-known form of "Ṣlayb."]

in Najd, in the furthest reaches of the Ḥijāz in the southwest beyond al-Ṭā'if, in the Dahnā' in the areas adjoining Kuwayt and the Aḥsā', and in the Iraqi Desert in the southeast.[2]

Modern Scholarship on the Ṣlayb

Scholars have been at a loss to account for the origins and descent of the Ṣlayb, and the confusion has not been limited to the European explorers and Western political figures who have had some contact with the Arab countries. It has also proliferated among others; and indeed, even the Arabs themselves, both settled folk and nomads, know no line of descent for this tribe. The uncertainty has even led some of the bedouins to call the Ṣlayb *khalwīya* or *khlāwīya*, "those who live in the wilderness," and sometimes to refer to them by the agnomen *kilāb al-khalā'*, "hounds of the wilderness."[3]

One of the first Arab authors to write about this tribe was Sulaymān al-Bustānī, who published in *Al-Muqtaṭaf* in 1887 a lecture on the bedouins which he read at the inaugural session of the Sun of Benevolence Society (*Jam'īyat shams al-birr*) in Beirut. In this lecture he divided the bedouins into groups: nomads, semi-nomads, and "nomads of the nomads" (*badw al-badw*), placing the Ṣlayb in this last category. He also advanced a theory which he was probably the first to propose. In it he attributes their origins to the Crusaders, who were scattered all about, he claims, after the shattering defeats inflicted upon them by the Ayyūbids, Mamlūks, and Mongols. He affirms that one group of them took refuge in the Syrian Desert and intermingled with some of its peoples and in time eventually assimilated with these desert

[2]See Guarmani, p. 92; also Doughty, I, 325, where he says that they roam to the horizons of all Arabia, from the Syrian highlands to Yemen beyond al-Ṭā'if. In his *The Penetration of Arabia* (New York, 1905), p. 314, David George Hogarth says of the British Resident in Būshīr that he hired a Ṣlaybī to serve as his guide on the way from Riyadh to the Gulf. Musil mentions (*Palmyrena*, p. 126) that the Ṣlayb are scattered throughout Arabia. Oppenheim (*Vom Mittelmeer zum Persischen Golf*, I, 221) states that they are spread out from Aleppo as far as the Persian Gulf south of the Euphrates.

[3]Doughty, I, 326, 327. [The names *khalwīya* and *khlāwīya* imply that those so called are obliged to wander in the wilderness (*al-khalā'*) because no matter where they go, they find no kin with whom they can rest for the night.]

folk.[4] Al-Bustānī returned to the subject in 1900 in an extended study in volume XI of the *Dā'irat al-ma'ārif* founded by Buṭrus al-Bustānī, and in this article he does not retreat from his view on the question of their Crusader origins.[5]

In the first edition of the *Encyclopaedia of Islam* there is an article by Professor W. Pieper in which he examines many of the ancient sources and modern authorities on the Ṣlayb and their various branches. However, he is unable to arrive at any precise informed conclusion concerning their origins, other than to reiterate the view that they are bedouins who were originally adherents of some religion other than Islam, and that they embraced Islam at a later time. He concludes with the statement that their manners and customs and their inferior sociopolitical standing indicate that they were the victims of some terrible ancient catastrophe or war, and that it was this that brought them to their current situation of ignominy and wretchedness.[6]

When the French became the Mandatory authorities in Syria and Lebanon they wrote a book on the bedouin tribes of Syria that was published in 1930 and reprinted in 1943. In this work they state that the Ṣlayb comprise an important group that is racially distinct from the Arab stock. Then the author states:

> Some attribute their origins to India and claim that they were brought to Baghdad as musicians for one of the 'Abbāsid caliphs. They base their view on the facts that the Ṣlayb dialect contains some Indian terms, that some of the folk tales and stories are similar to the narratives of the *Thousand and One Nights*, and that many of their clans camp in the land adjoining the Gulf.[7]

In the handbook on the bedouin tribes in Syria compiled by the English authorities in the last days of the Mandate, there are some

---

[4]Sulaymān al-Bustānī, "Al-Badw," *Al-Muqtaṭaf*, 12 (1887–88), pp. 141–47.

[5]*Idem*, "Al-Ṣulaba," in *Dā'irat al-ma'ārif*, edited by Buṭrus al-Bustānī (Beirut, 1876–1900), XI, 2–9.

[6]W. Pieper, "Ṣulaib," in *Encyclopaedia of Islam*, first edition, edited by T.W. Arnold *et al.* (Leiden, 1918–34), IV, 511–15.

[7]*Les Tribus nomades de l'état de Syrie* (Damascus, 1943), pp. 247–48.

reports on the Ṣlayb in which it is stated that with respect to "race," or rather origin, they are Arabs. But the compiler of the book continues to say of the Ṣlayb:

> The Sleib are a strange tribe whose origin is lost in legend. According to some they were brought from India to Baghdad by the Abbassid Caliphs as musicians. They themselves say they are descendants of the Crusaders and this is the generally accepted version. Bands of Crusaders remaining in Syria took up hunting as a means of existence and were driven into the desert by newcomers. Certain it is that the Sleib are great gazelle hunters. They claim that the name 'Sleib' is a corruption of the Arabic word 'salib' (cross) and for centuries they have worn jackets made of gazelle skin, the dark marks of which formed a cross. They are certainly not semitic and the prevalence of fair-haired and blue-eyed types amongst them appear to support their claim to Aryan descent. They are renowned as guides, being able to keep their route in the dark, or in a dust storm. They say they were forced to become Muslims, but their own code forbids polygamy and the wife has the right to repudiate her husband. They never contract marriages outside their tribe.[8]

It would not be surprising if the report on the Indian origin of the Ṣlayb, mentioned by the compilers of the English text and the French one that preceded it, had been taken up from the work of Oppenheim (already referred to above in note 2), where he asserts:

> The ethnographic descent of the Ṣlayb has yet to be established, but in all probability they are not Semites, but rather of Indian origin. It is said that some of the last caliphs in Baghdad brought to their court a group of musicians from India, some of whom fled into the desert at the time of Tamerlane's assault. I have heard the opinion expressed that the modern-day Ṣlayb are the descendents of these refugees.[9]

[8]Glubb, *Handbook*, pp. 65–66.
[9]*Vom Mittelmeer zum Persischen Golf*, I, 221.

Some of the European and Arab writers have thus been led to claim that the Ṣlayb are of either Crusader or Indian origin, because of the obscurity surrounding the question of their origins and because of the curious name attaching to them.[10] This name, however, comes from an era for which we have found no specific date in any of the sources we have consulted, and it is probably no more than 200 years old. I would do well to note here the example of the Italian explorer Lodovico di Varthema, one of the first to explore the peninsula and visit various parts of it. Dressed as a Mamlūk pilgrim, he set out from Egypt in 1503 and passed through the regions in the Syrian Desert where there could have been some of the Ṣlayb. But he says nothing in his book about the existence of such a tribe, although he does mention the presence in that period of a Jewish colony on a small mountain near Khaybar.[11] A similar case is that of Carsten Niebuhr, who set out with five other explorers in 1761, taking the sea route to the Ḥijāz to pursue geographical and other studies relating to the Bible.[12] He reached Yemen, and after that, in 1763, traveled to India; but in the narratives of his journey he does not mention that he met anyone from the Ṣlayb. In his book he wrote down all of the observations and reports he could gain from his comrades, all of whom—save Niebuhr himself—perished during the journey, felled by the hardships of travel and by illness.[13] It is possible, however, that they did not happen to pass through the regions where they could have seen some individuals from the tribe of Ṣlayb.

Between the journey of Varthema and that of Niebuhr many Western merchants (especially the English) and caravan leaders took to following the trade route between Aleppo and al-Baṣra, a state of affairs that continued until the end of the eighteenth century. But in all we have read of the diaries and memoirs of some of these travelers, no mention is made of the tribe of Ṣlayb. The memoirs of William Beawes, Gaylard Roberts, Bartholomew Plaisted, and John Carmichael have all

---

[10]See notes 4, 5, 6, 8 and 9 above.

[11]Lodovico di Varthema, *Travels*, translated by John Winter Jones and edited by George Percy Badger (New York, 1963), p. 23.

[12]Carsten Niebuhr, *Travels Through Arabia*, translated by Robert Heron (Edinburgh, 1792).

[13]Kiernan, pp. 88–103.

been published,[14] but in not any of them do we find any mention of the tribe of Ṣlayb or of individuals from it.

At the dawn of the nineteenth century, in 1809, the Swiss explorer John Lewis Burckhardt arrived in Aleppo. Donning Arab dress and calling himself Ibrāhīm ibn ʻAbd Allāh, he set out to visit various parts of the Arabian peninsula and left us a book on the Wahhābīs and bedouins that up until recent times ranked among the most important sources on them. Among the things he witnessed was a group whose name was "El Szoleyb," making him probably the first of all explorers and researchers—without exception—to make any reference to them. Burckhardt says of them:

> El Szoleyb, a tribe of the Ahl el Shemál [northern folk] living dispersed among all the neighbouring tribes of Aeneze, as well as of the Arabs el Shemál, and on friendly terms with all, because they are poor: they possess neither horses, camels, sheep, nor scarcely tents. . . .Their only property consists of a few asses, some cooking utensils, and a gun; their only means of subsistence, hunting and shooting. . . . They go about as beggars among the Arabs, and with whatever alms they get, purchase powder and shot.[15]

He does not indicate that they are of Crusader or Indian origin.

Following Burckhardt was a Finnish-Swedish explorer named Georg August Wallin who visited Arabia in 1845, passing through Suez across the desert via Maʻān and the Ḥamād under the assumed name of ʻAbd al-Walī. He saw some of the Ṣlayb himself and mentioned them by name in three places in his book. He indicated that they were the most despised clans of Hutaym and said that some of them lived in the Dahnā' in the summer; but like his colleague Burckhardt, he says nothing to suggest that their name has anything to do with Crusaders or Christians.[16]

After these two came Sir Richard Burton—al-Ḥājj ʻAbd Allāh—who undertook his journey in 1853. He mentions that he saw individuals

[14] *The Desert Route to India.*

[15] *Notes on the Bedouins and Wahábys*, I, 14–15.

[16] Wallin, *Ṣuwar min shamālī jazīrat al-ʻarab*, pp. 112, 184 [= *Travels in Arabia*, pp. 189, 337].

from this group, whom he called *khalāwīya* (plural of *khalawī*), as some of the bedouins call the Ṣlayb. He does not mention the name Ṣlayb, nor does he refer to any connection between them and Christians or Crusaders. Concerning them he says that they are as despised as the tribe of Hutaym, which has camps near Yanbu': "They are generally blacksmiths, have a fine breed of greyhounds, and give asses as a dowry, which secures for them the derision of their fellows."[17]

Probably the first to refer to a Christian origin for these Ṣlayb was the English explorer William Gifford Palgrave, who made his journey to Arabia in 1862 and published his book in 1866.[18] He mentions them in connection with his account of cautery and medical treatment among the bedouins, and claims that the tribe of Ṣlayb is the group most renowned for the practice of medicine among the bedouins, though they are "strangers to the Arab stem." They claim that they are from a "northern" tribe, and Palgrave mentions that their fair complexion, the handsome features of their faces, and their light eyes support this claim and point to a Syrian, not Arab, origin. Similarly, their careless gaiety of manner strongly contrasts with the cloudy and suspicious disposition that one finds among the other sons of the desert. Indeed, their name and customs confirm their descent from a Christian origin.[19] But Palgrave does not explicitly state or suggest that they are of Crusader or Frankish origin.

In 1864 Napoleon III sent an Italian named Carlo Guarmani, who knew the East and had earlier traveled in the Jawf region, and charged him with the task of purchasing Arabian horses for him. Assuming the name of Khalīl Āghā and claiming that he was a Turkish Muslim who trained horses for the governor of Damascus, he set out for Taymā' and Najd. In the course of his journey he saw some of the Ṣlayb, but took them for *ghajar*, that is, gypsies. Nothing about them interested him except for their donkeys, and in an appendix to his memoirs he states:

> When winter is past, many of the Saleib cross the Euphrates to hunt the wild ass in Mesopotamia, there being no more

[17]Sir Richard F. Burton, *Personal Narrative of a Pilgrimage to al-Madinah and Meccah* (London, 1893), II, 121.

[18]Palgrave, I, 150.

[19]*Ibid.*

> of these now in the Hammad. They take a certain number of them alive to breed with their own [she-asses].[20]

Nor does he fail to mention an important incident that befell him after drinking water from a pool hollowed out by dripping water in a grotto. He fainted and did not regain consciousness until several hours later, when he found himself in the house of a Ṣlaybī woman, or, as he calls her, a *zinjānī* ("gypsy") woman. Nursing him were four ugly-looking women; their menfolk looked the same, and he could see nothing beautiful around him other than the horses he had with him.[21]

Commenting on this incident, Carruthers wrote in a note on that page an explanation of the word *zinjānī*, stating that it means "gypsy" and adding that the Ṣlayb were a people of mysterious origin and were possibly older than the Semites and perhaps a remnant of the ancient inhabitants of Arabia. He then points out that:

> The principal characteristics of the Suluba do strike anyone knowing gypsy types in other countries. To mention a few: they are parasitic; feigning poverty, they are mostly well off; despised by resident folk, but are free to go where they will; of unknown lineage, and of no citizenship, skilled in hunting (or poaching); expert tinkers; have curious habits, and bury their money.[22]

In 1865 Colonel Lewis Pelly, the British Resident in Būshīr, one of the administrative districts of Persia, undertook a journey to Riyadh to meet Amīr Fayṣal ibn 'Abd al-Raḥmān Āl Su'ūd (grandfather of 'Abd al-'Azīz Āl Su'ūd) and on the return leg of his journey took along with him a Ṣlaybī guide from whom he gained unique and important information about his fellow tribesmen. For example:

> On certain festivals, and particularly on occasions of marriage and circumcision, they fix a wooden cross, dressed in

[20]Guarmani, p. 120.

[21]*Ibid.*, pp. 36–37.

[22]*Ibid.*, p. 37. See Doughty, I, 327, where we find that when the Ṣlaybī has more coins than he needs to buy tools for his trade and other requirements from the settled areas, he takes the surplus money and buries it somewhere in the desert and returns months or years later to dig it up.

> red cloth and adorned at the top with feathers, at the door of the person married or circumcised. At this signal the people collect and dance round the cross. They have a particular dance. The young men stand opposite their female partners, each advances, and the youth slightly kisses the shoulder of the maiden....

Pelly then says:

> The word "Seleeb" means a cross. But some of the caste derive their name from As-Solb-Al-Arab—i.e. from the back of the Arabs—meaning to assert that they are pure descendents of aboriginal Arabs. The Mohammedans, on the other hand, stigmatize them as outcasts....

He further states:

> No intermarriage takes place between the Selaib and the Arabs. Even a Bedouin will not stop to plunder a Selaib, nor to revenge a blood-feud against him. The Selaib are capital sportsmen. They live largely on gazelle's flesh,[23] and wear a long shirt of gazelle skin coming down to the feet. Their common diet is locusts and dates when procurable; but they will eat anything. They tend their sheep and camels, wander for pasturage during eight months of the year, and for the remainder seek some town or village where to exchange their produce for necessities of life. Their tents are black, of goat's hair, and are pitched separate from those of the Arabs. The Selaib are filthy in appearance; but the Arabs confess that, in point of features, the Selaib women are the most beautiful among them.

Pelly claims that the Ṣlayb wash their children 40 days after birth and close this rite by immersing them in the water seven times. As for

[23]The term in the original English is "deer's flesh," which is incorrect since deer were not so numerous as this, especially not in these regions.

marriage among the Ṣlayb, he said that this is concluded by agreement between the bride and groom after the two fathers give their consent.[24]

After discussing some of their customs concerning burial and prayer over the dead and their veneration of Mecca, he continues to say:

> They...state that their own proper place of pilgrimage is Haran, in Irak or Mesopotamia. They also say that their principal people have some psalms and other books written in Chaldean or Assyrian. They respect the Polar star, which they call Jah, as the one immovable point which directs all travelers by sea and land. They reverence also a star in the constellation, called Jeddy, corresponding with Aries. In adoring either of these heavenly bodies the Selaib stands with his face toward it, and stretches out his arms so as to represent a cross with his own body....They assert themselves to be a tribe of the Sabians emigrated to Nejd.

He states in conclusion:

> The Selaib eat carrion, and profess themselves to be the chosen people of God, who pay no tribute or tax, since no one will deign to receive it from them.[25]

Here we must note that this is a second explicit reference in the explorers' legacy suggesting that the Ṣlayb have some connection or quasi-connection with Christianity in their history, that they are of other than pure Arab stock, and that they have customs that would find no acceptance or place in Islam. But there is no reference or allusion to a Frankish origin or to any connection with the Crusaders themselves.

The last quarter of the nineteenth century witnessed an intensification of interest in Arabian exploration, especially on the part of the English. Some of them set out for the Arabian peninsula in search of

---

[24]Kiernan, p. 262. He observes that Pelly here says of the Ṣlayb that they raise camels, while Burckhardt does not hold this view. It is clear that in eastern Arabia in Burckhardt's day the Ṣlayb were not allowed to own camels.

[25]*Ibid.*, p. 263. [Cf. Pelly's "Note on the Selaib Tribe," Appendix XIII to his *Report on a Journey to the Wahabee Capital of Riyadh in Central Arabia* (Bombay, 1866; rep. Cambridge, 1983), pp. 90-96.]

Arabian horses, others went for tourism or to familiarize themselves with the bedouin and desert lands, and yet others came with other aims in mind. Thus we see Lady Anne Blunt undertaking a journey with her husband Wilfrid. She arrived in Baghdad, mixed with some of the heads of the tribes in the Syrian Desert, and met some of the Ṣlayb. Concerning one of the Ṣlayb families she says: "Two younger men, his relations, are exceedingly good looking, with delicately cut features, and the whitest of teeth." She then says:

> There is a boy, too, who is perfectly beautiful, with almond-shaped eyes, and a complexion like stained ivory. A little old woman not more than four feet high, and two girls of fourteen or fifteen, the most lovely little creatures I ever saw, complete the family.

With this she states:

> They are all very short, but in perfect proportion, their hands and feet exaggeratedly small, and all have a strange half-frightened smile, and an astonished look in the eyes, which remind one rather of wild creatures than of men and women.[26]

Despite the artistic-literary tendency that in this passage obviously leads Lady Anne to exaggerate in depicting the beauty of members of that family, she nowhere utters a word that would suggest that the Ṣlayb are of Crusader or Frankish origin. She also says that it is impossible that they could be Arabs, though some of the bedouins concede their Arabness while not accepting certain of their customs and disdaining to marry their daughters, their beauty notwithstanding. She says:

> That they are not mere gipsies is as certain as that they are not mere Arabs; but we suspect them of having the same origin with the gipsies, that is to say, that they came originally from India.[27]

---

[26] Blunt, p. 325.
[27] *Ibid.*, p. 326.

After Lady Anne Blunt we see William Wright visiting Tadmur in 1872 and 1874 and on his way there meeting some of the Ṣlayb in the mountainous region near 'Ayn al-Wu'ūl. He agrees with her on the matter of the beauty of the small children of this tribe,[28] but he does not indicate that they are of Crusader origin. Indeed, he tries to assess their origins in the Arabian peninsula and says:

> At a remote period this tribe was degraded from exercising the larger prerogatives of Bedawîn of the higher aristocracy. They do not make war on the weak, nor rob, except in a pilfering way, nor intermarry with any of the other tribes. Many wild stories relate the causes of their degradation, but that most common among the other Bedawîn is, that they ran away from the siege of Kerbela, leaving their friends to be butchered, "and the curse of Allâh still lies heavy upon them." As a part of their punishment, they were placed on the same footing with women, as unworthy to ride horses, and so they never ride anything but donkeys....[29]

We should note here that William Wright considered them to be Ishmaelite Arabs:

> The Suleib Arabs, unlike the other Ishmaelites of the desert, have their hand against no man, and no man's hand is against them. They live by the chase, and by the milk and wool of their flocks; and when they sell a donkey, its price supplies them with all they need from the outer world.

He describes how the Ṣlayb hunt the ibex, which lives in the mountains. They don clothing made of the animal's hides and follow it from rock to rock, crawling on their hands and knees until the ibex comes within range of their rifles, then they shoot it. Camouflaged in this manner, they were sometimes able to catch the ibex or gazelle alive with their own hands.[30]

---

[28] Wright, p. 53.
[29] *Ibid.*, pp. 48–49.
[30] *Ibid.*, p. 49.

In the same period there was a French Alsatian, Charles Huber, who lived in Syria and frequently visited the desert between 1878 and 1882, reaching the Jawf oasis and the city of Ḥā'il and seeing inscriptions on many of the rocks and stones. The French Ministère de l'Instruction Publique decided to send him and the German archaeologist Julius Euting on a voyage of exploration, and the two set out in 1883 and reached Taymā', where Euting copied the inscription on the famous Taymā' Stone, now in the Musée du Louvre. Huber completed arrangements to purchase the stone and sent it to Aleppo, and after that the two men separated. Huber continued his journey and reached Jeddah, and then tried to return to Ḥā'il, but on 29 July 1884 he was murdered at Rābigh by the guide accompanying him.[31]

At the beginning of his journey he had seen some of the Ṣlayb near Tadmur, and then continued and in the region of al-Hajr met other Ṣlaybīs. One of these, a man named Darbīsh, furnished him with a wealth of information on the wadis and gorges in these parts, and also on the Ṣlayb. All of this he recorded in a daily journal which survived among his personal effects and was handed over to the French consul in Jeddah. This *Journal* was published in 1891 by the Société Asiatique and the Société de Géographie, under the auspices of the French Ministère de l'Instruction Publique. Not surprisingly, many of the later authors and explorers looked through this diary when it was published and quoted from it, especially on matters pertaining to the description of Ṣlayb men and women, their clothing and customs, and regarding the eating of carrion, blood, and dog meat. Huber discussed the customs of the tribe at length, and spoke of the marriage of their daughters, the bride money paid, and divorce, and also on religious affairs, prayer whenever they were in the cities, and the differences between one clan and another. He also indicated that the Arab tribes generally consider them a degraded tribe or race. But in all his observations concerning them he does not suggest that anyone regarded them as descendants of the Crusaders.[32]

[31]Julius Euting, *Tagbuch einer Reise in Inner-Arabien*, edited by Enno Littmann (Leiden, 1896–1914), I, iv.

[32]Charles Huber, *Journal d'un voyage en Arabie, 1883–1884* (Paris, 1891), pp. 196–204; Kiernan, p. 265. Here it must be pointed out that among the foods eaten by the Ṣlayb, Charles Huber mentions gazelle's milk. This is incorrect. The source

Figure 75: A group of Ṣlayb tribesmen met by Oppenheim.

Three years prior to the publication of the *Journal* of Charles Huber, there appeared the greatest work describing bedouin life and the desert. This was *Travels in Arabia Deserta* (1888) by Charles Doughty, the great explorer known among the bedouins by the name Khalīl al-Naṣrānī. There were many subsequent reprintings of Doughty's work, and among many of the later explorers it rose to the position of the first word on bedouin life, a book of unrivaled authority. In Doughty's long study on the Ṣlayb, to which we shall return at the end of this chapter, we find that he, like most of the bedouins, regarded them as craftsmen from an inferior tribe with no deep-seated Arab lineage. Descended neither from Qaḥṭān nor from 'Adnān,[33] they were perhaps the descendants of one of the lost Jewish or Christian tribes from the eras preceding the rise of Islam.[34] Doughty does not refer to any connection between the Ṣlayb and the Crusaders.

Finally, it remains for us to mention Max Freiherr von Oppenheim, who referred to the Ṣlayb in his book *Vom Mittelmeer zum Persischen Golf*. He met a group of them in the summer of 1893, and said their origins were unknown and that in all probability they were non-Semites. They may have been from India, he said, since the last caliphs in Baghdad had brought to their court a group of Indian musicians, some of whom, in the wake of the attacks of Tamerlane and his sack of Baghdad, took refuge in the desert. From these the Ṣlayb may be descended.[35] For his part, Oppenheim too makes no reference to a Crusader origin.

The Views of al-Bustānī

In the late nineteenth and early twentieth centuries some studies on bedouin life began to appear from the pens of Arab litterateurs, at a time when printing was coming into general practice and newspapers and periodicals were widely circulated. The article published by Sulaymān al-Bustānī in *Al-Muqtaṭaf* and in the *Dā'irat al-ma'ārif* (the

of his error may have been that in certain homes of bedouins or settled folk he saw some gazelles that had been caught while still young and then domesticated, and so supposed that the Ṣlayb drink their milk.

[33][Qaḥṭān and 'Adnān were the respective eponymous ancestors of the southern and northern Arab tribes.]

[34]Doughty, I, 326.

[35]Oppenheim, pp. 220–21.

study to which we referred at the beginning of this chapter) thus had some influence in spreading his theory that in their origins the Ṣlayb are to be traced back to the Crusaders. The proofs he cites for this are the many cases of blue eyes that he claims occur among them, their fullness of face and abundant hair, their lack of affiliation with any particular religious confession, the claim made by some of them that their forefathers were Franks, the discrepancy between their form of livelihood and that of the other bedouin tribes, and the label they bear in the name "Ṣlayb" or "al-Ṣulaba." He also mentions that he saw in them a manifest difference in their manner of speaking and a profound lack of rigor in their mode of expression, which, he says, resembles that of the people of southern Lebanon. He also notices that they use certain Arabic expressions not used by the bedouins of the desert, such as *yā ḥazanī*, "O my grief," *yā 'aynī*, "O my precious one" (lit. "eye"), *yā bayyi*, "O my father," *yā khayyi*, "O my brother," *dakhlak*, "if you please," and so forth.[36]

It seems to me that his evidence, while it may distance the Ṣlayb from a bedouin Arab origin, does not constitute proof of a Crusader origin. And it is curious that while al-Bustānī concedes that they are the people most knowledgeable on the routes of the barren desert wastes—to such an extent that he states that the bedouin Arabs use them as guides on their long-distance journeys and calls them the "nomads of the nomads"—he at the same time attributes their origin to the Crusaders. I am afraid that it is al-Bustānī who has led astray, as I have mentioned, those who after him attributed the origin of the Ṣlayb to the Crusaders.[37]

In 1898, eleven years after the publication of al-Bustānī's article in *Al-Muqtaṭaf*, an article on the Ṣlayb by the Carmelite Father Anastase al-Karmalī was published in the first volume of the journal *Al-Mashriq*.[38] In it he set forth many reports on their origins, in not a one of which was there any reference to their descent from remnants of the Crusaders. Then he claims that he asked one of the elderly men of the tribe about their origins, saying: "He cleared his throat and wiped his

[36]Al-Bustānī, "Al-Badw," pp. 141–47; *idem*, "Al-Ṣulaba," pp. 2–9.
[37]W.B. Seabrook, *Adventures in Arabia* (London and Aylesbury, 1941), p. 43.
[38]Anastase al-Karmalī, "Al-Ṣulayb," *Al-Mashriq*, 1 (1898), pp. 673–81.

face, pondered and thought, and then said: 'Listen, my good man...,'" and here Father Anastase relates, in the words of this elderly man, a long account in rhymed prose similar to one of the *maqāmāt* of al-Ḥarīrī or al-Hamadhānī. Here it would be best for us to cite at least part of it, so the reader can see clearly for himself to what lengths imagination can go with certain authors:

> We are from the best of people, their choice elite; from the most eminent bedouins, their cream most sweet. Our forefather was an Arab of Ṣlayb, Ḍab'ān by name, this in a land of unsullied fame; a country to which that of the Arabs is close at hand, in which strange species do grow in the land. Then when the people became more and more, and the difference among stocks did wax full sore, our forefather Ḍab'ān to himself vowed, to go forth from a land where dwelled such a crowd.[39]

Father Anastase also quotes a long speech in this same type of rhymed prose by our friend Ḍab'ān, one in which there is not much of use to us on the Ṣlayb. Then he says: "I asked another one, and he said approximately the same thing as the former one did," and then states: "I asked a fourth man, and he said about the same as the earlier ones had."[40]

Objections to the Views of al-Karmalī

Here I would like to note that this is the first time I have ever seen a speech in classical Arabic, and in the rhymed prose style, delivered by a bedouin savant in modern times. I fear that Father Anastase, in a first article published for him in the esteemed journal *Al-Mashriq*, was trying to show how good he was at prose composition after the manner of the authors of the *maqāmāt*, and then attributed the speech to a Ṣlaybī, overlooking the fact that he was writing an article in a scholarly journal. It is interesting to note that he claims that this statement reported by him from the Ṣlaybī was one he either memorized or wrote down fifteen years before he wrote the article. Probably the best statement in his

[39] *Ibid.*, p. 675.
[40] *Ibid.*

article is this one: "As for the Ṣlayb themselves, they know nothing of their origins; or if they do, they have thought it up in their imaginations or invented it in their own minds."[41]

We have to contend with the fancies of Father Anastase, however, and not the imaginings or invention of the Ṣlayb themselves, when he says: "They keep chasing the gazelle until, when it becomes exhausted and stands like the thinker who has lost his wits, they open fire on it and pounce upon it."[42] And further: "They pursue the gazelle sometimes by running and at other times riding on a white donkey. When they draw close to the quarry they speak in a whisper to their donkey, which, understanding what is meant, kneels down like a camel. They then open fire from behind the beast of burden, using it in place of a covert so as to bag the gazelle."[43]

Not failing to mention their distinguishing characteristics, he describes the Ṣlayb as having:

> small heads, high broad foreheads, bluish-black or yellow eyes, beautiful arched eyebrows, sensitive noses, fair skin, oval-shaped faces, thin lips, fair hair, soft skin, slim waists, graceful figures, pure white teeth, healthy bodies, and excessively slim builds.

Had such attributes been in customary usage for judging beauty at the time he wrote this article, he would be setting before us an account making every Ṣlayb woman a world beauty queen. I have no idea how to bring Father Anastase's statement into harmony with that of Guarmani, who, as has already come to our attention, claimed that he has never seen women uglier than theirs.

Father Anastase further claims:

> The Ṣlayb absolutely abhor theft, deceit and duplicity, trickery, hypocrisy, and fraud in sales and trade. Lying is unknown among them. . . .Decency and chastity are second nature to them; they thus know nothing of adultery, and immoral sexual conduct occurs only rarely.[44]

[41] *Ibid.*, p. 674.
[42] *Ibid.*, p. 677.
[43] *Ibid.*
[44] *Ibid.*, p. 678.

All he leaves unsaid is that they are the saintly angels come down to earth! It is of interest to note here that many of the settled folk and bedouins did not agree with Father Anastase in these views and spoke ill of the Ṣlayb. Indeed, Shaykh Nūrī al-Sha'lān used to speak of the Ṣlayb to Musil himself when the latter complained about them to him, saying that they are vile rogues and scoundrels, grasping swindlers who ally among themselves against the stranger, despite the fact that Nūrī al-Sha'lān himself used to rely on Ṣlaybīs to scout out the land before the eastward migration and to inform him about his bedouin enemies whenever they saw hostile raiders in the desert as they passed from one tribal territory to another.[45]

It is curious that Father Anastase's statements on the Ṣlayb should have passed muster with some of the Orientalists, who accepted them and translated his article into their own languages, as is mentioned by Professor Gurgīs 'Awwād, who recorded this in his book on Father Anastase.[46] And it must be indicated here that there is enormous discrepancy between the view of Sulaymān al-Bustānī and that of Father Anastase on the issue of Ṣlayb origins.

In the twentieth century there was an increased interest among the European adventurers in studying the affairs, antiquities, and tribes of the Arabian peninsula. Political figures also devoted increasing attention to it in Europe when the Sick Man—Turkey—began to show signs of disintegration and enfeeblement.

There were many explorers, and they left behind them many works. Among the greatest of those who studied desert life was the Austrian scholar Alois Musil, professor of Oriental Studies of the University of Prague and known among the bedouins as Shaykh Mūsā al-Rwaylī since he camped with the Rwāla bedouins. Shaykh Mūsā visited many regions in northern Arabia, studied the geography of the peninsula and the affairs of its bedouins, and saw some of the Ṣlayb and wrote about them. He described their way of life, their dependence upon and methods of hunting, their raising of the donkeys for which they were famous, their knowledge of the steppes, wastelands, and places where water and

[45]Musil, *Arabia Deserta*, pp. 37, 212, 293, 296.

[46]Gūrgīs 'Awwād, *Al-Āb Anastās Mārī al-Karmalī: ḥayātuhu wa-mu'allafātuhu* (Baghdad, 1966), p. 66.

pasture could be found, and the reliance of the Rwāla upon them as guides. He described the devotion of some of their women to magic and sorcery and the way they tended the wounded in the battles that occurred between the warriors of different tribes, and he related some of their poems, recited in the manner of the bedouin *qaṣīd*. He confirmed their inferior social standing, but expressed no conclusive opinion on the question of their origins. He was content to say that once he saw some of them near al-Bakhrā', a district of Tadmur, and that these claimed some relationship to the Franks, who had left them behind in the desert when they emigrated (*sic.*) from Arabia to Europe.[47]

On another occasion he tried to gain information from others concerning their affairs, history, and customs. He thus invited one of them, a man named Sanad, into his tent, offered him food and tobacco, and spent about two hours with him, but to no avail since the man told him mutually contradictory stories. When Musil sent for another Ṣlaybī, a man named Faraj, who began to answer his queries with responses indicating some comprehension of the subject, his comrade Sanad, who was still in the open space beside the tent, noticed this and called out to him, saying: "Why do you teach him? He will be paid for every word in gold, but what will you get?" After this, Faraj in turn became reluctant to offer him information. Musil says: "Thereupon... I had to stop my work. When I complained to the Prince (Shaykh Nūrī al-Sha'lān) about it, he said, 'Do you not know, Mūsā, that the Ṣlayb are the worst scoundrels in the desert? Cursed be their ancestors for a progeny of such dogs!'"[48]

Views of Other Scholars

After Musil H.St. John Philby, who spent more than 40 years of his life in Arabia and was known as al-Ḥājj 'Abd Allāh Philby, tried to gain some knowledge of the truth about the Ṣlayb. In his book *The Heart of Arabia* he mentions that he met two of their shaykhs: Huwaydī ibn Bādī and Swaydān ibn Muḥārib from the clan of Ghnaymān-al-Jmayl. He also met others, but from none of them could he find out anything he could credit concerning their origins. What he does note is this:

[47]Musil, *Manners and Customs*, pp. 26, 77, 392, 406, 648–50; *idem*, *Palmyrena*, p. 90.

[48]Musil, *Arabia Deserta*, p. 293.

> The Suluba are a race apart, assimilated by environment to the Arabs, but not of them, a sort of lost tribe, whose origin is veiled by the mists of antiquity. Despised and patronised by the Arabs, to whom they pay a mild tribute in cash, kind or service for the right to breathe the desert air and for the complete immunity from molestation which they enjoy by the unwritten law, they are conscious of their low status in the social scale and are not ashamed of the current myth, which regards them as the surviving relic of some Christian tribe of the past, though at the present day they comport themselves in every respect as *Muslims* even to the practice of circumcision, with which they probably dispensed until comparatively recent times.

Philby then says:

> Whatever their origin may be, there is no doubt that they owe their privileged position in the desert to crafts of which they enjoy a practical monopoly, for in addition to being unrivaled hunters and expert guides—they are credited with knowing the positions of waterings in the desert unknown to any one else—they are the tinkers and smiths of the nomad community and as such indispensable. In this respect indeed they remind one strongly of the Sabaean community of the Euphrates valley and the Jews of Najran in the far southwest, who owe their continued existence in the midst of wild and intolerant *Muslim* tribes to the special services which they alone are capable of rendering to their neighbours in peace and war.[49]

It is to be noted that he does not refer to anything suggestive of a Crusader origin. Even in such later works of his as *The Land of Midian* and *Forty Years in the Wilderness* he makes absolutely no mention of the Ṣlayb, which may indicate that he was satisfied with what he had recorded about them in his earlier book.

[49]H.St. John Philby, *The Heart of Arabia* (London, 1922), I, 267–69.

In her book *The Syrian Desert* Mrs. Christina Grant took up the topic of the Ṣlayb in a note commenting on her account of some of the bedouin tribes. She claims that they are "a species of 'Gipsy' tribe... supposedly of Indian origin; at least they are not 'pure' Arab. Like the 'Aneza, the Suluba inhabit the inner Syrian Desert and range from Nejd in the south to northern Palmyrena." She also mentions that they are accomplished hunters and work at certain trades for the bedouins, and for further information on their affairs she refers the reader to some of the sources mentioned above.[50]

Before Grant, William Seabrook wrote about his adventures in the desert in a far from scholarly book called *Adventures in Arabia*, which I would have ignored had not certain later researchers relied upon it as a source for what they wrote about the desert. He claims that while he was in the camp of Shaykh Mithqāl Pāshā al-Fāyiz, the chief shaykh of the Banū Ṣakhr in Jordan, he met four men from the Christian bedouins known as Ṣlayb who had come to barter their donkeys for grain for their families.[51] He says:

> My friend, Amir Amin Arslan, who knew the Salib when he was desert governor under Turkish rule, had a theory that they were of mixed blood, dating back possibly to the last Crusades. They have no ritual, no contact with the Maronites or other native Christian cults, no symbols except a wooden cross. They believe in the divinity of Christ. Blue eyes are frequent among them, though not unknown among the pure Semitic tribes; a few of them are blond; some of their men are freckled and sandy-haired.[52]

He then continues to speak for himself concerning them: "These Christian nomads... speak Bedouin Arabic, but have certain special words which seem to be of French origin—or which at least trace back to

[50] Grant, p. 22.
[51] Seabrook, p. 43.
[52] *Ibid.*

Latin roots," and they "wear the skins of gazelles as shirts beneath their *abbas*."[53]

I am almost certain that Seabrook never saw a Ṣlaybī in his life; rather, he read about them or heard that they were a curious tribe among the bedouins, and so did not wish that his adventures should lack an account and description of them. Had he actually been familiar with the Ṣlayb, their customs, and their ways of life, he would have realized that they would not give up their donkeys so easily as this and would not want grain in exchange for them; indeed, they generally do not lay in supplies of grain as other bedouin tribes do. It would have been easier for such men as these, who, as Seabrook claims, came to Jordan from Syria, to sell their donkeys there and obtain their provisions from Syria and its towns, which are rich in grain. As for their deification of Christ, their Christianity, and their use of certain words of French or Latin origin, this is his own invention, or perhaps he heard it from persons who knew nothing of Ṣlayb affairs, and believed them. And add to this the fact that the theory he attributes to Amīn Arslān had already been proposed, as we have mentioned, by Sulaymān al-Bustānī.

> Sa'd watered them, but was still wearing his cloak.
> Camels are not to be watered thus, O Sa'd![54]

Later Europeans Who Wrote on the Ṣlayb

Among the later Europeans who wrote on the Ṣlayb was H.R.P. Dickson, who lived in Kuwayt in the 1950s and devoted a special chapter to the Ṣlayb in his book on the bedouins. In most of his material he agrees with earlier European researchers, and from Shaykh 'Abd Allāh al-Sālim al-Ṣabāḥ he reports that the Ṣlayb are descended from the European invaders who were taken captive during the wars of the Crusades and then carried into slavery among the bedouins of the desert.

[53] *Ibid.*, p. 44. The book is stuffed with mistakes, despite what it contains of the author's own experiences and his meeting with the Druze and the "Veiled Lady of Mukhtara" (pp. 129–76).

[54] Ibn 'Abd Rabbih, *Al-'Iqd (al-farīd)*, III, 108. The verse is by Mālik ibn Zayd Manāh and Sa'd was his brother. Comment on this verse has been made in our study of the camel [above, p. 203 n. 37].

Citing the words of His Highness the Shaykh as corroboration for this, he observes that the cross (in Arabic, *ṣalīb*) is the symbol of the tribe and that their name is Ṣlayb. But Dickson himself states: "It would be dangerous to form conclusions pending the collection of more data." He is content with the statement: "According to what is said of them they are the descendents of the Christian Crusaders."[55]

Interest in studying the bedouins and the desert did not cease in the first half of the twentieth century. Among those who wrote in this period on the Ṣlayb was the French officer Victor Müller, who in his book *En Syrie avec les bédouines* discusses the hunting of the gazelle and says:

> Hunting of the gazelle is above all a speciality of the Ṣlayb, a curious tribe of unknown origin who, up until our arrival, were subjected by the bedouins to draconian regulations. They live in corners of the desert where no one can live. All of the Ṣlayb, moreover, wear gazelle skins, rather badly tanned, that give off a nauseating odor.[56]

Another Western scholar was the anthropologist Henry Field, who undertook comprehensive studies to measure the head (skull) size of various peoples and tribes in the regions of the Near East. He saw more than 100 Ṣlayb tribesmen near Kuwayt and noted that they represented a special category different from the people of that region. They remained isolated and did not intermingle with the others, because of the contempt with which their Arab neighbors regarded them. He noticed that their eyes were generally black, likewise their hair, and that they had long narrow heads. He was not able to take measurements of their heads, however, because they did not consent when he tried to do this, and he gives no indication whatsoever that they had any connection to a Frankish or Crusader origin.[57]

---

[55]Dickson, pp. 515–25.

[56]Victor Müller, *En Syrie avec les bédouines: les tribus du désert* (Paris, 1931), pp. 92–93.

[57]Henry Field, *An Anthropological Reconnaissance in the Near East, 1950* (Cambridge, Mass, 1956), pp. 49–50.

There was also Hogarth, who made incidental mention of them in one of his books. He does not consider them to be Arab bedouins, but he does not refer to a Crusader origin.[58]

There is no need for us to mention all of these later European researchers and explorers, since we can observe that most if not all of them have copied their reports on the Ṣlayb from the earlier explorers and offer no new information worthy of mention. We must also note that the most important Arab authors to write about the Ṣlayb in this century have not accepted the Crusader origin theory. In his book *'Ashā'ir al-'Irāq*, 'Abbās al-'Azzāwī says of the Ṣlayb that they have no connection with the Crusaders, and states that their knowledge of the animals that live in the desert and of the plants used in drugs makes it inconceivable that they should be descended from the Crusaders.[59] Similarly, Aḥmad Waṣfī Zakarīyā took up the subject of the Ṣlayb in his books *'Ashā'ir al-Shām* and *Al-Rīf al-sūrī*[60] and devoted an elaborate discussion to their life and customs, based on his eyewitness experience and what he took from the European scholars before him, and he dismissed as nonsense the views of the later writers who attributed the origin of the Ṣlayb to the Crusaders.[61] "As for the statement by some that they have fair faces and blue eyes," he says, "there is no truth to this."[62] Fu'ād Ḥamza also mentions the Ṣlayb and says of them:

---

[58] *The Nearer East*, p. 255 n.

[59] Al-'Azzāwī, *'Ashā'ir al-'Irāq*, I, 312.

[60] Zakarīyā, *'Ashā'ir al-Shām*, II, 112–24; *idem.*, *Al-Rīf al-sūrī*, I, 322–26.

[61] *'Ashā'ir al-Shām*, II, 117; *Al-Rīf al-sūrī*, I, 324.

[62] *'Ashā'ir al-Shām*, II, 114. Here again he bases his statement on the assertion made to him by Mush'il Pāshā al-Fāris al-Jarbā, one of the most famous of the bedouin shaykhs. Zakarīyā is correct in denying that the Ṣlayb are of Crusader origin (p. 118), but he errs in his effort to reach an understanding of their origins and in his claim that they may be of Indian origin (p. 120). He also entangles himself in difficulty by copying information set forth earlier by Father Anastase al-Karmalī (without indicating that he is doing so), as in his statement (p. 117) that the Ṣlayb pursue the gazelle "until, when it becomes exhausted and stands like the thinker who has lost his wits, they open fire and pounce upon it. They pursue it sometimes by running and at other times riding on white donkeys. When they draw close to the quarry they speak in a whisper to their donkey, which understands what is meant and kneels down like a camel. They then open fire from behind the beast of burden, using it in place of a covert so as to bag the gazelle."

> The "sons of Ṣlaybī," or "sons of Ghānim": this is the name that is applied to the collectivity of tribes for which no line of descent is known. You will see them, because of their weakness and the obscurity of their descent, seeking refuge with well-known tribes and asking for their protection in exchange for the brother-right (*al-khāwa*), which they render to them with that aim in mind.

He reports that "the Ṣlayb claim that their origin is from the Ḥasā'."[63]

Here we can return to what Doughty wrote, based on information he heard from them pertaining to their origins. He asked one of the Ṣlayb about their origins, and the man responded: "What is this to inquire of us wretches dwelling in these deserts? We have no books, nor memories of things past; but read thou, and if anything of this be written, tell us."[64] Doughty mentions in another place that he met some of the Ṣlayb in the south and asked them about their origins. In reply they claimed that they were Arabs from an ancient tribe which they called Kafā', concerning which Doughty explains nothing. They also told him that in ancient times they had camels, sheep, and villages in Wādī l-Sidr, south of al-'Alā' and now in ruins, and that they used to be allies of Sālim ibn al-Zīr of Jabal al-Jahlah, a day's traveling distance from Medina.[65] Other Ṣlayb tribesmen made claims to Doughty, concerning their origins, that they were from the Banū Murra.[66] He was of the opinion that some of the bedouins believed this, saying of Ṣlayb that they were bedouins descended from Jassās ibn Murra al-Bakrī after they were destroyed at the hands of Kulayb ibn Wā'il (*sic*; perhaps they

---

[63] Ḥamza, pp. 166–68. See also Musil, *Arabia Deserta*, p. 233.

[64] Doughty, I, 326.

[65] *Ibid.*, I, 326–27.

[66] *Ibid.* Palgrave (II, 133) mentions that he saw a group from the Āl Murra in the middle of the Dahnā' and had never seen beings more savage-looking than these folk. Their hair was long and tangled, their clothes were in rags, and their look wildness personified. They were, on the other hand, eloquent in their speech. He says of them that they are the most widely distributed bedouins in Arabia. See also Donald Powell Cole, *Nomads of the Nomads* (Arlington Heights, Illinois, 1975).

mean al-Muhalhil—al-Zīr—the brother of Kulayb), and that having been laid so low they resorted to hunting, handicrafts, and smithing.[67]

The Emergence of the Ṣlayb

It is difficult for us to give our consent to such a statement as this and to accept that a group tracing its descent back to the one who killed Kulayb, one of the greatest Arabs of his time according to the consensus of the early transmitters—that is, back to the Bakrīs of Āl Murra—would sink to such a low social position among the Arab tribes. Anyone who reads the *mu'allaqa* of al-Ḥārith ibn Ḥilliza al-Bakrī would be aware of the pride, disdain, and strength of these Bakrīs.

Similarly, we can observe that most researchers agree that the Ṣlayb were originally adherents of a religion other than Islam. This religion—if it was not a Christian sect—was closer to Christianity than to any other faith, and up until a late date some of the Ṣlayb continued to adhere to certain rites and rituals of this religion. As a result of all this they came to be ostracized by the other bedouins, and the name Ṣlayb and its associated connections of servile, wretched, and contemptible status thus came to attach to them. This group was accordingly compelled to submit to a harsh system of regulations and to undertake special services in order to protect themselves and guarantee their survival.

One of the most important of these services was that they undertook to tend the wounded from the battles and raids that broke out between the warriors of quarreling tribes, to such an extent that it could be said of them that they were the Red Crescent or Red Cross in the desert. When a battle broke out between two tribes and a group of the Ṣlayb was nearby, they were the first to reach the wounded to rescue and treat them; carrying them to their humble tents, they tended them with no regard for the question of to which of the two parties any wounded man belonged. During their wanderings or hunting trips, if they saw any people stranded in the desert and on the brink of dying from thirst, regardless of whether they were bedouin raiders or others, they would immediately go to their assistance, mounting them on their donkeys, carrying them to their nearest camp, and treating them with butter and

[67]Doughty, I, 326.

water.[68] They were experts in medical treatment and materia medica, and because of this the injured felt assured that they were in the care of a group of experts.

The Ṣlayb accordingly enjoyed immunity in the desert: no one raided them, and they raided no one and did not have the right to own or ride horses. In certain regions they were compelled to pay a *khuwwa* in order to gain this immunity.

Today one sees them relying on donkeys in their wanderings in the desert, and also on camels, although up until recently they were not allowed to own camels and so depended primarily on donkeys. There would be nothing out of the ordinary in regarding their reliance upon the donkey as an indication that they are of settled origin and that they continued to raise and depend upon the donkey when, for reasons unknown, they were forced to move to the desert. The occasional shift from agricultural to nomadic life is a phenomenon that has come to be acknowledged among sociologists. Their dependence on asses in their wanderings proves that in certain cases bedouin life can be sustained in this way. In fact, donkeys were probably relied upon before camels were known, although the donkey cannot tolerate thirst or go without water for as long as the camel can.

It would seem that their shift to nomadic life was necessitated by their need to hunt in order to live in the Arabian peninsula, and this accounts for the fact that the Ṣlayb are the most expert hunters.

The Donkeys of Ṣlayb

Ṣlaybī donkeys are of two types: the ordinary breed, called *ḥaqāra* donkeys, and the special thoroughbred breed, called the *shahāra*.[69] The latter are usually white, swift, and extremely strong and agile. The Ṣlayb insist that in origin they are a crossbreed between onagers ("wild asses") and domestic she-donkeys; and they claim that when their she-donkeys go into heat late in winter, they leave them to graze at will out in the open countryside where onagers also graze, so that they will mate with the donkeys. Guarmani,[70] confirmed by Musil,[71] comments

[68]Musil, *Arabia Deserta*, pp. 181, 228.
[69]*Ibid*, p. 229.
[70]Guarmani, Appendix XIV.
[71]Musil, *Arabia Deserta*, p. 270; *idem*, *In the Arabian Desert*, pp. 187–88.

that the Ṣlayb used to cross the Euphrates to catch some onagers alive to mate with their she-donkeys. When I asked the Ṣlayb about this they did not deny it, but commented that the practice had become impossible since the turn of the century, when onagers began to disappear throughout the Arabian peninsula.[72] Whatever the truth of the matter may be, the donkey of the Ṣlayb continues up to the present day to be one of the liveliest and swiftest-running animals. It has a special gait like the trotting of a horse, and over a long distance it can outrun most animals. More than a hundred years ago these donkeys were being exported to distant lands: William Wright claims that they were shipped to England by way of Marrakesh.[73]

One of the most interesting stories told to me concerning the swiftness of the Ṣlaybī donkeys, an almost unbelievable tale, has it that some raiders saw from afar an old man whom they took for a warrior on a white charger, so they rushed forth toward him to rob him of his steed. When the man saw them, he in turn quickly jumped onto his mount and swiftly galloped toward some bedouins who were camped in the desert some few miles away behind a hill. The raiders rushed after him toward the bedouins' camp, each trying to beat the others to win the booty, but their horses were unable to catch up with him. When the Ṣlaybī got to the nomads' camp behind the hill ahead of his pursuers, he dismounted, betook himself to the tent of the shaykh, and sat down to rest. A little while later the members of the raiding party arrived and made their way to the tent of the shaykh to ask about the warrior who had been fleeing before them and who had sought refuge with the shaykh. Denying that there was any warrior camping with him, the shaykh said: "No one has come to camp with me except for this Ṣlaybī sitting by the tent, and he was on that white donkey of his." When they saw the Ṣlaybī they asked him if he was the one they had been pursuing. He admitted that he was, and asked for protection as the protégé of the shaykh. *Anta āman*, "You safety is assured," they said; but one of them pointed his rifle at the donkey and shot and killed it, saying: *lā 'āsha l-bahīm al-yafḍaḥ al-khayl*, "No brute beast

---

[72] Musil (*Arabia Deserta*, pp. 269–70) claims that some wild donkeys were still to be seen in the Wādī Sirḥān up until the first quarter of the nineteenth century.

[73] Wright, pp. 48–49.

may live that puts horses to shame!" He then paid the wergild for the donkey.

The Ṣlayb and Hunting

As we have already noted, the Ṣlayb are distinguished by their dependence upon hunting for their livelihood. They may use their donkeys to take them to the gazelles' grazing grounds, and for hunting they thus wear the hides of the gazelles they shoot. This manner of dress, which sets them apart from the rest of the bedouins, camouflages them from the quarry and serves them as a substitute for cloth. They stitch the skins, hair side outward, into a long robe with an attached hood covering the head, sleeves covering the arms down to the finger joints, and an opening at the neck and the front part of the chest. They put pieces of hide called *zanāniḥ* on the sleeves at the elbow and on the front of the robe at the knee, in order to protect the robe when the hunter or driver is crawling on his hands and knees after the game. One explorer says that he saw the trail left by a crawling Ṣlaybī hunter extending in the desert for the distance of about a mile.[74]

In the days when the desert teemed with onagers, ostriches, oryx, gazelles, rabbits, and other animals whose meat they ate, the Ṣlayb used to live by hunting. So it was in the days when hunting was with bow and arrow, and then similarly in the era of early firearms. Today they continue in like manner in their use of modern firearms, and as a result most of these animals have begun to die out. There was a time when gazelles, for example, grazed in herds in the deserts and along the desert fringes near the villages and farms. When the Ṣlaybī saw a herd of gazelles, he would take cover, select the animal he wanted from the herd, and kill it with an arrow, saying to himself: "Today I will content myself with this one; the herd is my herd, and tomorrow or the day after I will return to choose from it whatever I want," as if the herd was a flock of sheep in his paddock.[75] But when firearms were introduced and reached the hands of the Ṣlayb, they became meat vendors when they camped along the desert fringes near the villages, and the latter had no need for butchers or the meat of their slaughtered animals. I

[74][Kiernan, pp. 263–64.]

[75]See Doughty, I, 325.

have actually seen the Ṣlayb passing by on their donkeys, heading for the town in which I grew up loaded with gazelles taken in the hunt. One of them told me of a Ṣlaybī hunter who went out with a driver to hunt. When he saw a herd of gazelles he took cover downwind in a depression in the ground and sent his companion to drive the herd toward him. When the herd drew near he threw himself face down on the ground; the herd passed by him, and some of the gazelles almost trod on his legs. Then, when he sensed that he was in the midst of the herd, he calmly got up on his knees, aimed his rifle, and killed two bucks with two shots.

Doughty asserted that the Ṣlaybī could hit the quarry with the primitive means at his disposal, like the old matchlock firearm that obliged one to light its match before discharging it and firing it at the target.[76] Musil claimed that with his simple weapons the Ṣlaybī and his companion who drives the herd could take between 10 and 20 gazelles in a day.[77]

The Ṣlaybī also used to hunt ostriches. These birds used to graze in the Nafūd and in the southern plains, and then began to migrate in the late spring to the Ḥamād and the region of Wudyān, extending almost as far as the Ghūṭa region southeast of Damascus. In the autumn they returned south, and the Ṣlayb would take cover from them behind heaps of stones in locations downwind from the ostriches, so that it would be easy for the hunter to draw close and shoot them.[78]

I am not exaggerating when I assert that the Ṣlayb are to a large extent responsible for the disappearance of many such desert animals as the ostrich, oryx, gazelle, and onager, as a consequence of modern military firearms having fallen into their hands. Some responsibility for their disappearance must also be attributed to hunters from the villages and towns who throughout the Arabian peninsula hunted with motor vehicles and other such means.

In order to gain their livelihood the Ṣlayb, especially those clans living in the al-Manāẓir region and in the Syrian highlands, are dependent upon the raising of sheep and the sale of lambs and such sheep

---

[76] *Ibid.*, I, 406–407.
[77] Musil, *Manners and Customs*, p. 26.
[78] Musil, *Arabia Deserta*, p. 255.

products as clarified butter. Until recently this source of income was one of the most important ones for these clans. In the past the Ṣlayb had thousands of sheep, and it would be within their ability to become one of the richest tribes in Syria were their members to direct their attention to this resource alone, give up hunting, and seek government assistance in erecting storehouses for food and dry herbage and paddocks in which the sheep could spend the night on certain cold winter days.

The Ṣlayb and Handicrafts

The Ṣlayb have another source for their livelihood, and that is the simple handicrafts required by the bedouins: the repair of containers, utensils, and weapons, the smithing of the hoes used to dig out truffles (which in certain years could be another source of income for them) and uproot scrub for fuel, the making of shackles and shoes for horses, woodworking for the pack and riding saddles, pack frames, and litters that are tied onto the backs of camels during migration (or previously, on a raid), and for such wooden implements as pots, ladles, plates, poles upon which to raise the hair tents, and for the pegs to which the tent ropes are tied. This is why the bedouins consider them craftsmen and despise them. There is no space here for discussion concerning these crafts; but it is a Ṣlayb custom for only a small group connected by bonds of kinship to stay in any one camp, so that in one such camp there are rarely relatives more remotely related than the fifth generation.

Some of the Ṣlayb practice as physicians and veterinarians and earn a living from medicine. Both their women and their men have a knowledge of the many kinds of herbs and plants used in drugs. It is probably their knowledge of medicine and treatment of the wounded and the sick, coupled with their status as confederates or companions to all the bedouins, that has ordained that in the desert they should be the Red Cross or Red Crescent (as we have mentioned) for anyone wounded in raids, irrespective of the group or tribe to which he belongs. We have already observed how the four Ṣlaybī women treated the explorer Guarmani when their menfolk found him unconscious at a grotto pool on the mountain.

The Ṣlayb and Their Knowledge of the Desert

The Ṣlayb are also distinguished among the bedouins for their superior knowledge of the land, routes, pools, wadis, and dunes of the desert. They even claim that when a Ṣlaybī betakes himself to the settled areas to purchase what he needs, if he happens to have more than the required amount of cash he takes the surplus coins and buries them in a hiding place in the desert in a pile of rocks or elsewhere, and returns in a later season to retrieve them, as if he had hidden them in a garden of which he knows every single inch of ground.

They also know the places where water may be collected after a rainstorm, whether in a depression in the sandy soil in certain wadis, in rain pools sometimes left behind by torrents in the wadi beds, or in hollowed out rocks on certain mountain peaks. Indeed, after taking water from the small hollows in the rocks they may try to cover them with a rock or with brush, clay, and dirt, to hide the water they contain so that no one else will drink it while they are gone and it will remain there for them until they return.[79]

They are also knowledgeable in tracking and in recognizing the signs left behind on the surface of the ground by beasts and men, and when they hunt this knowledge helps them to follow the trail of game animals and pursue and kill them. Likewise, they have come to be experts in their knowledge of the desert lands and, by assent of the bedouins themselves, from all the various tribes, they act as guides in the unknown regions of the desert. It is common knowledge that the Rwāla—the bedouins of al-Shaʿlān—used to rely on the Ṣlayb in Syria to scout out resting places before their eastward migration, to ascertain the places where pasturage and water could be found after the first rainfall in the autumn, and to spy on their adversaries from the other tribes in their military campaigns. The Ṣlayb train their sons to acquire such skills, and hence this knowledge is passed on from the old to the young.

Poetry and Music

Another of the distinctive traits of the Ṣlayb is that they are well versed in music and in composing bedouin poetry, which they call the *qaṣīd*. At the beginning of this chapter I referred to the story which explains

[79]Doughty, II, 255–56.

the origins of the Ṣlayb with the tale that one of the ʻAbbāsid caliphs had their forefathers brought from India to Baghdad to serve as musicians in his court. Although it is difficult to credit this story, the Ṣlayb are in fact the desert masters of this art, as also of the *qaṣīd*. Just as poetry was in former times associated with song, the two of them proceeding together, the Ṣlayb have made the same connection. There are some Ṣlayb poets who have made of these two arts a trade and a livelihood, making their way to the tents of eminent bedouin shaykhs in both the desert and the settled lands to sing their praises in verse in the hope of receiving a present, just as many poets in medieval times used to do. They recite this poetry as a melody accompanied on the rebab, an instrument which they play better than all other bedouins. Many of their poets are parasites who impose themselves upon people; if they are not rewarded or honored they turn on them with verses of derision. One of the Ṣlayb told me that a poet of this kind camped by a man known as Ibn Maqṣūd, who was the headman (*mukhtār*) of the village of Ṣadad, near Ḥimṣ, and a woodworker by origin. Ibn Maqṣūd neither fed nor honored the poet, so the latter ridiculed him in verse:

> O rider on the back of a she-ass's daughter,
> Which is green and at twig-point jumps and starts:
> You come to the carpenter, the Christians' shaykh,
> For Ibn Maqṣūd's whiskers here are 2000 farts.

There is not space here to consider their poetry, but in brief it covers the forms of the panegyric, the lampoon, and the love poem, and takes up most of the poetic themes dealt with by the ancients. Shafīq al-Kamālī wrote a detailed study on bedouin poetry in general, referred to the impact of the Ṣlayb upon it, and quoted some Ṣlayb verse. One of these poems was a bedouin ode by a poet named Rāshid al-Khalāwī that al-Kamālī says was originally 1000 verses long, 96 of them rhyming with the same letter. The ode began:

> So says al-Khalāwī, who suffers not fatigue
> In the new composing of most extravagant odes.

Al-Kamālī asserted that this man Rāshid lived in the ninth century AH/fifteenth century AD, contemporary to Manīʻ ibn Sālim ibn ʻUrayʻar, chief of the al-Khawālid and one of the shaykhs of the Aḥsā'. He said that "al-Khalāwī" was an agnomen attached to Rāshid because he used to wander out in the open desert,[80] apparently not taking account of the fact that the bedouins in the north call every Ṣlaybī "al-Khalāwī," as we have mentioned above.

The Ṣlaybī Woman

The Ṣlaybī woman differs from her bedouin sister in that she enjoys a greater measure of freedom. She is not compelled to marry a man she does not like; rather, her consent must be granted, and it is only rarely that one sees a second wife in her tent. This is not due to poverty, as is generally the case in the desert, for the Ṣlayb are well-off compared to other bedouins. Rather, it arises from a custom their clans have been following traditionally for ages. If the woman is not content with life with her husband, it may happen that she will leave him and be awarded a share of the bride price. Guarmani claims that she may leave the tent and her husband will not ask her where she has been, even if she has been gone for months.[81]

The Ṣlaybī woman is also familiar with certain aspects of medicine: the dressing of wounds, the use of certain plants as medicaments, and serving as a nurse to tend to the wounded, as mentioned above. She developed this skill in a day when most of the tribes were in a constant state of conflict with one another. In recent years her assistance has been limited to dispensing to the sick the remedies and drugs that she keeps in a special box, and to helping people stranded or lost in the desert and who are on the brink of death.

She also has an artistic role as a dancer at the wedding and circumcision celebrations held by the bedouin shaykhs and other eminent men of the tribes camped nearby, and in the celebrations held by her own people. She dances so well that some have conjectured that the Ṣlayb are gypsies. When she dances by herself she lets her hair hang down and dances with her head uncovered, and sometimes begins to shake her head forward and back, right and left, so that her hair flies all around her face, as we see in the hip-shaking dance performed by

[80] Al-Kamālī, *Al-Shi'r 'inda l-badw*, p. 373.

[81] Guarmani, p. 37.

women dancers among the settled folk. A man may participate in the dance with her and kiss her, and her people see nothing objectionable in this. The other women may also dance with her, as we have already observed above.[82]

The Ṣlaybī woman will refuse to marry a slave, despite the humble social status of her people and her tribe, and she will also refuse a village craftsman, though most of the Ṣlayb are craftsmen themselves. The bedouins claim that some women of the Ṣlayb have a magical power enabling them to separate two people who love each other or join together two who are quarreling, to weaken the strong and strengthen the weak, to shorten or prolong life, or to stop the growth of a child. Bedouins who believe in such superstitions thus regard the Ṣlaybī woman as an omen of impending misfortune.

There are also women who, like their men, compose bedouin verse in the form of panegyrics, elegies, and love poetry. In his book ʿAbbās al-ʿAzzāwī cites examples of bedouin *qaṣīds* by women of Ṣlayb.[83]

The dress of the woman of Ṣlayb does not differ much from that of her bedouin sister, except that it is sometimes more delicate and more attractive. But she does not wear, like her husband the hunter, a robe of gazelle hide as some have imagined, unless her husband is so poor that he cannot afford the price of a robe. She sometimes decorates her cheeks by tattooing, as do many of the bedouin women of the semi-nomadic ʿArab al-Shawāyā. As the bedouin poet says:

> Were the young girls of Ṣlayb to venture hither
> On their full-blooded donkeys of pedigree fine,
> With their graceful cheeks all bearing the mark
> Of the tattooing needle in line after line,
> Still would I decide and select for my choice
> That young girl who is ever before my eyes,
> The beloved to whom my heart offers devotion
> And with whom my very soul soars off and flies.

[82]See Zakarīyā, *ʿAshāʾir al-Shām*, II, 122–24, giving a detailed account of a dancing party taken from the book of the French Captain Renaux after a visit of his to the Ṣlayb at the end of 1921; also Zakarīyā's *Al-Rīf al-sūrī*, I, 322–26, where he briefly reiterates what he had said in *ʿAshāʾir al-Shām*.

[83]Al-ʿAzzāwī, *ʿAshāʾir al-ʿIrāq*, I, 322–25.

When the group moves from one camping place to another she rides the donkeys (which abound in their camps) in a particular way that differs from the way village women ride. She lets both legs hang down over one side of the donkey, which is the easiest way to ride.

It hardly need be said that the Arab bedouin, especially the Rwaylī, looks upon the woman of Ṣlayb and her people with an attitude of contempt and scorn. He would disdain to allow himself, his son, or anyone in his charge to marry a Ṣlaybī girl, no matter how beautiful, and likewise the bedouin girl would haughtily refuse to marry a man of Ṣlayb, regardless of his wealth. If a Ṣlaybī passes by the tent of a bedouin woman and asks her for something to drink, she may even go so far as to refuse to allow him to drink from any of her vessels and instead pour water for him into his container, since in her eyes he is a filthy person who as an eater of carrion—as she and the other bedouins claim—would pollute her vessels.[84] Even among the Ṣlaybīs themselves there is a disparity in social status between the Ṣlaybīs of the north and those of the south. The Ṣlaybīs of the south are generally better off and regard themselves as nobler than the people of the north; one will notice that they do not intermingle with them and that the young men and women of the southerners disdain to marry the northerners.

Reference must here be made to the fact that most of the explorers and bedouins agree that the Ṣlaybī women are more beautiful than their bedouin sisters and that their complexion is fairer or less brown. Guarmani's comment concerning the four women who tended him must not be taken as a standard for judging the beauty or ugliness of the Ṣlaybī woman, since it would seem that he did not see any other Ṣlaybī women. The same applies to what has been said about the blue eyes, fair hair, and light complexion of some of them. It must not be supposed that this is a general feature of Ṣlaybī women or that it is found only among them. One time, in a bedouin camp of the ʻArab al-Shawāyā which I visited, I saw a girl whose facial features hardly differed at all from those of the faces of Scandinavian girls.[85]

---

[84]See Doughty, I, 324. This may be attributable to the fact that the Ṣlayb eat game without actually slaughtering it [i.e. by cutting its throat] after killing it and invoking the name of God over it, as the Muslims do.

[85]See Figure 45 on p. 263 above.

It now remains for us to consider the origins and descent of this tribe, matters that have provoked much contradictory opinion. Following al-Karmalī, Pieper says that the name of the Ṣlayb appears in the medieval Arabic sources, where it is "al-Za'ānīf,"[86] but he does not refer to any work that mentions this name, and in fact the Arabic sources do not mention the Ṣlayb by this or any other recognizable title. The Arabic word *za'ānīf* means the edge of a tattered robe, to which contemptible people are compared. Its meanings then came to include the tribe that has declined in numbers and broken up or come to be added to another, or any group not all of one origin. Hence the saying of the poet:

> We have recognized Ja'far and Banū 'Ubayd
> But we have denied the *za'ānīf* not of our own,[87]

We find it also in the saying of 'Amr ibn Maymūn: "Beware of these *za'ānīf*." Since he cites no source whatever, Father Anastase probably found that this word in the medieval Arabic dictionaries was applicable to the Ṣlayb and so claimed that their name appeared in this form in the ancient sources, despite the fact that the Arab genealogical works do not fail to make reference to the various bedouin tribes and the clans and sections into which they are divided.

Ṣlayb Origins: a View in Critique of al-Bustānī

We must first state that we reject the view of those who speak of a Crusader origin for the Ṣlayb. We have already noted that the first to refer to this in unequivocal fashion was Sulaymān al-Bustānī in his article in *Al-Muqtaṭaf*. He was certain on this point, and he was the only one who made an effort to adduce proofs for his view. As we have already mentioned, he was probably the original promulgator of this view among certain individuals, especially after he published it in the *Dā'irat al-ma'ārif*, of which he had become one of the editors after the death of its founder, Buṭrus al-Bustānī.

[86] "Ṣulaib," p. 512.

[87] [A verse by Jarīr in *Naqā'iḍ Jarīr wa-l-Farazdaq*, edited by Anthony Ashley Bevan (Leiden, 1905–12), I, 31.]

The proofs he adduces (referred to at the beginning of this chapter) are all untenable in our view and cannot sustain the argument that the Ṣlayb are of Crusader origin. As for the name "Ṣlayb" or "Ṣulaba," even if it were derived from the word *ṣalīb*, "cross," that would not necessarily demonstrate that the persons so called were descendents from the Frankish *ṣalībīyūn*, or "Crusaders," for it may well be that this lineage was from one of the sects of ancient Syrian Christians. As for his reference to the many Ṣlaybīs with blue eyes, this is untrue: it is rejected by many of those who made mention of the Ṣlayb in their works or who, like Waṣfī Zakarīyā, to whom we have referred above, met some of them. They have made it clear that this argument is devoid of foundation. I myself personally tried to find persons with blue eyes among the Ṣlaybīs I met; but I saw not a single one, though I had formerly been one of those who accepted the theory of the Crusader origin for this tribe. As for the laxity in their pronunciation, their use of special terms and expressions, their lack of affiliation to any particular confession of Islam, the disparity of their lifestyle, and the other reasons he mentions, these are matters that indicate their difference from the Arab bedouins, but they do not necessarily suggest a Crusader origin.

There remains the fact that some of the Ṣlayb, when asked about their origins, have replied: "We are descended from the Crusaders" or "from the Franks." Such responses are utterly worthless. They are refuted by the fact that most of the explorers who asked the Ṣlayb about their origins were told different stories: for example, they were originally the Christian inhabitants of these ancient lands; they were bedouins from this or that region; they were the bedouins of the Banū Murra; they were the bedouins of the Banū Ghānim; and so on with other origins. The fact of the matter is that the Ṣlayb, who for some reason or another came to their present level of lowliness, wretchedness, and fear, have resorted to dissimulation. They assign themselves an origin in accordance with the situation in which they find themselves. Among Christians they claim that they are of Christian origin, and among Muslims that they are Muslims like the other bedouins. When a Westerner visited them—and Westerners enjoyed a certain status in the nineteenth century—and they hoped to receive a present from him, they would claim that they were of Frankish origin. It may have been this dissimulation that led some to suppose that they were descended from Shīʿites who abandoned al-Ḥusayn at Karbalā' and that their punishment was thus to become outcasts.

Let us also note that the Ṣlayb are spread out in small groups in which a single camp does not amount to more than a few hair tents, that they are scattered in regions far removed from one another, and that they do not mix much either with the bedouins or with the people of the villages surrounding the desert. In such a situation it would have been difficult for their bedouin dialect—as it now exists—to assume any unified form had they really been of Crusader origin. Rather, it would have been natural for there to develop various dialects and small linguistic islands in the desert, some of which would have preserved traces of the language of the Franks. The reality, however, is otherwise. The Ṣlayb's use of the terms and expressions mentioned by al-Bustānī in fact makes it unlikely that they are of any Frankish origin and draws them closer to an indigenous origin within the Arab lands, as we shall see.

In addition to all this, the Crusaders who remained behind in these lands did not penetrate to the heart of the Arabian peninsula, but rather stayed close to the coasts of Syria and Lebanon. They may also have wandered to some of the Christian villages in Syria, and traces of this Western blood are still today evident in some of the residents of these two regions.

Further, we would assert that the Crusaders could not have penetrated to the heart of Arabia and spread throughout all of its northern parts, while at the same time not a single scholar, author, or historian was aware of their presence, no one wrote about them or paid any attention to them, every bit of information about them faded into oblivion, and nothing survived except for this strange name. And indeed, it is difficult for us to accept that a group of Frankish—or even non-Frankish—foreigners would have penetrated a land as vast as the Arabian peninsula, and then in a short span of time, historically speaking, become the people most knowledgeable on its quarters, deserts, routes, and water sources, and to such an extent that place names were known from them and repeated on their authority and that they came to be designated as those best able to find their way in Arabia's trackless wildernesses and as the foremost guides for its raiders. They also became the most eloquent of the bedouins in their language and the poets with the most ancient verse, thus forgetting their original language, of which no trace survives in their speech. Were they in truth to be described as the "nomads of the nomads," as Sulaymān al-Bustānī wished them to be, could they have been descended from the Crusaders? We say: No. But if not, then from what origin do they come? Is there anything that can assist us on this matter?

We have already mentioned above that the bedouins themselves are largely—if not entirely—agreed that the Ṣlayb are an ancient people. Doughty says that the first time he found out anything about them occurred when his guide pointed out a group of them and said: "Yonder I will show thee some of a people of antiquity."[88] At one time it seemed to me that they might be descended from the Nabataeans, for no reason other than the fact that they are the most renowned poets of the desert and their poetry is known as *al-shiʿr al-nabaṭī*, "Nabataean poetry," an appellation generalized in all Arab countries to refer to bedouin poetry. But I really do not find this reason sufficient grounds for concluding that the Ṣlayb descend from the Nabataeans. Although the Nabataeans were the connecting link in the commerce between East and West and knew the trade routes in the peninsula, there is in their history and military spirit enough to rule out the possibility that they would have declined to such a position as that occupied by the tribe of Ṣlayb. To the Arab in Islamic times the word *nabaṭ*, "Nabataeans," conveyed the sense of foreignness and remoteness from the Arab language more that it did a sense of degradation and abasement. The bedouins likewise agree that the Ṣlayb are not Arabs like themselves, but rather are of some obscure Christian or Jewish origin. Hence they are not allowed to intermarry with the Arab bedouins, even after converting to Islam. Nor, in times past, were they allowed to own horses or raid; and indeed, they were obliged to pay a *khuwwa* to the bedouin shaykhs who allowed them to move about in their tribal territory and practice the crafts we mentioned earlier. They thus live in the desert as people scorned and regarded with contempt.

---

[88]Doughty, I, 323. Musil, who does not rely much on their statements, in one place says of them (*Arabia Deserta*, p. 233) that among them there are those who claim that formerly their people used to occupy the Ḥasā' region.

A Theory on Their Origins

Someone could have asserted that these Ṣlaybīs are descended from the Jews who, as reported by the Italian explorer Varthema mentioned earlier in this chapter, remained in central Arabia near Khaybar until the early sixteenth century. But no one mentions this, and their name alone would be sufficient to refute such a claim. There thus remains no possibility other than that of a Christian or Sabaean origin. It is interesting for us to note that such an origin was referred to by some authorities, such as the British Resident Pelly, discussed above. Pelly also says that they practice certain strange religious rites, such as immersing their children in water seven times 40 days after their birth, veneration of the North Star and another star in the sign of Capricorn, and standing in veneration of these two stars with faces turned towards them and with arms extended to either side so that the body forms the shape of a cross. And they explicitly speak of themselves as a tribe of Sabaeans that migrated to Najd. Authorities other than Pelly related that up until recent times the Ṣlayb remained uncircumcised and did not know of circumcision. Indeed, some of them—as Palgrave claims—hated Islam and made no secret of this.[89] Musil asserts that there was a hill in the desert that the Ṣlayb regarded as sacred and claimed that it was or had once been the abode of a saint whom they called "Abū l-Ruḍama" and much exalted.[90] And in the same region there are graves which the Ṣlayb claim are remains of the ancients and regard as sacred.[91] Could the Ṣlayb be descended from the Sabaeans or members of the Ḥarrānian cult? Is there anything in the Arabic sources that would point in this direction?

In the *Kitāb al-Fihrist* Ibn al-Nadīm reports:

> In the year 215 (830 AD) al-Ma'mūn passed through Diyār Muḍar on his way to raid the land of the Greeks. The people received him, invoking blessings upon him, and among them there was a group of adherents of the Ḥarrānian cult whose manner of attire was to don full-length robes

[89]Palgrave, I, 150.
[90]Musil, *Arabia Deserta*, p. 74.
[91]*Ibid.*, p. 80.

with long sleeves and to wear their hair long. . . . Al-Ma'mūn disapproved of their appearance and said to them: "Of what protected religious community are you?" "We are Ḥarrānians," they replied. The caliph asked: "Are you Christians?" "No," they responded. "Are you Jews, then?" "No," came the reply. "So then are you Magians?" "No," they said. "Do you have a sacred scripture or prophet?," al-Ma'mūn asked, to which they mumbled an indistinct response. The caliph therefore told them: "You must then be unbelievers (*al-zanādiqa*) who worship idols. . . . The shedding of your blood is licit and there is no protection for you." "We will pay the *jizya*," they offered. "Of these persons who differ in faith from Islam," the caliph replied, "the *jizya* is taken only from the adherents of the religions that God—may He be praised and exalted—mentioned in His Book, people who have a sacred scripture and with whom the Muslims have concluded security arrangements on that basis. You, however, are neither the one nor the other. So choose, now, one of two alternatives: embrace Islam or one of the religions that God mentioned in His Book, otherwise I will slay you to the last man. I will wait for your decision until I return from this journey of mine. By then you will have embraced Islam or one of those religions which God mentioned in His Book; otherwise, I will order that you be killed and that your kind be exterminated."

Al-Ma'mūn then set out for the land of the Greeks, so the Ḥarrānians changed their attire, cut short their hair, and stopped wearing full long-sleeved robes. Many of them converted to Christianity and wore *zanānīr*,[92] one group embraced Islam, and all there was left of them was a small band who remained as they were. These were becoming anxious and distressed, but then a learned shaykh from the people of Ḥarrān presented himself to them and told them: "I have found for you something that will deliver you and

[92][The *zunnār* (pl. *zanānīr*) was a wide-girthed belt that identified the wearer as an adherent of one of the non-Islamic confessional communities under Islamic rule.]

> save you from being killed." So they gave him a huge amount of money... and he said to them: "When al-Ma'mūn returns from his journey tell him: 'We are Sabaeans.' This is the name of a religion which God—may His name be exalted—mentioned in the Qur'ān; embrace it, and in that way will you be delivered."
>
> As it happened, al-Ma'mūn died on that journey in al-Badhandūn, and the group adopted this name beginning at that time, since in Ḥarrān and its environs there was as yet no group called Sabaeans. When word reached them of the death of al-Ma'mūn, most of them who had converted to Christianity apostatized, returned to the Ḥarrānian cult, and grew their hair back to the length it had been before al-Ma'mūn had encountered them....Those who had embraced Islam could not apostatize, for fear of being killed, and so kept up a front of being Muslims. They had married Ḥarrānian women, and so made their sons Muslims and their daughters adherents of the Ḥarrānian cult.[93]

This account related by Ibn al-Nadīm on the persecution that befell the followers of the Ḥarrānian cult and their breakup into Ḥarrānian, Christian, and Muslim sects may be viewed in light of the reports that point to a Ḥarrānian or Christian origin for the Ṣlayb and name Ḥarrān as their place of pilgrimage, the customs and rites that some of the Ṣlayb practiced up until the end of the last century, their dispersal as small groups in northern Arabia, specially in the regions near the Euphrates not far from Ḥarrān itself and throughout the Syrian Desert in the north, and their dependence upon thoroughbred donkeys as a means of transportation and upon crafts for earning a living among the bedouin tribes. In all this there is enough to lead us to consider it likely that the Ṣlayb are in origin descended from Ḥarrānians who were compelled to emigrate from their homelands, embraced Christianity or the Sabaean cult, and then converted to Islam when they began to live with the bedouins and to stay permanently in the desert.

[93]Ibn al-Nadīm, *Fihrist*, I, 320–21.

It would not be surprising if some of them camped at al-Raqqa, near the Euphrates, and lived in the surrounding desert. In the *Mu'jam al-buldān* of Yāqūt one finds the following:

> *Al-Zawrā'*—Ruṣāfat Hishām, in which there is a marvelous monastery. There is no canal (*nahr*) or flowing spring there, and they can drink only from cisterns which they have within the walls. These sometimes run dry during the summer. Those of the people who are wealthy thus have slaves and donkeys, each of which set out for the Euphrates in the afternoon so as to return with water early the next morning, since he goes three or four leagues (*farsakh*s) and the same distance in return. They have long-drawing wells, each one of which is at least 120 cubits deep, despite which they are brackish and foul—this in the middle of the desert. The Banū Khafāja has the protection right (*khifāra*) over them, which the people pay to them as humbled protégés. Overall, were it not for the [people's] love of their homeland the town would have fallen to ruin. In it there is a group of wealthy folk, [who are there] either because they are merchants who travel to various parts or because they live there to do business with the bedouins. The town has a small market with some tens of shops. They have a talent for making garments: every man in the town, rich or poor, spins wool, and their women do the weaving.

He then says:

> The physician Ibn Buṭlān mentions this place in his epistle to Hilāl ibn al-Muḥassin, saying: "From al-Ruṣāfa to al-Raḥaba is a distance of four days' travel." He also says: "This compound"—meaning that of al-Ruṣāfa—"is a fortress of a lesser sort than the caliphal residence in Baghdad.[94] It is built of stone and in it there is a great church

[94][The reason for the comparison is that the imperial residence in Baghdad to which Ibn Buṭlān is referring was also called al-Ruṣāfa.]

> the outside of which is in gilded mosaic cubes. Constantine, son of Helen, built the compound, it was restored as al-Ruṣāfa, and Hishām ibn ʿAbd al-Malik lived there, going there for refuge from the gnats along the banks of the Euphrates. In the ground underneath the church there is a cistern built in the same manner as the church; it has vaults supported on marble columns, is paved in marble, and is full of rain water. The inhabitants of this fortress are desert folk (*bādiya*), most of them Christians, who earn their living by guarding the caravans and bringing in goods and merchandise. There are also vagabonds, as well as thieves. This compound is in the middle of the steppe. . . .One's field of vision does not extend to its extremities, which lie over the horizon. . . ." Ibn Buṭlān wrote this epistle in the year 440 (= 1048 AD).[95]

Here again I would consider it possible that the modern-day Ṣlayb are a group descended from these Christians near the Euphrates who, like many others, later converted to Islam. In their travels in their desert land their dependence continued to be on donkeys, and for their sustenance as bedouins they relied on hunting. Their knowledge of the desert lands from the times when they used to guard the caravans helped them to guide the bedouin tribes to places of pasturage and locations where rainfall collected, and the craftsmanship at which they were adept evolved into craftsmanship to serve the needs of the bedouins. They continued to be despised since they were craftsmen who paid a *khuwwa* to the bedouins, just as they had paid the Banū Khafāja for the right to protection as humbled protégés.[96]

---

[95] Yāqūt, *Muʿjam al-buldān* (Beirut, 1373–76/1955–57), III, 47–48. See also Hilāl al-Ṣābī, *Rusūm dār al-khilāfa*, edited by Mīkhāʾīl ʿAwwād (Baghdad, 1383/1964), pp. 19–20; *Khams rasāʾil li-Ibn Buṭlān al-Baghdādī wa-Ibn Riḍwān al-Miṣrī*, edited by Joseph Schacht and Max Meyerhof (Cairo, 1937), pp. 16–17. Ibn Buṭlān was a Christian physician who accompanied and learned from the Ḥarrānian physician Ibn Zahrūn (*Khams rasāʾil*, p. 23).

[96] We would do well to note here that every Ṣlaybī clan paid a *khuwwa* to the tribe that protected it, and the tribe would be responsible for warding off any element who would plunder the Ṣlaybī clan.

In the *Kitāb al-iʿtibār* of Usāma ibn Munqidh there is a third report concerning a small group in the time of the Crusades that may have been the Ṣlayb themselves before they came to be known by this name. In covering a military matter he says:

> When I reached al-Jafr, in which there were water, herbage, and trees, there arose from the brush a man wearing a black robe. We seized him, and my companions spread out and took another man, two women, and some boys. One of the women came and clutched my robe and said: "O shaykh, I am at your mercy!" "Your security is assured," I said, "What do you want?" She replied: "Your companions have taken from me a robe, a donkey (*nāhiq*), a dog (*nābih*), and a bead-stone." I said to my retainers: "He who has taken anything will return it." One brought forth a piece of garment, perhaps two cubits in length, and she said: "This is the robe." Another brought forth a piece of sandarac, and she said: "This is the bead-stone." "And what of the donkey and the dog?," I asked. They said: "The donkey they tied by its fore and back feet and it is now thrown down on the grass, and the dog has been turned loose and is running from place to place."
>
> So I collected them all together and saw in what desperate straits they were: one would think that their skins had dried on their bones. "Who are you?," I asked them, and they replied: "We are from the Banū Ubayy" (the Banū Ubayy being a grouping of the bedouins of the tribe of Ṭayyi' who eat nothing but carrion and yet say: "We are the best of the Arabs, for there is no one among us who is afflicted with leprosy, any chronic illness, or blindness." When a guest stops to camp with them, they slaughter an animal for him and give him to eat other than what they eat.) I said: "What is it that has brought you here?" "We have mounds of corn buried in the ground in the Ḥismā," they replied, "and we have come to take them."[97] "How

[97]The Ḥismā is an area in the Syrian Desert two days distance from Wādī l-Qurā. See Yāqūt, *Muʿjam al-buldān*, II, 258.

> long have you been here?," I asked. "We have been here since the feast of Ramaḍān," they said, "without setting eyes on any provisions." "And how have you been keeping alive?," I asked. "From carrion," they said, meaning old rotten bones that had been thrown away, "which we crush and boil in water with leaves of the *qaṭf* (a tree in that area); we have been living off that." "And your dogs and donkeys?," I asked. "The dogs we feed what we eat," they said, "and the donkeys eat grass." "But why haven't you gone to Damascus?," I asked, and they responded: "We were afraid of pestilence," though there is no pestilence more grievous than the situation already afflicting them. This was after the 'Īd al-Aḍḥā; so I stayed until the camels came, and then gave them some of the provisions we had. I also cut off the scarf that was on my head and gave it to the two women. They were almost mad with joy at the provisions, and I told them: "Do not stay here, otherwise the Franks will take you captive."[98]

As for the Sabaeans, reports have it that they were of Persian origin and were expelled from Persia in pre-Islamic times by the Zoroastrians and other Persian elements, who sought to wipe out every trace of this sect and burned their books. Some of them settled near the marshes that lay alongside the Euphrates. Some claim that these Sabaeans were the Christians of St. John because of the baptism they used to practice. There used to be large numbers of them living in Mesopotamia and near al-Baṣra. They are for the most part less brown in coloring than the Arabs, and some of them become bald-headed, as one sees with many Europeans.

While none of the texts we have discussed offers sufficient proof that the Ṣlayb are descended from these peoples, we do consider that they shed light on their origins and accord with reports passed down from some of them to the effect that they are from northern Syria from Christian or quasi-Christian elements or tribes. And in the final analysis we consider that there is nothing to sustain reports of their descent from a Crusader origin.

[98] Usāma ibn Munqidh, *Kitāb al-i'tibār*, pp. 11–12.

The Clans of Ṣlayb

Apropos of the names of the various clans of Ṣlayb and the calculation of their numbers of tents, there are a number of old computations from which it is difficult to derive any verifiably accurate information. The source of the discrepancies may be attributable to the time in which the data was compiled and the region in which it was recorded. If the Ṣlayb themselves were the ones who provided information to these explorers and authors, it would have been difficult for one group of them to know how many tents another group had if the latter lived in a different region. Be this as it may, the recording of some of these computations will give a general idea of the names of the Ṣlayb clans (which they call *badīda*, pl. *badāyid*), their numbers, and the regions they usually occupy.

From the tables it would seem that Fu'ād Ḥamza copied Musil and erred or made changes in the reading of some of the names.[99] He gives al-ʻArāqān instead of al-ʻArāqāt, al-Ḥiyāzīya for al-Ḥiyāḍīya, al-ʻAdādhla for al-Badhādhla, al-Ẓbayyāt for al-Ẓbībāt, al-ʻAnātir for al-ʻAnātra, Āl Rwway' for Āl Rway'ī, and al-Jahrā for al-Ja'ra or al-Qa'ra.[100] Similarly, we should observe that the table by the French command is the earlier one and was copied by the English command prior to their campaign to liberate Syria and Lebanon from the hands of the Vichy French.[101] The English command states that the number of Ṣlayb tents in Syria comes to 50, in Iraq 758, and in Najd 130, for a total of 938 tents, while their numbers in the table come to 963. This figure in turn differs from the table of Musil, which comes to 1460 tents. The book by the English command mentions that the Ṣlayb have 200 camels, 2000 sheep, and 150 donkeys in Syria alone. Concerning the shaykh of the Ṣlayb at the beginning of this century, a man named Mahdī ibn ʻAwaḍ, the command states that he alone owned about 1500 sheep, but owing to his generosity and his slaughtering of sheep for his guests, all he had left was about 100 ewes. Because of his generosity he was called *tall al-laḥm*, the "mountain of meat." The compiler of the

[99]Ḥamza, pp. 166–67.

[100]Cf. Musil, *Arabia Deserta*, p. 231; Ḥamza, pp. 166–67.

[101]Glubb, *Handbook*, p. 66.

TABLES OF THE ṢLAYB CLANS

Table of Alois Musil and Fu'ād Ḥamza			*English and French Tables*			
Clan	Tents	Area	Clan	Tents (Eng.)	Tents (Fr.)	Area
Āl Mājid	170	s. of Kuwayt	Āl Mājid	12	12	Iraq
Āl Rway'ī	60	w. of Kuwayt	al-'Imārāt	15	15	Iraq
al-Badhādhla	200	se of al-Samāwa	al-Dhubayḥ	29	29	Iraq
al-'Anātra	80	Shubayja to al-Najaf	al-Harīrāt	32	32	Iraq
Āl Jamīl	150	al-Quṣaym	al-Mwayhāt	22	22	Iraq
Āl Bannāq	50	Ḥā'il	al-Fāḍil	...	7	Syria
Āl Siyālān	60	s. of al-Ja'ra and al-Shanāfīya	al-'Ajlān	...	15	Syria
Āl Kabwān	...	same	al-Shaykh	...	22	Syria
al-'Arāqāt	30	al-Ruḥaymī, al-Ḥayāḍa	al-'Arqīya	40	40	Syria, Iraq
Āl Ṭarfa	100	al-Ḥazūl, the Jawf, the Ḥamād	al-Ṭarfa	57	58	Iraq
al-Sa'adāt	90	near Taymā'	al-Ṣṭayth	430	430	Iraq
Āl Msaylam	90	near Baghdad and al-Qub'a	al-Ṣṭayth	130	130	Najd
Āl Ḥazīm			Āl Ḥazīm	153	192	Syria,
Āl 'Īsā	80	al-Wudyān	(7 sections)			Iraq
Āl Mūsā						
al-Ẓbībāt	200	the Jazīra	...	...	...	
al-Ṣbayḥāt	100	al-Manāẓir	al-Ṣbayḥāt	43	43	Syria, Iraq
TOTAL	**1460**		**TOTAL**	**963**	**1047**	

book declares, as we have already mentioned, that the Ṣlayb are not Semites.[102]

Changes in Their Way of Life

It lastly remains for us to consider the changes that have overtaken the way of life of these folk over the last 70 years, for within this span of time the patterns of life in both the desert and settled lands have altered to a degree that the peninsula had not witnessed through the twenty centuries that had gone before it. The bedouins used to use lances in their raids, and as a boy I saw a large raiding party in the desert mounted on their thoroughbred camels and carrying no arms other than lances. Today lances are museum pieces and one rarely sees one in a bedouin camp. For hunting and shooting the Ṣlayb used to use bows and arrows; but when revolvers appeared they began to carry them and abandoned bows and arrows, doing likewise again when the Mauser rifle was introduced. Today they undoubtedly carry the modern firearms for which they find ammunition in the markets, but not for hunting, for game has entirely or almost entirely disappeared. They carry weapons only to protect their livestock—sheep, donkeys, and other animals—and to kill the wolves and hyenas of which even today there are still large numbers.

I say that game has entirely or almost entirely disappeared. The ostrich, wild ass (onager), and mountain goat (ibex) have been exterminated from the desert and from the mountains lying along its fringes or in its central areas. The oryx ("wild cow") would also be on the brink of extinction were it not for the fact that some have escaped the hunters' depredations by taking refuge in the Rubʿ al-Khālī. Some Arab rulers have taken steps to protect the oryx they have been able to collect by placing them in special preserves established for raising the animals. Concerning the gazelle, herds of them numbering in the hundreds once came into the heart of the settled lands in the areas around Ḥimṣ and Ḥamāh. This is no exaggeration, for with my own eyes I have seen herds of gazelles that were the size of flocks of sheep.

[102]The Ṣlayb make a special brand mark for their favorite camels which they call a *miẓba'*. They brand their donkeys with marks of various shapes, but do not brand their sheep.

Figure 76: A camp in which some of the people depend on the automobile for traveling to the cities.

Today, however, one only finds a very few gazelles in the Syrian Desert; and if the various governments in the Arab countries do not pass laws committing them to the prohibition of hunting gazelles, then one may as well bid farewell to this animal and it will pass into oblivion just as lions, ostriches, and onagers have done.

With the near or total extinction of those animals from which the Ṣlaybī made a living by hunting, there is no longer any motive for him to bear arms, other than to protect livestock. Nor is there any further reason for him to make his robe from gazelle hides, even were these of easy access to him. Security has also been established for them and for the bedouins so they can earn a living by raising livestock, especially sheep. In this respect the desert has been witnessing profound changes.

Motor vehicles of all kinds are playing a major role in this development by transporting water and food to the livestock when the animals are out in the desert and pasturage and water becomes unavailable. The motor vehicle has confirmed the bedouin's contact with the settled folk, and for the modern-day Ṣlaybī it may effect a similar connection and so lead to development and sedentarization. The Ṣlaybī is probably more receptive to this than his fellow Arab bedouin, who sees in nomadism a way of life more distinguished than that of settled folk. Ultimately, as the Ṣlaybī's sheep increase in numbers and he sometimes needs to carry water to them in tanker trucks, as is currently the case among sheep-raising folk in the villages along the desert fringes, the motor vehicle will lead the Ṣlaybī to dispense with the donkey.

Whatever the outcome of this proves to be, and despite the Ṣlaybī's superior knowledge of the desert and that firm attachment to nomadism which has earned him the title of "nomads of the nomads," he will be obliged by evolving conditions to incline toward sedentarization and living in the villages close to the desert. There he can work in various crafts and trades and by tending the sheep owned by the villagers, especially since the governments in all of the Arab lands surrounding the desert are seeking to encourage the bedouins to take up sedentary life and settle down. This they do by employing some in positions in companies and in the military, and by storing the water and fodder needed in years of drought in specified locations that in the future may become places for settlement. I have been told that in certain areas some of the Ṣlayb have in recent years begun to settle down in houses of mud-brick or stone.

CHAPTER XIX

THE HISTORY OF THE BEDOUINS IN NORTHERN ARABIA

In Ancient Times

It is extremely difficult to speak with certainty concerning the history of the Arab bedouins in the remote eras of prehistoric times. There is no doubt, however, that from the time the Arabs were first known by this name as a people distinct from other peoples, they were living the life of nomads and wandering from place to place in the various deserts of Arabia in search of the game and other things they needed in order to live. It is said that the ancient Semitic terms *'araba* and *'arab* used to denote only a "desert" or a "desolate region." As the Arab bedouin began to devote his labor to the raising of such animals as camels and sheep, his wandering in the desert came to be restricted to the limits of the areas that could provide these domesticated animals with sufficient water and pasturage. As for the Arabian peninsula, which today bears the name of the Arabs, this region is one of the world's most productive desert lands, although this may not have been so in the ages predating historically known times. Whatever the case may be, the northern desert known today as the Syrian Desert is now the richest and most fertile of the desert lands of the peninsula. At times when the central and fringe regions of Arabia became overpopulated or its lands were stricken by drought and its deserts turned into desolate wastes, some of its people were obliged to migrate. These people had no option open to them other than to move towards the Fertile Crescent; hence the Syrian Desert and the villages along its peripheries were (and continue to be) the geographical objective of peoples or tribes migrating from the heart and border lands of the peninsula.

Arabia was surrounded by seas on all sides but the north, where the land provided abundant means of subsistence. The migrating tribes thus proceeded to the region of the Fertile Crescent—to the Syrian Desert—or poured forth across Sinai to lands beyond the Fertile Crescent and settled in North Africa near the fertile banks of the Nile. It is interesting for us to note here that some of these southern regions are still today exposed to such drought or dearth. Agencies of the United Nations have in recent decades encountered drought conditions similar to these, as described in a World Health Organization report issued by the Regional Office for the Eastern Mediterranean. Some of these agencies had to send emergency supplies to the bedouins of Yemen after a nomadic region covering about 70,000 square miles—twelve times the area of all of Lebanon—along all of the southern fringes south of the sands of the Rubʿ al-Khālī was exposed to three consecutive years without rainfall, a continuous drought which brought about 40,000 bedouins to the brink of disaster.[1]

Historians agree that there have been numerous waves of this migration since remotest antiquity, and that such movement used to occur at widely spaced intervals. Among these waves was one that carried the Amorites, including the Canaanites, to the Fertile Crescent in about the middle of the third millennium BC. It should come as no surprise that some of the bedouin Arab tribes migrated at this remote time or several centuries later and settled in parts of the Syrian Desert close to Syria, Najd, and Iraq. These included the Hyksos "shepherd kings" who penetrated Egypt and North Africa and brought the horse with them to these lands.[2]

Assuming that it is true that the Arabs are descended from Ishmael, son of Hagar,[3] or that they are the people known as the Ishmaelites or

---

[1]World Health Organization, Regional Office for the Eastern Mediterranean, press release no. 24, 29 October 1969.

[2]Hitti, Jurji, and Jabbur, *Ta'rīkh al-ʿarab*, p. 48 [= Hitti, *History of the Arabs*, p. 20].

[3]The Torah mentions the Arabs and their land by the name of Kedar; Isaiah 21:16, Jeremiah 49:28. Kedar was the second son of Ishmael (Genesis 25:13); as for the first-born son of Ishmael, his name was Nabayot, and among his twelve sons were Duma and Tayma (Genesis 25:14–15). Al-Ṭabarī mentions Kedar, son of Ishmael, and says: "From Nābat and from Qaydar God propagated the Arabs;" *Ta'rīkh al-rusul wa-l-mulūk*, I, 351–52.

the sons of his son Kedar, then among the earliest references to them is in the Biblical story of Jacob's son Joseph, sold by his brothers to a caravan of Ishmaelites on their way to Egypt from Gilead with camels laden with spices and resins.[4] After this we hear of Moses and his marriage to an Ishmaelite (Midianite) girl in Sinai after his first exodus from Egypt.[5] This indicates that the Arab tribes were known in these northern regions in about the second millennium BC.

The Bible also makes clear reference to the presence of bedouin Arabs in the Syrian Desert in the days of King David and his son Solomon, i.e. prior to the first millennium BC.[6] Solomon mentions the tribe of Kedar and his black tents in the Song of Songs, when he says, quoting his young wife Balsan: "I am black and beautiful, O daughter of Jerusalem, black like the tents of Kedar, beautiful as the draperies of Solomon."[7] Shortly after this period it is again stated in the Bible that the Arab tribes brought Jehoshaphat, king of Judah (872–849 BC), taxes of sheep and goats: "of rams 7700 and of he-goats 7700."[8] Similarly, in Isaiah we see his words: "No bedouin will ever camp there, and no shepherd will make his flock to lie down there."[9] In the prophecy of Jeremiah, his words: "You wait for them as a bedouin waits in the desert"[10] indicate the presence of the bedouins in the Syrian Desert and incidents of raiding and highway robbery. In the Bible there is even a passage that explicitly mentions the bedouins participating with the Cushites and the Philistines in their attack on Jerusalem, the looting of its property, and the plundering of Jehoram, its king,[11] in the ninth century BC.

After the reports in the Bible, the earliest definite reference to bedouin Arabs occurs in an inscription of the Assyrian king Shalmaneser III, who in the sixth year of his reign led an expedition against

---

[4]Genesis 37:25–29.

[5]Exodus 2:22.

[6]II Chronicle 9:14.

[7]Song of Songs 1:5. As we have seen in Chapter IX, bedouin tents are up to this day still made from black goat's hair.

[8]II Chronicles 17:11.

[9]Isaiah 13:20.

[10]Jeremiah 3:2.

[11]II Chronicles 21:16–18.

the Aramaean king of Damascus and his two allies: Ahab, king of Israel, and Jundub, one of the Arab shaykhs. The two armies clashed at Qarqar, north of Ḥamāh, in 853 BC, and the inscription concerning the battle reports as follows:

> Qarqar, his royal city, I destroyed, I devastated, I burned with fire. 1200 chariots, 1200 cavalry, 20,000 soldiers of Hadad-ezer, master of Aram (Damascus)... 1000 camels of Gindibu' the Arabian... these twelve kings he brought to his support; to offer battle and fight they came against me.[12]

About a century and a half after Shalmaneser came Sargon II (722–705 BC), the conqueror of Carchemish and Samaria. In the seventh year of his reign he refers to his subjugation of certain peoples, including the tribes of Thamūd and Abādīd, who dwell in the desert and know neither high nor low officials. He made a severe example of them and exiled those who remained to Samaria.[13]

About a century after the time of Sargon, Ashurbanipal (668–626 BC) set out on an expedition against the Arab tribes and pursued them "in the parched and waterless desert, where you do not see the birds of the sky and where the onager is not found, nor even the gazelle."[14]

In the Assyrian annals there are many other references to bedouin leaders, including one stating that they kiss the feet of the kings of Nineveh, offer them presents, and give them camels and donkeys. There are reports of nine expeditions dispatched by Sargon II, Sennacherib, Esarhaddon, and Ashurbanipal to chastise the unconquerable bedouin tribes for harassing the Assyrian provinces in Syria and interfering with the commercial caravan routes.[15]

In Pre-Islamic Times

When we come to the era of the Persian and Roman empires and the strife between them, we find bedouin tribes spread throughout most

[12]Hitti, Jurji, and Jabbur, *Ta'rīkh al-'arab*, pp. 65–66 [= Hitti, *History of the Arabs*, p. 37], from Lukenbill, *Ancient Records*, I, 223, no. 611.

[13]Hitti, Jurji, and Jabbur, *Ta'rīkh al-'arab*, p. 66 [= Hitti, *History of the Arabs*, p. 37].

[14]*Ibid.*, p. 68 [= *ibid.*, p. 39].

[15]*Ibid.* [*ibid.*].

parts of the Arabian peninsula as far as the Roman frontier region in Syria. Among the reports on these tribes is the one given by al-Ṭabarī in his history concerning Shāpūr Dhū l-Aktāf when he tried to protect the frontiers of his kingdom from bedouin raids:

> He (i.e. Shāpūr) sent forces against them, and when these reached Hajar they found there bedouins of the tribes of Tamīm and Bakr. They spread death among them, and then turned toward the land of 'Abd al-Qays, where they exterminated all its people save those who fled from them and betook themselves to the sands. Then they came to al-Yamāma, where they wreaked a similar slaughter. They passed by no bedouin pool without ruining it, none of their wells without filling it with sand. When they approached Medina they killed or took captive any bedouins they found there. Then they turned toward the land of Bakr and Taghlib, in the region between the Persian Empire and the Roman frontier zone in the land of Syria, and killed or took captive any bedouin they found there and filled their water sources with sand.[16]

All this clearly indicates the presence of bedouin Arab tribes in the Syrian Desert in those pre-Islamic eras both before and after the birth of Christ. There can be no doubt that the flood of raiding and migrating nomads continued uninterrupted throughout the period that followed, up until the last years of the nineteenth century.[17]

These tribes migrating from the peninsula exerted pressure first on the tribes that had preceded them by several ages and had established

[16]Al-Ṭabarī, *Ta'rīkh al-rusul wa-l-mulūk*, I, 839.

[17]In his *Mu'jam al-buldān*, II, 494, Yāqūt refers to the territories (*diyār*) of Rabī'a as lying between Mosul, Nisibis, Ra's al-'Ayn, Dunaysir, and the Khābūr River; the lands of Bakr and those of Rabī'a have perhaps been grouped together and all called "Diyār Rabī'a" since all of these tribes were clans of Rabī'a. Yāqūt says: "This name for this land is an old one, the bedouins having occupied its desert areas before Islamic times. The name al-Jazīra applies to the whole area." Here we must make mention of such Arab tribes as Ghassān, Bakr, Taghlib, and Tanūkh, which migrated in pre-Islamic times and camped along the peripheries of Syria and Iraq.

themselves before them in the deserts and other lands of the Fertile Crescent. They either conquered these older tribes and subdued them to a subordinate status, or drove them across Sinai, or forced them to return to their original homelands, or obliged them to seek refuge in the settled lands. In this last case the displaced tribes kept sheep rather than camels, and hence became semi-sedentary tribes which then shared with the villagers in sheep-raising in the steppes and plains near the villages, not far out into the desert. For some of the tribes their situation ultimately led them to stop migrating and gradually to take up settled life in the villages and farms along the peripheries of the desert. It was also possible that the intruding tribe would itself be defeated and subdued by the tribe that had preceded it and would become one of its allies, or fall back unsuccessful to Najd or the south and wait for another opportunity to return.

The history of the bedouins in these times, extending over the long ages of the pre-Islamic era, was thus one of continuous strife. Some of this conflict was the result of personal rivalries in competition for leadership, as we see, for example, in their accounts of the War of al-Basūs between Taghlib and Bakr and the War of Dāḥis and al-Ghabrā', or was provoked by their disputes over such water sources as wells and pools, as in the battle days of al-Fayfā', Aqran, and al-Ghabīṭ. Strife could also arise between one great tribe and another genealogically far removed from it, as in the Day of Ḥalīma between the Ghassānids and the Lakhmids. Medieval Arab historians recorded accounts of these clashes and called them *ayyām al-'arab*, or "battle days of the Arab tribes," and in his *'Iqd* Ibn 'Abd Rabbih discusses some of them in an account that fills over 130 pages of his book.[18]

Strife would also sometimes break out between the bedouins and the settled folk near or within the settled lands themselves, since the settled folk from the villages surrounding the desert could not penetrate far into it. Abū 'Ubayda said:

> The bedouins were not afraid to raid in the fierce summer heat. At that time no one traveled and no one was able to cross these desert lands because of the long distance to be

[18]Ibn 'Abd Rabbih, *Al-'Iqd (al-farīd)*, V, 132–268.

> traveled without water and because of the intensity of the heat there.[19]

Strife would naturally occur in the wake of bedouin raids on the settled regions, inasmuch as these places were usually subject to looting and plunder: villages and farms were sometimes seized, and encroaching tribes could reach them without being stopped or confronted by any authority. This would occur when the state was weak or in conflict with a foreign enemy.

Hence, when we review the history of the Arabs from pre-Islamic times, or indeed, from the beginning of the Christian era, up until the twentieth century, we find that when state power weakened in the regions of the Fertile Crescent one would see the fractious bedouins making inroads on the peripheries of the settled lands, terrorizing the settled folk living in the villages surrounding the desert, plundering their livestock, threatening their security, destroying their fields, and wiping out their settled culture. Peake Pasha claimed that had it not been for the presence of strong state authority in Syria and Jordan after the end of the First World War, both would have reverted to tribal rule and poverty.[20]

This is the phenomenon to which Ibn Khaldūn long ago referred when he said of "the Arabs" (by which he means "the bedouins"):

> Due to their inherently barbarous nature, they are a people of pillage and ruination who plunder whatever they can lay their hands on without a fight or risk of danger, and then flee to their haven in the desert waste....The reason for this is that they are a barbarous nation deeply rooted in the customs and constituent elements of barbarism. For them, this has become a matter of character and natural disposition; they have come to relish such behavior since it means casting off the noose of authority and avoiding submission to government. This nature comprises the negation and antithesis of civilization. Further, the aim of all of their customary activities is traveling and the seizure of property,

[19] *Ibid.*, V, 225.
[20] C.S. Jarvis, *Arab Command* (St Albans, 1946), p. 61.

> which likewise comprise the antithesis and negation of the tranquility from which civilization arises. For example, the bedouins' only need for stones is for something upon which to set their cooking pots; so they carry them from buildings, which they demolish in consideration of their own need for the stones. Likewise, their only need for wood is for something upon which to erect their tents and to make into tent pegs for their dwellings, so they tear up roofs for that purpose. Hence, the very nature of their existence is the antithesis of building, which is the basis for civilization. Such is the general case with them. Further, it is their nature to plunder whatever other people possess, their subsistence consisting of anything across which the shadows of their lances fall....Their abode of Yemen is a ruin, save only a few towns. Bedouin-dominated Iraq has suffered likewise: the civilization for which the Persians were responsible has been utterly destroyed. Modern-day Syria has fallen victim to a similar fate, as also did Ifrīqiya and the Maghrib when the Banū Hilāl and the Banū Sulaym crossed over to these lands in the early fifth (eleventh) century.[21]

I have just said that by *al-'arab*, "Arabs," he means the people of the desert. The word "Arabs" was conventionally used in the sense of "bedouins," just as it continues to be used in certain village milieus in Syria when they say: "We went to the houses of the Arabs," by which they mean "to the tents of the bedouins." In the *Muqaddima* itself and in the history of Ibn Khaldūn there is evidence to confirm this, since in his chapter on the differing conditions of civilization he says: "and also like the Arabs who wander in the desert wastes,"[22] and also "not like the Arabs, the people of the desolate waste and the sand desert,"[23] meaning "like the bedouins."

Ibn Khaldūn was not alone in this usage; rather, it was the customary one before his time among many historians. We see this, for

---

[21]Ibn Khaldūn, *Muqaddima*, I, 269–72. [Medieval Ifrīqiya extended approximately over modern Tunisia and some surrounding lands.]

[22]*Ibid.*, I, 158.

[23]*Ibid.*, I, 161.

example, in the history of al-Ṭabarī himself, where he says concerning a shrine in the desert: "to one of the water sources of the Arabs,"[24] and states in another place: "one of the shaykhs of the Arabs."[25] The usage remained conventional among authors. Thus Usāma ibn Munqidh says in his memoirs: "When we went out from the Victory Gate, the tribes of the Arabs gathered together,"[26] "that was when the Arabs apostatized,"[27] and "when they arose the next morning they asked the Arabs who were offering them hospitality...."[28] In all these places "Arabs" has the meaning of "bedouins." In later times we see a similar usage in the history of Amīr Fakhr al-Dīn al-Ma'nī[29] and in scores of places in the history of Lebanon by Amīr Ḥaydar al-Shihābī.[30] Similarly, this also applies to what I said in the introduction to this book about how we understood the word "Arabs" in our village and in all of the villages lying in the highlands overlooking the desert.

Historical works are not lacking for reports on the battles that used to take place between the ruling authorities in the various parts of the Fertile Crescent and the bedouin tribes that wandered in the deserts and the lands nearby. Indeed, both the Persian and the Roman Empires used to form alliances with some of the tribes along their frontiers. The empires depended on these tribes for protection of the frontier zones from other tribes, and at the same time the bedouins also served the imperial regimes as spies on the movements of the armies of the other empire. The two powers thus turned these tribes into small quasi-statelets, some of which played a major role in the history of the struggle between East and West. These included the Ḍajā'ima and Tanūkh,[31] the

[24] *Ta'rīkh al-rusul wa-l-mulūk*, II, 289.

[25] *Ibid.*, II, 878.

[26] *Kitāb al-i'tibār*, p. 25.

[27] *Ibid.*, p. 37.

[28] *Ibid.*, p. 182.

[29] Aḥmad ibn Muḥammad al-Khālidī, *Lubnān fī 'ahd al-amīr Fakhr al-Dīn al-Ma'nī al-thānī*, edited by Asad Rustum and Fu'ād Afram al-Bustānī (Beirut, 1936), pp. 41, 42, 133, 153, 190.

[30] Ḥaydar Aḥmad al-Shihābī, *Lubnān fī 'ahd al-umarā' al-shihābīyīn*, edited by Asad Rustum and Fu'ād Afrām al-Bustānī (Beirut, 1933), index, III, 896.

[31] As is well known, the Tanūkhīs and the Ghassānids were Christians. It is said that the Tanūkhīs refused to pay the poll-tax (*jizya*) to the conquerors. When 'Umar ibn al-Khaṭṭāb tried to compel them to do so, they said: "Take the money

Ghassānids in the desert of Syria, and the Lakhmids on the frontiers of the Persian Empire when they occupied most of Mesopotamia. Along the Roman frontier in Syria before the time of the Ghassānids there was a Palmyrene state which enjoyed support from bedouin tribes and concluded alliance agreements with them, as we find recorded in historical accounts and attested by some of the various monuments from this era.

In Early Islamic Times up to the ʻAbbāsid Era

When the Islamic conquests began, there were thus many Yamanī and Qaysī bedouin tribes, apart from the Ghassānids and the Lakhmids, along the frontiers of the Persian and Roman Empires. These tribes continued to enjoy influence and prestige in the days of the Umayyads, since many of the tribesmen participated in the early conquests, which, even outside Arabia, made it an easy matter for them to indulge in activities consistent with their innate fondness for gain and plunder. The authorities relied to a great extent on desert horsemen from allied tribes and were on close terms with their leaders and shaykhs. The history of the conquest of Syria attributed to al-Wāqīdī reports that the caliph Abū Bakr summoned the Arab tribes from all the places in Arabia where they lived, and their forces marched to him from Yemen to participate in the campaigns. These tribes included Ṭayyi', Madhḥij, al-Azd, Qays, and Kināna, which came accompanied by their womenfolk, their children, and their herds of livestock (*amwāl*).[32] Indeed, some of the Umayyad caliphs sent their sons to the desert to mingle with the bedouins, live as nomads, become accustomed to the hardships of that way of life, take up the Arabic of the bedouins, and learn how to ride and shoot. Along the peripheries of the desert some of them built compounds (*quṣūr*) where they went to spend the spring and summer and to hunt desert animals and birds.

There is no space here for detailed discussion of the history of these bedouin tribes, their arrival in the Syrian Desert, and their struggle

from us in the name of alms (*ṣadaqa*) rather than poll-tax." ʻUmar at first refused, but then accepted that they should pay under the rubric of tax (*kharāj*).

[32]Al-Wāqidī (attrib.), *Futūh al-Shām* (Cairo, AH 1278), I, 3–8.

with other tribes in pre-Islamic times or even in the centuries following the Arab conquest. But it must be noted here that beginning in Umayyad times, when the conquests were completed, or indeed, while they were still in progress, some of the tribes continued to fight other tribes. The impact of this conflict was evident between the clans of Qays and those of al-Yaman, and it spread to the settled areas and regions in which these tribes later settled, as we can see in the historical reports for this era, in the verse of such Umayyad-period poets as Ka'b ibn Ju'ayl, al-Akhṭal, and al-Rā'ī,[33] and in reports for other periods in Islamic history.

When power passed from the Umayyads to the 'Abbāsids, the capital of the caliphate was transferred to Baghdad and actual power gradually shifted into the hands of non-Arab elements. The bonds between the ruling regime and the bedouin tribes were broken, and the former became much less dependent upon Arabs and men of the desert. The bedouins thus resorted to raiding, plundering, pillaging, and threatening the pilgrimage and communications routes far from the center of power in Baghdad. Anyone who leafs through the history of al-Ṭabarī will notice that after the reign of al-Mu'taṣim some of the bedouins began to wreak havoc along the pilgrimage routes. He informs us that in 230/844 the caliph al-Wāthiq received word that bedouins from the tribe of Sulaym had ravaged Medina and its environs. Al-Wāthiq sent an expedition against them to punish them; but the bedouins defeated the caliph's army and the Medinans (from Quraysh, the *anṣār*, and their clients) fighting with it, and the tribe of Sulaym gained possession of their livestock, weapons, and clothing. This only aroused their ruthlessness: they seized control of the villages and the springs between these villages and Mecca and Medina, and al-Wāthiq was forced

[33] It is said of the Taghlibī poet al-Akhṭal that one time he saw al-Jaḥḥāf, a warrior of Qays, in the audience chamber of the Umayyad caliph 'Abd al-Malik ibn Marwān, and so recited the ode of his in which he boasts about how the Taghlibīs wrought great slaughter among the Sulaym and 'Āmir, two clans of Qays, in one of their engagements. In the ode he says:

Do ask al-Jaḥḥāf whether he will seek revenge
For those struck down dead from the Sulaym and 'Āmir.

This led to al-Jaḥḥāf going out to his people and marshaling them to raid the Taghlib and kill some of their men. See al-Akhṭal, *Shi'r al-Akhṭal*, edited in the recension of al-Sukkarī by Antoine Ṣāliḥānī (Beirut, 1891), p. 286.

to send one of his generals, Bughā the Great, with a vast army to punish them.[34] Al-Ṭabarī's account relates the general's attack on them: some were killed, others were put to flight, and many were taken captive, a number of these being imprisoned in Medina as hostages.[35] He did the same in 231/845, when he sent his envoys to the tribes and about 3000 men, it is said, assembled together to meet him. Of these he cast about 1300 troublemakers into prison and allowed the others to go free.[36]

It would seem that after the reign of al-Wāthiq the depredations of the bedouins began to intensify, especially when weakness began to appear in the state. The tribe of Ṭayyi', which came from Yemen in the days of Abū Bakr, played a significant role in the breakdown of security along the pilgrimage routes and in plundering the populace.

The authorities in turn began to pursue bedouin raiders into the desert in order to maintain security and uphold their reputation. Making matters even worse was the fact that the 'Abbāsid empire relied upon an army of non-Arabs; a major source of livelihood was thus cut off from the bedouins who had participated in the conquests and who accordingly reverted to brigandage, raiding, and plundering. When matters reached the point that the caliphate broke up into statelets and principalities, bedouin power increased and they began to allocate spheres of influence for themselves, not only in the deserts of the Fertile Crescent, but also in the lands near the settled areas of Syria, Najd, and Iraq. They quarreled among themselves and waylaid caravans on the commercial and pilgrimage routes.[37] They likewise took to attacking the settled lands and seizing control of farms and villages. Many of the villages came to be totally uninhabited and turned into desolate wastelands, as is attested by their remains along the desert fringes of eastern Syria, Ḥimṣ, Ḥamāh, and Aleppo. The brigandage continued with impunity, and desolation prevailed in these villages until the end of the nineteenth century.

---

[34] Al-Ṭabarī, *Ta'rīkh al-rusul wa-l-mulūk*, III, 1335–38.

[35] *Ibid.*, III, 1338.

[36] *Ibid.*, III, 1342.

[37] *Aghānī*, IX, 111.

In the Era of the Declining 'Abbāsid Caliphate

Among the events for 249/863 recorded in his history, al-Ṭabarī informs us of how 'Alī ibn al-Jahm ibn Badr made his way from Baghdad to the frontier. But as he approached Aleppo, horsemen from the tribe of Kalb accosted and killed him and the bedouins took whatever he had with him.[38] Among reports for 250/864 there is an account of Yaḥyā ibn 'Umar and his revolt against the regime: he gathered around himself many bedouins who agreed to assist him and fought with him.[39] In 251/865 the bedouins attacked the villages and cut the caravan route, and al-Ṭabarī tells us of the regime's efforts to suppress them and how 300 of the bedouins were killed.[40] In reports for the same year we are told that as the bedouins were wreaking havoc an expedition was sent against them: 36 of them were taken prisoner and were carried off in 18 litters on the backs of the camels.[41]

For 285/898 al-Ṭabarī reports that bedouins of Ṭayyi' were cutting off the pilgrimage and in that year succeeded in capturing the pilgrimage caravan and took the property and trade goods it was carrying. He claims that these bedouins seized a number of women—free and slaves—and reports that the persons who were captured were worth a ransom of two million *dīnārs*.[42] Among reports for 286/899 he speaks of bedouins from the tribe of Shaybān and how they used to attack the villages, kill whomever they met, and drive off the livestock. The regime thus confronted them and its forces attacked them, but the bedouins defeated the army; many of the caliph's troops were killed, some drowned in the Euphrates, and the others scattered. Among the events of the same year, in the caliphate of al-Mu'taḍid (the husband of Qaṭr al-Nadā, daughter of Khumārawayh), he goes on to inform us that the bedouins were causing chaos, but that it was impossible to resist them.[43] For 295/908 he informs us that this was the year of the attack of al-Ḥusayn ibn Mūsā on the elite warriors of the bedouins

[38]See al-Ṭabarī, *Ta'rīkh al-rusul wa-l-mulūk*, III, 1514.
[39]*Ibid.*, III, 1516–17.
[40]*Ibid.*, III, 1618.
[41]*Ibid.*, III, 1594.
[42]*Ibid.*, III, 2183.
[43]*Ibid.*, III, 2188–89.

of Ṭayyi', who had been fighting Waṣīf ibn Ṣawārtakin; he killed 70 of their warriors, it is said, and took a number of their horsemen captive.[44]

Among events for the same year in his *Nahr al-dhahab fī ta'rīkh Ḥalab*, al-Ghazzī states:

> The tribe of Tamīm ravaged the land of Aleppo and caused great damage....Ibn Ḥamdān was at al-Raḥba; so he came forth looking for the Tamīm, encountered a group of them at Khunāṣira, attacked them, took some of them prisoner, and then returned.[45]

For 325/937 he then mentions the coming of the tribe of Kilāb from Najd and their attack on al-Ma'arra, a campaign in which they captured its governor and most of his troops. Abū l-'Abbās, the governor of Aleppo, therefore marched forth to fight them and rescued the governor of al-Ma'arra from them.[46] In this same period the situation of the governors weakened to such an extent that in 331/943 the Byzantines penetrated as far as the outskirts of Aleppo, plundered and ravaged the country, and took 15,000 people captive.[47]

The depredations of the bedouins thus increased as the 'Abbāsid empire broke up into principalities; some of the tribes grew in power, began to assert their authority over lands in various regions of the empire, and founded small statelets. Among the first of these tribes was the Banū Ḥamdān and its *amīr*s from the tribe of Taghlib. It founded a principality in Mosul in 317/929, and then shifted to Aleppo in the time of the renowned Sayf al-Dawla and his poet al-Mutanabbī. Sayf al-Dawla in turn undertook to protect his realm from the bedouins who had not settled and who continued to ravage, plunder, and loot, and at the same time he tried to ward off the Byzantines. In his reign some of the tribes of Ka'b ibn Rabī'a—'Āmir ibn Ṣa'ṣa'a, 'Uqayl, Qushayr, al-'Ajlān, and Kilāb—assembled and penetrated to the heart of the settled lands as far as Salamīya, near Ḥimṣ. Sayf al-Dawla himself led an expedition against them in 344/955; marching down from Aleppo

[44] *Ibid.*, III, 2279.
[45] Al-Ghazzī, *Nahr al-dhahab fī ta'rīkh Ḥalab* (Aleppo, AH 1342), III, 40.
[46] *Ibid.*, III, 42.
[47] *Ibid.*, III, 44.

to Salamīya, he defeated them, captured some of them, and took from them about 200 mares and the armor of their riders. The rest he routed and pursued eastward to al-Furqulus, and then to al-Ghunthur, al-Jabāh, al-Ghuwayr, al-Jifār, Nihyā, and all the way to Tadmur and the desert of al-Samāwa, where he fell upon them in a great battle. When he returned, he described what he had achieved there to his poet al-Mutanabbī, and the latter proceeded to immortalize his *amīr*'s victory over the ravaging bedouins in two poems, one of them his poem rhyming in *r*, which begins:

> The long spears can naught but lose their length
> When against them you turn your arms to fight,
> While your mote of favor or call for strength
> Soon swells to the like of the seas' roaring might.[48]

In this ode he refers to the fact that the tribe of Kilāb, like that of Ka'b, both of which were part of the Rabī'a ibn 'Āmir, had "broken the rod" of obedience to Sayf al-Dawla. But when the Kilāb saw what had happened to Ka'b and the disgrace it suffered, they became afraid that if they remained rebellious they would suffer the same fate, so they submitted and went with Sayf al-Dawla for the battle. On this al-Mutanabbī says:

> The Kilāb found themselves where the Ka'b had been,
> And so feared to suffer that which they had seen.
> In humility they acknowledged their master's might,
> And against Ka'b he and they went forth to fight,
> With cavalry he closed on the plains' broad flat,[49]
> On lean brand-marked steeds, neither scrawny nor fat.
> At Salamīya the horses raised such dust from the land,
> He'd know not that 'neath him, save for the brand.[50]

[48]Al-Mutanabbī, *Dīwān*, pp. 418–26. See the detailed story of Sayf al-Dawla's march in al-Ghazzī, *Nahr al-dhahab*, III, 52–54.

[49][That is, on the plains of Salamīya.]

[50]That is, the horses stirred up such rolling clouds of dust that the warriors would not have recognized the mounts beneath them had it not been for the brand by which they could identify them.

Al-Mutanabbī then describes how Sayf al-Dawla annihilated the bedouins and drove them in flight before him through these places we have mentioned, and goes so far as to speak of the bedouins' livestock—camels, sheep, and goats—and how they wept behind their fleeing masters, expressing their anguish in their various voices:

> They cried out behind them in their various voices,
> Lamenting with their roar, their bleat and their bray.
> At al-Ghunthur they spread out and covered the steppe
> As new-birthed and expectant were soon pulled away.[51]
> From thence to al-Jabāh did their course then run,[52]
> Where both armies gathered, and on all did dust lay.
> They came then to al-Ghuwayr, but no water did find
> Then Nihyā, al-Buwayda, and al-Jifār marked their way.[53]

---

[51]The base manuscript reads the place name as "al-'Ithyar," and in the commentary on this verse in the *Dīwān* it is noted that Ibn Jinnī reads it as "al-Ghunthur." Al-Yāzijī really should have accepted the reading of Ibn Jinnī and recorded it in the text rather than in the note, for this reading is the correct one. Today the place is still known by this name, and there was running water there when I last visited it some years ago. Al-Mutanabbī means that this livestock—roaring camels and bleating goats and sheep—were spread out over the plain of al-Ghunthur and covered the steppe. Of these Sayf al-Dawla's men selected the she-camels that had just recently borne young or were about to do so, as these were the camels most desirable to the bedouin.

[52]Al-Jabāh is a spring, still known today by this name, lying next to al-Ghunthur and a few kilometers from al-Qaryatayn. It would not be surprising if there had been a farm or small village around it in that period, though today there is no sign of settled life there.

[53]Such is the reading, "al-Ghuwayr," in the base manuscript; Yāqūt mentions the same place in his *Mu'jam al-buldān*, IV, 169, under "'Uwayr," and likewise at V, 328, where he refers to Nihyā. But the word *'uwayr* is meaningless, while *ghuwayr* is the diminuitive of *ghār*, "cave," and means a "small cave."

Were it not for the multitude of sources that read "al-'Uwayr" in place of "al-Ghuwayr," I would say that the correct reading should be "al-Ghadīr," referring to a pool. There are many pools between al-Jabāh and Tadmur. Indeed, there is one particular place which has water from a small spring and is called al-Ghadīr; I drank from its water during the summer and it is near al-Qaryatayn, not very far from al-Jifār, which al-Mutanabbī mentions. Who knows; Sayf al-Dawla perhaps mentioned these place names to al-Mutanabbī, who then did not cite them in the order of their locations on the route to Tadmur. It is also possible that al-Ghuwayr is a water source near al-Bakhrā', as Musil mentions in an appendix to *Palmyrena*,

Save Tadmur, there was now no place for their refuge,
And true to its name, here's where death won the day.[54]

The Ḥamdānid dynasty was a Shī'ite regime that remained in power approximately through the tenth century AD, that is, from 317/929 to 406/1002. It was followed by another bedouin regime, that of the 'Uqaylids, in Mosul from 386/997 to 489/1096; this Muḍarī regime was finally eliminated by the Turk Karbūqā, who incorporated its territories into the Seljuq empire. In Aleppo the Ḥamdānids were followed in the eleventh century, from 414/1023 to 472/1080, by the Mirdāsids; this regime was also Muḍarī, and its *amīr*s were from Kilāb ibn Rabī'a, the tribe that had submitted to Sayf al-Dawla. One of these *amīr*s was Naṣr ibn Ṣāliḥ ibn Mirdās, who in his defense of the Aleppo region inflicted a great defeat on the forces of the Byzantine emperor Romanos III. The Mazyadid regime, the *amīr*s of which were from the tribe of Asad, emerged in al-Ḥilla in Iraq and remained in power from about the early eleventh century to the mid-twelfth century. The appearance of these statelets, coupled with a further Byzantine expedition that attacked Islamic territory and captured the city of Aleppo in 351/962,[55] and Greek depredations in Syria and the Jazīra in 358/969 and 361/972,[56] contributed to the weakening of the power of the other bedouin tribes scattered in the desert far from the settled areas. All these factors

---

p. 255, or near al-Bārida (*loc. cit.*). It is evident that he was confused, since he does not know of the pool I have mentioned above.

Nihyā, al-Buwayḍa, and al-Jifār are names of water sources on the way to Tadmur, and al-Mutanabbī is asserting that the bedouins went there because of the thirst from which they suffered. Yāqūt (*Mu'jam al-buldān*, V, 328) says that Nihyā is a water source of the tribe of Kalb on the route to Damascus. He then states: "On the steppe between al-Ruṣāfa and al-Qaryatayn, on the road to Damascus, I myself saw a town called Nihyā that possessed both ancient ruins and inhabited areas, and had many cisterns, but there was no spring or canal there. Abū l-Ṭayyib [al-Mutanabbī] mentioned the place and said:

They came to 'Uwayr, but there was no *'uwayr*,
Then to Nihyā, and al-Buwayḍa, and al-Jifār."

[54] [Here al-Mutanabbī engages in a play on words, as if the name of Tadmur was derived from the verb *dammara*, "to destroy."]

[55] Ibn al-Athīr, *Al-Kāmil fī l-ta'rīkh*, ed. C.J. Tornberg (Leiden, 1851–76), VIII, 401.

[56] *Ibid.*, VIII, 454.

hindered the movement of the tribes towards the settled lands and led to their containment in the heart of the desert for about half a century. They continued to interfere with caravans of pilgrims, however, as the Banū Khafāja did in 402/1012.[57]

When the Mirdāsids captured Aleppo in 414/1022, the Fāṭimids in Egypt were already becoming weaker and the era of their decline had begun. As al-Ghazzī relates in his history of Aleppo, the Arabs of the desert in Syria and Arabia became ambitious. The bedouin shaykhs formed an alliance dividing up the desert amongst themselves, he says, it being agreed that the area from Aleppo to 'Āna would be reserved to Ṣāliḥ ibn Mirdās, the *amīr* of the Banū Kilāb, the region from al-Ramla to Egypt to Ḥassān ibn Mufarrij al-Ṭā'ī, and Damascus and its environs to Sinān ibn 'Alyān, *amīr* of the Banū Kalb.[58] The depredations of the bedouins increased in 446/1054, in the days of the commander al-Basāsīrī (d. 452/1060), who wrested Baghdad away for the Fāṭimids and attacked the bedouins and the Kurds in that year.[59] In 457/1065 war broke out between the bedouins and the Banū Ḥammād;[60] and in 493/1100 the *amīr* of the Banū Kilāb arrived with a great host of bedouins, and they grazed their livestock on the crops of al-Ma'arra, Kafr Ṭāb, Ḥamāh, Shayzar, al-Jisr, and elsewhere, and the country became desolate.[61] In 499/1106 their authority in the Iraqi Desert became so strong that they were able to plunder al-Baṣra,[62] and in 545/1151 they plundered the pilgrims.[63] Then war broke out between them and the forces of 'Abd al-Mu'min in 548/1153,[64] and in

---

[57] *Ibid.*, IX, 167.

[58] Al-Ghazzī, *Nahr al-dhahab*, III, 68. On this al-Ma'arrī says:

I see Aleppo by Ṣāliḥ now gained,
While Sinān at Jilliq is making his home,
And Ḥassān in glory has come forth and reigned,
Loosing the Ṭayyi' in Ablaq to roam.

See al-Ma'arrī's *Luzūm mā lā yalzum* (Beirut, 1381/1961), II, 201.

[59] Ibn al-Athīr, IX, 409.

[60] *Ibid.*, X, 29.

[61] Muḥammad Salīm al-Jundī, *Ta'rīkh Ma'arrat al-Nu'mān* (Damascus, 1963–64), I, 157.

[62] Ibn al-Athīr, X, 283.

[63] *Ibid.*, XI, 97.

[64] *Ibid.*, XI, 122.

558/1163 the tribe of Banū Asad was ousted from Iraq.[65] It is thus evident that bedouin depredations continued up until the emergence of the Ayyūbids (564–650/1169–1252). Ṣalāḥ al-Dīn (Saladin) sent forces to Yemen in 577/1181,[66] and in the following year crossed the Euphrates and occupied all of the lands of the Jazīra.[67]

In the Era of the Crusaders and Mongols

Here we must note that contingents of the Crusader hosts had already begun to penetrate the lands of Islam about 75 years before the emergence of the Ayyūbids. Some of their forces occupied Antioch, seized control of a large part of the Syrian coast, penetrated to the interior lands of Syria in the northern region of Edessa, and in 491/1098 also took al-Maʿarra, where some of the historians claim they killed about 100,000 of its people who had not surrendered.[68] They occupied Jerusalem in the south; but they did not penetrate very far toward the desert, where the bedouin tribes exercised a certain measure of authority. Their proximity to the great Syrian cities, from Aleppo in the north as far as Damascus in the south, was probably a factor that encouraged the bedouin tribes to fall back towards the Iraqi Desert and to withdraw for a time from the villages and towns close to the desert in Syria.

Their power meanwhile manifested itself between Mecca and Medina, for among the events for 545/1150 in his *Al-Muntaẓam* Ibn al-Jawzī relates that the bedouins, casting covetous eyes on the pilgrimage caravan, seized it between Mecca and Medina, looted the pilgrims of incalculable amounts of clothing, property, and camels, and stole many thousands of *dīnār*s from them:

> A group of merchants related how 10,000 *dīnār*s were taken from this one, 20,000 from that one, and 30,000 from another, and how property worth 100,000 *dīnār*s was taken from Khātūn, the sister of Masʿūd. The pilgrims scattered

[65] *Ibid.*, XI, 195.

[66] *Ibid.*, XI, 311.

[67] *Ibid.*, XI, 317.

[68] *Ibid.*, XI, 185–93; Ibn Taghrībirdī, *Al-Nujūm al-zāhira fī mulūk Miṣr wa-l-Qāhira* (Cairo, 1348–92/1929–72), V, 146, 161.

> and fled on foot into the desert, and so died of hunger, thirst, and exposure.[69]

Among the events for 553/1158, Ibn al-Jawzī reports that in that year he performed the pilgrimage. When he entered Medina he was told that the bedouins were lying in wait by the road, watching for the pilgrimage caravan. "The guide therefore took us by way of Khaybar," he says, "where I saw incredible mountains and other wondrous things."[70] It would seem that the ruling authorities were preoccupied with tending to the affairs of Syria, the struggle for leadership, and confronting the Crusader incursions. All this promoted a situation in which certain of the larger tribes continued to exercise such power and authority over the desert region that the urban authorities recognized their leadership and rule over the bedouins of the desert. Some of the shaykhs of the tribes were called *malik al-'arab*, "King of the Bedouins," or *amīr al-'arab*, "Amīr of the Bedouins;" similarly, agreements were concluded with some of the shaykhs for the maintenance of security in the desert, protection of the pilgrimage route to Mecca and Medina, and the rendering of assistance to the regime if the situation so required.

The Crusades led the Arab historians to pay greater attention to these wars than they did to affairs of the desert, the depredations of the bedouins, and their raids on the desert periphery and its villages. The historian Ibn al-Furāt does, however, relate for us some accounts concerning the bedouins in northern Arabia in the published parts of his history, which present events in an annalistic format: volume 4, covering the period extending from 563/1167 to 588/1192, and volumes 7–9, for the period 672–799/1273–1397. In his chapter on events of 563/1167 he says: "The Iraqi pilgrimage caravan arrived safely, but on the way to al-Ḥilla it was attacked by the Banū Khafāja, who cut off a part of the caravan, took the pilgrims' property, and killed a number of people."[71]

---

[69]Ibn al-Jawzī, *Al-Muntaẓam fī ta'rīkh al-mulūk wa-l-umam* (Hyderabad, AH 1357–58), X, 142–43.

[70]*Ibid.*, X, 182.

[71]Ibn al-Furāt, *Ta'rīkh*, IV.1, edited by Ḥasan Muḥammad Shammā' (Baṣra, 1386/1967), p. 1.

Among events for the same year Ibn al-Furāt states:

> The Banū Hudhaym from the tribe of Kalb happened onto King Shihāb al-Dīn Mālik ibn ʿAlī al-ʿUqaylī, master of the citadel of Jaʿbar, who had crossed the Euphrates to Syria in search of game. When they happened to encounter him there was a great battle between them and him. They emerged victorious and seized him after killing his advance guard and a number of his companions. They took him to al-Malik al-ʿĀdil Nūr al-Dīn, ruler of Syria, who placed him under arrest.[72]

It seems that security began to improve along the peripheries of the desert in the days of Ṣalāḥ al-Dīn; but the era of this great hero had no sooner come to an end than the dominion was divided up by his sons, none of whom possessed the power or shrewdness of their father. Incidents of civil strife and unrest broke out, and Ṣalāḥ al-Dīn's sons were succeeded by Ayyūbid clans that ruled in various parts of the Arab lands until the Mongols, under the leadership of Hülegü, put an end to whatever authority they still had.

In the Mamlūk Period

After the regime of the Ayyūbids came that of the Mamlūks, the foundations of whose dominion were laid by a woman, best known as Shajar al-Durr (the widow of the Ayyūbid al-Ṣāliḥ, d. 647/1249, the grandson of Ṣalāḥ al-Dīn's brother). The Mamlūk empire—in its two branches, the Baḥrī and the Burjī—endured for about three centuries (648–922/1250–1517), and most of the Mamlūks were of Turkish or Mongol descent. After the death of her husband, Shajar al-Durr married his army commander ʿIzz al-Dīn Aybak, who in the first years of his reign devoted his attention to the crushing of the Ayyūbid faction in Syria.[73] His authority expanded in the Jordanian desert to such an extent that in the region of al-Azraq in Jordan he left on the entrance

[72] *Ibid.*

[73] Hitti, Jurji, and Jabbur, *Ta'rīkh al-ʿarab*, p. 763 [= Hitti, *History of the Arabs*, pp. 671–72].

to an ancient Roman fortress an inscription bearing his name and proclaiming himself *malik al-ṣaḥrā'*, "King of the Desert."[74] Hülegü, as is well known, captured Baghdad in 656/1258. He then proceeded to northern Syria and conquered Aleppo, slaughtering many of its inhabitants. He then entered Ḥamāh and Ḥārim and sent one of his commanders to lay siege to Damascus. At 'Ayn Jālūt this army was confronted and defeated by the great Mamlūk *amīr* al-Malik al-Ẓāhir Baybars I, who occupied Syria and was able, with the occasional assistance of the bedouins, to defeat the Mongols.[75] Not content with defeating the Mongols, the Mamlūks also dealt the final blows to the Crusaders.[76]

In 672/1274 Ibn al-Furāt reports an account of the arrival of the Mongol army at al-Anbār. Al-Malik al-Ẓāhir Baybars had appointed the "Amīr of the Bedouins," 'Īsā ibn Muhannā, to attack the Mongols. They concluded that it was the Sultan himself who had suddenly fallen upon them, so Abāqā, the Mongol ruler, departed with his army, abandoning his plans and fleeing under very unfavorable circumstances.[77] For 673/1275 he relates an account of the procession of al-Malik al-Ẓāhir from Damascus to Ḥamāh, and reports that its governor came out in his own procession to attend the Sultan, who then proceeded with the military forces and all the bedouins attending him.[78]

In 679/1280 he relates an account of the arrival of the *amīr* 'Īsā ibn Muhannā, "ruler of the bedouins in the eastern lands," to assist the governor of Damascus, al-Malik al-Kāmil Sanqar al-Ashqar, to confront the Egyptian forces;[79] but Sanqar was defeated, his forces deserted him, and no one remained with him except for Amīr 'Īsā ibn Muhannā. Determined to attend the ruler, 'Īsā took him to his tents; he camped with him and those remaining with him in the desert of al-Raḥba, and

[74]See Philby, *Forty Years in the Wilderness*, p. 106, where he tries to set a date for the Mamlūk 'Izz al-Dīn Aybak and places him "in 1000 AD, it would seem, or earlier." In reality, the reign of 'Izz al-Dīn began with the year 648/1250, as we have mentioned.

[75]Hitti, Jurji, and Jabbur, *Ta'rīkh al-'arab*, p. 564 [= Hitti, *History of the Arabs*, p. 487].

[76]*Ibid.*, p. 746 [= Hitti, *History of the Arabs*, p. 655].

[77]Ibn al-Furāt, *Ta'rīkh*, VII, edited by Constantine Zurayk (Beirut, 1942), p. 6.

[78]*Ibid.*, p. 29.

[79]*Ibid.*, p. 169.

the ruler lived with the bedouins and their animals for a considerable length of time.[80] Here Ibn al-Furāt mentions that Sanqar corresponded with the ruler Abāqā ibn Hülegü, promising that he would side with him and informing him of the dissension that had broken out among the Islamic forces. Amīr ʻĪsā ibn Muhannā wrote along similar lines.[81] When Sultan al-Malik al-Manṣūr, the ruler of Egypt, heard of the Amīr ʻĪsā ibn Muhannā's disobedience and how he had befriended Sanqar, he entrusted the leadership of the Āl Faḍl and Āl ʻAlī to others and designated for these new *amīr*s the regions in which each one of them was camped.[82]

The Mongols were encouraged by these developments and attacked Aleppo; many of its inhabitants fled, and those who tarried the Mongols killed. They looted, took prisoners, and burned; and they did not withdraw until they realized that the Muslims were uniting to repulse them and that Sanqar and Ibn Muhannā had reached an agreement with the Egyptians.[83]

It was not very long before the Mongols who had attacked them returned to the fringes of the Aleppo region, led by Mankūdamar, the brother of Abāqā ibn Hülegü, who reached the outskirts of Ḥamāh and wreaked havoc there. The camp of the Muslims was on the outskirts of Ḥimṣ, and al-Malik al-Manṣūr arranged his army in battle order to meet the invaders, with the Sultan himself on the right flank, and at the head of the army, Amīr ʻĪsā ibn Muhannā, the Āl Faḍl, the Āl Murrī, the bedouins of Syria, and those affiliated with them. The narrator from whom Ibn al-Furāt takes the report claims that the Mongols numbered 100,000 horsemen and more, and that the army of the Muslims came to only half that and perhaps less. The place where the two sides met was between al-Rastan and the Orontes River (it is also said on the outskirts of Ḥimṣ), and the narrator gives a detailed description of the battle. Of this it is worth mentioning that the bedouin *amīr* ʻĪsā ibn Muhannā and his forces played a major role and that they killed many Mongols.[84]

---

[80] *Ibid.*, p. 170.
[81] *Ibid.*, p. 172.
[82] *Ibid.*, p. 177.
[83] *Ibid.*, p. 186.
[84] *Ibid.*, pp. 215–22.

When Amīr ʿĪsā ibn Muhannā died in 683/1285, the ruler of Egypt, al-Malik al-Manṣūr Qalāwūn, assigned the post of Amīr of the Bedouins to ʿĪsā's son, Amīr Ḥusām al-Dīn Muhannā.[85] Al-Malik al-Manṣūr died in 689/1290 and was succeeded as Sultan by his son al-Malik al-Ashraf, and before long the new ruler treacherously wronged Amīr Ḥusām al-Dīn, arresting him and his brothers and transferring the position of *amīr* to their cousin.[86] It was at the end of this century that the Crusaders made their final withdrawal from Syria and its coastal areas and their empire there came to an end. The Mongols returned to Aleppo,[87] and the bedouins reverted to ravaging and plundering and began to quarrel among themselves. In 748/1347 Sayf al-Dīn ibn Faḍl, Amīr of the Bedouins, began to fight near Salamīya with Aḥmad Fayyāḍ, one of the other *amīrs*. Sayf al-Dīn was defeated, and both his bedouin forces and those of Aḥmad Fayyāḍ subjected al-Maʿarra, Ḥamāh, and other towns to levels of pillaging and highway brigandage that defy description. They attacked Ḥamāh and al-Maʿarra, so the peasant cultivators fled, the villages were wiped out, and animals were grazed in the fields, vineyards, and gardens.[88]

There passes about a century for which we find in the sources available to us no significant information on the bedouin tribes. Among the reports for this period al-Ghazzī mentions nothing of importance concerning the tribes that had provoked chaos before that time in the vicinity of Aleppo. The volumes of the history of Ibn al-Furāt that cover this period are still unpublished, and in the published material (although it is volume 9) he begins with the events of 789/1387. Here we see that in those years the *imārat al-ʿurbān*, "*amīr*ship of the bedouins," as he says, was in the hands of Amīr Nuʿayr, who was of Āl Muhannā, and his bedouins of Āl Faḍl.[89] He was sometimes described as *malik ʿarab*

[85]Ibn al-Furāt, *Taʾrīkh*, VIII, edited by Constantine Zurayk and Najla Abū ʿIzz al-Dīn (Beirut, 1939), p. 8. Here we would do well to note that such agnomens as Ḥusām al-Dīn ("the sword edge of the faith," for the son of Amīr ʿĪsā) and Shihāb al-Dīn ("the shooting star of the faith," for his father) were ones that the rulers of Egypt used to bestow upon the shaykhs of the tribes.

[86]*Ibid.*, p. 156.

[87]Al-Ghazzī, *Nahr al-dhahab*, III, 170–72.

[88]Al-Jundī, *Taʾrīkh Maʿarrat al-Nuʿmān*, I, 184, 185.

[89]Ibn al-Furāt, *Taʾrīkh*, IX.1, edited by Constantine Zurayk (Beirut, 1936), pp. 57, 109, 111, 132.

al-Shām, "King of the Bedouins of Syria."[90] When Amīr Yalbaghā al-Nāṣirī rebelled against al-Malik al-Ẓāhir Barqūq, the latter called upon Amīr Nu'ayr for help against him. Among the events he relates for 792/1390, Ibn al-Furāt goes into great detail in presenting the reports concerning Amīr Nu'ayr, his dispute with Yalbaghā, and the fighting that took place between them on many occasions. In his reports for the same year he refers to an agreement concluded between Amīr Nu'ayr and another Turkoman *amīr* to fight the governors of Syria, and relates how Amīr Yalbaghā went out to fight Nu'ayr, met him and his bedouins, and routed them, killing some while the others fled. Ibn al-Furāt says that Yalbaghā did likewise with the bedouins of Āl 'Alī and plundered them of many of their camels and horses.[91] In his reports for 795/1393 he mentions an agreement between Nu'ayr and the Turkoman Minṭāsh to proceed together, at the head of a vast force, to raid Ḥamāh:

> So the governor (*nā'ib al-sulṭa*) of Ḥamāh and the governor of Tripoli came out to defend the city, but the bedouins routed the two governors and plundered Ḥamāh. When word of this reached the governor of Aleppo, he immediately set out with his forces, launched a surprise attack on the camps of Nu'ayr's bedouins, and took whatever he could lay his hands on of their property, livestock, horses, camels, men, women, and children. When word reached the bedouins of what the governor of Aleppo had done in their camps, they rushed back like madmen. But the governor's forces fell upon them from ambush and killed some and captured others.[92]

After this he mentions the submission of Nu'ayr and his tribe.[93] He relates that this bedouin *amīr* later met the Sultan, offered his submission, knelt down before him, and kissed the ground for him. Then he took the Sultan to his tents, made him camp there, and entertained him as his guest.[94] The Sultan al-Ẓāhir subsequently sent a robe of

[90] *Ibid.*, p. 139.
[91] *Ibid.*, pp. 217–19.
[92] *Ibid.*, p. 333.
[93] *Ibid.*, p. 342.
[94] *Ibid.*, p. 345.

honor to Nu'ayr, confirming him in his traditional position as *amīr* of the Āl Faḍl.[95] Before long, in 797/1395, he fell into dispute with the Turkomans, so they went to war against him, defeated him, and killed about a thousand of his men. A large number of his camels—3000, it is said—also died of thirst.[96] Six years later, however, Nu'ayr returned, descended upon Aleppo, besieged it, and reduced its inhabitants to dire straits. Its governor appealed to the Turkomans for aid, so they came to his assistance. There was fierce fighting between the two sides, and the people of Aleppo and the Turkomans were able to drive the bedouins back to the desert. The Turkomans pursued them, but were not able to defeat them.[97]

It was not long after this period that a new invasion swept over northern Syria: new Mongol hosts, again originating from the East, under the leadership of the famous Tīmūr Lang (Tamerlane), one of whose ancestors was reportedly a vizier to Hülegü, the grandson of Genghis Khān:

> Tīmūr at the head of his Tartar hordes initiated a long series of campaigns which gained for him Afghanistan, Persia, Fāris, and Kurdistān. In 1393 he captured Baghdad and in that and the following year overran Mesopotamia. . . .Like a cyclone his forces swept over northern Syria in 1401. They took Aleppo, and for three days the city was given over to plunder, captive-taking, and slaughter. The heads of those killed were built into round mounds about twenty cubits in circumference and about ten high, with the faces turned outward so passersby could see them.[98]

From Aleppo he then headed for Damascus, passing by and capturing Ḥamāh, Ḥimṣ, and Baalbek until he reached Damascus, which in turn also fell in 803/1401 after its citadel had held out for a month. Tīmūr

[95] *Ibid.*, p. 382.

[96] *Ibid.*, p. 405.

[97] Al-Ghazzī, *Nahr al-dhahab*, III, 217.

[98] Hitti, Jurji, and Jabbur, *Ta'rīkh al-'arab*, pp. 793–94 [= Hitti, *History of the Arabs*, pp. 699, 701]. See Ibn al-Furāt, IX, 343. In Ibn al-'Imād, *Shadharāt al-dhahab fī akhbār man dhahab* (Beirut, n.d.), VII, 63, it is said that the mother of Tīmūr Lang was a descendent of Genghis Khān.

stayed in Damascus, carrying away many of its inhabitants and burning its buildings; even the roofs of the Umayyad Mosque fell in the fire. He finally left Damascus, rushing to Baghdad to wreak vengeance on its people for killing certain of his officers. He made a frightful example of them, slaughtering a vast multitude and building 120 towers throughout the city with the heads of those killed.[99] The author of the *Shadharāt al-dhahab*, however, claims that he built 120 minarets from the heads of Baghdad's dead.[100]

There is no doubt that Tīmūr Lang struck fear in the hearts of the desert folk, for the bedouin tribes fell back to the heart of the desert. Fortunately for them, and for all the Arabs, Tīmūr died after a short time, in 807/1404, as he marched eastward in a bid to conquer China. His son, who succeeded him, was not able to subjugate the Mamlūks in Egypt, and civil strife began to erupt in the country.[101] The struggle subsequently developed into one between the Mamlūks, the Turks, and the bedouins.

Some of the tribes attained such levels of dominion that they sought, as was their wont, to terrorize the villages lying along the peripheries of the desert. One section of them reached the town of al-Ramla in the late fifteenth century. A traveler visiting Palestine in 1481 claims that in that year the bedouins raided al-Ramla and burned part of the town. The governor of Gaza thus came to its assistance, captured eleven bedouins, beheaded them, and sent the heads to Gaza. The bedouins accordingly launched a devastating attack against him and killed, as this traveler claims, 23,000 of his men.[102]

It is difficult to draw any informed conclusions about the origins of many of the tribes whose names are mentioned in accounts of events that transpired between one tribe and another or between one tribe and the ruling authorities. Generally speaking, it would seem that the leadership of the tribes in the Syrian Desert in the times prior to the eighteenth century was in the hands of Ṭayyi', which encompassed

---

[99]Hitti, Jurji, and Jabbur, *Ta'rīkh al-'arab*, p. 794 [= Hitti, *History of the Arabs*, p. 701].

[100]Ibn al-'Imād, *Shadharāt al-dhahab*, VII, 64–65.

[101]Hitti, Jurji, and Jabbur, *Ta'rīkh al-'arab*, p. 795 [= Hitti, *History of the Arabs*, p. 702].

[102]'Ārif al-'Ārif, *Ta'rīkh Ghazza* (Jerusalem, 1362/1943), p. 237.

other tribes under its leadership. Its shaykh was called *amīr 'arab al-Shām*, "Amīr of the Bedouins of Syria," in the Ayyūbid and Mamlūk periods, and in the latter era the leadership within Ṭayyi' devolved to an *amīr* named Rabī'a. The Āl Rabī'a later split into three tribes among which were divided influence and dominion in the desert and in the settled regions adjoining the desert, from the Ḥawrān and Jawlān as far as the Euphrates in the north of the country. Some of the clans that had come from Najd and the Ḥijāz began to affiliate themselves with the Ṭayyi'; hence the tribes increased in numbers and relations between them became more contentious.

Here we must note that with time the names of many of the tribes began to change. A tribe might produce a shaykh renowned for his martial skills and generosity and for his many sons and supporters; this man would emerge as a dominant figure and his clan would later trace its descent to him and give up attributing its roots to the original large tribe. Hence the phenomenon that emerges to our view in recent times of such new tribal names as al-Ḥadīdīyīn, al-Wahb, al-Bū Khamīs, al-Bū Salāma, al-'Abd Allāh, al-Sha'lān, and others, which makes it difficult for the researcher to draw well-informed conclusions about the tribe's origins or its relationship to the clans that had earlier established themselves in these northern desert lands. As we have already observed, some of these tribes are branches of the large and famous tribe of 'Anaza.

In Ottoman Times

In his *A'lām al-warā bi-man waliya nā'iban min al-atrāk bi-Dimashq al-Shām al-kubrā*, Ibn Ṭūlūn Muḥammad al-Ṣāliḥ al-Dimashqī gives a history of the events that transpired among the governors, and with these events the bedouins had some connection. The first part, ending in 865/1461, he excerpts from a book by Shams al-Dīn al-Zamlakānī, and in it there is nothing of concern to us here. The continuation of the book is Ibn Ṭūlūn's own work, and among the reports for 903/1497 he mentions that in those days word spread in Damascus that the governor, Karatbāy al-Aḥmar, had attacked the tribe (*ṭā'ifa*) of Mislib, one of the *amīrs* of Banū Lām, which had molested the pilgrimage caravan. He took much property from them, and it was also rumored that he went to the territory of the Banū Ṣakhr and wanted to build a citadel there,[103] the aim in doing so being the protection of the pilgrimage route from bedouin attacks.

Similarly, for 904/1498 Ibn Ṭūlūn relates that the new governor of Damascus traveled to the Ḥawrān, attacked the bedouins of Āl Mūsā, and seized many camels (2,000, it is said) from them.[104] Some of these he sold to the people of al-Qubaybāt, and the rest he handed over to the people of Damascus.[105] He proceeded to the bedouins of the Banū Hudhaym, plundered them, seized many sheep from them, and brought their womenfolk back to Damascus in the most miserable condition.[106] In the same year, the governor received word from the Commander of the Pilgrimage (*amīr al-wafd*) that the bedouins were so numerous that if the governor did not reach them quickly the bedouins would seize the entire pilgrimage caravan (*al-wafd*). The governor thus went to their aid with all of his army.[107] We then hear, in the reports for 905/1499, that the governor Qaṣruwa marched on the bedouins of Banū Ṣakhr with a large army, killed some twenty of them, caught others, and took many animals from them.[108] Among the reports for 906/1500, we find that the bedouins raided the pilgrimage caravan at the village of al-Ṣanamayn,[109] that the population was in a state of paralysis, and that beyond Damascus and its environs the roads were impassable due to the multitudes of bedouins from the tribes of al-Mafārja and Banū Lām.[110]

The bedouins continued to attack and plunder the outskirts of Damascus and to lay waste the surrounding villages, despite the governors' efforts to stop them. The governors in turn would plunder the bedouins, when they were able to do so, and at the same time plunder the villages, as we see in the reports of Ibn Ṭūlūn, a contemporary to these events.[111]

---

[103] Muḥammad ibn Ṭūlūn, *A'lām al-warā*, edited by Muḥammad Aḥmad Dahmān (Damascus, 1383/1964), pp. 88–89.
[104] *Ibid.*, p. 95.
[105] *Ibid.*, p. 96.
[106] *Ibid.*, p. 90.
[107] *Ibid.*, p. 98.
[108] *Ibid.*, p. 102.
[109] *Ibid.*, p. 115.
[110] *Ibid.*, p. 136.
[111] *Ibid.*, pp. 137–43.

Ibn Ṭūlūn continues to give accounts of relations between the provincial governors and the tribes as he presents events in the years of the first quarter of the tenth/sixteenth century. In many places in his book he refers to the journey of the pilgrims, their fear of brigandage along the route, their appeal to the governors for help, the marching forth of the army and militia to assist them, the outbreak of clashes between the al-Jabal bedouins and those of Āl ʻAlī, and the defeat of the army on some occasions and of the bedouins on others.[112] Among the reports for 916/1510 he gives an account of the bedouins of Āl Faḍl ibn Nuʻayr, saying that the governor of Damascus journeyed to the north country to assist the governor of Ḥimṣ against the bedouins of Ibn Nuʻayr, took them by surprise, plundered them of many camels and sheep, and killed many of the bedouins and their shaykhs.[113] For 917/1511 and 918/1512 he mentions the governor's victory over the bedouins of Āl ʻAlī, al-Jabal, and Āl Sirḥān, his plundering of Banū Ṣakhr, and his meeting with the *amīrs* Muslim, chief (*kabīr*) of the tribe of Banū Lām, and ʻAssāf, chief of the Āl Murrī, and their promise to protect the pilgrimage route and the pilgrims.[114] Nevertheless, it is clear that the pilgrimage route remained under threat and that bedouin depredations continued in those years on the outskirts of Damascus. They robbed travelers on the pilgrimage route, passed through many villages, burning the cereal crops they had produced, and killed many men from the governor's forces.[115]

Here Ibn Ṭūlūn begins to give reports for the Ottoman period and the arrival of the new governor, Yūnus Pāshā, in Damascus in 922/1516. He was followed in the same year by another governor who intended to make the pilgrimage that year, but could not do so because of bedouin unrest.[116] Nor could the Syrian pilgrimage be completed in 923/1517, for fear of the bedouins and the lack of water.[117] In 925/1519 the governor was finally forced to march to the Ḥawrān in search of the Amīr of the Bedouins, Jughaymān, and his group to keep them from molesting

[112] *Ibid.*, pp. 154, 161, 162, 165, 173, 175, 183, 189–93, 195, 198–200.
[113] *Ibid.*, p. 195.
[114] *Ibid.*, pp. 198–200.
[115] *Ibid.*, p. 202.
[116] *Ibid.*, pp. 219, 220.
[117] *Ibid.*, p. 225.

the pilgrimage caravan. The bedouins fled in fear from him to the Jawf, and the governor was able to take some of their camels and sheep. He then returned to Damascus, with the *maḥmal* of the pilgrimage[118] and a kinsman of Jughaymān leading the way. This relative, a man called Duway'ir who had taken the pilgrimage caravan in the previous year, was riding a camel and was bound by the neck with iron chains, and around him was a group of his men, also in chains.[119]

In 927/1521 the governor of Damascus traveled to the Ḥawrān to counter the bedouins of Amīr Dirbāgh ibn Muhannā. When he joined battle with them they put up a fierce fight, after which he reached an agreement with them guaranteeing the running of the pilgrimage, with bedouin hostages to be handed over to the governor.[120] In 931/1525 the new governor traveled to al-Marj to suppress the bedouins of Āl 'Alī, whose increasing aggressions had led to a great battle between them and the people of al-Marj.[121] In 937/1531 the governor of Damascus was forced to pay 75,000 *dīnār*s to merchants whose merchandise had been taken on the pilgrimage road two years earlier, and who had gone to the Sultan with their complaints against the governor. His accounts end in the year 942/1536.[122]

From the reports preserved in some of the historical works for the subsequent period, it is evident that the dominion of the desert Arabs began to increase. Some of the tribes began to reach to the heart of the settled regions, sometimes even to the coasts of southern Syria; and they began to conclude alliances and agreements with some of the district heads and governors in various places, especially for protection of the pilgrimage route, and were so effective that the individual exercising command of the pilgrimage was deemed a powerful man if he was able to come to terms with and appease the bedouin shaykhs so that they would not molest the procession of the pilgrims. In his account of the life of Qānṣūh al-Ghazzāwī, governor of 'Ajlūn and *amīr* of the Syrian pilgrimage for about fifteen years, al-Ghazzī states that

[118][The *maḥmal* was the heavily decorated tent-like litter carried on the back of a camel with the pilgrimage caravan on its way to Mecca.]

[119]*Ibid.*, pp. 230–31.

[120]*Ibid.*, p. 237.

[121]*Ibid.*, p. 243.

[122]*Ibid.*, p. 244.

anyone who performed the pilgrimage in his time could breathe easy on his journey; the bedouins obeyed and feared him, and thus he gained security and ease for the pilgrims. One of his friends was Amīr ʿAssāf, one of the bedouin shaykhs. Qānṣūh died in 1000/1594, and this report would thus seem to indicate—at the least—that in the final years of the tenth/sixteenth century the pilgrimage route was secure from bedouin attacks.[123]

Once we continue to the events of 1015/1606 in the same author's *Dhayl al-kawākib al-sā'ira*, however, we find reference to bedouin depredations, their influence in the struggles that broke out among the various district heads, their participation in the fighting and looting,[124] and how the governors returned to their territories and seized their livestock.[125] Similarly, in Shaykh Aḥmad ibn Muḥammad al-Khālidī's *Ta'rīkh Lubnān fī ʿahd al-amīr Fakhr al-Dīn al-Maʿnī al-thānī*, which covers reports about Amīr Fakhr al-Dīn al-Maʿnī between 1021/1612 and 1034/1624, we find evidence for many clashes—over a period of no more than thirteen years—between the tribes and the regime and among the tribes themselves. In the reports for 1021/1612, for example, we witness the domination of the Ḥawrān region by some of the tribes and strife between the bedouins of the Mafārja and Sardīya over the shaykhship in that region. The regime in Damascus intervened and joined one faction in fighting against the other, with the result that the Mafārja were driven out. They took refuge with Amīr Fayyāḍ al-Ḥiyārī, but it was not long before they returned to the Jawlān and Ḥawrān. Battles took place between them and the bedouins of the Sardīya, and the Mafārja accordingly sought the assistance of Amīr Fakhr al-Dīn. In 1022/1613 other clashes occurred in Mzayrīb in the Ḥawrān among the Syrian forces and the bedouins, with the Mafārja, their allies, and their supporter Amīr Fakhr al-Dīn emerging victorious over the other bedouins and the Syrian authorities. The victors despoiled their defeated enemies of 100 mares whose riders had been killed (*qalāyiʿ*) and the drums, flutes (*zumūr*), and flags (*bayāriq*) of

[123]Najm al-Dīn al-Ghazzī, *Al-Kawākib al-sā'ira bi-aʿyān al-mi'a al-ʿāshira*, edited by Jibrail Jabbur (Beirut, 1945–58), III, 201–202.

[124]Najm al-Dīn al-Ghazzī, *Luṭf al-samar wa-qaṭf al-thamar*, edited by Maḥmūd al-Shaykh (Damascus, 1981–82), I, 123–240.

[125]*Ibid.*, p. 304.

the Commander of the Pilgrimage, then made their way to the 'Ajlūn region.[126]

Al-Khālidī subsequently mentions that the Mafārja, under their leader Shaykh Rashīd, sought to pursue their campaign against the Sardīya, but some of his followers disagreed with him. They did know, however, that bedouins of Nāṣir al-Fuḥaylī were camped on the edge of the Lijāh along the peripheries of the Ḥawrān, so they attacked them by surprise and took them to the last man: "Not so much as a hobbling cord was left to them, and the booty taken amounted to 1,000 camels, not to mention the horses." The shaykh of the Mafārja maintained his alliance with Amīr Fakhr al-Dīn, and hence began to rely on his aid in subjugating the other bedouin tribes throughout the other surrounding regions.[127]

In the same year, 1022/1613, he mentions another clash between the bedouins of Mafārja (allies of Amīr Fakhr al-Dīn) and those of Sardīya. The nephew of the shaykh of the Sardīya was killed; about 200 thoroughbred riding she-camels (*dhalūl*) were taken from them, and ten horses were killed. He then records a battle between the Mafārja and the bedouins of the Wuḥaydāt in the vicinity of al-Karak in which three of the shaykhs of the Wuḥaydāt and some fine thoroughbred horses were killed.[128] In the same year there was a third battle between the bedouins of the Wuḥaydāt and their allies and all the bedouins of the Balqā and al-Karak; in this clash about 80 men and horses of Amīr Ḥamdān and the Wuḥaydāt were struck down.[129] He also refers to the march eastward by the son of Amīr Fakhr al-Dīn and the bedouins of the Mafārja Shaykh 'Amr to the territory of Amīr Fayyāḍ, *amīr* of the Āl Ḥiyār in Tadmur. When he realized that Fayyāḍ would not agree to them camping in his territory, he made his way to al-Qaryatayn and camped in its lands. After this he reports a great battle between them and the Syrian army; Nāṣir al-Fuḥaylī, who, along with his tribesmen, had lost their flocks to Shaykh 'Amr, accompanied them. Of the battle al-Khālidī says:

[126] *Lubnān fī 'ahd al-amīr Fakhr al-Dīn*, pp. 8–10.
[127] *Ibid.*, pp. 10–11.
[128] *Ibid.*, p. 26.
[129] *Ibid.*, p. 27.

> It was enough to turn the young man grey and lasted from the rising to the setting of the sun. In it Shaykh 'Amr displayed courage the like of which no one had ever shown, such that three horses were killed under him.[130]

All this indicates how powerful the bedouin dominion was in that period, for even the son of Amīr Fakhr al-Dīn could not travel in those parts without seeking the assistance of some of their shaykhs, who continued to accompany him even on his return journey to Ḥāṣbayyā.[131]

When al-Khālidī takes up events of 1024/1615, he cites reports indicating that an alliance was concluded between 'Amr, shaykh of the Mafārja, and Fayyāḍ al-Ḥiyārī, in agreement with a shaykh of the Āl Ṭūqān by the name of Amīr Sulṭān. They came to the Ḥawrān and fought with Shaykh Rashīd, shaykh of the Sardīya, and drove him out of the area. They left no bedouin of the Balqā or Jabal unplundered, and compelled all of the nomads to submit to them. Rivalry then broke out between Amīr Sulṭān and Amīr Fayyāḍ, obliging Sulṭān to seek refuge with the Sardīya. With that, Amīr Fayyāḍ launched an expedition from 'Araba, in the district of Salamīya, passed by the city of Damascus itself, marched on to the Ḥawrān, and made an attack on Amīr Sulṭān and his bedouins and seized their flocks. After doing so, however, they were defeated; some of the animals were recovered from them, and the bedouins of Sardīya subsequently made for the rocky terrain along the edge of the Lijāh. Compelled to seek a way to appease Fayyāḍ, Amīr Sulṭān and those with him headed north to al-Qaryatayn. Amīr Fayyāḍ thus took all of the herds and flocks of Sulṭān and drove them off. Sulṭān went to join Shaykh Nāṣir Āl Muhannā, shaykh of the land of Iraq, and from there began to raid the bedouins and the road traffic in Fayyāḍ's territory. It is even said that on one occasion he seized a caravan from Aleppo near Qāra, and that the people in it had cash and goods worth 50,000 piasters. When Amīr Fayyāḍ wearied of Sulṭān's vexations, he invited the latter's brothers—Amīr Najm, Amīr Abū Fāḍil, the sons of Amīr Aḥmad (the uncle of the first two *amīrs*), and Amīr Ḥasan ibn 'Arār—to come to visit him; he prepared a banquet for them in Salamīya, then seized

[130] *Ibid.*, p. 29.
[131] *Ibid.*, p. 31.

them, cast them into the citadel of Salamīya, and killed them.[132] Seeking to avenge his slain kinsmen, Sulṭān left the Āl Muhannā and came down to the Lijāh, where he fell upon the bedouins of Su'ayda by surprise and killed their shaykh. But they rallied against him, shot his horse out from under him, and passed judgment against him and his nephew, Amīr 'Alī ibn 'Arār. 'Awaḍ, the shaykh of the Su'ayda bedouins, killed them and they brought their heads to the city of Damascus in 1024/1615.[133]

With the passage of the years 1025–27/1616–19 al-Khālidī mentions nothing worthy of note on the bedouins, but with the advent of 1028/1619 he states that Amīr Fayyāḍ was still strong and would come from the Jazīra and interfere with traffic along the roads to Aleppo and Damascus.[134] We then read that in the autumn of 1031/1622, Amīr Ḥusayn ibn Fayyāḍ, having been driven out by Amīr Mudlij, came to see Amīr Fakhr al-Dīn. The latter graciously welcomed Ḥusayn and his group of bedouins, and before long Ḥusayn raided the bedouins of Sardīya and seized about 400 camels from them. He made his way on to the territory of the 'Anaza bedouins in Wādī Zubayda,[135] where the 'Anaza fell upon him and took many of his camels, since the terrain was very rugged, yet Ḥusayn still retained a good part of the booty. When Amīr Mudlij al-Ḥiyārī learned of Ḥusayn ibn Fayyāḍ's raid against the Sardīya, he forced Ḥusayn to return all of the plunder he had with him, since Amīr Mudlij had concluded a truce with the shaykh of the Sardīya. Amīr Ḥusayn thus went to Amīr Fakhr al-Dīn, and Amīr Mudlij sent his scribe bearing a letter to Fakhr al-Dīn in which he demanded the execution of Amīr Ḥusayn and promised to give his daughter in marriage to Fakhr al-Dīn's son, Amīr 'Alī. Fakhr al-Din's reply was that "this is not our custom, and it was not our hope that Amīr Mudlij would seek such a thing from us."[136] That was one of the most disastrous years in the desert and the land of Syria: most of the bedouins' herds starved to

[132] *Ibid.*, pp. 41–42.
[133] *Ibid.*, p. 42.
[134] *Ibid.*, p. 81.
[135] *Ibid.*, p. 131. Here we have one of the earliest references to the presence of the bedouins of 'Anaza on the peripheries of the Syrian Desert, going back to the eleventh century AH/seventeenth century AD
[136] *Ibid.*

death for lack of pasturage, and the thoroughbred horses died because of the high cost of barley.[137]

In the following year, 1032/1623, Amīr Fakhr al-Dīn, along with the bedouin *amīrs* and shaykhs, went to meet the pilgrimage caravan. Some of them went with it as far as Tabūk to protect it, and Fakhr al-Dīn and many of his bedouin horsemen allies returned to the Balqā', marched against the bedouins of al-Jaḥāwsha and al-Da'ja, attacked them by surprise, and seized all of their herds of camels and flocks of sheep, amounting to more than 15,000 head.[138] From the reports for this year it appears that the government was paying money to the shaykh of the Mafārja for protection of the pilgrimage route,[139] and that the bedouins of Shaykh Ḥusayn ibn 'Amr were buying all the provisions they needed from Jīnīn.[140] Amīr Fakhr al-Dīn and the bedouins of Shaykh Ḥusayn also attacked the tribesmen of Ibn Ṭarabāy and the Sawālma in the region of the River 'Awjā and seized their herds and tent furnishings (*athāth*); but their victims counterattacked, defeated them, killed about 30 or 40 of their men, and regained all that had been plundered from them.[141] From the reports for this year it appears that some of the bedouin shaykhs were so strong and powerful that they were able to penetrate as far as the Syrian coast in the south: it is stated that Amīr 'Alī ibn Ṭarabāy came with all his mounted tribesmen and launched an attack on the Acre coast, seized the flocks in the area, and returned to his own territory by way of Haifa. Naṣūḥ Bulūkbāshī, with his troops and flags, intercepted and attacked him, intending thereby to take the flocks from him and his men. But Ṭarabāy's men galloped on horseback down upon Naṣūḥ and his men, who were on foot. This Naṣūḥ was killed and his group fled down the coast in a ship to Acre. The bedouins of Amīr Aḥmad ibn Ṭarabāy then took to attacking the countryside around Kafar Kannā and seizing its flocks and crops, turning the area into a wasteland and continuing their depredations for some time.[142]

---

[137] *Ibid.*, p. 115.
[138] *Ibid.*, p. 119.
[139] *Ibid.*, p. 133.
[140] *Ibid.*, p. 140.
[141] *Ibid.*, p. 141.
[142] *Ibid.*, p. 142.

Among his reports for the year 1033/1624, al-Khālidī goes on to mention the dispute between Amīrs Mudlij and Ḥusayn of the Āl al-Ḥiyār. The reason for this quarrel was that at the death of Amīr Fayyāḍ, his son Amīr Ḥusayn had not yet come of age. His cousin Amīr Mudlij therefore assumed the position of shaykh, but gave him nothing in return as compensation. Ḥusayn thus launched a surprise attack by night on the tent of Amīr Mudlij in an attempt to kill him, but failed. Heading back toward Aleppo with a section of the bedouins of Āl Ḥiyār, Ḥusayn began to launch attacks on the bedouins of Mudlij and began to become so much more powerful than his cousin that the latter was forced to seek the assistance of Amīr Fakhr al-Dīn. Coming to the aid of Mudlij, Fakhr al-Dīn set out northward with a troop of his horsemen. They reached the village of Mhīn, plundered some bedouins of the Āl Birrī there, then passed by al-Ghunthur and from there went on to al-Furqulus, these being the same places where, as we have already seen at the beginning of this chapter, Sayf al-Dawla raided the bedouins during his reign. From al-Furqulus Fakhr al-Dīn proceeded on to the camps of Amīr Mudlij, where the latter received him and, in order to secure his favor, presented him with a gray mare named Saʿdā. The winter season did not allow for them to set out to raid Amīr Ḥusayn, Mudlij's cousin; so Amīrs Fakhr al-Dīn and Mudlij concluded an alliance and swore to act as one. Amīr Fakhr al-Dīn then returned to Baalbek after giving Mudlij 1000 pieces of gold.[143]

In the same year, Syrian bedouins of the Awlād Abī Qays clashed with government forces in the southern part of Syria; the bedouins were defeated, but subsequently launched a counterattack on the soldiers, defeated them, and seized their horses and weapons. The bedouins of al-Jabal did likewise when the governor of Damascus sent an expedition against them because of the great damage they were causing to the villages on the outskirts of Damascus. Proceeding as the Awlād Abī Qays had, they held back until the troops had gained a certain advantage, then counterattacked and defeated them, put them to flight, and killed many of them.[144] Also in the same year, an expedition sent by the governor of Aleppo, a friend of Amīr Mudlij, made an end of Amīr Ḥusayn

[143] *Ibid.*, pp. 156–58.
[144] *Ibid.*, p. 163.

ibn Fayyāḍ. The governor first sent an invitation to Ḥusayn and then betrayed him, raiding and plundering his bedouins. Ḥusayn's tribesmen counterattacked, defeated his army, and killed 300 of his mares; but deprived of their *amīr*, the greater part of Ḥusayn's forces went off to join Shaykh Nāsir ibn Muhannā in Iraq, and the rest attached themselves to Mudlij himself.[145]

In accounts of this same year we see many incidents and battles revealing the ascendancy of the bedouins, who were apparently well-versed in how to feign defeat and then counterattack and wipe out the government forces while the latter were engrossed with the spoils they had taken.[146] In this connection we hear of bedouins of Āl Faḍl, al-Sawālma, 'Āyid, Ghazza, Aḥmad ibn Ṭarabāy, Aḥmad ibn Ḥamdān, and others.[147]

Towards the end of that year the bedouin *amīr* Aḥmad ibn Ṭarabāy sent his brothers and sons to attack the territory of Amīr Fakhr al-Dīn ibn Ma'n. They seized the flocks, attacked his lands, laid waste his territory as far as the coast at Acre, and launched a surprise attack on some Turkomans camped at the River al-Mafshūkh, seizing all of their flocks. Kaywān Āghā-Sū, the Pāshā of Acre, took all of his horsemen, along with the people of the nearby villages, to a place there to oppose the bedouins. They joined battle with the tribesmen for about two hours, but broke ranks in the face of the bedouin cavalry. Some fled, some were killed, and some were plundered of their clothing and weapons; the number of those killed, according to al-Khālidī, was about 30. After that the bedouins continued their southward march and took all that came within their reach. After a time, matters reached the point where consultations and exchanges of letters and communications took place between Amīr Fakhr al-Dīn ibn Ma'n and Amīr Aḥmad ibn Ṭarabāy, and they reached an agreement whereby Amīr Aḥmad ibn Ṭarabāy would prevent his bedouins from spreading ruin in the land of Ṣafad while Amīr Fakhr al-Dīn would remove his troops from the citadel (*burj*) of Haifa. Amīr Aḥmad ibn Ṭarabāy sent men to demolish the citadel of Haifa after the troops had left: the roads

[145] *Ibid.*, pp. 164–65.
[146] *Ibid.*, pp. 187–91.
[147] *Ibid.*, pp. 185, 190.

between the lands of Ḥāritha and Ṣafad were patrolled, and no one any longer interfered with anyone else's movement.[148] Had al-Khālidī's history of Amīr Fakhr al-Dīn covered the 40–50 years after 1033/1624, we probably would have found many reports of how the bedouins laid waste, plundered, looted, and terrorized the centers of settled life in both southern and northern Syria.

When we return to al-Ghazzī's *Nahr al-dhahab*, we find him referring to bedouin depredations in 1085/1674 in the vicinity of Aleppo, where raiders were interfering with travelers. Their *amīr*, a man by the name of 'Assāf (not the 'Assāf mentioned above), had been taking a fixed stipend from the government; so when the oppressions of his bedouins increased the governor of Aleppo planned to use trickery to catch him, so as to dismiss him as Amīr of the Bedouins. The idea occurred to him to send an envoy to 'Assāf inviting him to a reception (*ḍiyāfa*) he was preparing for him in the district of Aleppo about five hours' traveling time away. The governor, a man by the name of Ibrāhīm Pāshā, went to the place he had specified with stores and troops, carrying presents and noising it about that this banquet was for the "Sultan of the Steppe" (*sulṭān al-barr*); i.e. Amīr 'Assāf. 'Assāf agreed to accept the invitation only after making certain from the envoy that no treachery was intended, and the envoy returned and warned the governor against any act of perfidy toward Amīr 'Assāf. Still fearful of treachery, 'Assāf came accompanied by a large number of bedouins, but the governor tried to assassinate him and opened fire on him. He failed to kill him, however, and 'Assāf fled and reverted to destruction and brigandage even more extreme than what he had done in the past.

When the regime heard of Ibrāhīm Pāshā's treachery, faithlessness, and misconduct, it dismissed him from Aleppo and replaced him as governor with Darwīsh Pāshā. This new governor came to Aleppo, redressed his tarnished image in the eyes of the bedouins, sent word to 'Assāf inviting him in courteous and gentle terms to submit to the Sultan, and sent costly presents with the envoy. The envoy arrived and gently chided him for his disobedience, while praising both him and his tribe. 'Assāf showed him the place where a bullet had struck his armor and where he had been wounded; so the envoy expressed his

[148] *Ibid.*, pp. 196–98.

commiserations, promised him safe-conduct, and told him: "The regime has only dismissed Ibrāhīm Pāshā because of his treachery toward you." This satisfied 'Assāf, who presented the envoy with horses and sent with him a number of horses to the government, as well as a payment order (*ḥawāla*) redeemable in Aleppo in the amount of 2000 gold pounds.[149]

Eight years later, in 1093/1682, both the governor and the bedouin *amīr* were replaced and, according to what al-Ghazzī says, the bedouins reverted to spreading ruin in the countryside around Damascus, causing tremendous damage and destruction. They committed such atrocious acts in their plundering and their attacks on caravans that the provinces were clamoring with demands for redress. The regime thus issued instructions ordering the governors of Aleppo, Damascus, Baghdad, and Tripoli to make every effort to catch Milḥim, the bedouins' *amīr*. Employing a ruse, the governor of Aleppo used treachery to capture Milḥim, kill a number of his party, and capture eighteen others whom he killed while they were his prisoners. Their *amīr* he sent to Edirne, where the Sultan was, and the latter ordered his execution. This made matters difficult for government officials, however, since they had been hoping to pardon him so he would serve as a guarantee that the bedouins, in view of his boundless courage, would cease their attacks.[150]

In the Ottoman period, matters reached the point where communications between the imperial capital and the centers of the Arab provinces were at the mercy of the sons of the desert and the notables of the tribes. And in about the middle of the eighteenth century, when new diverse tribes were beginning to come to the Syrian lands, there were at the same time many bedouin tribes along the lower Euphrates that concluded a truce amongst themselves and united under the name of al-Muntafiq. They began to cause many difficulties, not only for the *pāshā*s of Baghdad, but also for the inhabitants of the cities themselves and for the villages surrounding them.[151]

We may finally note that the power the bedouins enjoyed accrued to them for several reasons. First, they gained in strength by virtue of

[149]*Nahr al-dhahab*, III, 282–85.

[150]*Ibid.*, III, 288–92.

[151]Hitti, Jurji, and Jabbur, *Ta'rīkh al-'arab*, p. 835 [= Hitti, *History of the Arabs*, p. 738].

their participation in the Arab conquests in early Islam and during the Umayyad period. Second, the 'Abbāsid caliphate became weak, and rivalry among the princes in the statelets that took its place reached the point where, as we have seen, these princes in turn founded principalities in the settled areas. Finally, there was the weakness of the Ottoman caliphate, which inherited the sovereign authority at a later time. This debility was such that it was possible for one of the bedouin leaders in the eighteenth century to become shaykh over the region of Ṣafad, a position to which he had been appointed by the Shihābī ruler of Lebanon. The son of this bedouin shaykh became a local leader himself; in about 1151/1737, while he was still a young man, he was able to incorporate Tiberias into his domain and then went on to subjugate other cities. The year 1163/1750 had no sooner begun than this young man of bedouin origin—the famous Shaykh Ẓāhir al-'Umar—established his capital at Acre.[152]

It was in this period that the Western states again began to turn their attentions to the East—not for a religious cause or to protect the Holy Land, as was proclaimed in public, but rather for the region's importance from the economic standpoint. After the discovery of America, the discovery of the route around the Cape of Good Hope, and Portugal's monopolization of the maritime routes, England began to rise to prominence as a competitor to Portugal in the quest to reach India—in the European view the center for the treasures of the East—and initiated efforts to open a land route to India through the Arab countries. Explorers began to appear on the stage of historical events in Arabia, especially along the route between Aleppo and al-Baṣra; and in this period, the 300 years of the seventeenth through the nineteenth centuries, up until the digging of the Suez Canal, the development of the maritime routes down the Red Sea, and the following of a new land route between Damascus and Baghdad after the First World War, we

[152] *Ibid.*, p. 829 [= *ibid.*, pp. 731–32]. In 'Ārif, *Ta'rīkh Ghazza*, p. 183, it is stated that the family of Ẓāhir al-'Umar was called al-Zayādna, tracing his descent through his grandfather to a tribe by this name among the bedouins of al-Ṭā'if in the Ḥijāz. In the journal *Al-Jinān*, 24.15 (December 1877), pp. 847–53, there is a long article on the history of the Zayādna by Nu'mān Effendi al-Qasāṭlī. In this study he described the history of their coming to Palestine from the al-Ṭā'if region in 1102/1691 and their subsequent occupation of many villages there.

begin to hear reports of the bedouins and their efforts to cut the trade route.

It would be difficult to collect all that the explorers and others have left us over the last three centuries by way of reports on the bedouins and accounts of their obstruction of the merchants' caravans along the route to al-Baṣra. But here we must mention that on most occasions these caravans were of such strength and numbers that raiders did not run the risk of trying to plunder them unless they themselves were mounted and could attack the caravan by surprise far from the settled areas. To protect their caravans, the merchants would take along as their escorts a group of the bedouin leaders themselves. Here it will suffice for me to cite one of these explorers' description of the bedouin raiders. As he says:

> These robbers always appear on horseback, and though their numbers should be no more than thirty, they will be able to do a great deal of mischief to such a caravan as ours, and carry off a great booty; for they endeavour to come upon you unawares, and fall upon that part that is the least guarded, putting the camels into confusion. These being of a very timorous nature, some will run one way, and some another, dispersing themselves in the desert; and this is the very thing they aim at, for they can pick them up at their leisure. Besides those of the caravan who escape themselves give themselves little trouble about what becomes of the rest; or, if they did, they know it would be impossible to recover the loss. Besides, while they were assisting others, they themselves would be in danger of losing their own property.[153]

I have not encountered any source that gives a historical account devoted to the coming of any of the bedouin tribes, whether of ʿAnaza or others, to the Syrian Desert or to their occupation of the lands adjoining the great cities in Syria. It seems that the Mawālī were among the earliest bedouins in northern Syria, and that in the early seventeenth century tribes of Shammar began to come from Najd and clash with the

[153] *The Desert Route to India*, p. 95.

Mawālī tribe already living in the north. Then after that the tribes of 'Anaza came from Najd and in their turn began to exert pressure on the bedouins of the Mawālī and to try to drive them out of the regions near Ḥimṣ and Ḥamāh, some of the richest lands in pasturage and water. It seems to me that contingents of some of the 'Anaza tribes reached these areas in the early eighteenth century. Then other 'Anaza clans began to stream hither, with the result that 'Anaza was soon widely distributed in other parts of Syria and came to comprise the majority of the bedouins from among all the clans of Syria.

One of the earliest accounts to mention the penetration of 'Anaza from Najd to the Syrian Desert is that cited in Muḥammad al-Bassām's *Kitāb al-durar al-mafākhir fī akhbār al-'arab al-awākhir*, which contains many reports on the movement of the Wahhābīs between the years 1160/1746 and 1188/1774. At the beginning of the book he discusses the raids mounted by Su'ūd (I) with 20 men on she-camels and seven on mares, then continues to follow his raids as his army increased in size until, in his attack on Riyadh, it finally numbered about 3000 horsemen and infantry. At this point he indicates that when the Su'ūdīs gained power their policy with regard to the desert folk in Najd was to confirm their old *amīrs* in authority and to dismiss them only when one of them rebelled, in which case they would install his brother or cousin as shaykh. Al-Bassām then mentions that 'Abd al-'Azīz (I) forbade the bedouins from taking the *khuwwa* from the pilgrimage caravans. Referring to the bedouins of 'Anaza in this book, he states that they are the largest of the Arab tribes in Najd and as evidence for this cites a proverb of theirs: *kullu qawmin dūna 'Anaza*, "every tribe ranks below 'Anaza." He then says: "In the land of Najd there is no one who can oppose them."[154] After this he refers to the penetration by some 'Anaza clans into the Syrian Desert, to their wintertime migration to Wādī Sirḥān and the Ḥamad, and the camping of others in the steppelands near Aleppo, Ḥamāh, and Ḥimṣ. Referring to the Rwāla and calling them *shuj'ān al-jazīra*, the "heroes of Arabia," he says that they are a people with many camels, one individual owning perhaps four or five

[154]Muḥammad ibn Ḥamad al-Bassām, *Kitāb al-durar al-mafākhir fī akhbār al-'arab al-awākhir*, manuscript microfilm in the library of the American University of Beirut, p. 134. See also pp. 96–134.

hundred of them. He mentions that their territories lie in the Nuqra region between the Balqā' and the Ḥawrān;[155] and if this is correct, it indicates that the Rwāla migrated to the lands of Syria in this same period in which Muḥammad al-Bassām wrote.

In another book, a history by the priest Mikhā'īl Burayk al-Dimashqī entitled *Ta'rīkh al-Shām* and covering the years 1132–97/1720–82, it is said that word reached the city of Damascus that the military detachment (*jarda*) that went out to meet the pilgrimage caravan had been plundered by the Banū Ṣakhr, who had killed many of its soldiers; Mūsā Pāshā, governor of Sidon, had fled "stripped naked and barefooted." The place where the sack had occurred was the region of Ma'ān, this on 20 Dhū l-Ḥijja 1170/5 September 1757. He then says:

> Meanwhile, Damascus was in such a state of blockade, detriment, and anxiety for lack of word about the pilgrims and the paucity of those who had any information on how they had fared. Then, on the night of 16 Ṣafar 1171 (20 October 1757), the bad news arrived that the pilgrimage caravan had been plundered in its entirety, looted by Qa'dān al-Fāyiz, shaykh of the bedouins of the Banū Ṣakhr, and his tribesmen as well as some others. The cause of this was that when the pilgrims reached the citadel of Tabūk they were unable to proceed further, since they had heard that the above-mentioned bedouins were on the rampage along the route. They thus remained besieged in Tabūk for 22 days. . . .The Pāshā was not familiar with how to appease the bedouins and make good his escape, and instead, in his ignorance, loaded up the caravan and set out. When it drew near to Dhāt Ḥājj the bedouins attacked it by surprise: an untold number of people, both soldiers and pilgrims, were killed, the bedouins triumphed, and they plundered the caravan in its entirety and seized the *maḥmal*. The Pāshā fled with his head intact and returned to the citadel of Tabūk with only three other persons. These people and all these spoils fell as booty into the hands of the bedouins in Ṣafar

[155] *Ibid.*, p. 135.

> 1171 (October 1757). A number beyond counting died or were killed, most of the others starved to death, and none save a few reached Damascus....Damascus donned clothes of mourning and draped itself in the veil of disgrace.[156]

He also refers in his book to the bedouins of ʿAnaza in his reports for the year 1188/1774:

> In this year the Baghdad caravan, bearing wealth uncountable, was plundered at the hands of the bedouins of ʿAnaza, who had already taken the Mecca caravan. A mood of gloom and disgrace thus came to fall over Damascus.[157]

Similarly, in a work on the history of al-Maʿarra, we find that in 1189/1775 the governor of Ḥimṣ, ʿAbd al-Raḥmān Bey al-ʿAẓm, wanted to make an attack on the Mawālī bedouins with a small contingent from the army. There was a battle between them and the bedouins; the bedouins captured them, looted them even of their clothing, took the governor prisoner, and killed a colleague of his.[158] Among the events for 1276/1859, some of the last al-Ghazzī records on the history of the bedouins in the *Nahr al-dhahab*, his history of Aleppo, we find that in one of the collective volumes owned by his father he read:

> When sunset had passed on Wednesday, 5 Muḥarram (5 August 1859), there advanced on Aleppo bedouins of various tribes (*firaq*)—such as the ʿAnaza, Ḥadīdīyīn, Baqqāra, Ghasāsina, and others—numbering over 4000 coming to the aid of the insurgents. But the bedouins were defeated.[159]

Returning to al-Jundī's history of al-Maʿarra, we find among reports for 1317/1899 record of an incident of a very recent date:

> The army killed one of the *amīrs* of the Mawālī, a man by the name of ʿIzzū, whose oppression had weighed heavily

[156]Mikhāʾīl Burayk al-Dimashqī, *Taʾrīkh al-Shām* (Ḥarīṣā, 1930), pp. 45–46.
[157]*Ibid.*, p. 101.
[158]Al-Jundī, *Taʾrīkh Maʿarrat al-Nuʿmān*, II, 336.
[159]Al-Ghazzī, *Nahr al-dhahab*, III, 379–80.

> upon the people. He would come to a village and order its shaykh to bring forth to him whatever clothing, coffee, wheat, barley, and other things that he needed. If the shaykh refused or tarried, 'Izzū would put the village to the torch and kill any person or animal that came to his sight. He was finally killed, and his death was a relief for the region of Ḥamāh, al-Ma'arra, and Aleppo.[160]

The fullest Arabic source on the bedouins for this period after the era of Amīr Fakhr al-Dīn ibn Ma'n is probably Amīr Ḥaydar al-Shihābī's history of Lebanon in the time of the Shihābī *amīrs*, the period of 1109–1248/1697–1832. In this work he gives some information about the bedouins in the last part of the eighteenth century and the early years of the nineteenth. In reports for 1178/1764 we find him referring to an incident indicating that the bedouins were taking fees from government officials for matters pertaining to the pilgrimage: we are told that in this same year the Commander of the Pilgrimage, Ḥusayn Bey Kashkash, a bold and courageous man, set out with the pilgrimage caravan from Egypt and made both the outward and return journeys without paying any fees to the bedouins. Concerning him al-Shihābī states that he killed their shaykh, Shaykh Hazzā'.[161] Among reports for 1223/1808 he mentions that the pilgrimage caravan returned to Damascus without reaching Mecca, because of the people's fear of the Wahhābīs. He says:

> In that year one of the slaves of Shaykh Muhannā al-Fāḍil, shaykh of the 'Anaza bedouins, came to Damascus bearing word of the approach of the Wahhābīs and saying that the shaykh of the approaching warriors had sent letters to such other Wahhābī bedouins as the Banū Ṣakhr, Ghiyāth, Fid'ān, and Wild 'Alī, asking them to come to join him.[162]

Among his reports for 1228/1813 we read that war broke out between the bedouins of 'Anaza, led by their shaykh Muhannā al-Fāḍil,

---

[160] Al-Jundī, *Ta'rīkh Ma'arrat al-Nu'mān*, I, 211, 212.
[161] *Lubnān fī 'ahd al-umarā' al-shihābīyīn*, I, 65.
[162] *Ibid.*, II, 534, erroneously reading al-Fiyāt for the correct al-Ghiyāth.

and the bedouins of the Fid'ān; the bedouins of Muhannā suffered a tremendous defeat and the Fid'ān captured their womenfolk.[163] Unfortunately, however, Amīr Ḥaydar does not mention where in the Syrian lands this battle occurred. He states that in the same year another battle was fought between the Banū Ṣakhr and the Sardīya, on the one hand, and the Dūkhī l-Sumayr, accompanied by the forces of Dālātīya, on the other. The Banū Ṣakhr and Sardīya triumphed over Dūkhī and its supporters and inflicted a terrible defeat upon them; more than half of the Syrian army perished.[164]

Among his reports for 1230/1814 it is said that there came to the land of Ḥamāh from parts of Najd bedouins called by the name of the Fid'ān, and these camped on the eastern side of the Orontes. They were more than 20,000, including both horsemen and infantry, and were of diverse tribes (*ṭawā'if*): the Sbā'a, Āl Hadhdhāl, al-Jarbā, al-Nabī, and other people.[165] It was not their custom to come to this area, since it was the camping land of Shaykh Muhannā al-Fāḍil and his tribesmen and al-Dray'ī and his tribesmen, and between them and the Fid'ān bedouins there was long-standing hostility. Their arrival thus worried the vizier of Syria, and he accordingly ordered them to withdraw from the land of Ḥamāh. In defense of their action, however, they said that the reason they had come was the straitened living conditions in their own land, and that they were intending to stay in the grazing lands for two months during the spring, if the vizier would allow them to do so. They also promised him that they would undertake to protect the pilgrims, and for lower fees than those charged by their enemies. The vizier did not agree to this, however, and proceeded to muster the army to repel them and call for assistance from the governor of Sidon, the district head (*mutasallim*) of the 'Akkār region, and Muhannā al-Fāḍil and al-Dray'ī and their bedouins. His deputy Ibrāhīm Pāshā set out from Aleppo with 3000 men, the head of 'Akkār came with about 1000 horsemen to the city of Ḥamāh, and between them and the newly arrived bedouins there was fighting that lasted for a period of fifteen

[163] *Ibid.*, III, 592.

[164] *Ibid.*, reading Sakhr for Ṣakhr and al-Sa'īr for al-Sumayr, both of which are mistakes.

[165] *Ibid.*, III, 607, erroneously reading Fidh'ān for al-Fid'ān, al-Sabā'a for al-Sbā'a, and al-Jaryā for al-Jarbā.

days. Every day they fought one another near the waters of Salamīya from the morning until the evening. Ibrāhīm Pāshā and his forces were defeated, the head of 'Akkār and the bedouins of Muhannā held their ground, the shaykh of the Sbā'a and a number of his tribesmen were killed, and the Fid'ān occupied the area between Aleppo and Ḥamāh. Later they withdrew, then after a time raided the tribes of Muhannā, looted them of their tents and camels, and left them with nothing beyond the women and children.[166]

In accounts for 1233/1817 al-Shihābī mentions the victory of Ibrāhīm Pāshā, son of Muḥammad 'Alī Pāshā, over the Wahhābīs and refers to the coming of the 'Anaza to Ḥamāh and their agreement with Mullā Ismā'īl al-Dālātī through a group of bedouins living at that time in Ḥamāh. He also gives the names of their shaykhs: al-Ḍwayhī, al-Ḥmaydī, Nāṣir al-Muhannā, and Mish'āl al-Hadhdhāl. The district head of Ḥamāh found the bedouin alliance with Mulla Ismā'īl intolerable and so complained about the matter to the governor of Damascus. Meanwhile, the bedouins of 'Anaza attacked Ḥamāh, took captive the bedouin tribes living in the town, and plundered them of 45,000 sheep. These tribesmen were from the Banū Khālid, al-Ṭūqān, and al-Bashākim, and they had been paying the government taxes like the rest of the citizens of Ḥamāh. The vizier of Damascus fitted out an army to fight the 'Anaza and followed the bedouins as they fled before them to Zawr Baghdad.[167]

Among reports for 1234/1818 he mentions the return of Ṣāliḥ Pāshā, governor of Damascus, from Jerusalem. Upon his arrival, some of the bedouins living in the land of the Ḥawrān (there were the tribes of al-Sirḥān, al-Masālīkh, and Banū Ṣakhr) came to attend at his audience hall, and when they met him he ordered that three of their leading notables be seized and killed. He committed this outrage against them although no crime had been perpetrated by them against him. Then he sent the army against them, so they abandoned their tents and fled to the rugged countryside. The troops descended upon their tents in search of plunder and loot, and a troop of about 300 soldiers turned aside to the bedouins fleeing with their families to the rocky terrain,

[166] *Ibid.*, III, 607–608.
[167] *Ibid.*, III, 636–38.

hoping to pillage these people as well. But the bedouins rushed back at them, defeated them, and wreaked great slaughter among them; then they turned their attention to the soldiers who were in their tents and triumphed over them as well. That day the bedouins killed about 300 of the Pāshā's soldiers and took their weapons and horses as booty. The Pāshā, with his weakness exposed, returned to Damascus frustrated and defeated and was regarded as an object of great shame.[168]

Among his reports for 1236/1820, al-Shihābī states that during the stay of Darwīsh Pāshā, the governor of Damascus, and his retainers in the Ḥawrān, all of the leading notables of the ʿAnaza bedouins came to see him and an increasingly friendly relationship developed between them. These elders were Dūkhī, Ṣāliḥ, Ḥammūd al-Ḍwayḥī, Khalaf al-Ṭayyār, Nāyif al-Shaʿlān, and his cousin Midhwad, and from their tribesmen the governor and those with him bought a number of horses.[169]

It was in this period, then, that Muḥammad ʿAlī Pāshā rose to power in Egypt, put an end to the Mamlūks, carried out his conquests in Nubia and the Sudan, and achieved success in the expeditions in which he sent his son Ibrāhīm Pāshā to fight the Wahhābīs between 1816 and 1818. Then in 1831 he decided to send Ibrāhīm to occupy Syria, the Sublime Porte having failed to make good on its promise to make him governor of Syria. Here there is not space for studying the history of this campaign, in which, after Ibrāhīm's arrival in Syria, he brought along a contingent of Egyptian bedouins known as the Hanādī. The most important of his battles with the bedouins of Syria and his contacts with them find mention in the Syrian documents in the Egyptian royal archives published by Dr. Asad Rustum in four volumes (for the years from 1231/1816 to 1255/1839). I thus decided to keep to what was published in these documents, referring to their numbers in the sequence, along with the documents—recorded in their historical order—on the bedouins recorded by the English consuls in Aleppo, Damascus, and Jerusalem who consolidated their imperial and

[168] *Ibid.*, III, 630, 642, where he repeats an abbreviated version of the report and errs in giving the name of the tribe of al-Sirḥān. In one place he gives the name of this old established tribe of the Ḥawrān as al-Sirḥāl, and in another as al-Sirkhān.
[169] *Ibid.*, III, 674.

economic interests with the bedouins in that era.[170] These I have presented as appendices, and it will be noticed that some of them bear reference to the same developments mentioned in the reports we have cited from the Arab historians for the recent period.

[170]See Hitti, Jurji, and Jabbur, *Ta'rīkh al-'arab*, p. 832 [= Hitti, *History of the Arabs*, p. 734].

CHAPTER XX

THE TRANSFORMATION OF BEDOUIN LIFE

H.St. John Philby once spoke with me on the question of the evolution that was beginning to transpire in modern bedouin life. As he put it, whenever he passed by a bedouin encampment in his early days in Arabia, the people living there would refuse to allow him to continue past them without sampling a bit of life with them, or at least having a drink of milk from their she-camels. This he saw as a sign of their dedication to the values of noblehearted generosity and hospitality. He then said: "These days life has begun to change. When you pass near one of the camps, it now turns out that the bedouin boys are stopping you to get you to buy camel's milk from them, and in most cases this milk is mixed with water." This is not true of all bedouins, however, and one cannot take it as an indication that the bedouin has given up dedication to hospitality and noblehearted generosity: in saying this, Philby meant that whether we liked it or not, bedouin life was beginning to change.

The authorities in most parts of the Arab world have unquestionably facilitated the means for the sedentarization of the bedouin tribes in their lands, some of them making this one of the policy objectives pursued by their governments. But we must be aware of the fact that certain tribes in interior desert regions still adhere to their traditional ways, and that change has affected them only to a limited extent.

Manifestations of change are most clearly evident in the situation faced by the al-Shawāya bedouins, whom special circumstances have obliged to shift from camel tending to sheep herding. Such manifestations appear, before anything else, in the means of transport, and the automobile has become a familiar feature among them. It sometimes carries them to and from the towns when they are far removed from such centers, it transports water for their livestock if they are far away from water sources, and it may occasionally carry livestock and other cargo to the towns if the situation requires. This means of transportation has made it easy for the bedouins to make firmer contact with settled life and its lifestyles, and to borrow from them.

Perhaps the most important phenomenon of change, and the most drastic in its impact on their life, is their abandonment of raiding. Since their earliest times the raid had been an important factor in the lives of most bedouins. They used to teach their sons how to ride horses and to shoot so they could be warriors in expeditions, and a bedouin girl would look with favor on a man wishing to marry her if he was a warrior horseman known for his fortitude and strength on expeditions and his courage in battle. This state of affairs prevailed into the early 1940s, when Mandate and other government authorities, in order to put a complete stop to raiding, began to enact regulations prohibiting this practice, to conclude treaties with neighboring countries, and to arrange agreements among the shaykhs. One after another, each of the Arab states enacted laws proscribing raids and set down among the provisions of its constitution clauses aimed at sedentarizing the bedouins. Such was the action of Syria, for example, when the new Syrian Constitution of 5 September 1950 was promulgated, including in Article 158 one clause enjoining the government to act to settle the bedouins and another setting forth a phased program to ensure that this would be achieved.[1] Syria also acted to pass a special law for the tribes, the provisions of which were applicable to the tribes it listed in a special table.[2]

Here it must be mentioned that in 1956 an altercation occurred among some members in the Syrian Chamber of Deputies over the issue of fixing the proportion of settled individuals a tribe must have in order to be considered "sedentarized," and over the question of exempting from military service the young men of certain tribes considered to

[1]Aḥmad al-'Akkām, *Al-'Ashā'ir al-sūrīya wa-taḥḍīruhā* (Damascus, 1951), p. 117.

[2]*Ibid.*, pp. 124–33.

be sedentarized. The Chamber decided in favor of the tribes, despite the opposition of some deputies who saw this as a factor that would encourage landowning tribes to revert to nomadism, since they were treated differently from the settled folk themselves, and especially since lands amounting to hundreds of thousands of dunums in various places had already been distributed to them. The opposition claimed that every tribe that owned land should be considered as sedentarized, and should submit to the same regulations and laws that applied to the settled folk.

The socio-demographic impact of the bedouin element in society, where the question of land tenure is concerned, may be seen from some data on the areas of land utilized by the tribes in Syria, as compiled by Aḥmad al-ʻAkkām, representative of the Directorate of Tribes, for the Syrian Chamber of Deputies.[3] His figures calculate the numbers of individuals in the tribes and the land areas in dunums. As one can see from the table of this data below, the population of the landowning tribes three decades ago did not amount to more than 140,000, while they owned about three million dunums of land.[4]

It must also be pointed out here that the first ruler who sought to put an end to raids and prevented the tribes from attacking one another, disturbing the peace, or making trouble on the routes used by pilgrims, was King ʻAbd al-ʻAzīz Āl al-Suʻūd. He consolidated security in his kingdom and prevented the tribes of Najd and others in northern Arabia from causing trouble, as had occurred in centuries past when, because of drought or out of their fondness for the raid, tribes migrated with their families into the territories of other tribes. The situation eventually reached the point that if a supplicant made a request, no migration could take place without agreement being reached with the other tribes and with the state on whose lands the tribesmen were located. Once, for example, I actually saw tribes from the Najd grazing their camels in the pastures of the Syrian Desert, with the permission of the Syrian government and in agreement with their fellow bedouins. The government of Jordan, as we shall see later, followed a policy similar to that of King ʻAbd al-ʻAzīz.

[3]See the newspaper *Al-Ra'y*, 30 (April 1956), no. 581.

[4]Also mentioned are landless tribes whose members number only about 15,000.

Land Owned by Syrian Bedouin Tribes (1956)

Tribe	*No. of Individuals*	*Area of Land (dunums)*
Al-Rwāla	20,000	81,321
Al-Sbā'a Bṭaynāt	6,000	19,450
Al-Sbā'a al-'Abda	12,000	100,965
Al-Fid'ān Wild	13,000	129,095
Shammar al-Zawr	8,000	598,480
Shammar al-Khrāṣa	12,000	614,280
Banū Khālid	8,000	233,888
Al-Fawā'ira	3,000	145,105
Al-Ḥadīdīyīn	30,500	385,640
Al-Mawālī al-Shamālīyīn	10,000	55,300
Al-Mawālī al-Qiblīyīn	6,000	86,160
Al-Bū Khamīs	2,500	20,300
Al-Mhayd	2,000	91,865
Al-Byār	2,300	61,500
Al-Wahā	4,300	44,340

Another manifestation of change was that many bedouin youths known for their courage and fond of war enlisted in the army and served the state in which they were located. From these, tribal regiments—mounted on camels—were formed to assist the state in its role of maintaining security in the desert and elsewhere. The dress of these bedouin soldiers differed from that of their other nomadic brothers, and their food and drink to a great extent varied from that to which their fathers and forefathers had been accustomed. This trend spread to their families and offspring, and their children began to share in the lifestyle, upbringing, and also the schools of the children of the towns. In their dwellings one began to see types of food previously unknown to the bedouin, and their style of dress became similar to that of the people of the towns in or near which these bedouins lived.

Another feature of change has been the settlement of bedouins on farms, where they moved into homes of mud-brick or stone. Some of these farms, possessed of wells or small springs, were deserted, their earlier inhabitants having abandoned them in centuries past. This was due to the ravages of the bedouins themselves, whose depredations were such that they forced the local residents to move to the large villages and to abandon their farms. The authorities took over ownership of these places and made grants of some of them to bedouin shaykhs; or, when no one in the desert contested their right to do so, the shaykhs took possession of these sites themselves. On some such farms I myself have seen hair tents pitched near houses of stone or clay. By way of illustration, I recall the al-Bārida estate in Syria where cotton was cultivated, trees planted, and many kinds of vegetables grown, and where bedouin and settled cultivators intermingled. And I could point to more than twenty such farms and villages between al-Qaryatayn and Ḥimṣ. It is obvious that the governments in the Arab states took to encouraging this kind of change and settlement. They began to make grants of land for cultivation to some bedouins in order to settle them, and helped them to build stone houses. Similarly, on one of my visits to the desert of Jordan I also saw several places where hair tents were pitched in the open space adjoining a stone house or somewhere else close by.

When I began to study the actions taken by the Jordanian government on this matter, Ṣayyāḥ al-Rūsān, one of my students who

Figure 77: Bedouins in the Jordanian army.

graduated from the American University of Beirut and became an official for tribal affairs, sent me a long report on the steps taken to sedentarize the bedouins in Jordan. That was in 1959, and the report included the proposals made for the future, as well as a statement on the tribes and clans, the names of the new villages created and settled by bedouins, and the efforts exerted by the government to settle the others. In this report it was stated that the Desert Patrol (*Qūwat al-bādiya wa-l-ṣaḥrā'*) had been in existence in Jordan since 1927. But the maintenance of security and the prevention of raiding were not achieved until 1931, when the government conceived of the idea of taking drastic measures to put an absolute end to the raid and tried to find sources of livelihood for the bedouins. It admitted a large proportion of the tribes' young men to the Desert Patrol, and this helped to consolidate security and to put a stop to raiding. The second step was to grant to certain shaykhs who had a feel for settled life and tranquility government lands that they were to exploit and settle. The government also encouraged them to plow and plant the fields and to dig wells for drinking water.

When the bedouins took note of the authority of the regime and saw the gains their settled brothers were realizing, with government assistance, from agricultural production, they in turn spontaneously rushed to try to attain government lands for agricultural exploitation. They began to found new villages, eventually numbering about 150, and their eagerness for acquiring land and living off its yields reached such a point that incidents of unrest would break out over a plot of not more than a single dunum. This was what encouraged the bedouins to try to register the land in their own names, to exploit it, and to settle on it.

In turn, the government took the initiative of establishing schools to educate their children: the bedouins were agreeable to sending their children to these schools, especially since learning was offered free of charge and their children were likewise also sometimes given books, meals, and some clothing. Roads were built between these new villages and also between them and the capital. Further proposals were made for digging artesian wells between every three or four villages, ensuring that clean drinking water was available to the inhabitants, repairing old water sources, providing agricultural loans and modern agricultural equipment, establishing special clinics, and providing necessary medical treatment and services.

Al-Rūsān's report was accompanied by a table listing the tribes and their subsections one by one, and the numbers of villages they had settled in up to that year (1959). There were 112 villages for 112 clans from the tribes of Banū Khālid, al-Sirḥān, al-Sardīya, al-Masā'īd, al-'Uẓāmāt, al-Sharafāt, al-Shar'a, and Banū Ṣakhr, this in addition to the tribes, represented by 49 clans, residing in the district of Ma'ān and in the vicinities of Bethlehem, al-Karak, Hebron, Nablus, 'Ajlūn, and al-Balqā'. This was indeed a momentous change.

I myself witnessed some of these phenomena and traveled the roads laid down among those villages, where I was privileged to have the company of *'aqīd* Barakāt Ṭrād. A bedouin of the al-Khurshān tribe, he himself had earlier participated in raids with his father. His son had become a townsman holding an engineer's diploma and had married a girl from Amman who had a college preparatory high school graduation certificate.

The industrial ability of the bedouins also began to change, especially in the areas where companies were operating. In his book *Al-Badw wa-l-qabā'il al-raḥḥāla fī l-'Irāq*, Makkī al-Jumayyil states that 38 percent of the workers and technical employees of the Kuwait Oil Company were bedouins who had mastered machine skills, held decision-making positions in the company, and distinguished themselves in its administration.[5] At the same time, he pointed out that 900 workers lived in collective dwellings or in the villages close to their work.[6] And in his book he did not miss the opportunity to propose many ways for settling the bedouins, sedentarizing them, training specialists to lead the way in educational activity,[7] and involving the Ministry of Economic Affairs in the settlement program.[8]

Among the factors that have facilitated the bedouin's accommodation to sedentarization is the fact that his shaykhs are themselves generally the bedouins closest to sedentarization, and those who shift

[5]Makkī al-Jumayyil, *Al-Badw wa-qabā'il al-raḥḥāla fī l-'Irāq* (Baghdad, 1956), p. 133.

[6]*Ibid.*

[7]*Ibid.*, p. 64.

[8]*Ibid.*, pp. 172–74.

Figure 78: Bedouin women working picking cotton.

to it first. Hence, as he has followed the example of his shaykh, there is no disgrace in settling down, especially if it paves his way to a life better than what he had previously.

In some villages I have seen bedouin women working in the fields of wealthy villagers during the cotton-picking seasons (as we can see in Figure 78 above), apparently attracted by the wages. They find nothing wrong with such work, which would have been of only rare occurrence in previous generations.

A further manifestation of change is their concern for health and the sick, their faith in the preeminence of the urban medical profession, and their recourse to the health institutions and hospitals of the towns for treatment. As mentioned previously in this book, the records of the Danish hospital in the town of al-Nabk between 1953 and 1955 showed that in one year bedouins accounted for about a third of those treated. And to this we may additionally note the interest they take in the events occurring around them and the effort they make to understand them, thanks to the various broadcast media and the portable, economical, and readily available radios to which they can listen. I recall that in the

1940s I visited a Rwāla camp and saw only a single radio receiver, that in the possession of the townsman who repaired weapons, metal household effects, and other items for the bedouins. When I returned some years later there were many who owned transistor radios, which made it an easy matter for the bedouin to enrich his information concerning the world and his knowledge of its news and of events and discoveries that have occurred. The bedouin is inquisitive by nature, and when you meet him in the desert he will ask you for whatever news you may have. By the 1960s the transistor radio had placed at his disposal an informant that reports on command, furnishing him with various kinds of information and broadening his knowledge and culture.

Another development in the life of the bedouins is that when raiding came to an end, most of them gave up the horse-raising that had been done in centuries past. In a report compiled by one of the English consuls in the early 1860s, one reads that in all of the desert lands of northern Arabia the tribe of Rwāla had about 12,000 tents, and that there were other bedouins who, leaving out Shammar al-ʿIrāq, came to about 60,000 tents. Estimating that between one and three horsemen lived in each tent, the consul was led to the conclusion that the horses in bedouin possession numbered in the tens of thousands.

This number has dropped precipitously today. It would not be surprising to discover that today the horses in all of northern Arabia do not number a tenth of what they once did, and this applies not only to horses, but also to tents and desert dwellers. It may be that certain epidemic diseases wiped out many of the sons of the desert and some of their animals at a time when there was no means of protection against the epidemics. Whatever the case may be, the cost of raising horses in these recent days of bedouin life has been driven up by the high price of fodder. This expense cannot be avoided in certain seasons, but the bedouin is too poor to afford it. Horses have thus become rare; the bedouins used to raise horses for raiding, but raiding has come to an end. I noticed this for myself when I visited the camps of both camel-raising nomads and the ʿArab al-Shawāya, where in a tribe numbering about a hundred tents I saw no more than a few horses, not exceeding ten head.

What applies to horses applies to a certain extent to camels and to the number of tents. In times past there was in most parts of the Arab world a brisk market for camels to carry goods and supplies in the caravans and to work in certain agricultural sectors. The market for camels was especially lively in Egypt, where males too were sold, slaughtered, and their meat offered at fixed prices. The same occurred in Damascus itself and in other Syrian cities. But eventually the demand for camel meat slackened in Syrian cities, exports of it to Egypt came to a halt, and it ceased to be a required commodity in Syria. Demand for the meat of the camel has not disappeared entirely, but camel owners seeking to fill the needs of the settled folk have generally been compelled to shift to the raising of sheep to ensure their livelihood. This has caused them to give up trips into the heart of the desert and obliged them to keep to the desert fringes and the towns located nearby. This development has in turn further facilitated sedentarization, and with it the life of the old-style bedouin has evolved into a mode of nomadism in which the bedouin becomes semi-nomadic, and finally entirely sedentary.

There is something else that requires our consideration and attention for the impact it has had on the way nomadism has gradually evolved and shifted to a rather sedentary way of life. In the past, the desert used to be rich in wildlife that the bedouin liked to hunt and whose meat he enjoyed. Among these animals were gazelles, which were prevalent in large numbers in most parts of Arabia, especially in the north; oryx, onagers, and stags, which were to be found on most of the mountains surrounding the desert; rabbits, ostriches, and many kinds of birds, especially the bustard and the sand grouse. In hunting these animals and birds the bedouin found enjoyment and a sport rivaled only by that of the raid; the bedouins of Ṣlayb had the amplest share in the pursuit of hunting and in gaining part of their livelihood from it. Today, however, the gazelle is extinct, or nearly so, throughout northern Arabia. The ostrich has disappeared, no oryx survive except for those kept in government game preserves (and recently introduced into the wild), and the onager is gone. Naturally, the bedouin living in his tent began to turn to another source of subsistence in the towns, to life in a new environment, and to dependence on new ways of making a living. By way of illustration, I myself know families in my hometown some of whom are of bedouin origin and others of which are of Ṣlaybī origin—families such as Ṣlaybī, Sanad, and Nazzāl—not to mention the *za'īms* of the town in the last century who were descended from the bedouins of al-Jawf. Today their ranks have produced officers in the Syrian army and high officials of state, not to mention those who hold important posts in commerce and education.

Another factor that has had a major impact on the changing life of the bedouins is that of the oil companies, especially Aramco. This firm has eased the way for many bedouins who had stopped raiding and had contact with some of the towns in the peninsula to settle down and become familiar with townsmen, stone houses, and urban life. The company gave them positions amenable to their dispositions, and hence they began to realize that it is no disgrace for a man to take up certain tasks of manual labor, to supervise workers, to drive a car, and other similar tasks. I have actually seen some of them working in specialized positions in Aramco that they had learned without understanding the reasons or principles underlying their work, in addition to the sons of shaykhs and *amīr*s of bedouin origin who have studied and earned the highest degrees from various universities. Of late these now include the *amīr* who participated in the voyage of one of the space shuttles, the first Arab to take part in such a venture in the quest for knowledge.

There remains the matter of education. Most of the Arab states have adopted measures in their constitutions aiming at the education of the bedouins, and have begun to try through various simple means to spread some degree of education in the camps themselves, such as mobile schools or teachers who travel among the camps to teach the sons of the shaykhs. Some of the sons of the shaykhs have themselves taken to enrolling in the schools of the towns, living in the towns, and dressing like the townsmen, while preserving the customary bedouin headress, the *kūfīya* and *'iqāl* or the *shamla* without the *'iqāl*.

Long ago I saw in the tent of Amīr Fawwāz a teacher, accompanying his son Mut'ib, who was teaching the latter English. Previously the boy had studied in a school in Damascus, his father taking him out during the summer to live in the desert so he would keep in contact with it and with its people, the bedouins. In the tent of Shaykh Ḥadītha in Jordan I saw the sons of the shaykh, all of whom were studying in government schools in Amman, dressed in Western attire. When I was at the American University of Beirut I had the opportunity to teach senior-year students in the University's preparatory department, and among these students was Shaykh Ṣfūq al-Yāwir, son of Shaykh

Figure 79: A blacksmith in the desert. Note the radio antenna stretched between the two tent poles.

'Ajīl al-Yāwir, shaykh of the tribe of Shammar in Iraq, who became shaykh after his father. Indeed, during my university days I taught a student of bedouin origin, the late Farḥān Shbaylāt, who later became an ambassador for his country, Jordan; in addition, scores of sons of the tribes in Jordan came to differ not a whit from the townsmen.

In bringing this study to a close, and while discussing recent changes in bedouin life, I must draw attention to the fact that no matter how much the authorities in the Arab countries try to put an end to nomadism, or to settle the bedouins entirely, especially those tending camels, they will never achieve this so long as any part of the Arabian peninsula is covered by desert steppes or sands. Perhaps it is a good thing that there should be bedouins making use of these desert lands to raise camels: as the Rwāla claim, "When camels were created, the Rwāla were created to herd them." The demand for meat for human consumption has certainly not decreased from previous levels, and will rise with the increasing population in the cities, as we have witnessed over the past twenty years in all Arab countries. The best course of action for Arab governments to adopt would thus be to provide such bedouins as these with means of subsistence in the desert lands, marshaling all modern means possible to the promotion of this task. The possibilities include afforestation of the mountains near the desert and protection of the forested area (as at Jabal al-Bal'ās), in consideration of the increased level of rainfall in the winter; restoration of old ruined dams, like the al-Bārida dam, for example; construction, where possible, of new dams to hold back the waters of the flash floods flowing down from the mountains surrounding the desert; the creation of broad lakes, like those that once existed in some regions; and digging artesian wells where ground water is found.

At the same time, approximate territorial boundaries must be fixed for the various tribes in each region, especially in the northern desert, so that matters that arise among these tribes do not become causes for conflict. Other boundaries should be fixed between those regions set aside for grazing and bedouins and those suited to agriculture and settlement. Were this course of action to be followed, I see nothing that would prevent the entire Syrian Desert and its fringes from becoming one of the regions richest in both animal life and agriculture, and enjoying new resources in areas that the great rivers do not reach.

APPENDICES

APPENDIX I

Syrian Documents on the Bedouins from the Royal Egyptian Archives

1

From Asad Rustum, *Al-Uṣūl al-'arabīya li-ta'rīkh sūriyā fī 'ahd Muḥammad 'Alī Pāshā* (Beirut, 1933), I, on the bedouins, political documents for 1247/1831–32:

No. 30, I, 78–79, from Ibrāhīm Pāshā to Shaykh Maḥmūd and Shaykh Sulaymān 'Abd al-Hādī:

To the pride of our honored and esteemed shaykhs, Shaykh Maḥmūd and Shaykh Sulaymān 'Abd al-Hādī: We have previously sent Militia Commander Ḥusayn Āghā Qāzān, accompanied by 130 cavalrymen, to protect Nazareth and Tiberias, and we have dispatched to you our order that you are to act in unison with him on the matter of this protection, the safeguarding of the populace, and the prevention of bedouin depredations against them. We have now also sent Militia Commander 'Alī Āghā 'Awn Allāh with 94 cavalrymen to help Shaykh Burayk protect al-Marj, and Militia Commander Muḥammad Āghā al-'Aynāwī with 55 cavalrymen to take up positions in Jisr al-Majāmi' to protect the area. Likewise, as concerns the above-mentioned regions close by you, you must act in unison with the above-mentioned Militia Commanders on the matter of this protection, the safeguarding of the populace, and the prevention of bedouin depredations against them. We have accordingly issued to you this edict from the Army Bureau of

Acre, that you might act in accordance with and in fulfillment of it, on 20 Jumādā II 1247/[26 November 1831].

No. 74, II, 15–16, 10 Ṣafar 1248/[9 July 1832], from al-Ḥājj Ibrāhīm, Secretary of the Military Bureau, Cairo, announcing the capture of Ḥimṣ. In this document he states that the forces he had with him, which triumphed over the Ottomans at Ḥimṣ and captured the city, included bedouins. These pursued the fleeing Ottomans into the "desert of Ḥimṣ," as he calls it.

2

The most important reports on the bedouins in Syria in the Syrian documents of the Royal Egyptian Archives, published by Dr. Asad Rustum in 4 volumes, in consecutive order according to their date of issue, from 1231/1816 to 1256/1841:

No. 47, 11 Ramaḍān 1231/[7 July 1816], from an anonymous official to Muḥammad 'Alī Pāshā, telling him that the bedouins of 'Anaza in Syria are pleading that they are unable to send the required number of camels for the expedition against the Ḥijāz. His Highness' representative is returning with his mission unsuccessful.

No. 923, 16 Dhū l-Ḥijja 1247/[17 May 1832], from Muḥammad 'Alī Pāshā to his son Ibrāhīm Pāshā, commanding him to mount a strike against the bedouin tribes in order to take the camels from them.

No. 1377, 19 Ṣafar 1248/[18 July 1832], from Ibrāhīm Pāshā to the Khedivial Bureau, mentioning that some of the bedouins of the Hanādī, along with their shaykh, al-Ḥājj 'Alī Barakāt, are sojourning in Gaza.

No. 1790, 16 Rabī' II 1248/[12 September 1832], from Ibrāhīm Yakan Pāshā to Ibrāhīm Pāshā, concerning the bedouins of 'Anaza, their aggression against the pilgrims from Iran, and the appointment of Muḥammad Bey as leader of the clans of the Mawālī.

No. 1923, 4 Jumādā I 1248/[29 September 1832], from Salīm Bey Salaḥdār, the Khedivial Secretary, to Ibrāhīm Pāshā, with reference to Shaykh Ḍāhir Kulayb, shaykh of the Sardīya bedouins and District Resident in al-Mzayrīb, mentioning that he is dissociating himself from the bedouins of Banū Ṣakhr, offering his obedience, and saying that he is the servant of the Khedive.

No. 2710, 4–6 Shawwāl 1248/[24–26 February 1833], in the Register of Abstracts (*daftar al-khulāṣāt*), letters from the victorious army in which it is specified that the notables of the Banū Ṣakhr must be sent bound in chains to Acre for work in the ships.

No. 2765, 23 Shawwāl 1248/[15 March 1833], from Muḥammad ʻAlī Pāshā to his son Ibrāhīm Pāshā, seeking his opinion on whether he agrees that bedouin warriors should be sent from Egypt to Syria to punish the bedouins of ʻAnaza.

No. 2809, 5 Dhū l-Qaʻda 1248/[26 March 1833], from ʻAbd al-Bāqī Effendī to Sāmī Bey, advising him that the Secretary of the Military Bureau supports the plan proposing to send 900 bedouin warriors from Egypt to punish the bedouins of ʻAnaza in the Syrian Desert.

No. 2977, undated but filed among the documents for 1248/1832–33, from an anonymous official to Ibrāhīm Pāshā, drawing the attention of the headquarters of the High Command to information on the ʻAnaza and details on the current status of ʻAnaza tribes that had crossed the River Murād (*sic.*, probably the Euphrates, *al-Furāt*, is meant).

No. 2983, also undated, but filed under 1248/1832–33, from Aḥmad Bey, *qāʼimaqām* of Damascus, to Muḥammad ʻAlī Pāshā, a document in which he states the reason for his delay in submitting the necessary reports on the rebellion of Dūkhī l-Sumayr, one of the shaykhs of the ʻAnaza bedouins.

No. 2995, from the Adjutant Secretary of the Military Bureau to Muḥammad ʻAlī Pāshā on the question of the camels required from the ʻAnaza bedouins.

No. 3358, 23 Ramaḍān 1249/[3 February 1834], from Muḥammad ʻAlī Pāshā to Muḥammad Sharīf Bey, in which he states that he does not agree to the payment of purses from the Syrian treasury, as had been the custom in the past, to the bedouins of ʻAnaza, Wild ʻAlī, Ḥasan, Banū Ṣakhr, and other tribes.

No. 3387, 19 Dhū l-Qa'da 1249/[30 March 1833], from Muḥammad Sharīf Bey to Sāmī Bey, referring to the loss of the camels that had been taken from the Banū Ṣakhr and stating that the matter must be investigated.

No. 3429, 1250/1834–35, from Muḥammad 'Alī Pāshā to Muḥammad Rashīd Pāshā, complaining about the aggression of the 'Anaza bedouins.

No. 3567, 10 Rabī' I, 1250/[17 July 1834], from Ibrāhīm Pāshā to Muḥammad 'Alī Pāshā, a document in which he says that he appreciates the advantage to be gained by deciding to send a force under the command of the Ma'jūn Āghāsī[1] to Ḥamāh and Aleppo to subdue and pacify the 'Anaza bedouins.

No. 3568, 10 Rabī' I 1250/[17 July 1834], from Ibrāhīm Pāshā to Salīm Bey, assigning him to accompany the Ma'jūn Āghāsī and instructing the two to proceed with their horsemen to Ḥamāh to subdue the 'Anaza brigands (*sic.*, *luṣūṣ 'Anaza*).

No. 3595, 23 Rabī' I 1250/[30 July 1834], from Salīm Bey to Ibrāhīm Pāshā, in which he says that he is informed of the gist of the matter, and advises Ibrāhīm that he has sent certain persons to Mar'ash for purposes of espionage. He also states that the bedouins of 'Anaza have remained quiet since their flight into the interior.

No. 3839, 2 Sha'bān 1250/[4 December 1834], from Muḥammad Munīb Bey (Colonel of the Eleventh Cavalry Regiment) to Ibrāhīm Pāshā, giving reports the gist of which is that the bedouins of 'Anaza and those of Ṣfūf (*sic.*, meaning Ṣfūq, shaykh of the Shammar) are fighting one another in the desert near Karbalā'.

No. 5502, 1254/1838–39, from Muḥammad Sharīf Pāshā to Ibrāhīm Pāshā, concerning the bedouins of al-Ṣlūṭ and their march to the Lijāh.

[1][It is unclear what this official was in Ottoman times. The term *ma'jūn* in Ottoman Turkish (as in Arabic) should refer to pastes or doughy mixtures of various kinds—aphrodisiacs, opiates, or sweets—and the Ma'jūn Āghāsī may thus have been an Ottoman official in the imperial kitchens. But here, in the administration of Ibrāhīm Pāshā in Syria, he clearly has military duties. The title may thus have been an honorific one for commanders of irregular cavalry put to the task of controlling the bedouins. I am grateful to Professors Albert Hourani and Geoffrey Lewis for their suggestions concerning the interpretation of this title.]

They number between 250 and 260 and are afraid of being attacked by 'Anaza, for which reason they are not leaving the Lijāh. If they camp at the wells of al-Qasṭal, they will control the road between Damascus and the Ḥawrān. He therefore requests that a force of cavalry be sent to protect the road.

No. 5507, 23 Jumādā II 1254/[13 September 1838], from Ibrāhīm Pāshā to Ḥusayn Pāshā, informing him that after he had driven the bedouins of al-Ṣlūṭ from the Lijāh and sent them to the camp of Sharīf Bey, he wrote to him ordering him to tend personally to the task of driving them along for a distance of five or six hours' travel and then after that to hand them over to the cavalry so the latter could take them to al-Qunayṭara. He states in this letter that Sharīf Pāshā did not pay heed to his instructions, but rather sent them with an escort of 50 or 60 cavalry without going with them himself. It thus happened that the bedouins plundered the above-mentioned cavalrymen of their weapons, seized everything they had, and reentered the Lijāh, a matter that now causes us to write to Muḥammad Bey, Colonel of the First Ghārdayā Regiment, and to Aḥmad Bey, Colonel of the Infantry Regiment, ordering them to proceed with their forces and take control of the wells from which the bedouins draw their water. This letter is followed by another of the same date from the Secretary of the Military Bureau to Muḥammad Bey, Brigade Commander, concerning how essential it is that this task be carried out and that the bedouins be denied access to the water. The army is warned to be on vigilant watch by night, even if they have to sleep during the day. Under the same no. 5507 there is a long report of 21 Jumādā II [11 September] from one of the officers whose horses had been taken, a man named al-Ḥājj Muḥammad Bulūkbāshī, who submitted his report to the Secretary of the Military Bureau, who in turn sent it on to Muḥammad Sharīf Pāshā. In this report the author advises that the Ṣlūṭ are not rebelling, but rather reacting to the way in which matters pertaining to them are proceeding. If they are ordered to camp in the Ghūṭa region they will do so, or if they are ordered to move on to the Ḥawrān or to the desert, they will camp there; and if they remain in the Lijāh, they will be obedient and abide by all requirements made of them. But they cannot camp in the vicinity of al-Qunayṭara, because it does not have pasturage sufficient for their flocks and herds as well as those of ʻAnaza. If they are issued a command to camp in the Ghūṭa under guarantee of security they will do so; and in the winter, if they were to be issued a command to make their way to al-Qunayṭara they would do so, and during the summer camp in the Ghūṭa. This is what I have been given to understand by their shaykhs—Hantash, Bakhīt, and Rumaysh. With reference to the horses and weapons they have looted, they will keep them with them as security until we appear and present Your Grace with their petition. Should an order be issued guaranteeing their security in one of the specified places, they would abide by it and produce the above-mentioned horses and weapons. He also says:

> I understood from the shaykhs and elders (*al-ikhtiyārīya*) that their intent is to flee and camp among the ʻAnaza with Manṣūr al-Ḍuwayhī, but I replied to them that the ʻAnaza and Manṣūr al-Ḍuwayhī are already loyal subjects, and were you to go there they would seize you and treat you with the utmost severity. They replied: "We bedouins do not treat each other harshly."

With this is another report, dated 21 Jumādā II 1254/[11 September 1838], by Khalīfa Āghā al-Būṣaylī, advising that in light of the situation he made his way to the camps of the bedouins of the Lijāh so as to induce them to depart. He says:

> After the cavalry split up, with groups of ten proceeding each to a different bedouin band, ten cavalrymen and I made our way to the band of the Madālja. When we arrived, I alighted at the tent of Shaykh Rūmīṣ and we found the above-mentioned bedouins split into four groups. The shaykh explained to us that since the bedouins were divided up into four groups, they would flee during the night if we left them without supervision. The most appropriate course of action would thus be to post three cavalrymen with each group. So we split up the cavalrymen, according to his suggestion, so that no one would flee. Two cavalrymen and I remained in the tent of the shaykh. Then

> the shaykh left me, and then returned to say that he had been with Ḥamū Āghā and come back, that Ḥamū Āghā was calming down [the tribesmen], and that in the morning, God Almighty willing, they would set out with us. We thus remained on our guard until after the rising of the moon, when the shaykh arose from beside me and circulated among the bedouins of his group. They came to my group (*kūrla*), and after a time they came to us and seized our horses and weapons, the group including Hantash as well as a band of other bedouins. They and the rest of the bedouin bands struck their tents, set out, took us with them, and kept us—we and our cavalrymen who had split up among their bands—as their companions until we reached al-Zaytūn. There they returned to us some of our horses and weapons, while the rest remained with them. We originally had 55 horses, and they returned 18 of them to us, 37 remaining with them. Of army rifles they took 55, as well as all of the cavalry guns and three swords, except for a sword of mine, which they returned to us. What we understood from them was that they are still loyal, and even if they entered the Lijāh they did not do so in a spirit of rebellion. The only thing they will not do is camp at al-Qunayṭara. Were they to be authorized to camp in the Ghūṭa they would do so.

He states that they are prepared to return the horses and weapons on condition that they be given a guarantee of security, otherwise: "We are sitting amidst stones and will fight to defend ourselves with your rifles."

No. 5780, from Ibrāhīm Pāshā to Ḥusayn Pāshā, referring to a letter dated 26 Jumādā II 1254/[16 September 1838], in which the Chief Adjutant (*bāshmu'āwin*) states that the shaykhs of the Awlād 'Alī (the tribe of Wild 'Alī) and the Jumay'āt can send five or six thousand men and, if circumstances required and they were pressured to do so, they could even send 20,000. The Secretary of the Military Bureau refers to this letter and says: "Now is the time we need men, but we require of them not 20,000 but 500, whom we would undertake to equip with weapons and horses, since within the space of a few days we can have here more than enough horses and weapons for about 6,000 horsemen."

No. 5781, 21 Ṣafar 1255/[6 May 1839], from Muḥammad Bey [the Ma'jūn Āghāsī] to Ibrāhīm Pāshā, to provide the military authorities with news of the bedouin tribes in the vicinity of Aleppo and the Jazīra, informing them that Shaykh Ṣfūq, shaykh of the al-Jarba bedouins (i.e. Shammar), and all the men of his clan, as well as the bedouins of Fid'ān, had come up from Ra's al-Balīkh, near Aleppo, to Edessa. . . .He also advises them that the Sbā'a bedouins, some of the shaykhs of the Fid'ān, and a contingent of nomads from the Ḥawrān, had made camp at a place located between 'Āna and Jubb Dukhaynah.

No. 5950, 24 Jumādā I 1255/[5 August 1839], from Muḥammad Bey, the Ma'jūn Āghāsī, to Ibrāhīm Pāshā, providing the headquarters of the High Command with news of the attack by the clans of Ṣfūq, Fid'ān, and Sbāgh (*sic.*, probably meaning the Sbā'a) against the Syrian clans. The dispatch includes a report on the battle that had taken place between "Māwā" (*sic.*) and his group, on the one hand, and some of these bedouins, on the other, and the author advises that he is studying the possibility of marching against them. On the back of this letter is the following phrase, "Go and strike."

No. 5951, another letter, bearing the same date, from Muḥammad Bey to Ibrāhīm Pāshā, in which he mentions: "The 'Anaza bedouins have attacked the Baghdad caravan while it was on its way to Aleppo."

No. 5960, and in the same folder under the same number (article 12), an order from the Secretary of the Military Bureau to Muḥammad Bey, the Kaftān Āghāsī[2], dated 6 Jumādā II [17 August]: "When you reach Damascus do not take to leisure and idleness; rather, the moment you

[2][This is apparently another military title borrowed from Ottoman usage. In the sultan's court the Kaftān Āghāsī was the official in charge of the furs and robes given as tokens of honor; he was also the officer who went with the pilgrimage caravan to Mecca, charged with the task of investing with a kaftan the Sharīf of Mecca and anyone else the sultan wished to honor. In Ibrāhīm Pāshā's Syria, however, the Kaftān Āghāsī was clearly a military officer (like the Ma'jūn Āghāsī, see n. 1 above) in charge of irregular cavalry active along the desert fringes. I am again grateful to Professors Hourani and Lewis for their assistance with this title.]

reach there, set forth therefrom to punish the Banū Ṣakhr or other tribes there, this so as to intimidate these pigs (*sic.*) in the Ḥawrān."

No. 6028, in the same folder, a letter signed by Muḥammad Sharīf Pāshā, dated 25 Jumādā II [1255/5 September 1839], in which he refers to the bedouins' attack in a previous year on the properties and possessions in Jabal Druze and the Ḥawrān....Another letter signed by Muḥammad Bey, the Kaftān Āghāsī, and dated 19 Jumādā II/[31 August], advising that he had gone forth from Damascus, accompanied by Ismā'īl 'Āṣim Bey, to Jabal 'Ajlūn to punish the culprits, and that while he was passing through the Ḥawrān he learned that the bedouins of Banū Ṣakhr had gone to al-Karak and that the Awlād (Wild) 'Alī and the Rwāla had attacked the populace. He failed in his mission.

Another letter signed by Ma'jūn Āghāsī Muḥammad Bey, dated 29 Jumādā II [1255/[9 September 1839], advises that the bedouins of Ṣfūq had fled after turning many of their sheep loose among some of the clans living in the vicinity of the Khābūr, and that the Ma'jūn Bey will pursue them so as, with the help of God Almighty, to destroy them. Another of 22 Jumādā II [1255/2 September 1839], signed by Ismā'īl 'Āṣim, advises that the question of 'Ajlūn had been settled and that he will now set out for the Lijāh to erect guard towers and punish the bedouins. Another of 29 Jumādā II [1255/9 September 1839], signed by Ma'jūn Āghāsī Muḥammad Bey, advises that he has marched on the Afāḍila and has taken 3,000 head of sheep and goats and 160 rams (*kīsan*, probably meaning *kabshan*) from them. He then left that area, turning eastward to fight the Ṣfūq bedouins, only to learn after five days' march that they had migrated away to the vicinity of Baghdad. A third letter bears a military order, dated 7 Rajab [16 September] and sent to Ma'jūn Āghāsī Muḥammad Bey, which states as follows: "The clans that have submitted have only surrendered when they felt themselves under pressure. So do not let the talk of those of them who have submitted deceive you; rather, fight them until you have intimidated the notables of these clans."

There is a fourth letter, another which is also an order from the Secretary of the Military Bureau, dated 3 Rajab [12 September] and sent to Kaftān Āghāsī Muḥammad Bey. It commands him to launch an attack on the Rwāla, Sirḥān, and Banū Ṣakhr and to plunder their livestock, and sets forth the ways in which these goals are to be realized.

No. 6092, also in a folder containing letters, one of which was signed by Kaftān Āghāsī Muḥammad Bey and sent to Ibrāhīm Pāshā on 29 Sha'bān 1255/[7 November 1839]. The text is as follows:

> We had already destroyed the bedouins of Banū Ṣakhr, acting in accordance with military decree, and laid the current situation before His Majesty; and when we returned to al-'Ayn al-Zarqā', we received an order from the Honorable Sharīf Pāshā in which he said that he has sent three infantry commanders to Jabal 'Ajlūn, and that I am to go there and compel the rebellious shaykhs Barakāt and Ṣalāḥ to submit. I have obeyed his command.

He then relates how he devised a plan, calling upon the shaykh and bedouins of Balqah (meaning the Balqā') and the shaykhs of Jabal 'Ajlūn for assistance. Four days later they brought him the two shaykhs, who came willingly. He gave the two a guarantee of security as a token of benefaction, and also demanded that they surrender the weapons which they had. He took from them 81 rifles, one carbine, and two pistols, and also exacted their pledge of allegiance; in the Ḥawrān and in the environs of Damascus there remained no one who could rebel. In another letter he states that the shaykh called Nimr Salām, from the tribe of Banū Ṣakhr, requested a guarantee of security for himself and for those tenting with him; he granted this to him and ordered them to take up residence in the Old City of Damascus.

Cf. in the Index, under the following numbers:

On the payment of purses to the bedouins, **3358**.

On the Sardīya bedouins: the submission of their shaykh, **1923**.

On the bedouins: their treachery in Gaza, **350**.

On the Mawālī bedouins: their leader Muḥammad Bey, **1790**.

On the Sbā'a bedouins: their position on the struggle between the imperial authorities and the Pāshā, **5781**.

On the bedouins of Ṣfūq (Shammar): their attack on the clans of the Syrian Desert, **950**; their flight, **6028**.

On 'Anaza: the siege of Jaffa, **93**; the need to placate them and offer financial compensation to them, **838**; their attitude toward the Ottoman army, **850**; the need to mount a strike against them to take their camels, **923**; the Egyptian occupation, **1163**; measures taken to impress upon Shaykh Dūkhī the necessity to fulfill the undertakings to which he had pledged himself, **1452**; their aggression against the pilgrims, **1790**; their injurious actions, **2710**; their punishment, **2765**, **2809**; reports concerning them, **2977**; their insubordination, **2893**, **4295**; their camels, **2995**; they are not to receive the purse, **3358**; their acts of aggression, **3429**, **3567**, **3568**; their recourse to peace, **3595**; their fighting with the bedouins of Ṣfūq in the desert near Karbalā', **3839**; they attack the Baghdad caravan, **5951**.

On Shammar: their attitude toward the Egyptian regime, **5363**.

On Banū Ṣakhr: their recalcitrance, **890**; the sending of a force against them, **931**; the completion of preparations to strike them, **941**; transport of army supplies, **1535**; the expedition of Salīm Āghā al-Salaḥdār against them, **1726**; Salīm Bey al-Salaḥdār's victory over them, **1864**; Salīm Bey al-Salaḥdār and their punishment, **1928**; Ma'-jūn Āghāsī Muḥammad Āghā punishes them, **2752**; Shaykh Ḥumaydī al-Ṭurshān begs forgiveness, **2857**; they are not to receive the purse, **3358**; their concentration, **3387**; the problem of the Ḥawrān, **5915**; the march against them, **6028**; their pursuit **6088**; their destruction, **6092**.

On the Syrian Desert: the 'Anaza bedouins excuse themselves from sending camels, **47**.

On the Hanādī bedouins: the pardoning of their shaykhs, **662**; a number of their horsemen are organized and sent to Gaza, **783**; they take up residence in Gaza, **783**; they are agreeable to serve in the army, **912**; the flight of some of them to Egypt, **2163**, **2226**; the rebellion in Palestine, **3507**; their leader Ibrāhīm Āghā al-Ma'jūnī, **3516**; they leave for Gaza, **4738**.

On the Rwāla: the problem of the Ḥawrān, **5915**; the march against them, **6028**.

On the Fid'ān: their attitude toward the struggle between the imperial authorities and the Pāshā, **5781**; their rise against the clans of Syria, **5950**.

APPENDIX II

British Foreign Office Documents on the Bedouins

F.O. 195/170

The earliest of the documents of interest for our concerns here is probably a letter, dated 21 August 1835, from the English consul in Aleppo to the shaykh of the tribes of al-Jbūr, Shaykh Muḥammad Nāṣir. In this letter the consul asks the shaykh to come to an amicable agreement permitting the passage of steamships on the Euphrates, providing for access to al-Baṣra in affection and friendship, and facilitating buying and selling. He informs him that the English Empire has come to an agreement with the Ottoman regime and with Ibrāhīm Pāshā,[1] but that the English would also like to be on friendly terms with the bedouins, especially after an incident in which an Englishman has been wounded during one of the previous caravan journeys. The English have refrained from making a complaint to Ibrāhīm Pāshā, and have ascertained that the incident had occurred accidentally rather than by intent; otherwise, the English, the Ottoman Empire, the Sultan, and Muḥammad ʻAlī would have taken vengeance upon the perpetrators of the incident. The consul at the same time asks the shaykh to write to him and to inform him what he requires in order to facilitate compliance with these requests.

[1] Ibrāhīm Pāshā, son of Muḥammad ʻAlī, whose name is often encountered in the history of the bedouins. The beginning of the Egyptian attack on Syrian territories began in 1831, and by 1832 their occupation of most of the country was complete. They penetrated into Turkey and occupied Konya, and nearly took Istanbul when they reached Kütahya, only 175 kilometers from the Bosphorus.

In the second document, a letter dated October 1835 from the consul to his government, he reports on the migration of some of the 'Anaza tribes from the Syrian side of the Euphrates to Iraq. More than a month later, he follows it with another letter, dated 3 December 1835 and sent to the Foreign Office, in which he mentions that the bedouins of 'Anaza are in conflict with the tribe of Shammar and that the Euphrates is the dividing line between the two tribes, with 'Anaza firmly established on the Syrian side and Shammar on the Iraqi. In the same letter he indicates that 'Anaza is the strongest tribe in the Syrian Desert. It is also the tribe with the greatest fondness for warfare and raiding; in fact, it has begun, in connivance with the Wahhābīs, to mount certain attacks on the regions bordering the desert between Aleppo and the road to Damascus.

In another letter dated 19 December 1836, that is, more than a year after the previous letter, the same consul mentions that the caravan led by an Englishman named James has been subjected to search and plunder by the Iraqi tribes near the town of al-Ḥilla, and indicates that this caravan had been coming from the Gulf after the arrival of the steamer carrying the post from India. He states that the leader of the caravan hired camels and then directed his caravan along the route to al-Ḥilla, where the bedouins searched the postal bags. The people of the caravan then received word that Shammar was occupying the region through which the route to Hīt passed, and so took the route to 'Āna. They were exposed to a severe rainstorm that lasted four days, from 4 to 8 December, and then reached Tadmur ten days after they had left 'Āna and 23 days after their departure from Baghdad.

In another document, a letter by the same consul to the Foreign Office dated 10 February 1837, mention is made of an agreement between the Egyptian government and the bedouins in which the latter agree to provide the camels necessary to transport Syrian stores to the army in the interior. The letter also indicates that due to the presence of the Egyptian army, Syria is calm. About a year later, in another letter dated 22 March 1838, the consul goes on to mention that Ibrāhīm Pāshā has sent an expedition to overrun the Jabal Druze and subdue the Druze, who had previously put part of his army to flight. In another letter of 24 March he indicates that Ibrāhīm Pāshā has taken vengeance upon them; he then marched against the bedouins in the Lijāh and compelled them to surrender.

It is evident that the bedouins of 'Anaza had begun to wreak havoc in the regions they occupied and took to plundering livestock in the pastures. This reached the point that in a report which Consul F.H.S. Wherry submitted to Viscount Palmerston, we find that while the officer who set out to recover the animals seized by the bedouins came back and returned some of the livestock to its owners, he was unable to recover the animals taken by the 'Anaza bedouins, who had gone far out into the heart of the desert. At the same time, Wherry says that the tribe of the Ḥadīdīyīn has tendered their submission to the regime. This report is dated 15 February 1841.

Approximately three months after the date of this report, the same consul sent a letter dated 15 May 1841 in which he reports, concerning the bedouins of 'Anaza, that they are wreaking havoc in the country, and that when the governor, As'ad Pāshā, learned of their appearance on the plains, he sent for two of their shaykhs, Shaykh Ḥawrān and Shaykh Adham, in order to avert destruction in these lands. He came to an agreement with them providing for the appointment of a supreme shaykh to prevent the repetition of such incidents; but for some reason or another Shaykh Adham left Aleppo, gathered a force of about 2000–3000 of his tribesmen, attacked and plundered the Ḥadīdīyīn bedouins, and made off with about 30 herds of sheep. He then advanced on the city, near Indayhī, and said that should he be appointed first chief and allowed the rights formerly exacted by the "Raya" (*ra'āyā*, "flock-owning") shaykhs, he would be responsible for security. The officer in charge assured Adham that he would be the shaykh, but also that he would have to come to Aleppo in order to achieve this objective. Shaykh Adham, however, refused to do so.

On 25 June 1841, the same consul writes a report to the Foreign Office in which he mentions that As'ad Pāshā had decided to take revenge on Adham. He thus assembled a force from the army and on 25 May proceeded to a place near "Gebel Eess,"[2] about six or seven

[2]By this he means Jabal al-Bal'ās. There are those who consider that the name is a corruption of Ba'l Ḥith. The place is still known today as al-Bal'ās, and there are many terebinth trees there.

hours' journey from the city. The consul then says that he decided to mediate in the matter, knowing, as he did, that the army would cause destruction and that the populace would suffer from their presence. So he wrote to Shaykh Adham, asking him to come in person and on the consul's responsibility. He therefore came with 50 horsemen; but he came with the consul's envoys, and along the way they encountered an ambush set by supporters of Shaykh Ḥawrān and other clans. Their aim was to assassinate Adham, as they opposed his appointment as shaykh. The envoys returned and informed the consul of the situation, and said that they had almost been stripped because of their role in the invitation extended to Adham to become shaykh and assume the leadership, and in the agreement with the government. Wherry discussed the matter with the authorities, but its representatives made the excuse that the whole business had been planned without their knowledge; they decided to send a delegation with his envoy, to remain hostages in Adham's tent until his return from Aleppo. Adham was sick, however, so he sent his brother to be appointed as a chief under his command, and the matter ended with the acceptance of his excuse. The expedition returned without having achieved anything. The consul is now awaiting Adham's arrival so he can take him to the authorities for his official appointment, thus putting an end to these disagreements.

On 11 July of the same year, 1841, the consul informs his Prime Minister in a letter that there is no agreement in force between Shaykh Adham and the government to safeguard the desert frontiers and the trade routes that pass through these lands. A caravan of 20 camels carrying goods for delivery to the Euphrates steamer has thus been plundered by a group of about 1000 tribesmen of 'Anaza. He then states that when he informed Adham of the matter, the latter replied that this tribe is not presently in alliance with him, but said that he would try to force the raiders to return what they had plundered. At the same time, he indicated that his health was not conducive to his coming to Aleppo, and asked the consul to mediate with the government on the matter of relocating to the region of Nahr al-Dhahab, usually occupied by the leading shaykh and now occupied by Shaykh Ḥawrān and his supporters. The consul claims that he has communicated this to the authorities, and then says that Shaykh Adham proposed that his nephew Dhiyāb go with some representatives of the government and that they transfer the region from the other bedouins to him. Were this to be done, he would guarantee the protection of the region from unrest. Dhiyāb came and sent to the government a request written for him by the consul; but the government took no action, and Dhiyāb went back in a fury. The consul's report ends with his statement that a group of bedouins has intercepted a caravan coming from Ḥamāh and plundered many things from it.

In another letter of 13 July he mentions news of another caravan of 22 camels on a mission to the Euphrates that has been plundered by the bedouins of 'Anaza under the leadership of Shaykh Musnābī. The consul tried to recover the plundered goods through correspondence with the bedouins, but the raiders' leader refused. He is therefore writing to Istanbul, so that the Porte will in turn write to its representative in Aleppo to pay him the value of the plundered goods and assure the security of the lines of communication. This indicates that the Ottoman Empire was responsible to the English for the safeguarding of the caravans bearing their trade; in case of mishap they had to compensate the traders for their losses.

In another letter dated 2 August 1841, the consul goes on to state that a clash has occurred between the government and the supporters of Shaykh Ḥawrān (of 'Anaza), and that the latter has been killed, though he was the leader with whom the Porte had concluded an agreement and whom it had appointed as shaykh of 'Anaza. In the same letter, the consul points out that in warfare with the government the advantage always lies with the bedouins, first of all, by reason of the swiftness of their horses, and second, because they can endure hardship and live without food for a longer period than the regular army can. Furthermore, when they realize that they cannot persevere in a fight, they flee to the desert, where regular armies cannot overtake them. At the same time, the consul indicates that he has suggested to the primary parties that he himself mediate with the two factions for the sake of keeping the peace. He states that Captain Campbell has proposed that an order be issued to the shaykh of the Wlāda bedouins, allowing his expedition to land and erect an enclosure for the offloading of supplies from arriving steamers, and that the government and its bedouin allies be asked to permit English ships temporarily to unload their cargoes, so as not to overcrowd the river, and to permit commercial exchanges and transactions, responsibility for this to be borne by the shaykh and his bedouin supporters.

About a month and a half later, on 17 September, the consul writes in reference to the fact that the tribes of 'Anaza have begun to penetrate the frontiers of Syria in large numbers, and that they have launched an attack on the desert peripheries with a force of about 6000 men. To subdue them the government sent an army commanded by Aḥmad Pāshā. He made contact with them at Jabbūl, and when he opened fire on them with a first shot from a cannon they fled back across the Euphrates. They again infiltrated across the river into Syria in great numbers, however, and advanced into the area southeast of Aleppo. There they began to occupy regions that had been controlled by tribes, weaker and less influential than they, that were subject to the governor of Aleppo. The weak tribes have thus begun to fall back before the 'Anaza and to take refuge in the lands near the city of Aleppo in order to protect themselves from this tribe. The consul expresses his fear that 'Anaza will advance closer to Aleppo, that in the early spring their advance will extend to the point that it will be difficult for the governor to repel them, and that they will consequently pose a threat to the line of communications between Aleppo and Baghdad, and perhaps even threaten the route from Tripoli through Latakia to Alexandretta as well. He claims that these bedouins will spread out in every direction, the peasants will be forced to abandon their fields and flee before them, and the harvest will fall prey to the raiders. He states that the hirers of draught animals have themselves begun to refuse to hire their camels for the transport of certain common necessities, out of fear of the bedouins. These have actually begun to endanger the main road between Tripoli and Ḥamāh; they have killed some travelers and looted others, and the roads have become unsafe.

On 8 November 1841, Mr. Moore, the consul appointed to succeed Wherry, writes a letter to the Foreign Office concerning the 'Arab al-Shawāyā bedouins, who have camped in the region of Kafrā about four days' journey east of Aleppo. They have refused to submit to the authority of As'ad Pāshā, he reports, and have refused to pay taxes. He then says that an eyewitness told him that he attended a meeting at the tent of their leader, Shaykh Salāma Dandal, at which the *biyuruldu*, the decree requiring their tax payment, was read out to them. They laughed at the emissary, refused to pay, drove off the cavalrymen who were with him, and looted their property. The Shawāyā had earlier been a submissive tribe obedient to the state; but after their agreement with the powerful 'Anaza bedouins, they began to rebel against it. The messenger told Moore that the 'Anaza were beginning to cross the Euphrates with large numbers of camels and livestock which they had taken as booty from the Ghayara (Qayāra) bedouins in the region of Sakarīya, enemies of theirs with whom they were in a state of war, without a one of them paying any heed or attention to the presence of the Turkish authorities. At the end of this letter, the consul mentions that the messenger has been plundered of his property and clothing, but that the documents sent with him have arrived.

On 15 December of the same year, Consul Neale writes in reference to an expedition, of which he has written in previous reports to the Earl of Aberdeen, sent at the command of As'ad Pāshā, governor of 'Urfa, to subdue the bedouins, especially those who had rebelled east of Aleppo. The expedition consisted of 1200 men. The consul then reports receiving word from Tripoli that the trade route is threatened along the road to Ḥamāh, that travelers and caravans are at risk of plunder, and that the 'Anaza bedouins have attacked those of the Mawālī in a region eighteen hours' journey south of Aleppo, taken fifteen prisoners, killed four men, and seized livestock as booty.

On 30 December of the same year, the same consul writes from Aleppo a letter in which he confirms that, as already indicated in his previous reports, the governor in Aleppo cannot keep the peace among the bedouin tribes in that region. He then says to his minister that that Captain Lynch, from the Euphrates expedition, has written to him that the expedition has been compelled to employ some of the 'Anaza bedouins to protect it and its operations, since the governor himself cannot maintain security with his own forces.

F.O. 195/207

On 27 January 1842, the same consul reports that the 'Anaza bedouins have begun to infiltrate across the Euphrates and to advance in large numbers to the area southeast of Aleppo; they have also begun to take over the regions occupied by less important and weaker bedouins who had submitted to the governor of Aleppo. These vulnerable bedouins have thus sought refuge close to the city for protection from 'Anaza. The consul fears that when spring begins 'Anaza will advance in large numbers to the outskirts of Aleppo, and that it will be difficult for the governor to repel them. They will subsequently pose a threat to the Aleppo–Baghdad line of communications, and even to that between Tripoli, Latakia, and Alexandretta, since these bedouins will spread themselves, as he says, in every direction; the peasants will be forced to flee before them, leaving the harvests to fall prey to the bedouins. Even the hirers of draft animals have begun to refuse to hire their camels out for the carriage of goods out of fear of the bedouins ('Anaza). In fact, they already pose a menace to the main road between Tripoli and Ḥamāh: they have killed one person and looted many others, and the roads have become unsafe.

In a letter dated 13 August 1843, also from Aleppo, the consul states that a contingent of 'Anaza bedouins has attacked and plundered of their possessions 30 pilgrims on their way to Mecca. This occurred only a few hours from Aleppo itself.

In a letter sent from Aleppo on 22 April 1843, the consul reports news of the arrival from the desert of bedouins of 'Anaza and other tribes in large numbers, and advises that the semi-sedentary tribes are falling back before them to the settled region under the shelter of the mountains. The villages and routes of trade and communications lie open before the bedouins, and the government has been forced to send 200 cavalrymen to protect the post between Aleppo and Damascus.

In another letter of 22 May 1843, also sent from Aleppo, he again speaks of the coming of 'Anaza, their crossing of the Euphrates, their attacks on the bedouins of Shammar (under the leadership of Ṣfūq Bey), and how they plundered them of horses and livestock. He states that he has already received word that 150 of the Hanādī, once favorable to the governor and the government, have taken part in the fighting with the raiders. As for the bedouins of the Ḥadīdīyīn and other semi-sedentary tribes, they have come bearing gifts for the government.

On 7 June of the same year, the consul goes on to mention an incident in which pilgrims were plundered and their looted property was sold in Aleppo. He also indicates that the force sent by the governor to repel the bedouins near Ḥamāh forced them back to their frontiers between Jabbūl and the Euphrates, and mentions that Shaykh Ibn Muhayd has come offering his respects to the regime and the governor.

As for the ʻAnaza force, it was estimated, as the consul says in his letter, as comprising about 1500 horsemen armed with lances and daggers, about 700 of them carrying rifles; there were about 800 mounted on camels and carrying simple matchlock muskets. The regime sought to placate Sayyid Taḥsīn, who had joined the bedouins, so he would return to his home territory to protect the frontiers. Peace did not last long, however, for the ʻAnaza bedouins soon returned. As the consul says in a letter dated 12 August 1843, they again crossed the Euphrates and attacked some of the villages. A battle took place between the bedouins and the populace and the raiders returned back across the Euphrates, but the region has been under constant threat.

In his letter to the Foreign Office of 13 January 1844, the consul says that the people of many villages between Ḥamāh and Ḥimṣ and their environs, numbering about 400 families, have fled from their villages and taken refuge in other villages between Sarmīn and Khān Tūmān. They have submitted to the governor a petition stating that they are totally ruined, that they owe debts to the people of the city, and that the interest they must pay is 100 percent. The governor of Aleppo has sent word to ʻAlī Pāshā, governor of Damascus, advising him of their predicament. In the latter's reply he has advised that he should send them back to their villages, but the governor of Aleppo has in turn responded that they had left their women and children in the villages and have themselves scattered through the city.

On 9 March 1844, he writes that the shaykh of ʻAnaza, a man named Nāyif, is the one who plundered the Damascus–Baghdad caravan in the previous year, and that he is now twenty hours' traveling distance from Aleppo.

On 15 June 1844, he writes that ʻAnaza has attacked the Turkish garrison in the village of Jabbūl; they have routed the garrison, wounded its commander, and looted the village of its possessions. A contingent of the African Hanādī was with the garrison, and it is said that they sided with ʻAnaza and deserted the garrison. He also indicates that meetings are being held in the palace to formulate a plan to protect the frontiers from the attacks of ʻAnaza and to try to disperse them, this at the appeal of Ibn Ḥubayn and his clan of the Sbā'a, a branch of 'Anaza numbering about 1000 tents. The consul also reports that the shaykh has been won over, given a robe of honor, made responsible for the protection of the line of the Aleppo desert frontier, and charged with preparing for this purpose 200 horsemen who would provisionally take their living allowances and rations from the state for the whole of this season. But he goes on to say that he is not hopeful that this solution will prove successful, since the bedouins do not trust them—despite the fact that Dahhām, the former shaykh of 'Anaza, has left the tribe of 'Anaza and gone to another region. The consul also states that the African Hanādī cannot be trusted, nor can the Syrian army, which cannot stand up to the bedouins. He ends his letter with praise for Turkish rule, and says that while it once protected the land, it no longer does so now.

On 25 June 1844, the consul states in his letter that 'Anaza is retreating with its leader Dahhām and their other shaykhs, withdrawing from Jabbūl and heading for the desert.

On 10 August 1844, he writes to state that the bedouins of 'Anaza have made a fresh attack on the bedouins of the Ḥadīdīyīn at the village of Tall Ḥasan and have made off with five flocks of sheep.

In writing on 24 August 1844, he is content to allude to the fact that many of the bedouin tribes are at war among themselves.

On 4 January 1845, he writes and speaks at length of a plan to restrict the bedouins within that part of Syria near Aleppo. Martello towers would be constructed at specified intervals and guarded by garrisons; the population—both settled folk and crop-raising bedouins—would be obliged to help protect these frontiers. Responsibility for the failure of such schemes as these to bear fruit the consul places on the Turkish authorities in the cities and villages. He states that Ibrāhīm Pāshā had been able to protect the villages because his rule was better, and indicates that the bedouins only come to the villages and cities peaceably to buy things and then return to their camps in the surrounding areas. Among some of them an inclination for agriculture had once begun to emerge, but today this has entirely disappeared.

On 10 April 1845, he writes of the drought and famine in the north; he then refers to the movement of the 'Anaza bedouins to grazing lands near the town of Ḥamāh and the Orontes River, and to the fact that a force sent by the government has attacked them and, after seizing horses and camels from them, forced them to fall back to the vicinity of Jabbūl. In his letter he states that as they withdrew the bedouins ruined some of the fields.

On 6 September 1845, he writes that the governor of Aleppo, upon his return from an inspection tour of his province, has tried to organize and protect the villages, especially those inhabited in the days of Ibrāhīm Pāshā but subsequently abandoned.

On 4 April 1846, he writes to describe the bad condition of the trade routes, and likewise the desert frontiers, with respect to security, as a result of attacks by the bedouins of 'Anaza in the east and by the Nuṣayrīs from the mountains.

F.O. 195/302

On 29 April 1847, he writes of 'Anaza and says that as is their usual wont, they are threatening security and plundering villages and caravans. He indicates that the government sometimes sends expeditions to punish them, but to no avail. The bedouins withdraw when hard pressed, but before long they return, especially when drought prevails in the desert.

On 8 May 1847, he writes that the situation has deteriorated to the point that even Aleppo itself is practically blockaded by bedouins.

Two weeks later, on 22 May, he writes of the dispatching of a punitive expedition from Aleppo, Ḥamāh, and elsewhere against the bedouins. It clashed with the bedouins in a fight in which seven from each side were killed; having no desire to face artillery fire, the bedouins were compelled to fall back before the army.

On 19 June 1847, the consul writes that the situation is calm and that the garrison in Jabbūl has received from Shaykh Dahhām, the shaykh of the 'Anaza bedouins, the camels agreed upon in the pact.

Information on the bedouins in the consul's reports stops for about three years, after which, on 2 March 1850, he writes in reference to strife that has broken out between the Muslims and Christians in Aleppo. He states that the governor has sent a notice to all of the people of Aleppo calling upon them to throw down their arms and put a stop to the strife. He has also appeased the Muslims with many decrees, among them orders denying the Christians permission to strike the clappers in their churches, raise the Cross, or engage the services of servant girls and slaves. Those of the latter which they already have at present are to be released or freed immediately.

On 21 October a letter sent by the vice-consul in Alexandretta reports that the Christian villages around Aleppo have been pillaged by local folk, and that there are fears that the bedouins will come and pillage whatever is left. He then states, in another letter dated 20 November 1850, that the damage caused by the strife in Aleppo amounts to about 50 million piasters, that eighteen Christians have been killed and 60 wounded, that 450 houses have been looted and twelve burned, that three quarters have been looted, and that about 100 girls have been violated.

On 29 October of the same year (1850), he mentions the movement of ʿAnaza from Jabbūl and Safīrā and their vicinity to Aleppo in order to plunder and join forces with the Muslims of Bāb al-Nayrab. He says that the damage suffered by the Christians is great, and indicates that the government sent an expedition to punish the transgressing rebels—a number of them were killed and the leaders were captured, and in a proclamation it was stated that the criminal aggressors who had plundered the houses of the Christians and were guilty of mayhem and murder have been punished, and indicated that the number of those detained was about 600. Anyone who reads the petition of 22 November 1850 submitted by the Greek Orthodox and Maronites to the governor in Aleppo will realize the extent of the degradation suffered by these Christians.

On 5 April 1851, he reports the coming of Shaykh Jidʿān of ʿAnaza to Aleppo and the awarding to him of a robe of honor in view of the submission to the government by the bedouins of ʿAnaza in the region of Jabbūl. The men of his tribe have claimed that the ones who had stirred them up and incited them against the government were ʿAbd Allāh Bey and his lieutenant Ramaḍān Āghā. As for Dahhām, formerly the shaykh of the tribe recognized by the state, he is not on good terms with the governor and has left the region in which he had been and has made his way to the district of Ḥimṣ. In another letter the consul mentions that the situation is calm.

On 19 July 1851, he writes to state that the bedouins of the desert have staged an uprising for plunder in the Jabbūl area; but the semi-sedentary Mawālī bedouins, who are charged with the task of protecting the routes, have repelled the bedouins—with the assistance of regular army forces—and restored order to the region. He also indicates that this time of the year is the season for Arab bedouin inroads. From all these reports it is evident that the English were interested, above all else, in the establishment of order and the security of the route between Alexandretta and Aleppo, so as to ensure the free flow of trade.

About a year after this, on 12 June 1852, he writes in reference to the fact that Shaykh Jid'ān is still the recognized shaykh and the party charged with the maintenance of security along the frontiers between the villages and the desert.

On 11 September 1852, he writes to mention that Shaykh Dahhām has reverted to menacing the region of 'Urfa with a band of 'Anaza tribesmen.

After this, he writes on 30 October to state that the 'Anaza bedouins have left the northern regions and moved to southern Syria to the vicinity of Damascus, the Ḥawrān, and the Lijāh, taking advantage of the opportunity posed by the feud between Muḥammad Pāshā, the Druze, and the bedouins of al-Slūṭ in the Lijāh. With his letter he encloses a map of the region occupied by the bedouins in agreement with Farḥāt Pāshā. On the map, mention is made of ten villages near Jabbūl, east of Aleppo, extending as far as Ḥiṣn 'Alī and al-Luhayb, south of Aleppo.

F.O. 195/416

In a letter dated 13 January 1853, also from Aleppo, Consul N.W. Werry indicates that the harvests are excellent this year and that the situation is calm. Then two days later he again refers, in a second letter, to the fact that the situation is calm; in view of the strong authority granted by the Sublime Porte to the governor in Aleppo, he expects that this tranquillity will continue.

On 19 January 1853, he writes concerning the mountainous regions in the west that the situation there is chaotic; the area is practically independent and not subservient to Turkish rule. As for the northern region, although the situation there is calm conditions are in the final analysis dependent upon the Turkish regime. The government can maintain security from the bedouins only if the entire army (by which he means the militia responsible for security) remains in the area; otherwise, the bedouins will be plundering travelers between the villages from 'Urfa on throughout northern Syria. He says that the governor is a genial man, but irresolute, and that he seeks to rely upon the '*ulamā*' so as to gain their confidence and that of the "conservative reactionaries" in Istanbul.

On 27 August 1853, he writes in reference to incidents of a breakdown in security precipitated by a group of Muḥālī bedouins. An army force was sent to curb them, and they dispersed: some of them surrendered, and these included Shaykh 'Ārif, who, followed by many other shaykhs, sued for pardon. On 7 September he follows this up with another letter referring to the probability that the bedouins will submit to the regime, through the mediation of the Shaykh 'Ārif whose surrender he had already mentioned.

On 7 January 1854 he writes, concerning the governor, that he has implemented the measures necessary to curb the bedouins, check their encroachments, and protect the frontiers along the fringes of the desert. In another letter of 28 January he mentions that the frontiers of the desert are guarded by certain units of the army.

On 30 March 1854, he writes that the Turkoman tribes have begun to threaten communications and plunder travelers of whatever they have between Aleppo, Alexandretta, Antioch, and Latakia, and especially at the Baylān Pass. In another letter dated 14 April 1854 he indicates that the region of al-Khawr is paying taxes to 'Anaza, thus reducing it to poverty.

In his letter dated 16 April he refers to the dispatch of an agent to purchase horses for the British army. The man has chosen the required number (300 horses), but says that he must have time to complete the transaction, this because of the customary negotiations—i.e. haggling over the price demanded. His letter contains a note from Alexandretta from a Captain Nolan that pertains to the question of the purchase of horses; the latter claims that horses from Aleppo are stronger and larger in size, that he prefers Arabians if they are large ones, and that he will purchase thoroughbreds. He claims that bargaining with the bedouins will take a long time, hence he would prefer that a large number of horses be brought to Aleppo in order to choose a single purchase lot from them. The animal required is a horse at least four feet, nine inches tall; he wants, again, pure-blooded horses, and will pay between 30 and 40 English pounds for both stallions and mares. He reiterates his advice that Aleppo, ʻUrfa, and Qānā are the best centers for buying horses and the most preferable marketplaces for this.

In a letter dated 23 May 1854 he writes that tranquillity prevails throughout the desert, and that the tribe of ʻAnaza and its shaykh Dahhām are doing nothing that would disturb it. The tribe of Shammar, however, is harassing the villages in the vicinity of ʻUrfa, engaging in brigandage along the routes, and forcing the peasant cultivators to abandon their lands and fields. As soon as 20 July 1854, then, he is writing to complain about ʻAnaza and its shaykh, Dahhām, claiming that the bedouins have begun to make inroads against the fields of the peasants in the villages along the frontiers and are sharing with them in the crops of these villages.

On 16 September 1854, he writes concerning the Mawālī bedouins and states that they are beginning to cause unrest in the north. He says of them that they are not cultivators, but own certain agricultural lands and roam along the fringes of the desert. They were formerly allies of the government and used to protect the villages along the edges of the desert. They have between 350 and 400 horsemen. Since, like other bedouins, they were fond of plundering, when they became allies of the government it kept hostages from them in Istanbul. The consul states that in recent days they have begun to demand the return of the hostages. They have taken to plundering and have blockaded the saltworks at al-Jabbūla, and the government has dispatched a detachment from the army to check them, as well as an intermediary to negotiate a reconciliation.

On 19 September 1854, he writes to state, referring to the bedouins of ʻAnaza and their shaykh, Dahhām, that they have left the frontiers, crossed them, and headed southward to the regions where they usually spend the winter.

On 23 September 1854, he writes, concerning the Mawālī bedouins, that they have begun to flee before the imperial army and seek refuge with Shaykh ʻAbd Allāh Maṭar al-Jalīsī, asking for his mediation with the state so that it will pardon them. He has received word that the governor will grant them pardon on condition that they return what they have plundered.

On 4 October 1854, he writes to report an ambush perpetrated by the bedouins of Sbā'a on a detachment from the irregular army of Yūsuf Pāshā near Tādhif. He said that in this clash the shaykh of Tādhif was killed and the commander of the army, Kurd Yūsuf Āghā, was wounded. He also describes how the ambush was executed by some of the bedouins' stopping and falling back, and then the others attacking and devastating the troops as they pursued the fleeing bedouins into the ambush. He indicates that the expedition of the above-mentioned Yūsuf Pāshā was a failure because the troops who were with him had no military experience or talent.

In a second letter dated 11 November he returns to this topic and writes that the government sent an expedition to exact vengeance from the bedouins, but all the tribes of 'Anaza had withdrawn to the south. The commander of the expedition was thus able to collect the taxes from the villages along the frontiers.

On 13 December 1854, he writes that Yūsuf Pāshā is still lingering on the Euphrates frontier, negotiating with Shaykh Jid'ān of 'Anaza on the question of security in that region. In writing on 20 January 1855, he goes on to say that Yūsuf Pāshā has returned from this expedition of his and claims that he has succeeded in inducing some of the bedouins, known as "flock bedouins," to settle down and take up agriculture. In another letter, dated 15 March 1855, he indicates that the region is suffering from general poverty and its people are complaining of hunger, and that some people are living off of herbage and scrub.

On 7 May he writes to state that the route between Aleppo and Damascus has fallen under constant threat from the bedouins of 'Anaza and other tribes. The Mawālī have joined forces with 'Anaza, and the situation has reached the point that caravans do not dare to pass along this route without being accompanied by 20 to 50 cavalrymen; even the post itself is not secure unless it is guarded by 20 to 50 cavalrymen. In another letter, dated 17 July 1855, he indicates that the security situation continues to be disrupted in the north and also between Antioch and Baylān.

On 27 August 1855, he writes that the deputation sent to buy horses has purchased 657 of them. These have now arrived and are strong high-quality animals, although some of them have been lost.

On 9 October 1855, he writes that a number of the Mawālī who are agriculturalists fled on Sunday, 7 October, when they were attacked by bedouins of the "Haddadeen,"[3] who were themselves also tenders of crops. The Mawālī have sought refuge in the outskirts of the city (i.e. Aleppo). He states that apparently some of these Mawālī had insulted the women of the peaceful "Haddadeen;" the latter thus assembled in large numbers and attacked the Mawālī and pursued them as far as the gates of Aleppo. The governor dispatched a contingent of about 400 or 500 cavalry and infantry to support the Mawālī; but as they were not well armed, they were defeated and about ten of their men were killed and about twenty wounded. He states that although the Mawālī are few in number, they are marauders and notorious robbers. By granting the Mawālī protection the governor's aim has been to sedentarize them; but they have not taken to settled life, nor have they stopped looting, plundering, and committing acts of aggression. The "Haddadeen" thus ran out of patience and dealt with them as previously mentioned. The consul then indicates that the peasants supported the "Haddadeen," since they are peaceful bedouins and pay taxes to the state.

In a letter of 8 July 1856 he indicates that the Mawālī have plundered some officials of their property and killed one of them. In a letter dated 29 July he indicates that the 'Anaza bedouins have left the region and crossed the Euphrates, heading southward to find provisions. In another letter, dated 2 September 1856, he mentions that tranquillity prevails throughout the region.

It would seem that calm did not last long, and that subsequently security was not well established. In a letter that he wrote on 20 April 1857, he states that the authorities in Aleppo, including the governor, army commander, and others, have gathered together to study the question of security, with the aim of finding the best way to prevent the bedouin attacks that have been going on for about a century. They sent for Jid'ān and Dahhām, presented them with robes

[3]I.e. the Ḥadīdīyīn.

of honor, gave each one a sword, and gave presents to their followers in an effort to appease them and deter them from plundering. But they were all dissatisfied, and soon left, it seems, in indignant rage. The next day they attacked the tribe of al-Luhayb, which was submissive to the Sublime Porte, robbed it of nine mares and other plunder that took their fancy in two nearby villages, and carried off the loot, as well as a number of horses and sheep, to their camps. The consul states that he subsequently received word that these same bedouins also made off with the horses which the government had bought for crossbreeding and which were grazing in the lands along the fringes of the desert. The governor, ʻAzmī Pāshā, has been compelled to set out with an expedition of 400 regular troops and 200 irregulars to fight these bedouins.

On 12 May 1857, he writes of this expedition that had set out to fight the ʻAnaza bedouins, and indicates that certain shaykhs of bedouin clans allied with the government had joined the force. These included two shaykhs of the Luhayb bedouins, one named Ḥamādī al-Shayḥa and another named Fāris ibn Ḥusayn Shbāṭ, and a shaykh over the bedouins of the Ḥadīdīyīn named ʻAlāwī Rajū. They all conferred among themselves and agreed upon a surprise attack on ʻAnaza by night, but ʻAzmī Pāshā rejected this. By the time the army proceeded the next day, ʻAnaza had left the land where they had been camping and fled, since Baṭrān Āghā had privately sent a horseman who informed them of the movement of the expeditionary force, which was thus unable to catch ʻAnaza by surprise. Shaykh Dahhām subsequently separated from his comrade Jidʻān of ʻAnaza, withdrew, and sent envoys to offer his submission to ʻAzmī Pāshā. He told him that he was friendly and asked permission to come to Aleppo to offer his submission, but was told to remain where he was. In this letter the consul relates how the soldiers in turn plundered an Indian merchant's caravan, claiming that it belonged to the bedouins, and describes how they attacked the allied tribesmen of the Ḥadīdīyīn and the Luhayb because they are of ʻAnaza origin, despite the fact that they have come to the settled regions fleeing for refuge from ʻAnaza and are fearful of their depredations. The consul thus claims that the standing of the Sublime Porte has become weaker by reason of the declining position, indecision, and languor of the government in Aleppo.

Three days later, on 15 May, he writes to relate how sheep have been sold at public auction in Aleppo when, in fact, they are the property of the townsmen themselves, who had entrusted them to the peaceful bedouins whom the army have just plundered. He also mentions how the 'Anaza shaykh Jid'ān attacked the expedition as it made its way back to Aleppo, and killed a number of soldiers. Here Consul Barker claims that this policy will lead to the withdrawal of the entire expedition and the attacking and plundering of villages by the bedouins.

On 8 June 1857, Consul Skene writes in reference to negotiations between Shaykh Dahhām and the authorities, stating that Dahhām has visited him and shown him a copy of the agreement concluded with the governor. The agreement provides for recognition of Dahhām as sole shaykh of 'Anaza to the exclusion of his rival Jid'ān, and empowers Dahhām to call upon Jidān and all of the minor shaykhs to accept and affix their seals to this agreement. The accord stipulates that any bedouin bearing a pass from Shaykh Dahhām may enter the city of Aleppo; but without one, he may not. Skene then says that Dahhām has told him that during the last month five tribes of the 'Umayrāt known as the Dahāmsha, each tribe comprising about 600 families, have emigrated from central Arabia and camped on lands about 30 miles from Aleppo. These tribes are clans of 'Anaza that left Najd a century earlier for the same reason—lack of grazing lands, and these emigrants have placed themselves under the guardianship of Shaykh Dahhām. They are rich in livestock, especially sheep, but less so than the immediate followers of Dahhām, whose tribesmen have occupied a more productive part of the desert.

On 16 June 1857, he further writes that in that span of time the Mawālī have begun to mount attacks on the villages and to disrupt security. Warriors from this tribe have attacked two villages near Sarmīn and made off with fifteen camels and a number of sheep. After this, Aḥmed Bey, shaykh of all the Mawālī, attacked the village of Khān Tūmān, about ten miles from Aleppo, and made off with 50 camels. Lastly, the consul mentions that the government is preparing an expedition to retaliate against the Mawālī.

On 30 June he continues to write, saying that the governor has taken a decision prohibiting trade with all the bedouins. This is an unwise decision, he says, since it takes no account of the fact that the townsfolk do a brisk business with the bedouins: these latter sell the townsmen camels, sheep, and wool, and buy from them flour and other commodities which they will henceforth get by plundering them. The consul is thus complaining to the government about the defective policy pursued by the governor who represents the Turkish regime.

On 15 July of the same year the same consul writes a letter in which he reports a great three-hour desert battle that has taken place between the army and the bedouins in the valley of al-Dabislī, on the left bank of the Euphrates. The bedouin force comprised about 3000 warriors mounted on horses and camels, and the army was about 1500-strong. The bedouin shaykhs—Jid'ān, Dahhām, and Ju'ayyad—were all united together. The bedouins were defeated and fled and left between 300 and 400 dead on the field of battle; many drowned when they crossed the river. The Turks suffered the loss of eleven dead and twenty wounded, and the army seized 2500 camels and 100 sheep, these last being distributed among the troops. It appears that the bedouins came back and counterattacked on the next day; they attacked the contingent which was driving the camels, killed the officer in charge, and regained the camels. It would seem that the consul has reported the news of this battle from Turkish sources.

On 25 July of the same year, Consul Skene in Aleppo forwards to the ambassador in Istanbul and the Foreign Office a report sent to him from Colonel Sankey on the situation regarding the bedouins and the desert, and a letter in which the latter sets forth to the consul his recommendation for a course of action to subdue the bedouins and asks him for a force from the Ottoman army. The consul says that he has raised this matter with the government, and that it has agreed to provide the troops. Skene in turn praises Colonel Sankey and lauds him for his knowledge of and experience in Arab affairs and his understanding of the Oriental mentality, and respectfully requests that the English government accept this proposed course of action. Since this report is a long and important one, I have decided to paraphrase all of its contents, with consideration for abridgment in certain places. The date of the report is 19 July 1857.

In this report Sankey first discusses the perpetual strife in the desert and says that no benefit will accrue from continuing the struggle between the bedouins and the settled folk, nor any advantage from warfare and feuding: when defeated the bedouins will seek revenge, and when victorious their appetite will be whetted for further gain. He then speaks of the tribe of Hanādī, mention of which is more than once found in the consuls' letters, and says that they are of Berber and Egyptian origin and were brought in by Ibrāhīm Pāshā to fight the bedouins. They have a chieftain by the name of Baṭrān Āghā. They are brave, faithful, and well disposed toward Europeans, and they would undoubtedly be able to overcome the bedouins of ʿAnaza; this much is clear from past events, and ʿAnaza fears their leader.

As for ʿAnaza, they are bedouins who 60 years ago migrated from Najd to this country because of the scarcity of grazing lands in their home territories. In the regions around Aleppo they number about 15,000, and they have four shaykhs: Dahhām and Jidʿān, who camp with their clans opposite Qalʿat Jabbūr on the right bank of the Euphrates; Muḥammad al-Ḍulḥ ibn Ismāʿīl, who camps with his clan between Damascus and Aleppo; and finally Jlās ibn Fayṣal ibn Shaʿlān, leader of the tribe of Jlās and Rwāla.

These two tribes are scattered all over the country between Damascus and the Jawf; there are large numbers of minor shaykhs, both related to the major shaykhs and others dependent upon them. Between 50 and 200 tents may be found in each bedouin encampment, but not more. This is because of the enormous herds of camels requiring pasture (Sankey calculates an average of ten camels for every man). The bedouins do not remain more than three to five days in one place and have no regular beat. Their tents consist of strips of black camel-hair cloth[4] stretched over poles, and in the middle of the tent is a partition for the wife and children. Some of the large tents are 50 to 60 feet long. The wealth of the bedouins consists of horses, camels, and sheep, which they sell to the settled population, taking wheat and clothing in exchange. In the summer their food for the most part consists of dates steeped in melted butter. They are profoundly ignorant, have very limited reasoning faculties, and are greatly wanting in the

[4]He is mistaken when he claims that the tents are woven from camel's hair; of the hundreds of hair tents I have seen over the years of my travels to the desert, I have not seen a single one that was woven from camel's hair. The sole part of the tent that could possibly contain camel hair fabric is in the back or side panels hanging from the roof of the tent.

natural courtesy of the African bedouin. They are suspicious, deceitful, and perfidious, and while they see no shame in breaking trust with a European they may well be faithful one to another. That very day produced the proof. Sankey was a guest at the tent of the 'Anazī shaykh Dahhām, and when the latter bid him farewell he swore fraternity but sent no horseman to guard the British officer, saying that this was unnecessary. About twelve miles from his camp, however, the guide, his nephew, refused to proceed, and from his attitude Sankey understood that he wanted money. As Sankey was armed, he at first thought of resistance, but soon realized that he was surrounded by many 'Anaza bedouins who had left the camp before he had, and had gone ahead, armed with lances, to waylay him. Sankey therefore made the guide sit by him and tell him under what conditions he would allow him to take his leave of them quietly. The guide demanded 1000 dollars, and when Sankey refused the former intimated that refusal would be dangerous, since his men would be angry. Sankey then told him that he had the lives of twenty of his men in his belt, and that to enrage an armed European would have consequences more destructive than twenty 'Anazīs. He offered him 1000 piasters (eight gold pounds), payable in Aleppo provided that he accompany Sankey there, with a guarantee for his safety, to collect it. The guide was satisfied with this offer (to Sankey's surprise), but the latter did not know what role the revolver played in convincing him.

The 'Anaza are excellent horsemen, and they have the finest horses in the world. They do not use bits or stirrups, but rather ride on a saddle not firmly held in place. They depend upon their horses, esteem and glorify them, and would not like to be without them. It is said that Khedive 'Abbās Pāshā in Egypt paid fabulous sums for mares from 'Anaza. The endurance of these animals is wonderful, and it is well-known that they can run for 30 hours and more with very short intervals for rest. As contacts with the bedouins have been prohibited by the Turkish government and they do not grow crops or till the land, they cannot purchase barley for their horses. They have nothing for them other than the dry herbage of the *shīḥ* plant and camel's milk, to which latter they attribute the hardness of bone peculiar to their breed of horses. There are few of them who use firearms: their favored weapon is the lance, which can ward off any enemy swordsman.

It is considered a matter of honor to plunder an enemy of his horse in a fight. It is kept with them as if it was their own, as we would keep a trophy.

Obedience to the leader is optional, hence any undertaking with him is not binding upon them. Before the coming of ʻAnaza, the Mawālī bedouins were under the leadership of Shaykh Muḥammad Ḥurfān and were a more powerful tribe, but after numerous clashes they were forced to seek a truce and remained for some years as brokers between ʻAnaza and the villages, and agents or brokers for the village folk. Now, however, ʻAnaza handles its own trading affairs directly with Aleppo and its outlying districts, when the government permits it to do so.

ʻAnaza is now in a quasi-state of war with the government and the bedouins of the Ḥadīdīyīn, the Hanādī, the Mawālī, and Shammar. But the numerical strength of these tribes is meager compared to ʻAnaza; they would be able to overpower ʻAnaza only if they all united together. The Hanādī are the sole tribe which ʻAnaza fears. They have been kept out of the way by order of the government so that they will not revolt and join forces with the rebels, since the government knows that they are dissatisfied with it, and especially, that the pay due to them has been witheld for many years.

As for the Mawālī, they are a Syrian tribe. They were a more powerful tribe before ʻAnaza, and were compelled to become a brother-tribe of ʻAnaza in the time of Muḥammad Ḥurfān. They have, however, a history of perfidy. They invited 600 ʻAnaza warriors for a meal, and then, while they were eating, massacred all of them save one who fled because he did not trust them. There thus arose the proverb: "The tent of the Mawālī is the tent of shame."

Several years later ʻAnaza again tried to establish themselves in these lands. The Mawālī opposed them, and a battle broke out near Qalʻat Jabbūr. ʻAnaza took their revenge and killed the prisoners, since the Mawālī banquet was still fresh in their memories. This did not apply in one case, however. An ʻAnazī took one of the Mawālī prisoner and was willing to spare the life of his prisoner in return for the *diya*, or blood money. He was also willing to accompany the prisoner to a place where the latter could contact his comrades. When they arrived at that place, the prisoner told his captor that he was the son of Muḥammad Ḥurfān himself, the leader of the Mawālī. The ʻAnazī hesitated a short time, and then ordered the prisoner to mount and accompanied him to within sight of the Mawālī at a place called Spheria, and then released him, saying: "I bear your family nothing but hatred; but go, you are safe, the word of an Arab is sacred. I cannot receive ransom at the hands of Muḥammad Ḥurfān's son."

They have no such considerations and covenants toward the Europeans. Most of the plundering, looting, and killing around Aleppo is attributed to the Mawālī, and is in fact their work, though their numbers come to only about 1000 tents. As for the "Hadâdeen" (i.e. the Ḥadīdīyīn), they number about 800 tents and their camping grounds are always in the vicinity of Aleppo. They are well-disposed and harmless, and at present they are assisting the army against 'Anaza, since these have taken their best horses from them. This is the perennial cause of dissension among the bedouins. The "Hadâdeen" are herdsmen for sheepowners in Aleppo: they take charge of the sheep and supply the city with clarified butter. They are obedient to the Turkish government, in spite of how the authorities have recently dealt with them. When the Turkish army was not successful in subduing the 'Anaza bedouins, it plundered the "Hadâdeen" along its way, sold their sheep and those of the people of Aleppo in the markets of the city, and distributed the money among the troops.

As for the Shammar, this tribe is under the leadership of Shaykh 'Abd al-Karīm Ṣfūq. They camp on an island formed by a bend of the Euphrates 30 miles from Qal'at Jabbūr. Shaykh Dahhām, leader of 'Anaza, told Sankey that it was his intention to drive them off the island and occupy it. Shammar's numbers come to about 1500 tents. They migrated to this region from the Shammar mountains in northern Arabia at the time when 'Anaza migrated.

Their shaykh, 'Abd al-Karīm, has good qualities better than most of his followers, and he respects Europeans. A caravan belonging to a British merchant was plundered by a contingent from his tribe on the way from Mosul, and when the shaykh realized that it belonged to Europeans he gathered its goods from their tents and returned them all to their owners in Europe, carried on his own camels, and apologized for the action of his tribe.

Under existing circumstances, the imperial army can achieve nothing against 'Anaza, and greater damage and mischief may come to pass if this evil state of affairs continues. Were all the tribes to unite, Aleppo itself would be plundered, and Sankey hopes that the necessary steps will be taken to prevent damage to trade.

The proposal he sets forth to secure peace in the desert is to assign a particular region to each tribe and make it pay a rent to the government for its territory. In this way it will be possible to establish two points: first, the government's ownership of the land, which the bedouins generally do not concede; and second, the authority of the government or sultan. They would gain (by virtue of the tax they pay) the right to use the land, and they would become like Turkish subjects. This is a point they have yet to accept.

In order to gain their submission and payment of the tax, there will have to be an army of 1000 irregulars armed with rifles and revolvers. As the ʿAnaza bedouins fear weapons and military firearms, this should be sufficient. At the same time, this force will be able to protect the railroad and the telegraph lines. With such a force as this it will be possible to free the Pashalik of Aleppo from the depredations of the bedouins, whose submission to sedentarization and agriculture can be secured by no other means. This is due not only to their indomitable laziness, but also to the fact that they have been taught to regard any manual labor as shameful. This includes agriculture, which, when they are allocated land, can only gradually arise, without forcing them to settle down. Until these results are achieved, the bedouins, in the meantime, will be unable to engage in mischief and will become useful subjects. If the Turkish government is agreeable to this proposal, Sankey will help to implement it.

F.O. 195/595

Another report from Sankey to the British consulate, dated 7 June 1858, concerns the tribe of Qays. This is a tribe occupying the area between Ḥarrān and the Khābūr; its leading shaykh is a man named ʿAbd Allāh ʿUthmān, and he has 450 horsemen. For many years the clansmen of this tribe have not wandered much and have remained on the outskirts of ʿUrfa. They are more civilized than others, and their shaykhs have purchased lands to cultivate. Through judicious policy it would be possible for them to serve as a source of support for repelling the attacks of the other havoc-wreaking bedouins. They are excellent horsemen, and they are considered stronger than an equal number of horsemen from 'Anaza or Shammar, as they have proven on numerous occasions. The 'Urfa region was authorized to enlist 450 men for defense of the northern frontiers: 70 soldiers from the Kurds ("Melloo"), 45 from the leaders of the Qays, and the rest irregulars. These are based in the camps of the tribe of Qays and sow dissension, while in war they run away. As for the Qays warriors, since they were not strong enough to mount a defense by themselves they returned to 'Urfa and its outskirts, where they grazed their herds and caused damage to the ripening crops. If 400 of these recruits were assigned to Qays itself under the leadership of 'Abd Allāh al-'Uthmān, who could reinforce his army to 1000 horsemen, this would enable him to protect the northern frontier from al-Raqqa on the Euphrates to Ra's al-'Ayn at the source of the Khābūr. So long as they occupy these regions and settle in them, crops will increase between the frontier line and Ḥarrān, lands will be placed into cultivation, and harvests will increase twenty-fold. One sees the authorities, instead of trying to settle the Qays so they will take up agriculture, playing one tribal leader off against the other, with the result that the weaker ones appeal to Shammar or 'Anaza for assistance and actions taken to cure the problem instead make it worse. The position of Qays in 'Urfa is similar to that of the Ḥanādī in Aleppo, and they would form its best and ablest defense. To his report Sankey adjoins a plan for sedentarizing Qays and encouraging them to take up agriculture, and specific places for Qays settlements between al-Raqqa and Ra's al-'Ayn to prevent bedouin attacks. This demonstrates his understanding of the problem he has discussed for the revival of the interior lands and the prevention of bedouin attacks.

On 8 April 1858, Consul Skene mentions that the country is exposed to attacks by the bedouin tribes and observes that the return of fine weather has brought them back again to the vicinity of Aleppo. Their ranks have been swelled by the arrival of other tribes from central Arabia, and they apparently intend to use force against the trade they have been denied. Villages have been attacked, many people have been killed, herds of livestock have been taken, and some of the crops have been ruined and eaten by horses and camels.

Every year the 'Anaza bedouins return to their territory in the journey that brings them back to Aleppo in the summer, and takes them to 'Urfa, Diyārbakr, Mosul, and Baghdad in the winter. It takes them in a circuit around the southern part of the desert near Damascus, Ḥimṣ, Ḥamāh, and Aleppo. They lay in supplies of grain and manufactured commodities here, and dates in Baghdad, and sell their wool, clarified butter, camels, and horses in order to purchase these items. All of their requirements and needs are filled by the herds they tend, and it is these that require them to make this journey and oblige them to move in a great circle so as to avoid the central parts of arid Arabia and find new grazing lands around its fringes, moving on to them every time they finish grazing a pasture.

The value of the trade conducted with them is estimated to be five million piasters. The custom of the authorities had traditionally been to allow them to engage in trade, until, when they began to commit acts of aggression against the villages, the government sent a force to the villages to drive them back away from them, but ineffectually. Last spring they contacted the city for trade, according to their usual custom, but the governor dealt harshly with them. They went back furious with him and renewed their depredations, and decrees were thus issued prohibiting any dealings with them. The government sent an army expedition to subdue them; but they easily fled, and the expedition returned after plundering, on its way back, many of the allied tribes, and even the very caravans bearing the goods of the local traders, including one English subject. Amīn Efendī himself went out again and surprised 'Anaza and took camels from them; but the latter regrouped, counterattacked, and regained the camels from them by force. The expedition returned to its bases. Its concentration prevented further bedouin attacks, but the city suffered when it was deprived of the trade with them.

When the bedouins could not fill their needs, they tried to do so from Mosul; but as Shaykh 'Abd al-Karīm Ṣfūq, shaykh of Shammar, did not want them passing through his territories, he sent word to the governors of Diyārbakr, Mardīn, and Mosul that 'Anaza was heading northward, and offered to make a stand to stop them and prevent them from proceeding if he were offered assistance, since the men of his tribes alone were not sufficient to repel them. His proposal was not accepted;

and ten 'Anaza bands, each of 500 men, thus advanced, crossed the Euphrates, and attacked Shammar. After a battle that lasted for three days, Shammar was compelled to fall back before them, having suffered the loss, besides the dead and wounded, of about 1000 tents, 6000 camels, and 8000 head of sheep which were taken by 'Anaza. By this time, Shammar had been able to convince the Kurdish tribes and the inhabitants of the villages in northern Iraq to join them to repel 'Anaza. Battle broke out a second time in the north, and these contingents defeated the 'Anaza forces: they fell upon the plunder that had been taken from them, recovered their livestock, and in addition took 270 mares whose riders had been killed. The total number of those killed in this battle was about 704 from 'Anaza and 215 from Shammar, and 'Anaza was forced to retreat back across the Euphrates in January. 'Umar Pāshā was crossing the desert with two battalions of regular infantry on his way to Baghdad; and 'Anaza, fearful that he would cut off their retreat southward, thus made their way to the fortified village of al-Dayr. It seems that 'Anaza forced the inhabitants of al-Dayr to withhold supplies from the Pāshā; he therefore came and stormed the fort and declared al-Dayr open for the army to plunder. He lost seven of his men, among them the Hungarian colonel Nūrī Bey. 'Anaza then changed their route, slowly went back westward, and in these days have reached the outskirts of Aleppo in large numbers.

After the incidents of the past year and their debarment from trade, they may in future mount many acts of aggression. Skene has tried to convince the governor to permit them to trade with Aleppo and its villages, but he prefers to wait to see how they behave. His Excellency expects that his cavalry will be sufficient to keep them in check, although acts of plundering have already begun. Last week about 1000 'Anaza horsemen appeared in a place less than twenty miles from Aleppo, made off with some livestock, and killed five of the Hanādī irregulars who were guarding the flock. It is not to be expected that any steps will be taken to reach an agreement between the bedouins and the regime, since the bedouins do not trust the Turkish governors and seek the consulate's mediation. The British have promised that if they come to terms with the Turks the agreements will be kept, but Skene doubts that the Turks will be helpful in undertaking anything—not an agreement, and not in seeking assistance, at the same time, to confront them.

On 17 April 1858, there is another report in which he states that Jid'ān, shaykh of 'Anaza, has surprised him by visiting him with a merchant. He says that he was told that the merchant had been sent from the governor to secure the submission of Jid'ān: a promise guaranteeing his safety had been given in Skene's name, and had it not been for that Jid'ān would not have agreed to come with him. Skene told Jid'ān that he knew nothing of this arrangement and that the Turks had deceived him; it was up to him to decide for himself what to do. So Jid'ān went and came to terms with the governor; the latter pardoned him, and permitted the people of Aleppo to conduct trade with the bedouins.

Consul Skene writes again in Aleppo on 25 August 1858 to report aggression against peasants in the villages by Kurdish tribes and also bedouins, who have been quiet in recent months. He also writes another letter along the same lines on 2 September 1858. On 30 September he writes another letter in which he mentions that the bedouins are attacking the villages of Tādhif, fifteen miles from Aleppo, and that the horsemen of the village have defended it, driven off the bedouins, and incurred some losses: the bedouins lost three killed, four wounded, and some mares taken as plunder; five from Tādhif were wounded and they lost some sheep. The consul indicates that no assistance came to the people of Tādhif from the irregular army entrusted with the task of protecting the villages. These villages bear the burden of providing the subsistence and provisions for these troops, as they lack adequate supplies. Skene is appointing Sankey as a vice-consul.

News of the desert from the consul in Aleppo ceases for more than a year and a half, then on 21 April 1860 he writes a letter in which he mentions the contentment of some of the bedouins who have begun to incline toward agriculture. He says, however, that there are considerations which are causing them to abandon agriculture. One of the shaykhs, a man named Ḥajjī Baṭrān, the one to whom the government had paid a living allowance, saw that his stipend had ceased and so began to encourage Jid'ān, shaykh of 'Anaza, to plunder the cultivators. Jid'ān did not agree that this was a good time to do so, so Ḥajjī came to Aleppo, filled the authorities with fear of attacks that would be mounted on the peasants, and so convinced them that power and authority over the tribes have been placed in his hands. The consul states that he fears that with the authority vested in his hands Shaykh

Ḥajjī intends to lead astray the tribes of the "Weldeh," who have begun to take up settled life, cause them to revert to nomadism, and stand in the way of the sedentarization of other tribes. For this reason the consul proposes that he be exiled from the region entirely.

At the beginning of May 1860 he writes concerning a Frenchman by the name of Lascaris de Vintimille, whom Napoléon I had sent to the Arab countries in 1809 to effect a confederation among the Arab tribes in order to pave the way for Napoléon and facilitate his aim to occupy India. He says:

> Monsieur Lascaris spent three years in the desert, and before transmitting the results of his mission to the French Government he died in the year 1812 at Cairo, where Mr. Salt, then British Consul-General in Egypt, obtained possession of his papers. The Interpreter of Monsieur Lascaris, a native of Aleppo by the name Fathalla Sayer[5] states that these documents were subsequently claimed by him, and that Mr. Salt informed him in reply that he had forwarded them to Her Majesty's Government.

The consul in Aleppo therefore asks for the papers in order to facilitate his endeavors.

On 12 May 1860, he writes of the Mawālī tribe and says that they have begun to push the limits of their territory southward to the banks of the Orontes River. He fears that strife will break out between them and the cultivators in the villages. He states that the ruin of these regions dates about 80 years back, when the tribes of ʻAnaza appeared, driven by a famine from Arabia, and spread out along the eastern frontiers. He says:

> The villages have since then gradually receded before the tide of devastation, which in two places, near Acre, and between Lattakia and Tripoli, has at last reached the sea. Its progress has been more rapid of late years. . . .I have seen

[5][The reading of the text in the FO document is clear here, but it is nevertheless possible that the person intended was someone named Fatḥ Allāh Ṣāyigh rather than Fatḥ Allāh Sāyir.]

> this year twenty-five villages plundered, and deserted. The only remedy for this evil appears to me to be the formation of a line of located tribes, which might subsequently stretch eastward, by preventing the nomads from destroying the crops, and inducing them to follow the example of tilling the soil... this is the only course by which, I think, Syria can be saved, and the desert gained, to Turkey.

At the same time he suggests that positions be established for vice-consuls along the frontiers to facilitate communications between the bedouins and the authorities.

On 8 October 1860, he writes of a violent clash that has led to a war among the tribes, the cause being rivalry over tribal leadership, especially among the clans of Fid'ān between the shaykh and his nephew. The consul's letter also bears information about Jid'ān and his uncle Dahhām. It appears that Jid'ān was so much more powerful and generous that he was able to wrest the leadership of the tribe of Fid'ān from his uncle. This latter fell back on the Shammar bedouins for assistance, and Jid'ān pursued him with his allies, the Sbā'a and the Mawālī. They encountered Shammar, which the governor of 'Urfa had reinforced with his army, and there ensued a battle in which, as Skene says in his letter, upwards of 12,000 horsemen participated. Jid'ān was defeated and retreated back across the Euphrates; he appeared near Aleppo after having suffered the loss of his herds. The tribes which were near Aleppo gave him provisions and horses to make up for what he had lost, so he mounted a raid and recovered some of what had been plundered from him. Skene suggests that the situation thus may now remain quiet.

On 20 October 1860, he writes of the appearance of a new tribe that has begun to displace 'Anaza in the south, because of the war with Shammar. This tribe was near Damascus at the time of the massacre of 1860, and he states that he has heard that the 800 Christian women are in the custody of this tribe.

On 30 October 1860, he writes a report indicating that the bedouins of 'Anaza have suffered new losses of about 300 men in fighting with Shammar, and have been defeated. He has visited the tribe which he mentioned as holding the Christian women as prisoners, and found that most of these captives have passed on to the custody of the clan of 'Uqayl, since the bedouins no longer have sufficient food for themselves and for the women. On 13 June he writes from Damascus to report the arrival of bedouin tribes in the Ḥawrān region. These are the Sbā'a, 'Imārāt, Fid'ān, and the Dahāmsha; with them is Shaykh Ismā'īl, and at their head is Shaykh Fayṣal [al-Sha'lān].

On 14 April 1862, he writes concerning the arrival of Shammar under the leadership of Shaykh 'Abd al-Karīm, and with him Shaykh Dahhām, formerly one of the shaykhs of 'Anaza, at the banks of the Euphrates. He mentions that they have begun to advance toward Aleppo, and indicates that what seems to him to be the reason for their coming to Syrian lands in the north is that the harsh policy pursued by the governors of Baghdad and 'Urfa of denying them permission to enter the lands of Iraq has caused them to turn to the Aleppo area. He claims that if the same policy is pursued in Syria, there will remain no place for trading with the bedouins and buying what is needed from them or selling to them what they require. In such a situation they will be incited to looting and plundering. The consul reproaches the Turkish governors for their ignorance of the proper policy to pursue in bedouin affairs—personally, he favors the coming of the bedouins and trading with them.

On 2 May 1862, he writes to state that British trade is in peril, hence his concern for the issue of the desert, since Britain imports much wool from bedouin sheep. He is not pleased with the harsh policy pursued by the governors and military authorities: word has reached him that military expeditions are being sent to the desert to fight the bedouins, and he is upset by this. In his letter he complains about the governor of Aleppo, since he has built forts to repel the bedouins who sent word requesting permission for them to come into his district. At first he agreed, after stipulating the condition that they not engage in raiding. They accepted these terms, but then he demanded that hostages from them be placed in his custody; Skene noticed that before the governor arrived at an agreement there were already expeditions on the march against them in the provinces of both Baghdad and Damascus. Fearful of agreeing to their entry into the Aleppo area, he remained waiting for the arrival of orders from Istanbul. The consul then ends his letter by offering his own opinion, saying: "I suggest that permission be granted to them on condition that they remain tranquil and that there be a force nearby to deter them if they revolt."

On 30 May he writes to state that the governor-general of Aleppo has reached an agreement with the 'Anaza bedouins which may facilitate the means for trade with them. Then he say that he is glad that 'Iṣmat Pāshā has done this; he deserves praise, admiration, and encouragement. He has done what is appropriate and necessary, and, contrary to his colleagues in Baghdad and Damascus, he is following a wise policy.

On 15 September 1862, the tribes began to leave the region of Aleppo. There were no incidents of plundering or disturbance of security, and there came into being 28 villages inhabited by bedouins who in the previous period had been afraid to live in farms and villages. The consul then says that the governor is pleased with his policy of allowing the bedouins to come to the lands of Aleppo and of trading with them.

F.O. 195/761

Consul Skene writes a letter on 30 June 1863 in which he states that the bedouins have returned to the vicinity of the villages near the desert, and opines that, as it seems to him, that summer will not pass without the occurrence of some incidents. But up to the date of his letter nothing has happened. The harvests have been extremely bad, especially the cotton crop, ruined by locusts; and it seems that the country is, as he says, on the brink of poverty and destitution.

Here a British consul in Jerusalem sends a special letter dated 7 July 1863 in which he states that the tribes of Banū Ṣakhr and Banū Ḥasan, comprising about 2000–3000 tents, have entered the populated regions around Lake Tiberias and have begun to wreak havoc in the land, grazing their livestock on the crops awaited by the peasants. 'Uqayl Āghā, military protector of the region, went to meet their shaykhs, whom he knew, but they did not agree to withdraw. 'Uqayl Āghā thus resolved to drive them out by force. He asked the governor of Acre for military reinforcements, these were sent, and they all set out together to drive away the bedouins, who fled when they heard of the approach of the army. His letter ends with his statement: "The late energetic conduct of the authorities will act as a salutary check on these wandering bandits for some time to come."

F.O. 195/800

In a letter from a British consul in Aleppo dated 30 June 1864, he reports to a ministry of his government concerning the march of a force from the imperial army to the desert to prevent incidents of strife and contention between the two 'Anaza bedouin shaykhs Jid'ān and Dahhām, who are constantly quarreling over the overall shaykhship and the leadership of the entire tribe. He states that Dahhām gathered 2000 horsemen and advanced to the Aleppo area to uphold his right to the shaykhship, which the government had wrested away from him and given to Jid'ān. Despite the meager number of his men, Jid'ān was able in the first engagement to drive Dahhām back to the Euphrates, leaving 50 of his men dead behind him. Jid'ān, however, told Thurāyā Pāshā that Dahhām would come again with a larger force that Jid'ān alone might not be able to repulse, and for that reason he was requesting assistance. An army was then sent to help him. Dahhām tried on several occasions to attack the region, but his efforts to overpower its defenders met with no success, and he left. The military forces remain under the command of 'Umar Bey, an excellent leader.

On 30 September 1864, he writes to report on the march of an expedition under the leadership of Thurāyā Pāshā, governor of the region, and his adjutant 'Umar Pāshā, army commander for the desert. Their objective is to subdue the tribes, guarantee tranquil living conditions, collect the taxes from the clans which had begun to settle down and till the land, and open a new route for the caravans between Aleppo and Baghdad. He indicates that the question of the tribes is a vital one for this country, and that force alone will not suffice, since the bedouins, due to the superiority of their horses, will flee and then return.

On 31 December 1864, Consul Skene writes to state that the expedition of Thurāyā Pāshā has succeeded in subduing the crop-raising tribes, but that 'Anaza has gone back to Najd and central Arabia. He believes that they will return in the spring, hence he considers that it would be best to conclude an agreement with the ‘Anaza bedouins allowing them to return for trade and exchange and to safeguard the routes to Baghdad. Nothing would then remain save the problem of the bedouins of Baghdad.

On 31 March 1865, he writes to state that Jid‘ān, one of the shaykhs of ‘Anaza, has been appointed by the governor of Aleppo to protect the villages lying along the desert frontiers from attacks by other ‘Anaza bedouins and other tribes. He indicates that employing him for this task has detracted from his standing in the eyes of his ‘Anaza followers, who are fond of robbery and pillage. A part of them has thus abandoned him and joined his opponents and rivals, with the result that his power has weakened and he is no longer able to repel bedouin attacks. Some of them have accordingly attacked the villages near the camp of Jid‘ān and stolen from them some sheep belonging to the people of Aleppo. Jid‘ān has been unable to rescue them from them, so the governor suspects that he is acting in collusion with them. It is evident that the bedouin cannot submit entirely or accept half-measures like those employed by the government. Skene suggests that the only sure remedy would be to exclude the bedouins from the plains of the Syrian Desert by stationing troops along the frontiers from al-Qaryatayn to Tadmur, Manbij, and as far as the Euphrates, and forming a cordon along the Euphrates. The fertile plains would thus remain free from disturbance, and the migratory bedouins would be driven back to their homelands in Arabia. Or they should not be allowed to visit the plains of Syria except in exchange for certain guarantees and on condition that they be submissive to the government.

From Aleppo he also writes on 2 March 1866 to report that Shaykh Dahhām, the shaykh whose submission the governor tried to force in the previous year, has plundered the Turkish postal caravan between Baghdad and Aleppo, making off with $20,000 worth of goods belonging to the merchants of Aleppo. He has retained the documents sent through the post, in order to annoy the Turkish authorities.

In a letter of his dated 22 October 1866, he reports that all the tribes are rising in revolt and defying the government, and that there is no one who dares to resist them. One of the Indian merchants has been looted near Dayr al-Zūr. He states that Shaykh Dahhām has replaced Jid‘ān in the shaykhship over ‘Anaza, and that Jid‘ān, in turn, has consequently risen and begun to engage in brigandage. Even Dahhām is able to do nothing to stop him; and indeed, some of his own followers assist in the plundering.

Reference to the bedouins in the consul's reports ceases for about a year, then on 21 November 1867 he writes that the governor of Aleppo is Javdat Pāshā. On 3 December 1867, he writes that on 29 November 1000 bedouin horsemen have attacked the *'arab al-ra'īya* (i.e. the sheep-herding nomads) near the village of Qayārat Dayr Ḥāfir, 25 miles east of Aleppo; they have made off with more than 10,000 head of sheep and 30 mares, killed seven men, and wounded twelve others. The leader of the raiding expedition was Ibn Murshid, head of the al-Qmāṣa, a branch of the Sbā'a bedouins, which in turn is part of 'Anaza. None of the raiders was wounded except for a black slave belonging to the shaykh, and he has gone back with his master. The expenses incurred by the state to purchase camels and mules to carry the soldiers delegated to the task of checking bedouin attacks have been to no avail. About 50 horsemen under the leadership of Nāyif ibn Ḥajjī Baṭrān went forth to fight Ibn Murshid, but he repelled them and the thwarted troops took refuge in a fort in a nearby village.

F.O. 195/902

On 2 April 1868, he writes a report in which he sets forth the names and branches of the Arab, Kurdish, and Turkoman tribes of northern Syria, specifies their approximate numerical strengths, and also cites the names of the cities and important villages which comprise the majority of the population in the north.[6] Referring to the limits of the northern region frequented by the bedouins in the province of Aleppo, he specifies these as, in the north, the watershed of the Taurus Mountains at Gulek Boghaz (formerly the Cilician Gates), to the region beyond 'Urfa in Mesopotamia, then extending southward to the Euphrates

[6] [This report has now been published in Lawrence I. Conrad, "The Province of North Syria in 1868: a Foreign Office Perspective," in *Studies in History and Literature in Honour of Nicola A. Ziadeh*, edited by Ihsan Abbas, Shereen Khairallah, and Ali Z. Shakir (London, 1992), pp. 52–67. Opportunity is taken here to correct the readings of some of the tribal names given in the Arabic text.]

at Dayr al-Zūr, westward from there to Tadmur, then to the sea at the foot of Mt. Casius, and thence northward to Pompeiopolis. We would do well to cite these tables here, for they contain useful historical information, in addition to clarifying the relative numbers of village and city-dwellers throughout the province and of members of the tribes in the region itself in those years:

Number of inhabitants in the cities

Aleppo	110,000	Antioch	20,000
Baylān	3,500	Adana	40,000
Ṭarsūs	16,000	Mar'ash	18,000
Kalas	18,000	Idlab	12,000
'Ayntāb	25,000	Rūm Qāla	9,000
Nuzayb	6,000	Bīrādjak	15,500
'Urfa	27,000		

There are, in addition, 750,000 people living in villages and 140,000 desert-dwellers. The Christian population of Aleppo is 20,000. The tribal population consists of the following:

Arab bedouins	100,000
Turkoman bedouins	30,000
Kurdish bedouins	10,000
Total	**140,000**

The Arab nomadic population consists of these tribal units:

Ḥadīdīyīn	16,000
Wlāda	8,000
Shammar	25,000
'Anaza	40,000
small tribes	11,000
Total	**100,000**

In his report he states that only a few of the Ḥadīdīyīn and Wlāda bedouins have left the lands where they had been camping, and of these there are no sections elsewhere, while there are many branches of 'Anaza and Shammar in the Aleppo area and in other regions of the Syrian Desert and the Arabian peninsula. He gives the following table of the sections of the tribes:

Branches of Shammar: 1) Faddāgha, 2) Ṭayyi', 3)' Ubayd, and 4) 'Utayba. They have other branches in Iraq.

Branches of 'Anaza: the most important is the Sbā'a, which comprises the sections of 1) al-Qmāṣa, 2) al-Mawāyiqa, 3) al-'Abādāt, 4) al-Duwām, 5) al-Shafī', 6) al-Muwayni', and 7) "Fegheghi" (?). There is also the Fid'ān, which consists of 1) al-Muhīd, 2) al-'Aqāqira, 3) al-Khrāṣa, and 4) al-Rūs. There are also six large clans of 'Anaza which frequent the villages of the province of Aleppo in the spring in order to sell their products of milk and livestock and to buy grain. These are 1) al-'Amārāt, 2) "Erfuddi" (?), 3) 'Arab Ibn Hadhdhāl, 4) al-Jlās, 5) al-Rwāla, 6) al-Shmaylāt.

As for the small tribes to which he refers above, and which number 11,000 persons, their members have been included despite the fact that they are gradually becoming farmers who till and develop the land. The names of their clans are: 1) al-Qays, 2) al-Mawālī, 3) al-Fardūn, 4) al-Luhayb, 5) Banī Sa'īd, 6) al-Shuhamī, 7) al-Faḍḍāla, 8) Wild 'Alī, 9) al-Kiyār, 10) al-'Uqaydāt.

In his report he mentions the Turkoman and Kurdish tribes by their names, and says of the Kurdish bedouins that they till the land, but are the worst of the tribes for cruelty and malice.

On 12 April 1868, he writes concerning the government's resolve to fight the bedouins, repulse them, and prevent them from entering the settled lands, and also with reference to the onset of bedouin attacks on the frontiers. He indicates that a contingent of Fid'ān bedouins has entered and stolen 5000 head of sheep coming from Mosul to Damascus, at a distance of 60 miles from Aleppo. This contingent is under the leadership of Dahhām, shaykh of the Fid'ān.

On 12 May 1868, he writes that the Governor of the Desert has begun military operations against the bedouins, assisted by a unit of camel-mounted troops and other regular army units. The opening engagement of his expedition occurred on 3 May, when, at Ḥanta, 45 miles from Aleppo, he attacked a peaceful camp of ʻAqāqira bedouins. At the time they were there for purposes of pasturing and trade, and the people of that camp were not anticipating that they would be suddenly confronted with fighting or warfare. As soon as they saw the army coming toward their camp they took their women and children, mounted them on their horses, and fled, leaving behind their tents, camels, and personal effects. The army took all this as plunder, as well as their sheep which were in the nearby grazing lands, and brought it all back to Aleppo as proof of their victory. Such was their action, without distinguishing between the hostile tribes and the peaceful ones which did not commit acts of aggression and sought only to defend themselves. The aggression committed by the army against this tribe was without provocation. As for the 5000 head of sheep to which he earlier referred as having been stolen, they had been taken not by the ʻAqāqira bedouins, but by the Khrāṣa, who are now situated in Mesopotamia in Iraq. As for the other incidents of looting he has mentioned, these have been perpetrated by the tribe of Shammar. The military commander has thus exacted vengeance from those other than the perpetrators and made a scapegoat of them. The ʻAqāqira are peaceful bedouins and do not participate with the Sbāʻa and Fidʻān in raiding and plundering. After this, Skene would not be surprised were the tribes to rally together to attack the villages and take revenge upon them. The situation will worsen, security will disappear, and trade will cease, and all this will be due to the provocation of the bedouins by the government itself.

On 16 May—that is, four days after his first letter—he writes to state that what he predicted has come to pass. The ʻAqāqira have attacked the Ḥadīdīyīn and have driven off 40,000 head of sheep, most of these belonging to traders from Aleppo, and killed ten men. By its previous aggression against the ʻAqāqira, the government has thus caused losses to the people of Aleppo, disrupted security, reduced the situation to chaos, and by striking peaceful bedouins like the ʻAqāqira, goaded them into becoming very passable robbers.

It comes as no surprise to find this same matter being raised with the governor of Aleppo, or to see that the English ambassador in Istanbul, who, in addition to the Foreign Minister, was receiving these letters, advised the Sultanate in Istanbul to appoint a new military commander to protect the desert. In a letter dated 22 May and sent by the consul, we see him indicating that a new military commander has been appointed to protect the desert. Concerning this commander he says that he appears to be an intelligent judicious man, and he expects that matters will be restored to order during his tenure in office.

F.O. 195/927

It appears that the situation became somewhat calm in the desert of Aleppo, since nothing about the bedouins in that region appears in the letters of the consul throughout the period extending from 22 May 1868 to 8 March 1869, the date of the letter containing news of attacks by the bedouins. In his letter referring to these (the first letter of 1869 containing information about the bedouins), he reports an attack mounted on 3 March by Shaykh Jid'ān, leader of the Fid'ān bedouins of 'Anaza, on a number of villages about 20 miles from Aleppo. From these villages they stole about 5000 sheep and a large number of oxen which the peasants had acquired for plowing. The government has therefore dispatched an expedition of 500 troops armed with firearms (rifles) to oppose the advance of bedouin raiders. But these latter were more numerous, and in his letter the consul expresses his fear that the expedition that has been sent will be defeated and prove unsuccessful. He then says: "Jedaan has been for many years faithful to the Government, and his rebellion is attributed to the unwise treatment he has received of late at the hands of the Governor General."

However, in another letter dated four days later, on 12 March, he goes on to state that the shaykh of 'Anaza—i.e. Jid'ān—has been seen in a village 20 miles from Aleppo and was exposed to attack and defeat. He says:

> The Turks say they had fought with the horsemen of Jedaan, and having killed his nephew, Fadil, brought his head to their camp and placed it on a pole as an example. Bedouins, who have come from that neighbourhood, tell me, however, that it is the head of an obscure Anezi, who was found sick on the road....

In another letter which he wrote on the same day (i.e. 12 March), he states that there has come to him a letter from the bedouin leaders opposed to the Turks in which they ask him to meet them at a spot about 40 miles from Aleppo. He then says:

> I do not think there is any possibility of their wishing to take an unfair advantage, as I have known them long and intimately, and I hope it may be possible for me to induce them to give up their hostile intentions against the towns and villages. I mean therefore to proceed tomorrow morning to the desert, but I shall confine my endeavours to the exercise of any influence I may possess over the Arabs....One of the circumstances appears to me to be especially worthy of remark, which is the fact that the principal chief of the movement is the same Suleyman Ibn Mirshid [Sulaymān ibn Murshid], whose battle was fought by Colonel O'Reilly near Hama, but he is not with the chiefs asking to see me, and I shall try to detach them from him. If, however, I should not succeed in bringing about their unconditional submission to the Government....I shall withdraw from all further action in the matter, limiting it at present to the mere giving of advice.

On 23 March 1869, Skene writes to report that the meeting to which he had referred did not take place, this because the army had gone before him and attacked the bedouins, especially the tribe of "Rissali,"[7] near the place specified for the meeting with the bedouin leaders. These shaykhs thus withdraw. As for the tribe which the army attacked, it is the same one that the rebel Sulaymān ibn Murshid defeated with the help of Colonel O'Reilly and which subsequently has been submissive to the government. The result of this expedition, in which were taken livestock belonging to bedouins who had given no provocation to anyone, has been to join the bedouins of the "Rissali" tribe in alliance with the rebels:

[7][Probably the Rasālīn, a clan of the Sbā'a. See Max von Oppenheim, *Die Beduinen* (Leipzig and Wiesbaden, 1939–68), I, 116.]

> On my way I passed several villages, formerly populous and prosperous, now utterly deserted, not on account of the depredations of the Bedouins, but to avoid the exaction of the Turkish Government. The iniquitous and stupid measure of holding the cultivators responsible for the deficit alleged by the Contractor (i.e. the *multazims*, or "tax farmers") after their tithes had been collected in full by him, has had the effect of driving villagers in many parts of the Province to adopt nomadic habits. . . .The Troops are boldly attacked by the Bedouins, and on one recent occasion a detachment was kept for several hours on the defensive by repeated charges of Arab horsemen, who were repulsed only by the cool bravery of two officers in command of the party.

In this letter the consul praises the Turkish colonel 'Umar Bey, as well as Maḥmūd Āghā al-Barāzī, major of irregulars, for their services in the army delegated to protect the desert. He wishfully requests:

> The Porte would therefore, in my opinion, do well to transfer them from the district of Hama, where there is no danger, to the Province of Aleppo, and give them sole charge of the military operations against the Arab Tribes. . . .In this Province, the Turks are in point of fact greater robbers than the Arabs; they rob peaceful Bedouins of their flocks; they rob industrious cultivators of their crops; and they rob merchants, both native and foreign, of the advantages to be derived from trading with the nomads and the villagers.

On 31 March 1869, he writes and states that the expedition has returned from the desert, rejoicing over a great victory. He then says:

> The facts are, that the Troops never saw the revolted tribes at all, and they have brought back 300 tents, 350 camels, and 25,000 sheep. Colonel Omer Bey, who is favorably mentioned in my Despatch no. 19 of the 23d Ultimo, had been ordered to march from Hama for the purpose of acting in concert with the Commandant of Aleppo, who had marched

> out at the head of the troops here. Omer Bey had taken with him, besides his Regulars and Irregulars, the horsemen of a friendly Bedouin Tribe. The Expedition from Aleppo came to the camp of that tribe, where there were only women and children, took all the tents, and drove off all the flocks and herds grazing around it, which have been brought here for sale as spoil. Omer Bey protests strongly against the plundering of his men, but the Governor General of Aleppo retains the plunder on an unfounded plea, that the sheep had been robbed by the revolted tribes from the neighbourhood of Orfa, and left with Omer Bey's Arabs to be taken care of. Every one here knows that the latter are the enemies of the former; that the Bedouin Tribes are not in the habit of trusting their livestock, whether robbed or not, to the keeping of other Tribes, either friends or enemies; and that the flocks robbed by the revolted Arabs are all at a place called Bishiri beyond Palmyra, where the troops can never go....

On 3 April 1869, he writes to say that on the day on which the expedition returned, Jid'ān, one of the rebel leaders, appeared in Dayr Ḥāfir, 25 miles from Aleppo, accompanied by 900 warriors. He threatened the government in a letter in which he says that he will devastate the province from one end to the other; and if it is within their power to repulse him, then let them do so. The expedition thus returned to the desert to oppose him, but since then Jid'ān has stolen 15,000 sheep from the bedouins of the Twaymāt and Bū Khamīs tribes, clans of the Ḥadīdīyīn who are loyal to the government and entrusted with the sheep of the peasants, farmers, and the residents of Aleppo. They also stole 30 tents of the Twaymāt, and 20 of the Bū Khamīs, attacked the government collectors of the sheep tax and took their horses and money, and took captive four of the followers of the shaykh of the Shammar bedouins, 'Abd al-Karīm, who are in the service of the government. At the same time, two leading shaykhs of the 'Aqāqira, Ṭalāl ibn Jamājim and Khraymas, appeared and advanced into the region with 350 horsemen and from the tribe of al-Kiyār stole 2350 sheep belonging to the inhabitants of Aleppo.

On 12 April 1869, he writes to report that on 6 April Jid'ān and Ibn 'Īda, shaykh of the "Rissaly" tribe of 'Anaza, has attacked the tribe of Ghnāṣa of the Ḥadīdīyīn,[8] which is allied with the government, driven off a large number of sheep and camels, and on the following day come to within 30 miles of Aleppo. Though between 2000 and 3000 strong, they were pursued by the horsemen from the tribe of Ghnāṣa, who succeeded in regaining their livestock. The Ghnāṣa bedouins have firearms and killed some of the 'Anaza attackers; no one from the Ghnāṣa was killed, because they did not close with their opponents when they met them, and the 'Anaza bedouins had only lances. The army did not take part in either of the two battles, and in this incident there is a lesson for the government—that it would do well to leave it to the bedouins to attack their colleagues when there was a breakdown of security.

On 22 April 1869, he writes to state that the Turkish army has attacked a place called al-Hunaydī, where they found a herd of about 800 camels and some flocks of sheep, these latter being watered at the Euphrates by their tenders from the Bū Khamīs tribe, which in a partnership arrangement have been entrusted with the sheep of the people of Aleppo. The army stole these animals and were driving them off before them when Jid'ān suddenly appeared with 20 horsemen, attacked the army, and recovered 730 camels from them. As for the sheep and the rest of the camels, the army brought them to Aleppo, where they were sold in the market. These clashes with the 'Anaza bedouins do great harm to the reputation of the army and the government, but perhaps the situation will calm down now that the capable commander Osman Bey has begun to negotiate with the bedouin leaders for an agreement with them on conditions satisfactory to both sides.

He also writes in Aleppo on 22 July 1869 to state that the bedouins have all united in opposition to the Turkish government. Despite this, no incidents have occurred, since the two officers now in charge, Ḥusnī Pāshā in al-Dayr and 'Umar Bey in Ḥamāh, are excellent and capable men. Skene doubts that the bedouins will be able to wreak havoc in the land or do anything.

[8][I.e. the Ghanāṭisa; see Oppenheim, *Die Beduinen*, I, 301.]

F.O. 195/976

On 10 May 1871, Consul Skene writes to report the appearance of the tribes near Aleppo after having spent the winter in the desert. It has been a year of drought, most of the livestock and draught animals have perished, and the bedouins have nothing left but a few dates. Flour in the villages is expensive, the she-camels are giving little milk because of the dryness and drought, and there is no one who is helping the bedouins. In his letter he indicates that Aṣlān Pāshā, governor of the desert (as he calls him), is absent, and that the situation is bad because most of the Turkish officials are also absent. He then says that he has been informed that the Khrāṣa bedouins, who are a branch of ʻAnaza, have attacked the Ḥadīdīyīn and Mawālī (semi-sedentary) bedouins and that Shaykh Dahhām was slain after killing three of the Mawālī with his lance. As for his nephew Jidʻān, famous among the ʻAnaza, he has renewed the conflict to avenge his uncle. As the Ḥadīdīyīn and the Mawālī are unable to confront the multitudes of the Fidʻān, the situation has deteriorated.

Jidʻān is seeking his own selection for leadership of the Khrāṣa and Fidʻān (of ʻAnaza). There is, however, a son of Dahhām by the name of Nāyif who has a good reputation in his tribe and also seeks the shaykhship, although leadership in the tribe is by election more than by hereditary transmission. There is thus now a dispute between the two contestants for the position, and this dispute may lead to strife and fighting among the tribes of ʻAnaza, and hence to the disruption of agricultural affairs and the life of the villagers. Skene ends his letter by suggesting that the bedouins be given no encouragement or special concessions in exchange for their misdeeds.

On 31 May 1871, he writes to state that the Turkish government has granted Jidʻān the shaykhship over his bedouins in the desert around Aleppo, which is causing the situation to deteriorate since this appointment is unacceptable to the Mawālī. In fact, it has happened that about 20 horsemen from the following of Jidʻān were pursuing four of the Mawālī, two of which fled while the other two took refuge with a small tribe by the name of Fardūn, which granted them protection and prevented Jidʻān from taking them. Jidʻān therefore sought the aid of the Turkish government, which took the two men; one tried to flee and was killed, and the second was imprisoned. This was a course of action contrary to the law of protection in the desert. The Turks also imprisoned fifteen men from the peaceful Ḥadīdīyīn, and thus the peace-loving bedouins go to prison while the mischief-makers rejoice.

On 12 June 1871, he writes of a battle between the bedouins of ʻAnaza and Shammar and of many dead, and indicates that feuding in most cases breaks out in the spring, when ʻAnaza advances northward in search of grazing land. ʻAnaza tried to cross the Euphrates, but were confronted by about 400 horsemen [of Shammar], who forced ʻAnaza to fall back and pursued them. When the refugees of the Sbāʻa, a branch of ʻAnaza, sought the assistance of Jidʻān in his capacity as shaykh of all the ʻAnaza, the latter sent an army from all of ʻAnaza against these 400 horsemen, killing and wounding about 120 of them. This naturally renewed hostility, since among the bedouins the shedding of blood demands vengeance for the slain person as far as the fifth generation. The consul has demanded an end to this state of affairs, and hopes that circulating rumors about the appointment of Thurāyā Pāshā prove to be true, since he gave proof of his worthiness and his knowledge of bedouin affairs during his previous tenure in office.

On 8 July 1871, he writes in reference to the trial of the bedouins against whom Jidʻān had complained and who have been imprisoned. He states that they pleaded their innocence, but it has been said that two of them were led off in chains to Jidʻān. This is one of the evil consequences of appointing one shaykh from one faction as the leader responsible for the desert—the reputation of the government declines.

On 15 November 1871, he speaks of two units of ʻAnaza (both of the Khrāṣa bedouins) crossing the Euphrates, having come from Iraq, and attacking the government base at Maskana (Bālis); the garrison has repulsed them with the assistance of reinforcements that came to their aid. He then says: "It appears that this enterprise marks the beginning of the familiar pattern of encroachments." At the end of his letter he indicates that Shaykh ʻAbd al-Karīm, shaykh of Shammar, has been put in chains and taken to Istanbul.

Skene writes again on 17 November 1871 concerning another attack by the Khrāṣa bedouins on the village of Dibsa, twelve miles from the Abū Hurayra garrison post. The army repelled them, some of the attackers were killed, and the rest turned back in flight. He mentions the Turks' torture of the bedouins, especially those of them who were from the friendly tribes; this is a matter that will alienate all of the bedouins from the Turks. He suggests the appointment of a commander for the desert who is familiar with desert affairs.

On 23 November 1871, he writes to report on the hanging of Shaykh 'Abd al-Karīm in Mosul. On 13 December he reports on an attack by a new tribe, that of al-'Amūr, with the Khrāṣa on the Turkish garrison in the desert. He says that the 'Amūr are numerous and powerful, and then refers to a tribe called the "Sohani," near Tadmur, the people of which earn their livelihood by burning brushwood to make alkali to sell to soap factories in Aleppo, which use it in place of soda in the manufacture of soap.[9] The people of "Sohani" are reckoned among the wealthiest of tribes. He relates how the 'Amūr bedouins plundered the goods carried by a caravan belonging to the "Sohani", as well as their camels and the loads of flour they were bringing in exchange for saltwort or alkali. He also mentions that the Turks have a force in al-Safīrā, 80 miles from the place where the men of the caravan were plundered, and that one of the camel drivers in the caravan was able to flee and inform the men of the garrison: 200 horsemen came to repel the 'Amūr, and at this point the Khrāṣa bedouins arrived to assist the 'Amūr and a battle broke out near Salamīya, 30 miles from Ḥimṣ. At the end of his letter he refers to an article in the newspaper *Levant Herald* which states that the bedouin uprising is linked to the Turkish expedition against the Najd. This theory "is certainly without the least foundation," he says.

On 27 December 1871, Skene again writes, following up news on the Turkish garrison which set out. He relates that it returned to al-Safīrā without loss since its troops were carrying rifles; they repelled the bedouins from afar, despite the fact that on their way back the bedouins pursued them for four days.

F.O. 195/1027

Consul Skene apparently mentions nothing important on bedouin affairs in the year 1872, aside from the fact that Ṣubḥī Pāshā awarded

[9] [See above, pp. 75–77. "Sohani" is not a tribe, but al-Sukhna, a town near Tadmur.]

the bedouin shaykhs robes of honor. At this point they also became shaykhs of farm lands, since he granted them agricultural lands in the al-'Alā region which had previously been populated but has since then fallen into ruin. He offers a table of income and expenditures, as well as an agricultural report in which he mentions Syrian cattle and goats and the Baghdadi carrier pigeon. Concerning the bedouins, he says that since they have finally offered their willing submission to the government and dismantled their camps with their own hands, anyone who wishes to take up agriculture can turn a plot to profitable use if the government gives him the tools for plowing, oxen, seed, and other things. In this way they are forsaking their old customs and their plundering and "brother-right." In 1873 he is content with only a simple point, which he mentions in a letter he sent on 18 April concerning a dispute over some grazing lands between the people of the two villages of Ḥadar and 'Aysh al-Sitt. Along with his letter he sends an issue of the newspaper *Al-Akhbār*, 16th year, Thursday, 10 Sha'bān AH 1290, in four pages, two in Arabic and two in French.

Consul Skene writes again on 12 and 14 January 1875, concerning his purchase of seven Arabian horses, and asks that a vizierial order be obtained from the Ottoman government so the animals can be shipped.

On 18 March a new consul, Mr. Newton, writes concerning the purchase of land for a Protestant church in the town of 'Ayntāb. He says nothing about bedouin movements, and I refer to this letter of his because the letters subsequently coming from Aleppo are from him; he evidently took up his duties after Skene. The first letter from him in which there is something about the desert and the connection of the English with it is one he sent on 17 August 1875. In it he speaks of a journey he made to the desert to purchase horses. It is a long letter in which he recounts the Turks' efforts to subdue the bedouins and speaks of the establishment six years earlier of a government administration in Dayr al-Zūr independent of Aleppo, in order to force the migratory bedouins to settle and take up sedentary life, becoming farmers and cultivators tilling the land and making it productive. The administration has been successful in inducing, by persuasion, some "lower caste" bedouins to do so; but when it began to resort to coercion it failed, and the whole lot reverted to nomadism. They resist the collection of any tax or tithe from them, and say that the land was theirs before the Turks appeared from the region of the Caspian Sea, and that the desert has not previously been conquered or surrendered. He mentions in this letter that Jid'ān, shaykh of the Fid'ān after the death of his uncle Dahhām, has become shaykh of the Khrāṣa; and since Jmay'ān, shaykh of the 'Aqāqira, is hopelessly infirm, Jid'ān has in fact become shaykh of all 'Anaza. The other shaykh is Sulaymān ibn Murshid, and his leadership has been over the tribes of the Sbā'a, comprising al-Qmāṣa, al-'Mawāyiqa, al-Mawsana, al-'Amūr, al-Ashja'a, al-Duwām, and al-'Abādāt. Both shaykhs are capable intelligent men, and the number of their followers is estimated as about 40,000 families. At any moment they can marshal into the field a force of nearly 10,000 picked horsemen, leaving half as many more in the camps to protect them, or for sending on into battle if the situation requires. He states that the number of their camels and sheep is quite surprising: around one of the Qmāṣa camps, comprising 100 tents, one could roughly count about 20,000 camels. If these are valued at a very meager price, i.e. about five pounds for each camel, it would be as if each family possessed 1000 English pounds, this leaving out of consideration the horses and sheep, the numbers of which are greater than those of the camels.

The tribes of 'Anaza are tribes that love raiding and warfare, and they are forever in conflict with the tribe of Shammar over the grazing lands in the region lying beyond the limits of Mesopotamia. Shammar and 'Anaza are nearly equal in strength, and if one adds to 'Anaza the tribes of the Rwāla, Banū Ṣakhr, and Wild 'Alī, who between them can field a similar number of horsemen, the number becomes truly amazing. But these tribes are not directed or organized for the plundering of villages and caravans, as are the small tribes in the vicinity of the towns and villages, such as the Mawālī, Wlāda, Ḥadīdīyīn, Luhayb, and others, who give a bad name to the whole nomadic population of the desert. Jid'ān and Sulaymān ibn Murshid went to al-Dayr with the approval of their followers, but when the bedouins realized that the aim was only to collect taxes, the tribes all moved off to Najd in central Arabia. Jid'ān and Sulaymān were informed of the withdrawal of their tribes and were ordered to bring them back; Sulaymān went and Jid'ān remained as a hostage. When it became clear that neither Sulaymān nor the tribes were going to return, Jid'ān was tied to the mouth of a cannon and told that they were going to fire the cannon and blow him to atoms. Fortunately for him, the cannon was not loaded. Several hours later—with him all the while looking at those around him with contempt—his bonds were untied and he was taken to confinement.

This was sufficient cause to put the ʿAnaza bedouins on their guard, so they did not come near Dayr al-Zūr to sell their products on their northward journey when good weather returned and herbage grew in the desert. The government decided to grant Shaykh Sulaymān a full pardon if he and his followers would come to the region around Aleppo, but he refused and continued to frequent his grazing lands near Ḥamāh. He intimated his coming to the Ḥamāh area to the governor of the region, and asked permission to trade with its people. The governor of Ḥamāh raised the matter with his superior, the governor-general of Damascus, and the latter proposed that Sulaymān come to him for negotiations and an agreement on this issue. But Sulaymān refused, moved back to the area south of al-Dayr, and continued to communicate with Jidʿān through his own personal intermediaries. All this produced strange results. The latter—that is, Jidʿān—was appointed as a major in the Turkish army, both men consented to pay a sheep tax to the state, permission was granted to their tribes to trade with the towns, and Jidʿān was sent out with a unit of horsemen mounted on mules to collect the taxes (called the *aʿdād*) from the tribes. It was at that time that he arrived at the camp with Captain Upton. An agreement was reached providing that the bedouins pay camels instead of money, at the rate of five pounds per camel. When they began to collect the tax, however, the two tribes of al-Maska and al-Shwayja fled by night, their tribesmen driving their camels before them. A Turkish officer was thus delegated to pursue them, accompanied by the two shaykhs Jidʿān and Sulaymān. Also with them was Shaykh Ṣāliḥ ibn Sharḥ, shaykh of the Ḥadīdīyīn, and Muḥammad Bey, shaykh of the Mawālī. The former only rarely leaves the Aleppo area, since he is the agent responsible for protecting the herds belonging to the townspeople. He does not like the Turks. Muḥammad Bey had been in Istanbul as an officer for a period of two years with the Sultan's bodyguard; after that he returned to nomadic life.

Had the two withdrawing tribes wished to make good their escape it would not have been difficult for them to do so, for they had made a good head start and they knew that the army's pace would be slow. But the bedouins of the two tribes decided that the best course of action was to proceed slowly and confront them. The Turks pounced upon a herd of camels along their way and entrusted it to the bedouins of the Ḥadīdīyīn and the Mawālī to guard, on the advice of the shaykhs of the two above-mentioned tribes who were with the commander and left their tribes to observe the course of events from behind. At this point the bedouins of the Fid'ān, Khrāṣa, and 'Aqāqira—the tribes of Jid'ān—suddenly appeared on the field, and their men attacked the Ḥadīdīyīn and Mawālī and took the camels without killing or wounding a single one of them. After nightfall each tribe of 'Anaza recovered its camels from the tribe of Jid'ān and went far out into the desert where it would be difficult to seek and engage them.

As for the Turkish army, from which no one was injured, it seems that it, accompanied by Shaykh Sulaymān ibn Murshid, fought two of the tribes of Sbā'a, while the tribes of the Mawālī and the Ḥadīdīyīn, who were ostensibly on the side of the Turks, fought the Fid'ān, Khrāṣa, and 'Aqāqira. At the same time, the shaykhs of the tribes engaged—Jid'ān, Ṣāliḥ, and Maḥmūd—were accompanying the Turkish commander and orchestrating the maneuvers in this fake or sham fight by means of well-mounted messengers. And so ended the bedouin comedy starring Jid'ān, the one who accepted Turkish rank, and Sulaymān, who agreed to pay the taxes, and the curtain fell on the contingent of Turkish mule-mounted cavalry, who would return empty-handed, probably to claim that they had won splendid victories. The two shaykhs returned to their camps, families, and fellow tribesmen, who in the meantime had sold their produce.

Reports of the English Consul in Damascus Pertaining to Nomadism and Bedouins in the Province of Damascus, Beginning in 1861

E.T. Rogers writes from Damascus on 13 June 1861 to report on the camping of bedouin tribes in the Ḥawrān. There are four of these tribes: the Sbā'a, Fid'ān, 'Imārāt, and the Dahāmsha; Shaykh Ismā'īl is with them, and they are led by Shaykh Fayṣal. He states that they are said to number about 100,000, but one must be wary on the question of accepting such a figure. Some say they are in collusion with the Druze and will assist them against the government. He then says: "I think that the matter has something to do with the visit of Halim Pasha to Egypt; he has sent encouraging letters and presents to the shaikhs of Jordan in the Hauran."

On 20 June 1861, he writes to report concerning the appeal by Fu'ād Pāshā to the bedouin shaykhs, in order to reach an agreement with them providing for the allocation of inhabited lands to them for grazing their livestock; these lands would be specifically designated as theirs so that no one else would encroach upon them. They would have to become law-abiding herdsmen, without any consideration or query as to the question of their sedentarization; but Fu'ād Pāshā would be able to take men from them for the army, with their permission. It would be enjoined upon the shaykhs that they would prevent their tribes from committing acts of aggression against the populace in the farms and villages, and that bedouin hostages would remain with him to act as his aides in matters of disagreement and other affairs. The consul mentions that at first the shaykhs refused to accept the appeal, but before long they agreed to do so and came to Damascus, and went with him to Beirut. He ends his letter by saying that he hopes that this situation will serve to secure the hoped-for tranquillity and facilitate the flow of trade.

On 10 July 1861, he writes concerning a clash that has broken out between two tribes, those of Shaykh Muḥammad Dūkhī (Wild 'Alī) and Fayṣal al-Sha'lān (Rwāla), with the loss of some dead. He mentions that the military authorities intervened and separated the two sides. He also states that some sort of strife occurred between Ismā'īl al-Aṭrash and Shaykh Muḥammad Dūkhī because of an old quarrel, and that while some of the Druze in the Ḥawrān have sided with Shaykh Fayṣal in his struggle with Muḥammad Dūkhī, the senior shaykhs of the Druze have opted for complete neutrality.

He then writes on 12 July to state that the enmity between Shaykh Fayṣal al-Sha'lān, leader of the Rwāla, and Shaykh Muḥammad al-Dūkhī, leader of the Wild 'Alī, has recently intensified because of their dispute over grazing lands for their livestock. It seems that in years past it has been Fayṣal who has occupied the non-agricultural lands in the Ḥawrān, and that Shaykh Muḥammad al-Dūkhī has been content with the fringe and peripheral lands, even those upon which tax is payable. In order to put an end to the strife between them, Fu'ād Pāshā designated a territory for each tribe, as would seem from what the consul says in the report he wrote on 20 June. But this arrangement did not placate Shaykh Muḥammad Dūkhī, since he regarded it as a violation of his rights and a reduction in the grazing lands available for his use. He therefore raised objections to the plan, and the government accordingly altered this arrangement, increasing his territory and decreasing that of Fayṣal, which also lacked fertile grazing land and contained only a single source of water. Fayṣal thereupon requested that the government restore the lands to him according to the first division. The government refused to accede to his request, and he was told that if he was not satisfied, let him go back to the desert. When he saw that the *pāshā* in Mzayrīb harbored enmity against him, he withdrew about an hour's riding distance into the desert. The consul then says: "Grazing lands are extremely important to these bedouins, and I now fear that strife will arise because of them." It is said that the government forced Shaykh Fayṣal to return to the desert in view of his friendship with the Druze and his alliance with them, and that it would leave Shaykh Muḥammad to subdue the Druze when the situation required. The region east and south of Damascus is thus in a state of turmoil. The village of the Russian consul is under threat, as also is the village of 'Aqrabā, which is located about a half hour from Damascus. A contingent of bedouins has attacked the latter village and plundered it of its livestock; according to information reaching the consul from the following of Rasūl Āghā, there was a group of Kurds with the raiders.

On 23 December 1861, he writes from Damascus that infantry from the Turkish army arrested two bedouin shaykhs, beheaded them, and displayed the heads in Damascus.

F.O. 195/806

On 9 March 1864, he writes that Mrs. Digby, an English lady, purchased 250 camels and left them with herdsmen around Tadmur. They were then stolen by the bedouin shaykh Muḥammad al-Dūkhī, and she now demands compensation for their value, which she places at 250,000 piasters. The consul says that the governor of Damascus claims that he has written to Shaykh al-Dūkhī demanding that he return the camels; but the latter has not done so, and hence the lady has renewed her complaint. He then mentions that the army has attacked the tribe of al-Dūkhī and taken camels, some of which bear a brand which is that of the camels of Mrs. Digby.

On 10 March he writes of the death of Shaykh Fayṣal al-Sha'lān, whom he says he has mentioned frequently in his dispatches. Fayṣal was the most intelligent and most moderate of the shaykhs in the desert, he says, a leader at the head of one of the most powerful tribes. The consul states that Fayṣal was killed by a group of his distant relatives from "the tribe of Mash-hoor." Fayṣal was implicated in the killing of one of them at the hand of one of his slaves, and after the killing of Fayṣal the murderers fled on their horses and are presently with the bedouins of al-Rashīd and the Wahhābīs.

He also writes from Damascus to the ambassador in Istanbul on 12 March 1864 to report that Rushdī Pāshā, commander-in-chief of the Army of Arabia, has been dismissed from office and replaced by Ḥalīm Pāshā, who held this post before him and met with a most cordial reception.

On 14 March he writes concerning an Indian who has come to the Ḥawrān to purchase horses, and is carrying documents to the shaykhs of the oases of Qadmūs and al-Majīdīya in the desert. But so far he has bought nothing.

On 29 March 1864, he writes concerning a military inspector by the name of Samīḥ Pāshā who is eliminating many abuses in the part of the army that is based in the Arabian peninsula, cleaning up the hospitals and improving conditions in the army. He considers that thefts by embezzlement amount to 36,000 pounds sterling.

On 11 April 1864, he writes of an incident of plundering suffered by one of the merchants around Damascus, perpetrated by Amīr Salmān of the al-Ḥrāfsha group (the Ḥarfūsh tribe).

On 10 May 1864, he writes to report on the increase in the number of travelers, especially English ones. Plundering has become of lesser incidence and is limited to one case in a garden near Damascus; the government assisted in the above-mentioned case, exacted the money from the owner of the garden, and returned it, in the amount of 7000 piasters, to Mr. Blunt in Beirut.

On 16 August 1864, he writes concerning a woman from Rāshayyā, from the small community of Protestant Christians, reporting that she has been mistreated and beaten. Her face was smeared with honey, and she was put out in the sun to attract bees and flies. He describes the deed as barbarous, and says that the Pāshā has promised to institute an immediate inquiry. At the same time, however, the consul says that he cannot officially protect these Christians, since they are not British subjects.

On 11 October 1864, he writes to report on a meeting of Turkish governors and on the journey of the Damascus commander of the Army of Arabistan to the regions of Ḥimṣ and Ḥamāh, to organize an expedition to subdue some of the tribes.

On 27 January 1865, he writes that the Druze of the Ḥawrān and the Lijāh, who have taken it upon themselves to subdue the rebellious tribes, gathered and went to where it was claimed there were bedouins, but saw no one. This was probably a pre-arranged plan, for on their way back they plundered the Christian villages in their districts near Khabab and al-Baṣīr.

On 18 March 1865, he writes how the bedouins have collected the *khuwwa* and lodged as guests with the populace in the villages of the Ḥawrān. He also mentions that the Lijāh is a rallying point for rebels and the refuge of Bashīr Bey Abū Nakd, who has sought refuge in the mountains because of his participation in the massacre of Christians of 1860.

On 15 January 1866, Consul E.T. Rogers in Damascus writes a report on the trade situation in the year 1865. In it he states that the road between Damascus and Baghdad has been cut for years, and that it is his intention to meet some of the bedouin shaykhs to arrange for the reopening of the road. He indicates that the route followed by caravans to Iraq in the above-mentioned years was Mosul–Diyārbakr–Aleppo–Alexandretta, and then either to Beirut by sea or Damascus by land. By this route the journey takes from three to four months, while it would not take more than 40 days were there a direct route connecting Damascus and Baghdad. The consul mentions that merchants have imported 220,000 head of sheep from Anatolia to Damascus, 80,000 for Damascus itself and the remainder for other cities in Syria and for Egypt.

On 16 May 1866, he writes to relate that the bedouins of the al-Faḍl tribe have encroached upon the pastures and farm lands of Majdal Shams, and that there is strife between the bedouins of al-ʻAdwān, allied with a part of the Banū Ṣakhr and led by Nimr, son of Shaykh Rabāḥ al-Saʻīd, and the rest of Banū Ṣakhr and their acknowledged shaykh, whose name is Muṭlaq al-Saʻīd. Shaykh Muṭlaq was killed in this strife when his group was caught by surprise in a night attack. Many others from both sides were killed, and the government sent a force to prevent any further clash between these factions.

On 29 June 1866, he writes to report incidents of plundering in the desert east of the Ḥawrān and many raids on the villages. He indicates that the troops returning from accompanying the pilgrims have been ordered to remain in the town of Mzayrīb to protect the area.

On 30 August 1866, he writes that a punitive expedition has been sent in pursuit of bedouins near Ṣalkhad; but the bedouins knew that it was marching in their direction and so fled to the desert, and the army attacked the herdsmen who were tending the sheep of the Druze and stole the animals. The Druze were soon called to arms, took back their sheep, and killed and wounded a number of troops amounting to about 60. He also refers to reciprocal raids between the bedouins and the army.

On 27 October 1866, he writes to report the migration of a large number of Druze families from Ḥāṣbayyā and Rāshayyā and surrounding areas to the Ḥawrān during the last weeks prior to the date of his letter. The reason for the migration of these people, he says, is the poverty of the regions that have been devastated by locusts and the richness of the region of the Ḥawrān, which is full of abandoned villages. He states that the Druze have begun to populate these villages. Strife broke out between them and the tribe of Wild ʻAlī; a Druze was killed, and the other Druze attacked the tribe to exact vengeance for him. He also indicates that other reasons for the migration are the advantages enjoyed by the Druze in the Jabal, and the light taxes levied upon them there.

On 20 November 1866, he writes that the populace in the Jabal Ḥawrān has driven out the governor of the Jabal because the government no longer protects anyone, while at the same time taxes are levied upon them on the pretext of paying for their protection from the bedouins, and because the peasants are charged customs duty on the requisites they purchase from Damascus for their own use. This is the first protest clearly expressed by the Muslims and Christians of the Ḥawrān against taxes, and the consul says that they have called for an attack by the Slūṭ bedouins to help them. He then goes on to report that these bedouins killed the Christians who lodged them in the village of Khabab.

On 21 May 1867, he writes a long letter concerning the meeting of Rashīd Pāshā and Darwīsh Pāshā in Ḥimṣ and Ḥamāh with Jevdet Pāshā, governor of Aleppo, to discuss the establishment of a strike force of horse and camel-mounted cavalry, based at Tadmur, to deter the bedouins and protect the villages and fields. Its arm would extend like a cordon or fence as far as Aleppo to prevent the bedouins from grazing their herds west of that line. These decisions have been presented to the British consul in Damascus by Rashīd Pāshā, governor-general of Syria. The consul indicates that it would be best for the government to entice the bedouins with the prospect of gain rather than to intimidate them. It should also encourage relations between the bedouins and the peasants by establishing fairs in Tadmur and other villages located along the bedouins' path, places where the settled folk could sell provisions and clothing to the bedouins or barter them for such bedouin products as clarified butter, sheep, camels, and horses. He finally states: "I made similar observations to Darwish Pasha, and both these functionaries promised to take the suggestions into consideration."

On 12 June 1868, he writes concerning certain incidents and clashes that have occurred between the Druze and the Slūṭ bedouins. He says that the Druze suspect the government of taking sides with the Slūṭ bedouins, and from his letter it seems that he endorses the viewpoint of the Druze. He indicates that the Druze have lost a number of men killed and are seeking revenge; they have set out to raid the Slūṭ, but previously they killed the Christians who had lodged them in Khabab.

On 7 July 1868, he writes to state that the governor of Damascus, Rashīd Pāshā, motivated by a desire to rule the Ḥawrān as well, has encouraged the enmity between the Slūṭ bedouins and the Druze and has begun to allow the former to camp near the villages and ruin the fields, this with the connivance of his relative Yūsuf Ḍiyā Pāshā, district commissioner (*mutaṣarrif*) of the Ḥawrān. The Druze have noticed that they are under threat, and so have appealed to their kinsmen in Wādī al-Taym to protect them. The Druze claim that the Slūṭ killed twelve Druze individuals in al-Shafrā, and that the government has not curbed them or taken revenge upon them.

On 16 July 1868, in the wake of the above incidents, he writes that Ismā'īl al-Aṭrash has sent a letter to the shaykh of the Rwāla bedouins asking him to ally with them against the Slūṭ bedouins. He mentions in his letter that Ismā'īl al-Aṭrash leads the Druze.

In the last letter in which there is mention of the bedouins, dated 31 August 1868, he writes in defense of Muṣṭafā Pāshā, commander of the military forces in Arabistan, who has apparently been replaced by another commander.

F.O. 195/927

In a letter signed by Charles Wood, dated 3 April 1869, but included among the documents of the consul of Aleppo, he speaks about an attack by the al-Ghiyāth and al-Ḥasan bedouins north of the Ḥawrān on the trade route to Baghdad, where they accosted a caravan from which they stole 180 camels loaded with merchandise. He states that the governor-general ordered the Druze, through Hūlū Pāshā, governor of the Ḥawrān, to attack the bedouins to recover the stolen animals from them and exact a fine from them. The bedouins thus fled to the Lijāh and sought the aid of the Slūṭ; but the Druze threatened to attack the latter if they protected them, so the Ghiyāth and Ḥasan bedouins gave in and handed the stolen camels over to Shaykh Ismā'īl al-Aṭrash, who allowed them to withdraw without inflicting any punishment or fine upon them. Wood states that the commercial sluggishness of Damascus is attributable to the breakdown of security along the route to Baghdad.

On 16 July 1869, he writes to report that Shaykh Fandī al-Fāyiz, shaykh of the Banū Ṣakhr, set out at the head of 1500 warriors from his tribe, accompanied by Shaykh ʻAlī Diyāb at the head of 500 bedouins of ʻAdwān, and went to the village of al-Ranta on the Ḥawrān plain and plundered it. This they did because its people refused to pay the *khuwwa*, which had been abolished after an expedition launched by the government against the bedouins in 1867. When word of this reached the governor, he dispatched an army expeditionary force, accompanied also by Shaykh al-Dūkhī, shaykh of the Wild ʻAlī, and 800 horsemen from his tribe. He also persuaded Ismāʻīl al-Aṭrash to join the expedition, and the force advanced in three columns to the fringes of the desert. The consul was asked to accompany the expedition with the reserve unit, which consisted of Turkish infantry and cavalry, Druze infantry, and some tribesmen of the Balqā', as well as two cannons. The consul then says that he has heard that Fandī al-Fāyiz was defeated when he encountered Shaykh Dūkhī, and that the latter took spoils from him and his group of 2000 sheep, 300 camels, and 140 oxen. It is said that his group took most of the sheep before they could be handed over to the state. The leader of the ʻAdwān then offered his submission, which was accepted on condition that he pay 25,000 piasters—the value of the tribe's share of the goods plundered from the village. As for the Banū Ṣakhr, they did not capitulate and took refuge at the camp of the Ḥumaydī bedouins, who are camped in the passes between Ḥasbān and Karak.

The consul goes on to say that their line of march followed after Fandī down those twisting roads never previously reached by a Turkish army; they camped at a pool, thus forcing Fandī to seek a truce. This was granted on condition that he pay 200,000 piasters and hand over his son as a hostage. The rights to protect the pilgrimage route were revoked from Banū Ṣakhr and granted to the bedouins of Wild ʻAlī. As for the tribe of al-Ḥumaydī, which had protected Banū Ṣakhr, their tribesmen said that by their life they did not know that they were under the rule of a government; rather, their land has been theirs from time immemorial. Now, however, they recognize the Sultan's government and will pay taxes to the state. The task of collecting the taxes was entrusted to ʻUqaylī Āghā, who had joined us with 500 of his horsemen, and we returned. Before Wood took his leave and departed, however, Rashīd Pāshā, governor of Damascus, assembled all of the shaykhs of the tribes in the Balqā', and with them all present announced that any breach of security would lead to an expedition for which they themselves would pay the expenses.

There is a long letter, also from the consul of Damascus and dated 26 October 1869, in which he relates how the populace is obliged to till the ground with their guns loaded, and how the Banū Ṣakhr continues to compel the peasants to pay the *khuwwa* and other amounts of money. He reports the submission of the citadel of al-Salṭ to the government in 1867, and how it has been occupied and garrisoned and al-Salṭ itself made the seat of an administrative district (*qā'imaqāmīya*).

As for Karak, it too had not recognized the authority of the government, and in turn has also submitted. His excellency the governor has abolished the *khuwwa* throughout the region of the Balqā', added Jabal 'Ajlūn and the Nablus region to the Balqā', and promoted the governor, for whom al-Salṭ became his administrative seat. Discussing the lands, the consul says that they are suitable for cultivation and not desert; and he points to the remains of many ruined villages as proof of a former state of great prosperity and regards the wheat grown by the Banū Ḥasan in the north of the Balqā' as far superior to that of the Ḥawrān. As for the regions of 'Ajlūn, they are, as he says, comparable to the parks of England.

Of the bedouins he says that it is not within their ability to resist the regular army, and then classifies the bedouins into the categories of true bedouins, which include the Sbā'ā, the Rwāla, and the Wild 'Alī, and semi-bedouins, which include the other tribes. He sets forth a proposal for the establishment of blockhouses along the desert frontiers and for placing garrisons in them. Tadmur having been annexed to the province of Aleppo, its governor will establish a garrison there, and a garrison should also be stationed at al-Qaryatayn. He mentions that Rashīd Pāshā has also suggested that garrisons be established in blockhouses along the entire length of the pilgrimage route as far as the Jawf, where the tribes of 'Anaza spend the winter, and that a garrison be stationed in Petra—the bedouins would thus remain confined within this circle. He finally says that he is convinced that in such a situation as this the bedouins will gradually begin to settle. The Druze near the Lijāh will not submit if the bedouins do not also do so.

At the end of his report he provides a detailed table of the bedouin tribes and the numbers of their tents. We have thought it worthwhile to cite this table for comparison with the tables provided in a later period, for the benefit of those who may wish to peruse the names of the tribes and the numbers of their tents and members:

Small Clans

Tribe	*Tents*	*Shaykh*
al-Khrāṣa	4670	
al-Blādīya	100	
al-Masā'īd	100	al-Duray' Abū Ḥāmid
al-Ḥwayṭāt	300	Abū Ḥāzī
al-Nu'aym	100	
Banī Fahd	50	
al-Jaraband	50	
Total	5380	

Bedouins of the Balqā'

Tribe	*Tents*	*Location*
al-ʻAdwān al-Ṣāliḥ al-Qāyid ʻAbbād	450 500	al-Salṭ, Amman, and Jarash
Ḥasan	1000	Jabal ʻAjlūn
al-Waʻja	100	
al-ʻAjārima	150	
al-Ghanam (Banū) al-Ḥumayda (Banū) al-Ṣaqr	600 1000 200	s. of Ḥasbān, the domain of Ḥārithī ibn Fāyiz, who wields authority and influence over more than 1000 tents and receives the *khuwwa* from Banū Ḥumayda
al-Ghazāwiya	200	
Banū Ṣakhr	200	
Slayṭ	100	
al-Ḥajāyā	270	

Between one and three horsemen live in a single tent.

Bedouins of the Ḥawrān

Tribe	*Tents*	*Shaykh*	*Location*
al-Slūṭ	530		around the Lijāh
al-Ḥajāza			
al-Mrāshida			
al-Fawākhira			
al-Shar'a			
al-'Awārāt			
al-Zawf			
'Anaza			
Wild 'Alī	1000	Muḥammad ibn Samīr	w. of Buṣrā
al-Rwāla	3000	Hazzā' and Ṭalāl	e. of Buṣrā
al-Ma'jil	300	Ḥammūd ibn Ṣāliḥ	
al-Swālma	200	Ibn Jandal	
al-Blā'īs	300	Shīḥān	
al-Ghiyāth	200	Muṭlaq al-Hawwāsh	
al-Ḥasan	150	Tūhān al-Khaṭīr	
al-Masā'īd	250	Fraywān al-Sarūr	
al-'Uẓaymāt al-Fwā'ira	200		n. , e. , and s. of the Jabal Druze
al-Sardīya	200		
al-'Ujaylīya	100		
al-Faḍl	1000	Ḥasan al-Fā'ūr	
Turkomans	400	Ibn Diyāb Aghā	
al-'Isā	150	Khaṭṭāb	
al-Sirḥān	500	Nhār and Nkār	
al-Nu'aym	300	Barkīs al-Nādir	
Bakr	15	Ḥusnī al-'Ajlūf	

Originally Iraqi Tribes Frequenting Syria

Tribe	*Tents*	*Shaykh*	*Location*
ʻAnaza			
al-Rwāla	6,000	Ibn Shaʻlān	
al-Ḥsāna	1,000	Fāris al-Mazyad	around
al-Shāyiʻa	1,000	Ibn Muḥjin	
al-Swaylha	400	Ibn Jandal	
al-ʻAbd Allāh	500	Ibn Majīd	the
al-Raʻīya			Ḥamād
al-ʻAmārāt	8,000	Ibn Hadhdhāl	
al-Sbāʻa	6,000	Sulaymān al-Murshid and others	and
al-Fidʻān	4,000	Ibn Muhayd and Ibn Ghabīn	
al-Fwāʻira & al-Qamāqim	2,000	Aḥmad Bey and Amīr Fayyāḍ	Tadmur
al-Ḥadīdīyīn	4,000	Shaykh Ibrāhīm	
Banī Khālid	2,000	al-Zawwāf	
al-ʻAmūr	1,000	Ṭalī	
Ibn Shanbān	4,000	al-Nāṣir	
al-ʻAqaydāt	3,000	al-Ẓāhir	
Shammar			
Shammar	10,000	Farḥān Pāshā ʻAbd al-Karīm	
al-Jbūr	7,000	Muḥammad Amīn and ʻAbd Rabbih	around
al-Daym	4,000	ʻĪsā and Shāwshī	
al-ʻUbayd	4,000	Saʻdūn al-Muṣṭafā	Baghdad
al-Ẓafīr	4,000	Ibn Suwayṭ	
Maṭar	6,000	al-Duways	
al-Kastalīm	1,000	Dayyūs	

F.O. 195/965

Richard Burton was appointed as consul in Damascus in the summer of 1870 in replacement of Charles Wood. In a letter he sent on 1 September 1870 there is an enumeration of the number of the inhabitants of Damascus from the various confessional communities. There are 87,000 residents in the city: 4000 of them Jews, 13,000 Christians, and 70,000 Muslims. The letter refers to the effort by the Jews to sow the seeds of discord between the Christians and the Muslims, by drawing crosses on mosques by night. At the end of his letter he says that the Jews are profiteers and exploit everything for their own benefit. He follows this with another letter on 9 June 1871 in which he states that bedouin raids on the farmers are incessant; but he mentions nothing about any incident in these attacks, and between these two letters he makes no reference to bedouin affairs and desert life throughout the period of about an entire year. When a new consul named Thomas Jago was appointed after him, he states in his letter dated 28 September 1871 that the situation in the desert is calm, because of the leadership of Rashīd Pāshā and his expeditions into the desert. He indicates that the Pāshā took hostages from the bedouins after they devastated the frontiers in the desert, made attempts at plundering, and committed acts of agression. He also pursued the bedouins themselves to the interior of the desert.

F.O. 195/994

In 1872 a new consul, Mr. Green, was appointed. In a letter he writes on 28 February 1872 it is said that the governor in Damascus has proposed that pressure be brought to bear on the bedouins from the direction of both Egypt and Jordan in order to subdue them. In another letter dated 6 April 1872 he states that Ṣubḥī Pāshā, governor of Damascus, has displayed a noteworthy ability to deter the bedouins and defeat them in their numerous raids in the outlying districts around Tadmur. He is determined to make the bedouins understand Turkey's ability to check them and the impossibility of it acquiescing in these raids and in damage to its agricultural lands.

On 28 May 1872, he writes to state that Ṣubḥī Pāshā himself has decided that it would be a good idea to distribute certain state lands to the bedouins, and has actually given them 28 sites to till and render productive.

A month later, on 24 June, he writes that the Rwālā bedouins had invited the governor to visit their camp, and that the governor had invited Green to accompany him. He spent three days, he says, and it was the first time such a reception had been proffered to a Turkish governor, and the first time official permission was given to view their tribes. Their camp is located 35 miles east of Damascus, and their shaykh is Hazzā' al-Sha'lān. In the reception party for the governor were between 200 and 300 horsemen carrying lances, about fifteen feet long, and some of them clad in armor. As for the foot warriors, they were carrying matchlocks, scimitars, and clubs. They claim that they have between 2500 and 3000 horsemen and about 6000 foot warriors. He then says that the most important source of wealth among the Rwāla is camels, of which he says their tribe owns no less than 100,000, and "in the encampment we visited there were about thirty thousand." The governor gave their shaykhs revolvers as gifts, and one of the shaykhs opened fire with one of them and wounded himself in two fingers and also wounded a soldier. The bedouins have begun to consider that raids have already ended or are coming to an end, and they feel regret at that.

Green was also received by Shaykh Muḥammad al-Dūkhī, leader of 'Anaza, in his camp near the farm of 'Udhruh, and the celebration he held for him was no less warm than that which he received from the leader of the Rwāla, but not so imposing, this because only a fraction of his tribe was in 'Udhruh. The governor gained much information about their military power; it seems that they can send into battle about 60,000 horsemen and 180,000 foot warriors. The governor considered that were they to be released from demands for tribute and formally organized militarily, it would be possible to create an army like that of the Cossacks.

On 16 November he writes to state that the governor has informed him that he has been successful in making peace among the tribes living in Ma'ān, the Jawf, Karak, the Ghawr, Jabal Shahbah, Ṭafīla, and Wādī Mūsā, and prevailed upon them to give up their independence and submit to his governance. He also informed him that he has appointed Muḥammad Sa'īd Pāshā as district commissioner (*mutaṣarrif*) over them. The consul then says that the sedentaries in this region number about 40,000, accompanied by 100,000 bedouins; this agreement will accordingly place garrisons in special forts in the cities, 200 regular army troops in each town. He hopes that his project will prove successful, since it will establish security for traveling and touring foreigners.

F.O. 195/1027

On 27 January 1873, Consul Green writes from Damascus on the killing by the Druze of some bedouins who had frequently attacked the peasants and fields. He relates how about 4000 bedouins of the desert assembled in the region of Moab to seek vengeance. They concentrated near Ṣalkhad, which was under the control of the Aṭrash family. About 400 Druze horsemen under the leadership of Ibrāhīm al-Aṭrash rallied to confront the bedouins, attacked them by surprise, and seized from them 6000 sheep and 80 camels. There were then negotiations, in the wake of which all of the spoils that had been taken were returned. When the Druze returned to Ṣalkhad and were unprepared for fighting, the bedouins attacked them, began to open fire on them, and killed some of their horses. But the Druze immediately took to arms, rallied, counterattacked against the bedouins, and killed thirteen of their men. The Druze fear that it may have been the Turkish government that encouraged the bedouins.

On 20 February 1873, he writes to indicate that the Turkish government has decided to subdue all the tribes; then he writes again on 11 March and mentions that the bedouin tribes have begun to launch raids on the farms and villages, some of these attacks being on an extensive scale. On 16 April he writes again concerning the Jawf and the possibility of joining it to Ma'ān, and indicates that the Turkish government has abolished this sub-governorship because it considers the expenses of its maintenance excessive. He says that in the Jawf there are two oases, one with a population of 700 and the second with 400; the primary source of income in the larger oasis is dates.

In a letter dated 5 May of the same year, he mentions that there is news to the effect that the *mushīr* of Damascus has cleverly sent Shaykh Muḥammad al-Dūkhī, the famous leader of the tribe of Wild ʿAlī, on a secret mission to the Muslims of the Ḥawrān, who are rebelling against the Empire because of the government's attempt to enforce collection of the property tax. He says nothing further about this.

On 3 June 1873, he writes to say that the government is powerless even to settle affairs in Maʿān, Karak, and the Jawf, thus forcing the governor to request two army units for protection and two mountain howitzers. The government did not accede to his request, so this led him to resort to the local populace and conscript about 450 militia horsemen from them, some of whom deserted before he reached Maʿān. In the Jawf he encountered resistance from a group of about 4000 bedouin horsemen, launched a determined attack upon them, and unconditionally subdued them, killing about 30 of their horsemen. News of his victory and his destruction of the bedouins of the Jawf spread throughout Arabia, and the tribes offered their submission. Ibn Rashīd himself, ruler of Shammar, also came and offered his submission to the governor after it became clear to him that his claim to jurisdiction over the Jawf would avail him nothing; after returning to the tribe of Shammar he sent to the state horses and camels as an installment on the back taxes he owed. In the Jawf there are six townlets, and these can bring 4800 armed men into the field. The cities are Sakāka, al-Jawf, Qāra, Ṭuwayr, ʿAyṣarīya (in which there is a salt mine), and Kāf. The bedouin tribes of the Jawf are the Banū ʿAṭīya, Ibn Jāzī, al-Ḥwayṭāt, al-Hajāya, al-Saʿdīyīn, Ibn Rashīd, al-Manīn, and the al-Muḥammadīyīn; the members of these clans visit the Jawf to obtain supplies of dates and water, and for its grazing lands. By means of the taxes it takes from the bedouins the state can collect a sum a hundred times greater than the outlay for its maintenance. For more than two years the government has refused to provide escorts for visitors to Tadmur, and it has been up to the visitor to see to the matter of his own protection and to purchase the right of passage from the bedouins, which may cost a group of visitors between 200 and 300 English pounds. Now, however, some of the irregular army protects the routes, and the route to Baghdad is also safe. This is due to the resolve and tactics of Muḥammad Saʿīd Pāshā.

As for Karak, there are about 10,000 warriors in it. In praising Muḥammad Sa'īd Pāshā, the consul goes on to say that during his tenure of office in the Sinai and Petra area, western travelers could rest assured that they would be able to move about in safety. Perhaps he will also assure security for them in the Jawf, especially since he says that he has ordered the bedouins to maintain security and hopes that they will do so.

In a letter of 8 August 1873, sent by the same consul from his summer residence in Blūdān, he says of the bedouins of the Ḥawrān that they have rebelled against the government, and that in the last three days they have killed three Turkish soldiers. He refers to the movement of an army regiment to the Ḥawrān and its bivouacing in Dānūn.

In another letter sent from Damascus on 12 August, he states that another force of camel-mounted cavalry has been sent to the Ḥawrān since the bedouins have not submitted. Khālid Pāshā has asked the men of the expedition not to turn their attention to spoils and the gaining of camels and sheep; rather, he wants them to send him the heads of some of the rebels.

In another letter dated 3 October 1873, the consul states that security is still disrupted in the Ḥawrān region and that plundering is widespread. The English post sent by camel to Baghdad has been plundered.

In a letter of 29 October, also from Damascus, he indicates that the bedouins still persist in their disruption of security and in interfering with travelers and the post on its way to Baghdad. They have stripped the courier of his clothing, torn up the postal bags, and taken his camel. He says that if the bedouins are not punished, the situation will become worse and security will be lost.

The consul writes a letter from Blūdān on 31 August 1874 in which he states that about 200 bedouins from the Slūṭ and Ḥasan tribes have attacked the Ḥawrān town of Adhra', to which the garrison of Mzayrīb had been transferred and where some of the leaders of these bedouins were being held as hostages. The bedouins overwhelmed the garrison, stole 35,000 piasters from the treasury, wounded three officers of the garrison, and killed one as he tried to stop the bedouins. The governor-general in Damascus called on the Druze shaykhs to guarantee that they would not acquiesce in the withdrawal of the bedouins to the Jabal Druze, but none save a single Druze shaykh agreed to do so. The consul hopes that a punitive expedition will go forth to preserve the reputation of the government and restore its stolen funds.

Then on 19 September 1874 he writes to mention that the government is not taking the above-mentioned incident lightly, and to indicate that the governor of Damascus has been dismissed and that As'ad Pāshā has been appointed to take his place.

He then writes from Damascus in November 1874 to state that As'ad Pāshā has informed him of his intention to travel to the Lijāh to view the situation himself. A force from the army will escort him thither, since the bedouins continue to wreak havoc in the land, even up to the vicinity of Damascus and on the route to Baghdad. He then says that As'ad Pāshā has made the trip and gained the submission of the bedouins of the Lijāh and the support of the senior shaykhs of the Druze. He states that the Druze trust the English and heed their advice, and that they have promised to support the government in attacking and subduing the bedouins.

On 7 December 1874, he writes to mention the passage of As'ad Pāshā, governor of Damascus, returning from Ḥamāh and passing by al-Qalamūn, which in recent days has been subjected to continual bedouin attacks and the plundering of its livestock. He praises As'ad Pāshā for touring and inspecting the more removed parts of the country, and mentions the positive results of this course of action.

On 8 December 1874, he writes that the bedouins of Ghiyāth have accosted the Earl of Derby and stolen much of what he had with him. He indicates that an expedition has set out to subdue the bedouins of Slūṭ, but says that the bedouins who are the aggressors and troublemakers are those of Ghiyāth, al-Shaṭṭī, al-Ḥusayn, and al-'Amūr. Their territory is the Ṣafā, a volcanic region like the Lijāh surrounded by dry desert lands. An expedition against them would be very expensive, hence As'ad Pāshā sent a letter to them through Shaykh Muḥammad Dūkhī of the tribe of Wild 'Alī, and through some of the Druze, while the consul also offered his good offices. Shaykh Muṭlaq al-Hawwāsh, Shaykh Salāma, and Dayjal ibn Ṣwayna thus came to listen to the letter sent with Muḥammad al-Dūkhī. When the shaykhs of the Ghiyāth came As'ad Pāshā was in Tripoli, so the consul maintained the shaykhs as his guests for 20 days. When As'ad Pāshā returned he reached an agreement with them providing that they would return all of the plundered property and refrain from raids. The governor was able to convince them that it was within his power to subdue all of the Ṣafā and imprison them on their grazing lands. As'ad Pāshā thanked the consul for the role he had played in arranging this meeting.

APPENDIX III

Plants and Shrubs in Arab Desert Lands

IN THE FOLLOWING LIST the plants listed are in alphabetical order, according to the names by which they are known among the bedouins, followed by their Latin botanical names and a brief description. Different or variant names for the same plant are listed separately, but cross-referenced to one main entry or against one another.

A word of caution is in order with respect to the formal botanical names here provided for desert plants, which have been recorded on the basis of examination by botanists of actual plant specimens submitted by past researchers, as well as myself (see above, p. 81). The bedouin plant names imply no sense whatsoever of the strict botanical hierarchy and classification implied by the modern terminology, and as a result, the reader will find below numerous names (aside from the usual variants in pronunciation) that refer to the same plant.

1. ABŪ NASHR, *Galium ceratopodum* Boiss.: annual weed bearing bluish flowers.

2. 'ADDĪS, *Andrachne telephioides* L.: spurge-like plant.

3. 'ADHDHĀM, *Ephedra alata* Decne.: shrub resembling 'AJRAM. See also no. 12.

4. 'ADHĪR: a scented subshrub with pinnate leaves and small flowers.

5. 'ADHŪB: shrub with yellowish pinnate leaves.

6. ʿAḌĪD, *Reichardia picroides* (L.) Roth.: low annual weed with small greenish flower heads.

7. ʿAḌU: subshrub with small prickly leaves and greenish flowers.

8. ʿAFŪ: large bush with flexible branches and small leaves.

9. AḤḤAYM, *Silena gallica* L.: a kind of pink.

10. ʿAJRAM, *Anabasis setifera* Moq., *Anabasis articulata* (Forsk.) Moq.: a shrub with long stiff branches and scaled needle-shaped leaves; resembles rimth.

11. ʿAKRISH: dense thorny bush with green leaves.

12. ʿALANDA, *Ephedra alata* Decne.: shrub with leafless but scaled branches and small yellowish flowers forming round bunches. See also 3.

13. ʿALQA, *Scrophularia hypericifolia* Wydl.: bushy perennial with divided leaves and small purple flowers.

14. ʿANAM, *Alyssum anamense* Velen.: low herb with thin branches and small yellow flowers.

15. ʿANṢALĀN, *Ornithogalum* sp.: bulbous plant related to asphadol.

16. ʿAQŪL, *Alhagi maurorum* Medicus: spiny shrub bearing simple leaves and clusters of small reddish flowers.

17. ʿARĀD: shrub with thin branches and yellowish hairy leaves; resembles RŪTHA.

18. ARĀK, *Salvadora persica* L.: a shrub which camels, goats and gazelles eat.

19. ʿARANṬA, *Gaylussacia canescens* Meissn.: mignonette-like annual.

20. ʿARFAJ, *Musilia arabica* Velen.: bushy subshrub with white branches, small leaves, and heads of scented yellow flowers.

21. ARṬĀ, *Calligonum comosum* L'Hér.: nearly leafless shrub with articulated branches, clusters of small flowers, and nut-shaped hairy flowers.

22. 'AṢANṢAL, *Colchicum szovitsii* Fischer & C.A. Meyer: herb with brown scaled bulb and pink or white crocus-like flowers.

23. ATHL or ITHL, *Tamarix articulata* Vahl.: species of tamarisk, a tree with needle-shaped leaves.

24. AṬṬAYṬA: a plant that has small bulbs under the ground.

25. 'AWSAJ, *Lycium arabicum* Schweinf.: dense thorny shrub with sweet reddish berries.

26. BA'AYTHRĀN, *Artemisia judaica* L.: a kind of wormwood. See also no. 32.

27. BAKHĀTRĪ, *Erodium cicutarium* (L.) L'Hér.; *Erodium laciniatum* (Cav.) Willd.: gray herb with reddish flowers.

28. BANJĪ, *Hyoscyamus arabicus* Velen.: a kind of henbane.

29. BARWAQ, *Asphodelus pendulinus* Coss. et Dur.; *Asphodelus tenuifolius* Car. var.; *micranthus* Boiss.; *Asphodelus aestivus* Brot.: species of asphodel.

30. BASBĀS, *Echinosciadium arabicum* Zohary: annual of the parsley family.

31. BAṬṬŪSH: a plant with red fruits.

32. 'BAYTRĀN, *Artemisia judaica* L.: a kind of wormwood. See also no. 26.

33. BIZZ AL-'ANZ, *Stapelia* sp.: a cactus-like plant.

34. BRŪKĀN, *Centauria camelorum* Velen.: low bushy perennial with bristly bracts and yellowish flower-heads.

35. BURRAYD, *Bellevalia bracteosa* Velen.: species of hyacinth.

36. BUṢṢAYL, *Bellevalia* sp.: species of onion.

37. BUṬUM, *Pistacia terebinthus* L.: terebinth.

38. BWAYḌA, *Paronychia arabica* (L.) DC.: silver scaled herb with pinkish flowers.

39. BZĀR AL-SIMMAN, *Euphorbia rohlenae* Velen.: species of spurge.

40. DA'Ā', *Mesembryanthemum nodiflorum* (L.): a variety of SIMḤ.

41. DABGHA, *Erodium glaucophyllum* (L.) L'Hér.: perennial herb with prostrate stems and purple-colored flowers.

42. DA'LŪQ AL-JAMAL, *Scorzonera musili* Velen.: perennial with long roots, dense white branches, and hairy heads of yellowish flowers.

43. ḌAMRĀN, *Salsola tetrandra* Forsk.: intricately branched shrublet with minute scale-like fleshy leaves.

44. ḌARĪ', *Tricholaena teneriffae* (L.f.) Link.: a panic grass.

45. DAYDAḤĀN or ḤAYMARĀN, *Papaver laevigatum* Bieb.: a kind of poppy.

46. DHAMA, *Erodium laciniatum* (Cav.) Willd.: herb with very long roots, short stamens, and small purple flowers. See also no. 195.

47. DHANABNAB, *Reseda arabica* Boiss.: a species of mignonette.

48. DHĀNŪN, *Cistanche tubulosa* (Schenk) Wight: parasitic plant with root about two meters long and splendid flower spikes resting on sand.

49. DHAYL AL-ḤUṢNĪ, *Eremopyrum orientale* (L.) Jaub. et Spach: a wheat-like grass. See also no. 213.

50. DRAYHMA, *Alyssum homalocarpum* (Fisch et Mey.) Boiss.: a prickly hairy annual with small yellow flowers.

51. ḌURRAYṬ AL-NA'ĀM, *Cleome arabica* L.: semi-circular bush with purple flowers.

52. FIRS, *Traganum nudatum* Del.: scented shrub resembling wormwood.

53. FIṬR: mushroom.

54. FLAYFLA: low dark green strong-scented herb.

55. FRAYṬA, *Haplophyllum blanchei* Boiss.: shrub with straight branches, small leaves, and red or yellow flowers.

56. FUNŪN or KUḤḤAYL, *Echium longifolium* Del.: hairy and prickly annual with upright blue spikes and blue dye.

57. GHAḌĀ, *Haloxylon persicum* Boiss.: tree-like bush with long flexible boughs and lean needle-shaped leaves.

58. GHAḌRAF, *Salsola baryosma* (Roem. et Schult.) Dandy: subshrub with long roots, dense branches, and rosy flowers.

59. GHARAZ, *Pennisetum ciliare* (L.) Link.: a species of fountain grass.

60. GHASSA, *Ballota luteola* Velen.: a mint; subshrub with frilled leaves and bunches of white flowers.

61. GHAZZĀL, *Euphorbia retusa* Forsk.: a kind of spurge.

62. HAJĪN: bushy subshrub with thin branches, small leaves, and flowers.

63. ḤALBA, *Launaea mucronata* (Forsk.) Muschl.: bushy perennial with long thin roots, gray leaves, and yellow heads.

64. ḤALFA, *Imperata cylindrica* (L.) Beauv.: a kind of reed-like grass with silky, hairy, cylindrical spikes.

65. ḤALŪLĀ, *Leontodon autumnalis* (L.): fall dandelion. See also no. 127.

66. Ḥamāṭ, *Lithospermum callosum* Vahl.: hairy perennial bearing prickly leaves and blue flowers.

67. Ḥambāẓ or Ḥumbayẓ, *Emex spinosus* (L.) Campd.: a kind of sorrel known as prickly dock.

68. Ḥamḍ, *Haloxylon articulatum* (Cav.) Bge.: small bush with needle-shaped leaves and spikes of small whitish flowers. See also no. 204.

69. Ḥammā', *Erucaria uncata* (Boiss.) Asch. & Schweinf.: annual with small pinnate leaves and bunches of red flowers. See also no. 227.

70. Ḥamrā, *Pennisetum ciliare* (L.) Link.: a species of fountain grass with reddish spikes.

71. Ḥamṣīṣ, *Rumex pictus* Forsk.: a kind of sorrel.

72. Ḥanẓal, *Citrullus colocynthis* (L.) Schrad: colocynth.

73. Ḥarjal, see Ḥarmal.

74. Harm, *Zygophyllum simplex* L.: kind of bean caper.

75. Ḥarmal or Ḥarjal, *Peganum harmala* L.: African rue.

76. Ḥārra, *Sisymbrium irico* L.: a species of hedge mustard

77. Ḥarshaf, *Echinops ceratophorus* Boiss.: a tall thistle with white hairy leaves and large heads of bluish flowers. See also nos. 129–30.

78. Ḥasak, *Medicago aschersoniana* Urb.; *Medicago laciniata* (L.) Mill.: clover-like annual with spiny fruits.

79. Hashma: subshrub resembling 'arfaj.

80. Hawa', *Sonchus asper* (L.) Hill: a thistle wood.

81. Ḥawdhān, *Picris radicata* (Forsk.) Less.: bushy annual with hairy flower stalks and heads of yellow, scented flowers.

82. Ḥawwā', *Lagoseris sancta* (L.) K. Maly: annual with thin long root, long basal leaves, and long stalks bearing heads of yellowish flowers.

83. Ḥaymarān, see Daydaḥān.

84. Ḥazār, *Malcolmia crenulata* (DC.) Boiss.: low annual with small reddish flowers hidden in sand.

85. Hazzā': small grayish shrub with pinnate leaves.

86. Ḥillib, *Herniaria cinerea* Lam. et DC.: small, hairy, ash-colored herb which stains the hands.

87. Ḥimḥim, *Matthiola arabica* Boiss.; *Matthiola oxyceras* DC.: annual with tall hairy stem and yellow flowers.

88. Ḥinwa, *Calendula aegyptiaca* Desf.; *Calendula micrantha* Tinco et Guss.: a species of marigold.

89. Hlayba, see Rqayṭa.

90. Ḥlaywa, *Matricaria arabica* Velen.: chamomile-like annual.

91. Ḥrayẓa, *Frankenia hirsuta* L.: subshrub with long roots, prostrate branches, and violet flowers.

92. Ḥumbayẓ, see Ḥambāẓ.

93. Ḥuṣnīya, *Phalaris brachystachys* Link: bluish annual grass with spiked ends.

94. Idhn al-ḥmār, *Astragalus kahiricus* DC.: a subshrub with white hairy branches and leaves and with large yellow flowers.

95. Ijdayyān, *Solvia lanigera* Poir.: a species of sage.

96. Irbīyān, *Anacyclus alexandrinum* Willd.: a herb-like chamomile.

97. Irja', *Helianthemum lippii* (L.) Pers.: herb with hairy leaves and spikes of greenish-yellow flowers. See also no. 244.

98. ‘Irq, *Prosopis farcta* (Banks et Sol.) Macbride: mimosaceous shrub with bipinnate leaves and spikes of small flowers.

99. ‘Ishbit al-‘aqrab, *Anagallis arvensis* L. ssp. *latifolia* (L.) Arcangeli: pimpernel with blue flowers.

100. ‘Ishbit al-ghurāb, *Calendula aegyptiaca* Desf.: species of marigold.

101. ‘Ishbit al-ḥamām, *Arnebia hispidissima* (Lehm.) DC.: a prickly annual with long roots containing a violet pigment.

102. ‘Ishbit al-jaru, *Tephrosia musili* Velen.: subshrub with wooly stamens and leaves and racemes of white flowers.

103. ‘Ishbit al-rās, *Lappula spinocarpos* (Forsk.) Asch. ex Ktze: hairy and prickly annual with small flowers.

104. ‘Ishbit umm sālim, *Notoceras bicorne* (Ait.) Amo: low cress-like herb.

105. Ishnān, *Seidlitzia rosmarinus* (Ehrenb.) Solms-Laub.: scented subshrub with white branches, greenish leaves, and winged fruit; used instead of soap.

106. Islīḥ, *Cakile arabica* Bornm. et Velen.: bushy perennial with bare greenish branches and long clusters of pink flowers.

107. Ithl, see Athl.

108. Ja‘ada, *Teucrium polium* L.: scented, white wooly subshrub with hanging flower heads.

109. Jafna, resembles ‘arfaj, but with scaled branches.

110. Jamad, *Galium sinaicum* (Decne.) Boiss.: a hairy species of bedstraw.

111. Jamba, *Fragonia bruguieri* DC.; *Fragonia schimperi* Presl.: low spiny perennials with many branches.

112. JARAD or JIRRAYD, *Gymnocarpus decandrum* Forsk.: shrub with whitish-gray bark, narrow leaves, and small balls of flowers.

113. JAZAR, *Prangos arabica* Velen.: tall perennial with a vertical root, white hairy branches, and leaves and yellowish umbels.

114. JIRJĪR, *Senecio flavus* (Decne). Sch. Bip., var. *desfontainei* Bruce: species of groundsel, annual herbs with yellow heads.

115. JIRRAYD, see JARAD.

116. JITYĀT, *Francoeuria crispa* (Forsk.) Cass.: a bushy herb with small heads of yellow flowers.

117. JURAYBA, *Farsetia aegyptiaca* Turra: woody perennial covered with smooth white hairs and pink flowers.

118. JURB, *Onobrychis venosa* Desv.: wooly perennial legume with yellow flowers.

119. JURRAYS, *Atractylis cancellata* L.: low, annual, bushy herb, with large purple flower heads surrounded by silvery leaves.

120. KAFF AL-KALB, *Gymnarrhena micrantha* Desf.: low annual with scaled stamens bearing yellow heads which stick to soil and when dried become spoon-shaped.

121. KAFF MARYAM, *Anastatica hierochuntica* L.: rose of Jincho. See also no. 184.

122. KALKH, *Ferula sinaica* Boiss.: high perennial with deeply divided leaves and compound umbels of yellow flowers.

123. KALSHA, *Halimocnemis pilosa* Moq.-Tand.: small, bushy, gray, wooly herb with thin prickly leaves.

124. KARRĀTH, *Allium atroviolaceum* Boiss.: garlic with bluish purple flowers.

125. KHAFSH, *Diplotaxis harra* (Forsk.) Boiss.: hairy prickly subshrub with yellow flowers.

126. KHĀFŪR, *Schismus arabicus* Nees.; *Schismus barbatus* (L.) Thell.: an oat-like grass with dense stalks.

127. KHĀLŪLA, *Leontodon autumnalis* (L.): fall dandelion. See also no. 65.

128. KHARBAQA, *Helleborus vesicarius* Auch.: a kind of hellebore.

129. KHARSHAF, *Echinops ceratophorus* Boiss.: a tall thistle with white hairy leaves and large heads of bluish flowers. See also nos. 77, 130.

130. KHASHĪR, *Echinops ceratophorus* Boiss.: a tall thistle with white hairy leaves and large heads of bluish flowers. See also nos. 77, 129.

131. KHASHSHAYNĀ, *Carrichtera annua* (L.) Asch.: low hairy annual with violet-veined petals.

132. KHASHSHĪNAT AL-ḤASHĪSH, see QAṢBA.

133. KḤAYL, *Anchusa hispida* Forsk.: rough hairy annual with yellow flowers and root which produces a stain.

134. KḤAYL AL-NA'ĀM, *Astragalus hamrinensis* Hausskn. and Bornm: perennial subshrub with silver hairy winged leaves and violet flowers.

135. KHRAYMA, *Hippocrepis bicontorta* Lois.: a leguminous plant.

136. KHUBBAYZA, *Malva pusilla* Sm.: a species of mallow.

137. KHUDHRĀF, *Salsola spissa* Bieb.: bushy annual with large winged fruits.

138. KHUMṢĀN, *Isatis microcarpa* J. Gay: a wood-like herb.

139. KHUṬMĪ, *Polygonum equisetiforme* Sibth et Sm.: horsetail-like knotweed.

140. KHZĀMA, *Malcolmia arabica* Velen.: sappy annual with accented reddish flowers; sand sticks to it.

141. KSAYBRA, *Pimpinella cretica* Poir, var. *arabica* Boiss.: anise-like plant.

142. KUḤḤAYL, see FUNŪN.

143. KURM, *Pimpinella cretica* Poir: anise-like herb.

144. LAḤYAT AL-BIDIN, *Centaurea eryngioides* Lam.: knapweed-like perennial with spiny branches and heads of pink flowers.

145. LAḤYAT AL-TAYS, *Koelpinia linearis* Pall.: annual with thin upright stalks bearing little heads of yellow flowers.

146. LISĀN AL-GHRĀB, *Lycium barbarum*: box thorn.

147. LUBBAYNA, *Stachys aegyptiaca* Pers.; *Stachys musili* Velen.: subshrub with dense hairy branches and small red flower-racemes; of the mint family.

148. LWAYZA, *Amygdalus arabicus* Oliv.: an almond shrub.

149. MAKR, *Polycarpaea repens* Forsk. Asch. & Schweinf.: subshrub with long roots, small gray leaves, and white flowers.

150. MARRĀR, *Pyrethrum dumosum* Boiss.: chrysanthemum-like perennial with yellow flower heads.

151. MAṢA', see MṢA'.

152. M'ASSALA, *Launaea nudicaulis* (L.) Hook. f.: subshrub bearing many thin leafless branches and small yellowish-green flower heads.

153. MḤARŪT, *Scorodosma arabica* Velen.: scented herb with long root, tall stem, decompound hairy leaves, and many yellow flowers.

154. MIṢṢAY', *Cyperus conglomeratus* Rottb.: grass with strong brown roots, narrow scaled leaves, and spikelets.

155. MITNĀN, *Astragalus camelorum* Barb.; *Astragalus macrobotrys* Bge.: subshrub with prickly leaves and small flower heads.

156. MRĀR, *Centauria arabica* var. *musili* Velen.: annual centaury with bristly flower heads.

157. MṢA‘ or MAṢA‘, *Nitraria retusa* Forsk. Asch.: shrub with white branchy wedge-shaped leaves, hard spines, small yellowish flowers, and sweet fruit.

158. MSHA‘ or MASHA‘, *Scorzonera* sp.: with long narrow leaves and stalks bearing single heads of yellow flowers.

159. MWAṢṢALA, *Anarrhinum orientale* Benth.: coarse herb with flower thyrsus.

160. NA‘AYMA, *Pseudocrupina arabica* Velen.: bushy annual with divided leaves and small heads of reddish flowers.

161. NA‘AẒ, *Ephedra alata* Decne.: shrub with leafless branches and fasicles of small yellow flowers, shrubby horsetail.

162. NAJĪL, *Cynodon dactylon* (L.) Pers.: dog grass-like herb.

163. NA‘MĀN, *Glaucium arabicum* Fres.: poppy-like plant with yellow flowers.

164. NAṢĪ, *Aristida plumosa* L. (see SUBUṬ): dry sobol, smooth grass with roots to which sand sticks, and winged fruits.

165. NĀYMA, see R‘AYṢA.

166. NAYTŪL: perennial with high stem and green scented leaves.

167. NBAYṬA, *Reaumuria hypericoides* Willd.: subshrub with gray longish leaves and red flowers.

168. NIDD, *Suaeda salsa* (L.) Pallas: small annual with pink flowers.

169. NIFIL, *Trigonella hamosa* L.; *Trigonella monantha* C.A. Mey; *Trigonella stellata* Forsk.: clover-like plant.

170. NIQD, *Asteriscus graviolens* Less.: shrub with hard, gray, hairy branches and many heads of yellow flowers.

171. NQAYDA, *Euphorbia musili*: a species of annual spurge.

172. NUṢṢĪ, *Aristida lanata* Forsk.: a tall succulent grass.

173. QAḌQĀḌ, *Salsola inermis* Forsk.: subshrub with grayish leaves and small flowers.

174. QAFʿA, *Astragalus gyzensis* Del.; *Astragalus kofensis* Velen.; *Astragalus radiatus* Ehrenb. ex Bge.; *Astragalus tenuirugis* Boiss.; *Astragalus tribuloides* Del.; *Astragalus triradiatus* Bge.; *Astragalus tuberculatus* DC.: low annual with prickly leaves and fleshy husks or pods.

175. QAḤʿŪB: subshrub with bushy branches and dense flower heads.

176. QAṢBA or KHASHSHĪNAT AL-ḤASHĪSH, *Astenatherum forskalii* (Vahl) Nevski: tall grass with wool-covered scales.

177. QATĀD, *Astragalus spinosus* (Forsk.) Muschl.: bushy subshrub with long spines and white flowers.

178. QAṬAF, a species of *Atriplex* L.: subshrub with small drooping yellowish flowers.

179. QAYṢŪM, *Pyrethrum musili* Velen.: scented as asteraceous perennial with thin branches, hairy leaves, and many heads of blue flowers.

180. QAẒŪḤ, *Polygala scoparia* HBK.: subshrub with spiny branches and greenish-white flowers; species of milkwort.

181. QIRB, *Linaria aegyptiaca* (L.) Dum. Cour.: low perennial with small indented and yellow flowers.

182. QIRNĀ, *Hippocrepis ciliata* Willd.; *Hippocrepis biconcorta* Lois.: leguminous plant.

183. QLAYJLĀN, *Savignya longistyla* Boiss.: an annual with small pink flowers and circular husks.

184. QNAYFDHA, *Anastatica hierochuntica* L.: rose of Jincho. See also no. 121.

185. QRAYṬA, *Plantago coronopus* L.: a kind of plantain.

186. QṢĪṢ: low perennial with hairy prickly leaves.

187. QṬAYṬ, *Solanum sinaicum* Boiss.: bittersweet-like plant.

188. QURAYMA, *Jaubertia calyoptera* (Decne) Täckh.: subshrub with bare branches and winged fruits.

189. QURRAYṢ, *Trigonella hamosa* L.: bean-like annual.

190. QURẒĪ, *Pituranthos triaradiatus* (Hochst.) Asch. et Schweinf.: tall shrub with divided leaves and small greenish flowers.

191. QUṬAYYIN, *Bassia eriophora* (Schrad.) Ktze.: mallow-like herb.

192. RABL, *Pulicaria undulata* (L.) Kostel.: a wooly perennial with thick root and heads of yellow flowers.

193. RAḤĀB, *Heliotropium arbainense* Fres.: a perennial with hairy leaves and large flower spikes.

194. RAMRĀM, *Heliotropium luteum* Poir.; *Heliotropium persicum* Lam.: leaves wavy margined, the first wooly and the second prickly, flowers yellowish; species of heliotrope.

195. RAQMA, *Erodium laciniatum* (Cav.) Willd.: herb with very long roots, short stamens, and small purple flowers. See also no. 46.

196. RASHĀD, *Lepidium sativum* (L.): a species of pepperwort.

197. RATAM or RUTUM, *Lygos raetam* (Forsk.) Heywood: shrub with long rather stiff branches, long needle-shaped leaves, and hanging scented flowers.

198. R'AYṢA or NĀYMA, *Pteranthus dichotomus* Forsk.: low fleshy herb with many thick flower heads and winged fruit.

199. RBAḤLA, *Scorzonera papposa* DC.: a bulbous plant with lilac flower heads.

200. RGHAYLA, *Atriplex dimorphostegia* Kar. et Kir.: annual herb with leaves beset with crystalline papilli and small yellowish flowers.

201. RIBLA, *Plantago cylindrica* Forsk.; *Plantago gintlii* Velen.: species of plantain.

202. RĪḤĀN, *Ocimum basilicum* L.: sweet basil.

203. RIJLAT AL-GHURĀB, *Senecio gallicus* Choix: herb with alternate leaves, white hairy heads, and small flowers.

204. RIMTH, *Haloxylon articulatum* (Cav.) Bge.: a bush with jointed green stems and scale-like leaves; flowers small and whitish. Plant serves as fuel and has sweet juice. See also no. 68.

205. RKHĀMA, *Convolvulus reticulatus* Choisy: long woolly perennial resembling bindweed with thick woody roots and pinkish white flowers.

206. RQAYJA, *Zygophyllum simplex* L.: prostrate herbaceous annual with small leaves and yellow flowers; a species of bean caper. See also no. 207.

207. RQAYJA or RQAYSHĪ, *Zygophyllum simplex* L.: prostrate herbaceous annual with small leaves and yellow flowers; a species of bean caper. See also no. 206.

208. RQAYṬA or HLAYBA, *Carduus getulus* Pomel: an annual thistle with reddish heads.

209. RUGHL, *Atriplex leucoclada* Boiss.: subshrub, silvery-white, with loose clusters of small yellowish flowers.

210. RŪTHA, *Salsola lancifolia* Boiss.: subshrub with thin acute leaves and small pinkish flowers.

211. RUTUM, see RATAM.

212. SA'DĀN, *Neurada procumbens* L.: woolly prostrate herb with rounded, large spiny fruits.

213. SAFSŪF, *Eremopyrum orientale* (L.) Jaub. et Spach: a wheat-like grass. See also no. 49.

214. SA' 'ĪD, *Iris sisyrinchium* L.: a small iris with blue flowers.

215. ṢAM', *Stipa tortilis* Desf.: a grass with a much twisted very long awns.

216. SAMMĀ', *Bufonia multiceps* Decne.: a low plant with shrubby base and short thread-like leaves.

217. SAMN: annual with longish branches and small white flowers.

218. SAMUR, *Acacia tortilis* (Forsk.) Hayne: a low spiny shrub.

219. ṢFĀR, *Barbarea arabica* Velen.: low annual with many branches of small yellow flowers. See also no. 240.

220. SHAḤḤŪM, *Gagea reticulata* (Pall.) A. & H. Schultes: small bulbous herb with linear leaves and green flowers with yellow margins.

221. SHAJARAT AL-NAKHL, *Pterocephalus pulverulentus* Boiss. et Bl.: perennial with shrubby base, whitish, and heads of yellow flowers.

222. SHA'RĀN, *Suaeda* a shrub with small greenish flowers.

223. SHIBRI', *Pergularia tomentosa* L.: a milkweed climber with woolly leaves and greenish yellow flowers.

224. SHIDD AL-JAMAL, *Paronychia arabica* (L.) DC.: bushy herb with resplendent scales and very small flowers.

225. SHĪḤ, *Artemisia inculta* Del.: a kind of wormwood.

226. SHILWA, *Linaria tenuis* (Viv.) Spreng.: a low flax-like plant.

227. SHIQQĀRA, *Erucaria uncata* (Boiss.) Asch. & Schweinf.: annual with small pinnate leaves and bunches of red flowers. See also no. 69.

228. SHJARA: subshrub with brown branches and prunate leaves.

229. SHUBRUM, *Zilla spinosa* (Turra) Prantl.: a thorny shrub.

230. SIDR, *Ziziphus spina-christi* (L.) Willd.: a shrub with thorny stipules.

231. SIJJĪL, *Koeleria phleoides* (Vill.) Pers.: a grass with soft, hairy, flat, linear leaves.

232. SIL‘, *Convolvulus pilosellifolius* Desr.: a perennial species of bindweed with pink flowers.

233. SILLA, *Zilla spinosa* (Turra) Prantl.: a thorny shrub.

234. SIMḤ or SEMḤ, *Mesembryanthemum forskahlei* Hochst.: a low sappy annual with green fleshy leaves and small green flowers, seeds used as substitute for bread.

235. ṢIRR, *Noaea mucronata* (Forsk.) Asch. & Schweinf.: shrub with thorny twigs.

236. SLAYLA, *Aristida obtusa* Del.: a very low perennial grass.

237. SLAYQA, *Scorpiurus subvillosus* L.: small beet-like herb or subshrub with small green leaves.

238. ṢLAYYĀN, *Aristida ciliata* Desf.: a low perennial grass.

239. SUBUṬ, *Aristida plumosa* L.: a species of grass called NAṢĪ (or NAYṢĪ) when dry.

240. ṢUFFĀRA, *Barbarea arabica* Velen.: low annual bearing many branches of small yellow flowers. See also no. 219.

241. SUKUB, *Fumaria parviflora* Lam.: small-flowered fumitory.

242. SUNAYSLA, *Bupleurum semicompositum* Höjer: a small green weed resembling a grass.

243. SWĀS: a high plant similar to the KALH.

244. SWAYQA, *Helianthemum lippii* (L.) Pers.; *Helianthemum sessiliflorum* (Desf.) Pers.; *Helianthemum ventosum* Boiss.: weed-like species of sun-rose. See also no. 97.

245. SWAYS: brownish subshrub.

246. SYĀL, *Acacia seyal* Del.: a kind of acacia.

247. ṬAḤMA, see ṬḤAMA.

248. ṬALḤ, *Acacia raddiana* Savi.: one of the species called ṬALḤ; round irregular crown with scented cream-colored flowers.

249. TANḌUB, *Capparis decidua* (Forsk.) Edgew.: yellow-green shrub with deciduous leaves before flowering.

250. TARBA, *Eremobium nefudicum* (Velen.) Burtt et Rech. f.: early annual with very narrow leaves and pink flowers.

251. ṬARBA, *Malcolmia nefudica* Velen.: early annual with very narrow leaves and pink flowers.

252. ṬARFA or ṬARFĀ', *Tamarix hampeana* Boiss.; *Tamarix nilotica* (Ehrenb.) Bunge: a number of species of tamarisk may be known by the general name ṬARFA.

253. ṬARTHŪTH, *Cynomorium coccineum* L., var. *gigantium* Velen.: parasite with root more than two meters long and innumerable yellow and pink flowers forming a large spike; grows on root of GHAḌĀ bush and is edible.

254. ṬḤAMA or ṬAḤMA, *Suaeda vermiculata* Forsk.: bushy perennial with green fleshy leaves and very small flowers.

255. THMĀM, *Pennisetum dichotomum* (Forsk.) Del.: a tall grass.

256. TUMMAYR, *Erodium bryoniaefolium* Boiss.; *Erodium ciconium* (L.) L'Hér: species of hemlock stork's-bill.

257. 'UFAYNA, *Cleome arabica* L.: herb with reddish flower-heads.

258. UMM RUWAYS, *Scabiosa palaestina* L.: high annual with hairy flower, stalks, and leaves, and heads of yellowish flowers; a species of scabions.

259. 'UNAYBA, *Solanum sinaicum* Boiss.: bittersweet-like plant.

260. URAYNBA, *Bassia muricata* (L.) Murr.: white hairy herb covering the sand.

261. WARDIT AL-IKHWA, *Sternbergia colchiciflora* Waldst. et Kit.: bulbous herb with a large spike of yellow flowers.

262. WASHM: plant considered to indicate that truffles may appear in that place.

263. WḤIRRA, *Orobanche aegyptiaca* Pers.: a leafless root-parasite herb.

264. WRAQA, *Fagonia glutinosa* Del.: bushy subshrub with hairy and spiny branches, pink flowers, and green pods.

265. YANAMA, see YINIM.

266. YASĪḤ, *Erucaria hispanica* (L.) Druce: bushy herb with thin branches and yellowish flowers.

267. YINIM or YANAMA, *Plantago cylindrica* Forsk.: a species similar to the plantain.

268. ZAHR, *Brassica tournefortii* Gouan: a turnip-like herb.

269. ZAYTA, *Lavandula coronopifolia* Lam.: a species of lavender with blue flowers.

270. ZIBB AL-DHĪKH, *Orobanche cernua* Loefl.: leafless root parasite with a thick fleshy base and spicate flowers.

271. ZRAYQA, *Lotus angustissimus* L.; *Lotus gebelia* Vent.: two species of birds-foot trefoil.

Bibliography of Works Cited

The listing below includes all primary sources (documents, manuscript materials, and printed editions) and modern works cited in the text and notes. The Arabic definite article (*al-*) is ignored for purposes of alphabetization.

'Abd al-'Azīz, Nabīl Muḥammad. *Al-Khayl wa-riyāḍatuhā fī 'aṣr salāṭīn al-mamālīk*. Cairo, 1976.

'Abd Allāh ibn Ḥamza. *Ta'rīkh al-khuyūl al-'arabīya*, with the commentary of his son Aḥmad. Sanaa, 1979.

'Abd al-Malik, Buṭrus, Thompson, John Alexander, and Maṭar, Ibrāhīm. *Qāmūs al-Kitāb al-muqaddas*. Beirut, 1964.

Abū Māḍī, Ilīya. *Dīwān*. Beirut, 1982.

Abū Nuwās al-Ḥasan ibn Hāni' al-Ḥakamī. *Dīwān*. Volumes 1–2, edited by Ewald Wagner. Beirut, 1378–92/1958–72.

Abū Tammām Ḥabīb ibn Aws al-Ṭā'ī. *Dīwān al-ḥamāsa*. 2 volumes. Cairo, AH 1335.

Abū 'Ubayda, Ma'mar ibn Muthannā. *Kitāb al-khayl*. Hyderabad, AH 1358.

———. [*Naqā'iḍ Jarīr wa-l-Farazdaq*. Edited by Anthony Ashley Bevan. 3 volumes. Leiden, 1905–12.]

Aḥmad ibn Ḥanbal. *Musnad*. 6 volumes. Cairo, AH 1311–13.

al-Akhṭal, Ghiyāth ibn Ghawth. *Shi'r al-Akhṭal*. Edited by Antoine Ṣāliḥānī. Beirut, 1891.

al-'Akkām, Aḥmad. *Al-'Ashā'ir al-sūrīya*. Damascus, 1951.

Al-'Ālam, London, May 1959.

Albright, William Foxwell. *From the Stone Age to Christianity*. Baltimore, 1940.

Allen, Mark. *Falconry in Arabia*. London, 1980.

Almagro, Martin, *et al*. *Qusayr 'Amra: Residencia y baños omeyas en el desierto de Jordania*. Madrid, 1975.

Arabia. Published by British Foreign Office. Report no. 61. London, 1920

al-'Ārif, 'Ārif. *Al-Ḥubb wa-l-sharī'a wa-l-taqālīd 'inda l-badw*. Jerusalem, 1944.

________. *Al-Qaḍā' bayna l-badw*. Jerusalem, 1351/1933.

________. *Ta'rīkh Bi'r al-Sab' wa-qabā'iluhā*. Jerusalem, 1934.

________. *Ta'rīkh Ghazza*. Jerusalem, 1362/1943.

al-'Arjī, Abū 'Umar 'Abd Allāh ibn 'Umar. *Dīwān*. Edited by Khiḍr al-Ṭā'ī and Rashīd al-'Ubaydī. Baghdad, 1375/1956.

'Awwād, Gurgīs. *Al-Ab Anastās Mārī al-Karmalī: ḥayātuhu wa-mu'allafātuhu*. Baghdad, 1966.

al-'Azzāwī, 'Abbās. *'Ashā'ir al-'Irāq*. 4 volumes. Baghdad, 1937–56.

al-Balādhurī, Abū l-'Abbās Aḥmad ibn Yaḥyā. *Futūḥ al-buldān*. Edited by M.J. de Goeje. Leiden, 1866.

al-Bassām, Muḥammad ibn Ḥamad. *Kitāb al-durar al-mafākhir fī akhbār al-awākhir*. American University of Beirut, Ms. no. 7358.

Bazyar al-'Azīz bi-l-lāh al-Fāṭimī. *Kitāb al-bayzara*. Edited by Muḥammad Kurd 'Alī. Damascus, 1371/1952.

Bible, Protestant and Catholic printings.

Bietenholz, Peter G. *Desert and Bedouin in the European Mind*. Khartoum, 1963.

Blunt, Lady Anne. *Bedouin Tribes of the Euphrates*. New York, 1879.

________. *A Pilgrimage to Nejd*. 2nd edition. 2 volumes. London, 1881.

Boris, G. *Le Chameau chez les Maraziq*. Tunis, 1951.

Boucheman, Albert de. *Matériel de la vie bédouine*. Damascus, 1934.

Brickwood, E.D. "Horse: History," in *Encyclopaedia Britannica*, 11th edition (Cambridge, 1910–11), XI, 717–23.

Brown, William R. *The Horse of the Desert*. New York, 1929.

al-Buḥturī, Abū 'Ubāda al-Walīd ibn 'Ubayd. *Dīwān*. Edited by Ḥasan Kāmil al-Ṣayrafī. 4 volumes. Cairo, 1963–64.

al-Bukhārī, Abū 'Abd Allāh Muḥammad ibn Ismā'īl. *Al-Jāmi' al-ṣaḥīḥ*. Edited by Ludolf Krehl and Th.W. Juynboll. 4 volumes. Leiden, 1862–1908.

Bulliet, Richard W. *The Camel and the Wheel*. Cambridge, Mass., 1975.

Burckhardt, John Lewis. *Notes on the Bedouins and Wahábys*. 2 volumes. London, 1831.

________. *Travels in Arabia*. London, 1829.

Burton, Sir Richard F. *Personal Narrative of a Pilgrimage to al-Madinah and Meccah*. 2 volumes. Memorial Edition. London, 1893.

al-Bustānī, Buṭrus. *Muḥīṭ al-muḥīṭ*. 2 volumes. Beirut, 1867–70.

al-Bustānī, Sulaymān. "Al-Badw," *Al-Muqtaṭaf*, 12 (1887–88), pp. 141–47.

———. "Al-Ṣulaba," in *Dā'irat al-ma'ārif*, edited by Buṭrus al-Bustānī (Beirut, 1876–1900), XI, 2–9.

Carruthers, Douglas. *Arabian Adventure*. London, 1935.

———, ed. *The Desert Route to India*. London, 1929.

Cheesman, R.E. *In Unknown Arabia*. London, 1926.

Cole, Donald Powell. *Nomads of the Nomads*. Arlington Heights, Illinois, 1975.

[Conrad, Lawrence I. "The Province of North Syria in 1868: a Foreign Office Report," in *Studies in History and Literature in Honour of Nicola A. Ziadeh*, edited by Ihsan Abbas, Shereen Khairallah, Ali Z. Shakir (London, 1992), pp. 52–64.]

al-Damīrī, Kamāl al-Dīn Muḥammad ibn Mūsā. *Ḥayāt al-ḥayawān al-kubrā*. 2 volumes. Cairo, AH 1274.

Dhū l-Rumma, Abū l-Ḥārith Ghaylān ibn 'Uqba. *Dīwān*. Edited by Carlile Henry Hays Macartney. Cambridge, 1919.

Dickson, H.R.P. *The Arab of the Desert*. London 1949.

al-Dimashqī, Mikhā'īl Burayk. *Ta'rīkh al-Shām*. Ḥarīṣā, 1930.

Dostal, W. "The Evolution of Bedouin Life," in *Ancient Bedouin Society*, edited by Francesco Gabrieli (Rome, 1959), pp. 11–34.

Doughty, Charles M. *Travels in Arabia Deserta*. 2 volumes, new and definitive edition. London, 1936.

Euting, Julius. *Tagbuch einer Reise in Inner-Arabien*. 2 volumes. Edited by Enno Littmann. Leiden, 1896–1914.

al-Farazdaq, Abū Firās Hammām ibn Ghālib. *Dīwān*. Edited by 'Abd Allāh al-Ṣāwī. 2 volumes. Cairo, 1354/1936.

Feilberg, C.G. *La Tente noire*. Copenhagen, 1944.

Field, Henry. *Among the Beduins of North Arabia*. Chicago, 1931.

———. *An Anthropological Reconnaissance in the Near East, 1950*. Cambridge, Mass., 1956.

Gaury, Gerald de. *Arabian Journey and Other Desert Travels*. London, 1950.

Gauthier-Pilters, Hilda, and Dagg, Anne Innis. *The Camel*. Chicago and London, 1981.

al-Ghazzī, Kāmil ibn Ḥusayn. *Nahr al-dhahab fī ta'rīkh Ḥalab*. Aleppo, AH 1342.

al-Ghazzī, Najm al-Dīn Muḥammad ibn Muḥammad. *Al-Kawākib al-sā'ira fī manāqib a'yān al-mi'a al-'āshira*. Edited by Jibrail Jabbur. 3 volumes. Beirut, 1945–58.

———. *Luṭf al-samar wa-qaṭf al-thamar*. Edited by Maḥmūd al-Shaykh. 2 volumes. Damascus, 1981–82.

Glubb, John Bagot. [*The Empire of the Arabs*. London, 1965;] Arabic translation by Khayrī Ḥammād, *Imbirāṭūriyat al-'arab*. Beirut, 1966.

———. *Handbook of the Nomad, Semi-nomad, Semi-sedentary and Sedentary Tribes of Syria*. British Ninth Army, 1942.

———. *Peace in the Holy Land*. London, 1971.

———. *The Story of the Arab Legion*. London, 1948.

Grant, Christina Phelps. *The Syrian Desert*. New York, 1938.

Guarmani, Carlo. *Northern Najd*. Translated by Lady Capel-Cure with introduction and notes by Douglas Carruthers. London, 1938.

Hall, H.R. *The Ancient History of the Near East*. 7th edition, revised. London, 1927.

Hamilton, R.W. *Khirbat al-Mafjar*. Oxford, 1959.

Ḥamza, Fu'ād. *Qalb jazīrat al-'arab*. Cairo, 1352/1933.

Hardy, M.J.L. *Blood Feuds and the Payment of Blood Money in the Middle East*. Beirut, 1963.

Harrison, David L. *The Mammals of Arabia*. 3 volumes. London, 1964–72.

Ḥassān ibn Thābit al-Anṣārī. *Dīwān*. Edited with commentary by Muḥammad 'Inānī. Cairo, AH 1331; edited by Walīd 'Arafāt. 2 volumes. Leiden and London, 1971.

al-Ḥāyik, Iskandar Yūsuf. *Al-Badawī*. Beirut, n.d.

Hilāl ibn al-Muḥassin al-Ṣābi'. *Rusūm dār al-khilāfa*. Edited by Mīkhā'īl 'Awwād. Baghdad, 1383/1964.

al-Hilālī, Ḥamīd ibn Thawr. *Dīwān*. Cairo, AH 1371.

Hill, Donald R. *The Termination of Hostilities in the Early Arab Conquests A.D. 634–656*. London, 1971.

Hitti, Philip K. *History of Syria*. London, 1951.

———. [*History of the Arabs*.] Expanded edition and Arabic translation by Philip K. Hitti, Edward Jurji, and Jibrail Jabbur, *Ta'rīkh al-'arab*. Beirut, 1965. [Tenth English Edition. London, 1971.]

———. *Lebanon in History*. London, 1957.

Hogarth, David George. *The Nearer East*. New York, 1915

———. *The Penetration of Arabia*. London, 1905.

Huber, Charles. *Journal d'un voyage en Arabie, 1883–84*. Paris, 1891.

al-Ḥuṣrī, Abū Isḥāq Ibrāhīm ibn 'Alī. *Zahr al-ādāb*. Edited by 'Alī Muḥammad al-Bijāwī. 2 volumes. Cairo, 1372/1953.

Ibn 'Abd Rabbih, Abū 'Umar Aḥmad ibn Muḥammad. *Al-'Iqd al-farīd*. Edited by Aḥmad Amīn, Aḥmad al-Zayn, and Ibrāhīm al-Ibyārī. 7 volumes. Cairo, 1359–69/1940–50.

Ibn al-Athīr, 'Izz al-Dīn Abū l-Ḥasan 'Alī ibn Abī l-Ḥusayn. *Al-Kāmil fī l-ta'rīkh*. Edited by C.J. Tornberg. 11 volumes. Leiden, 1851–76.

Ibn Buṭlān al-Baghdādī and Ibn Riḍwān al-Miṣrī. *Khams rasā'il*. Edited and translated by Joseph Schacht and Max Meyerhof. Cairo, 1937.

Ibn Dirham, 'Abd al-Raḥmān. *Nuzhat al-abṣār bi-ṭarā'if al-akhbār wa-l-ash'ār*. 3 volumes. Beirut, AH 1345.

Ibn Fāris, Aḥmad, *Mutakhayyar al-alfāẓ*. Edited by Hilāl Nājī. Baghdad, 1390/1970.

Ibn al-Furāt, Nāṣir al-Dīn Muḥammad ibn 'Abd al-Raḥīm. *Ta'rīkh Ibn al-Furāt*. Volumes 4.1–2, edited by Ḥasan Muḥammad al-Shammā'. Basra, 1386–89/1967–69; volume 7, edited by Constantine Zurayk. Beirut, 1942; volume 9, edited by Constantine Zurayq and Najla Abū 'Izz al-Dīn. Beirut, 1936.

Ibn Hishām, Abū Muḥammad 'Abd al-Malik. *Sīrat rasūl Allāh*. Edited by Ferdinand Wüstenfeld. 2 volumes. Göttingen, 1858–60.

Ibn al-'Imād al-Ḥanbalī, Abū l-Falāḥ 'Abd al-Ḥayy ibn Aḥmad. *Shadharāt al-dhahab fī akhbār man dhahab*. 8 volumes. Beirut, n.d.

Ibn al-Jawzī, Abū l-Faraj 'Abd al-Raḥmān ibn 'Alī. *Al-Muntaẓam fī ta'rīkh al-mulūk wa-l-umam*. 10 volumes. Hyderabad, AH 1357–58.

Ibn al-Kalbī, Abū l-Mundhir Hishām ibn Muḥammad. *Ansāb al-khayl*. Edited by Aḥmad Zakī Pāshā. Cairo, 1946.

Ibn Khaldūn, Abū Zayd 'Abd al-Raḥmān ibn Muḥammad. *Al-Muqaddima*. Edited by E.M. Quatremère. 3 volumes. Paris, 1858.

Ibn Khallikān, Abū l-'Abbās Aḥmad ibn Muḥammad. *Wafayāt al-a'yān wa-anbā' abnā' al-zamān*. Edited by Iḥsān 'Abbās. 8 volumes. Beirut, 1968–72.

Ibn Manẓūr, Abū l-Faḍl Muḥammad ibn Mukarram. *Lisān al-'arab*. 15 volumes. Beirut, 1374–76/1955–56.

Ibn al-Nadīm, Abū l-Faraj Muḥammad ibn Isḥāq. *Al-Fihrist*. Edited by Gustav Flügel. Leipzig, 1871–72.

Ibn Qutayba, Abū Muḥammad ʿAbd Allāh ibn Muslim. *ʿUyūn al-akhbār*. 4 volumes. Cairo, 1343–49/1925–30.

Ibn Saʿd, Muḥammad. *Kitāb al-ṭabaqāt al-kabīr*. Edited by Eduard Sachau *et al.* 9 volumes. Leiden, 1904–40.

Ibn Taghrībirdī, Abū l-Maḥāsin Yūsuf. *Al-Nujūm al-zāhira fī mulūk Miṣr wa-l-Qāhira*. 16 volumes. Cairo, 1348–92/1929–72.

Ibn Ṭūlūn, Muḥammad. *Aʿlām al-warā*. Edited by Muḥammad Aḥmad Dahmān. Damascus, 1383/1964.

Imru' al-Qays ibn Ḥujr. *Dīwān*. Edited by Muḥammad Abū l-Faḍl Ibrāhīm. Cairo, 1958.

al-Iṣfahānī, Abū l-Faraj ʿAlī ibn al-Ḥusayn. *Kitāb al-aghānī*. Edited by Naṣr al-Hūrīnī. 20 volumes. Cairo/Būlāq, AH 1285.

Jabbur, Jibrail. "Abu-al-Duhūr. The Ruwalah Uṭfah," in *The World of Islam: Studies in Honour of Philip K. Hitti*, edited by James Kritzeck and R. Bayly Winder (London, 1960), pp. 195–98.

———. Essays written under the pseudonym of *fatā l-bādiya* in the newspaper *Al-Aḥrār*. Beirut, 1925–26.

———. [*Min ayyām al-ʿumr*. Beirut, 1991.]

———. *ʿUmar ibn Abī Rabīʿa*. 3 volumes. Beirut, 1935–71.

al-Jāḥiẓ, Abū ʿUthmān ʿAmr ibn Baḥr. *Al-Bayān wa-l-tabyīn*. Edited by Ḥasan al-Sandūbī. 3 volumes. Cairo, 1351/1932.

Jarīr ibn ʿAṭīya. *Dīwān*. Edited by Nuʿmān Amīn Ṭāhā. 2 volumes. Cairo, 1969–71.

Jarvis, C.S. *Arab Command*. St Albans, 1946.

———. *Three Deserts*. cheap edition. London, 1941.

al-Jumayyil, Makkī. *Al-Badāwa wa-l-badw fī l-bilād al-ʿarabīya*. Sars al-Liyān, 1962.

———. *Al-Badw wa-l-qabāʾil al-raḥḥāla fī l-ʿIrāq*. Baghdad, 1956.

al-Jundī, Muḥammad Salīm. *Taʾrīkh Maʿarrat al-Nuʿmān*. 2 volumes. Damascus, 1963–64.

Kaḥḥāla, ʿUmar Riḍā. *Muʿjam qabāʾil al-ʿarab*. 3 volumes. Damascus, 1949.

al-Kamālī, Shafīq. *Al-Shiʿr ʿinda l-badw*. Baghdad, 1384/1964.

al-Karmalī, Anastās Mārī. "Al-Ṣulayb," *Al Mashriq*, 1 (1898), pp. 673–81.

al-Kaylānī, Mu'ayyad. *Muḥāfaẓat Ḥamāh*. Damascus, 1964.

al-Khālidī, Aḥmad ibn Muḥammad. *Lubnān fī 'ahd al-amīr Fakhr al-Dīn al-Ma'nī*. Edited by Asad Rustum and Fu'ād Afram al-Bustānī. Beirut, 1936.

Kiernan, R.H. *The Unveiling of Arabia*. London, 1937.

Kingdom of Iraq, published by a Committee of Officials. Baltimore, 1946.

Kitāb al-'īd (American University of Beirut Festival Book). Edited by Jibrail Jabbur. Beirut, 1967.

Al-Kumayt ibn Zayd al-Asadī. *Dīwān*. Edited by Dawūd Sallūm. 3 volumes. Baghdad, 1969–70.

Kurd 'Alī, Muḥammad. *Khiṭaṭ al-Shām*. 6 volumes. Damascus, 1343–47/1925–28.

Kushājim, Abū l-Fatḥ Maḥmūd ibn al-Ḥusayn. *Adab al-nadīm*. Cairo, AH 1298.

________. *Dīwān*. Edited by Khayrīya Muḥammad Maḥfūẓ. Baghdad, 1390/1970.

________. *Al-Maṣāyīd wa-l-maṭārid*. Edited by Muḥammad As'ad Ṭalas. Baghdad, 1954.

Kuthayyir 'Azza ibn 'Abd al-Raḥmān. *Dīwān*. Edited by Iḥsān 'Abbās. Beirut, 1391/1971.

Lammens, H., "Mecca," in *Encylopaedia of Islam*, 1st edition, edited by T.W. Arnold *et al.* (Leiden and London, 1918–34), III, 437–42.

Lancaster, William. *The Rwala Bedouin Today*. Cambridge, 1981.

Lawrence, T.E. *Seven Pillars of Wisdom*. Aylesbury, 1926.

Leonard, Arthur G. *The Camel*. London and New York, 1894.

Leopold, A. Starker. *The Desert*. New York, 1961.

"Locust," in *Encyclopaedia Britannica*, 15th edition (Chicago, 1978), Micropaedia, VI, 293.

Luckenbill, Daniel D. *Ancient Records of Assyria and Babylonia*. 2 volumes. Chicago, 1926–27.

McClure, Harold A. *The Arabian Peninsula and Prehistoric Populations*. Miami, 1971.

al-Ma'arrī, Abū l-'Alā' Aḥmad ibn Muḥammad. *Luzūm mā lā yalzam*. 2 volumes. Beirut, 1381/1961.

________. *Saqṭ al-zand*, with the commentary of Abū Ya'qūb Yūsuf ibn Ṭāhir al-Khūwī, *Sharḥ al-tanwīr*. 2 volumes. Cairo, 1342/1924.

Majnūn Laylā. *Dīwān*. Edited by 'Abd al-Sattār Aḥmad Farrāj. Cairo, n.d.

Ma'lūf, Amīn. *Mu'jam al-ḥayawān*. Cairo, 1932.

Mashāqa, Mīkhā'īl. *Muntakhabāt min al-jawāb 'alā iqtirāḥ al-aḥbāb.* Edited by Asad Rustum and Ṣubḥī Abū Shaqrā. Beirut, 1955.

al-Mas'ūdī, Abū l-Ḥasan 'Alī ibn al-Ḥusayn. *Murūj al-dhahab wa-ma'ādin al-jawhar.* Edited by Charles Pellat. 7 volumes. Beirut, 1966–79.

Merrill, Selah. *East of the Jordan.* London 1881.

Montagne, Robert. *La Civilisation du désert.* Paris, 1947.

al-Mubarrad, Abū l-'Abbās Muḥammad ibn Yazīd. *Al-Kāmil.* Edited by William Wright. 2 volumes. Leipzig, 1864–92.

Mughīr, Yāsīn. "Al-Waḍ' al-qabalī fī Sūriya". MA thesis. American University of Beirut, 1946.

Müller, Victor. *En Syrie avec les bédouins.* Paris, 1931.

Musil, Alois. *Arabia Deserta.* New York, 1927.

———. *In the Arabian Desert.* New York, 1931.

———. *The Manners and Customs of the Rwala Bedouins.* New York, 1928.

———. *The Middle Euphrates.* New York, 1927.

———. *The Northern Hegaz.* New York, 1926.

———. *Northern Negd.* New York, 1928.

———. *Palmyrena.* New York, 1928.

al-Mutanabbī, Abū l-Ṭayyib Aḥmad ibn al-Ḥusayn. *Dīwān.* Edited by Nāṣīf al-Yāzijī. Beirut, 1887.

al-Nābigha al-Dhubyānī, Ziyād ibn Mu'āwiya. *Dīwān.* Edited by Shukrī Fayṣal. Beirut, 1968.

Nabk Hospital, manuscript records for 1953–55.

News Review (Beirut), reports in volume VII.32 and X.42 (1959)

Nicholson, Reynold A. *A Literary History of the Arabs.* London 1907.

Niebuhr, Carsten. *Travels Through Arabia.* Translated by Robert Heron. 2 volumes. Edinburgh, 1792.

[Oppenheim, Max von. *Die Beduinen.* 4 volumes. Volumes 3–4 edited by Werner Caskel. Leipzig and Wiesbaden, 1939–68.]

———. *Vom Mittelmeer zum Persischen Golf.* 2 volumes. Berlin, 1899–1900.

———. *Der Tell Halaf.* Leipzig, 1931.

Palgrave, William Gifford. *Narrative of a Year's Journey Through Central and Eastern Arabia, 1862–1863.* 2 volumes. 3rd edition. London and Cambridge, 1866.

Philby, H. St. John. *The Empty Quarter*. New York, 1933.

________. *Forty Years in the Wilderness*. London, 1957.

________. *The Heart of Arabia*. 2 volumes. London, Bombay, and Sydney, 1922.

________. "The Land of Midian," *The Middle East Journal*, 9.2 (1955), pp. 117–29.

________. *The Land of Midian*. London, 1957.

Pieper, W. "Sulaib," in *Encyclopaedia of Islam*, 1st edition, edited by T.W. Arnold *et al.* (Leiden, 1918–1934), IV, 511–15.

Podhajsky, A.W., "Horse," in *Encyclopaedia Britannica*, 15th edition (Chicago, 1978), Macropaedia, VIII, 1088–92.

Poidebard, A. *La Trace de Rome dans le désert de Syrie*. Paris 1934.

Qasāṭlī, Nu'mān, "Mulakhkhaṣ ta'rīkh al-zayādina," *Al-Jinān*, 24 (15 December 1877), pp. 847–53.

al-Qusūs, 'Awda. *Kitāb al-qaḍā' al-badawī*. Amman, 1936.

al-Qazwīnī, Zakarīyā ibn Muḥammad. *'Ajā'ib al-makhlūqāt wa-gharā'ib al-mawjūdāt*. Beirut, 1978.

Qur'ān.

al-Quṭāmī, Umayr ibn Shuyaym. *Dīwān*. Edited by Jacob Barth. Leiden, 1902.

Raswan, Carl R. *Black Tents of Arabia*. Boston, 1935.

al-Rāwī, 'Abd al-Jabbār. *Al-Bādiya*. Baghdad, 1368/1949.

al-Rīḥānī, Amīn. *Mulūk al-'arab*. 2 volumes. Beirut, 1924–25.

Ripinksy, Michael, "Camel Ancestry and Domestication in Egypt and the Sahara," *Archaeology*, 36 (1983), pp. 21–27.

________, "The Camel in Ancient Arabia," *Antiquity*, 49 (1975), pp. 295–98.

________, "Pleistocene Camel Distribution in the Old World," *Antiquity*, 56 (1982), pp. 48–50.

Romer, Alfred Sherwood. *Vertebrate Paleontology*. 2nd edition. Chicago, 1945.

Rustum, Asad, ed. *Al-Maḥfūẓāt al-malakīya al-miṣrīya fī wathā'iq al-Shām*. 4 volumes. Beirut, 1940–43.

________. *Al-Uṣūl al-'arabīya li-ta'rīkh Sūriya fī 'ahd Muḥammad 'Alī Pāshā*. 5 volumes. Beirut, 1933.

Sābā, George, and Rūkaz ibn Zā'id al-'Azīzī. *Ṣafaḥāt min al-ta'rīkh al-urdunnī wa-min ḥayāt al-bādiya*. Amman, 1961.

Ṣābir, Muḥyī l-Dīn, and Malīka, Louis Kāmil. *Al-Badw wa-l-badāwa*. Sars al-Liyān, 1966.

Salmān, Archimandrite Būlus. *Khamsat a'wām fī sharqī l-Urdunn*. Ḥarīṣā, 1929.

Schmidt-Nielsen, Knut, "The Physiology of the Camel," *Scientific American*, 201 (6 December 1959), pp. 140–51.

Seabrook, William. *Adventures in Arabia*. London and Aylesbury, 1941.

Shanklin, William M. "The Anthropology of the Rwala Bedouins," *The Journal of the Royal Anthropological Institute*, 65 (1935), pp. 375–95.

al-Sharīf, Munīr. report in the newspaper *Al-Ḥayāt*, no. 2094 (Beirut, 1953).

al-Shihābī, Ḥaydar Aḥmad. *Lubnān fī 'ahd al-umarā' al-shihābīyīn*. Edited by Asad Rustum and Fu'ād Afram al-Bustānī. 3 volumes. Beirut, 1933.

Simpson, George G. *Horses*. New York 1951.

al-Sukkarī, Abū Sa'īd al-Ḥasan ibn al-Ḥusayn, compiler and commentator. *Dīwān al-hudhalīyīn*. Edited by 'Abd al-Sattār Farrāj. 3 volumes. Cairo, 1384/1965.

al-Suyūṭī, Jalāl al-Dīn 'Abd al-Raḥmān ibn Abī Bakr. *Ḥusn al-muḥāḍara*. 2 volumes. Cairo, AH 1321.

al-Ṭabarī, Abū Ja'far Muḥammad ibn Jarīr. *Jāmi' al-bayān 'an ta'wīl āy al-Qur'ān*. 30 volumes. Cairo, 1373/1954.

________. *Ta'rīkh al-rusul wa-l-mulūk*. Edited by M.J. de Goeje *et al.* 15 volumes. Leiden, 1879–1901.

al-Ṭāhir, 'Abd al-Jalīl. *Al-Badw wa-l-'ashā'ir fī l-bilād al-'arabīya*. Cairo, 1955.

Talbot, Lee Merriam, article in *Time Magazine*. vol. 66, 21 November 1955, p. 32.

al-Tawḥīdī, Abū Ḥayyān 'Alī ibn Muḥammad. *Al-Baṣā'ir wa-l-dhakhā'ir*. Edited by Wadād al-Qāḍī. 10 volumes. Beirut, 1408/1988.

Thesiger, Wilfred. *Arabian Sands*. London and Colchester, 1959.

________. *Desert, Marsh and Mountain*. London, 1979.

Thomas, Bertram. *Arabia Felix*. London, 1932.

al-Tibrīzī, Yaḥyā ibn 'Alī. *Sharḥ al-qaṣā'id al-'ashr*. Edited by Charles James Lyall. Calcutta, 1894.

al-Ṭirimmāḥ ibn Ḥakīm al-Ṭā'ī. *Dīwān*. Edited by Fritz Krenkow. Leiden and London, 1927.

Les Tribus nomades de l'état de Syrie. Damascus, 1943.

Twitchell, K.S. *Saudi Arabia*. Princeton, 1947.

'Umar ibn Abī Rabī'a. *Dīwān*. Edited by Paul Schwarz. 3 volumes. Leipzig, 1318–27/1901–1909.

United Kingdom, Foreign Office. *Embassy and Consular Archives: Turkey Correspondence*. F.O. 195, volumes 170–1027. London, 1835–74.

'Urwa ibn Ḥizām al-'Udhrī. *Dīwān*. Ms in the author's possession, undated but copied from an ancient codex.

Usāma ibn Munqidh. *Kitāb al-i'tibār*. Edited by Philip K. Hitti. Princeton, 1930.

Varthema, Ludovico di. *Travels*. Translated from the original Italian edition of 1510 by John Winter Jones and edited by George Percy Badger. New York, 1963.

Volney, M.C.-F. *Travels Through Syria and Egypt, 1783–1785*. 2 volumes. London, 1787.

Wahba, Ḥāfiẓ. *Jazīrat al-'arab fī l-qarn al-'ishrīn*. Cairo, 1365/1946.

Wallin, Georg August. ["Notes taken During a Journey Through Part of Northern Arabia in 1848," *Journal of the Royal Geographical Society*, 20 (1850), pp. 293–344; = *idem*, *Travels in Arabia (1845 and 1848)* (London, 1979), pp. 15–146]. Arabic translation by Samīr Salīm Shiblī, *Ṣuwar min shamālī jazīrat al-'arab fī muntaṣaf al-qarn al-tāsi' 'ashar*. Beirut, 1971.

al-Wāqidī, Abū 'Abd Allāh Muḥammad ibn 'Umar (attrib.). *Futūḥ al-Shām*. Cairo, AH 1278.

Wilson, R.T. *The Camel*. London and New York, 1984.

Wirth, Eugen. *Syrien. Eine geographische Landeskunde*. Darmstadt, 1971.

World Health Organization. Regional Office for the Eastern Mediterranean. Press release nos. 24–29. October 1969.

Wright, William. *Palmyra and Zenobia*. London, 1895.

Yāqūt ibn 'Abd Allāh al-Ḥamawī. *Mu'jam al-buldān*. 5 volumes. Beirut, 1374–76/1955–57.

Zakarīyā, Aḥmad Waṣfī. *'Ashā'ir al-Shām*. 2 volumes. Damascus, 1363–66/1945–47.

________. *Al-Rīf al-sūrī*. 2 volumes. Damascus, 1374–76/1955–57.

al-Zamakhsharī, Abū l-Qāsim Maḥmūd ibn 'Umar. *A'jab al-'ajab fī sharḥ lāmiyat al-'arab*. Cairo, AH 1300.

al-Zawzanī, al-Ḥusayn ibn Aḥmad. *Sharḥ al-mu'allaqāt*. Beirut, 1382/1963.

al-Ziriklī, Khayr al-Dīn. *'Āmān fī 'Ammān*. Cairo, 1343/1925.

________. *Mā ra'aytu wa-mā sami'tu*. Cairo, 1923.

General Index

In the arrangement adopted here, the Arabic definite article *al-* and the differences between Arabic letters with the same basic Latinized form (e.g. a and ā, d and ḍ) have been ignored for purposes of alphabetization.

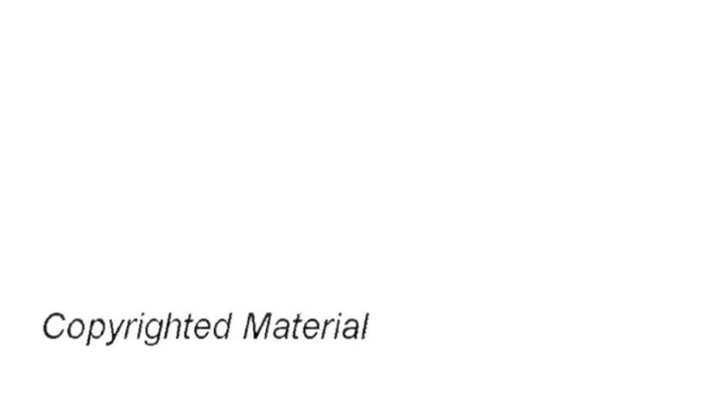

1623340R20378

Made in the USA
San Bernardino, CA
09 January 2013